Bolivia

Anja Mutić
Kate Armstrong, Paul Smith

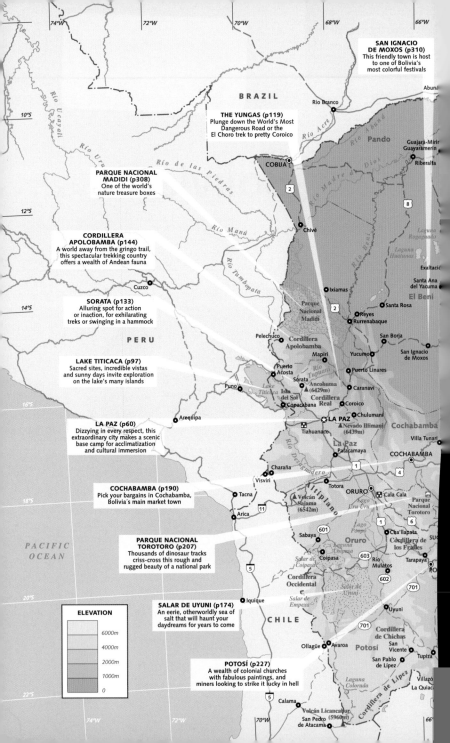

SAN IGNACIO DE MOXOS (p310)
This friendly town is host to one of Bolivia's most colorful festivals

THE YUNGAS (p119)
Plunge down the World's Most Dangerous Road or the El Choro trek to pretty Coroico

PARQUE NACIONAL MADIDI (p308)
One of the world's nature treasure boxes

CORDILLERA APOLOBAMBA (p144)
A world away from the gringo trail, this spectacular trekking country offers a wealth of Andean fauna

SORATA (p133)
Alluring spot for action or inaction, for exhilarating treks or swinging in a hammock

LAKE TITICACA (p97)
Sacred sites, incredible vistas and sunny days invite exploration on the lake's many islands

LA PAZ (p60)
Dizzying in every respect, this extraordinary city makes a scenic base camp for acclimatization and cultural immersion

COCHABAMBA (p190)
Pick your bargains in Cochabamba, Bolivia's main market town

PARQUE NACIONAL TOROTORO (p207)
Thousands of dinosaur tracks criss-cross this rough and rugged beauty of a national park

SALAR DE UYUNI (p174)
An eerie, otherworldly sea of salt that will haunt your daydreams for years to come

POTOSÍ (p227)
A wealth of colonial churches with fabulous paintings, and miners looking to strike it lucky in hell

ELEVATION

6000m
4000m
2000m
1000m
0

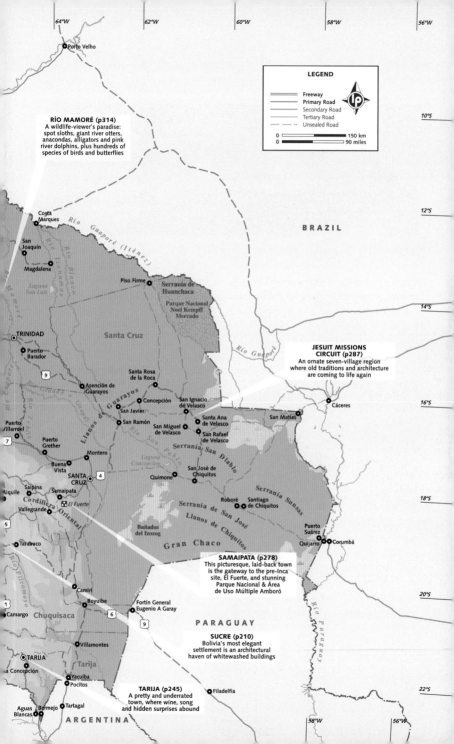

LEGEND

Freeway
Primary Road
Secondary Road
Tertiary Road
Unsealed Road

0 — 150 km
0 — 90 miles

BRAZIL

RÍO MAMORÉ (p314)
A wildlife-viewer's paradise:
spot sloths, giant river otters,
anacondas, alligators and pink
river dolphins, plus hundreds of
species of birds and butterflies

Porto Velho

Costa
Marques

San
Joaquín

Magdalena

Río Guaporé (Iténez)

Piso Firme

Serranía de
Huanchaca

Parque Nacional
Noel Kempff
Mercado

TRINIDAD

Puerto
Barador

Santa Cruz

Río Guaporé

**JESUIT MISSIONS
CIRCUIT (p287)**
An ornate seven-village region
where old traditions and architecture
are coming to life again

Santa Rosa
de la Roca

Asención de
Guarayos

Concepción

San Ignacio
de Velasco

San Javier

Santa Ana
de Velasco

Cáceres

San Ramón

San Miguel
de Velasco

San Rafael
de Velasco

San Matías

Puerto
Villarroel

Puerto
Grether

Montero

Buena
Vista

Serranía San Diablo

SANTA
CRUZ

Laguna
Concepción

San José
de Chiquitos

Aiquile

Saipina

Samaipata

El Fuerte

Quimone

Serranía de San José

Roboré

Santiago
de Chiquitos

Serranía Sunsas

Vallegrande

Cordillera
Oriental

Bañados
del Izozog

Llanos de Chiquitos

Puerto
Suárez

Quijarro

Corumbá

Tarabuco

Gran Chaco

SAMAIPATA (p278)
This picturesque, laid-back town
is the gateway to the pre-Inca
site, El Fuerte, and stunning
Parque Nacional & Área
de Uso Múltiple Amboró

Camiri

Boyuibe

Fortín General
Eugenio A Garay

Camargo

Chuquisaca

PARAGUAY

SUCRE (p210)
Bolivia's most elegant
settlement is an architectural
haven of whitewashed buildings

Villamontes

Tarija

TARIJA

TARIJA (p245)
A pretty and underrated
town, where wine, song
and hidden surprises abound

Yacuiba

Pocitos

Filadelfia

a Concepción

Aguas
Blancas

Bermejo

Tartagal

ARGENTINA

Río Paraguay

On the Road

ANJA MUTIĆ Coordinating Author

Here I am standing on the crusty salts of Salar de Uyuni (p174), in awe of my surroundings but at the same time wondering if I'll reach my destination for the night. It's the rainy season and the jeep driver is nervously navigating the salty terrain riddled with water puddles and cracks. I've heard of people getting stuck in the Salar for days during the rains so I'm quite happy and relieved once we reach solid ground at the edge of salt.

KATE ARMSTRONG I'm at heady heights overlooking La Paz (p60), amazed at the incongruity of this thriving city, the melting pot of both the modern and traditional. I love its harsh environment. In awe of its sprawling urbanization, I am also conscious that this reflects both the threats and opportunities of globalization. On the edge of La Paz, I ponder how the city, too, is on a rocky precipice in a quest to balance both its future and its past.

PAUL SMITH Here I am killing time in the 40°C heat of the Chaco (p256) as the bus drivers try to dig us out of the hole they have just driven us into. Everybody seemed to have a helpful piece of advice on how to get us out of the fix, but nobody was prepared to put their money where their mouth was and physically help dig the bus out of the deep sand it was trapped in. It was far too much like hard work!

For full author biographies see p372

Bolivia Highlights

Bolivia equals adventure. Often called the Tibet of the Americas for its altitude and isolation, Bolivia beckons intrepid travelers with its rugged landscapes and vibrant indigenous cultures. The variety of things to see and do here can be daunting – where should you begin? Scaling a snowcapped Andean peak? Gliding through the steamy Amazon jungle in search of reclusive wildlife? Exploring magnificent colonial cities? Joining in the festivities for the Aymará solstice? Here, a selection of Lonely Planet travelers, authors and staff share their most memorable experiences.

KARL LEHMANN

1 TUPIZA – BOLIVIA'S WILD WEST

The laid-back and friendly town of Tupiza (p180) is smack-bang in the middle of a region blessed with spectacular canyons, *quebradas*, rocky hills and other curious geologic formations, all waiting to be explored. So grab a cowboy hat and throw your leg over a horse, lace up your hiking boots, pump up the tires of your mountain bike or line up a 4WD, and head off for some adventures of your own in Bolivia's Wild (South) West.

Annelies Mertens, Lonely Planet Staff, Australia

JAMES LYON

POTOSÍ

It may claim to be the highest city in the world (p227) but thin air aside, Potosí's wealth was enough to leave visitors dizzy. Rivers of silver were said to run beneath the Cerro Rico (Rich Mountain), for centuries enriching Europe and, more recently, mining multinationals. Colonial-era buildings exude wealth wrought from the mines, and legend has it the mark of Potosí's mint gave us the '$' sign. Get some perspective by visiting the mines and witness how a country so resource-rich has come to be so poor.

Debra Herrmann, Lonely Planet Staff, Australia

2 SALAR DE UYUNI

A trek through Salar de Uyuni (p174) is full of oddities: a graveyard of rusted, graffitied trains on tracks leading nowhere; a large expanse of salt flats that gives the appearance of 'floating' with the right camera perspective; an 'island' of 12m-high cacti; and the skulls of little people buried in caves. You can't help but be mesmerized by the moon-like landscape sitting at 4000m.

Monique Smith, Traveler, Canada

3

KRZYSZTOF DYDYNS

JAUME BALAN

4 ISLA DEL SOL, LAKE TITICACA

After a long boat trip the island (p109) finally appears. When you land you see the Inca steps which are needed to get to the top of the island. After a very tiring climb you finally see the small town where you are going to pass the night, so far away from civilization but so mystical that your tired body feels renewed.

Camilo Blanco, Traveler, Colombia

PARQUE NACIONAL & ÁREA DE USO MÚLTIPLE AMBORÓ

Perfectly placed where the lush, leafy Amazon meets the thorny, dusty Chaco, and the sweltering lowlands greet the refreshing highlands, Amboró National Park (p276) teems with wildlife. Everything from anteaters to aracaris and jaguars to jararás make their home in this immense tropical paradise. It's a wilderness just begging to be explored.

Paul Smith, Lonely Planet Author, Paraguay

JAMES BALOG

5

TRAVELSCAPE IMAGES/ALAMY

LA PAZ'S MARKETS

A far better alternative to the tourist-oriented Sagárnaga strip are the markets nearby (p71). Wander through the streets and alleys to marvel at the vast variety of produce, from maca, a turnip-like vegetable (and natural Andean Viagra) to electronic devices, agricultural tools and exotic fruits. The best part is interacting with the *cholita* vendors who are always ready for a quick sale.

Kate Armstrong, Lonely Planet Author, Australia

BRENT WINEBRENNER

6

7

RIVER TRIPS ON THE RÍO BENI

After a dusty drive across barricades we finally reached the Río Beni (p304) near Rurrenabaque. Within moments of being on the boat we saw our first croc – within 15 minutes we'd seen hundreds, and plenty of families of rotund capybaras grazing on the banks. To then jump into the murky water at the wide bends of the river took a leap of faith, but was well worth it when we heard the squawks of river dolphins underwater, keeping the crocs away for us as they frolicked and rolled about in the water nearby.

Sarah Charnaud, Traveler, Australia

SUCRE

Beautiful Sucre (p210), birthplace of independent Bolivia and the nation's judicial capital, is a stunning white city in the foothills of the Andes. It's an eclectic mix of the old and the new, where you can while away your days perusing historic buildings and museums, and your nights enjoying the city's famous nightlife.

Paul Smith, Lonely Planet Author, Paraguay

8

MICHAEL BOYN

TREKKING IN THE CORDILLERA REAL

I did a 25-day trek in April and May along the Cordillera Real (p141) – the best experience of my life! If you are a trek enthusiast like me and like mountains, you all must do this trek or part of it.

antdave, Traveler

10

WOODS WEATCBC

IMAGEBROKER/ALAMY

9

LAGUNA COLORADA – BOLIVIA

On the border of Bolivia and Chile exists a natural feature that will take your breath away. The lake (p176) harbors an algae that produces a red-colored hue and during certain times of the year, flocks of pink flamingos congregate on its waters. The magical combination creates a colorful experience that makes you feel like you're on another planet.

Lou La Grange, Lonely Planet Staff, USA

Contents

On the Road 4

Bolivia Highlights 5

Destination Bolivia 12

Getting Started 13

Itineraries 17

History 21

The Culture 32

Food & Drink 42

Environment 49

Outdoors 54

La Paz 60
History 61
Orientation 61
Information 63
Dangers & Annoyances 66
Sights 67
Activities 74
Courses 74
Tours 74
Festivals & Events 76
Sleeping 77
Eating 81
Drinking & Clubbing 84
Entertainment 84
Shopping 85
Getting There & Away 87
Getting Around 88
AROUND LA PAZ 89
Valle de la Luna 89
Mallasa 90
Valencia & Mecapaca 90

Muela del Diablo 91
Valle de las Ánimas 92
Cañón de Palca 92
Chacaltaya 93
Tiwanaku 93

Lake Titicaca 97
Copacabana 99
Copacabana to Yampupata 107
Isla del Sol 109
Isla de la Luna (Koati) 114
Islas de Wiñaymarka 114
Around Lake Titicaca 115
Estrecho de Tiquina 116

The Cordilleras & Yungas 117
THE YUNGAS 119
Coroico 119
El Choro Trek 124
Yolosita 126
Yolosa 126
Takesi (Taquesi) Trek 127
Yunga Cruz Trek 129
Chulumani 129
Around Chulumani 132
Sorata 133
El Camino del Oro (Gold Digger's Trail) 136
Mapiri Trail 138
Guanay 139
Aucapata & Iskanwaya 140
Caranavi 140
CORDILLERA REAL 141
Huayna Potosí 141
Illimani 142
Condoriri Massif 143
Ancohuma 144
CORDILLERA APOLOBAMBA 144
Charazani 144
Área Natural de Manejo Integrado Nacional (Anmin) Apolobamba 146
Lagunillas to Agua Blanca (Curva to Pelechuco) Trek 147
CORDILLERA QUIMSA CRUZ 150
Activities 150
Getting There & Away 150

Southern Altiplano 151

Oruro	153
Around Oruro	162
Parque Nacional Sajama	163
Around Parque Nacional Sajama	165
SOUTHWESTERN BOLIVIA	165
Uyuni	166
Around Uyuni	173
THE SOUTHWEST CIRCUIT	173
Salar de Uyuni	174
Other Southwest Attractions	177
Tupiza	180
Around Tupiza	185

Central Highlands 188

Cochabamba	190
Parque Nacional Tunari	201
Cochabamba Valley	202
Incallajta	205
Totora	206
Mizque	206
Aiquile	207
Parque Nacional Torotoro	207
Sucre	210
Tarabuco	222
Candelaria	223
Cordillera de los Frailes	223
Potosí	227
Around Potosí	241

South Central Bolivia & the Chaco 243

SOUTH CENTRAL BOLIVIA	245
Tarija	245
San Jacinto Reservoir	253
San Lorenzo	253
El Valle de la Concepción	254
Padcaya & Chaguaya	254
Reserva Biológica Cordillera de Sama	254
Reserva Nacional de Flora y Fauna Tariquía	255
THE CHACO	256
Yacuiba	256
Villamontes	257
Parque Nacional y Área Natural de Manejo Integrado Aguaragüe	258
Reserva Privada de Patrimonio Natural de Corbalán	259
Camiri	259

Santa Cruz & Gran Chiquitania 261

Santa Cruz	263
Buena Vista	273
Parque Nacional & Área de Uso Múltiple Amboró	276
Santa Cruz to Samaipata	278
Samaipata	278
Around Samaipata	283
Vallegrande	283
Pucará	284
La Higuera	285
GRAN CHIQUITANIA	286
Jesuit Missions Circuit	287
Far Eastern Bolivia	291
Quijarro	292

Amazon Basin 294

CHAPARE REGION	297
Villa Tunari	297
Parque Nacional Carrasco	300
Puerto Villarroel	300
WESTERN BOLIVIAN AMAZON	301
Rurrenabaque	301
San Buenaventura	307
Parque Nacional Madidi	308
San Borja	308
Reserva Biosférica del Beni	309
San Ignacio de Moxos	310
EASTERN BOLIVIAN AMAZON	312
Trinidad	312
Puertos Almacén & Varador	317
Santuario Chuchini	317
Reserva de Vida Silvestre Ríos Blanco y Negro	318
Parque Nacional Noel Kempff Mercado	318
THE NORTHERN FRONTIER	323
Guayaramerín	323
Riberalta	324
Riberalta to Cobija	326
Cobija	326

Directory 328

Accommodations	328
Activities	329
Business Hours	330
Children	330
Climate Charts	330
Customs	331
Dangers & Annoyances	331
Discount Cards	331
Embassies & Consulates	331
Festivals & Events	332
Food	333
Gay & Lesbian Travelers	333
Holidays	333
Insurance	334
Internet Access	334
Legal Matters	334
Maps	334
Money	334
Photography & Video	336
Post	336
Shopping	336
Solo Travelers	337
Telephone	337
Time	339
Toilets	339
Tourist Information	339
Travelers with Disabilities	339
Visas	339
Women Travelers	340
Work & Volunteering	341

Transportation 342

GETTING THERE & AWAY	342
Entering the Country	342
Air	342
Land & River	345
GETTING AROUND	346
Air	346
Bicycle	347
Boat	347
Bus	347
Car & Motorcycle	348
Hitchhiking	349
Local Transportation	349
Train	350
Tours	350

Health 352

BEFORE YOU GO	352
Insurance	352
Medical Checklist	352
Online Resources	353
Further Reading	353
IN TRANSIT	353
Deep Vein Thrombosis	353
Jet Lag & Motion Sickness	354
IN BOLIVIA	354
Availability & Cost of Healthcare	354
Infectious Diseases	354

Travelers' Diarrhea 358
Environmental Hazards 358
Traveling with Children 359
Women's Health 360

Language 361

Glossary 368

The Authors 372

Behind the Scenes 374

Index 380

GreenDex 391

Map Legend 392

Regional Map Contents

AMAZON BASIN
p296

THE CORDILLERAS
& YUNGAS
p118

LAKE TITICACA
p98

LA PAZ
pp62–3

SANTA CRUZ &
GRAN CHIQUITANIA
p262

CENTRAL
HIGHLANDS
p189

SOUTHERN
ALTIPLANO
p152

SOUTH
CENTRAL BOLIVIA
& THE CHACO
p244

Destination Bolivia

A place of mind-boggling superlatives, landlocked Bolivia really packs a punch. The hemisphere's highest, most isolated and most rugged nation, it's among the earth's coldest, warmest and windiest spots, with some of the driest, saltiest and swampiest natural landscapes in the world. It's also a land of paradoxes: South America's poorest country, Bolivia is the richest on the continent in natural resources. But the superlatives don't end here. Over 60% of the population claim indigenous heritage, including Aymará, Quechua and Guaraní, making it South America's most indigenous country.

Bolivia's natural treasures are many and marvelous, from soaring mountain peaks and surreal salt flats to steamy jungles and wildlife-rich grasslands. Exploring the cultural aspect – the country's vibrant ancient traditions and preserved colonial cities – offers unparalleled delight. Most visitors stick to the well-worn paths of the Altiplano, but there's plenty to see and do elsewhere, from dense rainforests to snowcapped cordilleras. While Bolivia is now well and truly on the travelers' radar, it's still largely raw and undeveloped. This may be a boon for intrepid travelers, but it's a perennial source of problems for Bolivians – notable changes have been sweeping Bolivia's formidable landscapes in the last few years.

Since 2005, Bolivia has been undergoing a revolution of sorts virtually synonymous with former *cocalero* (coca grower) Evo Morales, Bolivia's first indigenous president. In January 2009, he pushed through a groundbreaking new constitution. Approved in a nationwide referendum by 67% of the population, it grants previously unheard-of rights to the country's indigenous majority and allows the president to seek a second five-year term in office.

This was stellar news for the working classes and the indigenous population of the western highlands but not for everyone in Bolivia. In fact, many middle- and upper-class Bolivians, especially in the energy-rich eastern provinces, are vehemently critical of Morales' anticapitalist stands and socialist ideologies. This opposition led to violent protests in autonomy-hungry Santa Cruz in September 2008 (with 11 dead), and the alleged attempt at presidential assassination in April 2009.

Another hot topic is the trial of former president, 'Goni' Sánchez de Lozada, who stands accused, together with 16 members of his cabinet, for 67 deaths during the 2003 protests in La Paz. The trial opened in May 2009 in absentia; Goni still lives in Maryland and the unheeded request to the US for extradition is one of several sore points (including the controversial coca) between Bolivia and the USA. Since the diplomatic talks in spring 2009, the worn ties between the two have been on the slow mend.

In addition to Bolivia's internal strife, Morales has other things on his plate, such as the management of Bolivia's so far untapped lithium reserves (the world's largest) and the election in December 2009. With his approval ratings still high, at presstime it looked like he was in for a second term. How he will manage to keep his polarized country in check remains to be seen. As the Bolivians themselves say, *vamos a ver...*

Getting Started

Travelers can no longer be smug about 'discovering' Bolivia; it's well and truly on the traveler's map for those who visit South America. Having said that, most stick to the more accessible and well-worn routes and don't give it the attention it warrants. For the more motivated and curious traveler, this means there will be plenty of stimulation if you venture off the tourist track – it's so easy to do. All travelers to Bolivia will be delighted by the multilayered, rich and varied cultures, stunning natural beauty, and unforgettable experiences and characters. Adventure nuts will also be well sated: there are plenty of opportunities for outdoor action, with a wide variety of luxury levels and travel choices on offer. The going isn't always easy, but the rewards are well worth the effort.

See climate charts (p330) for more information.

WHEN TO GO

Travelers will encounter just about every climatic zone, from stifling humidity and heat to arctic cold. Summer (November to April) is the rainy season, when overland transportation becomes difficult if not impossible in some areas. The most popular, and arguably most comfortable, time for exploring the whole country is during the dry, clear days of winter (May to October).

Most of Bolivia lies as near to the equator as Tahiti or Hawaii, but its elevation and unprotected expanses result in unpredictable weather. Bolivia's two poles of climatic extremes are Puerto Suárez with its overwhelming heat, and Uyuni with its icy, cold winds. But there are no absolutes; there are times when you can sunbathe in Uyuni and freeze in Puerto Suárez.

Summer (rainy season) in the lowlands can be utterly miserable, with mud, high humidity, biting insects and relentless tropical downpours. However, washed-out roads means there is an increase in river transportation, making this the best time to hop on a cargo boat. Winter in the Altiplano means extreme heat during the day, and freezing winds and subzero temperatures at night. The highland valleys are refuges, having a comfortable climate and little rain year round.

DON'T LEAVE HOME WITHOUT

- Checking the visa situation (p339)
- Checking travel advisory warnings (p330)
- Proof of vaccination for yellow fever (p356)
- A copy of your travel insurance policy details (p334)
- Plug adaptor for your camera battery charger (p329)
- Binoculars for wildlife watching
- Sunscreen and a hat for the clear skies at 4000m
- First aid kit (p352)
- Ear plugs for disco nights you want to sleep through
- A pack lock or other luggage security for peace of mind
- Your sense of humor – both patience and courage will be tested in queues and on bus rides

August is the most popular month of the high tourist season, which runs from late May to early September. High season sees the most reliable weather and coincides with European and North American summer holidays. It's also when most of Bolivia's major festivals take place, so many Bolivians and South Americans travel at this time as well. This can be an advantage if you are looking for people to form a travel group, but prices are generally higher than during the rest of the year.

COSTS & MONEY

Overall, prices are slightly lower here than in neighboring countries. The biggest cost in any trip to Bolivia will be transportation, especially getting there (and, to a lesser extent, getting around, as the distances involved are great).

While ultrabudget travelers can get by on less than US$17 per day, most people will spend between US$25 and US$50. Visitors who want to enjoy the best Bolivia has to offer can easily travel comfortably for US$150 a day (this would include hire of private transportation). Most prices in this book are quoted in bolivianos (B$). Avoid over-bargaining with local people for goods and services just for the sake of it. While Bolivians themselves might bargain among their friends at markets, bargaining is not actually a common cultural practice. In any case, be realistic about how much you are actually saving – the few bolivianos you might save can be worth a great deal more to the locals than to you. If you feel uncomfortable about pricing issues, ask locals for a ballpark idea of what you can expect to pay for something, including taxis. Always agree on food, accommodations and transportation prices beforehand to avoid any unpleasant situations.

HOW MUCH?

Dorm bed US$2-8

Almuerzo (set lunch) US$1-2.50

Internet per hour US$0.15-2

Hotel room (double) US$25

City taxi fare US$0.75-1.50

See also the Lonely Planet Index, inside front cover.

TRAVEL LITERATURE

Sitting at the top of the South American travelogue list is the humorous and well-written *Inca-Kola,* by Matthew Parris. It follows the meanderings of several Englishmen on a rollicking circuit throughout Peru and parts of Bolivia.

A great read, especially if you're traveling in the lowlands, is *Jungle: A Harrowing True Story of Survival* (originally published as *Back from Tuichi*) by Yossi Ghinsberg; it's about an Israeli traveler who gets lost in the Parque Nacional Madidi in the early 1980s and how he finds his way out of the jungle. Other travel books that are worth noting include *Chasing Ché: A Motorcycle Journey in Search of the Guevara Legend,* by Patrick Symmes, and *The Incredible Voyage: A Personal Odyssey,* by Tristan Jones, which follows the intrepid sailor's journey through landlocked Bolivia on Lake Titicaca and beyond. An offbeat historical character is portrayed in *Lizzie: A Victorian Lady's Amazon Adventure,* compiled by Anne Rose from the letters of Lizzie Hessel, who lived in the Bolivian Amazon settlement of Colonia Orton during the rubber boom of the early 20th century. *Exploration Fawcett,* by Percy Fawcett, is a fabulous jungle travel book from the early 20th century.

Less travelogue and more history book is the comprehensive synthesis of recent Bolivian political history, *Bolivia: Between a Rock and a Hard Place,* by Pete Good, which provides the most up-to-date commentary on Bolivia. You can find copies for sale in many travel agencies and hotels in La Paz. *The Fat Man from La Paz: Contemporary Fiction from Bolivia,* a collection of short stories edited by Rosario Santos, is a widely recommended read. For a good synopsis of Bolivian history, politics and culture, check out *Bolivia in Focus,* by Robert Werner.

Some good suggestions for books in general are available if you look on the excellent website www.libreriaboliviana.com (in Spanish).

Top PICKS

BOLIVIA

FESTIVALS & EVENTS

Thanks to their rich culture, imbibed with tradition, Bolivians are big on celebrating. There's almost always something fascinating going on, from saints' days in small villages to nationwide events. The following is a list of our favorites. See p332 for more details of festivals and events throughout the country.

- El Gran Poder (La Paz), May/June (p76)
- Carnaval (nationwide, p332; best in Oruro, p157, and Tarija, p249), February/March
- Pujllay (Tarabuco), March (p223)
- Fiesta de la Cruz (Lake Titicaca), May 3 (p104)
- Fiesta del Santo Patrono de Moxos (San Ignacio de Moxos), July 31 (p311)

- Fiesta de San Bartolomé; Chu'tillos (Potosí), August (p236)
- Fiesta del Espíritu (Potosí), June (p235)
- Fiesta de la Virgen de Urkupiña (Quillacollo), August 15–18 (Cochabamba; p197)
- International Theater Festival (Santa Cruz), April (p268)
- International Festival of Baroque Music (Santa Cruz), April (p268)

EXTREME ADVENTURES

Bolivia's rugged landscape and outgoing, knowledgeable tour guides offer innumerable thrilling adventures. Whether you want to hang off a precipice or walk on the wild side in the jungle, Bolivia's got it all.

- Hike the Mapiri trail, a demanding but superb walking trek (p138)
- Do the tandem mountain bike and raft trip from Sorata to Rurrenabaque (p135)
- Tackle the remote Quimsa Cruz range – not to be missed if you're a serious climber (p150)
- Shoot the rapids from Class II–V in the Yungas (p121)
- Float the Río Mamoré through pristine Amazon jungle (p314)

- Conquer the 6088m Huayna Potosí (p141)
- Soak in hot springs at the base of Nevado Sajama (p164)
- Go wild by heading upriver to a jungle-based community ecolodge (p306)
- Trek the Trans Cordillera route from Sorata to Huayna Potosí and Illimani (p134)
- Head to the most remote of remote national parks, Noel Kempff Mercado, for an awesome nature experience (p318)

MOUTH-WATERING EATS

There are some excellent countrywide eateries, as well as plenty of must-try local Bolivian specialties. To tantalize your taste buds, try the following five eateries and five taste sensations.

- El Huerto, Sucre – a classy garden-party eating experience (p220)
- La Estancia, Cochabamba – for lovers of meat, this is hard to beat (p198)
- Casa Típica de Camba, Santa Cruz – for an authentically Bolivian experience (p270)
- La Comedie Art-Café Restaurant, La Paz – French/Bolivian fusion cuisine with a touch of class (p82)

- Nayjama, Oruro – renowned for the local Oruro specialty, boiled sheep's head (p160)
- *Salteñas* – heavenly pastry parcels filled with chicken, beef and vegetables (p42)
- *Tamales* – those from the Tupiza market are especially scrumptious (p184)
- *Trucha* – the famed (and now farmed) Lake Titicaca trout satisfies any fish cravings (p105)

INTERNET RESOURCES

Bolivia.com (www.bolivia.com, in Spanish) Current news and cultural information.

Bolivia web (www.boliviaweb.com) Good portal with a variety of cultural and artistic links, and more.

Bolivian.com (www.bolivian.com, in Spanish) Spanish-language portal with a slew of links and some travel info.

Boliviacontact.com (www.boliviacontact.com) Thorough, searchable index of Bolivian sites.

GBT Bolivia (www.gbtbolivia.com) Solid commercial site with travel links.

Noticias Bolivianas (www.noticiasbolivianas.com, in Spanish) Comprehensive news site with links to major media.

South America Explorers Club (www.saexplorers.org) Interesting trip reports and travel bulletins.

Itineraries

CLASSIC ROUTES

CULTURE VULTURES & NATURE NOMADS Two to Three Weeks

Stimulate your senses around the streets of **La Paz** (p60) before heading by bus to **Sucre** (p210). It's worth going via **Cochabamba** (p190), a great place to eat and get your cultural fill. Sucre is *the* place to visit churches and museums, and offers fascinating short sojourns to nearby villages, famous for their craftworks; try **Tarabuco** (p222). From here, head by bus to **Potosí** (p227), a starkly beautiful Unesco World Heritage city, situated at 4070m. Visit and learn about the cooperative mines, still in operation. You can thaw your chills in the nearby Tarapaya **hot springs** (p242). Jump on an overnight bus to **Tupiza** (p180), former territory of Butch Cassidy and the Sundance Kid. Here, there's a choice of hikes and horseback or bike rides among the colored rocks of the surrounding *quebradas* (ravines). Join a tour from here to **Uyuni** (p166) and to cruise your way around a three- or four-day Southwest Circuit tour of the **Salar de Uyuni** (p174) and the **Reserva Nacional de Fauna Andina Eduardo Avaroa** (p173). From Uyuni make your way up to **Oruro** (p153), famed for its Carnaval. Alternatively, from Tupiza head to **Tarija** (p245) and its surrounds, a relaxing town and region, and Bolivia's heart of paleontology and viticulture. From Tarija you can fly or bus to La Paz; from Oruro it's an easy three-hour bus ride.

For those who love a mix of culture and action, Bolivia has it all. A visit to colonial towns, craft centers and mining regions will tantalize your traveling taste buds. You can skate across salt plains one day, and dance with the devils the next.

FROM HIGH TO LOW
Two to Three Weeks

The most popular way to enter Bolivia is to come in overland from Peru, following the exciting tourist path, with a developed tourist infrastructure. Start by enjoying the views of Lake Titicaca from white-washed **Copacabana** (p99), eating the local trout dishes and getting some R&R. After a day or two, hike to the tiny port of **Yampupata** (p109), visiting the villages along the way for a reed-boat ride. From Yampupata (or nearby villages) or Copacabana, you can take a boat across Lake Titicaca to tranquil **Isla del Sol** (p109). Walk from the island's north to south and explore the Inca ruins. Marvel at Illampu in the distance over Isla de la Luna and then head back to the mainland.

Back on the mainland, jump on a tourist bus for a trip across the stunning Cordillera Real toward **La Paz** (see p60). For a side trip to the remarkably tranquil **Sorata** (p133), catch another bus at the Sorata turn-off. Chill in this oasis or do some serious hiking or downhill mountain biking. Once in La Paz, spend a few days acclimatizing and absorbing the smells and sights in the hectic markets, fascinating museums and top-class restaurants and cafés. Take a day out to take in the ancient ruins of **Tiwanaku** (p93).

From here, the adventurous can take on the **Takesi** (p127) or **Choro Treks** (p124), or ride a bike (or bus) down the **World's Most Dangerous Road** (p75) to **Coroico** (p119) in the Yungas. Alternatively, you could fly to **Rurrenabaque** (p301) and spend a few days chilling in a hammock and exploring the surrounds (add on an extra five to seven days for this to allow for 'plane delays' and jungle visits).

The area around La Paz is jam-packed with highlights and activities, including the sun-filled Lake Titicaca, ancient Inca ruins and tranquil oases. Two weeks will give you a brief taste of adventure and relaxation, and the opportunity to experience a diverse range of environments.

ROADS LESS TRAVELED

AMAZONIAN ADVENTURE   **10 Days to Two Weeks**

A wonderful way to get off the beaten tourist track (but still enjoy an element of comfort) is to start in **Santa Cruz** (p263), a sophisticated and cosmopolitan city with a dreamy (sometimes steamy) climate and tropical atmosphere. From here, fly or catch the overnight bus to **Trinidad** (p312), a sleepy town with a pretty plaza. After whirling around on a motorcycle, take a side trip to **Puerto Varador** (p317) for a local fish meal, a visit to a museum or two and a much-needed siesta or three – it gets hot. A three-hour bus ride will take you to the Jesuit mission village of **San Ignacio de Moxos** (p310) – plan your trip around the town's colorful, not-to-be-missed festival in July. Take a side trip into **Reserva Biosférica del Beni** (p309) and then make the long slog via **San Borja** (p308) to **Rurrenabaque** (p301), hammock country, from where you can set out for a couple of days on a jungle or pampas tour. Alternatively, get your jungle fill at the **San Miguel del Bala** (p307) ecoresort, just upriver from Rurrenabaque. Whatever you do, don't miss a trip to **Madidi National Park** (p308), a wild, little-trodden utopia and a must for wildlife-watchers. Finally, leave enough time to stay in the highly regarded, community-run **Chalalán Ecolodge** (p306).

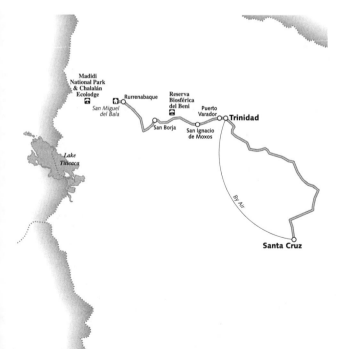

The sights and sounds of the jungle make for a once-in-a-lifetime experience. Start sophisticated and go wild, with a tour from the city to the remote reserves. After a few rough but adventurous trips, you can laze away the days in a hammock in tropical temperatures.

TAILORED TRIPS

NATIONAL PARKS & RESERVES

Bolivia has protected 18% of its territory in 22 national parks and re-serves. From **Reserva Biológica Cordillera de Sama's** (p254) slice of the Al-tiplano, to the inundated savannas of the remote, but spectacular, **Parque Nacional Noel Kempff Mercado** (p318), flora and fauna fans will be in their element. Although some of these protected areas can be difficult to access, the following places are worth every ounce of the effort they take to reach.

Parque Nacional Sajama (p163) with its vicuñas, soaring volcanoes (including Bolivia's highest peak) and heavenly hot springs was Bolivia's first reserve. **Parque Nacional Madidi** (p308) is possibly now the best known,

encompassing one of the most biodiverse habitats in the world and featuring numerous protected species.

Parque Nacional Carrasco (p300) and **Parque Nacional Tunari** (p201) are two of the more accessible, middle-altitude cloud forests, while **Parque Nacional y Área de Uso Múltiple Amboró** (p276) is a prime place for bird-watching.

Área Natural de Manejo Integrado Nacional Apolobamba (p146) is one of the least visited national parks, while the most popular, **Reserva Nacional de Fauna Andina Eduardo Avaroa** (p173), receives tens of thousands of visitors per year and is part of the Southwest Circuit.

PLANES, TRAINS & CAMIONES

In Bolivia, getting there is an important part of the travel experience, and often half the fun! The means of transportation can be the highlight (okay, and sometimes lowlight) of your adventure.

From the sluggish **Trans-Chiquitano train** (p292) to the most remote **Río Mamoré river journeys** (p314), you're spoiled for choice when it comes to mobility options.

Foolhardy mountain-bike adventurers shouldn't pass up the chance to conquer the **World's Most Dangerous Road** (p75) or settle instead for single-track pistes around **La Paz** (p60), **Sorata** (p133) and **Sucre** (p210). **Flying** (p322) in a small plane into remote Parque Nacional Noel Kempff Mercado will satisfy the most snap-happy traveler. In Trinidad, piling yourself and your gear on to a chauffeured **moto-taxi** (p315) is as much fun as renting one independently.

Several days of bumping around the **Southwest Circuit** (p173; including the Salar de Uyuni) by 4WD is worth it for the scenery alone. Romantic reed-boat journeys or hydrofoil cruises on **Lake Titicaca** (p97) provide a tranquil change of pace. Or, for those wanting a rush, you can **raft** (p297) into the Amazon Basin.

Let's not forget our humble feet, the best form of mobility in Bolivia. Awe-inspiring trekking includes via Inca trails to the **Yunga Cruz trek** (p129). As for the inevitable travel on buses or *camiones* (flatbed trucks)? This can be as adrenaline-inducing as anything.

History

Tangible history lives on in most of Bolivia's best-known destinations. From pre-Hispanic archaeological sites and living indigenous traditions to colonial architecture and the more recent headline-making political upheaval, the country's history reflects the influences that have shaped South America as a whole.

For more information on the fascinating Tiwanaku site, read Alan Kolata's *A Valley of Spirits* (Wiley & Sons, 1996).

The great Altiplano (which literally means high plateau), the largest expanse of arable land in the Andes, extends from present-day Bolivia into southern Peru, northwestern Argentina and northern Chile. While it's been inhabited for thousands of years, the region's early cultures were shaped by the imperial designs of two major forces: the Tiwanaku culture of Bolivia and the Inca of Peru.

Most archaeologists define the prehistory of the Central Andes in terms of 'horizons' – Early, Middle and Late – each of which was characterized by distinct architectural and artistic trends. Cultural interchanges between the early Andean peoples occurred mostly through trade, usually between nomadic tribes or as a result of the diplomatic expansionist activities of powerful and well-organized societies. These interchanges resulted in the Andes' emergence as the cradle of South America's highest cultural achievements.

During the initial settlement of the Andes, from the arrival of nomads, probably from Siberia, until about 1400 BC, villages and ceremonial centers were established, and trade emerged between coastal fishing communities and farming villages of the highlands.

EARLY & MIDDLE HORIZONS

The so-called Early Horizon (1400–400 BC) was an era of architectural innovation and activity, most evident in the ruins of Chavín de Huantar, on the eastern slopes of the Andes in Peru. Chavín influences resounded far and wide, even after the decline of Chavín society, and spilled over into the Early Middle Horizon (400 BC–AD 500).

The Middle Horizon (AD 500–900) was marked by the imperial expansion of the Tiwanaku and Huari (of the Ayacucho Valley of present-day Peru) cultures. The Tiwanakans produced technically advanced work, most notably the city itself. They created impressive ceramics, gilded ornamentation, engraved pillars and slabs with calendar markings and designs representing their bearded white leader and deity, Viracocha.

By 700 BC, Tiwanaku had developed into a thriving civilization. Considered as advanced as ancient Egypt in many respects, it had an extensive system of roads, irrigation canals and agricultural terraces. This system is

TIMELINE

1400 BC–AD 400	500–900	1000–1200
The first peoples settled in the Bolivian Altiplano, followed by a wave of Aymará Indians who swept across the Andes from central Peru into Alto Perú (Bolivia), driving out most of the Altiplano's original settlers.	The ceremonial center of Tiwanaku, on the shores of Lake Titicaca, grew and developed into the religious and political capital of the Alto Peruvian Altiplano.	Tiwanaku's power wanes, the population disperses and the ceremonial site is largely abandoned due to mysterious reasons – possibly climate change (drought), an earthquake or foreign invasion.

believed to have supported a population of tens of thousands of people in the 83-sq-km Tiwanaku Valley.

Tiwanaku was inhabited from 1500 BC until AD 1200, but its power lasted only from the 6th century BC to the 9th century AD. One speculation is that Tiwanaku was uprooted by a drop in Lake Titicaca's water level, which left the lakeside settlement far from shore. Another theory postulates that it was attacked and its population massacred by the warlike Kollas (also known as the Aymará) from the west. When the Spanish arrived, they were told an Inca legend about a battle between the Kollas and 'bearded white men' on an island in Lake Titicaca. These men were presumably Tiwanakans, only a few of whom were able to escape. Some researchers believe that the displaced survivors migrated southward and developed into the Chipaya people of the western Oruro department.

Today the remains of the city lie on the plain between La Paz and the southern shore of Lake Titicaca, and collections of Tiwanaku relics can be seen in several Bolivian museums. For further information, see p93.

LATE HORIZON – THE INCA

The period between 900 and 1475 is known as the Late Intermediate Horizon. Little is known about this era apart from the fact that it was marked by a clutch of regional states, each one with a distinct culture. The Late Horizon (1476–1534), in contrast, marked the zenith of Inca civilization. The Inca, the last of South America's indigenous conquerors, arrived shortly after the fall of Tiwanaku. They pushed their empire from its seat of power in Cuzco (Peru) eastward into present-day Bolivia, southward to the northern reaches of modern Argentina and Chile, and northward through present-day Ecuador and southern Colombia.

The Inca inhabited the Cuzco region from the 12th century and believed they were led by descendents of the Sun God. The 17th-century Spanish chronicler Fernando Montesinos believed that the Inca were more likely descended from a lineage of Tiwanaku sages.

Renowned for their great stone cities and skill in working with gold and silver, the Inca also set up a hierarchy of governmental and agricultural overseers, a viable social welfare scheme and a complex road network and communication system that defied the difficult terrain of their far-flung empire.

Around 1440 the Inca started to expand their political boundaries. The eighth Inca, Viracocha (not to be confused with the Tiwanaku leader/deity of the same name), believed the mandate from the Sun God was not just to conquer, plunder and enslave, but to organize defeated tribes and absorb them into the realm of the benevolent Sun God. The Kollas (Bolivians) living around the Tiwanaku site were essentially absorbed by the Inca and their religion was supplanted; they were permitted to keep their language and social traditions.

It is believed that between 1200 and 1475 the Incas used the essential oil of the coca plant to remove brain tumors.

1440s	1520s	1531
The Inca, based in Cuzco, Peru, extend their political boundaries by pushing eastward into Kollasuyo (present-day Bolivia) and assimilating local tribes by imposing taxation, religion and their own Quechua language.	Internal rivalries herald the beginning of the end for the Inca state, a political force for less than a century. In a brief civil war, Atahualpa defeats his half brother, Huáscar, and assumes the emperor's throne.	The Spanish, led by conquistador Francisco Pizarro, arrive in Ecuador. After a bitter fight with the Incas, they claim Alto Perú, which would later become Bolivia.

By the late 1520s internal rivalries began to take their toll on the empire, marking the beginning of the end of the Inca political state, having thrived for less than a century. In a brief civil war over the division of lands, Atahualpa, the true Inca emperor's half-brother, imprisoned the emperor and assumed the throne himself.

SPANISH CONQUEST

The arrival of the Spanish in Ecuador in 1531 was the ultimate blow to the Inca. Within a year, Francisco Pizarro, Diego de Almagro and their bands of conquistadores arrived in Cuzco. Atahualpa, while still the emperor, was not considered the true heir of the Sun God. The Spanish were also aided by the Inca belief that the bearded white men had been sent by the great Viracocha Inca as revenge for Atahualpa's breach of established protocol. In fear, Atahualpa ordered the murder of the real king, which not only ended the bloodline of the Inca dynasty but brought shame on the family and dissolved the psychological power grip of the Inca hierarchy. Within two years the government was conquered, the empire dissolved and the invaders had divided the Inca lands and booty between the two leaders of the Spanish forces.

Alto Perú (which later became Bolivia) fell briefly into the possession of Diego de Almagro, who was assassinated in 1538. Three years later, Pizarro suffered the same fate at the hands of mutinous subordinates. But this didn't deter the Spanish, who kept exploring and settling their newly conquered land. In 1538 La Plata (later known as Sucre) was founded as the Spanish capital of the Charcas region.

The Legacy of Potosí

By the time Diego Huallpa revealed his earth-shattering discovery of silver at Cerro Rico in Potosí in 1544, Spanish conquerors had already firmly implanted their language, religion and customs on the remnants of Atahualpa's empire.

Spanish Potosí, or the 'Villa Imperial de Carlos V,' was officially founded in 1545 and quickly grew to have a population of 160,000, making it the largest city in the western hemisphere. The Potosí mine also became the world's most prolific, and the silver extracted from it underwrote Spain's economy, particularly the extravagance of its monarchy, for at least two centuries.

Atrocious conditions in the mines of Potosí guaranteed a short life span for the local indigenous conscripts and African slaves who were herded into work gangs. Those not actually worked to death or killed in accidents succumbed to pulmonary silicosis within a few years. Africans who survived migrated to the more amenable climes of the Yungas northeast of La Paz, and developed into an Aymará-speaking minority (see p131). The indigenous peoples became tenant farmers and were

History buffs can get stuck into *A Concise History of Bolivia* by Herbert S Klein (Columbia University Press, 2003).

1544	1545	1809
The wandering Indian Diego Huallpa discovers silver in Potosí's Cerro Rico (Rich Mountain), which leads to the development of the world's most prolific silver mine.	Potosí is founded as a mining town but, due to the incredible wealth of its silver mine, it grows rapidly and gains a mint, 86 churches and a population approaching 200,000 by 1672.	In May 1809, Bolivia proclaims its independence from Spain by establishing the first juntas (autonomist governments); the first in Chuquisaca (later renamed Sucre) and then in La Paz.

required to supply their Spanish lords with food and labor in exchange for subsistence-sized plots of land.

Coca, ace at numbing nerves and once the exclusive privilege of Inca nobles, was introduced among the general populace in order to keep people working without complaint (see p298).

INDEPENDENCE

The first coins in the Americas were minted in Potosí.

By May 1809, Spanish America's first independence movement – sparked by the criollos (people of Spanish ancestry born in the Americas) and mestizos (people of both indigenous and Spanish ancestry) – had gained momentum, and was well underway in Chuquisaca (later renamed Sucre), with other cities quick to follow suit. By the early 1820s, General Simón Bolívar had succeeded in liberating both Venezuela and Colombia from Spanish domination. In 1822 he dispatched Mariscal (Major General) Antonio José de Sucre to Ecuador to defeat the Royalists at the battle of Pichincha. In 1824, after years of guerrilla action against the Spanish and the victories of Bolívar and Sucre in the battles of Junín (August 6) and Ayacucho (December 9), Peru won its independence.

Sucre then incited a declaration of independence from Alto Perú and, in 1825, the new Republic of Bolivia was born. Bolívar and Sucre served as Bolivia's first and second presidents but, after a brief attempt by the third president, Andrés Santa Cruz, to form a confederation with Peru, things began to go awry. One military junta after another usurped power from its predecessor, setting a pattern of political strife that haunts the nation to this day.

Few of Bolivia's 192 governments to date have remained in power long enough to have much intentional effect.

SHRINKING TERRITORY

At the time of independence Bolivia's boundaries encompassed well over 2 million sq km. Its neighbors soon moved to acquire its territory though, removing coastal access and much of the area covered by its ancient Amazonian rubber trees.

The coastal loss occurred during the War of the Pacific, fought against Chile between 1879 and 1884. Many Bolivians believe that Chile stole the Atacama Desert's copper- and nitrate-rich sands and 850km of coastline from Peru and Bolivia by invading during Carnaval. Chile did attempt to compensate for the loss by building a railroad from La Paz to the ocean and allowing Bolivia free port privileges in Antofagasta, but Bolivians have never forgotten this devastating *enclaustramiento* (landlocked status).

The next major loss was in 1903 during the rubber boom when Brazil hacked away at Bolivia's inland expanse. Brazil and Bolivia had both been ransacking the forests of the Acre territory – it was so rich in rubber trees that Brazil engineered a dispute over sovereignty and sent

1822	1825	1865–71
After a series of battles, General Simón Bolívar succeeds in liberating Venezuela, Ecuador, Colombia and Panama. He is made president of a short-lived new nation, Gran Colombia (1819–31).	As a result of General Sucre inciting a declaration of independence for Alto Perú, the new Republic of Bolivia is born, loosely modeled on the US, with legislative, executive and judicial branches of government.	General Mariano Melgarejo once drunkenly set his army off on an overland march to aid France at the outset of the Franco-Prussian War. A sudden downpour made him sober up and abandon the project.

in its army. Brazil then convinced the Acre region to secede from the Bolivian republic, and promptly annexed it.

There were two separate territory losses to Argentina. First, Argentina annexed a large slice of the Chaco in 1862. Then, in 1883, the territory of Puna de Atacama also went to Argentina. It had been offered to both Chile and Argentina, the former in exchange for return of the Litoral, the latter in exchange for clarification over Bolivia's ownership of Tarija.

After losing the War of the Pacific, Bolivia was desperate to have the Chaco, an inhospitable region beneath which rich oilfields were mooted to lie, as an outlet to the Atlantic via the Río Paraguay. Between 1932 and 1935, a particularly brutal war was waged between Bolivia and Paraguay over the disputed territory (more than 80,000 lives were lost). Though no decisive victory was reached, both nations had grown weary of fighting, and peace negotiations in 1938 awarded most of the disputed territory to Paraguay.

> The Chaco War (1932–35) between Bolivia and Paraguay inspired several books, including *Aluvión de fuego* (1935) by Oscar Cerruto, *Sangre de mestizos* (1936) by Augusto Céspedes and *Laguna* (1938) by Costa du Rels.

CONTINUING POLITICAL STRIFE

During the 20th century wealthy tin barons and landowners controlled Bolivian farming and mining interests, while the peasantry was relegated to a feudal system of peonage known as *pongaje*. The beating Bolivia took in the Chaco War made way for reformist associations, civil unrest among the *cholos* (indigenous people who dress traditionally but live in cities) and a series of coups by reform-minded military leaders.

The most significant development was the emergence of the Movimiento Nacionalista Revolucionario (MNR) political party. They united the masses behind the common cause of popular reform, sparking friction between peasant miners and absentee tin bosses. The miners' complaints against outrageous working conditions, pitifully low pay and the export of profits to Europe raised the political consciousness of all Bolivian workers. Under the leadership of Víctor Paz Estenssoro (commonly referred to as Víctor Paz), the MNR prevailed in the 1951 elections, but a last-minute military coup prevented it from actually taking power. What ensued was a period of serious combat, which ended with the defeat of the military and Paz Estensorro's rise to power. He immediately nationalized mines, evicted the tin barons, put an end to *pongaje* and set up Comibol (Corporación Minera de Bolivia), the state entity in charge of mining interests.

> In 1935, just over a century after Bolivia's independence, Bolivia had lost more than half of its territory.

The miners and peasants felt they were being represented, enabling the MNR to stay in power for 12 years under various leaders. But even with US support, the MNR was unable to raise the standard of living or increase food production substantially. Its effectiveness and popularity ground to a halt and Víctor Paz Estenssoro was forced to become increasingly autocratic; in 1964 his government was overthrown by a military junta headed by General René Barrientos Ortuño.

1879–84	1903	1932
The War of the Pacific, in which Bolivia loses her coastline to Chile, is a sore point to this day that the government uses as a rallying cry to unite the people behind a common cause.	During the rubber boom, Brazil annexes the remote Acre area, which stretched from Bolivia's present Amazonian borders to halfway up Peru's eastern border. Brazil's promise to build a railroad into Bolivia was never kept.	Bolivia enters the Chaco War against Paraguay over a border dispute for control of the potentially huge deposits of oil eyed by rival foreign oil companies.

Five years later Barrientos died in a helicopter accident and a series of coups, military dictators and juntas followed. Right-wing coalition leader General Hugo Banzer Suárez eventually took over in 1971 and served a turbulent term through 1978, punctuated by reactionary extremism and human-rights abuses.

The next three years were filled with failed elections, appointed presidents, military coups and hideous regimes, and a rash of tortures, arrests and disappearances, as well as a marked increase in cocaine production and trafficking.

Keen Ché Guevara fans should definitely grab a copy of *Ché Guevara: a Revolutionary Life* (Bantam Press, 1997).

In 1982 Congress elected Hernán Siles Zuazo, the civilian left-wing leader of the Communist-supported Movimiento de la Izquierda Revolucionaria (MIR). His term was beleaguered with labor disputes, ruthless government spending and huge monetary devaluation, resulting in a truly staggering inflation rate that at one point reached 35,000% annually.

When Siles Zuazo gave up after three years and called general elections, Víctor Paz Estenssoro returned to politics to become president for the fourth time. He immediately enacted harsh measures to revive the shattered economy: he ousted labor unions, removed government restrictions on internal trade, slashed the government deficit, imposed a wage freeze, eliminated price subsidies, laid off workers at inefficient government-owned companies, allowed the peso to float against the US dollar and deployed armed forces to keep the peace.

Inflation was curtailed within weeks, but spiraling unemployment, especially in the poor Altiplano mining areas, caused enormous suffering and threatened the government's stability. Throughout his term, however, Paz Estenssoro remained committed to programs that would return the government mines to private cooperatives and develop the largely uninhabited lowland regions. To encourage the settlement of the Amazon, he promoted road building (with Japanese aid) in the wilderness and opened up vast indigenous lands and pristine rainforest to logging interests.

CHAOS PREVAILS

Free from the threat of military intervention, the 1989 presidential elections were characterized mostly by apathy. Hugo Banzer Suárez of the Acción Democrática Nacionalista (ADN) resurfaced, the MIR nominated Jaime Paz Zamora and the MNR put forth mining company president and economic reformist Gonzalo Sánchez de Lozada ('Goni'). Although Banzer and Sánchez were placed ahead of Paz Zamora, no candidate received a majority, so it was left to the National Congress to select a winner. Congress selected Paz Zamora as the new president (meanwhile, rivals Banzer and Paz Zamora formed a coalition). The Paz Zamora presidency, while generally peaceful and fairly successful, introduced no major changes to the political climate.

1935	1942	1952
A ceasefire in the Chaco War is negotiated on June 10, 1335, at which time Paraguay controls much of the region. This is ratified by a 1938 truce, awarding Paraguay three quarters of the Chaco.	Hundreds of laborers who had formed a trade union are shot down by government troops at a Catavi tin-mining complex while striking for better wages and conditions.	A military coup provokes a popular armed revolt by the miners, known as the April Revolution. After heavy fighting, the military is defeated and Víctor Paz Estenssoro takes power.

In the 1993 election, Sánchez was elected. Sánchez's Aymará running mate, Victor Hugo Cárdenas, appealed to *cholos* and *campesinos* (subsistence farmers), while European urbanites embraced Sánchez's free-market economic policies. This administration attacked corruption and began implementing *capitalización* by opening up state-owned companies and mining interests to overseas investment. Officials hoped privatization would stabilize and streamline companies, making them profitable. Overseas investors in formerly state-owned companies received 49% equity, total voting control, license to operate in Bolivia and up to 49% of the profits. The remaining 51% of the shares were distributed to Bolivians as pensions and through Participación Popular, a program meant to channel spending away from cities and into rural schools, clinics and other local infrastructure.

In late 1995, reform issues were overshadowed by violence and unrest surrounding US-directed coca eradication in the Chapare. Even the establishment of a Spanish-managed private pension scheme and a subsequent payment of US$248 to each Bolivian pensioner – with the promise of future payments from the less-than-fluid plan – did little to boost the administration's popularity.

In 1997 voters, upset by the reforms, cast 22.5% of the ballot in favor of comeback king and former dictator General Hugo Banzer Suárez. Congress deemed Banzer the victor, and he was sworn in on August 6 to a five-year term, up from four by a 1996 constitutional amendment.

In the late 1990s Banzer faced swelling public discontent with his coca eradication measures and widespread corruption, and unrest in response to increasing gas prices, a serious water shortage and economic downturn in the department of Cochabamba. In 2000, public protests over increasing gas prices versus government-controlled transportation fares resulted in the blockade of the Yungas Highway for several weeks, and several issues inspired marches, demonstrations and occasional violence, which sporadically halted all traffic (in some cases even vendor and pedestrian traffic) in La Paz and other cities.

Following a successful campaign advised by a team of US political consultants that he hired, 'Goni' Sánchez de Lozada was appointed president in August 2002. In February 2003 his International Monetary Fund (IMF)-endorsed economic policies, including steep tax hikes and the exportation of gas out of Bolivia for processing elsewhere, were met with widespread demonstrations and the loss of 67 lives during a police lockdown in La Paz. In October 2003, Goni resigned amidst massive popular protests and fled back to the States, where he lives today in Maryland. Bolivia's government accused Goni and 16 members of his cabinet for the deaths caused by the military crackdown in 2003. In 2008 the request for extradition was formally served to the US government but has so far been unheeded. The trial opened in La Paz in May 2009 in absentia, with only eight of 17 accused politicians in attendance.

Goni was the first Bolivian president to have introduced 'shock therapy', an economic theory introduced by Harvard economist Jeffrey Sachs used to drastically cut hyperinflation in a short period of time.

1964	**1967**	**1978**
After trying and failing for twelve years to raise the standard of living and increase food production, the MNR's popularity wanes, and Victor Paz' government is finally forced out by a military junta.	Argentine revolutionary Ernesto 'Ché' Guevara, having failed to foment a peasant revolt in Bolivia, is executed by a US-backed military squad in the hamlet of La Higuera.	Hugo Banzer Suárez schedules general elections and loses. He ignores the results and accuses the opposition of ballot-box tampering but is forced to step down in a coup led by General Juan Pereda Asbún.

The earliest references to the use of the coca leaf is found in *chulpas* (mummies) in north Peru (2500–1800 BC).

After Goni's resignation, his vice president and respected historian Carlos Mesa automatically took office. Although the unrest continued, Mesa remained a popular leader during his first two years as president. In 2004 he held a referendum on the future of Bolivia's natural gas reserves – Bolivians overwhelmingly advocated Mesa's proposals to exert more control over the foreign-owned gas companies. But in 2005, rising fuel prices led to major protests. Tens of thousands of Bolivians took to the streets. Mesa resigned in June 2005, and Supreme Court Judge Eduardo Rodriguez took over as interim president.

THE MORALES ERA

In December 2005, Bolivians elected their country's first indigenous president. Former llama herder and *cocalero* (coca grower) activist Juan Evo Morales Ayma (more commonly known as Evo Morales, or endear-

---

THE COCA CONTROVERSY

Born to a poor indigenous family in the outskirts of Oruro, Evo Morales picked a political battle that is dear to the Aymará and Quechua – coca cultivation. The culture clash is simple: the West sees coca as a raw product in the manufacturing of an addictive drug; the indigenous peoples of the Andes view it as a sacred crop that has sustained them for centuries in its unprocessed form. The government estimates that as many as 1.2 million kilos of coca leaf are consumed monthly in Bolivia for traditional uses such as chewing the leaf, drinking it in *mate* and using it in religious ceremonies. In fact, its mild alkaloids are said to provide an essential barrier against altitude sickness and fatigue for farm workers and miners in the highlands.

Morales' hard-line stance against the 1990s' US-led Plan Dignidad (a coca eradication program) won him some political battle scars; intransigence on both sides led to the loss of many lives, *cocaleros* (coca growers) and soldiers alike, in the Chapare region. Morales continues to claim that the West should confront the demand for cocaine in the developed world (at his first address to the UN, he held up a coca leaf, remarking that it was green, not white).

In the new constitution, Morales declared coca an intrinsic part of Bolivia's heritage and Andean culture. Following the expulsion of the US ambassador in September 2008, the US State Department placed Bolivia on its 'drug blacklist' for their unwillingness to cooperate on the drug trafficking problem. In retaliation, Morales suspended the activities of the US Drug Enforcement Agency in Bolivia. At a UN meeting in March 2009, he announced that Bolivia would start the process to remove the coca leaf from the 1961 Single Convention that prohibits the traditional chewing of coca leaf. Evo has been hard at work attempting to establish a new industry of legal coca-based by-products such as tea, medicines and cosmetics, in hopes of creating a growing market and boosting the income of coca growers. Some see this as opting out of the war on drugs. But, using the motto 'coca yes, cocaine no', he has cracked down on illegal drugs; in April 2009, a new anti-corruption unit was established in Bolivia mainly to fight drug trafficking and related crime.

For more on coca, see p298.

1982	1985	1987
The Bolivian Congress appointed a woman, Lidia Gueilar, as interim president during the tumultuous period of several presidential elections and coups. The rule of Bolivia's first woman president was brief.	Víctor Paz Estenssoro's New Economic Policy promotes spending cuts and privatization, resulting in strikes and protests by the miners' union; massive unemployment follows the crash of the price of tin.	The USA begins sending Drug Enforcement Administration anti-coca squadrons into the Beni and Chapare regions, where coca has generated substantial income for the growers and traffickers.

ingly, Evo) of Movimiento al Socialismo (MAS) won nearly 54% of the vote, having promised to alter the traditional political class and to empower the nation's poor (mainly indigenous) majority. After the election, Morales quickly grabbed the lefty spotlight, touring the world and meeting with Venezuela's Hugo Chávez, Cuba's Fidel Castro, Brazil's Lula de Silva and members of South Africa's African National Congress. Symbolically, on May Day 2006, he nationalized Bolivia's natural gas reserves – the second largest in South America, after Venezuela's – and raised taxes on energy investors in a move that would consolidate Bolivian resources in Bolivian hands.

In July 2006, Morales formed a National Constituent Assembly to set about rewriting the country's constitution. The assembly sat for the first time on August 6, 2006 (Bolivia's Independence Day). In January 2009, the new socially-focused constitution was approved by 67% of voters in a nationwide referendum. The first constitution in Bolivia approved by popular vote, it gave greater power to the country's indigenous majority and allowed Morales to seek a second five-year term. For the first time in Bolivia's history, the 36 formerly marginalised groups were granted the right to territory, language and community justice. Echoing the land reform bill passed by the Senate in November 2006, the constitution also limited the size of landholdings in order to redistribute Bolivia's land from large ranchers and landowners to poor indigenous farmers, and to promote social and economic equality.

> Tune into *Our Brand in Crisis* (2005), Rachel Boynton's documentary about a team of high-profile US political consultants hired to market the 2002 election campaign of Gonzalo 'Goni' Sánchez de Lozada.

BOLIVIA SPLITS OVER EVO

Having redefined indigenous identity and empowered the underprivileged majority in a land where '*Indio*' (Indian) is still a common insult, Evo has near-universal support among the indigenous people of Bolivia. But his radical social changes aren't without resistance. In the eastern part of the country, in the four departments known as La Media Luna (Half Moon, for their geographic shape), where much of the natural resources lie, a strong right-wing opposition has been standing up to Morales, often accusing him of being an ethnocentric despot. Since 2006, there have been a series of violent protests sweeping the four lowland provinces – these culminated with street battles in Santa Cruz in September 2008, killing 11 people and wounding 50 in a clash between anti-government activists and the military troops sent in to guard natural gas pipelines to ensure continued export to Brazil and Argentina. Sparked by Evo's attempts to redirect gas revenues of the energy-rich eastern provinces to the poor highlands, the conflict also rests on the other sore point for La Media Luna – the new constitution, particularly for its land reform and for allowing Morales to run for re-election.

The polarization in Bolivia is very real, with the province of Santa Cruz constantly requesting more autonomy and threatening to secede from the

1989	1993	1995
With no candidate winning a majority in the presidential election, the National Congress is left to select Jaime Paz Zamora of the MIR as the 73rd President of Bolivia.	Gonzalo Sánchez is elected president on a centre-left free-marketeering ticket and, with his government, proceeds to introduce landmark social, economic and constitutional reforms.	Labor grievances over the new privatization policies result in a 90-day state-of-siege declaration and the arrest of 374 labor leaders. By mid-year, measures were relaxed.

BOLIVIA: SET TO BECOME THE SAUDI ARABIA OF LITHIUM?

Bolivia holds the key to an environmentally sustainable future – 50% of the world's lithium deposits (about 5.4 million tonnes), a mineral essential for hybrid and electric vehicles, is found in the salt flats of Uyuni. Unlike metals such as lead, nickel and cobalt traditionally used in batteries, lithium is energy efficient and quickly rechargeable. Lithium-ion batteries already power mobile phones, digital cameras and laptops.

Several major players in the global auto industry have their eyes set on this untapped potential. And while Bolivia's previous governments would have happily sold off its lithium reserves to foreign companies, it's not going to happen under Evo Morales. He takes a firm stand on this topic: Bolivia's natural bounty will not be subject to foreign exploitation again, like the plundering that occurred with silver, gold and tin. Instead, the idea is to maximize the benefits for Bolivian people. Faithful to his anti-capitalist rhetoric, he has continually rejected bids from international mining companies and, so far, successfully warded off outside involvement in this precious mineral. With an investment of US$6 million, Comibol, the state agency that oversees mining projects, is currently constructing a pilot plant in the salt flats, slated to produce about 1.2 kilotonnes per year at first, to be increased to 30 kilotonnes by 2012.

Car manufacturers predict that the world will need 500 kilotonnes per year to service a niche market, with that figure to rise if electric cars become the norm. If the demand for eco-vehicles does rise, the world's supply of lithium will be outstripped by 2015. Critics claim that Bolivia doesn't have the technology to extract lithium quickly and efficiently enough, which may thwart its plans to become the Saudi Arabia of lithium. State control over the lithium reserves may be a good social move in order to lift Bolivians out of poverty and keep the wealth inside the country. Whether it's a practical move remains to be seen.

western highlands. However, Morales has been surprisingly successful in pushing his initiatives through despite the fervent opposition. Following the September 2008 protests, he even expelled the US ambassador, Philip S Goldberg, reproaching him for fuelling the right-wing separatists.

In April 2009, more opposition drama ensued as Morales and his ideological allies went on a five-day hunger strike to protest the opposition minority in the Senate that tried to sabotage the new constitution by reducing the number of indigenous seats in the Assembly. Despite the opposition leaders calling this hunger strike 'political blackmail', the Congress did pass the law guaranteeing 14 congressional seats and allowing expatriates the right to vote in the general elections in December 2009. Soon after, an elite police force shot dead three men in Santa Cruz who reportedly tried to assassinate Morales. He later implied that this thwarted murder plot was linked to the recent vote in Congress and his expulsion of the American ambassador.

While popular with the traditionally oppressed 'little people' who have been in the shadows throughout Bolivia's history, Morales has seriously alienated the hard-working businessmen and industrialists

2000	2002–03	2005
The World Bank forces the Bolivian government to sell Cochabamba's water utility to the private US-company Bechtel. When the water rate is hiked, local people take to the streets and Bechtel is forced out.	Gonzalo Sánchez de Lozada ('Goni') wins the presidency with only 22.5% of the vote. After his unpopular economic policies lead to massive protests and over 60 deaths, he resigns in October 2003.	After a string of more than 70 presidents throughout its tumultuous history, Bolivia elects the country's first indigenous leader, Evo Morales, who wins with nearly 54% of the vote.

of the eastern provinces. The country has perhaps never been as split along economic, cultural and ethnic lines. Some claim that Morales has disguised authoritarian tactics under the name of rectifying historic injustice. Furthermore, economists argue that the government's socialist-flavored nationalizations have scared off potential investors from abroad. Morales has also managed to antagonize the US with his radical moves and his ties with the leftist governments of Venezuela and Cuba. In spring 2009, the US and Bolivia started to mend the frayed diplomatic ties, a process fraught with controversial issues such as the 'war on drugs' (see p28) and Goni's extradition.

While Morales undoubtedly sparked off a cultural and social revolution, he in turn estranged a solid chunk of his country's population. Bolivia continues to struggle as one of South America's poorest countries, despite the nationalization policies intended to bring about an economic boost. The December 2009 election was, at presstime, predicted to bring an easy victory for Evo but, even so, what will happen with the country's deep internal divide and its continued economic strife? Even his own people's patience may be limited after centuries of ineffectual rule.

A worthwhile read for its articles on history, culture and the environment (less useful for the practical details, which are now out of date) is Peter McFadden's *An Insider's Guide to Bolivia*.

2006	2008	2009
On August 6, Bolivia's Independence Day, the Morales-created National Constituent Assembly, sits for the first time. It stated aim is to allow Bolivia's marginalized communities to design a new constitution for their nation.	Right-wing factions' opposition to Morales' re-nationalization of Bolivian gas wealth culminates in pitched street battles in Santa Cruz that leave 11 dead and more than 50 wounded.	The new constitution was approved in a nationwide referendum by more than 60% support, giving more rights to the majority indigenous population and allowing Morales to run for second term.

The Culture

THE NATIONAL PSYCHE

In Bolivia, attitude depends on climate and altitude. *Cambas* (lowlanders) and *kollas* (highlanders) enjoy expounding on what makes them different (ie better) than the other. Lowlanders are said to be warmer, more casual and more generous to strangers; highlanders are supposedly harder working but less open-minded. While the jesting used to be good-natured, regional tensions have increased over the past few years, with Santa Cruz's threats of succession constantly in the news.

Over the last 30 years, the Aymará (a cultural group of highlanders and descendents of the Tiwanaku empire) in particular have increasingly embraced their ethnicity with pride and their status has increased with economic success, mostly in the urban areas. In La Paz, there has been a resurgence of traditional Aymará dress among some younger women (see p37 for more on this phenomenon). So strong are the trends that the annual contest to elect a Miss Cholita Paceña is attracting contestants who have ditched their designer jeans in favor of new-found *cholita* fashions and status. The image of the *chola* (a city-dwelling Aymará woman who wears traditional dress; *'cholita'* is sometimes considered more polite) is altering dramatically. The traditional image of a market trader is rapidly being superseded by that of a businesswoman or politician (there are even *cholas* in government); her attitudes and behavior are said to represent the contemporary Aymará bourgeoisie. See p36 for more on Bolivian women.

Bolivian identity and national psyche have been in a state of flux over the last few years. Thanks in part to Bolivia's first indigenous president, Evo Morales, many Bolivians have been 'redefining' and even questioning what it means to be Bolivian. From the beginning, Morales vigorously stressed that Bolivian identity was based on an individual's ethnic origins. Despite his claims that all Bolivians were equal, Morales was quick to espouse the status of indigenous groups. Some accuse him of political maneuvering and of polarizing the country according to race, class, economic status and skin color. He has been seen as favoring indigenous groups over Bolivian and foreign 'whites' and mestizos who, as descendants of the Spanish colonists and indigenous people, are rightly proud of their Bolivian status.

At a social level, Bolivians are keen on greetings and pleasantries. Every exchange is kicked off with the usual *Buen día* or *Buenos días* (Good morning), but also with a *¿Cómo está?* or *¿Qué tal?* (How are you?). Bolivian Spanish is also liberally sprinkled with endearing diminutives referring to everyday items such as *sopita* (a little soup) and *pesitos* (little pesos, as in 'it only costs 10 little pesos').

Bolivians are extremely proud of their regional foods and cultural practices, including dances. In fact, most Bolivians love any excuse to *festejar* (party).

Collectively, Bolivians have a landlocked longing for the sea and unerringly mark El Día del Mar (Day of the Sea) to commemorate the Chilean annexation of Bolivia's only stretch of coastline on March 24, 1879, during the War of the Pacific.

LIFESTYLE

Day-to-day life varies from Bolivian to Bolivian, mostly depending on whether they live in the city or in the country. Many *campesinos* (subsistence farmers), including those in the north of Potosí, live without

Quechua is spoken by 2.6 million Bolivians, nearly 30% of the population.

Many Bolivians will greet a person – including a stranger being introduced – with a kiss on one cheek (in the country's north) or on two cheeks (in the country's south).

running water, heat or electricity, and some wear clothing that has hardly changed in style since the Spanish arrived. But in the Bolivian cities, especially Santa Cruz (the country's richest city), La Paz, Cochabamba and Sucre, thousands of people enjoy the comforts of contemporary conveniences and live very modern lifestyles.

Still, for the vast majority of Bolivians, standards of living are alarmingly low, marked by substandard housing, nutrition, education, sanitation and hygiene. Bolivia suffers from a Third World trifecta: a high infant mortality rate (45 deaths per 1000 births), a reasonably high birth rate (3.17 per woman) and a low literacy rate (86.7%).

Overall, 87% of primary school-aged children are enrolled in classes, but attendance isn't necessarily a high priority. On the higher-education front there are 30 universities in the country, 10 of which are public. The growing ranks of well-educated college graduates are frustrated by the lack of domestic employment opportunities and are increasingly seeking work abroad, especially in Spain, Argentina and the US. However, a positive push toward educating the indigenous populations was made by the Morales government when they announced the opening of three indigenous universities (for Aymarás, Quechuas and Guaranís) in April 2009, in order to boost intercultural and multi-language exchange.

In 2006, US software giant Microsoft launched its Windows and Office software in the Quechua language.

Since Morales rose to power, he has put an accent on improving the social welfare system, funded largely by profits generated by the nationalization of the country's natural gas reserves. There are now stipends for primary education and food vouchers for the elderly and children. However, this has been far from smooth sailing, and the disabled, mentally ill and underemployed still sometimes take to the streets, hoping to arouse sympathy. One ethnic group in the department of Potosí is known to have organized a begging syndicate; they send older women into larger cities around the country, provide accommodations and supply them with suitably grubby-looking children.

In the highlands, the concept of *ayllu*, the traditional peasant commune that dates back to the Inca times, is still very much linked to Bolivia's close-knit families of today. These sociopolitical structures were extended family groups that worked the land together. In some ways, this concept still exists today, with old people predominantly provided for by their relatives. Evo often refers to the concept of *ayllu* in his speeches, thus promoting community values.

The recent trend of gold teeth of indigenous groups – in the shapes of stars, moons and other symbols – is a sign of wealth and status.

Homosexuality is legal in Bolivia but isn't openly flaunted in this society of machismo. Despite a growing number of gay bars in some larger cities, gay culture remains fairly subtle. For more details, see p333.

ECONOMY

Despite its rich natural resources, Bolivia is one of the poorest countries in Latin America. Estimates put 64% of the population below the poverty line; this figure goes up to 80% in rural areas. The average annual earnings is around US$900 and GDP is around US$36 billion or US$3937

ARE YOU LOST, MY FRIEND?

Rather than give no response at all, some Bolivians will provide you with incorrect answers or directions. They're not being malicious; they merely want to appear helpful and knowledgeable. It's also worth remembering that street numbers are hardly used – people give directions by landmarks instead. Sometimes it's best to ask several people the same question – the most common response is likely to be correct.

per capita (2009 estimate). Current inflation is around 8.7% and the unemployment rate is 7.5%.

Bolivia's main exports include natural gas (with Argentina and Brazil as the main buyers) and zinc. The country's agricultural products include soybeans (also a major export), coffee, sugar, cotton, corn and timber. Coca, sunflower seed (for oil) and organic chocolate are also growing industries.

There is widespread underemployment; a large percentage of the underemployed supplement their income by participating in the informal street-market economy, which employs more than 60% of the workforce and involves large amounts of contraband. Street vendors seem to be omnipresent all over Bolivia, hawking anything from medicine to art works and household machines. Coca production, mainly in the Yungas and the Chapare, provides subsistence for about 10% of Bolivia's working population.

Striking and protests have been part of the socio-economic landscape for years, although the tables have turned more recently and instead of coca farmers and poor highland workers, it's now the wealthy landowners and industrialist elites of the lowland regions who are displeased. Political change is still a fact of life in Bolivia; some locals have felt that this has been more damaging than constructive to the economy.

With the nationalization of natural gas reserves in 2006, Bolivia has been relying more on its own resources than on foreign aid and keeping the profits in the hands of the Bolivian people. If managed well, Bolivia's untapped lithium reserves could prove to become a boost to the economy; see p30.

Most recent UNICEF child-labor data reports that 21% of Bolivian children aged five to 14 are working to support themselves and their families, a staggering total of 850,000 young people. Most work in the mines or in the streets as *lustrabotas* (shoe-shiners) who have become ubiquitous in larger cities (they make a meagre B$10 per day at best).

Despite the agrarian reform agenda that Morales has been pushing since his election, forced labor is still very present in the lowlands where landowners hire the indigenous people to work the land under appalling conditions – workers are given food, the cost of which is then deducted from the average daily wage of B$15.

POPULATION

Bolivia is thinly populated, with around 9.8 million people occupying approximately 1,098,580 sq km. The Altiplano supports nearly 70% of the population – despite its frigid climate and frequently simmering social and political strife – mostly in the La Paz, Lake Titicaca and Oruro regions.

Bolivia has 36 identified indigenous groups, but there are varying figures regarding the indigenous population. According to the 2001 national census, about half of Bolivia's population claims indigenous heritage, while most sociologists and anthropologists cite figures of just over 60%. A mere 1% is of African heritage, mostly descendants of slaves conscripted to work in the Potosí mines (see p131). The remainder of Bolivia's citizens are largely of European extraction. Not all are descendants of the early Spanish conquerors; there are some Mennonite colonies, Jewish refugees from Nazi Europe, Eastern European refugees and hordes of researchers, aid workers and missionaries. Small Middle Eastern and Asian minorities, consisting mainly of Palestinians, Punjabis, Japanese and Chinese, have also immigrated.

The vast majority of those who identify themselves as indigenous are Aymará (about 25%) and Quechua (about 30%), many of whom are

The Fat Man from La Paz: Contemporary Fiction from Bolivia, edited by Rosario Santos, is a collection of 20 short stories offering perspectives about typical Bolivians and their lives.

The Wiphala flag (square-shaped and consisting of 49 small squares in a grid with graduating colors of the rainbow) has been adopted as a symbol of the Aymará people. Whether the colors used originate from Inca times, or more recently, is cause for debate.

Despite the high prevalence of llama fetuses in the markets (used for sacrificial offerings), llamas are not killed especially for them. About 3000 llamas are slaughtered daily on the Altiplano for wool and meat; the fetuses are removed from those animals subsequently found to be pregnant.

located in the highlands. The remaining groups (including Guaraní and Chiquitano) are located almost entirely in the lowlands.

SPORTS

Like its Latin American neighbors, Bolivia's national sport is *fútbol* (soccer). La Paz's Bolívar and The Strongest usually participate (albeit weakly) in the Copa Libertadores, the annual showdown of Latin America's top clubs. Bolivian teams typically fare well in *futsal* or *fútbol de salon* (five-vs-five mini-soccer) world championships. Professional *fútbol* matches are held every weekend in big cities, and impromptu street games are always happening. While small towns lack many basic services, you can be sure to find a well-tended *cancha* (football field) almost everywhere you go – and you'll be welcome to join in. Some communities still bar women from the field, but in the Altiplano, women's teams have started popping up, where they play clad in *polleras* (skirts) and jerseys. There is a national women's team, and the game is becoming more popular among females.

Several times a year La Paz locals put aside concerns about the weather, the price of tickets and other worldly matters for a game that's guaranteed to swell the Hernando Siles (Map pp68-9) soccer stadium to its near 50,000 capacity: El Clásico, the showdown between La Paz's (and the nation's) two big *fútbol* teams, Bolívar and The Strongest. The intracity rivalry stretches back more than a quarter-century, to Club Bolívar's founding in 1925 (The Strongest are the country's oldest team, started in 1908). The Strongest (nicknamed the 'Tigres' for their bold yellow-and-black striped uniform) have more support in the working-class and poorer neighborhoods, while the 'Celestes' of Club Bolívar (dubbed for their sky-blue uniforms) are more of a rich-man's team.

El Alto is home to the rough-and-ready, athletic and extremely choreo-graphed 'free-style' *lucha libre* (wrestling matches). Less of a sport and more an entertainment for audience voyeurs, 'good guy' and 'bad guy' wrestlers fight it out in the ring wearing outfits that Superman and Spiderman would envy. More recently, much to the delight of the crowds, women have joined the fray, some dressed as innocent looking *cholitas,* others in devilish costumes. Anything goes, from eye gouging to head-locks and, occasionally, dwarf-throwing (not for the politically correct or sensitive viewer). See p73 for more details.

In rural communities, volleyball is a sunset affair, with mostly adults playing a couple of times a week. Racquetball, billiards, chess and *cacho* (dice) are also popular. The unofficial national sport, however, has to be feasting and feting – the competition between dancers and drinkers knows no bounds.

RELIGION

Roughly 95% of Bolivia's population professes Roman Catholicism and practices it to varying degrees. The remaining 5% are Protestant, agnostic and belonging to other religions. Strong evangelical movements are rapidly gaining followers with their fire-and-brimstone messages of the world's imminent end. Despite the political and economic strength of Western religions, it's clear that most religious activities have mixed Inca and Aymará belief systems with Christianity. Doctrines, rites and superstitions are commonplace, and some *campesinos* still live by a traditional lunar calendar.

Based on animism, indigenous religions believe in natural gods and spirits, which date back to Inca times and earlier. Pachamama, the

The Aymará and Quechua spiritual worlds embrace three levels: Alajpacha (the world above or eternal sky, representing light and life, the center or the earthly world); Akapacha (located between the sky and hell, and between life and death); and Mankapacha (located below, symbolizing death and obscurity).

FIESTA DE LAS ÑATITAS

One of the most bizarre and fascinating Aymará rituals is the **Fiesta de las Ñatitas** (Festival of Skulls), which is celebrated one week after Day of the Dead. *Ñatitas* (skulls) are presented at the cemetery chapel in La Paz to be blessed by a Catholic priest. Parish priests shy away from associating this rite with mass, but have begrudgingly recognized the custom. The skulls are adorned with offerings of flowers, candles and coca leaves, and many even sport sunglasses and a lit cigarette between their teeth. While some people own the skulls of deceased loved ones and friends (who they believe are watching over them), many anonymous craniums are believed to have been purchased from morgues and (so it is claimed) medical faculties. After the blessings, the decorated *ñatitas* are carted back to the owners' houses to bring good luck and protection. This ancient Aymarán ritual was practiced in secret but, nowadays, the chapel's head count is growing every year.

ubiquitous earth mother, is the most popular recipient of sacrificial offerings, since she shares herself with human beings, helps bring forth crops and distributes riches to those she favors. She has quite an appetite for coca, alcohol and the blood of animals, particularly white llamas. If you're wondering about all the llama fetuses in the markets, they are wrapped up and buried under new constructions, especially homes, as an offering to Pachamama.

Among the Aymará and Quechua mountain gods, the *apus* and *achachilas* are important. The *apus,* mountain spirits who provide protection for travelers, are often associated with a particular *nevado* (snowcapped peak). Illimani, for example, is an *apu* who looks over inhabitants of La Paz. *Achachilas* are spirits of the high mountains; believed to be ancestors of the people, they look after their *ayllu* (loosely translated as 'tribe') and provide bounty from the earth.

Ekeko, which means 'dwarf' in Aymará, is the jolly little household god of abundance. Since he's responsible for matchmaking, finding homes for the homeless and ensuring success for businesspeople, he's well looked after, especially during the Alasitas festival in La Paz (p76).

Talismans are also used in daily life to encourage prosperity or to protect a person from evil. A turtle is thought to bring health, a frog or toad carries good fortune, an owl signifies wisdom and success in school, and a condor will ensure a good journey.

WOMEN IN BOLIVIA

Machismo is alive and well in Bolivia, but women's rights and education organizations are popping up, most notably in El Alto, and in the strong activist women's movement Mujeres Creando (www.mujerescreando .org) in La Paz. Women began to play a role in the political arena back in 1982 when the Bolivian congress appointed a woman as interim president. Then, in 1989, Remedios Loza became the first indigenous woman who sat in Congress. Today, under the Morales government, many women, including *cholas,* have been elected as members of the 2006 national legislature and as representatives to the Constitutional Assembly.

More recently, a new lingo has emerged to describe Bolivian *cholas,* whose status, thanks partly to the support of the indigenous president, is increasing. While the *chola* is a woman who wears traditional dress (see opposite), the *chota* is a woman who has ditched her *chola* dress and converted to Western-style dress, a *birlocha* is a Western-style woman who opposes the *chola,* and '*chola* transformers' are females who assume the role of *cholas* when they feel like it, such as in cultural events and fiestas.

ARTS

Bolivia is rich in artistic expression, whether it be through music and textiles or film and literature. While traditional music and textiles are more prevalent than contemporary gallery art, La Paz's Museo de Arte Contemporaneo (p72) represents a growing appreciation of contemporary art. The **Casa de la Cultura** (Map pp68-9; ☎ 2-240-6877; Mariscal Santa Cruz & Potosí) in La Paz is an excellent place to view art exhibits, as well as find out information on the art scene. In the way of performances, formal theater is limited to larger cities and traditional *peñas* (folk-music programs). You can catch lively dance and theatrical performances almost anywhere during festivals and parades.

Textile weaving methods have changed little in Bolivia for centuries. During the colonial period, woven cloth was one of the most important tribute items (after gold, silver and other minerals) required by the crown. In rural areas girls learn to weave before they reach puberty, and women spend nearly all their spare time with a drop spindle or weaving on heddle looms. Prior to colonization, llama and alpaca wool were the materials of choice, although now sheep's wool and synthetic fibers are also prominent.

Bolivian textiles come in diverse patterns. The majority display a degree of skill that results from millennia of artistry and tradition. The most common piece is a *manta* or *aguayo*, a square shawl made of two handwoven strips joined edge to edge. Also common are the *chuspa* (coca pouch), *chullo* (knitted hat), the *falda* (skirt), woven belts and touristy items such as camera bags made from remnants.

Regional differences are manifested in weaving style, motif and use. Weavings from Tarabuco often feature intricate zoomorphic patterns,

Librería Boliviana (www .libreriaboliviana.com, in Spanish) stocks an extensive collection of books, videos, traditional instruments and music, and ships worldwide.

A common petty crime in La Paz is the theft of bowler hats – valued upwards of US$8 – from *cholitas'* heads in crowded markets.

CHOLA DRESS

The characteristic dress worn by many Bolivian indigenous women was imposed on them in the 18th century by the Spanish king, and the customary center parting of the hair was the result of a decree by the Viceroy Toledo.

This distinctive ensemble, both colorful and utilitarian, has almost become Bolivia's defining image. The most noticeable characteristic of the traditional Aymará dress is the ubiquitous dark green, black or brown bowler hat. These are not attached with hat pins, but balance on the *cholitas'* heads.

The women normally braid their hair into two long plaits that are joined by a tuft of black wool known as a *pocacha*. The *pollera* skirts they wear are constructed of several horizontal pleats, worn over multiple layers of petticoats. Traditionally, only a married woman's skirt was pleated, while a single female's was not. Today, most of the synthetic materials for these brightly colored *polleras* are imported from South Korea.

The women also wear a factory-made blouse, a woolen *chompa* (sweater/jumper), a short vest-like jacket and a cotton apron, or some combination of these. Usually, they add a shawl known as a *manta*. Fashion dictates subtleties, such as the length of both the skirt and the tassels on the shawl.

Some sling an *aguayo* (also spelled *ahuayo*), a rectangle of manufactured or handwoven cloth decorated with colorful horizontal bands, across their backs. It's used as a carryall and is filled with everything from coca or groceries to babies.

The Quechua of the highland valleys wear equally colorful but not so universally recognized attire. The hat, called a *montera*, is a flat-topped affair made of straw or finely woven white wool. It's often taller and broader than the bowlers worn by the Aymará. The felt *monteras* (aka *morriones*) of Tarabuco, patterned after Spanish conquistadores' helmets, are the most striking. Women's skirts are usually made of velour and are shorter in length.

MARINA NÚÑEZ DEL PRADO

Bolivia's foremost sculptor, Marina Núñez del Prado, was born on October 17, 1910 in La Paz. From 1927 to 1929 she studied at the Escuela Nacional de Bellas Artes (National School of Fine Arts), and from 1930 to 1938 she worked there as a professor of sculpture and artistic anatomy.

Her early works were in cedar and walnut, and represented the mysteries of the Andes: indigenous faces, groups and dances. From 1943 to 1945 she lived in New York and turned her attentions to Bolivian social themes, including mining and poverty. She later went through a celebration of Bolivian motherhood with pieces depicting indigenous women, pregnant women and mothers protecting their children. Other works dealt largely with Andean themes, some of which took appealing abstract forms. She once wrote, 'I feel the enormous good fortune to have been born under the tutelage of the Andes, which express the richness and the cosmic miracle. My art expresses the spirit of my Andean homeland and the spirit of my Aymará people.'

During her long career she held more than 160 exhibitions, which garnered her numerous awards, and she received international acclaim from the likes of Pablo Neruda, Gabriela Mistral, Alexander Archipenko and Guillermo Niño de Guzmán. In her later years Marina lived in Lima, Peru, with her husband, Peruvian writer Jorge Falcón. She died there in September 1995 at the age of 84.

---

while distinctive red-and-black designs come from Potolo, northwest of Sucre. Zoomorphic patterns are also prominent in the wild Charazani country north of Lake Titicaca and in several Altiplano areas outside La Paz, including Lique and Calamarka.

Some extremely fine weavings originate in Sica Sica, one of the many dusty and nondescript villages between La Paz and Oruro, while in Calcha, southeast of Potosí, expert spinning and an extremely tight weave – more than 150 threads per inch – produce Bolivia's finest textiles.

Vicuña fibers, the finest and most expensive in the world, are produced in Apolobamba and in Sajama National Park.

Music

While all Andean musical traditions have evolved from a series of pre-Inca, Inca, Spanish, Amazonian and even African influences, each region of Bolivia has developed distinctive musical traditions, dances and instruments. The strains of the Andean music from the cold and bleak Altiplano are suitably haunting and mournful, while those of warmer Tarija, with its complement of bizarre musical instruments, take on more vibrant and colorful tones. Original Andean music was exclusively instrumental, but a recent trend toward melody has inspired the addition of appropriately tragic, bittersweet or morose lyrics.

Surf the Bolivian Educational & Cultural network's site www.llajta .org to hear samples of a wide range of traditional and modern Bolivian music.

The instrument Bolivia is most known for, and understandably proud of, is the *charango,* considered the king of all stringed instruments. Modeled after the Spanish *vihuela* and mandolin, it gained initial popularity in Potosí during the city's mining heyday. It has five courses of two strings and is not usually picked, but rather played in a flailing manner, called *rasqueado,* much like a banjo. Thanks to conservation efforts, the *charango* is no longer made of *quirquinchos* (armadillos) or tortoises. Bolivia hosts two *charango* festivals: the biannual Encuentro Internacional del Charango, held every other April in different cities, and the annual Sede Nacional del Charango, a competitive event that takes place every November in Aiquile (near Cochabamba). If you're there at the time, stop by to see who wins the Golden Charango.

Another instrument commonplace in the gringo markets is the *quena,* a small flute made of cane, bone or ceramic. The instrument predates

Europeans by many centuries and the earliest examples, made of stone, were found near Potosí. A curious instrument known as a jaguar-caller comes from the Amazon region. This hollowed-out calabash, with a small hole into which the player inserts his hand, seems to do the trick in calling the big cats to the hunt.

Of the contemporary Andean music groups, perhaps the best known is Kalamarka – watch out for their concerts. Young Bolivians have found a voice in El Alto's hip-hop movement with Bolivia's most popular group Ukamau y Ké. The band and its frontman Abraham Bojorquez was spreading a social message to international audiences, blending ancient Andean folk and modern hip-hop with lyrics criticizing corporate media, demanding justice for victims of the 2003 gas conflict, and urging change of the harsh realities of life in El Alto and the rest of Bolivia. Abraham was killed by a speeding bus in El Alto in May 2009, leaving a void in the contemporary political music and activism scene in Bolivia. To find out more about what's hot on the hip-hop scene in Bolivia, check out the happenings at Wayna Tambo cultural centre (http://perso.wanadoo.es/web_osqui/index.htm) in El Alto, which has a radio station and a café.

Los Kjarkas are one of the best-known and loved Andean music groups in South America. The group has introduced the world to the sounds of the *zampoña,* the *quena* and the *charango.*

Visit www.mamani.com to find out more about contemporary Aymará artist Mamani Mamani.

Dance
Traditional Altiplano dances celebrate war, fertility, hunting prowess, marriage and work. After the Spanish arrived, European dances and those of the African slaves were introduced, resulting in the hybrid dances that now characterize many Bolivian celebrations. Several postcolonial dances were traditionally performed as a satire, making fun of the colonists. This includes the dance of the *doctorcitos,* who wear small round glasses and fake hooked noses, imitating the colonial lawyers.

The country's geography and climate has traditionally influenced the style and costumes of the different dances – those in the highlands are generally more melancholy, with more cumbersome costumes than their counterparts in the warmer lowlands. Some costumes can weigh up to 50kg and are worn for more than 10 hours of dancing. Popular pre-Hispanic dances include La Sicuriada, La Morenada and La Tarqueada. The Spanish had some influence on dance, introducing their salon dances, the Cueca and Bailecito; both are still popular in most of Bolivia. They are danced by handkerchief-waving couples, primarily during fiestas.

The most unusual and colorful dances are performed at Altiplano festivals. Oruro's Carnaval draws huge local and international crowds who watch the many *fraternidades* (groups) perform most dances, including the well-known Diablada, and Llamerada, Sicuris and Incas. Huge amounts of money are spent on the costumes and it provides an industry in Oruro (see p157). Potosí is famed for *tinku* (see p237), recreating the region's *tinku* fight tradition, while La Paz is renowned for La Morenada, which re-enacts the dance of African slaves brought to the courts of Viceroy Felipe III. The costumes consist of hooped skirts, shoulder mantles and devilish dark-faced masks adorned with plumes.

Architecture
Tiwanaku's ruined structures and Inca roads, especially around northern La Paz, and the Altiplano architecture in Bolivia, are interesting examples of pre-Colombian architecture. The classic Inca polygonal-cut stones that distinguish many Peruvian sites are rare in Bolivia, found only on Isla del Sol and Isla de la Luna in Lake Titicaca.

While modernization, earthquakes and a depressed economy have resulted in the loss of many colonial buildings throughout Bolivia, fine colonial-era houses and street facades survive, notably in Potosí, Sucre and La Paz. Most remaining colonial buildings, however, are religious, and their styles are divided into several major overlapping periods. Look carefully at church fronts, as they often possess icons of pagan religions that were incorporated by the indigenous artisans trained by European craftsmen.

Renaissance (1550–1650) churches were constructed primarily of adobe, with courtyards and massive buttresses. One of the best surviving examples is in the village of Tiwanaku (p93). Renaissance churches indicating *mudéjar* (Moorish) influences include San Miguel in Sucre and the cathedral in Copacabana (p102).

For a comprehensive rundown on the history of Bolivian film, see www .embolivia-brasil.org.br/ cultura/cine/menu _cine .htm

Baroque (1630–1770) churches were constructed in the form of a cross with an elaborate dome. One of the best examples is the Iglesia de San Agustín (p231) in Potosí. Potosí has a long-term renovation project sponsored by the Spanish government to rehabilitate churches and other colonial buildings.

Mestizo style (1690–1790) is defined by whimsical decorative carvings including tropical flora and fauna, Inca deities and designs, and bizarre masks, sirens and gargoyles. See the amazing results at the San Francisco church in La Paz (p71) and San Lorenzo (p233) in Potosí.

In the 18th century, the Jesuits in what is now known as the Beni and Santa Cruz lowlands, went off on neoclassical tangents, designing churches with Bavarian rococo and Gothic elements. Their most unusual effort was the bizarre mission church at San José de Chiquitos (p290).

Since the 1950s many modern high-rises have appeared in the major cities. Though most are generic, there are some gems. Look for triangular pediments on the rooflines, new versions of the Spanish balcony, and the use of hardwoods of differing hues. The cathedral in Riberalta (p324) sings the contemporary gospel of brick and cedar like nobody's business.

Newer modern architecture in La Paz, especially that in Zona Sur, with its reflective glass and anything-goes style, leaves much to be desired.

Visual Arts

In the early colonial days Bolivian art was largely inspired by religion, the major contribution being represented by the Escuela Potosina Indígena. Hallmarks of this tradition include gilded highlights and triangular representations of the Virgin Mary.

Notable modern artists include Alejandro Mario Yllanes, an Aymará tin miner turned engraver and muralist, and Miguel Alandia Pantoja who, in the late 1940s, painted scenes of popular revolution.

Contemporary Aymará artist Roberto Mamani Mamani from the village of Tiwanaku strives to portray the true 'color' of the Altiplano – not the landscape but rather the images that inspire the people. The *paceño* artist Gil Imana brings out the stark, cold and isolated nature of life in the Andes, using only tiny splashes of color on drab backgrounds to hint at the underlying vibrancy of the culture.

Other contemporary artists to look out for are Gaston Ugalde, Edgar Arandia, Roberto Valcarcel and Patricia Mariaca.

Check out www .thedevilsminer.com for information about the award-winning film *The Devil's Miner* (2005), an American-directed film about the life of child miners in current-day Potosí.

Film

Bolivian film includes an impressive list of names and titles that cannot be done justice here. Film buffs should make their way to La Paz's Cinemateca Boliviana (p85).

One of the most important films in Bolivian history is the documentary *Vuelve Sebastiana* (The Return of Sebastiana; 1953), directed by Jorge Ruiz. It follows a group of people in the Altiplano who are facing extinction.

Later, Ruiz managed the Institute of Cinematography in Bolivia, set up after the 1952 April Revolution to develop national cinema. Between 1953 and 1966 it was one of the top five producers of film in Latin America. In 1964, Jorge Sanjinés took over as manager. After making propaganda films for the government, Sanjinés then outraged the government by shooting *Ukamau* (And So It Is; 1966), the tale of the rape and murder of an Aymará woman and her mestizo landowner. Today, Sanjinés is regarded as the most important director and prolific filmmaker in Bolivian cinema. His 1969 film *Yawar Mallku* (The Blood of the Condor) was a controversial affair for its open criticism of US imperialism; it is today considered one of the stellar examples of Latin American militant cinema.

Worth seeing is the Bolivia episode of Art Wolfe's *Travels to the Edge* PBS series, in which the acclaimed photographer travels to the Altiplano.

As well as the films listed here, look out for: *El Triángulo del Lago* (2000; Mauricio Calderón), *El Atraco* (2004; Paolo Agazzi), *Di Buen día a Papá* (Say Good Morning to Dad; 2005; Fernando Vargas), *Cocalero* (2007; Alejandro Landes) and *Alicia en el País* (2008; Esteban Larraín). Or look out for one of the following:

Amargo Mar (Bitter Sea; 1984) By highly regarded director Antonio Eguino, looks at the loss of Bolivia's coastline to Chile.

American Visa (2005; Juan Carlos Valdivia) Tells the story of a Bolivian professor who, on being denied a visa to the US, finds himself involved in a web of unsavory activities.

Dependencia Sexual (Sexual Dependency; 2003; Rodrigo Bellot) An award-winning film following five troubled teenagers and shot in an unconventional split-screen double angle.

Jonas y la Ballena Rosada (Jonah & the Pink Whale; 1995; Juan Carlos Valdivia) Deals with the drug trade around the Santa Cruz region.

Sayari (1995; Mela Márques) A breakthrough film with an all-indigenous cast and a female director.

One of the best-known Bolivian films is *Cuestión de Fé* (1995; Marcos Loayza), the story of three marginalized urbanites transporting a statue of the Virgin Mary from La Paz to the northern Yungas.

Literature

Bolivia has an extraordinarily rich literary tradition, starting with the 19th-century modernist poets, Rubén Dario, Ricardo Jaimes Freyre, Gregorio Reynolds and Franz Tamayo. Other notable poets include the 20th-century poet Oscar Cerruto and feminist poet Adela Zamudi (1854–1928). Award-winning poet and novelist Yolanda Bedregal (1916–99) is still considered one of the most prolific and important authors in Bolivia.

In the 1920s, Bolivian literature developed an indigenous theme, with stories such as *La Misk'isimi* ('Sweet Mouth' in Quechua) by Adolfo Costa du Rels and *La Ch'askañawi* (Eyes of Stars) by Carlos Medinaceli. The Chaco War (1932–35), between Bolivia and Paraguay, is examined in *Aluvión de fuego* (1935), by Oscar Cerruto, *Sangre de mestizos* (1936), by Augusto Céspedes, and *Laguna* (1967), by Costa du Rels.

Subversive literature came to the fore in the 1960s with the death of Ché Guevara in 1967; the best-known publication is *Los fundadores del alba*, by Renato Prado de Oropeza. By the end of the '60s, fiction, rather than realism, dominated the literature scene. The '70s and '80s saw critical literature restricted by the period's military dictatorships; *Antología del terror político* (1979) was one of the only titles to come out during that period, a short story collection about the effects of the dictatorship. The 1990s gave rise to urban literature, including *American Visa* (1994) by Juan de Recacochea and *The Fat Man from La Paz: Contemporary Fiction from Bolivia* (2003), edited by Rosario Dantos.

Two contemporary books speak about the Morales regime. *De la revolución al Pachakuti* (2008), by Filemón Escóbar, looks at Evo's policies with a critical eye. *Jefaso* (2008), by Martin Sivak, is a sympathetic biography of the controversial leader.

Bolivian literature first hit the literary psyche at the end of the 19th century with the modernist poets Ricardo Jaimes Freyre, Gregorio Reynolds and Franz Tamayo.

Food & Drink

Food lovers will be well sated in Bolivia. While the Bolivian national cuisine might not have an international profile, it deserves one, not least for its admirable versatility derived from the country's staple foods. Most Bolivian cuisine uses the freshest of fresh, locally grown ingredients and, unlike many other countries, Bolivia still produces a large share of its food. While pesticides and synthetic fertilizers are on the rise, many growers still cultivate with age-old practices that minimize the use of these substances. We can thank the central Andes for our potatoes and peanuts – it's the center of origin for these important crop plants.

Bolivian diets reflect its regional, ecological and cultural diversity – ingredients are particular to where you are. Altiplano fare tends to be starchy and loaded with carbohydrates, while *charque* (jerky), rice and tropical fruits are popular in the tropics. In the lowlands, fish, fruit and vegetables feature more prominently.

Meat invariably dominates and is usually accompanied by rice, a starchy tuber (usually potato or oca) and shredded lettuce. Often, the whole affair is drowned by *llajhua* (a fiery tomato-based salsa). The soups are a specialty and must be consumed as the locals do – watch how much *llajhua* they do (or don't) add. Learning how to consume Bolivian dishes is integral to their enjoyment.

In the cities, sophisticated world cuisine has well and truly hit the market; many restaurants have created delicious fusions of international dishes and local fare. Asian and European restaurants are increasingly prevalent and popular.

STAPLES & SPECIALTIES

Desayuno (breakfast) consists of little more than coffee and a bread roll, and is often followed by a mid-morning street snack such as a *salteña* (meat and vegetable pasty), *tucumana* (an *empanada*-like pastry) or *empanada*. Restaurants in tourist-oriented towns offer more elaborate Western-style breakfasts.

Lunch is the main meal of the day. Most restaurants offer an *almuerzo* (set lunch), which consists of soup, a *segundo* (main course) and tea or coffee; sometimes you'll get a salad and dessert as well. Depending on the class of the restaurant, *almuerzos* cost anywhere from B$7 to B$30; meals from the à la carte menu cost roughly twice as much. *La cena*, the evening meal, is mostly served à la carte. Many highlanders prefer a light *te* (tea) instead of an evening meal.

Snacks

Salteñas, tucumanas or *empanadas*, common streetside snacks, are football-shaped and consist of a pastry shell stuffed with juicy, spiced mixtures of meat and vegetables. Each has a distinct flavor and texture.

Originating from Salta (Argentina), *salteñas* are crammed with beef or chicken, olives, eggs, potatoes, onions, peas, carrots, raisins and sundry spices. The best ones are juicy and dribble all over the place. The *tucumana* has a puffier pastry shell that is filled with a piquant mix of egg, potatoes, chicken and onions. *Salteñas* tend to be sweeter, while *tucumanas* pack a spicy punch. *Empanadas* have a slightly more bready encasement that is sometimes deep-fried rather than baked. A cheesey and yuca (manioc or cassava) bun called *cuñape* is popular in Santa Cruz.

Cook up a Bolivian storm – browse www.boliviaweb.com/recipes for mouth-watering Bolivian blends of flavors and dishes.

Bolivia is the center of origin for many crops including quinoa, *cañawa*, oca and potato.

The South American Table, by Maria Baez Kijac, includes hundreds of recipes from Latin America and is flavored with a touch of history as well.

Other scrumptious street snacks include *tamales* (cornmeal-dough pockets filled with spiced beef, vegetables, potatoes and/or cheese) and *humintas* (or *humitas;* cornmeal filled with cheese, onion, egg and spices, baked in the oven or boiled). For a hearty snack, try *anticuchos* (grilled cow heart on skewers), served at markets or street stalls.

Soup

A large bowl of *sopa* – whether vegetarian or meat based – is the start of every great Bolivian meal. Two of the most popular soups are the delicious *maní* (peanut) soup and *chairo*, a hearty soup using many Andean ingredients including *chuños* (freeze-dried potatoes), meat and vegetables, and often topped with crispy fried pigskin. *Chupe, cha'que* and *lawa* (aka *lagua*) are the most common thick, stew-like soups. Quinoa and *maní* are often used to thicken broth.

Quinoa was baptized 'seed mother' by the Incas. Used in cooking, especially soups, it is renowned for its taste but, even more so, for its high protein levels.

Meat & Fish

Llamas, alpacas and guinea pigs are the only animals domesticated in the Andes for meat production and are generally consumed during feasts and special occasions. Beef, chicken and fish are the backbone to nearly all Bolivian dishes; *carne de chancho* (pork) is considered a delicacy, often eaten deep-fried as *chicharrón,* or roasted as *lechón. Campesinos* (subsistence farmers) eat more *cordero* or *carnero* (mutton), *cabrito* or *chivito* (goat), or llama.

Beef is typically *asado* or *parrillada* (barbecued or grilled) in various cuts (*lomo, brazuelo* and *churrasco*). Jerked beef, llama or other red meat is called *charque*. A popular dish is *pique a lo macho,* a plate of chopped grilled beef and sausage served with potatoes, onions, lettuce, tomatoes and *locoto* (chili peppers). On the Altiplano, beef is often served with *choclo* (corn), corn on the cob, or *mote* (rehydrated dried corn kernels); in the lowlands it's served with yuca or mashed plantain. In the Beni, beef may be served as *pacumutus,* enormous chunks of grilled meat accompanied by yuca, onions and other trimmings.

Pollo (chicken) is either *frito* (fried), *al spiedo* or *a la broaster* (cooked on a spit), or *asado* (barbecued) or *dorado* (broiled). Cheap chicken restaurants are ubiquitous in Bolivia, where a meal of chicken and potatoes costs around B$7.

On the Altiplano the most deservedly popular *pescado* (fish) are *trucha* (trout) and *pejerrey* (kingfish), introduced species from Lake Titicaca. The lowlands have a wide variety of other freshwater fish; *surubí,* a catfish caught throughout the lowlands, is arguably the best of the lot. Try to find out which river your lowland fish might have come from, as some rivers may have been polluted with mercury cast-offs from mining. Fish from the Pilcomayo River, for example, is considered to be contaminated and unfit for consumption.

Tubers

Tuberous plants make up the bulk of the Bolivian diet and are native to the region; there are over 200 potato varieties. *Chuños* or *tunta (*freeze-dried potatoes) are rehydrated, cooked and eaten as snacks or with meals. Although bland on their own, in soups such as *chairo* they can be delicious. They are also a testament to the resourcefulness of Andean peoples, who developed the complicated freeze-drying process to be able to survive the cold and dry Andean winters. The raw potatoes are left out for several nights to freeze, after which they're stepped on to squeeze out the water, and then set in the sun to dry further.

Potato lovers may enjoy consuming the weighty tome *The Potatoes of Bolivia: Their Breeding Value and Evolutionary Relationships* by JG Hawkes, an in-depth treaty to the humble spud.

Ocas are delicate, purple, potato-like tubers, which taste best roasted or boiled. In the lowlands, the potato and its relatives are replaced by plantain or the root of the yuca.

Cereals & Pulses

The white and pink *pasankalla* (corn puffs) that you see in giant bags may be too chewy for some, but they use an age-old and sophisticated food preservation technique.

Other common foods include *choclo,* a large-kernel corn (maize) that's ubiquitous on the Altiplano, and *habas,* similar to the domesticated fava beans that are eaten roasted or added to stews. In Cochabamba, ask for the delectable *habas con quesillo* (beans with cheese).

Quinoa, a unique Andean grain, is massively high in protein and is used to make flour and to thicken stews. Recent research has shown that it's the only edible plant that contains all essential amino acids in the same proportions as milk, making it especially appealing to vegans. Packed with protein and fiber, it's considered a 'super food' and is deservedly experiencing a resurgence these days. Look for quinoa cookies, cakes, chocolate, croquettes, soups and bread.

Cañawa is another high-protein grain, typically roasted and ground into a powder.

Fruit

The humble soybean is one of Bolivia's most important exports but (sadly for vegetarians) is one of the most environmentally unfriendly crops to grow, causing havoc to the Bolivian landscape.

Many deliciously juicy South American fruits are cultivated in Bolivia. Most notable are the *chirimoya* (custard apple), *tuna* (prickly pear cactus) and *maracuya* and *tumbo* passion fruits.

In the lowlands, the range of exotic tropical fruits defies middle-latitude expectations. Among the more unusual are the human hand-shaped *ambaiba;* the small, round, green-and-purple *guaypurú;* the spiny yellow *ocoro;* the lemon-like *guapomo;* the bean-like *cupesi;* the *marayau,* which resembles a bunch of giant grapes; the currant-like *nui;* the scaly onion-looking *sinini;* and the stomach-shaped *paquio.*

DRINKS
Nonalcoholic Drinks

Most common international drinks such as coffee, soda and bottled water are widely available. But don't leave the country without trying any of the local specialty drinks; many are gastronomic highlights.

Api and *mate de coca* are heated morning-time treats. *Api* is made from a ground purple corn while *mate de coca* is an infusion of water and dried coca leaves. Another wonderful hot drink is *trimate,* a combination of chamomile, coca and anise. A must try is a *mocochinche,* a sugary peach drink made from boiled cane sugar, cinnamon sticks and featuring a floating dried peach (another Andean food-preservation marvel). Also popular are the sweet and nutty *tostada* and the corn-based *horchata* and *licuados* (fruit shakes blended with water or milk).

Throughout most towns and cities, juice vendors ply their trade from their fruit carts. For a mere B$3, you can enjoy an orange or grapefruit taste sensation.

Alcoholic Drinks

Beer poured at high altitude generally has a frothier head. A local superstition is that the frothier your beer, the more money you have. The person with the frothiest lager head must take a pinch of the froth and put it in their pocket.

When Bolivians gather for recreational drinking – beer or something harder – they intend to get plastered. Remember that altitude increases both froth and effect. Bolivia produces its own wines, lagers and local concoctions of varying qualities.

Enjoyable Bolivian regional lagers include the fizzy and strange-tasting Huari, the good but rather nondescript Paceña (they have also introduced a delicious dark porter), the pleasant but weak-flavored Sureña, the

---

SPIRITS FOR THE SPIRITS

The Andean inhabitants believe their world is populated by well-respected supernatural beings, the *apus* and *achachilas* (mountain spirits said to be ancestors of the people). These beings, prone to both favorable behavior and fits of temper, are believed to pervade wild areas. The indigenous people see themselves as descendants of the much respected and venerated earth mother, Pachamama.

The spirits are taken into consideration in facets of everyday life, and certain things are done to keep on their better side. Before a person takes the first sip of alcohol from a glass, it's customary to spill a few drops on the ground as an offering, or *t'inka*, to Pachamama. This demonstrates to Pachamama that she takes precedence over her human subjects (and she likes to drink a drop, too). Alcohol is also splashed or sprinkled over homes and cars as a *cha'lla* (blessing).

---

refreshing Taquiña, the robust Potosina, the slightly rough Ducal and the cold and tasty Tropical Extra.

Wines are fermented around Tarija and are increasingly being recognized in the world of viticulture. The best – and most expensive – is Bodega La Concepción's Cepas de Altura, from some of the world's highest vineyards, which sells for around B$70 for a 750ml bottle. Other good wineries are Kohlberg and Aranjuez.

Drunk more for effect than flavor, and created by fermenting corn, *chicha cochabambina* is favored by the Bolivian masses. It's produced mostly around Cochabamba, where white plastic flags on long poles indicate that the *chichería* is open for business (you can even bring your own bottle for a fill-up).

Bolivia's national liquor is Singani, a white grape brandy produced around Tarija and typically mixed with a soda or lemonade to create the popular cocktail *chuflay*.

Campesinos rarely consider taste or personal health when looking for a cheap and direct route to celebration (or inebriation) – thus their willingness to swill the head-pounding *puro* or *aguardiente* (firewater). This burning, gut-wrenching stuff is essentially pure alcohol so, if you're offered a glass, you may wish to make a particularly generous offering to Pachamama (see above).

> Tarija's vines are grown at high altitude, which speeds up the maturing process of the grape. The wine producers are trying to establish whether the wine deteriorates faster due to these natural factors.

CELEBRATIONS

Bolivians love to eat and drink, and festivals and celebrations provide the perfect excuse. On the Día de los Muertos (Day of the Dead), families prepare the favorite dishes of their loved ones, along with little sweet breads, with plaster-cast faces, representing their dead relatives. Very ornate and brightly iced cakes adorn cake shops and are a favorite for birthdays – the fancier the better. *Confites* are sugar candies (surrounding coconut, dried peach or nuts) made by traditional candy makers; they're consumed during Carnaval time or for feasts such as Alasitas in La Paz (p76). There are several kinds of *confites,* one of which is brightly colored and not consumed, but instead is used as an offering at a *cha'lla* (blessing).

> Maca, a small turnip-type root vegetable, is considered the Viagra of the Andes.

WHERE TO EAT & DRINK

Larger towns and cities have a range of eateries, from family-run operations to upscale cloth-napkin restaurants. All towns have cheap food stalls in the market *comedores* (dining halls) that serve filling and tasty meals and snacks.

Disappointingly, there are a growing number of Western-style fast-food joints in the big cities – to eat in these is sometimes seen as a status

Much coca is sprayed with insecticide and other chemicals. There is a strong organic coca movement in Bolivia, promoting the benefits of organic coca for chewing and other consumption. Support the movement and seek out the organic varieties – experts can taste the difference.

symbol. Restaurants serving typical European or North American foods are found around larger hotels or in middle-class districts of larger cities. Increasingly popular in larger cities are Italian restaurants, *chifas* (Chinese restaurants), and Mexican, Swiss and Japanese eateries. Peruvian *cevicherías* (specialized seafood restaurants) and vegetarian options are also on the rise. Best of all are the Bolivian/international restaurants, serving international dishes with a Bolivian twist, using ingredients such as quinoa and the vast range of fresh ingredients that Bolivia should be so famous for. Get your taste buds working, your juices flowing and absorb the wonderfully diverse tastes and flavors of Bolivia. *¡Buen provecho!*

Quick Eats

Markets and street stalls are the best places for cheap, on-the-go bites and local specialties. Hygiene at some of these places isn't a top priority so your internal plumbing may need time to adjust. You should be fine if you choose a stall that seems clean and well organized.

Confiterías and *pastelerías* sell little more than snacks and coffee. *Heladerías* (ice-cream parlors) are becoming increasingly worldly, offering pizza, pasta, doughnuts, *salteñas,* coffee specialties and even full (if bland) meals.

VEGETARIANS & VEGANS

Vegetarians may well be delighted by what they find on offer. Many soups are prepared with vegetables and noodles, and often *chuño*. More flexible vegetarians (who can put up with meat stock or pick meat out of a dish) will be fine. Vegans will find themselves eating a lot of potatoes in the highlands, and fresh fruits and vegetables elsewhere. Bigger cities and popular tourist areas have at least one vegetarian restaurant. The typical *plato paceño* (La Paz dish) is traditionally served without meat – it's just fried cheese, fresh corn and fava bean and, of course, potatoes. Check first, though, as many restaurants will include a piece of meat with the dish.

HABITS & CUSTOMS

Nearly everything stops from noon to at least 3pm when families get together and loll over a multi-hour lunch. It's the main meal of the day and no one rushes through it. *Campesinos* may eat with their fingers among family, but Bolivians in general use Western-style utensils. Tipping up to 10% is standard at upscale restaurants when service is up to snuff; locals leave small change, if anything at all, elsewhere.

EAT YOUR WORDS

Want to know a *pacumutu* from a *pique a lo macho*? *Chupe* from *chaque* or *charque*? Get behind the *comida* (food) scene by getting to know the lingo. For pronunciation guidelines, see p361.

Useful Phrases

Do you have a menu in English?
¿Tienen una carta en inglés?   tye·nen oo·na kar·ta en een·gles
What do you recommend?
¿Qué me recomienda?   ke me re·ko·myen·da
Do you have any vegetarian dishes?
¿Tienen algún plato vegetariano?   tye·nen al·goon pla·to ve·khe·ta·rya·no
Not too spicy please.
No muy picoso/picante, por favor.   no mooy pee·ko·so/pee·kan·te por fa·vor

I'll try what he/she is having.
Voy a pedir lo que el/ella pedío.   voy a pe·*deer* lo ke el/e·ya pe·*dyo*
I'd like the set lunch.
Quisiera el almuerzo, por favor.   kee·*sye*·ra el al·*mwer*·so por fa·*vor*
This food is delicious.
Esta comida está exquisita.   es·ta ko·*mee*·da es·*ta* ek·*skee*·see·ta
The bill (check), please.
La cuenta, por favor.   la *kwen*·ta por fa·*vor*

Food Glossary

ají	a·*khee*	chili condiments
anticuchos	an·tee·*koo*·chos	beef-heart shish kebabs
api	a·pee	syrupy form of *chicha* made from sweet purple corn, lemon, cinnamon and white sugar
brazuelo	bra·*zwe*·lo	shoulder
buñuelo	boo·nyoo·*we*·lo	sticky type of doughnut dipped in sugar syrup
cabrito	ka·*bree*·to	goat
camote	ka·*mo*·te	sweet potato
carne	*kar*·ne	beef
carne de chancho	*kar*·ne de *chan*·cho	pork
cerveza	ser·*ve*·sa	beer; Taquiña is the best, Huari the fizziest
chairo	*chai*·ro	mutton or beef soup with *chuños*, potatoes and *mote*
chajchu	*chakh*·choo	beef with *chuño*, hard-boiled egg, cheese and hot red pepper sauce
chanko	*chan*·ko	chicken with yellow pepper and a tomato and onion sauce; a Tarija specialty
chaque	*cha*·ke	like *chupe* but much thicker and contains more grain
charque	*char*·ke	meat jerky (often llama meat); the source of the English word 'jerky'
charquekan	*char*·ke·kan	meat jerky served with *choclo*, potato and boiled egg
chicha	*chee*·cha	popular beverage that is often alcoholic and made from fermented corn
chicharrón de cerdo	chee·cha·*ron* de *ser*·do	fried pork
chirimoya	chee·ree·*mo*·ya	custard apple; a green scaly fruit with creamy white flesh
choclo	*chok*·lo	large-grain corn (maize)
chuños	*choo*·nyos	freeze-dried potatoes
chupe	*choo*·pe	thick meat, vegetable and grain soup with a clear broth flavored with garlic, *ají*, tomato, cumin or onion
churrasco	choo·*ras*·ko	steak
cordero	kor·*de*·ro	lamb or mutton
cuñape	koo·*nya*·pe	cassava and cheese roll
despepitado	des·pe·pee·*ta*·do	(aka *mocachinchi*) a dried and shriveled peach in a boiled cane sugar and cinnamon liquid
empanada	em·pa·*na*·da	meat or cheese pasty
escabeche	es·ka·*be*·che	vinegar pickled vegetables
fricasé	free·ka·*se*	pork soup; a specialty from La Paz
fritanga	free·*tang*·ga	spicy-hot pork with mint and hominy
haba	a·ba	bean of the *palqui* plant found on the Altiplano, similar to fava beans
huminta	oo·*min*·ta	(aka *humita*) like a *tamale* but filled with cheese only and normally quite dry

kala purkha	*ka·la poor·ka*	soup made from corn that is cooked in a ceramic dish by adding a steaming chunk of heavy pumice; a Potosí and Sucre specialty
lawa	*la·wa*	(aka *lagua*) meat-stew broth thickened with corn starch or wheat flour
licuado	*lee·kwa·do*	fruit shake made with either milk or water
llajhua	*lya·khwa*	spicy-hot tomato sauce
llaucha paceña	*lyow·cha pa·se·nya*	a doughy cheese bread
locoto	*lo·ko·to*	small, hot pepper pods
lomo	*lo·mo*	loin (of meat)
maní	*ma·nee*	peanuts
maracuya	*ma·ra·koo·ya*	a sweet and delicious fruit (aka passion fruit); also see *tumbo*
masaco	*ma·sa·ko*	*charque* served with mashed plantain, yuca and/ or corn; a Bolivian Amazonian staple sometimes served with cheese
mate	*ma·te*	herbal infusion of coca, chamomile, or similar
milanesa	*mee·la·ne·sa*	a fairly greasy type of beef or chicken schnitzel (see *silpancho*)
mote	*mo·te*	freeze-dried corn
oca	*o·ka*	tough edible tuber similar to a potato
papas rellenas	*pa·pas re·ye·nas*	mashed potatoes stuffed with veggies or meat, and fried; especially tasty when piping hot and served with hot sauce
parrillada	*pa·ree·ya·da*	meat grill or barbecue
pastel	*pas·tel*	a deep-fried *empanada*; may be filled with chicken, beef or cheese
pescado	*pes·ka·do*	generic term for fish
pollo	*po·yo*	chicken
pomelo	*po·me·lo*	large, pulpy-skinned grapefruit
pucacapa	*poo·ka·ka·pa*	circular *empanada* filled with cheese, olives, onions and hot pepper sauce and baked in an earth oven
queso	*ke·so*	cheese
quinoa	*kee·no·a*	nutritious grain similar to sorghum
saíce	*sai·se*	hot meat and rice stew
salteña	*sal·te·nya*	delicious, juicy meat and vegetable pasty; a popular mid-morning snack
silpancho	*seel·pan·cho*	a schnitzel pounded till very thin and able to absorb even more grease than a *milanesa*. A properly prepared *silpancho* is said to be perfect to use when viewing a solar eclipse!
tallarines	*ta·ya·ree·nes*	long, thin noodles
tamale	*ta·ma·le*	cornmeal dough filled with spiced beef, vegetables and potatoes then wrapped in a corn husk and fried, grilled or baked
tarhui	*tar·wee*	legume from Sucre
thimpu	*teem·poo*	spicy lamb and vegetable stew
tomatada de cordero	*to·ma·ta·da de kor·de·ro*	lamb stew with tomato sauce
tucumana	*too·koo·ma·na*	*empanada*-like pastry stuffed till bursting with meat, olives, eggs, raisins and other goodies; originated in Tucumán, Argentina
tumbo	*toom·bo*	a variety of passion fruit
tuna	*too·na*	prickly pear cactus
witu	*wee·to*	beef stew with pureed tomatoes
yuca	*yoo·ka*	cassava (manioc) tuber

Environment

When people think of the Bolivian environment, they often think high (La Paz), dry (Altiplano) and salty (Uyuni salt plains). While these cover large regions of the country, there's much more scope to the Bolivian landscape.

The country's varying altitude – between 130m in the jungles of the Amazon Basin and 6542m in the rugged Andes mountain range – means that a huge variety of ecological and geological spheres support a large number of plants and animals. Giant anteaters shelter here, as do anacondas and armadillos, and the plants range from the much-lauded mahogany to palms. In 2005 a new species of monkey, the titi, was discovered in Madidi National Park (see p50).

The country's 1000 neotropical bird species and 5000 plants species rank among the highest numbers in the world; it's also among eight countries with the most diverse range of reptiles (16 of which exist only in Bolivia), and is home to 13 endemic mammals.

The 1990s saw a dramatic surge in international and domestic interest in ecological and environmental issues in the Amazon region. Since the creation of the government-run **Servicio Nacional de Áreas Protegidas** (SERNAP; www.sernap.gov.bo, in Spanish, see p63 for more information) in 1997, 22 national protected areas have been declared, covering 18% of the national territory. This represents significant strongholds for rarer and regionally threatened wildlife such as spectacled bears, giant otters, Andean condors and jaguars. Local and international NGOs have worked with SERNAP to craft innovative ways to preserve select habitats.

Unfortunately, however, much of the Bolivian environment is being destroyed or is under threat and many regions risk exhaustion of their forest and wildlife resources; see p52.

THE LAND

Despite the huge loss of territory in wars and concessions (see p24), at 1,098,581 sq km, landlocked Bolivia is South America's fifth-largest country, 3.5 times the size of the British Isles.

Two Andean mountain chains define the west of the country, with many peaks above 6000m. The western Cordillera Occidental stands between Bolivia and the Pacific coast. The eastern Cordillera Real runs southeast, then turns south across central Bolivia, joining the other chain to form the southern Cordillera Central.

The haunting Altiplano, which ranges in altitude from 3500m to 4000m, is boxed in by these two great cordilleras. It's an immense, nearly treeless plain punctuated by mountains and solitary volcanic peaks. At the Altiplano's northern end, straddling the Peruvian border, Lake Titicaca is one of the world's highest navigable lakes. In the far southwestern corner, the land is drier and less populated. The remnants of two vast ancient lakes, the Salar de Uyuni and the Salar de Coipasa, are there as well.

East of the Cordillera Central are the Central Highlands, a region of scrubby hills, valleys and fertile basins with a Mediterranean-like climate.

North of the Cordillera Real, the Yungas form a transition zone between arid highlands and humid lowlands. More than half of Bolivia's total area is in the Amazon Basin, with sweaty tropical rainforest in the western section, and swamps, flat savannas and scrub in the east.

Bolivia will never forget 1879, the year it lost its outlet to the sea. Each year on March 23 it stages marches and events; discussion is still ongoing as to how it can regain access to the Pacific.

The *bolivianita* is a rare semiprecious stone made up of citrine and amethyst and has a pretty pinky-yellow color.

The Altiplano makes up only 10% of Bolivia's land mass, yet is the country's most densely populated zone.

In the country's southeastern corner is the flat, nearly impenetrable scrubland of the Gran Chaco.

WILDLIFE
Animals

Thanks to its varied geography, sparse human population and lack of extensive development, Bolivia is one of the best places on the continent to observe wildlife. Even the most seasoned wildlife observers will be impressed by Parque Nacional Madidi and Parque Nacional Noel Kempff Mercado.

The Andean condor, the world's heaviest bird of prey, has a 3m wingspan and can effortlessly drag a 20kg carcass.

The distribution of wildlife is largely dictated by the country's geography. The Altiplano is home to vicuñas, flamingos and condors. The elusive jaguars, tapirs and white-lipped and collared peccaries occupy the nearly inaccessible, harsh expanses of the Chaco in relatively healthy numbers. The Amazon Basin contains the richest density of species on earth, featuring an incredible variety of lizards, parrots, monkeys, snakes, butterflies, fish and bugs (by the zillions!).

The southern Altiplano is the exclusive habitat of the James flamingo. The versatile rhea or *ñandú* (the South American ostrich) inhabits the region from the Altiplano to the Beni, the Chaco and the Santa Cruz lowlands. In the highlands, lucky observers may see a condor; highly revered by the Inca, these rare vultures are the world's heaviest birds of prey.

River travelers are almost certain to spot capybaras (large amphibious rodents), turtles, alligators, pink dolphins and, occasionally, giant river otters. It's not unusual to see anacondas in the rivers of the department of Beni, and overland travelers frequently see armadillos, rheas, sloths and *jochis* (agoutis).

You won't have to travel very far to spot the most common Bolivian fauna – the llama and the alpaca – as these have been domesticated for centuries.

ENDANGERED & RARE SPECIES

Amateur birdwatchers should get their binoculars out to catch a glimpse of South American Birds: A Photographic Aid to Identification by John Stewart. Experts will want to spot Jon Fjeldsa's Birds of the High Andes.

The extremity of the landscape has kept many areas uninhabited by people for a long time, preserving pristine habitats for many exotic species.

Vicuñas, which fetch a bundle on the illicit market for their fuzzy coats, are declining in the wild, but in a couple of Bolivian reserves their numbers have been increasing. Other precious wild highland species include foxes and *tarukas* (Andean deer), the mysterious Andean cat and the titi monkey.

In Bolivia, guanacos are found exclusively in a remote part of the Bolivian Chaco. The viscacha, a rabbit-like creature with a long tail, spends most of its time huddled under rocks in the highlands.

The tracks of pumas, native throughout the Americas, are occasionally seen in remote mountain ranges and in the Amazonian regions, but the

---

GOLDEN OPPORTUNITY

When a team of researchers from the Wildlife Conservation Society, led by biologist Dr Robert Wallace, discovered a new species of titi monkey in the park, they came up with a novel idea. As discoverers of the species, they had the rights to name it (it was spotted in 2000, but proceedings were formalized in 2005). Wallace and his team decided to auction the rights to the name, with all proceeds going to Fundesnap, a nonprofit foundation that protects the monkeys' habitat in Madidi National Park. The lucky winner? A Canadian online casino paid $650,000 for the rights to name the monkey *callicebus avrei palatti* (Golden Palace).

NATIONAL PARKS, RESERVES & PROTECTED AREAS

Twenty-two national parks, reserves and protected areas administered by SERNAP are officially functioning although, in reality, some have better infrastructure than others. The following parks vary in their levels of isolation and infrastructure, including the activities on offer. Consult relevant chapters and guides before visiting these protected areas on your own.

Protected Area	Features	Activities	Best Time to Visit	Page
Amboró	Home to the rare spectacled bear, jaguars and an astonishing variety of bird life	Hiking, wildlife, waterfalls, endangered species	Any	p276
Apolobamba	Extremely remote park on the Peruvian border, home to typical Andean fauna	Trekking, climbing	May-Sep	p146
Carrasco	Extension to Amboró protects remaining stands of cloud forest in the volatile Chapare region	Birdwatching, hiking, tours	Any	p300
Madidi	Protects a wide range of wildlife habitats and over 900 officially registered bird species	Hiking, boating, plant- and wildlife-watching, swimming	Mar-Oct	p308
Noel Kempff Mercado	Remote and spectacular, with Amazonian fauna and flora, and waterfalls	Hiking, mountain biking, canoeing, wildlife-watching	Mar-Oct	p318
Reserva Nacional de Fauna Andina Eduardo Avaroa	A highlight of the Southwest Circuit tour; wildlife-rich lagoons, pink flamingos, endangered species	4WD tour of Southwest Circuit, climbing	Mar-Oct	p173
Sajama	Adjoins Chile's magnificent Parque Nacional Lauca; contains Volcán Sajama (6542m), Bolivia's highest peak	Climbing, mountaineering, hot springs, trekking	Jun-Sep	p163
Torotoro	Rock formations with dinosaur tracks, caves and ancient ruins	Paleontology, hiking, caving (spelunking)	Apr-Oct	p207
Tunari	Within hiking distance of Cochabamba, features the Lagunas de Huarahuara; lovely mountain scenery	Climbing	Apr-Nov	p201

elusive character of this species means there's little chance of spotting one without mounting a special expedition.

Rarer still, but present in national parks and remote regions, are jaguars, maned wolves, giant anteaters and spectacled bears. These animals can be seen in the Parque Nacional Noel Kempff Mercado.

Plants

Because of its enormous range of altitudes, Bolivia enjoys a wealth and diversity of flora rivaled only by its Andean neighbors.

In the overgrazed highlands, the only remaining vegetable species are those with some defense against grazing livestock or those that are unsuitable for firewood. Much of what does grow in the highlands grows slowly and is endangered. While there's remarkably little forest above 3000m elevation, rare dwarf *queñua* trees live as high as 5300m. The uncommon giant *Puya raimondii* plant is found only in Bolivia and southern Peru.

The lower elevations of the temperate highland hills and valleys support vegetation similar to that of Spain or California. Most of southeastern

The national flower of Bolivia is the *kantuta*; not only is it aesthetically beautiful, but it reflects the color of the country's national flag.

Bolivia is covered by a nearly impenetrable thicket of cactus and thorn scrub, which erupts into colorful bloom in the spring.

The moist upper slopes of the Yungas are characterized by dwarf forest. Further down the slopes stretches the cloud forest, where the trees grow larger and the vegetation thicker.

Northern Bolivia's lowlands are characterized by true rainforest dotted with vast wetlands and open savannas. The Amazon Basin contains the richest botanical diversity on earth, with thousands of endemic species.

> The Andean sacred animals include the condor, titi, puma, guinea pig, llama and frog.

NATIONAL PARKS & RESERVES

Bolivia has protected 18% of its total land by declaring 22 national protected areas and additional regional reserves under what is known as the Sistema Nacional de Áreas Protegidas (SNAP), home to much of Bolivia's most amazing landscapes and wildlife. The administrative body SERNAP manages the 22 national protected areas.

> The solstices are important dates for the people of the Andes. Winter (June 21), when the earth is prepared, dictates the agriculture; spring (September 21) is seed-sowing time; and summer (December 21) sees the start of the harvesting season.

The idea as of the last couple of years has been to encourage local involvement and co-management of protected areas in an effort to attract tourists to community-based, ecotourism experiences, as well as to produce commercially viable natural products, including medicinal patents. Some of the success stories include the San José de Uchupiamonas community in Parque Nacional Madidi (p308) and the Tomarapi community in Parque Nacional Sajama (p163). A comprehensive guide to such initiatives in Bolivia was published in 2008: *Deep Inside Bolivia* (*Desde Adentro*).

ENVIRONMENTAL ISSUES

Bolivian environmental problems are increasing rapidly and, while these have not yet reached apocalyptic proportions, NGOs and environmentalists are concerned that they are not being accompanied by the necessary measures to maintain a sound ecological balance.

While Bolivia lacks the population pressures of Brazil, it is promoting indiscriminate colonization and development of its lowlands. In the past decades, settlers have continued to leave the highlands to clear lowland forest and build homesteads. Slash-and-burn agricultural techniques (see opposite), overgrazing and soil erosion all serve to create serious problems in many areas. There is also hydrocarbon exploration and illegal logging in the area just outside the Parque Nacional Madidi, and the possible threat of a new road that will bisect the park.

Further east, particularly around the Santa Cruz and Beni departments, soybean crops continue to cause havoc. Huge tracts of land are cleared for soybean agriculture, but without crop-rotation programs the soil doesn't have enough time to recover. Similarly, cattle ranches are responsible for the destruction of vast areas of forest. Tracts of the Amazon are being exploited by both companies and individuals to fulfill international demand.

Many water supplies used for irrigation and drinking are polluted, particularly those around La Paz; much of this pollution ends up in the Amazon Basin. In fact, the Chipaya in the southern Altiplano are threatened by water pollution (p179). Glacial retreat on peaks due to global warming is an ongoing issue – in 2009, the 18,000 year-old Chacaltaya glacier, one of the highest in South America at 5421m, melted away entirely. Scientists predict that the handful of glaciers on the colossal Illimani that looms over La Paz will melt within 30 years. These glaciers are a major supply of water for La Paz, and their disappearance could cause some serious water shortage problems.

EL CHAQUEO: THE BIG SMOKE

Each dry season, from July through September, Bolivia's skies fill with a thick pall of smoke, obscuring the air, occasionally canceling flights, aggravating allergies and causing respiratory strife, especially in the lowlands. Illimani is a blurry blob against the La Paz skyline, visitors to Lake Titicaca are deprived of spectacular views and there is the odd aviation problem.

This is all the result of *el chaqueo*, the slashing and burning of the savannas (and some rainforest) for agricultural and grazing land – including cattle ranches and soybean crops. A prevailing notion is that the rising smoke forms rain clouds and ensures good rains for the coming season. In reality, the hydrological cycle, which depends on transpiration from the forest canopy, is interrupted by the deforestation, resulting in diminished rainfall. In extreme cases deforested zones may be sunbaked into wastelands. The latest World Bank records (from studies done between 2000 and 2005) estimate that each year Bolivia loses 0.45% of its forests in this manner, which is approximately 300,000 hectares per year.

Ranchers in the Beni department have long set fire to the savannas annually to encourage the sprouting of new grass. Now, however, the most dramatic defoliation occurs along the highways in the country's east. In the mid-1980s, this was largely virgin wilderness, accessible only by river or air, but the new roads connecting the region to La Paz have turned it into a free-for-all. Forest is consumed by expanding cattle ranches and only charred tree stumps remain. Although the burned vegetable matter initially provides rich nutrients for crops, those nutrients aren't replenished. After two or three years the land is exhausted and it takes 15 years to become productive again. That's too long for most farmers to wait; most just pull up stakes and burn larger areas.

Ironically, all this burning is prohibited by Bolivian forestry statutes – but such laws are impossible to enforce in an area as vast as the Bolivian lowlands. When relatively few people were farming the lowlands, *el chaqueo*'s effects were minimal, but given Bolivia's annual population growth rate of 1.38%, the country must feed a hefty number of additional mouths each year. Because much of this population growth is rural, more farmers' children are looking for their own lands.

Although the long-term implications aren't yet known (hint: take a look at the devastated Brazilian states of Acre and Rondônia), the Bolivian government has implemented a program aimed at teaching forest-fire control and encouraging lowland farmers to minimize *el chaqueo* in favor of alternatives that don't drain the soil of nutrients. Despite these efforts, it seems that *el chaqueo* will be a fact of life in Bolivia for many years to come.

Many nonprofit groups are working on countrywide environmental conservation efforts. Contact the following for further information.

Asociación Armonía (www.armonia-bo.org, in Spanish; www.birdbolivia.com) Everything you need to know about Bolivian birding and bird conservation.

Conservación Internacional (CI; www.conservation.org.bo, in Spanish) Promotes community-based ecotourism and biodiversity conservation.

Fundación Amigos de la Naturaleza (FAN; www.fan-bo.org, in Spanish) Works in Parques Nacionales Amboró and Noel Kempff Mercado.

Protección del Medioambiente del Tarija (Prometa; www.elgranchaco.com/prometa) Works in Gran Chaco, Sama, Tariquía and El Corvalán reserves and Parque Nacional Aguaragüe (p258).

Trópico (www.tropico.org, in Spanish) Works with communities in areas of conservation, sustainable development and environmental and resource management.

Wildlife Conservation Society (WCS; www.wcs.org) Works with local institutions and communities in applied wildlife research, natural resource management, and land-use planning and administration through conservation programs in the Madidi and Kaa-Iya regions.

Parque Nacional Amboró is under threat by human encroachment and slash-and-burn farming techniques.

Outdoors

Bolivia is all about getting breathless. If the beauty hasn't already taken your breath away, then the high altitude might, at least when you first arrive. Then there is the outdoor fun; the country offers an awesome mix of activities that get the lungs working and the heart pumping. Adventure companies are entering the market faster than a downhill bike plunge, offering a great mix of trekking, climbing and mountain-biking activities. Adventurers can opt for hikes of all levels, from climbs up snowcapped mountains in the Cordillera Real, to low-key wanders along Inca trails or through the jungle. Do you want to retrace the steps of Butch Cassidy and the Sundance Kid on horseback? Cruise in a 4WD across deserts? Shoot down a river in a raft or tube? No problem: it's all here, plus more; basic skiing, wildlife-watching and even ziplining (see boxed text, p306) are yours for the doing.

HIKING & TREKKING

Hiking and trekking are arguably the most rewarding Andean activities. Bolivia rivals Nepal in trekking potential, but has only relatively recently been discovered by enthusiasts. Some of the most popular hikes and treks in Bolivia begin near La Paz, traverse the Cordillera Real along ancient Inca routes and end in the Yungas. These include the well-known and well-used Choro (p124), Takesi (p127) and Yunga Cruz (p129) treks. Sorata is a trekker's dream-come-true, with a variety of trails, from don't-leave-home-without-a-machete–type hikes – the Mapiri Trail (p138) among them – to more pleasant walks on Inca trails. The Área Natural de Manejo Integrado Nacional (Anmin) Apolobamba (p146) is becoming more popular for medium-standard trekking, including the four- to five-day Lagunillas to Agua Blanca trek (p147), thanks to improved access from La Paz and a growing number of accommodations options.

National parks are hikers' paradises, with opportunities in Parque Nacional & Área de Uso Múltiple Amboró (p276) and, for anyone who makes it there, in Parque Nacional Noel Kempff Mercado (p318). Birdwatching and endemic plants are just part of the magic.

Less hardcore trekkers can enjoy the cultural and historical sites and hot springs around Cordillera de los Frailes (p223).

Muggings and robberies continue to be reported in some regions, so be sure to inquire locally about the safety of trails before heading out.

MOUNTAINEERING & CLIMBING

Climbing in Bolivia is an exercise in extremes – like the country itself. In the dry southern winter (May to October) temperatures may fluctuate as much as 40.5°C in a single day. Once you're acclimatized to the Altiplano's relatively thin air (you'll need at least a week), there is still 2500m of even thinner air lurking above.

A plus for climbers is the access to mountains; although public transportation may not always be available, roads pass within easy striking distance of many fine peaks.

The most accessible and spectacular climbing in the country is along the 160km-long Cordillera Real northeast of La Paz. Six of its peaks rise above 6000m and there are many more gems in the 5000m range. Because of the altitude, glaciers and ice or steep snow, few of the peaks are 'walk-ups,' but some are within the capability of the average climber, and many can be done by beginners with a competent guide. Huayna Potosí (p141)

In 1925, Colonel Percy Fawcett disappeared, searching for the 'lost city' of the Incas. Keen treasure hunters should seek out *Exploration Fawcett* by the man himself, Lt Col PH Fawcett.

RESPONSIBLE TREKKING

To help preserve the ecology and beauty of Bolivia, consider the following tips when trekking.

- Carry out all your rubbish. Okay, so many tracks in Bolivia are already littered, but this doesn't mean that you should contribute to it. Don't overlook easily forgotten items, such as silver paper, orange peel, cigarette butts and plastic wrappers.

- Never bury your rubbish: digging disturbs soil and ground cover and encourages erosion. Buried rubbish will likely be dug up by animals, who may be injured or poisoned by it. It may also take years to decompose.

- Contamination of water sources by human feces can lead to the transmission of all sorts of nasties. Where there is a toilet, please use it. Where there is none, bury your waste. Dig a small hole 15cm (6 inches) deep and at least 100m (320ft) from any watercourse. Cover the waste with soil and a rock. In snow, dig down to the soil.

- Don't use detergents or toothpaste in or near watercourses, even if they are biodegradable.

- Hillsides and mountain slopes, especially at high altitudes, are prone to erosion. Stick to existing trails and avoid short cuts.

- Don't depend on open fires for cooking. The cutting of wood for fires in popular trekking areas can cause rapid deforestation. Cook on a lightweight kerosene, alcohol or Shellite (white gas) stove and avoid those powered by disposable butane gas canisters.

- Do not feed the wildlife as this can lead to animals becoming dependent on handouts, to unbalanced populations and to disease.

- Always seek permission to camp from landowners or villagers.

For further information, contact Servicio Nacional de Áreas Protegidas (SERNAP; see p63).

is one of the most popular climbs for nonprofessionals, but be aware that although it's on the La Paz agency circuit, it's no walk (or climb) in the park! La Paz operators also take climbs up the magnificent Volcán Sajama (p163), Bolivia's highest peak.

Around Cordillera Quimsa Cruz (p150) there are a variety of lesser-known climbing opportunities. Volcán Illimani (p142) is for serious climbing expeditions and popular among advanced climbing groups.

The dangers of Bolivian climbing are due to ill-equipped or poorly trained guides, the altitude and the difficulties in mounting any sort of rescue. Mountaineering insurance is essential to cover the high costs of rescue and to ensure medical evacuation out of the country in the event of a serious accident. Note that helicopters cannot fly above 5000m. There is a small but potentially serious avalanche danger. For information on dealing with potentially fatal altitude problems, it's wise to carry the practical and easily transportable *Mountain Sickness*, by Peter Hackett, whenever you ascend to high altitude. See p358 for information about altitude sickness.

The **Asociación de Guias de Montaña** (☎ 2-214-7951; www.agmtb.org, in Spanish; Edificio Doryan, Sagárnaga 189, La Paz) is an internationally certified association of registered mountain guides; they also have a group of professional high-altitude rescuers.

A useful website for climbers' logs and accounts on climbs in the Andes is www .andeshandbook.cl.

MAPS

Historically, maps of Bolivian climbing areas have been poor in quality and difficult to obtain. Even now, elevations of peaks are murky, with reported altitudes varying as much as 600m – it seems the rumor that Ancohuma is taller than Aconcagua won't die.

Before you head off on your own into the Amazonian jungle, take heed from Yossi Ginsberg's *Back from Tuichi: the Harrowing Life and Death Story of Survival in the Amazon Rainforest.*

Maps are available in La Paz (p63), Cochabamba (p191) and Santa Cruz (p265) through Los Amigos del Libro and some bookstores. In La Paz try the trekking agents and tourist shops along Sagárnaga, or watch for ambulatory vendors prowling the Prado.

The *Travel Map of Bolivia,* one of the best country maps, and *New Map of the Cordillera Real,* which shows mountains, roads and pre-Hispanic routes, are published by O'Brien Cartographics and are available at various gringo hangouts, including the postcard kiosks within the La Paz central post office.

Government 1:50,000 topographical and specialty sheets are available from the Instituto Geográfico Militar (IGM), which has offices in most major cities, including two offices in La Paz (p63). These sheets cover roughly two-thirds of the country, with notable exceptions including the areas north of Sorata, the Cordillera Apolobamba and Parque Nacional Noel Kempff Mercado. Walter Guzmán Córdova has produced 1:50,000 colorful contour maps of Choro–Takesi–Yunga Cruz, Mururata–Illimani, Huayna Potosí–Condoriri and Sajama, but those other than the Choro–Takesi–Yunga Cruz map are in short supply. The Deutscher Alpenverein (German Alpine Club) produces the excellent and accurate 1:50,000 maps *Alpenvereinskarte Cordillera Real Nord (Illampu),* which includes the Sorata area, and *Alpenvereinskarte Cordillera Real Süd (Illimani),* which centers on Illimani.

GUIDEBOOKS

Sorata Guides & Porters Association (p135) can arrange treks in Sorata.

The best mountaineering guide is *Bolivia – A Climbing Guide,* by Yossi Brain; the late author worked as a climbing guide in La Paz and also served as secretary of the Club Andino Boliviano. *The Andes of Bolivia,* by Alain Mesili, was recently translated into English.

AGENCIES & GUIDES

Many travel agencies in La Paz and larger cities organize climbing and trekking trips in the Cordillera Real and other areas (see p350 for a list of recommended tour companies). Not all, however, are everything they claim to be. Some guides have gotten lost, several have died, and others have practiced less-than-professional tactics, such as stringing 10 or more climbers on the same rope. Always do your research and go with professionally accredited guides such as those registered with Asociación de Guias de Montaña (p59); you'll find them to be more expensive than independent guides, but it's worth the cost.

Specialist agencies can do as much or as little as you want – from just organizing transportation to a full service with guide, cook, mules, porters, a full itinerary and so forth. Professional trekking guides generally charge US$40 to US$60 per day (plus their food) for challenging treks such as volcano climbs. Note that you may be able to find something cheaper in the agencies along Sagárnaga but these 'guides' are often in reality porters and cooks. In addition you need your food, technical equipment and clothing, and – often the most expensive part of any trip – transportation to and from the base camp or the start of the trek. Some people do resort to public transportation or hitchhiking on *camiones* (flatbed trucks), but this requires more time, patience and logistics.

The highest mountain in Bolivia is Sajama at 6542m, followed by Ancohuma at 6427m and Illampu at 6362m.

In addition to the agencies – one of the best is the high-quality **Bolivian Mountains** (☎ 2-249-2775; www.bolivianmountains.com; Rigoberto Paredes 1401, San Pedro, La Paz) – mountain guide information is available from the Asociación de Guias de Montaña (p54).

MOUNTAIN BIKING

Bolivia is blessed with some of the most dramatic mountain-biking terrain in the world: seven months every year of near-perfect weather and relatively easy access to mountain ranges, magnificent lakes, pre-Hispanic ruins and trails, and myriad ecozones connected by an extensive network of footpaths and jeep roads.

The Bolivian Andes are full of long and thrilling descents, as well as challenging touring possibilities. One of the world's longest downhill rides will take you from Parque Nacional Sajama (p163) down to the Chilean coast at Arica. In the dry season you can even tackle the mostly level roads of the vast Amazon lowlands. Parque Nacional Noel Kempff Mercado (p318) also offers the chance to explore on a treadly.

Some rides from La Paz can be done by riders of any experience level. There are more combinations than a bike lock: trails follow Inca roads, tropical tracks, jeep roads and scree chutes. The best known (but not necessarily the best ride for serious riders as there's lots of traffic and dust) is the thrilling 3600m trip down the World's Most Dangerous Road (see boxed text, p74) from La Cumbre to Coroico. Another popular route near La Paz is the lush Zongo Valley ride (p121), which can be started at the 5395m Chacaltaya.

The town of Sorata is emerging as the mountain-bike mecca of Bolivia, with scores of downhill single-track trails and jeep road rides near town, including a combination bike-and-boat trip from Sorata to Rurrenabaque (see boxed text, below). For the hardcore rider, scree chutes to biker-built single track and jump zones abound. Every year, typically in October, Sorata is host to the longest downhill race on a hand-built course, the Jach'a Avalancha (Grand Avalanche) Mountain Bike race. Other epic descents begin in Sorata and head into the hinterland of the Cordillera Muñecas, or start in Copacabana and La Paz and head to Sorata. For descriptions of these routes, see boxed text, p121.

Each year the Jach'a Avalancha (Grand Avalanche) Mountain Bike race is held in Sorata, attracting local and international participants to its two hand-built downhill tracks. Contact Andean Epics Ride Company (p135).

GO WITH THE FLOW

Keen adventurers can experience a double-action whammy – a five-day ride-and-river jaunt from Sorata to Rurrenabaque. This full-on adventure includes a two-day cycling trip, an exciting 4000m descent on single track via Consata and Mapiri, followed by three days of floating down Beni River on a riveting expedition in a motorized dugout canoe, with side hikes to the waterfalls and looking for wildlife in Madidi National Park. This trip is offered every Monday by Andean Epics Ride Company in Sorata.

Another possible longer trip is a two-day riding adventure from Sorata to Charazani, where you construct a *balsa de goma* (tube raft with wooden platform) to float downstream on either the Tuichi, Kamata or Aten rivers toward Rurrenabaque, which takes up to 10 days depending on which river you take.

The 10-day Tuichi trip, for example, heads through the heart of the glorious Madidi National Park, where there are jungle excursions, community visits at San José and fishing and swimming opportunities aplenty. Accommodations for all trips is camping in tents on the river banks. This is a class-IV river in one of the most remote and wild areas in South America, so experienced, knowledgeable and responsible guides are vital, as your life is in their hands.

For those more or less keen on the people-powered component of the trip, itineraries can be custom-made; the cycling section can be completed by 4WD and you can choose the length of your trip.

Andean Epics Ride Company (p135) offers the above options as well as other action-packed trips that are designed to get you off the gringo trail and into the wild areas of the Cordilleras Real, Muñecas and Apolobamba.

More and more travelers are taking up the cycling challenge and heading on two wheels from the north of the country to the south, or vice versa. Those with their own bikes need to consider several factors. During part of the rainy season, particularly December to February, some roads become mired in muck, and heavy rain can greatly reduce visibility, creating dangerous conditions. Also worth noting is Bolivia's lack of spare parts and shortage of experienced mechanics. Comprehensive repair kits are essential. In the Southern Altiplano and Uyuni regions, water is very scarce; you must be able to carry at least two days' worth of water in some places.

4WD

Before heading out on any adventure trips, make sure you acclimatize in either La Paz or Lake Titicaca. See the Health chapter for advice (p358).

Heading out in 4WD vehicles is becoming an increasingly popular activity. It allows you access to places that are tricky to get to and, although sometimes on the pricier side, may be the only feasible way of visiting a region. As well as the standard Southwest Circuit tours (setting off from Uyuni, Tupiza or La Paz), you can cruise out to the *quebradas* (ravines or washes, usually dry) and beyond Tupiza (p185), visit the Tarabuco market (p222; by tour from Sucre, see p218) or the Inca ruins near Cochabamba (p202).

Tours in 4WDs are a great way to enter some of the country's national parks. Current trips include those around Parque Nacional Torotoro (from Cochabamba; p210) and Parque Nacional Sajama (from La Paz; see p350) or into the Cordillera de los Frailes (from Sucre; p217).

For those keener to arrange trips themselves, consider hiring a driver. This can be an efficient and good-value way of seeing specific areas, especially if you are in a group. See p348 for a list of drivers.

WHITEWATER RAFTING & KAYAKING

Bolivia is the 12th most biodiverse country on earth with 2194 known species of amphibians, birds, mammals and reptiles, and more than 14,000 species of plants.

One of Bolivia's greatest secrets is the number of whitewater rivers that drain the eastern slopes of the Andes between the Cordillera Apolobamba and the Chapare. Here, avid rafters and kayakers can enjoy thrilling descents. While access will normally require long drives and/or treks – and considerable expense if done independently – there are a few fine rivers that are relatively accessible.

Some La Paz tour agencies can organize day trips on the Río Coroico (p121). Other options include the Río Unduavi (p132) and numerous wild Chapare rivers (p297). Wilderness canoeing is offered in Parque Nacional Isiboro-Sécure (p298).

A more gentle but fun rush in the Chuquisaca region is a float downriver in rubber inner-tubes. This trip is often coupled with mountain biking (p218). One of the greatest thrills along the same biathlon idea, is to cruise 4000m downhill on mountain bike to Mapiri and then raft your way for several days, camping en route, to Rurrenabaque (see boxed text, p57). Check the Andean Epics Ride Company in Sorata (p135) for a variety of whitewater rafting trips.

HORSEBACK RIDING

For some, a horse saddle sure beats a bus seat. It's a great way to absorb the sights, sounds and smells of a country. Horseback-riding trips are a new and increasingly popular way to see inaccessible wilderness areas. The best place to get your butt into a saddle is in Tupiza, former territory of 'Butch Cassidy and the Sundance Kid' (p182). Here, you can bounce, cruise and walk your way through the areas in triathlon tours, where horses, 4WD and foot are the methods of transportation. You get to see the multicolored desertscapes, *quebradas* and cacti-potted countryside. Other pleasant options to trot are through cloud forest in Coroico (p120), around La Paz (see Calacoto Tours, p351) and in Reserva Biosférica del Beni (p309).

WILDLIFE WATCHING

Bolivia is the Botswana of South America. Fauna and flora fanatics are spoilt for choice in this extraordinary country; world-class wildlife-watching abounds. The diversity of intact habitats throughout the country accounts for the huge number of surviving species.

Parque Nacional Madidi (p308), for example, harbors 1200 bird species, the world's most dense concentration of avifauna species. It is home to wildlife endemic to all Bolivian ecosystems, from tropical rainforest and tropical savanna to cloud forest and alpine tundra. Birding hot spots include the highlands around La Paz and Cochabamba, Parque Nacional & Área de Uso Múltiple Amboró (p276) and Parque Nacional Noel Kempff Mercado (p318), and the Reserva Biosférica del Beni (p309).

Agencies, often run by scientists or environmentalists, offer nature trips run out of Santa Cruz, Cochabamba and Samaipata and, to a lesser extent, La Paz. Contact **Asociación Armonía** (www.birdbolivia.com), the Bolivian partner of BirdLife International, for further birding information. Other organizations with birding knowledge include **Fundación Amigos de la Naturaleza** (FAN; ☎ 3-355-6800; www.fan-bo.org, in Spanish; Km 7.5, Carretera a Samaipata, Santa Cruz) and **Michael Blendinger Tours** (Map p279; ☎ /fax 3-944-6227; www.discoveringbolivia .com; Bolívar s/n, Samaipata).

OTHER ACTIVITIES

Paragliding is a recently introduced activity, so should be done with care – not all local guides are experts of years' standing (or flying!). Most paragliding is done around Sucre (p218).

Other hot spots, and far more relaxing ones, are the many *termas* (hot springs) that bubble away in various parts of the country. You don't have to go to the ends of the earth to immerse yourself in this less energetic activity – there are springs in Tarapaya (p242) just outside of Potosí, Talula (p227), San Xavier (p287) and Sajama (p164).

The 18,000-year-old Chacaltaya glacier in Bolivia, one of the highest in South America, has entirely melted away in 2009.

La Paz

La Paz is dizzying in every respect, not only for its well-publicized altitude (3660m), but for its quirky beauty. Most travelers enter this extraordinary city via the flat, sparse plains of the sprawling city of El Alto, an approach that hides the sensational surprises of the valley below. The first glimpse of La Paz will, literally, take your breath away. The city's buildings cling to the sides of the canyon and spill spectacularly downwards. On a clear day, the imposing showy, snowy Mt Illimani (6402m) looms in the background.

Although Sucre still hangs on to its status as the constitutional capital, La Paz – Bolivia's largest city and centre for commerce, finance and industry – is the country's seat of government. Meanwhile, El Alto is the Aymará capital of the world. Although in reality an extension of urban La Paz, El Alto's ongoing influx of immigrants – mostly looking for work – means it has morphed into one of Latin America's fastest-growing cities.

La Paz must be savored over time, not only to acclimatize to the altitude, but to experience the city's many faces. Wander at leisure through the alleys and lively markets, marvel at the interesting museums, chat to the locals in a *comedor* (dining hall) or relax over a coffee at a trendy cafe.

Since La Paz is sky-high, warm clothing is desirable most of the year, at least in the evenings. In summer (November to April) the climate can be harsh: rain falls most afternoons, the canyon may fill with clouds and steep streets often become torrents of runoff. In winter (May to October) days can be slightly cooler, but the sun (and its UV rays) is strong and temperatures reach the high 60s; at night it often dips below freezing.

HIGHLIGHTS

- Tantalize your taste buds on a **walking tour** (p75) with a difference – where you consume the city's food, ecology and culture
- Wander through the sprawling markets of **El Alto** (p73) for the sights and sounds of indigenous La Paz (p71)
- **Shop** (p85) till you drop in fair-trade shops around Illampu, El Prado and Zona Sur
- Marvel at the recent finds in the ancient ruins of **Tiwanaku** (p93)
- Eat to the beat of a **peña performance** (p84) for a night of traditional dancing and folk music

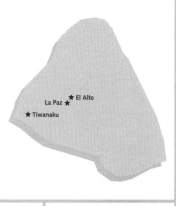

| ■ TELEPHONE CODE: 2 | ■ POPULATION: 829,000 | ■ ELEVATION: 3660M |

HISTORY

La Ciudad de Nuestra Señora de La Paz (the City of Our Lady of Peace) was founded and named on October 20, 1548, by a Spaniard, Captain Alonzo de Mendoza, at present-day Laja situated on the Tiwanaku road. Soon after, La Paz was shifted to its present location, the valley of the Chuquiago Marka (now called the Río Choqueyapu), which had been occupied by a community of Aymará miners.

The 16th-century Spanish historian Cieza de León remarked of the newfound city: 'This is a good place to pass one's life. Here the climate is mild and the view of the mountains inspires one to think of God.' But despite León's lofty assessment (perhaps he mistakenly got off at Cochabamba), the reason behind the city's founding was much more terrestrial. The Spanish always had a weakness for shiny yellow metal, and the now-fetid Río Choqueyapu, which today flows underneath La Paz, seemed to be full of it.

The Spaniards didn't waste any amount of time in seizing the gold mines, and Captain Mendoza was installed as the new city's first mayor. The conquerors also imposed their religion and their lifestyle on the indigenous people, and since most of the colonists were men, unions between Spanish men and indigenous women eventually gave rise to a primarily mestizo population.

If the founding of La Paz had been based on anything other than gold, its position in the depths of a rugged canyon probably would have dictated an unpromising future. However, the protection this setting provided from the fierce Altiplano climate and the city's convenient location on the main trade route between Lima and Potosí – much of the Potosí silver bound for Pacific ports passed through La Paz – offered the city some hope of prosperity once the gold had played out. By the time the railway was built, the city was well enough established to continue commanding attention.

In spite of its name, the City of Our Lady of Peace has seen a good deal of violence. Since Bolivian independence in 1825, the republic has endured over 190 changes of leadership. An abnormally high mortality rate once accompanied high office in Bolivia; the job of president came with a short life expectancy. In fact, the presidential palace on the plaza is now known as the Palacio Quemado (Burned Palace), owing to its repeated gutting by fire. As recently as 1946 then-president Gualberto Villarroel was publicly hanged in Plaza Murillo.

See the History chapter (p21) for more on Bolivia's history, much of it centered around La Paz, as seat of government and ever-expanding city.

ORIENTATION

It is just about impossible to get yourself lost in La Paz. There is only one major thoroughfare and it follows the Río Choqueyapu canyon (fortunately for your olfactory system, the river flows mostly underground). The main thoroughfare changes names several times from the top to the bottom: Avs Ismael Montes, Mariscal Santa Cruz, 16 de Julio (the Prado) and Villazón. Quite often the section is simply referred to as 'El Prado.' At the lower end of the thoroughfare, the street divides into Avs 6 de Agosto and Aniceto Arce.

The business districts and the wealthier neighborhoods – with their skyscrapers, colonial houses and modern glass constructions – occupy the city's more tranquil lower altitudes (which is the reverse of many US and European cities). The best preserved colonial section of town is near the intersection of Calles Jaén and Sucre, where narrow cobbled streets and colonial churches offer a glimpse of early La Paz. The most prestigious neighborhoods are found further down in the canyon in Zona Sur (Southern Zone, which includes the neighborhoods of Obrajes, La Florida, Calacoto, San Miguel and Cotacota, as well as a growing throng of other barrios. Numbered streets run perpendicular to the main road in Zona Sur, making navigation easier; the numbers increase from west to east.

Above the city center and Zona Sur, and still very much part of La Paz, are the cascades of cuboid, mud and brick dwellings and ever-growing neighborhoods, which literally spill over the canyon rim and down the slopes on three sides. This is where much of the daily hustle and bustle takes place, with all sorts of sights, sounds and smells. Above all this, stretching for miles away from the canyon's rim across the Altiplano, is the city of El Alto. If you find yourself becoming disoriented up here and want to return to the center, just head downhill.

LA PAZ

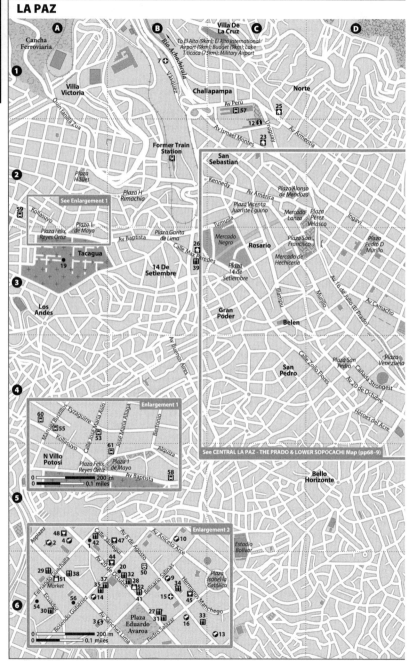

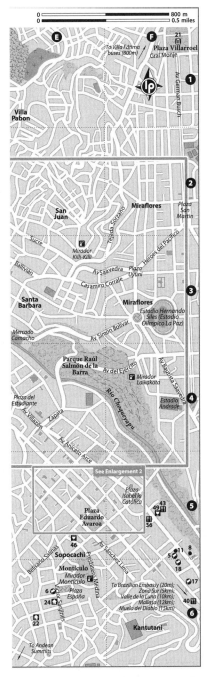

Maps

Free city maps are available at the tourist offices. Inside the central post office, opposite the *poste restante* counter, there are gift shops that sell a range of maps.

La Paz is the place to stock up on maps for the rest of your trip. For information on buying topographic sheets and climbing maps, see also p55 and p334.

Instituto Geográfico Militar (IGM; Map pp68-9; ☎ 237-0118; Oficina 5, Juan XXIII 100; ☀ 8:30am-12:30, 2:30-6:30pm Mon-Fri) In a blind alley off Rodríguez, IGM offers original 1:50,000 topographic maps (B$40) or photocopies (B$35) if a sheet is unavailable. Another outlet is located at Saavedra, Estadio Mayor, Miraflores.

Lectura (Map pp68-9; Camacho & Loayza) Stocks books and maps on Bolivia.

Librería Olimpia (Map pp68-9; ☎ 240-8101; Galería Handal, Mariscal Santa Cruz, Local 14) A stationery store that stocks a small but worthwhile collection of maps.

Servicio Nacional de Áreas Protegidas (SERNAP; ☎ 242-6272; www.sernap.gov.bo, in Spanish; Francisco Bedregal 2904, Sopocachi) Provides information and maps of Bolivia's 22 protected national areas.

INFORMATION
Bookstores & Book Exchanges

To trade books, the best library is Oliver's Travels bar (p84), but some readers don't appreciate the higher charges for 'trading' a book (in their defense, these are good quality books). Or try Gravity Assisted Mountain Biking (p74), or Cafe Sol y Luna (p84).

Andean Base Camp ('Ex-Etnic'; Map pp68-9; ☎ 246-3782; www.andeanbasecamp.com; Illampu 863) This helpful place (see p86) stocks a large range of Lonely Planet guides and excellent maps.

Librería Olimpia (Map pp68-9; ☎ 240-8101; Galería Handal, Mariscal Santa Cruz, Local 14) Stationery store with a good map selection.

SpeakEasy Institute (Map pp68-9; ☎ 244-1779; www.speakeasyinstitute.com; Arce 2047) Stocks hundreds of fantastic reads including classics and blockbusters. Fifty per cent of earnings goes to a local knitters association to provide their children with homework support.

Spitting Llama Bookstore & Outfitter (Map pp68-9; ☎ 7039-8720; www.thespittingllama.com; Calle Linares 947) Stocks new and used guidebooks, including heaps of Lonely Planets, plus Spanish and foreign-language books. Inside La Posada de la Abuela.

Cultural Centers

Alianza Francesa (Map opposite; ☎ 242-5004; www.afbolivia.org; Guachalla 399) Offers language classes, exhibitions and promotes cultural events.

INFORMATION		
Alianza Francesa	**1**	A5
Argentine Embassy	**2**	A5
ATM	**3**	A6
Australian Consulate	**4**	A5
British Embassy	**5**	F5
Canadian Consulate	**6**	E6
Centro Epidemiológico Departamental La Paz	**7**	B1
Dr Jorge Jaime Aguirre	**8**	F5
Dutch Embassy	**9**	B6
German Embassy	**10**	B5
Goethe Institut	**11**	F5
Information Kiosk	**12**	C2
Italian Embassy	**13**	C6
Japanese Embassy	**14**	A6
Medicentro	**15**	B6
Paraguayan Embassy	**16**	B6
Peruvian Embassy	(see 9)	
Spanish Embassy	**17**	F6
US Embassy	**18**	F6

SIGHTS & ACTIVITIES		
Cemetery	**19**	A3
ie instituto exclusivo	**20**	B6
Museo de la Revolución Nacional	**21**	F1

SLEEPING 🏠		
A La Maison Appart-Hotel	**22**	E6
Adventure Brew Hostal	**23**	C2
Alcalá Apart Hotel	**24**	E6
Hostal Tambo del Oro	**25**	C1
Hotel La Joya	**26**	B3
La Loge	(see 38)	

EATING 🍴		
Alexander Coffee & Pub	**27**	B6
Arábica	**28**	B6
Arco Iris	**29**	A6
Armonía	**30**	A6
Cafe Blueberries	**31**	B6
Café La Terraza	**32**	B6
El Arriero	**33**	B6
Fridolin	**34**	B6
Hipermaxi	**35**	A6
Ketal Hipermercado	**36**	F5
Kuchen Stube	**37**	A6
La Comédie Art-Café Restaurant	**38**	A6
La Guinguette	(see 1)	
Mercado Uruguay	**39**	B3
New Tokyo	**40**	F6
Paceña La Salteña	**41**	B6
Restaurant Paladar	**42**	A5
Wagamama	**43**	F5

DRINKING & CLUBBING 🍸		
Diesel Nacional	**44**	B6
Mongo's	**45**	B6
Ram Jam	**46**	E5
Reineke Fuchs	**47**	B5
Thelonius Jazz Bar	**48**	A5
Traffic	**49**	F5

ENTERTAINMENT 🎭		
Cine 6 de Agosto	**50**	B6

SHOPPING 🛍		
Irupana	**51**	A6
Tecnología Fotográfica	**52**	B6

TRANSPORT		
Autolíneas Ingavi	**53**	A4
Budget	**54**	A6
Buses to Huarina & Huatajata	**55**	A4
Kolla Motors	**56**	A6
Main Bus Terminal	**57**	C1
Micros to Center	**58**	B5
Trans Altiplano	**59**	A2
Trans-Unificado Sorata	**60**	A4
Transportes Manco Kapac	**61**	B5
TransTurs 2 de Febrero	(see 61)	

Centro Boliviano-Americano (CBA; ☎ 243-0107; www.cba.edu.bo; Parque Zenón Iturralde 121) Language classes and US periodicals library.

Goethe Institut (Map pp62-3; ☎ 243-1916; www .goethe.de; Arce 2708, cnr Campos) Films, language classes and good German-language library.

Emergency

Numbers for emergency services (police, fire and ambulance) are the same throughout the country: see the Quick Reference, on the inside front cover.

Tourist Police (Policía Turística; Map pp68-9; ☎ 222-5016; Plaza del Estadio, Puerta 22, Miraflores) Next to Disco Love City. English-speaking. Report thefts to obtain a *denuncia* (affidavit) for insurance purposes – they won't recover any stolen goods.

Immigration

Migración (Map pp68-9; ☎ 211-0960; Camacho 1468; ⏱ 8:30am-4pm Mon-Fri) Some call this place 'Migraineation' but this is where you must obtain your visa extensions.

Internet Access

La Paz has nearly as many cybercafes as shoeshine boys. Charges range from B$1 to B$3 an hour, and connections are generally fastest in the morning or late evening. Many of the smarter cafes have wi-fi access.

Internet Alley (Map pp68-9; Pasaje Iturralde) Just off the Prado near Plaza del Estudiante. Fast, cheap connections with several places open until late.

Internet Resources

For Spanish readers, the following are useful:

Bolivia Travel Guide (www.gbtbolivia.com) A privately run site with excellent coverage of La Paz.

Visit Bolivia (www.visitbolivia.org) Produced by OGD (Organización de Gestión de Destino), a government-run organization, this site has some excellent information.

www.lapaz.bo La Paz's municipal website has good cultural and tourism sections.

Laundry

Lavanderías (laundries) are the cheapest and most efficient way of ensuring clean (and dry) clothes in La Paz.

Calle Illampu, at the top of Sagárnaga, is lined with laundries. Many hotels and some *residenciales* (budget accommodations) offer cheap hand-washing services. For quick, reliable same-day machine-wash-and-dry service (B$5 to B$10 per kilo), try the following:

Lavandería Aroma (Map pp68-9; Illampu 869)

Lavandería Maya (Map pp68-9; Hostal Maya, Sagárnaga 339)

Limpieza Express (Map pp68-9; Aroma 720)

Left Luggage

Most recommended sleeping places offer inexpensive or free left-luggage storage, especially if you make a return reservation. The main bus terminal (p87) has a cheap *depósito*, but think twice about leaving anything valuable here.

LA PAZ IN...

Two Days

Given the altitude and hills, La Paz is to be explored at leisure, allowing a day to acclimatize. Over the next two days, slowly make your way through these suggestions. Start the mornings with breakfast on the Prado or a snack – try *salteñas* (filled pastry shells) – around Plaza Avaroa, both perfect spots for watching one of the world's highest cities wake up. Stroll the historic cobblestone streets around **Iglesia de San Francisco** (p71) and the historic Calle Jaén, home to the wonderful **Calle Jaén Museums** (p71). Tie some cultural threads together at the **Museo de Textiles Andinos Bolivianos** (p72), or wander through the interesting (if tourist-ready) **artesanía alley** (Calle Linares; p85) and **Mercado de Hechicería** (Witches' Market; p70). From here, head up to the **markets** (p71) sprawled along many street blocks, to wander among the people, merchandise and delicious foodstuffs.

Head back downhill along the Prado and treat yourself to fine dining at an international eatery in Sopocachi on one night, and in the trendy Zona Sur on another (see p82). Alternatively, kick back in one of the many popular bars around town (see p84) or enjoy a taste of traditional music at one of the **peñas** (p84).

Four Days

Follow the two-day itinerary, then on your third day do a **guided walking tour** (p75) of La Paz or its surrounds, getting a taste of local food and its origins. On the fourth day take a day trip out to **Tiwanaku** (p93) to explore the excavated ruins. Or, depending on the season, you could visit **Chacaltaya** (p93) or do a day's **bike trip** on the outskirts of La Paz (p74).

Media

La Razón (www.la-razon.com), *El Diario* (www.eldiario.net) and *La Prensa* (www.laprensa.com.bo) are La Paz's major daily newspapers. National media chains **ATB** (www.bolivia.com) and **Grupo Fides** (www.radiofides.com, in Spanish) host the most up-to-date online news sites.

Medical Services

For serious medical emergency conditions, contact your embassy for doctor recommendations. The 24-hour **Medicentro** (Map pp62-3; ☎ 244-1717; 6 de Agosto 2440) has been recommended for general care. For emergencies, there's **Clínica Sur** (☎ 278-4001; Hernando Siles, Zona Sur).

There's a well-stocked 24-hour pharmacy (Map pp68-9) at the corner of 16 de Julio and Bueno. Other *farmacias de turno* (after-hours pharmacies on rotation) are listed in daily newspapers.

A reader-recommended optical outlet providing glasses and contact lenses is **Techno Vision** (☎ 240-9637; Calle Comercio 844).

The following are reputable medical and dental contacts:

Centro Epidemiológico Departamental La Paz (Centro Piloto; Map pp68-9; ☎ 245-0166; Vásquez at Perú; ⏱ 8:30-11:30am Mon-Fri) Off upper Ismael Montes near the brewery. Anyone heading for malarial areas can pick up antimalarials, and rabies and yellow fever vaccinations, for the cost of a sterile needle – bring one from a pharmacy.

Dr Elbert Orellana Jordan (☎ 242-2342, 7065-9743; asistmedbolivia@hotmail.com) Gregarious and caring English-speaking doctor makes 24/7/365 emergency house calls.

Dr Fernando Patiño (☎ 7724-3765; curare27@gmail.com; Edificio CURARE, Calle 10, 8090, cnr Julio C Paiño, Calacoto) US-educated, English-speaking general practitioner.

Dr Iturri Stroobandt Igor (☎ 221-876, 7195-8595; bolivianmedicine@latinmail.com) French- and English-speaking, reader-recommended doctor.

Dr Jorge Jaime Aguirre (Map pp62-3; ☎ 243-2682; 1st fl, Edificio Illimani, Arce 2707) Frequently recommended dentist for everything from routine cleaning to root canals.

High Altitude Pathology Institute (off Map pp68-9; ☎ 224-5394, 7325-8026; www.altitudeclinic.com; Saavedra 2302, Miraflores) Bolivian member of the International Association for Medical Assistance to Travelers (Iamat). Offers computerized high-altitude medical checkups and can help with high altitude problems. English spoken.

Money

ATMS

Cash withdrawals of bolivianos and US dollars are possible at numerous ATMs at major intersections around the city. For

LA PAZ

cash advances (bolivianos only, amount according to your limit in your home country) with no commission and little hassle, try the following:

Banco Mercantil (Map pp68-9; cnr Mercado & Ayacucho)

Banco Nacional de Bolivia (Map pp68-9; cnr Colón & Camacho)

MONEY TRANSFERS
Try **Western Union/DHL** (Map pp68-9; ☎ 233-5567; Pérez 268), which has other outlets scattered all around town, for urgent international money transfers.

MONEYCHANGERS
Casas de cambio (exchange bureaux) in the city center can be quicker and more convenient than banks. Most places open from 8:30am to noon and 2pm to 6pm weekdays, and on Saturday mornings. If desperate, try Hotel Gloria (p79).

Be wary of counterfeit US dollars and bolivianos, especially with *cambistas* (street moneychangers) who loiter around the intersections of Colón, Camacho and Santa Cruz. Outside La Paz you'll get 3% to 10% less for checks than for cash. The following places change US and euro traveler's checks for around 2% to 3% commission:

Cambios América (Map pp68-9; Camacho 1223)

Casa de Cambio Sudamer (Map pp68-9 Colón 206 at Camacho; ☺ 8:30am-6:30pm Mon-Fri, 9:30am-12:30pm Sat) Also has Moneygram service for money transferral.

Post
Ángelo Colonial (Map pp68-9; Linares 922; ☺ 8:30am-7:30pm Mon-Fri, 8:30am-6pm Sat, 9am-noon Sun) This small post office, in the same building as Ángelo Colonial restaurant (p81), offers both incoming and outgoing mail services.

Central Post Office (Ecobol; Map pp68-9; Santa Cruz & Oruro; ☺ 8am-8pm Mon-Fri, 8:30am-6pm Sat, 9am-noon Sun) A tranquil oasis off the Prado, *lista de correos* (*poste restante*) mail is held for two months for free here – bring your passport (see p336). A downstairs customs desk facilitates international parcel posting (see p336).

Telephone & Fax
Convenient *puntos* (privately run phone offices) of various carriers – Entel, Cotel, Tigo, Viva etc – are scattered throughout the city. Street kiosks, which are on nearly every corner, also sell phone cards, and offer brief local calls for around B$1 per minute.

You can buy cell phone sim cards (known as *chips*) for around B$10 from Entel (see below) or any carrier outlet. International calls can be made at low prices from the international **call center** (Galería Chuquiago, Sagárnaga, cnr Murillo; ☺ 8:30am-8pm).

Entel office (Map pp68-9; ☎ fax 213-2334; Ayacucho 267; ☺ 8:30am-9pm Mon-Fri, 8:30am-8:30pm Sat, 9am-4pm Sun) The main Entel office is the best place to receive incoming calls and faxes.

Tourist Information
Information kiosks Main bus terminal (Map pp62-3); Casa de la Cultura (Map pp68-9; Mariscal Santa Cruz & Potosí)

InfoTur (Map pp68-9; ☎ 265-1778; www .visitbolivia.org, in Spanish; Av Mariscal, with Columbia; ☺ 8:30am-12:30 & 3-7pm Mon-Fri, 9am-1pm Sat) Part of a chain of information points run by the OGD (see p64), with friendly staff and limited information on La Paz and Bolivia, this office is in a handy spot on the Prado.

Tourist Information Office (Map pp68-9; ☎ 237-1044; Plaza del Estudiante; ☺ 8:30am-12:30pm & 3-7pm Mon-Fri) This is the original tourist office, where English-speaking staff provide good verbal information as it's a bit short on printed matter, including free city maps. Ask to see a copy of *Jiwaki*, a listing of the month's activities.

DANGERS & ANNOYANCES
Fake police officers and bogus tourist officials exist. Note: authentic police officers will always be uniformed (undercover police are under strict orders not to hassle foreigners) and will never insist that you show them your passport, get in a taxi with them or allow them to search you in public. If confronted by an imposter, refuse to show them your valuables (wallet, passport, money etc), or insist on going to the nearest police station on foot. If physically threatened, it is always best to hand over valuables immediately.

In the last few years, there have been many incidents of fake 'taxi drivers' assaulting or kidnapping unsuspecting travelers and extorting ATM PIN details. Always take a radio cab; these have a radio in the car and a promo bubble on its roof (do not take the informal cabs which merely have a 'taxi' sticker). At night, ask the restaurant or hotel to call a cab – the cab's details are recorded at a central base. Don't share cabs with strangers and beware of accepting lifts from drivers who approach you (especially around dodgy bus areas). See p102 for a warning on traveling between La Paz and Copacabana.

La Paz is a great city to explore on foot, but take the local advice *'camina lentito, come poquito…y duerme solito'* (walk slowly, eat only a little bit…and sleep by your poor little self) to avoid feeling the effects of *soroche* (altitude sickness).

In the last couple of years, it seems traffic has increased tenfold due in part to second-hand car imports – take care in crossing roads and avoid walking in busy streets at peak hours when fumes can be overwhelming.

Scams

Sadly, La Paz seems to have caught on to South America's common ruses. The bogus tourist is a popular one: on engaging you in conversation in English, the 'tourist' is confronted by fake 'tourist police.' The 'tourist' abides by an 'order' to show the tourist police his bag/papers/passport, and 'translates' for you to do the same. During the search, the cohorts strip you of your cash and/or belongings.

Psst my friend! This popular scam involves someone spilling a substance on you or spitting a phlegm ball at you. While you or they are wiping it off, another lifts your wallet or slashes your pack; the perpetrator may be an 'innocent' granny or young girl. Similarly, make sure that you don't bend over to pick up a valuable item which has been 'dropped.' You risk being accused of theft, or of being pickpocketed. See also p330.

SIGHTS

When the sun shines, La Paz cries out for leisurely exploration. Bolivia's governmental capital has its share of cultural and historical museums, most of which are found in the city center or close surrounds. Yet much of the enjoyment comes from observing the rhythms of local life. Much of the daily action takes place in the upper central regions of La Paz, where a mass of irregular shaped steep streets and alleys wind their way skywards. Here, locals embrace their frenetic daily life. Women, sporting long black plaits, bowler hats and vivid mantas, attend to steaming pots or sell everything from dried llama fetuses to designer shoes, while men, negotiating the frenetic traffic (and its fumes), push overladen trolleys. Keep your eyes peeled for fantastic glimpses of Illimani's triple peak towering between the world's highest high-rises. Many visitors allow another day or two to acclimatize during a day trip to Tiwanaku (p93) or Lake Titicaca (p97).

Most official sites, including museums, are closed over the Christmas holiday period (December 25 to January 6).

Cathedral & Plaza Murillo

Although it's a relatively recent addition to La Paz's collection of religious structures, the 1835 **cathedral** (Map pp68-9) is an impressive structure – mostly because it is built on a steep hillside. The main

---

WARNING: SAN PEDRO PRISON

It's likely you won't be in La Paz long before you'll hear about 'tours' to San Pedro prison – from other travelers, or sometimes operators and hostels. We strongly advise against participating in one of these unofficial – and, in fact, illegal – 'tours', which are organized by inmates, guards and dodgy operators. There are high risks associated with entering San Pedro prison. First, it's illegal, and the Bolivian authorities are cracking down on unofficial visits. In 2009 the government restricted visiting hours to try to stop prison tourism; this had a negative impact on many people, including the wives and children of inmates. In response, prisoners rioted.

Inside the prison, there's no protection or guarantee of your safety. If you're robbed, assaulted or worse, you are unlikely to be defended and will have no possible recourse. While most visitors to the prison go for curiosity's sake – which can border on voyeurism – others undoubtedly visit to purchase cocaine. The danger of doing so cannot be overstated. Despite its ubiquity, cocaine is illegal, and if you're caught with it, you could end up staying at San Pedro prison for much longer than an afternoon; Bolivian drug penalties are severe. The altitude in La Paz compounds the effects of the drug, and defective cocaine can cause serious medical consequences, including death.

The UK Foreign & Commonwealth Office has issued a travel advisory against visiting the prison. We concur with their advice.

CENTRAL LA PAZ - THE PRADO & LOWER SOPOCACHI

INFORMATION
24-hour Pharmacy...........................**1** D4
Andean Base Camp.....................(see 97)
Ángelo Colonial.............................(see 68)
Banco Mercantil (ATM)..................**2** D3
Cambios América............................**3** D3
Casa de Cambio Sudamer................**4** D3
Central Post Office..........................**5** D3
Entel Office.....................................**6** D3
Information Kiosk...........................(see 87)
Instituto Geográfico Militar
  (IGM)...**7** C4
Internet Alley.................................**8** E5
Lavandería Aroma.........................(see 35)
Lavandería Maya............................(see 42)
Librería Olimpia..............................**9** C3
Limpieza Express...........................**10** B2
Migración.......................................**11** D4
SpeakEasy Institute.......................**12** F6
Spitting Llama Bookstore &
  Outfitter....................................(see 60)
Techno Vision................................**13** C2
Tourist Information Office..............**14** E5
Tourist Police.................................**15** H3
Western Union/DHL........................**16** E6

SIGHTS & ACTIVITIES
Academia de Música Helios.......**17** D2
America Tours...............................**18** D4
Cathedral.......................................**19** D3
Club Andino Boliviano...................**20** D5
Gravity Assisted Mountain
  Biking..(see 18)
Iglesia de San Francisco...............**21** C3
Magri Turismo...............................**22** F6
Mercado de Hechicería.................**23** B3
Mercado Lanza..............................**24** C2
Museo de Arte
  Contemporáneo.........................**25** E5
Museo de Etnografía y
  Folklore......................................**26** D2

Museo de Instrumentos
  Musicales....................................**27** C1
Museo de la Coca..........................**28** B3
Museo Nacional de
  Arqueología...............................**29** E5
Museo Nacional del Arte...............**30** D2
Museo San Francisco.....................**31** C2
Museo Tambo Quirquincho............**32** C2
Presidential Palace........................**33** D2
SpeakEasy Institute.....................(see 12)
Templete Semisubterráneo............**34** G4
Turisbus......................................(see 58)
Zig-Zag...**35** B3

SLEEPING
Arcabucero Hostal Inn...................**36** C3
Arthy's Guesthouse.......................**37** C1
Ayni..(see 58)
Cafe El Consulado......................(see 70)
Estrella Andina Hotel....................**38** B2
Hospedaje Milenio........................**39** D1
Hostal Austria...............................**40** D2
Hostal Maximiliano........................**41** B1
Hostal Maya.................................**42** B3
Hostal Naira..................................**43** C3
Hostal República...........................**44** E3
Hostel Provenzal........................(see 86)
Hotel Berlina.................................**45** B2
Hotel Brisas..................................**46** B2
Hotel Continental..........................**47** B2
Hotel España.................................**48** F6
Hotel Europa.................................**49** E5
Hotel Fuentes...............................**50** B3
Hotel Gloria...................................**51** C2

Hotel La Valle...............................**52** C2
Hotel Madre Tierra.......................**53** E6
Hotel Majestic...............................**54** B4
Hotel Milton..................................**55** B4
Hotel Presidente...........................**56** C2
Hotel Radisson Plaza.....................**57** F6
Hotel Rosario................................**58** B2
Hotel Sagárnaga............................**59** B3
La Posada de La Abuela..................**60** C3
Loki La Paz....................................**61** E3
Onkel Inn......................................**62** D4
Plaza Hotel....................................**63** E5
Residencial Sucre..........................**64** C5
Wild Rover.....................................**65** E3

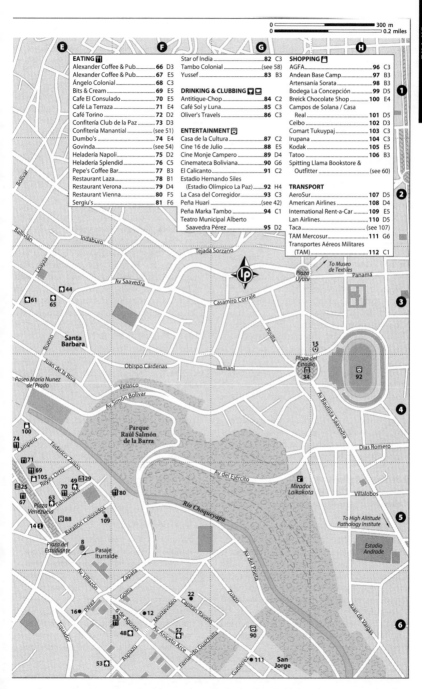

EATING 🍴
Alexander Coffee & Pub.............. **66** D3
Alexander Coffee & Pub.............. **67** E5
Ángelo Colonial............................ **68** C3
Bits & Cream................................. **69** E5
Cafe El Consulado........................ **70** E5
Café La Terraza............................. **71** E4
Café Torino................................... **72** D2
Confitería Club de la Paz **73** D3
Confitería Manantial .... (see 51)
Dumbo's... **74** E4
Govinda....................................... (see 54)
Heladería Napoli.......................... **75** D2
Heladería Splendid...................... **76** C5
Pepe's Coffee Bar........................ **77** B3
Restaurant Laza............................ **78** B1
Restaurant Verona....................... **79** D4
Restaurant Vienna....................... **80** F5
Sergiu's.. **81** F6
Star of India................................. **82** C3
Tambo Colonial......................... (see 58)
Yussef... **83** B3

DRINKING & CLUBBING 🍷 🖥
Antique-Chop................................ **84** C2
Café Sol y Luna............................. **85** C3
Oliver's Travels............................. **86** C3

ENTERTAINMENT 🎭
Casa de la Cultura........................ **87** C2
Cine 16 de Julio........................... **88** E5
Cine Monje Campero **89** D4
Cinemateca Boliviana.................. **90** G6
El Calicanto.................................. **91** C2
Estadio Hernando Siles
  (Estadio Olímpico La Paz)........ **92** H4
La Casa del Corregidor................ **93** C3
Peña Huari.................................. (see 42)
Peña Marka Tambo **94** C1
Teatro Municipal Alberto
  Saavedra Pérez......................... **95** D2

SHOPPING 🛍
AGFA.. **96** C3
Andean Base Camp...................... **97** B3
Artensanía Sorata......................... **98** B3
Bodega La Concepción................. **99** D5
Breick Chocolate Shop **100** E4
Campos de Solana / Casa
  Real... **101** D5
Ceibo.. **102** D3
Comart Tukuypaj........................ **103** C3
Irupana.. **104** C3
Kodak... **105** E5
Tatoo... **106** B3
Spitting Llama Bookstore &
  Outfitter................................. (see 60)

TRANSPORT
AeroSur....................................... **107** D5
American Airlines........................ **108** D4
International Rent-a-Car **109** E5
Lan Airlines................................. **110** D5
Taca... (see 107)
TAM Mercosur............................ **111** G6
Transportes Aéreos Militares
  (TAM).. **112** C1

entrance is 12m higher than its base on Calle Potosí. The cathedral's sheer immensity, with its high dome, hulking columns, thick stone walls and high ceilings, is overpowering, but the altar is relatively simple. Inside, the main attraction is the profusion of stained-glass work; the windows behind the altar depict a gathering of Bolivian politicos being blessed from above by a flock of heavenly admirers.

Beside the cathedral is the **Presidential Palace** (Map pp68–9), and in the center of Plaza Murillo, opposite, stands a **statue of President Gualberto Villarroel**. In 1946, he was dragged from the palace by vigilantes and hanged from a lamppost in the square. Interestingly enough, don Pedro Domingo Murillo, for whom the plaza was named, met a similar fate here in 1810.

Museo Nacional de Arqueología

Two blocks east of the Prado, this **museum** (National Archaeology Museum; Map pp68-9; ☎ 231-1621; Tiahuanacu 93; admission B$10; ☺ 9am-12:30pm & 3-7pm Mon-Fri, 9am-noon Sat) holds a small but well-sorted collection of artifacts that illustrate the most interesting aspects of the Tiwanaku culture's five stages (p94) – those that weren't stolen or damaged during the colonial days. Some of the ancient stonework disappeared into Spanish construction projects, while valuable pieces found their way into European museums or were melted down for royal treasuries. Unfortunately there are no explanations in English, only Spanish. Also holds excellent temporary exhibitions.

Mercado de Hechicería

The city's most unusual market, the **Witches' Market** (Map pp68–9), lies along Calles Jiménez and Linares between Sagárnaga and Santa Cruz, amid lively tourist *artesanías* (stores selling locally handcrafted items). What is on sale isn't witchcraft as depicted in horror films and Halloween tales; the merchandise is herbal and folk remedies, plus a few more unorthodox ingredients intended to manipulate and supplicate the various malevolent and benevolent spirits of the Aymará world. An example of these types of ingredients is dried toucan beaks, intended to cure ills and protect supplicants from bad spirits.

If you're building a new house, for example, you can buy a llama fetus to bury beneath

the cornerstone as a *cha'lla* (offering) to Pachamama, encouraging her to inspire good luck therein. If someone is feeling ill, or is being pestered by unwelcome or bothersome spooks, they can purchase a plateful of colorful herbs, seeds and assorted critter parts to remedy the problem. As you pass the market stalls, watch for wandering *yatiris* (witch doctors), who wear dark hats and carry coca pouches, and offer (mainly to locals) fortune-telling services.

Inquiries and photographs taken here may be met with unpleasantness – ask politely first.

Museo de la Coca

Chew on some facts inside the small, slightly tired **Coca Museum** (Map pp68-9; ☎ 231-1998; Linares 906; admission B$10; ☺ 10am-7pm), which explores the sacred leaf's role in traditional societies, its use by the soft-drink and pharmaceutical industries, and the growth of cocaine as an illicit drug. The displays (ask for a translation in your language) are educational, provocative and evenhanded.

Museo Nacional del Arte

Near Plaza Murillo, this **museum** (National Art Museum; Map pp68-9; ☎ 240-8600; www.mna.org.bo; cnr Comercio & Socabaya; admission B$10; ☺ 9:30am-12:30pm & 3:30-7pm Tue-Sat, 9:30am-12:30pm Sun) is housed in the former Palacio de Los Condes de Arana. This stunning building was constructed in 1775 of pink Viacha granite and has been restored to its original grandeur, in Mestizo (mixed) baroque and Andino baroque styles. In the center of a huge courtyard, surrounded by three stories of pillared corridors, is a lovely alabaster fountain. The various levels are dedicated

---

LUSTRABOTAS

Around La Paz and the rest of Bolivia *lustrabotas* (shoeshine men and boys) are a familiar sight and hound everyone with footwear, even those sporting sandals. Many *lustrabotas,* especially the older ones, wear ski masks and baseball caps – it's said that they often do so to avoid social stigma, as many are working hard to support families or pay their way through school – you can support their cause for between B$2 and B$3.

to different eras, from pre-hispanic works to contemporary art, with an emphasis on religious themes. Highlights include works by former Paceño Marina Nuñez del Prado. There are regular temporary exhibitions on the ground floor.

Calle Jaén Museums

These four, small, interesting **museums** (Map pp68-9; ☎ 228-0758; combo admission B$4; ⏰ 9:30am-12:30pm & 3-7pm Tue-Fri, 9am-1pm Sat & Sun) are clustered together along Calle Jaén, La Paz's finest colonial street, and can easily be bundled into one visit. Buy tickets at the Museo Costumbrista (below).

Also known as Museo del Oro (Gold Museum), the **Museo de Metales Preciosos** (Museum of Precious Metals; Jaén 777) houses four impressively presented salons of pre-Colombian silver, gold and copper works and pieces from Tiwanaku.

Sometimes called the Museo de la Guerra del Pacífico, the diminutive **Museo del Litoral** (Jaén 798) incorporates relics from the 1884 war in which Bolivia became landlocked after losing its Litoral department to Chile. The collection consists mainly of historical maps that defend Bolivia's emotionally charged claims to Antofagasta and Chile's Segunda Región.

Once the home of don Pedro Domingo Murillo, a leader in the La Paz Revolution of July 16, 1809, the **Casa de Murillo** (Jaén 790) displays collections of colonial art and furniture, textiles, medicines, musical instruments and household items of glass and silver that once belonged to Bolivian aristocracy. Other odds and ends include a collection of Alasitas miniatures (p76). Murillo was hanged by the Spanish on January 29, 1810, in the plaza now named after him. The most intriguing painting on display is *The Execution of Murillo*.

The **Museo Costumbrista Juan de Vargas** (cnr Jaén & Sucre) contains art and photos, as well as some superb ceramic figurine dioramas of old La Paz. One of these is a representation of *akulliko*, the hour of coca-chewing; another portrays the festivities surrounding the Día de San Juan Bautista (St John the Baptist's Day) on June 24; another depicts the hanging of Murillo in 1810. Also on display are colonial artifacts and colorful dolls wearing traditional costumes. A pleasant cafe is on the premises.

Museo Tambo Quirquincho

This intriguing **museum** (Map pp68-9; ☎ 239-0969; admission B$3; ⏰ 9:30am-12:30pm Tue-Fri, 9am-1pm Sat & Sun), off Evaristo Valle at Plaza Alonzo de Mendoza, is a former *tambo* (wayside market and inn). It houses temporary exhibitions (past ones have included cultural photos of Mexico and Peruvian art).

Iglesia de San Francisco

The hewed stone basilica of San Francisco (Map pp68–9), on the plaza of the same name, reflects an appealing blend of 16th-century Spanish and mestizo trends. The church was founded in 1548 by Fray Francisco de los Ángeles, and construction began the following year. The original structure collapsed under heavy snowfall around 1610, but it was reconstructed between 1744 and 1753. The second building was built entirely of stone quarried at nearby Viacha. The facade is decorated with stone carvings of natural themes such as *chirimoyas* (custard apples), pinecones and tropical birds.

The mass of rock pillars and stone faces in the upper portion of Plaza San Francisco is intended to represent and honor Bolivia's three great cultures – Tiwanaku, Inca and modern.

The cloisters and garden of the recently opened **Museo San Francisco** (Map pp68-9; ☎ 231-8472; Plaza de San Francisco; adult/concession B$20/15; ⏰ 9am-6pm Mon-Sat), adjacent to the basilica, beautifully revive the history and art of the city's landmark. There are heavenly religious paintings, historical artifacts, an interesting anteroom and a God-like, if quirky, view from the roof.

Museo de la Revolución Nacional

The first question to ask when approaching this **museum** (Museum of the National Revolution; Map pp62-3; Plaza Villarroel; admission B$2; ⏰ 9:30am-12:30pm & 3-7pm Tue-Fri, 10am-noon Sat & Sun) is 'Which Revolution?' (Bolivia has had more than 100 of them). The answer is that of April 1952, the popular revolt of armed miners that resulted in the nationalization of Bolivian mining interests. It displays photos and paintings from the era. Located at the end of Av Busch.

Markets

The entire section of town from Plaza Pérez Velasco uphill (west) to the cemetery – past Mercado Lanza, and Plazas Eguino and

Garita de Lima – has a largely indigenous population and is always bustling. The streets are crowded and noisy with traffic honking its way through the narrow cobbled streets, *cholitas* (Quechua or Aymará women living in the city but continuing to wear traditional dress) rushing about socializing and making purchases, and pedestrians jostling with sidewalk vendors. The market stalls sell all manner of practical items from clothing and fast foods to groceries, health-care products and cooking pots. The focus of activity is near the intersection of Buenos Aires and Max Paredes, especially on Saturdays.

The markets sprawl along various streets – especially on the weekends – and are a great way to see daily life. More interesting markets for tourists include those around the streets of Graneros ('designer' clothes), Tumusla (anything and everything) and Isaac Tamayo, between Santa Cruz and Sagárnaga (tools and building materials). The best place for electronics is along Eloy Salmón. Be especially careful when wandering around this part of town: it's notorious for light fingers.

North of Plaza San Franciso, on Calle Figueroa, a new construction will house **Mercado Lanza** (Map pp68–9), one of La Paz's main food markets (the other major one is Mercado Camacho). It will sell foodstuffs of every type. It will also house the **Flower Market** (at the time of research, this was temporarily located in the Plaza de San Francisco).

Museo de Etnografía y Folklore

This free **museum** (Ethnography & Folklore Museum; Map pp68–9; ☎ 240-8640; www.musef.org.bo; cnr Ingavi & Sanjinés; ☻ 9am-12:30pm & 3-7pm Mon-Sat, 9am-12:30pm Sun) is for anthropology buffs. The building, itself a real treasure, was constructed between 1776 and 1790, and was once the home of the Marqués de Villaverde. The highlight is the Tres Milenios de Tejidos exhibition of stunning weavings from around the country – ask a guide for a look inside the drawers beneath the wall hangings. It also has a fine collection of Chipaya artifacts from western Oruro department, a group whose language, rites and customs have led some experts to suggest that they are descendants of the vanished Tiwanaku culture, and the Tarabucos, from near Sucre.

Museo de Arte Contemporáneo

Better modern art may be found in various other collections around town, but this private **museum** (MAC; Contemporary Art Museum; Map pp68-9; ☎ 233-5905; 16 de Julio 1698; admission B$15; ☻ 9am-9pm) wins the gold star for the most interesting building: a restored 19th-century mansion (only one of four left on the Prado) with a glass roof and stained-glass panels designed by Gustave Eiffel. The museum's eclectic collection housed over three floors is a mix of reasonable – but not mind-blowing – Bolivian and international work. You might catch an interesting temporary exhibition.

Museo de Instrumentos Musicales

The exhaustive, hands-on collection of unique instruments at this **museum** (Museum of Musical Instruments; Map pp68-9; ☎ 240-8177; Jaén 711; admission B$5; ☻ 9:30am-1pm & 2-6:30pm) is a must for musicians. The brainchild of *charango* master Ernesto Cavour Aramayo, it displays all possible incarnations of the *charango* (a traditional Bolivian ukulele-type instrument) and other indigenous instruments used in Bolivian folk music and beyond. If you don't happen on an impromptu jam session, check out Peña Marka Tambo (p85) across the street. You can also arrange *charango* and wind instrument lessons here for around B$50 per hour.

Museo de Textiles Andinos Bolivianos

Fans of Bolivia's lovely traditional weaving consider this small **textile museum** (off Map pp68-9 ☎ 224-3601; Plaza Benito Juárez 488, Miraflores; admission B$15; ☻ 9:30am-noon & 3-6pm Mon-Sat, 10:30am-noon Sun) a must-see. Examples of the country's finest traditional textiles (including pieces from the Cordillera Apolobamba, and the Jal'qa and Candelaria regions of the Central Highlands) are grouped by region and described in Spanish. The creative process is explained from fiber to finished product. The gift shop sells museum-quality originals; 90% of the sale price goes to the artists. To get there, walk 20 minutes northeast from the Prado or catch *micros* (small buses or minibuses) *131* or *135*, or minibuses marked 'Av Busch.'

Arte al Aire Libre

La Paz's mayor, Juan del Granado, has created **Arte al Aire Libre** (Map p76; on the Kantutani btwn Calles 16 & 14, Obrajes, along the river, Zona Sur).

This wonderful open-air art gallery features around 15 giant artworks that focus on La Paz and surrounds, from images of Illimani to notable painters of La Paz. Works change every three months.

Lookouts

For some great views of La Paz from different perspectives head to any of a number of lookout points around the city (getting there on foot is half the fun, remember!). The small park of **Monticulo** (Map pp68–9) in Sopocachi is just down the hill from the Plaza España. Alternative vistas are great from **Killi Killi** (Map pp68–9) and **Laikakota** (Map pp68–9).

Templete Semisubterráneo & Museo al Aire Libre

The open-pit **Museo al Aire Libre** (Map pp68-9; admission free) opposite the stadium contains replicas of statues found in Tiwanaku's Templete Semisubterráneo (p95). The showpiece Megalito Bennetto Pachamama (Bennett monolith) was moved to Tiwanaku's new site museum to avoid further smog-induced deterioration. This place is only worth seeing if you aren't able to visit the actual site.

El Alto

A billboard in El Alto announces: 'El Alto is not part of Bolivia's problem. It's part of Bolivia's solution.' Not all would agree, but visiting here is an experience. Having once been a melting pot for *campesinos* (subsistence farmers) and people from all around the country, and with a population of 648,400, El Alto is now a city in its own right. It has a 5% to 6% growth rate per year and is considered the Aymará capital of the world.

If you arrive by air, below you are dozens of white church spires soaring up from the brown earth. These were built by a German priest, Padre Obermaier, renowned in the city for his past and current works (and longevity). From the canyon rim at the top of El Alto Autopista (toll-road) or the top of the free route at Plaza Ballivián, the streets hum with almost perpetual activity. It's hard to distinguish one street from another – the miles of orange brick and adobe houses, shops, factories and *cholita*-filled markets create a hectic atmosphere at every corner.

In the lively La Ceja (Brow) district, which commands one of the highest real-estate prices in the region for its commercial value, you'll find a variety of electronic gadgets and mercantile goods. For an excellent market experience don't miss the massive **Mercado 16 de Julio** (☼ 6am-3pm Thu & Sun), which stretches for many blocks along the main thoroughfare and across Plaza 16 de Julio. This shopaholic's paradise has absolutely everything, from food and electronics, to vehicles and animals, all at reasonable prices. You'll have to fight your way through the crowds, though (warning: watch your wallet in both senses of the phrase).

To fighting of a different kind, one of the most popular local attractions in El Alto is the **Lucha Libre** (☼ shows 4pm), which are wrestling matches where theatrical males and acrobatic *cholitas* play to the crowds. It's on at the Polifuncional de la Ceja de El Alto, a multifunctional sports stadium. You can go on your own, but for ease and convenience, **Coca Travels** (☎ 246-2927; Sagárnaga 139 & Jimenes 818) organizes trips to the Sunday shows (B$80), departing at 4pm and returning to central La Paz at 8pm.

For a great view of La Paz from the Alto rim, head in a taxi to the Tupac Katari Mirador, situated right on the edge of the rim that plunges down the valley to La Paz. It was – and is – a sacred Inca site and ritual altar where Tupac Katari is believed to have been drawn and quartered by colonialists. The colonialists constructed and interred a statue of Christ on the same site, but that didn't stop locals from performing spiritual rituals here.

Around the *mirador* (lookout) and as far as the eye can see is a long line of small identical blue booths, distinguished only by a number. These house *curanderos* or *yatiris*, who provide sage advice. Note: a *yatiri's* counsel is taken extremely seriously; please be sensitive to this – both photos and tourist appointments are considered inappropriate and are not appreciated.

Taxis to El Alto charge around B$50 from the center.

La Paz Cemetery

As in most Latin American cemeteries, bodies are first buried in the traditional Western way or are placed in a crypt. Then, within 10 years, they are disinterred and cremated. After cremation, families purchase or rent glass-fronted spaces in the cemetery walls for the ashes, they affix plaques and mementos of the deceased, and place flowers behind the glass door. Each wall has hundreds of these doors, and some of the walls have been expanded upward to such an extent that they resemble three- or four-story apartment blocks. As a result the **cemetery** (Map pp62–3) is an active place, full of people passing through to visit relatives and leave or water fresh flowers.

It's possibly most interesting on November 2, the Día de los Muertos (Day of the Dead), when half the city turns out to honor their ancestors. Be aware that the area around the cemetery is a little unsavory.

ACTIVITIES

You'll get plenty of exercise hoofing up and down the Prado but you don't have to head far out of town for a real adrenaline rush.

Mountain Biking

For a thrilling experience, zoom down the 'World's Most Dangerous Road' (see boxed text, opposite) from La Cumbre to Coroico or from Chacaltaya to Zongo, where extra thrills are the awesome views of La Paz and the Cordillera Real. Serious single-track cyclists can choose from a range of great rides in the valleys around La Paz.

Many different operators offer a range of rides. One of the best known is **Gravity Assisted Mountain Biking** (Map pp68-9; ☎ 231-3849; www .gravitybolivia.com; Edificio Avenida, 16 de Julio 1490 No 10), a knowledgeable, highly regarded and professional outfit that has an excellent reputation among travelers. In addition to the trip to Coroico (B$600 per person), it offers a Ghost Ride (*whooo!* in every respect – think riding to a 'castle' in the jungle at night; B$680) plus several rides around La Paz, including road and single-track trips around the Zongo Valley, Sorata and beyond (from B$600). Discounts are offered on second rides.

Also recommended for the Coroico trip (B$440 to B$480 per person) in particular is **B-Side** (off Map pp68-9; ☎ 211-4225; www.bside -adventures.com; Pablo Caballero 47 or Linares 943), which receives positive reports from travelers.

Hiking & Climbing

Except for the altitude, La Paz and its environs are made for hiking. Many La Paz tour agencies offer daily 'hiking' tours to Chacaltaya, a rough 35km drive north of La Paz, and an easy way to bag a high peak. This formerly offered the world's highest downhill skiing run (5320m down to 4900m). Some companies offer hiking trips with a fascinating cultural, environmental and/or nature-based focus (opposite).

COURSES
Language

Note that not everyone advertising language instruction is accredited or even capable of teaching Spanish, however well they speak it, so seek local and personal recommendations, and examine credentials before signing up. Plan on paying around B$60 per hour.

ie instituto exclusivo (Map pp62-3; ☎ 242-1072; 20 de Octubre 2315, Sopocachi) Specialized courses for travelers and professionals.
Instituto de la Lengua Española (ILE; off Map pp62-3; ☎ 279-6074; www.spanbol.com; Calle 14, cnr Aviador 180, Achumani) Offers private and group lessons.
SpeakEasy Institute (Map pp68-9; ☎ 244-1779; www.speakeasyinstitute.com; Arce 2047) Specialized courses for travelers and professionals.

Music

For musical instruction (in Spanish) on traditional Andean instruments (such as the *zampoña, quena, charango*), see Professor Heliodoro Niña at the **Academia de Música Helios** (Map pp68-9; ☎ 240-6498/99; Indaburo 1166; per hr from B$40) or inquire at the Museo de Instrumentos Musicales (p72).

TOURS

Many of Bolivia's tour agencies are based in La Paz. Some are clearly better than others (note: many are not formally registered; check carefully if choosing between those on Sagárnaga) and many specialize in particular interests or areas. Most agencies run day tours (US$10 to US$60 per person) in and around La Paz, to Lake Titicaca, Tiwanaku, Zongo Valley, Chacaltaya, Valle de la Luna and other sites. See p351 for a list of mostly La Paz–based agencies.

Inexpensive agency transfers to Puno can be the most straightforward way of getting to Peru, and they allow a stopover in Copacabana en route. Agencies are also useful for arranging climbing in the Cordilleras; many rent equipment.

The following is a selection of some recommended agencies and tour operators.

DEADLY TREADLIES & THE WORLD'S MOST DANGEROUS ROAD

Many agencies offering La Cumbre to Coroico mountain-bike plunge give travelers the T-shirts boasting about surviving the road. Keep in mind that the gravel road is narrow (just over 3.2m wide), with precipitous cliffs with up to 600m drops and few safety barriers.

In March 2007 a new replacement road opened. Prior to this, the road between La Paz and Coroico was identified as 'The World's Most Dangerous Road' (WMDR) by an Inter-American Development Bank (IDB) report. Given the number of fatal accidents that have occurred on it over the years, the moniker was well deserved. An average of 26 vehicles per year disappeared over the edge into the great abyss.

Crosses (aka 'Bolivian caution signs') lining the way testify to the frequency of vehicular tragedies from the past. The most renowned occurred in 1983 when a *camión* (flatbed truck) plunged over the precipice, killing the driver and 100 passengers in the worst accident in the sordid history of Bolivian transportation.

Over the past few years, a new paved route has been constructed on the opposite wall of the valley, thanks to a US$120 million loan from the IDB. This means the old road – the WMDR – is now used almost exclusively by cyclists, support vehicles and the odd tourist bus.

Around 15 cyclists have died doing the 64km trip (with a 3600m vertical descent) and readers have reported close encounters and nasty accidents. Ironically, the road – now traffic-free – can be more dangerous to cyclists, especially for kamikaze freewheeling guides and overconfident cyclists who think they don't have to worry about oncoming vehicles. (One fatal accident occurred during our research period.) Other accidents are due to little or no instruction and preparation, and poor-quality mountain bikes; beware bogus rebranded bikes and recovered brake pads.

Unfortunately, even though it is such an adventurous activity, there are no minimum safety standards in place for operators of this trip, and no controls over false advertising, or consequences for unsafe operating practices. In short, many agencies are less than ideal. As such the buyer has to be aware, even a bit paranoid; this is one activity where you don't want to be attracted by cheaper deals. Experienced and trained guides, high-quality bikes, well-developed risk-management systems, and adequate rescue equipment all cost money, and cheaper companies may stretch the truth about what they provide if it means making another sale. Cost cutting can mean dodgy brakes, poor-quality parts and literally, a deadly treadly. This, plus inexperienced and untrained guides and little or no rescue and first-aid equipment, is a truly scary combination on the WMDR.

For a more comprehensive list of tour agencies, refer to p351.

Andean Summits (off Map pp62-3; ☎ 242-2106; www.andeansummits.com; Calle Muñoz Cornejo 1009, cnr Sotomayor, Sopocachi) Offers a variety of outdoor activities from mountaineering and trekking to 4WD tours in Bolivia and beyond. The owners are professional UIAGM/IFMGA mountain guides.

America Tours (Map pp68-9; ☎ 237-4204; www .america-ecotours.com; 16 de Julio 1490 No 9) This recommended English-speaking agency offers a wide range of ecotourism projects and tours around La Paz and Bolivia, including an interesting trip to Tiwanaku (shared tour US$12 per person, private tour US$42 to US$110 depending on group size) and Uyuni (US$70 to US$262 per person). Also takes bookings for Chalalán (see p306).

La Paz on Foot (Map p76; ☎ 211-8442, 7154-3918, 7153-9753; www.lapazonfoot.com; Calle Rene Moreno, E22, Calacoto, Zona Sur) Run by the passionate English-speaking ecologist, Stephen Taranto, who offers a range of activities, including walks in and around La Paz, the Yungas, Chulumani and Titicaca. The fascinating, fun and interactive La Paz urban trek (half-day tours US$23 to US$25, day tours US$42 to US$45, depending on group size) heads from the heights of El Alto to the depths of Zona Sur. Other tours include: art and architecture, living history and a stimulants tour (think coca, cocoa and coffee). Trips further afield include a three-day Pacha Trek, four-day Condor Trek, a Yungas Coca Tour as well as various nature trails. Multilingual guides; call for more information and reservations.

Magri Turismo (Map pp68-9; ☎ 244-2727; Capitán Ravelo 2101) Organizes a range of tours around Bolivia.

Mundo Quechua (off Map p76; ☎ 279-6145; www .bolivia-travel.net; Circunvalación 43, Achumani, Zona Sur) French- and English-speaking owners who offer tailor-made tours around Bolivia, including Salar de Uyuni, Tiwanaku, Sajama – whatever you want. Prices vary according to group size and trip.

Turisbus (☎ 244-1756; www.turisbus.com; Hotel Rosario, Calle Illampu) Organizes a large range of day and multiday tours for groups and individuals around Bolivia.

Zig-Zag (Map pp68-9; ☎ 245-7814, 7152-2822; www .zigzagbolivia.com; Office 5, Illampu 867) Offers a range of trekking tours (including Choro and Takesi), beginners' climbs and custom-made adventures around Bolivia.

Bus Tours

Viajes Planeta (☎ 279-1440) runs tours of the city and Zona Sur in a red, double-decker, city-tour bus (B$50 per person; around three hours). Stops on the Zona Sur trip include Valle de la Luna (admission B$15). The recorded narration is in seven languages. Tickets can be purchased in many travel agencies, or on the bus. Buses depart from Plaza San Isabel Católica at 9am and 3pm for city tours, and 10:30am and 1:30pm for Zona Sur.

FESTIVALS & EVENTS

La Paz is always looking for an excuse to celebrate. Check with the Tourist Information Office (p66) for a complete list of what's on.

January

Alasitas During Inca times the Alasitas (Aymará for 'Buy from me', in Spanish it's *Cómprame*) fair coincided with the spring equinox (September 21), and was intended to demonstrate the abundance of the fields. The date underwent some shifts during the Spanish colonial period, which the *campesinos* weren't too happy about. In effect they decided to turn the celebration into a kitschy mockery of the original. 'Abundance' was redefined to apply not only to crops, but also to homes, tools, cash, clothing, cars, trucks, airplanes and even 12-story buildings. The little god of abundance, Ekeko ('dwarf' in Aymará), made his appearance and modern Alasitas traditions are now celebrated on January 24.

May/June

La Festividad de Nuestro Señor Jesús del Gran Poder Held in late May or early June, El Gran Poder began in 1939 as a candle procession led by an image of Christ through the predominantly *campesino* neighborhoods of upper La Paz. The following year the local union of embroiderers formed a folkloric group to participate in the event. In subsequent years other festival-inspired folkloric groups joined in, and the celebration grew larger and more lively. It has now developed into a unique La Paz festival, with dancers and folkloric groups from around the city participating. Embroiderers prepare elaborate costumes for the event and upwards of 25,000 performers practice for weeks in advance. El Gran Poder is a wild and exciting time, and offers a glimpse of Aymará culture at its festive finest. A number of dances are featured, such as the *suri sikuris* (in which the dancers are bedecked in ostrich feathers), the lively *kullasada*, *morenada*, *caporales* and the *inkas*, which duplicates Inca ceremonial dances.

Ayamará New Year & San Juan The winter solstice is celebrated across the Altiplano around June 21, the longest and coldest night of the year. Festivities feature huge bonfires and fireworks in the streets, plus lots of drinking to stay warm.

San Juan (June 24) The Christian version of the solstice celebration. The solstice celebrations are most lively at Tiwanaku (p93).

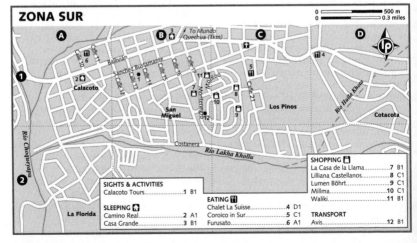

EKEKO

Ekeko is the household god and the keeper and distributor of material possessions. During Alasitas his devotees collect miniatures of those items they'd like to acquire during the following year and heap them onto small plaster images of the god. He's loaded down with household utensils, baskets of coca, wallets full of miniature currency, lottery tickets, liquor, chocolate and other luxury goods. The more optimistic devotees buy miniature souped-up *camiones* (flatbed trucks), 1st-class airline tickets to Miami and three-story suburban homes! Once purchased, all items must be blessed by a certified *yatiri* (witch doctor) before they can become real. If this apparent greed seems not to be in keeping with Aymará values – the community and balance in all things – it's worth noting that Ekeko is also charged with displaying that which a family is able to share with the community.

July

Fiestas de Julio This month-long cultural series at the Teatro Municipal features much folk music.

Virgen del Carmen The patron saint of the department of La Paz gets her own public holiday (July 16), which includes many dances and parades.

Entrada Folklórica de Universitaria Held on the last Saturday in July, and with an atmosphere alluding to Carnaval, hundreds of dance groups made up of students from around the country perform traditional dances through the streets of La Paz.

August

Independence Day This lively public holiday (August 6) sees lots of gunfire in the air, parades galore and mortar blasts around the city center.

November & December

Día de los Muertos (All Saints Day) Colorful celebrations of ancestors fill cemeteries around the city and country.

New Year's Eve Look out for the fireworks – many at eye level – which are best seen from high above the city at a *mirador*.

SLEEPING

Most backpackers beeline for central La Paz to find a bed. The downtown triangle between Plazas Mendoza, Murillo and 14 de Septiembre is full of popular budget hostels, *residenciales* (hostels) and midrange hotels, the vast majority of which are around Sagárnagaand to the east of upper Montes. The area around the Witches' Market (Mercado de Hechicería; between Illampu, Santa Cruz and Sagárnaga) is about as close as Bolivia gets to a travelers ghetto. If you want to live closer to movie theaters, a wider array of restaurants and a bar or two, consider staying closer to Sopocachi around Plaza San Pedro. For more upmarket luxury, look along the lower Prado and further south in Zona Sur.

All places reviewed here claim to have hot water at least part of the day; few have it all the time.

Many are cheaper outside high season.

West of the Prado & Mariscal Santa Cruz

BUDGET

Hotel Continental (Map pp68-9; ☎ 245-1176; hotel continental626@hotmail.com; Illampu 626; r per person B$50, with bathroom B$60) This older, two-star HI-affiliate is clean, well located and popular among thrifty tour groups. It's hard to meet people due to its unsociable hotel-style design. Lucky, then, that rooms have cable TV.

Hostal Maya (Map pp68-9; ☎ 231-1970; mayahost_in@hotmail.com; Sagárnaga 339; s/d/tr B$55/110/150, with bathroom B$80/140/180; 🖳) This is a friendly, if basic, place. The most appealing rooms have windows (note: a few don't), although rooms at the front can be a little noisy, especially as it's a *charango* strum away from Peña Huari (p85); the music may annoy some. Breakfast is included.

Hotel Sagárnaga (Map pp68-9; ☎ 235-0252; www.hotel-sagarnaga.com; Sagárnaga 326; Category B s/d/tr B$60/100/140, Category A s/d/tr B$140/180/220) The knight in shining armor at the front desk (and no, we're not talking about the reception-ist, although he *is* friendly) and the mirrors are the brightest things in this otherwise slightly tarnished, yet adequate, '80s-style place. Category A rooms are newer and more pleasant; Category B rooms are older and unrenovated.

Hostal Provenzal (Map pp68-9; ☎ 231-0479; Murillo 1014; s B$90, d B$160-165) This place offers pleasant light and breezy rooms in neat surroundings and with good storage. Being so close to Oliver's Travels (see p84) can mean noise. Rooms without cable TV are slightly cheaper.

Arcabucero Hostal Inn (Map pp68-9; ☎ /fax 231-3473; arcabucero-bolivia@hotmail.com; Viluyo 307; s/d/tr with bathroom B$90/180/240) The nine quiet rooms at this restored colonial home are arranged around an ornate, plant-filled indoor courtyard. The saggy mattresses, however, should be relegated to the inn's otherwise quirky antique decorations. Breakfast costs B$10.

Hotel Majestic (Map pp68-9; ☎ 245-1628; Santa Cruz 359; s B$100, d B$145-160, tr B$220) Its pink bathrooms, smart parquet floors and cable TV provide some distraction from its nondescript, genuinely retro, yet clean surrounds in the heart of things.

MIDRANGE

Hotel Berlina (Map pp68-9; ☎ 246-1928; www .hotelberlina.com; Illampu 761; s/d/tr B$125/185/220; 🖳) This is one of a plethora of new Rosario wannabes in this area. While the lobby promises shiny things, the spacious rooms are stark, if clean. It lacks a bit of personality, but seems a reliable bet, although the jury is still out, given that it only opened at the end of 2008.

Hotel Brisas (Map pp68-9; ☎ 246-3691; www.hotel brisas.net; Illampu 742; s/d/tr B$125/185/220; 🖳) Since opening in 2008, the management here has been trying hard with a 'modern Bolivia' style – think stark, but neat rooms (some with internal windows), a few shabby bits and external glassy walls. Rooms at the front have excellent views and staff are friendly.

Hotel La Joya (Map pp62-3; ☎ 245-3841; www .hotelajoya.com; Max Paredes 541; s/d/tr US$8/16/24, with bathroom US$14/27/35) A clean, friendly and frilly three-star '80s-style option amid the bustle of the street markets. It includes a basic breakfast in the disco-lit dining area, cable TV and good hot showers. Head to the roof top at night for a sparkling view.

Hotel Fuentes (Map pp68-9; ☎ 231-3966; www .hotelfuentesbolivia.com; Linares 888; s/d/tr B$140/195/250; 🖳) In the heart of tourist mecca nestles this cozy place, recommended by readers for its friendly, helpful management. Rooms are basic, but neat, with original parquet floors. Some rooms on higher levels have superlative views.

Hotel Milton (Map pp68-9; ☎ 235-3511; Illampu 1126-1130; s/d/tr US$18/24/36) Tune in, drop out! This '70s pad features red vinyl–studded

walls, painted murals and funky wallpaper. Darker rooms at the back are a bit dingy, but the higher and lighter front rooms afford stupendous views over La Paz. The associated Milton Tours runs buses to Tiwanaku and Copacabana.

Estrella Andina Hotel (Map pp68-9; ☎ 245-6421; www.estrellaandina.com; Illampu 716; s/d/tr with bathroom US$24/34/45) The rooms in this clean and well-run place are chock-a-block with Andean murals, Inca-themed paraphernalia and, for a touch of the 21st century, cable TV. It's central and good value for this price range.

La Posada de la Abuela (Map pp68-9; ☎ 233-2285; Linares 947; s/d/tr US$28/36/46) Readers praise this pleasant oasis in the heart of artisan and tourist mecca. The rooms are sterile and clean (some have internally facing windows), and the plant-filled courtyard adds a colorful, if potentially noisy, touch. Reserve ahead – it's popular with groups.

Hostal Naira (Map pp68-9; ☎ 235-5645; www .hostalnaira.com; Sagárnaga 161; s/d/tr B$200/256/340; 🖳) At the bottom of Sagárnaga, near Plaza San Francisco, Naira is popular for its location, cleanliness and heating – it can be noisy, however. Breakfast is served in the downstairs eatery, Cafe Banais.

our pick Hotel Rosario (Map pp68-9; ☎ 245-1658; www.hotelrosario.com; Illampu 704; s/d/tr B$350/440/560; 🖳) The professional, English-speaking staff at La Paz's best three-star hotel pamper you with five-star treatment. The ultraclean rooms in the well-maintained colonial residence all have solar-powered hot showers, cable TV and heaters. There is free internet and a generous breakfast buffet at the Tambo Colonial (p81). Groups love it, so reserve ahead.

East of the Prado & Mariscal Santa Cruz
BUDGET

Hospedaje Milenio (Map pp68-9; ☎ 228-1263; hospedajemilenio@hotmail.com; Yanacocha 860; r per person B$27) A simple, laid-back joint, run by friendly staff. The best rooms are upstairs and outward facing (note: most single rooms have internal windows). Laundry service is available.

Hostal Austria (Map pp68-9; ☎ 240-8540; Yanacocha 531; dm B$35, s/d/tr B$45/70/105; 🖳) This shabby, rambling and friendly number could almost be relegated to a history museum, it's been around so long. It has short beds (some in windowless cells) and dicey shared bathrooms. Hot showers and cooking facilities are available.

Hotel La Valle (Map pp68-9; ☎ 245-6085, annex 245-6053; www.lavallehotel.com; Evaristo Valle 139 & 153; annex s/d/tr with bathroom B$50/80/110, newer s/d/tr with bathroom & breakfast B$75/120/150) This good-value place is particularly popular with locals for its clean rooms at fair prices. There are two sections: the older annex with simple, but adequate, no-frills rooms, and next door, the newer Hotel La Valle with fancier rooms (in the frilly bedspread kind of way) and cable TV. While the front rooms (all double) are the best, street traffic can be noisy.

Only mentioned because they'd be obvious by their absence:

Wild Rover (Map pp68-9; ☎ 211-6903; www.wildroverhostel.com; Comercio 1476; dm B$40-56, d without/with bathroom B$70/75)

Loki La Paz (Map pp68-9; ☎ 211-9034; www.lokihostel.com; Calle Loayza 420; dm B$45-55, d B$120-140) Self-promoting, party pumper and one of a chain of insomnia-crowd-attracting hostels. Upfront warning: if you don't already know about it, you probably shouldn't stay here.

MIDRANGE

Hostal República (Map pp68-9; ☎ 220-2742; www.angelfire.com/wv/hostalrepublica; Comercio 1455; s/d/tr US$13/19/25, with bathroom US$21/31/42; 💻) Three blocks from the historic heart of the city, this hostel occupies a lovely historic building that was once home to one of Bolivia's first presidents. Its two large courtyards are a pleasant oasis, although the place could do with an all-round spruce-up. All the rooms are fairly basic (those downstairs can be dank and musty) but will make for a pleasant, if unremarkable, stay. Family rooms and a spacious *casita* (separate apartment) are also available. Discounts for longer stays.

Cafe El Consulado (Map pp68-9; ☎ 211-7706; www.topas.bo; Calle Bravo 299; r US$40, with bathroom US$50) You'll feel every bit the VIP in one of these five delightful rooms, housed in a converted consulate and stunning colonial building, above the cafe of the same name. This boutique place oozes European style (it's Danish run), with large, airy and spacious rooms in a quiet location. Those with private bathrooms have clawed baths. A relaxing B&B experience and a welcome addition to this category.

Hotel Gloria (Map pp68-9; ☎ 240-7070; www.hotelgloria.com.bo; Potosí 909; s/d/tr B$320/420/490) At the lower range of the top-end towers, and above the snarling traffic of the Prado. It's got a red shagpile look and slightly stale smell about it, but the helpful and friendly staff make this place good value.

TOP END

Plaza Hotel (Map pp68-9 ☎ 237-8311; www.plazabolivia.com.bo; 16 de Julio 1789; s/d US$99/119; 💻) Friendly and convenient, this is a smart, if ever-so-slightly frayed at the edges, place. Has cable TV and a continental buffet breakfast.

Hotel Presidente (Map pp68-9; ☎ 240-6666; www.hotelpresidente-bo.com; Potosí 920; s/d/ste US$140/160/200; ⚅ 💻 🏊) Once you get past the unconsciously retro furnishings, this venerable *grande dame* gives a pleasant, if '80s-style, room-with-a-view experience. Its small casino will chew up any of your remaining pennies.

Hotel Europa (Map pp68-9; ☎ 231-5656; www.hoteleuropa.com.bo; Tiahuanacu 64; s/d/ste US$150/170/370; ⚅ 💻 🏊) The city's sleekest biz-focused place, whose executive amenities include wi-fi, radiant bathroom heating and humidification system (on request). The two suites on the 12th floor have amazing city views. Nonguests can use the spa, heated pool and fitness center for B$80 per day.

San Pedro & Sopocachi

BUDGET

Residencial Sucre (Map pp68-9; ☎ 249-2038; Colombia 340; r per person B$40, s/d with bathroom B$80/120) This place hasn't been refurbished since the '50s, it seems. But management is helpful and the spotless, old rooms – with the squeakiest of squeaky-clean floors – are around a secure and pleasant colonial courtyard (good for cycling storage). Some rooms have cable TV.

Onkel Inn (Map pp68-9; ☎ 249-0456; www.onkel-inn-highlanders.com; Colombia 257; r per person B$60-200, d B$160-250; 💻) This bright, HI-affiliated place is in a fabulous spot between San Pedro and El Prado. Its location, behind a small shopping arcade, means it avoids the street noise, although the inside bar is close to a couple of the rooms. Choose between a private single, double or triple room, or one of two dorms (the upstairs one is more airy). Generally rooms are bright, light and modern.

MIDRANGE

Hotel España (Map pp68-9; ☎ 244-2643; 6 de Agosto 2074; s/d/tr B$190/270/360; 💻) This place is a bit like a great aunt – friendly with a colorful personality but ever-so-slightly worse for wear. It's a slightly overpriced colonial place, with a lovely, sunny courtyard and garden, and worn rooms. It's within an easy stroll of many of the city's best restaurants. Rates include cable TV. The attached restaurant also offers inexpensive lunches and dinners (B$12).

Hotel Madre Tierra (Map pp68-9; ☎ 241-9910; www.hotelmadretierra.com; Av 20 de Octubre; s B$260, d B$300-340, tr B$510) One of the newer additions in this area, this modern, slightly daggy, yet reliable place is in a great location, handy for Plaza del Estudiante, without the surrounding chaos. They've gone to town with the paintbrush, and all rooms are light, with generous windows, carpet and cable TV.

A La Maison Appart-Hotel (Map pp62-3; ☎ 241-3704; www.alamaison-lapaz.com; Pasaje Muñoz Cornejo 15; s/d B$280/350; 🖳) Several artistic and bright serviced apartments add a creative flair to this neck of the woods, located in a tranquil area a couple of blocks from Plaza España. With a kitchenette, wi-fi and cable TV, you'll feel very much indeed 'at home.' Even breakfast is thrown in.

TOP END

La Loge (Map pp62-3; ☎ 242-3561; www.lacomedielapaz.com; La Comédie Art-Cafe Restaurant, Pasaje Medinacelli 2234, Sopocachi; apt B$400; 🖳) *Oooh la la!* This one is tops. The attention to detail in these light, bright and airy self-catering, serviced apartments is French in flavor – and that means *bon goût*. The four apartments have modern and stylish trimmings, a small kitchen with a coffee percolator, a microwave and cupboards stocked with basic foodstuffs. Not that you'll want to cook with La Comédie Art-Cafe Restaurant (p82) below you. The rooms even include cable TV and your own internet connection.

Alcalá Apart Hotel (Map pp62-3; ☎ 241-2336; www.alcalapartamentos.com; Víctor Sanjines on Plaza España; s/d/tr B$400/475/550) Come here for an alternative to the standard hotel scene. These good-value, fully equipped and very roomy apartments overlook leafy Plaza España and are away from the cut and thrust of noisy downtown. You're in walking distance of the Sopocachi cafes.

Hotel Radisson Plaza (Map pp68-9; ☎ 244-1111; www.radisson.com/lapazbo; Arce 2177; s/d US$160/180, ste US$240-280; 🖳 🖳 🖳) The Radisson has everything you'd expect in a five-star hotel,

even if its pink walls are c 1980s. There's a range of more luxurious options, from studios to luxury suites. The top-floor restaurant affords a superb view over the city and surrounding mountains.

Near the Main Bus Terminal
BUDGET

Hostal Maximiliano (Map pp68-9 ☎ 246-2318; hostalmaximiliano@yahoo.com; Inca Mayta Kapac 531; s B$35, d with bathroom B$90) An extremely basic, but secure place, and the type of place you come for little, or no, action. It's in a handy location for Plaza San Francisco and the bus terminal. The doubles are more pleasant.

Hostal Tambo del Oro (Map pp62-3; ☎ 228-1565; Armentia 367; s/d B$40/70, with bathroom B$70/100) A pleasantly quiet, cozy and colonial-style place, with good-value, slightly run-down carpeted rooms and gas showers.

Adventure Brew Hostel (Map pp62-3; ☎ 246-1614; www.theadventurebrewhostel.com; Ismael Montes 533 & 641; dm B$46-49, dm with bathroom B$60, d/tr with bathroom B$160/210) The name says it all. This popular abode offers designer-style rooms, funky communal spaces, pancake breakfasts (included in price), barbecues, as well as activities and fun on tap. Yes, there's an authentic microbrewery on site. It's so popular that the owners opened another one just down the road, appropriately named Adventure Brew Hostel Too. You'll need to book ahead to score a bed in either place.

Arthy's Guesthouse (Map pp68-9; ☎ 228-1439; www.arthyshouse.tripod.com; Ismael Montes 693; r per person B$70) This clean and cozy place hidden behind a bright orange door deservedly receives rave reviews as a 'tranquil oasis,' despite its location on one of La Paz's busiest roads. The friendly, English-speaking owners will do all they can do to help you. It offers single, twin and quadruple rooms. Kitchen facilities are available. Note: it has a midnight curfew.

Zona Sur
Tarapari La Paz (off Map p76; ☎ 7154-3918; www.lapazonfoot.com; per person US$12) Fourteen kilometers from Zona Sur, in the very authentic village of Chicani, is this tranquil escape: an ecofriendly apartment in a secure location. It's made of adobe and its kitchen and bathroom is operated by solar water. Guests can even access fresh veggies from the organic vegetable garden. It's the perfect place

to base yourself for day and overnight hikes into the Cordillera Real – the owner (of La Paz on Foot tours fame; p75) says you can be at the base of a glacier within eight hours. Access is by an unsealed road, 45 minutes by minibus from central La Paz (B$4).

Camino Real (Map p76; ☎ 279-2323; www.caminoreal .com.bo; Ballivián 369, cnr Calle 10, Calacoto; s/d US$115/135, family ste US$165) Another of Zona Sur's five-star hotels with all the luxury trimmings: a pool, a business center and restaurants.

Casa Grande (Map p76; ☎ 279-5511; www.casa -grande.com.bo; Ballivián, with Calle 17; s/d/f US$140/ 150/190) Spic and span, modern and luxurious, this is a reliable upmarket choice.

EATING

La Paz enjoys an abundance of inexpensive and upmarket eateries offering everything from local treats to more Western-style dishes. For local fare, your cheapest (and sometimes tastiest) bets are the *almuerzos* (set lunches) in the countless hole-in-the-wall restaurants; look for the chalkboard menus out front. As a general rule, the higher you climb from the Prado, the cheaper the meals will be.

Vegetarians are increasingly well catered for these days and there are some excellent vegetarian restaurants.

Calle Sagárnaga is lined with dozens of cafes of reasonable price and quality.

Many midrange and upmarket restaurants are concentrated at the lower end of town: on the lower Prado around 16 de Julio and in Sopocachi around Avs 20 de Octubre and 6 de Agosto. Zona Sur is considered among wealthier locals *the* place to go for a weekend coffee. While there's a good mix of cafes, restaurants and a few eateries that sell Bolivian food, the more upmarket places have a definite Western flavor.

Restaurants
BUDGET

There are heaps of acceptable budget restaurants on Evaristo Valle, near Mercado Lanza (p72); also cheap are the several places along the lower (eastern) end of Calle Rodríguez, which also boasts a handful of excellent, cheap Peruvian-style *ceviche* (an appetizer of raw fish marinated in lime or lemon juice) joints in the block.

Coroico in Sur (Map p76; Juli Patino 1526; almuerzo B$15; ☯ lunch & dinner Mon-Sat, lunch only Sun) A

great place to join the locals for typical Bolivian lunch dishes of *plato paceño* (a dish of fried cheese, corn, beans and potato) and set lunches in a tranquil garden setting.

Paceña La Salteña (Map pp62-3; 20 de Octubre 2379, Sopocachi; ☯ 8:30am-2pm) Eating a *salteña* (no, we won't tell you what it is, here) is a not-to-be-missed local experience. The peach walls, chintz curtains and gold trimmings give the fare a gilded edge at this award-winning *salteñería*. Vegetarian *salteñas* are available on weekends only.

Join the locals for cheap eats at the following authentic joints:

Restaurant Laza (Map pp68-9; Bozo 244; lunch B$8)

Restaurant Verona (Map pp68-9; Colón near Santa Cruz; mains B$15-20)

MIDRANGE

Yussef (Map pp68-9; Sagárnaga 380; mains B$20-45; ☯ lunch & dinner) Good Middle Eastern food with mixed vegetarian plates of Lebanese specialties like hummus, falafel, tabouli and *baba ganoush*. The extensive menu also has many meaty choices.

Restaurant Paladar (Map pp62-3; ☎ 244-4929; Guachalla 359; mains B$40-60, almuerzo Tue-Fri B$20; ☯ lunch Tue-Sun) This cavernous place serves recommended Brazilian fare, including *feijoada* (a bean and meat casserole, typical of Portugal and Brazil). Heavy drapes, bow-tied waiters and smartly dressed locals would have you think it's a pricey joint. And you'd be fooled – all this for a mere B$20. À la carte dishes are served at weekend lunches.

Ángelo Colonial (Map pp68-9; ☎ 236-0199; Linares 922; mains B$2.50-5) This quirky, darkened colonial-style restaurant features a ramshackle collection of antiquities – pistols, swords and antique portraits, plus excellent soups, salads and luscious veggie lasagna. You don't want to be in a hurry – service is slow.

Tambo Colonial (Map pp68-9; ☎ 245-1658; Hotel Rosario, Illampu 704; mains US$3-6; ☯ breakfast & dinner) Known for its salad bar and excellent mains such as trout in white-wine sauce, llama medallions with mushroom sauce, and veggie lasagna. Afterward indulge in what may be the best chocolate mousse south of the equator. Nonguests of Hotel Rosario are welcome to eat at the breakfast buffet.

Star of India (Map pp68-9; ☎ 211-4409; Calle Cochabamba 170; mains B$30-40; ☯ 9am-11pm Mon-Fri,

4-11pm Sat & Sun) Worthy of a London curry-house (the owner is British), this place is hot. It receives rave reviews by foreign residents and travelers for its broad menu of tasty Indian foods. Also serves lassi breakfasts and snacks.

Cafe El Consulado (Map pp68-9 ☎ 211-7706; Bravo 299; mains B$35-55; 🕙 9am-10:30pm Tue-Sun) A stylish cafe-restaurant, housed in a stunning, refurbished colonial building (formerly the Consulate of Panama), surrounded by green lawns and gardens. You can enjoy a range of contemporary-style international and local dishes sitting in a delightful glasshouse-cum-terrace or inside, in a choice of cozy spaces. Not surprisingly, given its Danish ownership, it has an all-round European influence.

TOP END

Japan seems to have hit La Paz in a big way. The Japanese listings below are worth their weight in sushi and the remaining choices serve up top-quality nosh.

Restaurant Vienna (Map pp68-9; ☎ 244-1660; www .restaurantvienna.com; Zuazo 1905; mains B$30-65; 🕙 lunch & dinner Mon-Fri, closed Sat, lunch only Sun) Arguably La Paz's best continental restaurant, classy (in an old-fashioned kind of way) Vienna serves traditional, Central European cuisine and unique takes on Bolivian criollo classics. Also has live piano music.

Furusato (Map p76; ☎ 279-6499; Inofuentes 437; mains B$40-70; 🕙 lunch & dinner Tue-Sun, dinner only Mon) This place is neater than an origami figure – and fittingly so. It's very formal, with exquisite Japanese fare, although friendliness isn't always on the menu.

La Comédie Art-Cafe Restaurant (Map pp62-3; ☎ 242-3561; Pasaje Medinacelli 2234, Sopocachi; mains B$40-70; 🕙 lunch & dinner Mon-Fri, dinner Sat) Cruise in to this ship-shape place (note the building) – it's hard to beat for its bar and restaurant ambience, food and French je ne sais quoi. The chocolate mousse is not to be missed. The experience isn't the cheapest, but it's the perfect place to anchor yourself at any time.

El Arriero (Map pp62-3; ☎ 243-5060; 6 de Agosto 2535; mains B$45-75; 🕙 lunch & dinner) This Argentine grill restaurant is a spacious, cheery place for a serious protein injection. The chunky meat is kept warm on a table-side grill, while a series of even larger cuts (B$140) feed three or four. There's a decent

salad bar, but it's no vegetarian hangout! Good, if pricey, wine selection.

Wagamama (Map pp68-9; ☎ 243-4911; Pinilla 2257; meals B$45-90; 🕙 lunch & dinner Mon-Sat) This Japanese joint, hidden up a lane, reveals classy atmosphere and impeccably presented food. Treat yourself to a *teishoku* (a feast featuring 'everything'; B$80).

Chalet La Suisse (Map p76; ☎ 279-3160; www .chaletlasuisse.com; Muñoz Reyes 1710, Calacoto; mains B$60-120) This Swiss-run restaurant is as upscale as the name sounds – it's seriously expensive (by Bolivian standards), has a very old-style atmosphere and is extremely good. Imported cheeses, top local wines and trout dishes are merely part of the experience. Don't go here if you're after Bolivian atmosphere – it would be as at home in New York or London – but it's good fare.

Cafes & Quick Eats

Few places that serve breakfast open before 8am or 9am, but early risers desperate for a caffeine jolt before they can face the day will find bread rolls and riveting coffee concentrate at the markets for B$5. The *salteñas* and *tucumanas* (like a *salteña*, but with fluffier pastry) sold in the markets and on the streets – even cheaper than those in sit-down cafes – are normally excellent.

The following cafes are open all day and serve breakfast and snacks. Some are closed on Sundays and most are open until early evening (exceptions are stated).

Cafe Torino (Map pp68-9; Hotel Torino, Socabaya 457; snacks B$5-30; 🕙 7am-11pm Mon-Fri, 7am-3pm Sun; 🖳) A somewhat quirky, olde-worlde cafe with '80s music, internet and a good selection of snacks. Good-value *almuerzos* cost from B$20 to B$30.

Kuchen Stube (Map pp62-3; Gutiérrez 461; cakes B$8-20) A favorite for sweet snacks with decadent German pastries, reasonable coffee, fresh juices and quiche lorraine. Each day they have a special lunch – from vegetarian to Italian fare – for B$25.

Pepe's Coffee Bar (Map pp68-9; Jiménez 894; snacks B$10-25) This cheery, inviting, arty little cafe is tucked away on a sunny bend in the Witches' Market. It's a cozy place for coffee or cocktails. Big breakfasts and veggie lunch options go down easily while browsing the library of guidebooks and English-language periodicals.

Alexander Coffee & Pub (Prado Map pp68-9; 16 de Julio 1832; Socabaya Map pp68-9; Calle Potosi 1091; Sopocachi Map pp62-3; 20 de Octubre 2463; www .alexandercoffee.com; ✆ until 1am; mains B$10-40) A popular chain cafe serving java drinks, good fruit juices and tasty snacks, from pastries to vegetarian quiche. It's a good place for a caffeine hit. Their delicious offerings promote Andean food products where possible – don't miss the *torte de quinoa*.

Cafe La Terraza (mains B$10-40; ✆ late; Prado Map pp68-9; 16 de Julio 1615; Sopocachi Map pp62-3; 20 de Octubre 2331; Montenegro Bloque) This stylish chain offers quality espresso and other coffee treats, as well as rich chocolate cake and cooked breakfasts that include North American–style pancakes and *huevos rancheros* (spicy eggs).

Confitería Club de La Paz (Map pp68-9; cnr Camacho & Mariscal Santa Cruz; mains B$10-30) For a quick coffee or empanada, join the well-dressed elderly patrons in their daily rituals. The cafe was formerly renowned as a literary cafe and haunt of politicians (and, formerly, of Nazi war criminals); today, it's better known for its strong espresso and cakes.

Fridolin (Map pp62-3; ✆ 215-3188; 6 de Agosto 2415; snacks B$18-60; ✆ 8am-10pm) This Austrian-flavored place has several branches around town and it's easy to see why – the sweet-toothed love its large variety of *postres* (cakes, pastriesand desserts) and everything in between, from salads to breakfasts. Worth coming here to fill the stomach.

Sergiu's (Map pp68-9; 6 de Agosto 2040; snacks from B$20; ✆ from 5pm) Popular among students, this evening-only hole-in-the-wall near the Aspiazu steps serves up a reasonable pizza and fast foods.

Cafe Blueberries (Map pp62-3; ✆ 243-3402; Plaza Avaroa; mains B$30-50; ✆ closed Sun) Tea lovers will enjoy this relaxed Japanese-owned place – it has a good selection of infusions and accompanying snacks, from salads to cakes. The pleasant front terrace overlooks Plaza Avaroa, and the back sunroom overlooks a pretty rose garden. There's even wi-fi connection.

La Guinguette (Map pp62-3; Guachalla 399; ✆ 9am-2am) Hang out with the Sopocachi cool cats at this chic spot below the Alianza Francesa. At the time of research, it was in the process of opening under new management of the owners of La Comédie (see opposite). If that's anything to go by then this place will be well worth checking out.

Arábica (Map p62-3; ✆ 211-3293; 20 de Octubre 2355) A great place to chill thanks to its wi-fi, newspapers and good lunches, including sandwiches and salads, among which are excellent vegetarian options. It has a happy hour (think cheap cocktails) every day between 7pm and 9pm.

A good choice for Italian ice cream is **Heladería Napoli** (Map pp68-9; Ballivián; ✆ 8:30am-10:30pm) on Plaza Murillo's north side and **Heladería Splendid** (Map pp68-9; cnr Nicolas Acosta), which has been scooping up splendid ice cream for nearly 50 years. In addition to ice-cream concoctions, it serves breakfasts, pastries, cakes and other snacks. There are also several popular ice-cream parlors along the Prado, such as the circus-like **Dumbo's** (Map pp68-9; 16 de Julio s/n; mains B$15-45) and seductively named Bits & Cream (Map pp68-9). We promise! It really does serve ice cream.

VEGETARIAN

Armonía (Map pp62-3; Ecuador 2284; buffet B$25; ✆ lunch Mon-Sat) A recommended all-you-can-eat vegetarian lunch is found above Libería Armonía in Sopocachi. Organic products where possible.

Confitería Manantial (Map pp68-9; Hotel Gloria, Potosí 909; buffet B$25; ✆ lunch Mon-Sat) This place has a good-value and popular veggie buffet. Arrive before 12:30pm or you risk missing the best dishes.

Govinda (Map pp68-9; Hotel Majestic, Santa Cruz 359; almuerzo B$14; ✆ 9am-9pm Mon-Fri, 9am-3pm Sat & Sun) This cavernous place has a touch of the Hari Krishna, and has been blessed with a good chef who serves up a buffet lunch which changes daily but always includes soup, salad, main dish and dessert.

GROCERIES

If you don't mind the hectic settings, your cheapest food scene is the markets. The *comedor* at Mercado Uruguay (Map pp62–3), off Max Paredes, sells set meals (of varying standards and in basic surrounds), including tripe and *ispi* (similar to sardines), for less than B$8. Other areas to look for cheap and informal meals include the street markets around Av Buenos Aires.

In Sopocachi, the northwest border of Plaza Avaroa is lined with *salteña* stands. Cheap DIY meals can easily be cobbled together from the abundance of fruit, produce and bread at the markets.

If you're headed off for a picnic, load up on everything from olives to cheese, crackers and beer at **Ketal Hipermercado** (Map pp62-3; Arce nr Pinilla, Sopocachi). There's also the decent but more basic **Ketal Express** (Map pp62-3; Plaza España). Just up the road from Kuchen Stube is **Hipermaxi** (Map pp62-3), a well-stocked supermarket. Opposite Sopocachi Market, **Arco Iris** (Map pp62-3; Guachalla 554; 8am-8pm Mon-Sat) has an extensive *pastelería* (cake shop) and deli featuring fine specialty regional meat and dairy treats like smoked llama salami, plus products such as fresh palm hearts and dried Beni fruits.

DRINKING & CLUBBING

There are scores of inexpensive, local drinking dens where men go to drink *singani* (distilled grape spirit, the local firewater), play *cacho* (dice) and eventually pass out. Unaccompanied women should steer clear of these dens (even accompanied women may have problems).

There are plenty of elegant bars, which are frequented by foreigners and middle-class Bolivians. Local, gilded youth mingle with upmarket expats at clubs along 20 de Octubre in Sopocachi and in Zona Sur, where US-style bars and discos spread along Av Ballivián and Calle 21. These change as often as fashions, so it's best to ask around for the latest in-spot.

Ram Jam (Map pp62-3; Presbitero Medina 2421; 6pm-3am) A trendy hot spot with the lot: great food and drinks, mood lighting and live music. There are vegetarian options, English breakfasts and microbrewed beer. They are proud of the reputation: 'come for a meal and stay until far too late…'

Oliver's Travels (Map pp68-9; Murillo 1014) The worst (or best?) cultural experience in La Paz is to be had at this pub, thanks to its crowd of mainly foreign revelers, beer, football, typical English food (including curries) and popular music. It has a good, if pricey (according to some readers, at least) book exchanges around. **Mongo's** (Map pp62-3; Manchego 2444; mains B$30-60; 6pm-3am) is La Paz's long-standing hip, hot (it gets crowded) and happening spot that seems to stand the test of time for both tourists and locals alike. There's after-dinner music, and live salsa music on Tuesdays.

Cafe Sol y Luna (Map pp68-9; cnr Murillo & Cochabamba; breakfast, lunch & dinner Mon-Fri, dinner Sat & Sun) A low-key, Dutch-run hangout

offering cocktails, good coffee and tasty international meals. It has three cozy levels with a book exchange and an extensive guidebook reference library (many current Lonely Planet titles), talks, salsa nights, live music and other activities.

Thelonious Jazz Bar (Map pp62-3; 20 de Octubre 2172; cover charge around B$25; 7pm-3am Mon-Sat) Bebop fans love this charmingly low-key bar for its live and often impromptu performances and great atmosphere. A flier on the wall promotes forthcoming sessions.

Reineke Fuchs (Map pp62-3; Jáuregui 2241; from 6pm Mon-Sat) Sopocachi *brewhaus* featuring imported German beers, *schnappsladen* and hearty sausage-based fare. Also in Zona Sur.

Antique-Chop (Map pp68-9 Pichincha off Ingavi) Opposite the Mormon church, the rustic interior, retro photographs from the '20s and '30s, Western pop music and pitchers/jugs of beer make La Choperia a favorite with middle-class locals.

Diesel Nacional (Map pp62-3; 20 de Octubre 2271; from 7:30pm Mon-Sat) The postmodern place to escape reality for an overpriced drink with the rich kids. It doesn't really get going until late.

Traffic (Map pp62-3; www.trafficsanjorge.com; Arce 2549) Has lost some pizzazz in recent times, but still popular for cocktails, live music – from world music to disco – and all the attitude and dancing you can muster. You can linger until late.

ENTERTAINMENT

Pick up a copy of the free monthly booklet *Kaos* (available in bars and cafes) for a day-by-day rundown of what's on in La Paz. Otherwise, watch hotel notice boards for bar and live music posters, or check the *Jiwaki,* a monthly brochure providing arts and theater listings. The Tourist Information Center (p66) and **Casa de la Cultura** (Map pp68-9; cnr Mariscal Santa Cruz & Potosí) has a free monthly cultural and fine arts schedule, and the **Teatro Municipal** (Map pp68-9; cnr Sanjinés & Indaburo) has an ambitious theater and folk-music program.

Peñas

Typical of La Paz (and most of Bolivia) are folk-music venues known as *peñas*. Most present traditional Andean music, rendered on *zampoñas, quenas* and *charangos,* but also often include guitar shows and song recitals. Many *peñas* advertise nightly shows, but in reality most only have shows on Friday and Saturday nights, starting at 9pm or 10pm and lasting until 1am or 2am. Admission ranges from B$30 to B$80 and usually includes the first drink; meals cost extra. Check newspapers for advertisements about smaller unscheduled *peñas* and other musical events.

The following are central *peñas*:

El Calicanto (Map pp68-9; ☎ 240-8008; Sanjinés 467; mains B$25-50, dinner buffet B$30)

Peña Marka Tambo (Map pp68-9; ☎ 228-0041; Jaén 710; cover charge B$30, mains B$4; ☽ from 8pm Thu-Sat)

Peña Huari (Map pp68-9; ☎ 231-6225; Sagárnaga 339; cover charge B$105, buffet dinner B$100; ☽ show 8pm nightly)

Peña Parnaso (Map pp68-9; ☎ 231-6827; Sagárnaga 189; cover charge B$80, mains B$35-40; ☽ show 8:30pm) Also open for lunch (B$35) with no show.

La Casa del Corregidor (Map pp68-9; ☎ 236-3633; Murillo 1040; cover charge B$25, food & show B$80; ☽ 7pm-late Mon-Sat)

Cinema

Your best chance of catching a quality art film is at the cutting-edge **Cinemateca Boliviana** (Map pp68-9; ☎ 244-4090; cnr Zuazo & Rosendo Gutiérrez), which shows an excellent selection of new art-house Bolivian and subtitled foreign films regularly.

German films are screened regularly at the Goethe Institut (p64). Modern cinemas on the Prado show recent international releases, usually in the original language with Spanish subtitles, for around B$25. The following are recommended movie houses:

Cine 6 de Agosto (Map pp62-3; ☎ 244-2629; 6 de Agosto, btwn Calles Gutiérrez and Salinas.

Cine 16 de Julio (Map pp68-9; ☎ 244-1099; 16 de Julio)

Cine Monje Campero (Map pp68-9; ☎ 212-9033, 212-9034; cnr 16 de Julio & Bueno)

Theater

The **Teatro Municipal Alberto Saavedra Pérez** (Map pp68-9; cnr Sanjinés & Indaburo; tickets B$20-50) has an ambitious program of folklore shows, folk-music concerts and foreign theatrical presentations. It's a great old restored building with a round auditorium, elaborate balconies and a vast ceiling mural. The newspapers and municipal tourist office (p66) have information about what's on here.

Spectator Sports

The popularity of *fútbol* (soccer) in Bolivia is comparable to that in other Latin American countries. Matches are played at Estadio Hernando Siles (Estadio Olímpico La Paz; Map pp68-9). Sundays (year-round) are the big game days, and Wednesdays and Saturdays also have games. Prices vary according to seats and whether it's a local or international game (B$10 to B$60). You can imagine what sort of advantage the local teams have over mere lowlanders; players from elsewhere consider the high-altitude La Paz games a suicide attempt! Check newspapers for times and prices.

SHOPPING
Souvenirs & Artesanía

La Paz is a shopper's paradise; not only are prices very reasonable, but the quality of what's offered can be astounding. The main tourist shopping area lies along the very steep and literally breathtaking Calle Sagárnaga (Map pp68-9) between Santa Cruz and Tamayo, and spreads out along adjoining streets. Here, you'll also find Calle Linares, an alley chock-a-block with artisans' stores.

Some stores specialize in *oriente* wood-carvings and ceramics, and Potosí silver. Others deal in rugs, wall-hangings, woven belts and pouches. Amid the lovely weavings and other items of exquisite craftsmanship, you'll find plenty of tourist kitsch, an art form unto itself: Inca-themed ashtrays, fake Tiwanaku figurines, costume jewelry and mass-produced woolens.

Music recordings are available in small stores along Valle Evaristo and more established places on Linares. Or you can try your luck in the Mercado de Hechicería (p70) where there are figurines and Aymará good-luck charms, including frogs.

For less expensive llama or alpaca sweaters, bowler hats and other non-tourist clothing items, stroll Calles Graneros and Max Paredes.

Ayni (Map pp68-9; www.aynibolivia.com; Illampu 704) This fabulous shop, a fair-trade project supporting groups of *artesanatos* in La Paz, stocks beautiful textiles and good-quality handicrafts. There's a second branch in Hotel Rosario (p78).

LA PAZ

Artesanía Sorata (Map pp68-9; ☎ 239-3041; www .artesaniasorata.com; Sagárnaga 363 & Linares 900) A community-focused project that specializes in export-quality handmade dolls, original alpaca products and other beautiful items.

Comart Tukuypaj (Map pp68-9; ☎ 231-2686; www. comart-tukuypaj.com; Linares 958) Offers export-quality, fair-trade llama, alpaca and *artesanías* from around the country. Upstairs the Inca Pallay women's weaving cooperative has a gallery with justly famous Jal'qa and Candelaria weavings.

Clothing

Reflecting its status as the more upmarket area, Zona Sur opts for designer clothing. Several stores sell stunning llama and alpaca fashion items. Try the following:

Liliana Castellanos (Map p76; ☎ 212 5770; www .lilianacastellanos.com; Montenegro 810, Bloque H, San Miguel)

Millma (Map p76; ☎ 231-1338; www.millma.com; cnr Sagárnaga 225 & Claudio Aliaga 1202, San Miguel)

La Casa de la Llama (Map p76; ☎ 279-0401; Montenegro, Bloque E, No 2, Calacoto)

Lumen Böhrt (Map p76; ☎ 277-2625; Montenegro 910, San Miguel)

Waliki (Map p76; www.waliki.com; Calle Rene Moreno, E22, Calacoto, Zona Sur) An alpaca artisan outlet that supports community employment and offers stylish contemporary clothing.

Musical Instruments

Many La Paz artisans specialize in *quenas*, *zampoñas*, *tarkas* and *pinquillos*, among other traditional woodwind instruments. There's a lot of low-quality or merely decorative tourist rubbish around. Visit a reputable workshop where you'll pay a fraction of gift-shop prices, and contribute directly to the artisan rather than to an intermediary. Several shops sell instruments along Sagárnaga, Linares and Illampu.

Photography & Film

For the few photographers who use slide and/or print films nowadays, these are available in some camera shops; be cautious about buying film at street markets where it is exposed to strong sun all day.

Many photo shops cluster around Plaza Venezuela (El Prado); some of these do digital processing.

AGFA (Map pp68-9; ☎ 240-7030; Mariscal Santa Cruz 901) Perfect for passport photos in a flash.

Kodak (Map pp68-9; ☎ 211-7606; 16 de Julio s/n, Edificio Alameda)

Tecnología Fotográfica (Map pp62-3; ☎ 242-7402, 7065-0773; www.tecnologiafotografica.com; 20 de Octubre 2255) For camera problems, Rolando's your man.

Outdoor Gear

For all kinds of backpack protection – plastic sacks, chains, padlocks etc – check the street stalls along Calle Isaac Tamayo.

Andean Base Camp (Map pp68-9; ☎ 246-3782; Illampu 863) For equipment rentals, this is the place. Stocks top-quality Swiss-made gear, including gas-stove canisters. Ask for Christian – he will kit you out with exactly what you need.

Tatoo (Map pp68-9; ☎ 245-1265; Illampu 828) Part of a South American chain, this outdoor outlet stocks the lot – good-quality equipment and clothing of well-known brands.

Spitting Llama Bookstore & Outfitter (Map pp68-9; ☎ 7039-8720; www.thespittingllama.com; Linares 947) Inside Posada de la Abuela, this friendly one-stop shop stocks everything from maps and gear, including tents, backpacks and hiking boots.

Wine & Food

Irupana (Map pp62-3; Murillo 1014, cnr Tarija) Don't miss this shop, which sells locally made organic produce including sugar-free muesli and some of the most delicious chocolate in Bolivia. There is another branch near the corner of Fernando Guachalla and Av Sanchez Lima.

El Ceibo (Map pp68-9; www.elceibo.org; Potosí 1147; Cañada Strongest 1784) Chocoholics mustn't miss El Ceibo, an ecologically friendly producer of fantastic local chocolates (all natural ingredients).

Breick Chocolate Shop (Map pp68-9; Zuazo at Bueno) Also not to be missed, Breick is where Bolivia's top-quality chocolate is for sale for ridiculously reasonable prices.

FARE HIKES IN TRANSPORTATION

At the time of research the government was proposing an increase of between 20% and 30% in public transportation fares. If this proposal is passed, then there will be differences between the public transportation fares quoted in this book and the fares you will actually pay.

Bodega La Concepción (Map pp68-9; ☎ 248-4812; Cañada Strongest 1620 at Otero de la Vega, San Pedro) Award-winning, high-altitude vintages are available at wholesale prices from this outlet of the Tarija-based winery.

Campos de Solana/Casa Real (Map pp68-9; ☎ 249-1776; Otero de la Vega 373, at 20 de Octubre) A Tarija winery best known for its Malbec and Riesling.

GETTING THERE & AWAY
Air
El Alto International Airport (LPB; ☎ 281-0240) is 10km via toll-road from the city center on the Altiplano. At 4050m, it's the world's highest international airport; larger planes need 5km of runway to lift off and must land at twice their sea-level velocity to compensate for the lower atmospheric density. Stopping distance is much greater too, and planes are equipped with special tires to withstand the extreme forces involved.

Airport services include a news-stand, ATMs, internet, souvenir stores, a bookstore, a coffee shop, fast food, a bistro and a duty-free shop in the international terminal. The currency-exchange desk outside the international arrivals area gives poor rates on traveler's checks – if possible, wait until you're in town. The domestic departure tax is B$14, while the international departure tax is B$170.

AIRLINE OFFICES
AeroSur (Map pp68-9; ☎ 244-4930; www.aerosur.com; Edificio Petrolero, 16 de Julio 1616)

Amaszonas (Map pp68-9; ☎ 222-0848; Saavedra 1649, Miraflores)

American Airlines (Map pp68-9; ☎ 237-2009; www.aa.com; Edificio Hernann, Plaza Venezuela 1440)

Lan Airlines (Map pp68-9 ☎ 235-8377; www.lan.com; Suite 104, Edificio Ayacucho, 16 de Julio 1566)

Taca (Map pp68-9; ☎ 215-8202; www.taca.com; Edificio Petrolero, 16 de Julio 1616)

TAM Mercosur (Map pp68-9; ☎ 244-3442; Heriberto Gutiérrez 2323)

Transportes Aéreos Militares (TAM; Map pp68-9; ☎ 268-111, 277-5222; www.tam.bo; Ismael Montes 738)

Bus
The **main bus terminal** (Terminal de Buses; Map pp62-3; ☎ 228-0551; Plaza Antofagasta; terminal fee B$2) is a 15-minute uphill walk north of the city center. Fares are relatively uniform between companies. This full-service terminal

serves all destinations south and east of La Paz, as well as international destinations. Other destinations are served mainly by *micros* and minibuses departing from the cemetery district (below) and Villa Fátima (p88). Prices quoted in this section increase during high season and festival holidays.

MAIN TERMINAL – SOUTHERN & EASTERN BOLIVIA
Buses to Oruro run about every half-hour (B$15 to B$45, 3½ hours) between 5am and 9:30pm. The best way to get to Uyuni is on the overnight buses (US$35) of **Todo Turismo** (☎ 268-111, 277-5222, 211-9418; www.touringbolivia.com; Plaza Antofagasta 504, Edificio Paula Piso 1), although the times they go seem to vary; at the time of research they were not travelling on Sunday nor Wednesday. Several companies serve Cochabamba (B$45 to B$90, seven to eight hours) daily. Buses to Santa Cruz generally leave in the evening at 5pm or 7pm (B$170, 16 hours). El Dorado runs a direct service.

Most overnight buses to Sucre (B$70 to B$135, 14 hours) pass through Potosí (B$40 to B$70, eight hours) and some require a layover there. Have warm clothes handy for this typically chilly trip. Some Potosí buses continue on to Tarija (B$90 to B$180, 24 hours), Tupiza (B$115, 20 hours) or Villazón (B$115 to B$140, 23 hours).

MAIN TERMINAL – INTERNATIONAL SERVICES
Several companies offer daily departures to Arica (B$100 to B$150, eight hours) and Iquique (B$150 to B$200, 11 to 13 hours); to Cusco (B$100 to B$150, 12 to 17 hours) via either Desaguadero or Copacabana, with connections to Puno (B$50 to B$80, eight hours), to Lima (B$350, 27 hours) and Arequipa; and to Buenos Aires (normal/ *bus cama* or sleeper, 50 hours), via either Villazón or Yacuiba.

CEMETERY DISTRICT – LAKE TITICACA, TIWANAKU & PERU (VIA DESAGUADERO)
Several bus companies, including **Transportes Manco Kapac** (Map pp62-3; ☎ 245-9045) and **TransTurs 2 de Febrero** (Map pp62-3; ☎ 245-3035), run frequent services to Copacabana (B$15 to B$20, three to 3½ hours) between 5am and 8pm from Calle José María Aliaga near Plaza Felix Reyes Ortiz (Plaza Tupac Katari).

Alternatively, there are more comfortable tourist buses (B$25 to B$30, three hours) that do hotel and hostel pickups; you can book them at most La Paz travel agencies. Most companies offer daily services to Puno (with a change in Copacabana) for about B$80, including hotel pickup. The trip takes nine to 10 hours, including lunch in Copacabana and the border-crossing formalities. If a company doesn't fill its bus, passengers may be shunted to another company so no one runs half-empty buses. All companies allow stopovers in Copacabana.

Between 5am and 6pm, **Autolíneas Ingavi** (Map pp62-3; José María Asín) has departures every 30 minutes to Desaguadero (B$10, two hours) via Tiwanaku (B$10, 1½ hours) and Guaqui. Nearby is **Trans-Unificado Sorata** (Map pp62-3; ☎ 238-1693; cnr Kollasuyo & Bustillos), which operates daily buses and minibuses to Sorata (bus B$13-20, minibus B$15). You need to reserve buses on weekends, so book your ticket early. Sit on the left for views. Buses to Huarina and Huatajata (B$10, two hours) leave nearby from the corner of Calles Bustillos and Kollasuyo.

Trans Tours Tiwanaku (☎ 7191-4889; Calle José María Aliaga) offers trips to Tiwanaku (B$10, two hours).

Be sure to watch your bags in this area, especially while boarding or leaving buses.

VILLA FÁTIMA – YUNGAS & AMAZON BASIN

Several *flotas* (long-distance bus companies) offer daily bus and minibus services to the Yungas and beyond. **Flota Yungueña** (☎ 221-3513) has two offices; the one at Yanacachi 844, behind the *ex-surtidor* (former gas station), serves Coroico; the one at Las Américas 341, just north of the former gas station, serves Amazon Basin routes. Nearby **Trans Totaí** (San Borja) and **Trans San Bartolomé** (☎ 221-1674) serve Chulumani. Other companies serving the region are clustered along Virgen del Carmen, just west of Av Las Américas. Expect frequent delays in the rainy season. For all services, it's wise to reserve seats in advance.

Sample fares include Coroico (B$15 to B$25, three hours), Chulumani (B$15 to B$20, four hours), Guanay (B$60, eight hours), Rurrenabaque (B$50 to B$80, 18 to 20 hours), Guayaramerín (B$160 to B$180, 35 to 60 hours), Riberalta (B$140,

35 to 60 hours) and Cobija (B$180, 50 to 80 hours).

Train

La Paz's old train station is defunct. Trains for Chile and the Argentine border, via Uyuni and/or Tupiza, all leave from Oruro (p161). For information and bookings, contact the **Empresa Ferroviaria Andina** (FCA; Map pp68-9; ☎ 241-6545/46; www.fca.com.bo, in Spanish; Guachalla 494; ✆ ticket office 8am-noon Mon-Sat).

For information about rail services within Peru, contact **Peru Rail** (www.perurail.com).

GETTING AROUND
To/From the Airport

There are two access routes to El Alto International Airport: the *autopista* (B$3) toll-road and the sinuous free route, which leads into Plaza Ballivián in El Alto.

Minibus 212 runs frequently between Plaza Isabel la Católica (Map pp68–9) and the airport between around 7am and 8pm. Heading into town from the airport, this service will drop you anywhere along the Prado.

Radio taxis (around B$50 for up to four passengers) will pick you up at your door; confirm the price with the dispatcher when booking, or ask the driver to verify it when you climb in. For a fifth person, there is an additional B$10 charge. Transportes Aéreos Militares (TAM) flights leave from the **military airport** (☎ 237-9286, 212-1585) in El Alto. Catch a Río Seco *micro* from the upper Prado. Taxi fares should be about the same as for the main El Alto airport.

To/From the Bus Terminals

The main bus terminal is 1km uphill from the center. We strongly recommend that you take a taxi – ironically, if there's more than one of you, it's just as cheap and will save you both the hassles of squeezing in swollen backpacks and the danger of robberies. If you insist on public transportation, crowded *micros* marked 'Prado' and 'Av Arce' pass the main tourist areas. If walking (not recommended with a backpack), snake your way down to the main drag, Av Ismael Montes, and keep descending for 15 minutes to the center.

Micros and minibuses run to the cemetery district constantly from the center. Catch them on Av Santa Cruz or grab *micro*

2 along Av Yanacocha. Heading into the city from the cemetery by day you can catch *micros* along Av Baptista. Don't accept a ride from anyone who approaches you (see Dangers & Annoyances, p66).

You can reach Villa Fátima by *micro* or minibus from the Prado or Av Camacho. It's about 1km uphill from Plaza Gualberto Villarroel.

Car & Motorcycle

Driving the steep, winding, frenetic one-way streets of La Paz may be intimidating for the uninitiated, but for longer day trips into the immediate hinterlands, you could consider renting a car (but hiring a driver is probably easier and just as economical; p348). For rental rates and policy details, see p349.

Avis (Map p76; ☎ 211-1870; www.avis.com.bo; Calle 20 y Costañera 23, Zona Sur)

Barbol (☎ 282-0675; www.hertzbolivia.com; santacruz@hertzbolivia.com; Av Héroes del Km 7, 777) The official agent for Hertz.

Budget (Map pp62-3; ☎ 241-8768; www.budget bolivia.com; Fernanda Guachalla 639) Also a branch at the airport.

Kolla Motors (Map pp62-3; ☎ 241-9141, fax 241-1344; www.kollamotors.com; Gutiérrez 502)

Petita Rent-a-Car (☎ 242-0329; www.rentacarpetita .com; Valentín Abecia 2031, Sopocachi Alto) Swiss-owned and specializing in 4WDs.

Rent-a-Car International (Map pp68-9; ☎ 244-1906; Zuazo 1942)

Public Transportation

MICRO AND MINIBUS

La Paz's sputtering and smoke-spewing *micros*, the older three-quarter-sized buses, mock the law of gravity and defy the principles of brake and transmission mechanics as they grind up and down the city's steep hills. They charge around B$1 per trip. Minibuses service most places as well, for a slightly higher price. In addition to a route number or letter, *micros* plainly display their destination and route on a signboard posted in the front window. Minibuses usually have a young tout screaming the stops. You can simply wave both down anywhere except for near policed intersections.

TRUFI

Trufis are shared cars or minibuses that ply set routes. Destinations are identified on placards on the roof or windscreen. They charge approximately B$3 around town and B$4 to Zona Sur.

TAXI

Although most things worth seeing in La Paz lie within manageable walking distance of the center, the bus terminals are all rather steep climbs from the main hotel areas. Especially considering the altitude, struggling up the hills through traffic with bulky luggage isn't recommended.

Radio taxis (with roof bubbles advertising their telephone numbers) are recommended as the safer option. They charge about B$4 around the center, B$8 to B$10 (more in peak hours) from Sagárnaga to Sopocachi or Sopocachi to the cemetery district and B$15 to B$20 to Zona Sur. Charges are a little higher after 11pm.

Most regular taxis are also collective taxis and charge a per-person rate. This means that the driver may pick up additional passengers, and that you can flag down a taxi already carrying passengers. Regular taxis charge B$6 per person around the center (a bit more for long uphill routes).

If possible, ask your hotel or restaurant to ring for a taxi (see Dangers & Annoyances, p66). Otherwise, taxis can be waved down anywhere, except near intersections or in areas cordoned off by the police. If you're traveling beyond the city center, or your journey involves a long uphill climb, confirm the fare with the driver before climbing in (it will usually be slightly more than the regular fare), and try to carry small change at all times.

Pre-ordered or radio taxis to the airport cost from around B$50 to B$70.

AROUND LA PAZ

VALLE DE LA LUNA

About 10km down the canyon of the Río Choqueyapu from the city center, **Valle de la Luna** (Valley of the Moon; admission B$15) is a slightly overhyped place, though it's a pleasant break from urban La Paz. It could be easily visited in a morning or combined with another outing such as a hike to Muela del Diablo (p91) to fill an entire day. It isn't a valley at all, but a bizarre, eroded hillside maze of canyons and pinnacles technically known as badlands. Several species of cactus

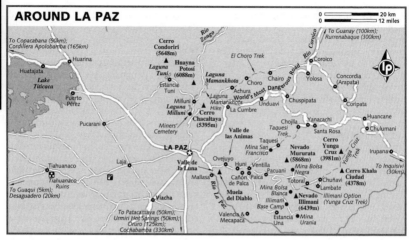

grow here, including the hallucinogenic *choma* (San Pedro cactus). Unfortunately, urban growth has caught up to the area, making it less of a viewpoint than it otherwise might be. Note: readers have reported muggings in recent years, even while in the site's confines.

Getting There & Away

If you visit Valle de la Luna as part of an organized tour, you'll have only a five-minute photo stop. If on your own, from Av México in La Paz, which parallels the Prado, catch any form of transportation marked 'Mallasa' or 'Zoológico.' These will drop you off several meters from the entrance.

For a taxi from the center, you'll pay around B$80 for up to three people, and the driver may wait for an hour or so while you look around.

MALLASA

After a traipse around Valle de la Luna, you can also visit the village of Mallasa, popular among *paceños* on weekends. Just east of Mallasa is La Paz's spacious, but sorely underfunded, **Vesty Pakos Zoo** (☎ 274-5992; admission B$3.50; ☺ 10am-5pm). Animal lovers may be upset by the poor conditions, however.

From the overlook immediately behind the zoo, you can take the clearly marked walking track that descends to and crosses the fetid Río Choqueyapu, before beginning a lung-bursting 600m climb to the Muela del Diablo.

The Swiss-run **Hotel Restaurant Oberland** (☎ 274-5040; www.h-oberland.com; Calle 2, Mallasa; s/d/ste US$38/46/54; ☐ ☒) is a slightly worn but friendly country-style hotel 30 minutes by minibus from the center of La Paz. It sits at an altitude of just 3200m, so it's warmer than central La Paz. It has a pleasant cactus garden and lots of family features: an indoor pool and a sauna, squash and beach-volleyball courts, and table tennis. Transfers from La Paz cost B$30 per person. Most pleasant is the outdoor eating area, popular on weekends, serving a range of Swiss and local food (B$30 to B$50).

To get to Mallasa from La Paz, take minibus 231 from Sagárnaga, or any form of transportation marked 'Mallasa' or 'Zoológico.' From the top of Valle de la Luna, catch a *micro* headed downvalley or continue a couple of kilometers on foot to Mallasa.

VALENCIA & MECAPACA

About 30km south of La Paz, and 15km from Mallasa, are two quaint, if increasingly urbanized, villages worth visiting for their authenticity and beautiful landscapes. Mecapaca boasts a beautifully restored church in its plaza (ask for Sra Ninfa Avendaño for keys; if you buy something from her store and add a donation to the church box, she'll likely oblige). The church is perched on the hillside of the small plaza with wonderful views of the fertile valley beyond. The village's terracotta color is notable, thanks to the 'generosity' of a local cement baron,

LA PAZ

who wanted to prettify the village and had it painted. He resides in La Paz, but has built a large complex for weekend use (look for it down on the right as you enter town). On the plaza, there are two small super-simple restaurants for lunch (mains B$15).

A great treat on the way back to La Paz is to stop for an Italian meal at **Trattoria Sant' Aquilina** (☎ 274-5707; ☯ weekends only), a Greek island–style restaurant, just before or after Jupapina, depending which direction you are coming from. The restaurant is renowned for its wood-fired pizza and gelato and is popular among the trendy *paceñan* crowds who converge on a Sunday. If this doesn't take your fancy, join the *paceñans* at a number of other weekend eateries that have sprung up along the increasingly urbanized road south of La Paz.

Take minibus 253 to Macapaca/Valencia from Plaza Belso in San Pedro (B$4) or from Mallasa. To return to La Paz take the same minibus 253 from Mecapaca; from anywhere else, catch anything that moves back up the valley. On weekends, *trufis,* minibuses and radio taxis leave constantly from Plaza Humboldt (Zona Sur) for points south.

MUELA DEL DIABLO

The prominent rock outcrop known as the Devil's Molar is actually an extinct volcanic plug that rises between the Río Choqueyapu and the suburban sprawl of Pedregal and Calacoto. A hike to its base makes a pleasant, half-day walking trip from La Paz; it offers incredible views of the city and valley of La Paz, and can be easily combined with a visit to Valle de la Luna. Warning: several robberies have been reported here; inquire locally about safety before heading out and travel in pairs or groups.

From the cemetery in Pedregal, the trail climbs steeply (several times crossing the new road that provides access to the hamlet near the base of the *muela*). After a breathless hour or so, you'll reach a pleasant grassy swale where the 'tooth' comes into view, as well as some precarious pinnacles further east.

At this point the walking track joins the road and descends through the hamlet. About 300m further along, a side route branches off to the left and climbs toward the base of the *muela*. From the end of this route you can pick your way with extreme caution up to the cleft between the double summit, where there's a large cross. Without technical equipment and expertise, however, it's inadvisable to climb further.

After descending to the main track, you can decide whether to return the way you came, or follow the steep track that circles the *muela* in a counterclockwise direction and descends to the Río Choqueyapu before

---

RÍO CHOKE

If statistics are anything to go by, the name of the Río Choqueyapu, which flows through La Paz, might as well be shortened to the Río Choke (or 'Omo River,' after the quantity of laundry soap flowing in it). This fetid stream, which provided the gold that gave La Paz its present location, is now utterly dead and beyond help. According to one source, 'the Río Choqueyapu receives annually 132,000 gallons of urine, 200,000 tons of human excrement and millions of tons of garbage, animal carcasses and industrial toxins.' The industrial toxins include cyanide from tanneries and a cocktail of chemicals and dyes from textile and paper industries, which cause the river to flow bright orange in places, or red topped with a layer of white foam.

The Choqueyapu fortunately flows underground through the city, but it emerges in Zona Sur. Further down, it's used by *campesinos,* who take water for washing, consumption and agriculture. Most people heat the water before drinking it, but few boil it, and even boiling wouldn't eliminate some of the chemical pollutants from industrial wastes. Several years ago there was an outbreak of cholera in La Paz, prompting people to blame the *campesinos* in a nearby valley, who grow vegetables in the fertile valley.

Currently no one can be fined or cited for dumping waste into the river because, incredibly, the city has no laws against it. In 2000 the mayor's Environmental Quality office proposed a raft of projects aimed at controlling water pollution, vehicle emissions, rubbish dumping and noise. As always, the problem with implementation has been funding, and still the foul stream continues to flow, most of it ending up in the Amazon Basin.

climbing the other side of the valley to the zoo in Mallasa. The latter option will turn this hike into a full-day trip, as it takes about six hours for the hike between Pedregal and Mallasa.

Getting There & Away

From La Paz the best access to the start of the hike is on minibus 288, marked 'Pedregal,' from the lower Prado. The end of the line is the parking area a couple of hundred meters downhill from Pedregal's cemetery. Returning from Valle de la Luna, you can board these minibuses at Zona Sur's Plaza Humboldt or follow the difficult walking track from near the zoo in Mallasa, which involves a descent to the Río Choqueyapu and then a stiff 600m ascent to the eastern side of the *muela*. To return to La Paz from Pedregal, catch a 'Prado' minibus from the parking area.

VALLE DE LAS ÁNIMAS

The name Valley of Spirits is used to describe the eerily eroded canyons and fantastic organ-pipe spires to the north and northeast of the barrios of Chasquipampa, Ovejuyo and Apaña (which are rapidly being absorbed into the Zona Sur neighborhoods of La Paz). The scenery resembles that of Valle de la Luna, but on a grander scale. It's worth just getting out here.

There are two (long-day) walking routes through the valley: the Río Ovejuyo Route and the Quebrada Negra Route. The Río Ovejuyo walk requires a compass and 1:50,000 topography sheet *5944-II* and, for a very short section, topo sheet *5944-I* (see p63 for details on where to get maps). This option can be challenging, especially because of the altitude. Make sure you carry plenty of water, a hat and snacks.

The Quebrada Negra Route heads up Quebrada Negra, over Cerro Pararani and down to Huni. Although only 7km, it's a demanding day hike that requires six to seven hours. It begins at the Quebrada Negra ravine, which crosses the road at the upper (eastern) end of Ovejuyo village. *Micro* 'Ñ' and minibus 385 (marked 'Ovejuyo/ Apaña') or minibus 42 (marked 'Apaña') all travel right past the ravine mouth.

The easy-to-follow 4km route up Quebrada Negra will take you through the most dramatic of the eroded Valle de las Ánimas

pinnacles. Near the head of the ravine, you need to traverse southeast around the northern shoulder of Cerro Pararani, until you find the obvious route that descends steeply to Huni village (not Huni chapel, which is also marked on topo sheets). In fine weather, you'll have good views of Illimani along this section. For this route you'll need a compass and the 1:50,000 topo sheets *5944-I* and *6044-III*.

To return to La Paz, follow the road for 2km up over Paso Huni and then for another 1.5km downhill to Apaña, where you'll catch up with regular *micros* and *trufis* returning to the city.

CAÑÓN DE PALCA

The magnificent Palca Canyon (marked on topo sheets as Quebrada Chua Kheri) brings a slice of Grand Canyon country to the dramatic badland peaks and eroded amphitheaters east of La Paz. A walk through this gorge makes an ideal day hike from La Paz. Note: go only in groups as assaults on single hikers at the time of research have been reported here. Check the safety status before setting out.

A good, safe alternative is to head out with **La Paz on Foot** (p75), which offers excellent guided day hikes through the canyon (US$45 per person including transportation and lunch).

Sleeping & Eating

Palca is a pleasant, basic town located relatively close to the exit of the canyon. It has a simple **hostal** (r per person B$20-40), which offers set meals and is popular with Bolivian tourists on weekends. Alternatively, you can camp around Palca or nearby Ventilla. Beware of the badly polluted surface water, and ask permission before you set your tent up in a field or pasture.

Huni is a small town above the entrance to Cañón de Palca. It has a store selling basic supplies, including bottled water and snack foods, and also provides Bolivian set-menu meals at lunchtime.

Getting There & Away

For the start of this hike, you need to reach Huni, which is served only by *micros* and *trufis* headed for Ventilla and Palca. These leave at least once daily from near the corner of Boquerón and Lara, two blocks north of Plaza Líbano in the San Pedro district of La Paz. There's no set schedule, but most leave in the morning – be there by 7am. You'll have the best luck on Saturday and Sunday, when families make excursions into the countryside. Alternatively, take *micro 42* or minibus 385, marked 'Ovejuyo/Apaña,' get off at the end of the line, and slog the 1.5km up the road to Paso Huni.

From Palca back to La Paz, you'll find occasional *camiones, micros* and minibuses, particularly on Sunday afternoon, but don't count on anything after 3pm or 4pm. Alternatively, you can hike to Ventilla, an hour uphill through a pleasant eucalyptus plantation, and try hitchhiking from there.

If you arrive in Palca geared up for more hiking, you can always set off from Ventilla along the Takesi trek (p127).

CHACALTAYA

The 5395m-high Cerro Chacaltaya peak, atop a former glacier (it diminished over several decades and, tragically, had melted completely by 2009), is a popular day trip. Until the 'big melt,' it was the world's highest 'developed' ski area. It's a steep 90-minute ride from central La Paz, and the accessible summit is an easy 200m ascent from there.

You can get your thrills, spills (well, hopefully not) and great views on a 60km-plus mountain-bike trip from Chacaltaya to Zongo and beyond at descents of up to 4100m (vertical drop). Gravity Assisted Mountain Biking (p74) runs trips starting at B$600 per person.

For visitors and hikers, Chacaltaya offers spectacular views of La Paz, Illimani, Mururata and 6088m Huayna Potosí. It's a high-altitude, relatively easy (but steep) 100m or so climb from the lodge to the summit of Chacaltaya. Remember to carry warm clothing and water, and take plenty of rests, say, a 30-second stop every 10 steps or so, and longer stops if needed, even if you don't feel tired. If you start to feel light-headed, sit down and rest until the feeling passes. If it doesn't, you may be suffering from mild altitude sickness; the only remedy is to descend.

From Chacaltaya it's possible to walk to Refugio Huayna Potosí, at the base of Huayna Potosí (p141), in half a day. Before you set out, you must obtain maps from Instituto Geográfico Militar (p63) and instructions.

If it's open, snacks and hot drinks are available at Club Andino's lodge; if you want anything more substantial, bring it from town. Also bring warm (and windproof) clothing, sunglasses (100% UV proof) and sunscreen.

For overnight stays at Chacaltaya, you can crash in Club Andino's ski lodge, a '50s-style, stone ski lodge. A warm sleeping bag, food and some sort of headache/*soroche* (altitude sickness) relief are essential for an overnight stay.

Those who fly into La Paz from the lowlands will want to wait a few days before visiting Chacaltaya or other high-altitude places. For guidelines on avoiding or coping with altitude-related ailments, see p358.

Getting There & Away

There's no public transportation to Chacaltaya. Most La Paz tour agencies take groups to Chacaltaya for around B$50 to B$80 per person.

The **Club Andino Boliviano** (Map pp68-9; ☎ 7126-0958; México 1638, La Paz) occasionally organizes transportation to Chacaltaya on weekends for groups for around B$60 per person (transportation only).

TIWANAKU

Little is actually known about the people who constructed the great Tiwanaku ceremonial center on the southern shore of Lake Titicaca more than a thousand years ago. Archaeologists generally agree that the civilization which spawned Tiwanaku rose around 600 BC. Construction on the ceremonial site was under way by about AD 700, but around 1200 the group had melted into obscurity, becoming another 'lost' civilization. Evidence of its influence, particularly its religion, has been found throughout the vast area that later became the Inca empire.

The treasures of Tiwanaku have literally been scattered to the four corners of the earth. Its gold was looted by the Spanish, and early stone and pottery finds were sometimes destroyed by religious zealots who considered them pagan idols. Some of the work found its way to European museums; farmers destroyed pieces of it as they turned the surrounding area into pasture and cropland; the Church kept some of the statues or sold them as curios; and the larger stonework went into Spanish construction projects, and even into the bed of the La Paz–Guaqui rail line that passes just south of the site.

Fortunately, a portion of the treasure has been preserved, and some of it remains in Bolivia. A few of the larger anthropomorphic stone statues have been left on the site. Others are on display at the Museo Nacional de Arqueología (p70) in La Paz. New finds from the earliest Tiwanaku periods are being added to the collection of the new onsite **Museo Lítico Monumental** (admission US$10; ☺ 9am-5pm). The star of the show is the massive **Monolito Bennetto Pachamama**, rescued in 2002 from its former smoggy home at the outdoor Templete Semisubterráneo (p73) in La Paz.

Pieces from the three more recent Tiwanaku periods may be found scattered around Bolivia, but the majority are housed in archaeological museums in La Paz and Cochabamba. The ruins themselves have been so badly looted, however, that much of the information they could have revealed about their builders is now lost forever.

Labeling at the onsite museums is sparse and almost exclusively in Spanish. The single admission ticket includes the site, the **Puma Punku** excavation site (not included in many tours), the new museum and the visitors center. Guides must be registered and can be hired.

A major research and excavation project is ongoing, which means that some of the main features may be cordoned off during your visit.

History

Although no one is certain whether it was the capital of a nation, Tiwanaku undoubtedly served as a great ceremonial center. At its height the city had a population of 20,000 inhabitants and encompassed approximately 2.6 sq km. While only a very small percentage of the original site has been excavated – and what remains is less than overwhelming – Tiwanaku represents the greatest megalithic architectural achievement of pre-Inca South America.

The development of the Tiwanaku civilization has been divided by researchers into five distinct periods, numbered Tiwanaku I through V, each of which has its own outstanding attributes.

The Tiwanaku I period falls between the advent of the Tiwanaku civilization and the middle of the 5th century BC. Significant finds from this period include multicolored pottery and human or animal effigies in painted clay. Tiwanaku II, which ended around the beginning of the Christian era, is hallmarked by ceramic vessels with horizontal handles. Tiwanaku III dominated the next 300 years, and was characterized by tricolor pottery of geometric design, often decorated with images of stylized animals.

Tiwanaku IV, also known as the Classic Period, developed between AD 300 and 700. The large stone structures that dominate the site today were constructed during this period. The use of bronze and gold is considered evidence of contact with groups further east in the Cochabamba valley and further west on the Peruvian coast. Tiwanaku IV pottery is largely anthropomorphic. Pieces uncovered by archaeologists include some in the shape of human heads and faces with bulging cheeks, indicating that coca leaf was already in use at this time.

Tiwanaku V, also called the Expansive Period, is marked by a decline that lasted until Tiwanaku's population completely disappeared around 1200. Pottery grew less elaborate, construction projects slowed and stopped, and no large-scale monuments were added after the early phases of this period.

When the Spaniards arrived in South America, local indigenous legends recounted that Tiwanaku had been the capital of the bearded, white god-king called Viracocha, and that from his city Viracocha had reigned over the civilization.

Visiting the Ruins

Scattered around the Tiwanaku site, you'll find heaps of jumbled basalt and sandstone slabs weighing as much as 25 tons each. Oddly enough, the nearest quarries that could have produced the basalt megaliths are on the Copacabana peninsula, 40km away beyond the lake. Even the sandstone blocks had to be transported from a site more than 5km away. It's no wonder, then, that when the Spanish asked local Aymará how the buildings were constructed, they replied that it was done with the aid of the leader/deity Viracocha. They could conceive of no other plausible explanation.

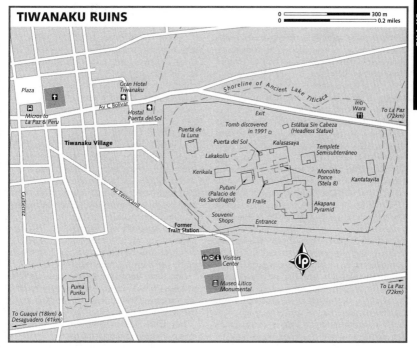

TIWANAKU RUINS

0 — 300 m
0 — 0.2 miles

Shoreline of Ancient Lake Titicaca

Plaza

Gran Hotel Tiwanaku

Av C Bolívar

Micros to La Paz & Perú

Hostal Puerta del Sol

Tiwanaku Village

Guitérrez

Av Ferrocarril

Puma Punku

Former Train Station

Puerta de la Luna

Puerta del Sol

Lakakollu

Kerikala

Putuni (Palacio de los Sarcófagos)

Souvenir Shops

Exit

Tomb discovered in 1991

Kalasasaya

El Fraile

Estátua Sin Cabeza (Headless Statue)

Templete Semisubterráneo

Monolito Ponce (Stela 8)

Akapana Pyramid

Entrance

Inti-Wara

To La Paz (72km)

Kantatayita

Visitors Center

Museo Lítico Monumental

To La Paz (72km)

To Guaqui (18km) & Desaguadero (41km)

Tiwanaku's most outstanding structure is the **Akapana pyramid**, which was built on an existing geological formation. At its base this roughly square 16m hill covers a surface area of about 200 sq meters. In the center of its flat summit is an oval-shaped sunken area, which some sources attribute to early, haphazard, Spanish excavation. The presence of a stone drain in the center, however, has led some archaeologists to believe it was used for water storage. In the past few years, archaeologists have changed their minds. At the time of research, the pyramid was undergoing excavations in various stages; the most recent findings include craniums, assumed to be war trophies, leading archaeologists to believe the pyramid was, in fact, a ceremonial temple.

North of the pyramid is **Kalasasaya**, a partially reconstructed 130m-by-120m ritual-platform compound with walls constructed of huge blocks of red sandstone and andesite. The blocks are precisely fitted to form a platform base 3m high. Monolithic uprights flank the massive entrance steps up to the restored portico of the enclosure, beyond which is an interior courtyard and the ruins of priests' quarters. Note the size of the top stair – a massive single block.

Other stairways lead to secondary platforms, where there are other monoliths including the famous **El Fraile** (priest). At the far northwest corner of Kalasasaya is Tiwanaku's best-known structure, the **Puerta del Sol** (Gateway of the Sun). This megalithic gateway was carved from a single block of andesite, and archaeologists assume that it was associated in some way with the sun deity. The surface of this fine-grained, gray volcanic rock is ornamented with low-relief designs on one side and a row of four deep niches on the other. Some believe these may have been used for offerings to the sun, while others maintain that the stone served as some kind of calendar. The structure is estimated to weigh at least 44 tons.

There's a smaller, similar gateway carved with zoomorphic designs near the western end of the site that is informally known as the **Puerta de la Luna** (Gateway of the Moon).

East of the main entrance to Kalasasaya, a stairway leads down into the **Templete**

Semisubterráneo, an acoustic, red sandstone pit structure measuring 26m by 28m, with a rectangular sunken courtyard and walls adorned with 175 crudely carved stone faces. In the 1960s archaeologists tried to rebuild these and used cement between the stones.

West of Kalasasaya is a 55m-by-60m rectangular area known as **Putuni** or Palacio de los Sarcófagos, which is still being excavated. It is surrounded by double walls and you can see the foundations of several tombs. (It's said that of the artifacts collected by amateur enthusiast Fritz Buck in the early 20th century from these tombs, or funerary rooms, around 90% are located in the Museo de Metales Preciosos (p71).)

The heap of rubble at the eastern end of the site is known as **Kantatayita**. Archaeologists are still trying to deduce some sort of meaningful plan from these well-carved slabs; one elaborately decorated lintel and some larger stone blocks bearing intriguing geometric designs are the only available clues. It has been postulated – and dubiously 'proven' – that they were derived from universal mathematical constants, such as pi, but some archaeologists simply see the plans for a large and well-designed building.

Across the railway line southwest of the Tiwanaku site, you'll see the excavation site of **Puma Punku** (Gateway of the Puma). In this temple area megaliths weighing more than 130 tons have been discovered. Like Kalasasaya and Akapana, there is evidence that Puma Punku was begun with one type of material and finished with another; part was constructed of enormous sandstone blocks and, during a later phase of construction, notched and jointed basalt blocks were added.

Note also, in the distance of the site's northern boundary, the *sukakollo*, a highly sophisticated system of terraced irrigation.

Festivals & Events

On June 21 (the southern hemisphere's winter solstice), when the rays of the rising sun shine through the temple entrance on the eastern side of the complex, the **Aymará New Year** (Machaq Mara) is celebrated at Tiwanaku. As many as 5000 people, including a large contingent of New Agers, arrive from all over the world. Locals don colorful ceremonial dress and visitors are invited to join the party, drink *singani* (alcoholic spirit), chew coca, sacrifice llamas and dance until dawn. Artisans hold a crafts fair to coincide with this annual celebration.

Special buses leave La Paz around 4am to arrive in time for sunrise. Dress warmly because the pre-dawn hours are bitterly cold at this time of year.

Smaller, traditional, less tourist-oriented celebrations are held here for the other solstices and equinoxes.

Sleeping & Eating

You'll find several basic eateries near the ruins. Tiwanaku village, 1km west of the ruins, has several marginal restaurants and an incredibly colorful Sunday market. As a tour participant you may want to carry your own lunch; otherwise you'll likely be herded into an overpriced restaurant.

Hostal Puerta del Sol (r per person B$25) This very basic option, at the La Paz end of the village, is the closest to the ruins (and looks like it should be part of them). Simple meals available.

Gran Hotel Tiwanaku (☎ 289-8548; Bolívar 903; r per person B$105) This is the nicest place to stay, with rooms that are clean, breezy and comfortable. There's a restaurant open daily.

Inti Wara (☎ 289-8543; mains around B$25; 🕑 lunch) The best eating option, on the northeastern side of the ruins.

Getting There & Away

Many La Paz agencies offer reasonably priced, guided, full- and half-day Tiwanaku tours (US$10 to US$20 per person), including transportation and a bilingual guide. These tours are well worth it for the convenience and most travelers visit Tiwanaku this way.

For those who prefer to go it alone, **Transportes Ingavi** (Map pp62-3; José María Asín, La Paz) leaves for Tiwanaku (B$10, 1½ hours) about eight times daily, as does **Trans Tours Tiwanaku** (☎ 7191-4889; Calle José María Aliaga, La Paz) for the same price (two hours).

Minibuses, which are often crowded, pass the museum near the entrance to the complex. To return to La Paz, catch a minibus from the village's main plaza. Sometimes minibuses will pass the museum entrance if they're not full, looking for passengers. *Micros* to Guaqui and the Peruvian border also leave from the plaza in Tiwanaku village, or may be flagged down just west of the village – again, expect crowds.

Taxis to Tiwanaku from La Paz cost from B$210 to B$280 for the round trip.

Lake Titicaca

Lake Titicaca is deservedly awash with gushing clichés. This incongruous splash of sapphire amid the stark plains of the Altiplano is one of the most beautiful sights in the region. Covering 8400 sq km and sitting at 3808m, it's the world's largest high-altitude lake.

The lake straddles both Peru and Bolivia, and is a remnant of the ancient inland sea known as Lago Ballivián, which covered much of the Altiplano before geological faults and evaporation brought about a drop in the water level.

The traditional Aymará villages along the lakeshore, with the snow-topped peaks of the Cordillera Real in the background, provide a magical landscape. Even more fascinating for the visitor are the colorful and historical communities that inhabit the lake's many tiny islands. Integral to any visit is learning about the region's ancient legends, which can enhance the travel experience.

Long rumored to be unfathomable, the depth of the lake has now been measured at up to 457m. Trout were introduced into it in 1939, but are now largely farmed in special hatcheries.

LAKE TITICACA

HIGHLIGHTS

- Visit the tiny island of **Pariti** (p115), whose lovely museum features exquisite finds from a recent excavation

- Discover vestiges of the Inca culture in and around **Copacabana** (p103)

- Check out a baptism (or even a vehicle blessing!) at **Copacabana cathedral** (p102)

- Visit **lakeside villages** (p107) between Copacabana and Sampaya, and take a spin in a reed boat

- Explore **Isla del Sol** (p109) and **Isla de la Luna** (p114) and enjoy spectacular lake views, ancient ruins and landscapes straight out of the Mediterranean

Map labels: Yumani, Isla del Sol ★ · Sampaya ★ · ★ Isla de la Luna · ★ Copacabana · ★ Isla Pariti

▪ TELEPHONE CODE: 2	▪ ELEVATION: 4810M	▪ AREA: 8500 SQ KM

History

When you first glimpse Lake Titicaca's crystalline, gemlike waters, beneath the looming backdrop of the Cordillera Real in the clear Altiplano light, you'll understand why pre-Inca people connected it with mystical events. Those early inhabitants of the Altiplano believed that both the sun itself and their bearded, white god-king, Viracocha, had risen out of its mysterious depths. The Incas, in turn, believed that it was the birthplace of their civilization.

When the Spanish arrived in the mid-16th century, legends of treasure began to surface, including the tale that some Incas had flung their gold into the lake to prevent the Spanish carting it off. Distinct fluctuations in the water level of the lake have led treasure hunters to speculate that the ruins of ancient cities might lie beneath its surface.

From year to year, changes in the water level of Lake Titicaca are not uncommon; previous fluctuations may even have inundated settlements and ruins. In the floods of 1985–86, highways, docks, fields and streets all disappeared beneath the rising waters, adobe homes turned to mud and collapsed, and 200,000 people were displaced. It took several years for the Río Desaguadero, the lake's only outlet, to drain the flood waters.

Although evidence of submerged cities remains inconclusive, archaeologists are still unearthing exquisite finds around the lake. At Isla Koa, north of Isla del Sol, they found 22 large stone boxes containing a variety of artifacts: a silver llama, some shell figurines and several types of incense burners. And in 2004, the tiny island of Pariti hit world headlines when a team of Finnish and Bolivian archaeologists discovered elaborate and beautiful pottery there, which is now housed in a small museum on the island, and in La Paz.

Climate

From February to November the climate around Lake Titicaca is mostly pleasant and sunny, but there's often a cool wind off the lake and nights can be bitterly cold. Most rainfall occurs in midsummer (December and January).

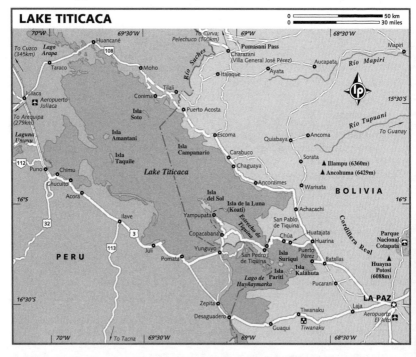

Getting There & Away

Lake Titicaca is a focal point for visitors from both Peru and Bolivia. The road journey between La Paz and Copacabana is impressive. It follows a scenic route with the Cordillera Real on one side and, after the Altiplano, the lake shoreline on the other. Vehicles are ferried by barge across the Estrecho de Tiquina (Tiquina Straits) while passengers ride in launches (p116).

COPACABANA

pop 54,300 / elevation 3800m

Nestled between two hills and perched on the southern shore of Lake Titicaca, Copacabana (Copa) is a small, bright and enchanting town. It was for centuries the site of religious pilgrimages, and today local and visiting Peruvian pilgrims flock to its fiestas (p103).

Although it can appear a little tourist-ready, the town is a pleasant place to wander around. It has scenic walks along the lake and beyond, is the launching pad for visiting Isla del Sol and Isla de la Luna, and makes a pleasant stopover between La Paz and Puno or Cuzco (Peru).

History

After the fall and disappearance of the Tiwanaku culture, the Kollas (Aymará) rose to power in the Titicaca region. Their

---

> ### 'DOING' THE LAKE
>
> If you are not on a strict budget, an efficient and more luxurious way to 'do' Titicaca is to choose from several La Paz-based companies that offer guided lake excursions on hydrofoils, catamarans or motor boats. The most popular companies are **Balsa Tours** (☎ 244-0620; www.turismobalsa.com; Manchego 2526, La Paz), which offers motor excursions around the lake based from its resort at Puerto Pérez; **Crillon Tours** (☎ 233-7533; www.titicaca.com; Camacho 1223, La Paz), an upmarket agency with a hydrofoil service offering various day and multiday packages; **Transturin** (☎ 242-2222; www .transturin.com; Arce 2678, La Paz), which runs day and overnight cruises in covered catamarans and has luxury accommodation on Isla del Sol; and **Turisbus** (☎ 244-1756; www .turisbus.com) at Hotel Rosario, Illampu, La Paz, or Hotel Rosario, Copacabana (p114).

---

most prominent deities included the sun and moon (who were considered husband and wife), the earth mother Pachamama and the ambient spirits known as *achachilas* and *apus*. Among the idols erected on the shores of the Manco Capac peninsula was Kota Kahuaña, also known as Copacahuana (Aymará for 'lake view'), an image with the head of a human and the body of a fish.

Once the Aymará had been subsumed into the Inca empire, Emperor Tupac Yupanqui founded the settlement of Copacabana as a wayside rest for pilgrims visiting the *huaca* (shrine) known as Titi Khar'ka (Rock of the Puma; p112), a former site of human sacrifice at the northern end of Isla del Sol.

Before the arrival of Spanish priests in the mid-16th century, the Incas had divided local inhabitants into two distinct groups. Those faithful to the empire were known as Haransaya and were assigned positions of power. Those who resisted, the Hurinsaya, were relegated to manual labor. It was a separation that went entirely against the grain of the community-oriented Aymará culture, and the floods and crop failures that befell them in the 1570s were attributed to this social aberration.

This resulted in the rejection of the Inca religion, and the partial adoption of Christianity and establishment of the Santuario de Copacabana, which developed into a syncretic mishmash of both traditional and Christian beliefs. The populace elected La Santísima Virgen de Candelaria as its patron saint, and established a congregation in her honor. Noting the lack of an image for the altar, Francisco Tito Yupanqui, a direct descendant of the Inca emperor, fashioned an image of clay and placed it in the church. However, his rude effort was deemed unsuitable to represent the honored patron of the village and was removed.

The sculptor, who was humiliated but not defeated, journeyed to Potosí to study arts. In 1582 he began carving a wooden image that took eight months to complete. In 1583 *La Virgen Morena del Lago* (the Dark Virgin of the Lake) was installed on the adobe altar at Copacabana, and shortly thereafter the miracles began. There were reportedly 'innumerable' early

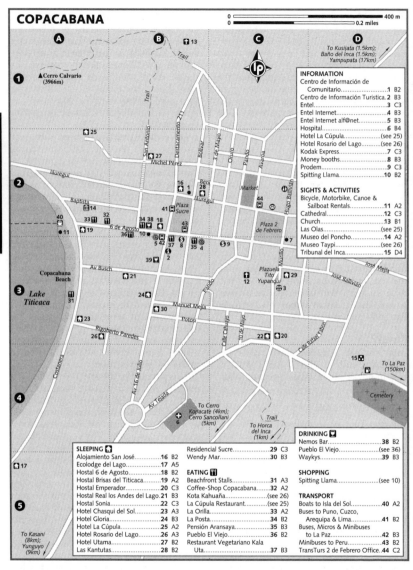

INFORMATION
Centro de Información de
  Comunitario..........................**1** B2
Centro de Información Turística.**2** B3
Entel.......................................**3** C3
Entel Internet........................**4** B3
Entel Internet alf@net.............**5** B3
Hospital.................................**6** B4
Hotel La Cúpula..............(see **25**)
Hotel Rosario del Lago.......(see **26**)
Kodak Express........................**7** C3
Money booths..........................**8** B3
Prodem..................................**9** C3
Spitting Llama.......................**10** B2

SIGHTS & ACTIVITIES
Bicycle, Motorbike, Canoe &
  Sailboat Rentals.................**11** A2
Cathedral..............................**12** C3
Church...................................**13** B1
Las Olas..........................(see **25**)
Museo del Poncho.................**14** A2
Museo Taypi.....................(see **26**)
Tribunal del Inca...................**15** D4

SLEEPING
Alojamiento San José.............**16** B2
Ecolodge del Lago.................**17** A5
Hostal 6 de Agosto................**18** B2
Hostal Brisas del Titicaca.......**19** A2
Hostal Emperador..................**20** C3
Hostal Real los Andes del Lago.**21** B3
Hostal Sonia..........................**22** C3
Hotel Chasqui del Sol............**23** A3
Hotel Gloria...........................**24** B3
Hotel La Cúpula....................**25** A2
Hotel Rosario del Lago..........**26** A3
Hotel Utama..........................**27** B2
Las Kantutas.........................**28** B2

Residencial Sucre...................**29** C3
Wendy Mar...........................**30** B3

EATING
Beachfront Stalls....................**31** A3
Coffee-Shop Copacabana.......**32** A2
Kota Kahuaña...................(see **26**)
La Cúpula Restaurant........(see **25**)
La Orilla...............................**33** A2
La Posta................................**34** B2
Pensión Aransaya..................**35** B3
Pueblo El Viejo.....................**36** B2
Restaurant Vegetariano Kala
  Uta....................................**37** B3

DRINKING
Nemos Bar............................**38** B2
Pueblo El Viejo.................(see **36**)
Waykys................................**39** B3

SHOPPING
Spitting Llama...................(see **10**)

TRANSPORT
Boats to Isla del Sol..............**40** A2
Buses to Puno, Cuzco,
  Arequipa & Lima...............**41** B2
Buses, Micros & Minibuses
  to La Paz...........................**42** B3
Minibuses to Peru.................**43** B2
TransTurs 2 de Febrero Office..**44** C2

healings and Copacabana quickly became a pilgrimage site.

In 1605 the Augustinian priesthood advised the community to construct a cathedral commensurate with the power of the image. The altar was completed in 1614, but work on the building continued for 200 years. In 1805 the *mudéjar* (Moorish-style) cathedral was finally consecrated, although construction wasn't completed until 1820. In 1925 Francisco Tito Yupanqui's image was canonized by the Vatican.

Orientation

Copacabana is set between two hills that offer high-altitude views over the town and the lake. Much of the action in Copa centers around Plaza 2 de Febrero and 6 de Agosto, the main commercial drag, which runs east to west. The transportation hub is in Plaza Sucre. At its western end is the lake and a walkway (Costañera), which traces the lakeshore. Most items of interest within the town center are within walking distance. Some attractions outside the town centre can be easily reached by minibus or taxi.

MAPS
The best map of Copacabana and Lake Titicaca is *Lago Titikaka* by Freddy Ortiz. It is available for sale at some hotels and the Tourist Information Center (B$25).

Information
BOOK EXCHANGE
Hotel La Cúpula (☎ 862-2029; www.hotelcupula.com; Michel Pérez 1-3), **Hotel Rosario del Lago** (☎ 862-2141, La Paz 2-245-1341; www.hotelrosario.com/lago; Paredes at Costañera) and the **Spitting Llama** (☎ 259-9073; Av 6 de Agosto) have the best book exchange and lending libraries (with many Lonely Planet guides).

INTERNET ACCESS
Entel Internet alf@net (6 de Agosto; per hr B$10; ☻ 9am-11pm) The best connections (and cheap video rentals and a book exchange) are available at this friendly place.
Entel Internet (6 de Agosto; per hr B$10; ☻ 8:30am-11pm) A second, smaller branch.

BEWARE RIOTOUS REVELRY
Copacabana is generally a very safe and tranquil place. Unfortunately, though, during festival time (p103), and especially during the Festival of Independence (first week of August) and Semana Santa (Easter week), robberies and muggings are as riotous as the reveling. Local people are quick to point the finger at their Peruvian neighbors, who flood into Copacabana on religious pilgrimages. But whoever the culprits may be is irrelevant to the victims of crime, usually tourists. Hotels and businesses display strong warnings to travelers to be extra cautious in the days leading up to and including festivals: don't carry valuables, take only the money you need, and never go out alone at night.

LAUNDRY
Lavanderías are noticeably scarce, although many hotels now offer a laundry service (B$10 to B$20 per kilo). Laundry services are offered along 6 de Agosto. Note: in most cases, the sun is the drying machine.

LEFT LUGGAGE
Most hotels will hold luggage free of charge for customers for a few days while they visit Isla del Sol.

MEDICAL SERVICES
There is a basic hospital on the southern outskirts of town with medical and dental facilities, but for serious situations don't think twice – head straight to La Paz.

MONEY
Travelers beware: there's no ATM in town. Calle 6 de Agosto is the Wall Street of Copacabana with many money booths. **Prodem** (6 de Agosto & Pando; ☻ 2:30-6pm Tue, 8:30am-12:30pm, 2:30-6pm Wed-Fri, 8:30am-3pm Sat & Sun) gives cash advances on Visa and MasterCard (5% commission). Note that it's closed on Mondays and even when it's open the machine is not always reliable. Numerous *artesanías* (handicraft stores) also change US dollars and (if you're lucky) traveler's checks, but watch out for excessive commissions. You can buy Peruvian *soles* at most *artesanías*, but you'll normally find better rates in Kasani, Bolivia, or Yuguyo, just beyond the Peruvian border.

PHOTOGRAPHY
Vendors in front of the cathedral sell 36-exposure print film. Reasonably priced, one-hour developing, plus digital prints, are available at **Kodak Express** (Plaza 2 de Febrero; ☻ 8am-8pm).

POST & TELEPHONE
Entel (Plazuela Tito Yupanqui; ☻ 7am-11pm) In a modern building behind the cathedral. Entel, Cotel, Tigo and Viva *puntos* (privately run phone offices) are dotted along 6 de Agosto and around town.
Post office (☻ 8:30am-noon & 2:30-4pm Tue-Sun) On the north side of Plaza 2 de Febrero, but often closed or unattended.

TOURIST INFORMATION
Centro de Información de Comunitario (Plaza Sucre; ☻ 9am-1pm & 3-7pm) An NGO-sponsored project encouraging tourism to three communities in the area:

LAKE TITICACA

Isla de la Luna (p114), Cha'llapampa (p111) and Las Islas Flotantes (see boxed text, p107). It has an excellent photographic exhibit (English labeling), a short screening and a community shop.

Centro de Información Turística (☎ 7191-5544; 16 de Julio, nr Plaza Sucre; ☺ 9:30am-5pm Tue-Sat) Another attempt at a municipal information office – this time they seem to be getting it right. Helpful English-speaking attendant, although rudimentary information available.

Dangers & Annoyances

In 2005–06 there were several particularly nasty incidents involving travelers on illegal minibuses and taxis – where lifts were offered between Copacabana and La Paz. Syndicates, posing as fellow passengers, kidnapped and held tourists bound and blindfolded for over 24 hours while their bank accounts were depleted to the maximum amount permitted.

In recent years, this has not occurred but, in any case, the smaller minibuses are more dangerous – they tend to be packed with people and are prone to speed. Travelers are encouraged to take the formal tourist buses (or the larger buses; p106). These drop passengers at major hotels such as those in Calle Illampu, and can be organized through any of the tour agencies in Copacabana. The cost is slightly higher (B$25 to B$30) but is worth the investment.

Tourists should also be especially careful during festivals (see boxed text, p101). Stand well back during fireworks displays, when explosive fun seems to take priority over crowd safety, and be wary of light-fingered revelers.

The thin air, characteristically brilliant sunshine, and reflection off the water combine to admit scorching levels of ultraviolet radiation. Wear a hat and sunscreen in this region.

Sights

Copacabana's central attractions can be visited in one long but relaxed day, but there are some great trips further afield, including to the surrounding peninsulas (see p107).

CATHEDRAL

The sparkling white *mudéjar* cathedral, with its domes and colorful *azulejos* (blue Portuguese-style ceramic tiles), dominates the town. Baptisms take place every Satur-

---

BENEDICIÓN DE MOVILIDADES

The word *cha'lla* is used for any ritual blessing, toasting or offering to the powers that be, whether Inca, Aymará or Christian. On most mornings during the festival season (opposite), from around 10am (and reliably on Saturday and Sunday), cars, trucks and buses hover in front of Copacabana's cathedral decked out in garlands of real or plastic flowers, colored ribbons and flags. They come for a *cha'lla* known as the Benedición de Movilidades (Blessing of Automobiles). Petitions for protection are made to the Virgin, and a ritual offering of alcohol is poured over the vehicles, thereby consecrating them for the journey home. Between Good Friday and Easter Sunday, the *cha'lla* is especially popular among pilgrims and long-distance bus companies with new fleets. The priest slips owner donations into his vestments faster than you can say Hail Mary, but per vehicle it's still a cheap alternative to insurance!

---

day at 4pm; check the notice board in front of the entrance for the mass schedule.

The cathedral's black Virgen de Candelaria statue **Camarín de la Virgen de Candelaria**, carved by Inca Tupac Yupanqui's grandson, Francisco Yupanqui, is encased above the altar upstairs in the niche *(camarín)*; note, visiting hours can be unreliable. The statue is never moved from the cathedral, as superstition suggests that its disturbance would precipitate a devastating flood of Lake Titicaca.

The cathedral is a repository for both European and local religious art and the **Museo de la Catedral** (per person B$8, minimum 4; ☺ all day) contains some interesting articles – offerings from hopeful individuals. Unfortunately, the museum is open only to groups of four or more (unless, of course, you're happy to pay) and you'll most probably need to chase down a sister to arrange your visit.

COPACABANA BEACH

While Bolivia's only public beach can't hold a candle to the better-known beach of the same name in Rio de Janeiro, on weekends the festive atmosphere is a magnet for families. You can take a pew at one of the many little eateries along the (unfortunately) drain-ridden shore front. More appealingly, you can soak up sun, trout and beer. Or, you can rent all manner of boating craft, bicycles (B$70 per day) and motorbikes (B$50 per hour).

CERRO CALVARIO
The summit of Cerro Calvario can be reached in half an hour and is well worth the climb, especially in the late afternoon to watch the sunset over the lake. The trail to the summit begins near the **church** at the end of Calle Destacamento 211 and climbs past the 14 Stations of the Cross.

HORCA DEL INCA
The fascinating **Horca del Inca** (admission B$5) is a pre-Inca astronomical observatory. This odd trilithic gate perched on the hillside is surrounded by pierced rocks that permit the sun's rays to pass through onto the lintel during the solstice of June 21, the Aymará New Year (this predicts everything from the amount of rain to the crop yields). During this time locals venture up before sunrise to celebrate.

These weirdly rugged rock formations merit an hour or so of exploration. From near the end of Calle Murillo, a signposted trail leads uphill to the site.

A further 4km down this road, toward Kasani (near the turnoff to the floating islands), lies **Cerro Kopakati**, a carved stone featuring pre-Inca ruins and pictographs. The best known, but difficult to distinguish, is the **Escudo de la Cultura Chiripa**, a unique icon attributed to the pre-Inca Chiripa culture.

TRIBUNAL DEL INCA (INTIKALA)
North of the cemetery on the southeastern outskirts of town is the sadly neglected site of artificially sculpted boulders known as the **Inca Tribunal** (admission B$5). Its original purpose is unknown, but there are several carved stones with *asientos* (seats), basins and *hornecinos* (niches), which probably once contained idols.

KUSIJATA & BAÑO DEL INCA
A 3km walk northeast along the shoreline from the end of Calles Junín or Hugo Ballivián leads to the community of **Kusijata** (admission B$5), where there's a former colonial hacienda, housing a small, dusty (read

untouched) archaeological display. If you can see in the semi-dark – there's no electricity – seek out the long-deceased mummified corpse *(chullpa)* sitting in an upright fetal position, as he was buried. If no one is at the entrance, simply ask around. You can also enter the now-unkempt gardens where there's a pre-Columbian irrigation channel, originally used to access the subterranean water supply. Head past the first gushing pipe and follow the path to the carved-stone water tank, the **Baño del Inca** (Inca Bath), whose origins and meanings are a little unclear.

MUSEUMS
A visit to the **Museo del Poncho** (Baptista, cnr Costañera; 🕑 9:30am-12:30pm & 3-6pm Mon-Sat, 9:30am-4pm Sun) will help you unravel the mysteries of the regional textiles. The exhibits, spread over two floors, give a clear insight into the origins and meanings of the poncho and their associated regions. Labels are in both English and Spanish. At the time of research, hours were irregular; ring the bell on the side and try your luck (the curators say the door is closed for security).

Museo Taypi (Hotel Rosario del Lago; admission free) is a small, private cultural museum within the grounds of Hotel Rosario (p105) with a small, but lovely collection of antiquities and cultural displays on the region. Here, too, is Jalsuri, a fair-trade craft shop selling quality *artesanía*.

Tours
There are several combinations of getting to, from and around the island in a day or longer. See p113 for a description of the trips to Isla del Sol. Note: although the agencies label them 'tours,' these are not tours in the formal guided sense of the word. For more formal tours, see boxed text, p99.

Festivals & Events
Copacabana hosts several major annual fiestas. The town also celebrates **La Paz departmental anniversary** on July 15. Thursday and Sunday are lively market days.

JANUARY
Alasitas festival (see also p332) One local tradition is the blessing of miniature objects, such as miniature cars or houses. Supplicants pray that the real thing will be obtained in the coming year. Held on January 24.

FEBRUARY
Fiesta de la Virgen de Candelaria (see also p332) Honors the patron saint of Copacabana and all Bolivia. Copacabana holds an especially big bash, and pilgrims and dancers come from Peru and around Bolivia. There's much music, traditional Aymará dancing, drinking and feasting. On the third day celebrations culminate with the gathering of 100 bulls in a stone corral along the Yampupata road, and the town's braver (and drunker) citizens jump into the arena and try to avoid being attacked. From February 2 to 5.

MARCH/APRIL
Semana Santa As part of this festival (p332), on Good Friday the town fills with pilgrims – some of whom walk the 158km journey from La Paz – to do penance at the Stations of the Cross on Cerro Calvario. Beginning at the cathedral at dusk, pilgrims join a solemn candlelit procession through town, led by a statue of Christ in a glass coffin and a replica of the Virgen de Candelaria. Once on the summit they light incense and purchase miniatures representing material possessions in the hope that they will be granted the real things by the Virgin during the year.

MAY
Fiesta de la Cruz (Feast of the Cross; p332) Celebrated over the first weekend in May (or on May 3 – check, as dates change) all around the lake, but the biggest festivities are in Copacabana.

AUGUST
Bolivian Independence Day (p333) Copacabana stages its biggest event during the first week in August. It's characterized by round-the-clock music, parades, brass bands, fireworks and amazing alcohol consumption. This coincides with a traditional pilgrimage that brings thousands of Peruvians into the town to visit the Virgin.

Sleeping

Hotels (many shoddy) are springing up like reeds in Copacabana. During fiestas accommodations fill up quickly and prices increase up to threefold. Ironically, given its lakeside position, Copacabana's water supply is unpredictable. Better hotels go to extreme efforts to fill water tanks in the morning (the supply is normally switched off at some time between 8am and noon).

BUDGET
A host of budget options abound charging around B\$25 per person (significantly more in high season and festivals), especially along Calle Jáuregui.

Hostal Emperador (☎ 862-2083, La Paz 2-242 4264; Murillo 235; r per person B\$20, with bathroom B\$25) This budget travelers' favorite is a basic, albeit lively and colorful, joint, with hot showers, a laundry service, a small shared kitchen and luggage storage. A newer wing at the back has brighter rooms with bathrooms and a sunny terrace, ideal for lounging and views.

Alojamiento San José (☎ 7150-3760; Jáuregui 146; r per person B\$20-25) This place is as rudimentary but as clean as they come – it's always a good sign when the floors smell like a polish factory. Perfectly adequate for a budget traveler, although the claims of constant hot water are a little dubious.

Hostal Sonia (☎ 862-2019; Murillo 256; r per person from B\$25) This lively spot has ever-so-slightly run-down, but bright and cheery, rooms. In 2009, new renovations were under way. A kitchen, a terrace and laundry service make it an excellent budget choice.

Hostal 6 de Agosto (☎ 862-2292; 6 de Agosto; r per person B\$25) A rosy and very central place with a sunny outlook over a garden and clean, if standard, rooms. A good restaurant is also on the premises (*almuerzo* menu around B\$15).

Residencial Sucre (☎ 862-2080; Murillo 228; r per person B\$25, with bathroom B\$35, f B\$140) Clearly a smart hotel in former days, this place – now a little tired but perfectly adequate – has color local TV, carpeted rooms, reliable hot water, a courtyard and a restaurant (breakfast costs extra). Some rooms are cell-like, but all have external windows.

Hostal Brisas del Titicaca (☎ 862-2178, La Paz 2-245-3022; www.hostellingbolivia.org; 6 de Agosto at Costañera; r per person B\$50; ▢) Situated right on the beach, this popular HI-affiliate has amenable (albeit retro-1970s) rooms. A few rooms with shared bathrooms have teeny-weeny windows with no outlook, but several others with private bathrooms have their own lake-view terraces with good vistas.

MIDRANGE & TOP END
Ecolodge del Lago (☎ 862-2500, La Paz 2-245-1138; r per person B\$100) Situated 20 minutes on foot along the Costañera (or a quick taxi ride), this ecofriendly place, right on the lake in a wonderful nature paradise, offers a tranquil experience. The quirky adobe rooms and self-equipped apartments are self-heated thanks to the mud bricks, and have solar-

powered water. The rambling garden of dahlias and gladioli affords great views of the lake. (The downside: no doubt these introductory prices will have risen by the time you read this.)

Hostal Real los Andes del Lago (☎ 862-2103; Busch s/n; s/d/tr B$100/120/180) Although nothing fancy, this central place is neat and clean, light and breezy, polished and professional. The top-floor rooms offer good views (although a rival hotel obscures some of them). There's cable TV and gas – yay, not electric – showers. Good value.

Las Kantutas (☎ 862-2093; Jáuregui, cnr Bolívar; d/tr B$120/180) A good and safe option with friendly staff. It's popular with tour groups (book ahead) for its spacious, airy rooms, all with external-facing windows and cable TV. Excellent family rooms, in the hotel's corner with large windows, are available. Breakfast costs B$10 extra.

Wendy Mar (☎ 862-2124; 16 de Julio; d/tr B$120/180) It's new and modern (in a frilly, shiny, Bolivian kind of way), and offers shiny bed covers, plus clean and neat rooms with a motel feel.

Hotel La Cúpula (☎ 862-2029; www.hotel cupula.com; Michel Pérez 1-3; s US$10-12, d US$16-18, tr US$20, with bathroom s US$12-22, d US$22-28, tr US$36) International travelers rave about this inviting oasis, marked by two gleaming white domes on the slopes of Cerro Calvario, with stupendous lake views. Its 17 individual, creatively designed rooms provide one of Bolivia's best-value and most pleasant stays. Bonuses include a TV room, a library, a shared kitchen and laundry facilities, and the cozy La Cúpula Restaurant (p106). Sculptures and hammocks are throughout its pretty gardens. The helpful staff speak several languages. Best to reserve ahead.

our pick Las Olas (☎ 862-2112; www.hostallasolas .com; Michel Pérez 1-3; s US$30, d US$36-38, tr US$48-53) To say too much about this place is to spoil the surprise, so we'll merely give you a taste: quirky, creative, stylish, individual, kitchenettes, flowers, outdoor Jacuzzi, hammocks, ecofriendly, million-dollar vistas. You get the idea – a once-in-a-lifetime experience, and well worth the splurge. Reserve ahead. Enter through La Cúpula's premises.

Hotel Rosario del Lago (☎ 862-2141, La Paz 2-245-1341; www.hotelrosario.com/lago; Paredes at Costañera; s/d/tr/ste B$350/440/560/850; ▣) One of the smartest places in town, the neocolonial, three-star

sister of Hotel Rosario in La Paz has charming motel-style rooms with solar-heated showers, double-glazed windows and lake views. Extras include magnetic locks, room safes and excellent service. The Altiplano light streams in and there's a pleasant sun terrace. A new museum (p103), an excellent shop and a travel agency, Turisbus, adds to the experience.

Other comfortable options:

Hotel Utama (☎ 862-2013; cnr Michel Peréz & San Antonio; s US$10-15, d with bathroom US$10-20) Clean and reliable and popular with groups.

Hotel Chasqui del Sol (☎ 862-2343; www.chasqui delsol.com; Costañera 55; s/d US$20/35) Massive vistas of the lake and friendly staff.

Hotel Gloria (☎ 286-2294, La Paz 2-240-7070; www .hotelgloria.com.bo; 16 de Julio & Manuel Mejía; per person with bathroom & breakfast s/d/tr B$290/360/440) A bit like a large spacious and airy boarding house but with better views.

Eating

Copa hardly sets the culinary world on fire. Your best bets are the daily *almuerzos* (set lunches) served at some of the more local eateries.

The specialty is *trucha criolla* (rainbow trout) and *pejerrey* (king fish) from Lake Titicaca. The trout were introduced in 1939 to increase protein content in the local diet. Today, trout stocks are mainly grown in hatcheries; *pejerrey* stocks are seriously depleted. The catch of the day is served ad nauseam to varying degrees of taste; some resemble electrocuted sardines, while others are worthy of a Michelin restaurant rating.

The best trout dishes seem to be served at La Cúpula Restaurant and Kota Kahuaña, or along the beachfront stalls (these cost as little as B$20). Here you can sip a drink and observe the quintessential Bolivian beach life, though the nearby drains detract a little from the experience.

Nearly every place in town serves breakfast – *Americano* (with an egg or two), *continental* (drink, bread and jams) or muesli with fruit.

CAFES & RESTAURANTS

A Groundhog Day horde of eateries is along 6 de Agosto. The following is a selection, but by no means a gourmand's compendium.

Restaurant Vegetariano Kala Uta (6 de Agosto at 16 de Julio; mains B$20-30) An artsy, appealing Andean atmosphere pervades this place. It serves up passable, if slightly bland, vegetarian choices. The breakfasts are more imaginative; try the *poder Andino* (Andean power) – quinoa crêpes topped with jam, banana, yogurt, Brazil nuts, raisins and coconut. Its opening hours are a bit unreliable.

Pueblo El Viejo (6 de Agosto 684; mains B$20-50) Readers love this rustic, cozy and chilled cafe-bar, with its ethnic decor and laid-back atmosphere. It serves up a good burger and pizza, and is open until late (thus breakfast clients sometimes eat here in a stale haze of smoke, courtesy of the previous evening's clients).

La Cúpula Restaurant (☎ 862-2029; www .hotelcupula.com; Michel Pérez 1-3; mains B$20-50; ☺ closed lunch Tue) Inventive use of local ingredients make up an extensive international and local menu. The vegetarian range includes a tasty lasagna, and there's plenty for carnivores too. Dip your way through the cheese fondue with authentic Gruyère cheese – it's to die for…which leaves the Bolivian chocolate fondue with fruit platter beyond description. The glassy surroundings admit lots of Altiplano light and maximize the fabulous view of the lake.

Pensión Aransaya (6 de Agosto 121; almuerzo B$15, mains B$25-40; ☺ lunch) Super-friendly local favorite for a tall, cold beer and trout heaped with all the trimmings. It's neat, clean, very traditional and popular with the locals.

Coffee-Shop Copacabana (6 de Agosto s/n; mains B$25-45) Laid-back in more ways than one – eat quickly before the great-value *almuerzo* (B$15) slides off your plate. Extensive list of teas and good coffees (proper espresso!), breakfasts, pastas, nachos and everything served in your choice of two environments.

Kota Kahuaña (☎ 862-2141; Paredes at Costañera; mains B$25-55) Based at Hotel Rosario del Lago's restaurant, this place is one of the more expensive in town, but is a higher standard than some of its counterparts. Stuffed trout, an excellent salad bar, and satisfying main courses and Bolivian wines ensure a fine-dining experience.

Also recommended:

La Posta (☎ 7252-1244; 6 de Agosto s/n; ☺ dinner) Tasty pizzas in a cozy, tango-themed setting.

La Orilla (☎ 862 2267; 6 de Agosto; mains B$25-45; ☺ 10am-10pm, closed Sun) Serves up tasty local and international dishes.

The bargain basement is the market *comedor* (dining hall), where you can eat a generous meal of *trucha* (trout) or beef for a pittance, or an 'insulin shock' breakfast or afternoon tea of hot *api morado* (hot corn drink; B$2) and syrupy *buñuelos* (donuts or fritters; B$1).

Drinking

New nightspots come and go as frequently as tour boats. As well as Pueblo El Viejo (left) – the following were among the reliable options.

Waykys (www.waykys.com; 16 de Julio, at Busch) A friendly, warm den of a place with cozy corners, graffiti-covered walls and ceilings (you can add what you want), a billiards table, book exchange and a varying range of music.

Nemos Bar (6 de Agosto 684) This dimly lit, late-night hangout is a popular place for a tipple.

Shopping

Local specialties include handmade miniatures of *totora*-reed boats and unusual varieties of Andean potatoes. Massive bags of *pasankalla*, which is puffed *choclo* (corn) with caramel, the South American version of popcorn, abound. Dozens of stores sell llama- and alpaca-wool hats and sweaters; a reasonable alpaca piece will cost around B$80. Vehicle adornments used in the *cha'lla*, miniatures and religious paraphernalia are sold in stalls in front of the cathedral.

Spitting Llama (☎ 259-9073; Av 6 de Agosto) This welcome addition stocks an extensive range of books and maps (including guidebooks and many Lonely Planet editions), plus outdoor gear, hiking boots and camping equipment.

Getting There & Away

TO/FROM LA PAZ

The booking offices of **Trans Manco Kapac** (☎ 862-2234, in La Paz 2-245-9045) and **TransTurs 2 de Febrero** (☎ 862-2233, in La Paz 2-245-3035) are near Plaza 2 de Febrero, but buses sometimes arrive at and depart near Plaza Sucre. The more comfortable nonstop tour buses from La Paz to Copacabana – including Milton Tours and Combi Tours – cost from around B$25 to B$30 and are well worth the investment (p102). They depart from La Paz at around 8am and leave Copacabana at 1:30pm (3½ hours). Note, at the time of research, these were departing from the top of 16 de Julio, several blocks south of Plaza Sucre. Tickets can be purchased from tour agencies.

TO/FROM PERU

Many tour buses go all the way to Puno (Peru), and you can break the journey in Copacabana and then continue with the same agency. You can do just the Copa– Puno leg (B$30, three to four hours) or go all the way to Cuzco (B$85 to B$150, 15 hours) – changing buses in Puno. These buses depart and arrive in Copacabana from Av 6 de Agosto.

Alternatively, catch a public minibus from Plaza Sucre to the border at Kasani (B$3, 15 minutes). Across the border there's frequent, if crowded, onward transportation to Yunguyo (five minutes) and Puno (2½ hours). If you're headed straight to Cuzco, many Copacabana agencies offer tickets on the daily buses. They also offer bus journeys to Arequipa (B$95 8½ hours), Lima (B$400) and other Peruvian destinations. All buses will wait until the last person has completed immigration formalities.

Note that Peruvian time is one hour behind Bolivian time.

TO/FROM ISLA DEL SOL

All agencies sell tickets to Isla del Sol for boat companies Titicaca and Andes Amazonia. Alternatively, you can buy tickets on the morning of departure (B$20 to B$25) from one of the beach offices. Local community boats (Mallku and Sol Tours) also run less frequent trips. For details, see p103.

COPACABANA TO YAMPUPATA

An enjoyable way to reach Isla del Sol is to walk or travel in taxi or minibus (p109) along the lakeshore to the village of Yampupata, which lies just a short boat ride from the ruins of Pilko Kaina on Isla del Sol.

Main Route

If walking, this trek is road-bound, making it a fairly hot and hard slog (allow seven hours if you're stopping along the way), although with lovely views and interesting village visits. Take your own snacks; there's little, if anything, along the way.

From Copacabana, head northeast on the road around the lake for around 1½ hours until the **Gruta de Lourdes** (aka Gruta de Fátima), a cave that for locals evokes images of its French and Portuguese namesakes, respectively. For a shortcut, turn right immediately after the small bridge leading to the Virgin and follow the Inca path.

TREATS BEYOND TOWN

Throw away the guidebook and discover some of Copa's wonderful surrounds on your own.

- Visit Las Islas Flotantes (floating reed islands), a community project at Sahuiña, approximately 6km from Copa, for a delightful spin on one of the most tranquil parts of the lake, in a row boat or a *totora*-reed boat (B$10 to B$15 per person per island). Hint: take the minibus towards Kasani (B$2.50) and ask to be let off at the entrance (a 10-minute ride). The office is 15 minutes on foot from here, and it's another 15 minutes to the boats.

- Ask the Centro de Información Turística (p102) for a list of Inca ruins and strike out on your own. Hint: some, but not all, Inca sites are listed here. Admittedly, many are now neglected or rarely visited. Let us know what you find!

- Hike around the stunning peninsula south of town; this offers a different perspective of the lake. Head 6km out of town to the village of J'iska Q'ota, near the *ex-pista* (former airport strip). To get there, catch a minibus marked 'Kasani,' and after about 10 minutes you'll arrive at the *ex-pista* (B$2.50). Follow the road towards the lake heading in a northeasterly – and then northerly – direction around the peninsula and back to Copa.

- Hire a bike at Copacabana Beach (p102) and head off into the hills or in the direction of Yampupata – yes, a hilly, but beautiful journey.

LAKE TITICACA

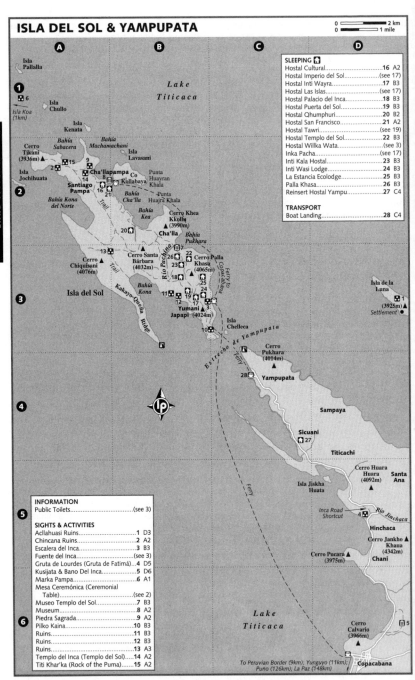

ISLA DEL SOL & YAMPUPATA

SLEEPING	
Hostal Cultural....................................16 A2
Hostal Imperio del Sol...................(see 17)
Hostal Inti Wayra..............................17 B3
Hostal Las Islas...............................(see 17)
Hostal Palacio del Inca......................18 B3
Hostal Puerta del Sol........................19 B3
Hostal Qhumphuri.............................20 B2
Hostal San Francisco.........................21 A2
Hostal Tawri....................................(see 19)
Hostal Templo del Sol........................22 B3
Hostal Willka Wata..........................(see 3)
Inka Pacha....................................(see 17)
Inti Kala Hostal................................23 B3
Inti Wasi Lodge................................24 B3
La Estancia Ecolodge.........................25 B3
Palla Khasa.....................................26 B3
Reinsert Hostal Yampu........................27 C4

TRANSPORT	
Boat Landing...................................28 C4

INFORMATION	
Public Toilets................................(see 3)

SIGHTS & ACTIVITIES	
Acllahuasi Ruins................................1 D3
Chincana Ruins.................................2 A2
Escalera del Inca...............................3 B3
Fuente del Inca..............................(see 3)
Gruta de Lourdes (Gruta de Fatimá)....4 D5
Kusijata & Baño Del Inca.....................5 D6
Marka Pampa....................................6 A1
Mesa Ceremónica (Ceremonial
Table)......................................(see 2)
Museo Templo del Sol.........................7 B3
Museum..8 A2
Piedra Sagrada..................................9 A2
Pilko Kaina.....................................10 B3
Ruins...11 B3
Ruins...12 B3
Ruins...13 A3
Templo del Inca (Templo del Sol)........14 A2
Titi Khar'ka (Rock of the Puma).......15 A2

When the path peters out head directly up-hill to rejoin the main road at the crest of the hill. Note: to save an hour or so and avoid the flat and litter-strewn outskirts of town, you can catch a minibus (B$5) or taxi (one way/return B$40/70) from Copa to the Gruta de Lourdes (9km), from where the more picturesque hiking begins.

At the fork just below the crest of the hill bear left and descend to the shore and into the village of **Titicachi**, where, if it's open, there's a basic *tienda* (shop) selling soft drinks. For die-hard archaeologists, in and around Titicachi are some pre-Inca walls and the abandoned **Tiahuanacota Inca cemetery**, but these are not obvious to the visitor. The community currently boasts two privately run **floating islands** (B$10 per person per island), although at the time of research the return trip to Isla del Sol with both boat companies incorporated a visit here (check with Centro de Información in Copa).

At the next village, **Sicuani**, Juan Mamani runs the **Hostal Yampu**, offering very basic accommodations with bucket showers. Hikers can pop in for a beer or soft drink. Slightly further on in the same village, don't go past the gregarious, quirky and very photogenic Hilario Paye Quispe. Señor Paye Quispe is happy to take you for a spin around the bay in a *totora*-reed boat or via motorboat to the peninsula opposite (prices negotiable), where he's constructed fine walking trails to a hidden 'tunnel.' (He claims there is a series of underground tunnels on the island.) For those who want to spend the night in isolation, you can camp here for the night. He offers trips to Isla del Sol (around B$85, 30 minutes) or in a row boat (minimum two people B$40, 1½ hours). He also has basic rooms for rent (price negotiable).

Five to six hours from Copacabana, you'll reach **Yampupata**, a collection of lakefront adobe houses. If you ask around, you'll find rooms for rent. Asociación Yamputours Lacustre Terrestre takes passengers across the **Estrecho de Yampupata** to Pilko Kaina or Yumani, both in the island's south (p110), in a motorboat (minimum B$70 to B$90) or a row boat (B$20 to B$30). Prices start from B$200 to head to the island's north and south, or to the south plus Isla de la Luna.

Alternative Routes

An alternative hiking option, especially for those who don't want to head to Isla del Sol, is to catch a taxi (B$180) from Copacabana along the main road and stop at villages along the way. You finish at the beautiful and unspoiled cobblestone village of **Sampaya**, 5km from Yampupata. At the time of research, the community was building a series of stylish huts, plus a museum; check their progress with Turisbus at Hotel Rosario del Lago (p105) or Copacabana's Centro de Información Turística (p102). You can return on foot to Copacabana via the higher eastern route (four hours). Although this road doesn't pass through main villages, it affords magnificent views and a more nature-bound experience.

Getting There & Away

For those who don't want to walk or catch a taxi, the easiest way to travel between Yampupata and Copacabana is by minibus (B$5, 40 minutes). At the time of research, these were leaving Copacabana from near the market (Monday to Saturday) and from Plaza Sucre (Sunday) at 10am, noon and 5pm; add approximately 40 minutes for the return times from Yampupata. Times change, however; first check with the minibus company 6 de Junio.

ISLA DEL SOL

The Island of the Sun was known to early inhabitants as Titi Khar'ka (Rock of the Puma), from which Titicaca takes its name. This island has been identified as the birthplace of several revered entities, including the sun itself. There, the bearded, white god-king Viracocha and the first Incas, Manco Capac and his sister-wife Mama Ocllo, mystically appeared under direct orders from the sun. In fact, most modern-day Aymará and Quechua peoples of Peru and Bolivia accept these legends as their creation story.

Isla del Sol's 2500 permanent residents are distributed between the main settlements of **Cha'llapampa**, near the island's northern end; **Cha'lla**, which backs up to a lovely sandy beach on the central east coast; and **Yumani**, which straddles the ridge above the Escalera del Inca.

With a host of ancient ruins, tiny traditional villages, beautiful walking routes and a distinctly Aegean look, magical Isla del Sol definitely merits a night or two – you can then devote a day each to the northern and southern ends. While the day tour gives you a decent introduction to the island (you can do a walking circuit of the main sights in a long day), whirlwind half-day tours are strictly for the been-there-done-that crowd.

Visitors who have time can wander through the ruins at the island's northern and southern ends; explore the island's dry slopes, covered with sweet-smelling *koa* (incense) brush; and hike over the ancient *pampas* (terraces), which are still cultivated.

There are no vehicles on Isla del Sol, so visitors are limited to hiking along rocky trails (some are now paved in Inca style) or traveling by boat. The main ports are at **Pilko Kaina**, the **Escalera del Inca** in Yumani and near the **Templo del Inca** and **Chincana ruins** at Cha'llapampa. There's also a small port at **Japapi** on the southwest coast.

Extensive networks of walking tracks make exploration fairly easy, though the 4000m altitude and sun may take their toll. Hikers should carry lunch and ample water. The sun was born here and is still going strong; a good sunscreen is essential, particularly by the water.

Southern Half
PILKO KAINA

This prominent **ruins complex** (for information about admission fees, see boxed text, right) near the southern tip of the island sits well camouflaged against a steep terraced slope. The best-known site is the two-level **Palacio del Inca**, which is thought to have been constructed by the Incan Emperor Tupac-Yupanqui. The rectangular windows and doors taper upward from their sill and thresholds to narrower lintels that cover them on top. The arched roof vault was once covered with flagstone shingle and then reinforced with a layer of mud and straw.

FUENTE DEL INCA & ESCALERA DEL INCA

About 30 minutes' walk north of Pilko Kaina, incongruous streams of fresh water gush from the natural spring Fuente del Inca and pour down three artificial stone channels alongside a beautifully constructed Inca-era staircase, the Escalera del Inca (for information about admission fees, boxed

text, below); the springs feed a lovely terraced and cultivated water garden.

Early Spaniards believed Yumani's spring was a fountain of youth, and for the Incas the three streams represented their national motto: *Ama sua, Ama llulla, Ama khella*, meaning 'Don't steal, don't lie and don't be lazy.' Today, the fountain is a crucial source of water for locals, who come daily to fetch water and carry it up the steep trail.

YUMANI

Yumani's small church, **Iglesia de San Antonio**, serves the southern half of the island. Nearby you'll find an exploding cluster of guesthouses and fabulous views over the water to Isla de la Luna. You can also climb to the ridge for a view down to the deep sapphire-colored **Bahía Kona** on the western shore. (Or you can walk to here – about half an hour from the village heading north, a track to the left leads to its shore; the one to the right descends to Bahía Kea Cucho.) From the crest you'll also find routes leading downhill to the tiny, pretty village of **Japapi** and north along the ridge to the Chincana ruins and Cha'llapampa.

With extra time you can make your way over the isthmus and up onto the

COIN COLLECTION ON THE ISLA DEL SOL

In 2008, to overcome the inequity of the spread of tourist spending on the island, and to provide a means of upkeep to the main walking route, local communities introduced a system of entry fees for visitors to the island. At the time of research, visitors had to pay a total of B$20 at various points: in the north at Cha'llapampa, B$10 for entrance to the museum and the Chincana ruins (a guide will accompany you to both); at the half-way mark of Ch'alla, B$5 to pass through the island's center (regardless of which direction you are coming from); and in the south, B$5 to enter Yumani and visit the Escalera del Inca and Pilko Kaina. Note, as with all prices in this book, these admission fees are a guide only – both prices and where you pay may have altered by the time you read this. Please be respectful of these (ongoing) changes; check with the tourist office prior to departing.

prominent **Kakayo-Queña Ridge**, the island's southwestern extremity. The serene walk along the ridge to the **lighthouse** on the southern tip takes at least half a day (return) from Yumani.

CHA'LLA

This agreeable little village stretches along a magnificent sandy beach that appears to be taken straight out of a holiday brochure for the Greek islands. Note: the village is spread out – it extends over the hill to the south. There's a small kiosk and a guesthouse, Hostal Qhumphuri (p113).

In the pastoral flatlands over the low pass between Cha'lla (for information about admission fees, see boxed text, opposite) and Yumani is the **Museo Étnico**, with some dusty exhibits including Inca pots. It's an hour's walk north of Yumani along the lower path (or on the western route if coming from the north). It's worth it for the stunning bay and valley views; the museum itself is disappointing and you will have to ask around to be let in (the B\$5 paid at Cha'lla covers admission).

Northern Half

There are two major routes between the northern and southern ends of Isla del Sol. The lower route winds scenically through fields, hamlets and villages, and around the bays and headlands above the eastern coast. The most commonly used route follows the dramatic ridge path that runs between Cha'llapampa in the north and Yumani in the south. In the north are the Chincana ruins that sit on top of an uninhabited ridge (for information about admission fees, see boxed text, opposite). The views down to both coasts of the island are nothing short of spectacular.

CHA'LLAPAMPA

Most boat tours visiting the northern ruins land at Cha'llapampa, which straddles a slender isthmus.

The **small museum** (admission B\$10) contains artifacts excavated in 1992 from Marka Pampa, referred to by locals as La Ciudad Submergida (Sunken City). The museum's current dusty exhibits include anthropomorphic figurines, Tiwanaku-era artifacts, animal bones, skull parts, puma-shaped ceramic *koa* censers, and cups resembling

---

A BOLIVIAN ATLANTIS?

At low tide an innocuous-looking column of rock peeps just a few centimeters above Lake Titicaca's surface, north of Isla del Sol. Most locals dismiss it as a natural, stone column, similar to many others along the shoreline. In 1992 stone boxes containing artifacts (including several made of pure gold) were discovered at the underwater site known as **Marka Pampa** (aka La Ciudad Submergida). In August 2000 further excavations near the site revealed a massive stone temple, winding pathways and a surrounding wall, all about 8m underwater. Although it remains unclear who was responsible for the structures, it has been postulated that they are of Inca origin. Investigations are ongoing.

Monty Python's Holy Grail. For more information about admission fees to the museum, see the boxed text, opposite.

PIEDRA SAGRADA & TEMPLO DEL INCA

From Cha'llapampa, the Chincana route continues parallel to the beach, climbing gently along an ancient route to the isthmus at **Santiago Pampa** (Kasapata).

Immediately east of the trail is an odd carved boulder standing upright in a small field. This is known as the **Piedra Sagrada** (Sacred Stone). There are theories that it was used as an execution block for those convicted of wrongdoing.

Over the track and in a field, just southwest of the Piedra Sagrada, are the ancient walls of the complex known as the **Templo del Inca** (or Templo del Sol). Although little remains of this temple, built for an unknown purpose, it contains the only Bolivian examples of expert Inca stonework comparable to the renowned walls found in Cuzco.

CHINCANA RUINS & TITI KHAR'KA

The island's most spectacular ruins complex, the **Chincana ruins** (admission B\$10, see boxed text, opposite), lies near the island's northern tip. Its main feature is the **Palacio del Inca**, a maze of stone walls and tiny doorways, also known as El Laberinto (Labyrinth) or by its Aymará name, Inkanakan Utapa. Within the labyrinth there is a small well, believed by Inca pilgrims to contain sacred water with which they would purify themselves.

About 150m southeast of the ruins is the **Mesa Ceremónica** (Ceremonial Table), which also happens to be a convenient picnic spot. It's thought to have been the site of human and animal sacrifice. East of the table stretches the large rock known as Titicaca – or, more accurately, **Titi Khar'ka**, Rock of the Puma – which is featured in the Inca creation legend. The name is likely to derive from its shape, which, when viewed from the southeast, resembles a crouching puma.

Three natural features on the rock's western face also figure in legend. Near the northern end is one dubbed the **Cara de Viracocha** (Face of Viracocha) – the guide will point it out with the help of a mirror (and some imagination). At the southern end are four distinctive elongated niches. The two on the right are locally called the **Refugio del Sol** (Refuge of the Sun) and those on the left, the **Refugio de la Luna** (Refuge of the Moon). According to tradition it was here during the Chamaj Pacha ('times of flood and darkness') that the sun made its first appearance, and later Manco Capac and Mama Ocllo appeared and founded the Inca empire.

In the surface stone immediately south of the rock you'll pass the **Huellas del Sol** (Footprints of the Sun). These natural markings resemble footprints and have inspired the notion that they were made by the sun after its birth on Titi Khar'ka.

If you've the energy, climb nearby Cerro Uma Qolla for a great view.

Sleeping

The most scenic place to stay is Yumani – high on the ridge – where guesthouses are growing faster than coca production. Ch'allapampa and Ch'alla have basic options. If camping, it's best to ask permission from the local authority and then set up away from villages, avoiding cultivated land.

Water is a precious commodity. The island does not yet have access to water mains and supplies are carried by person or donkey. Please bear this in mind; think twice before taking showers (after all, we're all in – and on! – the same boat).

Note: in high season (June to August and during festivals) prices listed here may double.

YUMANI
Budget
Inti Wasi Lodge (☎ 7196-0223; museo_templodelsol@ yahoo.es; dm per person B$25, cabins with bathroom & breakfast per person B$70) Four basic, but cozy cabins with en suite and smashing views and a recommended restaurant, Palacio de la Trucha, attached. Turn right just before Hostal Illampu as you head up the hill.

Inka Pacha (☎ 289-9160; inkapachaecologica@ hotmail.com; r per person B$25, s/d/tr with bathroom & breakfast B$70/140/200) What this HI-affiliated place lacks in luxury (read: simple rooms), it makes up for in friendliness and service. A continental breakfast is served in an airy, communal area.

Hostal Imperio del Sol (☎ 7196-1863; r per person B$35, with bathroom B$100) This peachy, modern and central place has rooms with bathroom, or plainer ones without. It's spotless – but there may be a reason: guests in the budget category report that, disappointingly, the shower room is rarely open due to limited water supplies.

Hostal Inti Wayra (☎ 7194-2015, La Paz 2-246-1765; r per person from B$45) The amicable and rambling Inti Wayra affords great views from most rooms; these vary a great deal – some are larger and more open. Can be a bit unreliable with opening times.

Other basic, budget options – all charging from around B$25 to B$30 (more in high season) – include, in geographical order from south to north:
Hostal Willka Wata (☎ 7325-0242)
Hostal Las Islas (☎ 7193-9047)
Hostal Tawri (☎ 7352-7194)
Hostal Puerta del Sol (☎ 7195-5181)
Hostal Templo del Sol (☎ 7122-7616)
Hostal Palacio del Inca (☎ 7151-1046)

This list is by no means exhaustive. Within this category (B$25 to B$30), hostel standards (read: basic) and prices (read: fair price-to-quality ratio) are almost identical. This is a fun place for DIY exploring.

Midrange & Top End
Palla Khasa(☎ 7622-9180; palla-khasa@hotmail.com; per person with bathroom & breakfast B$80) This small, tasteful and professionally run place stands on its own in every respect – it's about 400m before or after Yumani, depending on which direction you're coming from. There's more: views to make a grown man

weep, a pleasant ambience (it's worth persevering up the hill if northbound), simple yet comfortable rooms, plus a really wonderful restaurant.

Inti Kala Hostal (☎ 7194-4013; javierintikala@hotmail.com; r per person with bathroom & breakfast B$80) This place has a massive deck, and small, neat rooms. At the time of research it was expanding (we feel at the expense of maintaining existing rooms – these had lost some of their former zing) but readers give it the thumbs up.

La Estancia Ecolodge (☎ 7156-7287, La Paz 2-244-2727; www.ecolodge-laketiticaca.com; s/d with bathroom US$60/90) Magri Turismo's delightful adobe cottages are set above pre-Inca terraces facing snow-capped Illampu. They are authentically ecological with solar-powered showers, sun-powered hot-boxes for heaters, and Aymará thatched roofs. The price includes breakfast and dinner. La Estancia is a 15-minute walk from Yumani.

CHA'LLA
On the hill behind the beach at Cha'lla is the simple, family-run **Hostal Qhumphuri** (☎ 7152-1188, La Paz 02-284-3534; hostalqhumphuri@hotmail.com; s/d B$20/40), a mustard-colored construction that offers clean rooms.

CHA'LLAPAMPA
The neatest of a choice of very basic options is the flowery **Hostal San Francisco** (r B$25). It's to the left of the landing site. **Hostal Cultural** (☎ 7190-0272; r per person B$20, with bathroom B$35) behind the beach is the only option with private bathrooms. Other budget options are on the beach behind the museum. For boat shuttles around the island, as well as to Isla de la Luna, ask around (there are three companies – Wara Tours, Chasqui Tours and Wiracocha Tours).

There are several restaurants in the village that serve good fish dishes.

Eating
There are more cafes in Yumani than Titicaca has *trucha*. We suggest you follow your nose and taste buds, plus fellow travelers' recommendations (and see how far your feet can take you) and choose what appeals to you. Most midrange and top-end accommodation options have good eateries. Most restaurants are blessed with good views, and those on the ridge are special for the sunset.

Nearly all menus are identical; *almuerzos* and set dinners cost between B$25 and B$30. Pizzas are the go; Isla del Sol rivals Rome for its per capita number of pizzerias.

Getting There & Around
BOAT
From the beach in Copacabana, two main boat companies (and, in high season, several private *lanchas*, small boats) offer transportation to/from Isla del Sol. In addition to the main boat companies, community boats service Yumani (Mallku and Sol Tours) and Cha'llapampa (Chasqui Tours, Wara Tours and Wiracocha Tours).

A daily return trip costs around B$25; a half day to the south or a one-way trip costs from around B$15 to B$20 (there is no overnight return – you buy two one-way tickets).

Tickets may be purchased at the ticket kiosks on the beach or from Copacabana agencies. Boats to the northern end of the island land at Cha'llapampa, while those going to the southern end land at either Pilko Kaina or the Escalera del Inca (Yumani).

Launches embark from Copacabana beach around 8:30am and 1:30pm daily. Depending on the season and the company, they may drop you off at a choice of the island's north or south (check with the agency).

Most full-day trips go directly north to Cha'llapampa (two to 2½ hours). Boats anchor for 1½ hours only – you'll have just enough time to hike up to the Chincana ruins, and return again to catch the boat at 1pm for the Escalera del Inca and Pilko Kaina in the island's south. Here, you'll spend around two hours before departing for Copa.

Half-day trips generally go to the south of Isla del Sol only.

Those who wish to hike the length of the island can get off at Cha'llapampa in the morning and walk south to the Escalera del Inca (Yumani) for the return boat in the afternoon.

Alternatively, you can opt to stay overnight or longer on the island (highly recommended), then buy a one-way ticket to Copacabana with any of the boat companies, including the local boat associations (including Mallku Tours and Sol Tours in Yumani and Chasqui Tours and Wayra

Tours in Cha'llapampa; check departure times on arrival).

At the Hotel Rosario del Lago (p105), **Turisbus** (www.turisbus.com), offers half-day tours to the south of Isla del Sol (B$695 per person, less if more people) and full-day tours (B$1155 per person, less if more people) to both north and south.

For boat tours see p99.

WALKING

A more adventurous alternative is to walk to Yampupata (four to seven hours), just across the strait, and hire a boat to the north or south of the island. See route info, p107.

ISLA DE LA LUNA (KOATI)

A visit to Isla de la Luna is a true, if tranquil, adventure. Legend has it that the small Island of the Moon was where Viracocha commanded the moon to rise into the sky. A walk up to the eucalyptus grove at the summit, where shepherds graze their flocks, is rewarded by a spectacular vista of aquamarine waters, Cerro Illampu and the entire snow-covered Cordillera Real. It's lost some popularity in recent times thanks to the aggressive marketing of neighboring Isla del Sol and transportation operators who stopped heading there, but offers a genuine experience for those who make the effort.

The **ruins** (admission B$10) of an Inca nunnery for the Vírgenes del Sol (Virgins of the Sun), also known as Acllahuasi or Iñak Uyu, occupy an amphitheater-like valley on the northeast shore. It's constructed of well-worked stone set in adobe mortar, and was where chosen girls (believed to be around eight years old) were presented as an offering to the sun and moon.

Before visiting, be sure to check out the new Centro de Información de Comunitario in Copacabana (p101), an organization established to help community tourism. Here, there are exhibits (with English labels), a 10-minute explanatory video about the island and community, and a small shop.

Several recently constructed, basic **hostels** (B$25 per person) offer a unique new way to stay on the island. Bring some supplies with you, but you will support the locals (25 families) by buying their local produce (yes, there are some tiny, basic *tiendas*).

At the time of research, no tour boats were heading to Isla de la Luna from Isla del Sol (but check this status). The cheapest option is to charter a launch from Yampupata or the Escalera del Inca (Yumani, Isla del Sol; B$200). Alternatively, the Centro de Información de Comunitario (p101) can help arrange transport, as can tour agencies (it pays to get a group together to reduce the costs).

ISLAS DE WIÑAYMARKA

Lago de Wiñaymarka's most frequented islands, Kalahuta and Pariti, are easily visited in a half-day trip. Tourism has become an economic mainstay, but it has not been entirely beneficial to the Kalahuta people who reside on the islands. Please behave sensitively; ask permission before taking photos and refuse requests for money or gifts.

CONSTRUCTION OF A TOTORA-REED BOAT

The construction of *totora*-reed boats is an art form. Green reeds are gathered from the lake shallows and left to dry in the sun. Once free of moisture, they are organized into fat bundles and lashed together with strong grass. In former days, often a sail of reeds was added. These bloated little canoes don't last long as far as watercraft go; after several months of use they become waterlogged and begin to rot and sink. In former times, in order to increase their life span, the canoes were often stored some distance away from the water. Now the boats are made and used mainly for tourism purposes.

In the early 1970s Dr Thor Heyerdahl, the Norwegian adventurer and ethnographer, solicited the help of Suriqui's shipbuilders, the Limachi brothers and Paulino Esteban, to design and construct his vessel *Ra II* to sail from Morocco to Barbados.

Dr Heyerdahl wanted to test his theory that migration andearly contact occurred between the ancient peoples of North Africa and the Americas. He planned to show the feasibility of traveling great distances using the boats of the period, in this case, papyrus craft.

ENTERING/LEAVING PERU

Most travelers enter/exit Peru via Copacabana (and the Tiquina Straits) or the scruffy town of Desaguadero (avoiding Copacabana altogether).

Via Copacabana

Micros to the Kasani–Yunguyo border leave Copacabana's Plaza Sucre regularly, usually when full (B$3, 15 minutes). At Kasani you obtain your exit stamp at passport control and head on foot across the border. On the Peruvian side, *micros* and taxis will ferry you to Yunguyo (around 6 Peruvian *soles*, 15 minutes). From here, you can catch a bus heading to Puno. An efficient alternative is to catch a tourist bus from/to La Paz to Puno via Copacabana (from B$60); some allow you a couple of days' stay in Copacabana. Note: even if you've bought a ticket to Cusco or elsewhere in Peru, you'll change buses in Puno. Here, buses to Cusco depart from the international terminal; this is located about three blocks from the local terminal.

Via Desaguadero

A quicker, if less interesting, route is via Desaguadero, on the southern side of the lake. Several bus companies head to/from this border from/to Peru. The crossing should be hassle-free: you obtain your exit stamp from the **Bolivian passport control** (8:30am-8:30pm), walk across a bridge and get an entry stamp at *migración* in Peru. Frequent buses head to Puno hourly (around 3½ hours).

It's possible to camp overnight, particularly on sparsely populated Pariti, however camping is not recommended on Kalahuta – you will probably draw some criticism from locals, who believe in night spirits.

Isla Kalahuta

When lake levels are low, Kalahuta ('stone houses' in Aymará) becomes a peninsula. Its shallow shores are lined with beds of *totora* reed, the versatile building material for which Titicaca is famous. By day fisherfolk ply the island's main bay in their wooden boats; just a few years ago you'd also have seen the *totora*-reed boats, and men paddling around to gather the reeds to build them, but they are no longer used.

During Inca times, the island served as a cemetery, and it is still dotted with stone *chullpas* (funerary towers) and abandoned stone houses. Legends abound about the horrible fate that will befall anyone who desecrates the cemetery, and locals have long refused to live in the area surrounding the island's only village, Queguaya.

Isla Pariti

This tiny island, surrounded by *totora*-reed marshes, made world news in 2004 when a team of Bolivian and Finnish archaeologists discovered ancient Tiwanaku ceramics here

in a small circular pit. While the American archaeologist Wendell Bennet was the first to excavate the island in 1934, the more recent finds uncovered some extraordinary shards and ceramics, believed to be ritualistic offerings, and many of which are intact. Today, many of these stunning pots and *ch'alladores* (vases) are displayed in the recently opened **Museo de Pariti** (admission B$20), while the remainder are displayed in the Museo Nacional de Arqueología in La Paz (p70). These stunning exhibits reflect the high artistic achievements of Tiwanaku potters. Don't miss the *Señor de los patos*. For that matter, don't miss a visit here.

Getting There & Around

Many tour agencies in La Paz (p74) offer day tours to the islands. For a more local option, try the Spanish-speaking **Catari Bros brothers** (7197-8959; Hostal Puerto Inti Karka) based in Huatajata. They run informative day visits to Isla del Sol, Isla de la Luna and Copacabana for around B$1000 (minimum of five people).

AROUND LAKE TITICACA

Huarina

This nondescript but pleasant little village, midway between Copacabana and La Paz, serves as a road junction, particularly for

LAKE TITICACA

WORTHWHILE WANDERINGS

For an extremely genuine cultural experience, don't miss an overnight stay at **Santiago de Okola** (www.santiagodeokola.com), a tiny, traditional fishing and farming community on the shores of Lake Titicaca, approximately three hours from La Paz on the road to Apolobamba, and 1½ hours from the Isla del Sol by boat. With the support of external funding bodies, 'Okola' has formed a community-based agro-tourism company to both conserve its rich agricultural heritage and generate income for members. Visitors stay with families in basic, but specially designated rooms and participate in daily life. Great beaches, walks and hikes abound, including a short climb to the crest of a magnificent rock outcropping behind the village with spectacular lake views known as the Sleeping Dragon. Other activities include weaving classes, a medicinal plant walk and Andean cooking classes (at extra cost). Bookings (B$160 per person per night all inclusive) can be made via email (info@santiagodeokola.com).

---

the town of Sorata. If you're traveling between Sorata and Copacabana, you'll have to get off at the intersection with the main road (500m from the town itself), and wait here to flag down the next bus, usually from La Paz, going in your direction.

ESTRECHO DE TIQUINA

The narrow Tiquina Straits separate the main body of Lake Titicaca from the smaller Lago de Wiñaymarka. Flanking the western and eastern shores respectively are the twin villages of San Pedro and San Pablo. Vehicles are shuttled across the straits on *balsas* (rafts), while passengers travel across in small launches (B$1.50, 10 minutes). It seems unlikely that a bridge will be built as the ferries ensure that locals remain in business. Bus travelers should carry all valuables onto the launch with them.

Small restaurants and food stalls on both sides serve people caught up in the bottleneck of traffic. Note that occasionally, foreigners traveling in either direction may have to present their passports for inspection at San Pedro, which is home to Bolivia's largest naval base.

The Cordilleras & Yungas

Two of South America's icons – the Amazonian jungle and the peaks of the Andes – meet in this fabulously diverse zone of soaring highlands and misty valleys. It offers the traveler unrivaled opportunities for adventure, from serious assaults on 6000m summits to trekking in some of Bolivia's most remote uplands.

The region packs a lot into what isn't, on a map at least, a very large area. However, although some of the attractions are but a short condor flight from La Paz, by the time your bus has twisted and turned its way along the tortuous roads, seeming to detour up every valley, you'll envy the bird. The destinations here offer an isolated, outpost-like feel, whether you are buried in the jungle at the river port of Guanay, or lost in the ranges in sleepy Chulumani.

The Cordillera Real contains most of Bolivia's iconic mountains. Though there are no easy climbs, peaks like Huayna Potosí can be scaled by any reasonably fit person with a decent guide. For the allure of untrodden routes up barely known mountains, head to the Quimsa Cruz.

The drop from the Altiplano to the jungle is an almost sheer one in parts, and the Yungas towns are reached by breathtaking (literally) roads that plunge downwards, losing kilometers in altitude. The trees (remember them?) rush up to meet you, and moisture hangs heavy in the air under the floppy-leaved foliage. It's an exhilarating descent on a bike and, at the bottom, warm, jungle towns await, perfect for hammock-swinging or pool-lounging.

THE CORDILLERAS & YUNGAS

HIGHLIGHTS

- Head down the paved paths and plunging scenery on the **Choro** (p124), **Takesi** (p127) and **Yunga Cruz** (p129) treks
- Treat yourself to a hammock and a poolside drink in **Coroico** (p119)
- Swing over to **Sorata** (p133), which offers almost as much trekking as it does relaxing
- Meet delicate wild vicuñas and the renowned Kallawaya healers in the remote **Cordillera Apolobamba** (p144)
- Strap on your crampons and swing your ice axe to climb one of the fabulous peaks of the **Cordillera Real** (p141)

★ Cordillera Apolobamba

★ Sorata

★ Cordillera Real

★ Coroico

Choro, Takesi ★ & Yunga Cruz treks

▦ TELEPHONE CODE: 2	▦ POPULATION: 547,600	▦ ELEVATION: 600M TO 6429M

History

The first settlers of the Yungas were inspired by economic opportunity. In the days of the Inca empire, gold was discovered in the Tipuani and Mapiri valleys, and the gold-crazed Spanish immediately got in on the act. To enrich the royal treasury, they forced locals to labor for them, and the region became one of the continent's most prolific producers of gold. Today the rivers of the lower Yungas are ravaged by hordes of wild-cat prospectors and bigger mining outfits.

During October 2003, in what were to be the dying days of President Sánchez de Lozada's government, the Yungas was the scene of roadblocks and violent clashes between police, the military and *campesino*

protestors angry at the selling of the nation's natural resources (principally gas) and the mistreatment of the indigenous population. More than 100 tourists found themselves trapped in the town of Sorata for over a week during the demonstrations, until a misguided military mission was launched to 'rescue' them, sparking violent clashes that left six people dead. The fall-out from the violence and the mismanagement of the situation led to the resignation of Sánchez de Lozada and ultimately to the election of Evo Morales, a former coca farmer.

The sweet Yungas' coca is the most often consumed in Bolivia and as a result, the region has been at the forefront of Morales's 'coca revolution' with the *cocaleros* (coca farmers) finding themselves newly empowered as a political force. However, they have been unable to find a united voice, with two main factions forming; *Las Proteccionistas*, the more established highland farmers who want to defend the localized economy, and the more numerous *Nacionalistas*, from newly colonised lower altitude areas who seek to expand the coca economy. *Las Proteccionistas* claim that coca is the only viable crop at the altitudes at which they live and that Morales's policies actually threaten their livelihoods by opening coca cultivation up to the multitudes.

Climate

The Yungas' physical beauty is astonishing, and although the hot, humid and rainy climate may induce lethargy, it's nevertheless more agreeable to most people than the chilly Altiplano. Winter rains are gentle, and the heavy rains occur mainly between November and March. The average year-round temperature hovers in the vicinity of 18°C, but summer daytime temperatures in the 30s aren't uncommon. As a result, the region provides a balmy retreat for chilled highlanders, and is a favorite R&R hangout for foreign travelers. The mountains of the cordilleras, on the other hand, are serious, lofty beasts and conditions can be extreme, with warm days, and nights that drop well below zero.

Getting There & Around

Access is entirely overland and the region's unpaved roads can get mucky and washed out in the rainy season. Scheduled public transportation is infrequent to many trekking

THE CORDILLERAS & YUNGAS

0 — 45 km
0 — 30 miles

PERU

Moho, Agua Blanca, Pelechuco, Ulla, Ulla, Area Natural de Manejo Integrado Nacional (Amini) Apolobamba, Parque Nacional Madidi, Cordillera Apolobamba, Lagunillas, Curva, Río Cavini, Conima, Tilali, Italaque, Charazani (Villa General José Pérez), Apolo, Isla Soto, Puerto Acosta, Isla Campanario, Lake Titicaca, Escoma, Aucapata, Iskanwaya, Isla del Sol, Puerto Carabuco, Consata, Río Mapiri, Sorata, Limitada, Quiabaya, Ancoma, Ancoraimes, Mapiri, Isla de la Luna (Koati), Sorata, Ancohuma (6427m), Illampu (6362m), Río Tipuani, Achacachi, Tipuani, Guanay, Huatajata, Lago de Huyñaymarka, Huarina, Cordillera, BOLIVIA, Puerto Pérez, La Paz, Batallas, Real, Tiwanaku, Pucarani, Huayana Potosí (6088m), To Rurrenabaque, Tiwanaku, Parque Nacional Cotapata, Caranavi, Milluni, Chairo, Yun, Laja, La Cumbre, Coroico, Viacha, El Alto Airport, Unduavi, Yolosa, Chuspipata, Ventilla, Palca, Yanacachi, Chuñavi, Chulumani, Illimani (6439m), Laza, Río La Paz, Irupana, Cordillera Quimsa Cruz, Mina Viloco, Mina Caracoles, Quimé

TREKS

1 Lagunillas to Agua Blanca (Curva-Pelechuco) Trek
2 Mapiri Trail
3 El Camino del Oro
4 El Choro Trek
5 Takesi (Taquesi) Trek
6 Yunga Cruz Trek

and mountaineering base camps, so chartered private transportation from La Paz is used more often here than in other regions of the country.

If you are scared of heights, or just don't have much faith in Bolivian bus drivers, ask for an aisle seat. Roads are narrow, drops are steep and some of the routes, such as the one to Chulumani, are particularly hairy.

Traveling between towns in the region often necessitates backtracking to La Paz, a frustrating business.

THE YUNGAS

The Yungas – the transition zone between dry highlands and humid lowlands – is where the Andes fall away into the Amazon Basin. Above the steaming, forested depths rise the near-vertical slopes of the Cordillera Real and the Cordillera Quimsa Cruz, which halt Altiplano-bound clouds, causing them to deposit bounteous rainfall. Vegetation is abundant and tropical fruit, coffee, coca, cacao and tobacco grow with minimal tending. The Yungas is composed of two provinces in La Paz department, Nor and Sud Yungas (oddly, most of Sud Yungas lies well to the north of Nor Yungas), as well as bits of other provinces. Coroico and Chulumani are the main population centers.

COROICO
pop 2360 / elevation 1750m

While Coroico is a metropolis by Yungas standards, it feels like a sleepy hilltop village and maintains a relaxed ambience despite being one of the more popular destinations for weekending *paceños* (La Paz locals) and chilling travelers. Perched eyrie-like on the shoulder of Cerro Uchumachi, it commands a far-ranging view across forested canyons, cloud-wreathed mountain peaks, patchwork agricultural lands, citrus orchards, coffee plantations and dozens of small settlements. When the weather clears, the view stretches to the snow-covered summits of Mururata, Huayna Potosí and Tiquimani, high in the Cordillera Real.

Coroico is derived from the Quechua word *coryguayco* meaning 'golden hill.' The town's biggest attraction is its slow pace, which allows plenty of time for swimming, sunbathing and hammock-swinging. The hill-walking around here is more strolling than trekking, which appeals to stiff-legged hikers from the Choro trail or those nursing bruised bottoms after the hectic mountain-bike descent from La Paz.

Coroico is relatively warm year-round, but summer storms bring some mighty downpours. Because of its ridgetop position, fog is common, especially in the afternoon when it rises from the deep valleys and swirls through the streets and over the rooftops. The town festival is on October 20, and Saturday and Sunday are market days. On Monday the town closes down, with most stores and restaurants re-opening Tuesday morning.

Information

There's a basic regional hospital near Hostal El Cafetal, but for serious medical treatment you'll be happiest in La Paz (p65). There are no foreign-card-accepting ATMs in Coroico. For tourist information online try www.coroi.co.cc.

Lavandería Nancy Vega (Zuazo Cuenca; per kg B$13) For machine washing; it's a couple of blocks east of the plaza.
Prodem (☎ 213-6009; Plaza García Lanza; ⊙ 8:30am-noon & 2:30-6pm Tue-Fri, 8:30am-4pm Sat & Sun) Changes dollars at a fair rate and does cash advances for 5% commission.
Tourist office (☎ 7401-5825; Plaza García Lanza; ⊙ 8am-8pm) Can provide guides for local hikes. There's also a small information kiosk at the bus terminal.
Únete (Plaza García Lanza; per hr B$3; ⊙ 10am-10pm) Offers the most reliable internet access in town.

Activities
HIKING

For pretty views, head uphill toward Hotel Esmeralda and on up to **El Calvario**, an easy 20-minute hike. At El Calvario the Stations of the Cross leads to a grassy knoll and chapel. There are two good trailheads from El Calvario. The one to the left leads to the **cascadas**, a trio of waterfalls two hours beyond the chapel. The trail to the right leads to **Cerro Uchumachi** (five hours round-trip), which affords terrific valley views.

A good day's walk will take you to **El Vagante**, an area of natural stone swimming holes in the Río Santa Bárbara. Follow the road toward Coripata to Cruce Miraflores, 750m beyond the Hotel Don Quijote. Here, turn left at a fork in the road and head steeply downhill past Hacienda Miraflores;

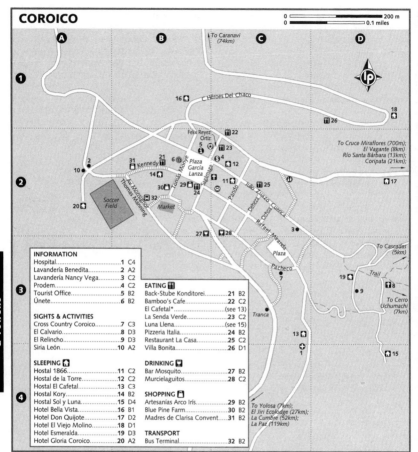

COROICO

INFORMATION
Hospital.............................1 C4
Lavandería Benedita.................2 A2
Lavandería Nancy Vega...........3 C2
Prodem..............................4 C2
Tourist Office.........................5 B2
Únete.................................6 B2

SIGHTS & ACTIVITIES
Cross Country Coroico..........7 C3
El Calvario............................8 D3
El Relincho...........................9 D3
Siria León...........................10 A2

SLEEPING
Hostal 1866.........................11 C2
Hostal de la Torre.................12 C2
Hostal El Cafetal...................13 C3
Hostal Kory........................14 B2
Hostal Sol y Luna.................15 D4
Hotel Bella Vista...................16 B1
Hotel Don Quijote.................17 D2
Hotel El Viejo Molino.............18 D1
Hotel Esmeralda...................19 D3
Hotel Gloria Coroico.............20 A2

EATING
Back-Stube Konditorei...........21 B2
Bamboo's Cafe.....................22 C2
El Cafetal*.........................(see 13)
La Senda Verde....................23 C2
Luna Llena.........................(see 15)
Pizzeria Italia.......................24 B2
Restaurant La Casa...............25 C2
Villa Bonita.........................26 D1

DRINKING
Bar Mosquito.......................27 B2
Murcielaguitos.....................28 C2

SHOPPING
Artesanías Arco Iris...............29 B2
Blue Pine Farm.....................30 B2
Madres de Clarisa Convent....31 B2

TRANSPORT
Bus Terminal.......................32 B2

---

at the second fork, bear right (the left fork goes to Santa Ana). After two hours along this route, which features a stretch with some pre-Columbian terraces, you'll reach a cement bridge. Turn right before the bridge and follow the river downstream for 20 minutes to a series of swimming holes and waterfalls. The water isn't drinkable, so carry water or purification tablets – and bear in mind that the return route is uphill all the way.

It can get extremely hot while hiking, so carry plenty of water.

HORSEBACK RIDING

A recommended spot for horseback riding is **El Relincho** (☎ 7192-3814; per person per hr incl guide

B$50). Trips sometimes include a barbecue lunch. The owner, Reynaldo, also offers a two-day trip round Uchumachi for B$700 per person, all-inclusive. El Relincho is between Hotels Esmeralda and Sol y Luna, a 10-minute walk above town.

MOUNTAIN BIKING

The area around Coroico is great for mountain biking. Friendly **Cross Country Coroico** (☎ 7127-3015; www.mtbcoroico.com; cxc_mtb@yahoo.com; Pacheco 2058) offers day trips to attractions in the region for all levels of rider from B$280 per person, including a guide and packed lunch. Readers have reported the trips as being good-natured if a little disorganized.

WHITEWATER RAFTING

About three hours north from Coroico is the **Río Coroico**, which flows through the Nor Yungas. This is the country's most popular commercially rafted river, and is the most convenient to La Paz. The river features well over 30 rapids, great surfing holes, dramatic drops and challenging technical maneuvers (most of these can be scouted from the river and from several bridges). It alternates between calm pools and 50m to 900m rapids, with sharp bends, boils, mean holes, undercurrents, sharp rocks and rather treacherous undercuts.

The whitewater normally ranges from Class II to IV, but may approach Class V

DOWNHILL THRILLS

The vertical scenery in the spectacular Cordillera Real will prove a sort of nirvana for mountain bikers who prefer sitting back and letting gravity do the work! The following descriptions of the most prominent rides should start your wheels spinning. For further information on mountain biking in Bolivia, as well as choosing an operator, see p57 and p74.

'The World's Most Dangerous Road' – La Cumbre to Coroico

Quite deservedly this ride is Bolivia's most popular, made so by travelers wishing to combine a long and thrilling downhill run with a very appealing destination. It features an incredible range of scenery and a spectacular 3600m descent from the Altiplano, down between snow-capped peaks into the steaming Yungas. The dramatic, cliff-hugging descent is billed as 'The World's Most Dangerous Road,' though now that motorized traffic uses the new Coroico road it is quite a lot safer than it once was. That said, choose your operator carefully: accidents do happen and not all companies are prepared for them – cheaper does not mean better.

After this thrilling day trip, riders can relax poolside in the quiet Yungas town of Coroico. From here, it's possible to continue to Rurrenabaque, in the Amazon Lowlands, or return to La Paz on public transportation.

To reach La Cumbre from La Paz, catch any Yungas-bound transportation from Villa Fátima. Many La Paz–based agencies offer this as an organized day trip, either leaving you in Coroico or taking you back to La Paz.

Sorata

Sorata is not only Bolivia's trekking capital but it's also saturated with mountain-biking opportunities, and the fun begins with a descent into the town from the mountains astride Lake Titicaca. From La Paz, take a Sorata-bound bus to the pass north of Achacachi and then choose either the main road or any of the downhill routes along unpaved roads. Most routes eventually lead to Sorata – or at least in view of it (but some don't, so it's wise to have a map). Throughout the ride you're presented with superb views of towering snow-capped peaks, plunging valleys and tiny rural villages. This route is organized (as are others) by Andean Epics (p135).

Zongo Valley

This ride includes a descent from the base of spectacular Huayna Potosí (6088m) past Zongo Dam, and then along a dramatic 40km, 3600m descent into the lush and humid Yungas. This is a dead-end road that lacks a great destination at its finish, but there's little vehicular traffic, so you tend to have the road to yourself and can open up the throttle a little more.

Chacaltaya to La Paz

This trip begins with a drive up to the world's highest developed ski slope at 5345m. After taking in the incredible view across the Cordillera Real, riders descend along abandoned mine roads. Along the way you'll have marvelous vistas across the mountain ranges, the Altiplano and the city of La Paz nestling in the bottom of the Choqueyapu canyon. This route is nearly all downhill, descending more than 2000m from Chacaltaya back to central La Paz. For more on Chacaltaya, including access from La Paz, see p93.

during periods of high water (when it becomes too dangerous to raft). There are few spots to take out and rest, so stay focused and be prepared for surprises.

Access is from the highway between Yolosa and Caranavi; the best put-ins are 20 minutes north of Yolosa and near the confluence with the Río Santa Bárbara, 50 minutes by road north of Yolosa. Just look for any track that winds down from the road toward the river and find one that provides suitable access. Trips average three to five hours. For the take-out, look on the right side of the river for a devastated steel bridge (destroyed in a 1998 flood) across a normally diminutive creek. Don't miss it because after this the climb to the road up the steep jungled slopes is practically impossible, and it's a long, long way to the next possible exit.

The **Río Huarinilla** flows from Huayna Potosí and Tiquimani down into the Yungas to meet the Río Coroico near Yolosa, and is best accessed from Chairo, at the end of El Choro trek. Although it's normally Class II and III, high water can swell it into a much more challenging Class IV to V. The full-day trip is best suited to kayaks and narrow paddle rafts. The new Yungas Hwy passes right by the take-out at the confluence of the Ríos Huarinilla and Coroico.

The whitewater is great, but unfortunately the high tourist season coincides with the dry season. Several agencies around the plaza offer day-long rafting trips for B\$250 to B\$350 per person.

MASSAGE & YOGA
Ninfa at Villa Bonita (opposite) gives yoga classes and meditation sessions, normally on Monday afternoons. Classes are free, but a gift of fruit is appreciated.

Courses
Coroico is a relaxed place to learn Spanish. A recommended teacher is **Siria León** (☎ 7195-5431; siria_leon@yahoo.com; Tomás Manning) who charges B\$35 an hour for private lessons. Her house is at the junction behind the soccer field. With Hotel Gloria Coroico down the road to your left, head through the tiny black gate to the right of the building that immediately faces you. The first door on your left is Siria's.

Sleeping
On weekends from June to August hotels are often booked out. It's possible to make advance reservations, but there's no guarantee that all hotels will honor them. On holiday weekends prices may increase by as much as 100%. See also p126 for some appealing choices in the forests of the Coroico area.

BUDGET
Hostal Sol y Luna (☎ 7156-1626, in La Paz 2-244-0588; www.solyluna-bolivia.com; campsite B\$20, s/d B\$70/120, with bathroom B\$110/160, apt or cabañas with bathroom s/d B\$110/116; 🏊) Set on a jungly hill above town, this inspiring spot offers appealingly rustic accommodations in a variety of *cabañas* (cabins) situated some distance apart on the steep slope. They vary in size and style; palm-thatched Jatata is one of the most charming. There are also apartments (one has a kiln!), comfortable rooms with shared bathroom, and a grassy area to pitch a tent. Other delights include shiatsu massages, two pools, a small outdoor hot tub, a good restaurant and a book exchange. Sol y Luna is a 20-minute uphill walk from town, or B\$12 in a taxi.

Hostal de la Torre (☎ 289-5542; Cuenca s/n; r per person B\$25) Sunny and clean, this is the cheapest acceptable accommodation, but don't be jealous when you hear other travelers splashing around in their hotel pool. At the time of writing all rooms had shared bathrooms, but a newer, more modern block of mini-apartments for up to five people was soon to open (apartment B\$250).

Hostal El Cafetal (☎ 7193-3979; danycafetal @hotmail.com; Miranda s/n; r per person with bathroom B\$35; 🏊) In addition to the superb eatery here, there are several clean, secure rooms with splendid views. The lush grounds encourage lazing in a hammock or chilling in the pool.

Hostal 1866 (☎ 7159-5607; Cuenca s/n; r per person B\$35, with bathroom B\$60) This curious building just up from the plaza – a hybrid of medieval and Moorish style – is a decent choice. The interior rooms are windowless and dingy, but the rooms with bathroom are spacious, light and breezy, especially on the higher floors.

Hotel Esmeralda (☎ 213-6017; www.hotel -esmeralda.com; Julio Suazo s/n; r per person B\$50, with balcony B\$90, with bathroom B\$100, ste B\$150; 🖳 🏊) There's a variety of rooms; the cheapest are tiny and dark, with shared bathrooms, but the suites are nicer, with balconies with great views and hammocks to swing in. The hotel has good facilities – pool table, laundry and a buffet restaurant – but some readers report that service can been erratic.

Hostal Kory (☎ 7156-4050; Kennedy s/n; s/d with bathroom B$60/100; ☯) Right in the center of town, this is the best choice in this price range. There are fabulous views of the valley and Cordillera peaks. Rooms are clean, spacious and modern. The large pool is available to nonguests for B$10, and the restaurant, although usually empty, serves decent food in smallish portions.

MIDRANGE

Hotel Don Quijote (☎ 213-6007; Iturralde s/n; s/d with bathroom B$80/150; ☯) A 10-minute (1km) walk east of the plaza, this friendly pad is popular with Bolivian families. It looks more expensive than it is and makes a good alternative to staying in town. It's clean and has all the amenities of a solid midrange option – including an inviting pool. Staff will pick you up for free from the plaza. Breakfast included.

Hotel El Viejo Molino (☎ /fax 220-1519; www.hotel viejomolino.com; s/d with bathroom B$140/210, superior B$250/350; ☯) Coroico's most luxurious option is a 15-minute downhill walk northeast of town on the road toward the Río Santa Bárbara. All rooms have private bathroom and TV, and include breakfast and access to the temperamental sauna and Jacuzzi, as well as the sizable pool.

Hotel Gloria Coroico (☎ /fax 289-5554, in La Paz 2-240-7070; www.hotelgloria.com.bo; s/d with bathroom B$260/320; ☯) At the bottom of town, this attractive old resort hotel has a likeable colonial ambience, with its spacious lounges, high ceilings and grandiose halls. The rooms are simple but comfortable enough; the ones with a bathroom boast cunning floor-to-ceiling two-way mirrors for windows. Rooms share a wide veranda; make sure you get a room on the pool/valley side, rather than the car-park side.

Eating

The plaza is ringed by a number of inexpensive local cafes and pizzerias; all have ordinary menus, acceptable fare and a typically tropical sense of urgency and service. Local volunteers swear that the average Pizzeria Italia (C Ortiz) is the best of the mediocre bunch.

La Senda Verde (Reyes Ortíz; snacks B$5) Serving home-produced coffee from a refuge in nearby Yolosa, this little cafe is a great place for breakfast. It's set in a quiet courtyard.

Villa Bonita (☎ 7192-2917; Héroes del Chaco s/n; mains B$12-30; ☯ 10am-6pm) This delightfully peaceful garden-cafe is 600m from town but feels a world away. The relaxed, personable owners offer delicious homemade ice creams and sorbets bursting with fresh fruit, tasty sundaes with unusual local liqueurs, and an eclectic range of vegetarian dishes. Meals are served outside where you can appreciate the valley views.

Luna Llena (☎ 7156-1626; mains B$15-35) The small outdoor restaurant at the Hostal Sol y Luna is run with a motherly hand by doña María, and has a well-priced, tasty menu of Bolivian and European dishes including vegetarian options. An extraordinary treat if you have a group – or can muster one – is the Indonesian buffet (B$35 per person) for eight to 20 people, which must be booked a day in advance.

El Cafetal (☎ 7193-3979; Miranda s/n; mains B$15-40) This secluded lean-to has unbeatable views, as well as cane chairs and slate-topped tables where you can enjoy some of the Yungas' finest food. There's a large range of dishes prepared with a French touch. The menu includes sweet and savory crêpes, soufflés, steaks, sandwiches, curries, vegetarian lasagna and regular specials that might include llama goulash. It's near the hospital, a 15-minute walk uphill from the plaza.

Bamboo's Café (Iturralde 1047; mains B$20-40) A friendly place that offers good-value, *picante* (spicy) Mexican food (tacos, burritos and veggie refried beans). Later in the evening it's also a cozy, sociable spot for a candlelit drink or two.

ourpick Back-Stube Konditorei (Kennedy s/n; mains B$22-40; ☯ breakfast & lunch only) One of the best places to eat in town, this welcoming bakery-restaurant has excellent breakfasts, tempting cakes and pastries as well as pasta, vegetarian plates and memorable *sauerbraten* (marinated pot-roast beef) with *spätzle* (German dough noodles). There's also a great terraced area, and a book exchange.

Restaurant La Casa (☎ 213-6024; Cuenca s/n; mains B$30-40) While not quite what it was in its glory days, this home-style, candlelit restaurant is still a good choice for its friendly management and selection of fondue and *à la carte* meals. There are also small but tasty steaks, pasta dishes and a range of scrumptious pancakes. For the sweet of tooth, the sinful chocolate fondue is the way forward.

Drinking

After midnight, with the resto-bars shut, it's time for **Murcielaguitos** (☎ 7122-9830; Pacheco s/n; ☺ Fri & Sat night), in the Residencial 20 de Octubre, where students from the agricultural college join others to dance to loud Latin music and sing karaoke. If you prefer to let the professionals do the singing then try **Bar Mosquito** (Sagárnaga s/n; ☺ 6pm onwards) where you can play pool and enjoy the two-for-one happy hour.

Shopping

For quality handmade jewelry visit **Artesanías Arco Iris**, on the south side of the plaza. It isn't cheap, but most items are unique. During the high season the plaza is frequented by itinerant craftspeople selling a wide range of *artesanías* (locally handcrafted items).

For natural and organic produce **Blue Pine Farm** is just off the plaza on Tomás Monye. The **Madres de Clarisa Convent** (☺ 8am-8pm) sells homemade brownies, orange cakes, creatively flavored biscuits, and wines. You'll find it down the steps off the southwest corner of the plaza; ring the bell to get into the shop area.

Getting There & Away

The La Paz–Coroico road is now open, replacing the 'World's Most Dangerous Road' as the town access route. It's asphalted along its whole length, but in the short time it's been open several landslides have cut up some sections. Buses and *micros* from La Paz arrive at the bus terminal on Av Manning. It's a steep walk uphill to the plaza, or you can hop in a taxi (B$5). **Turbus Totaí** run comfortable taxi services to La Paz from the terminal, leaving when full (B$20, two hours).

BICYCLE

An exhilarating, adrenaline-filled option is to descend by mountain bike from La Paz to Coroico. The thrilling one-day descent from the top at El Cumbre is a memorable experience, but not for the faint-hearted. An ever-increasing number of operators run the trip (p74). Choose carefully – if your company cuts corners, it's a long way down (p75). There have been many fatalities on this route, the vast majority caused by over-eager bikers going too fast. However, if you're sensible and follow instructions, there's no great risk.

BUS

From the Villa Fátima area in La Paz, buses and *micros* leave for Coroico (B$20, 3½ hours) at least hourly from 7:30am to 8:30pm, with extra runs on weekends and holidays. En route they stop in Yolosita where you can connect with buses and *camiones* (flatbed trucks) north to Rurrenabaque (B$100, 15 to 18 hours) and further into Bolivian Amazonia.

For Chulumani, the quickest route is to backtrack to La Paz. Although the junction for the Chulumani road is at Unduavi, few passing *micros* have spare seats at this point.

EL CHORO TREK

The La Cumbre to Coroico (Choro) trek, which traverses Parque Nacional Cotopata, is one of Bolivia's premier hikes. It begins at La Cumbre (4725m), the highest point on the La Paz–Coroico highway, and climbs to 4859m before descending 3250m into the humid Yungas and the village of Chairo. Along the 57km route (which is in best condition during the April to September dry season), you'll note a rapid change in climate, vegetation and wildlife as you leave the Altiplano and plunge into the forest.

Energetic hikers can finish the trek in two days, but it's a demanding walk more comfortably done in three days. Many people allow even more time, or organize a stay of a few days in the *albergue* (basic accommodation) at Sandillani.

Prepare for a range of climates. It can be pretty cold, even snowy, on the first day, but you'll soon be in sweatier climes. For the lower trail, light cotton trousers will protect your legs from sharp vegetation and biting insects. The Inca paving can be pretty slippery, so make sure you've got shoes with grip.

Dangers & Annoyances

Travelers have occasionally been robbed doing this trek solo, with most thefts reported below Choro village. Though these appear to be isolated incidents, it's a better idea to go

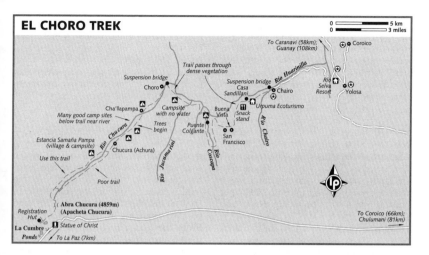

EL CHORO TREK

0 _____ 5 km
0 _____ 3 miles

To Caranavi (58km);
Guanay (108km)

Coroico

Trail passes through
dense vegetation

Suspension bridge   Suspension bridge   Río Huarinilla
                Choro   Casa   Río
                           Sandillani   Chairo   Selva
                                          Urpuma Ecoturismo Resort   Yolosa
        Cha'llapampa   Campsite   Buena   Snack
Many good camp sites   with no water Vista stand
below trail near river   Trees   San
Estancia Samaña Pampa   begin   Puente   Francisco
(village & campsite)   Colgante
              Chucura (Achura)

Use this trail

            Poor trail

Abra Chucura (4859m)
(Apacheta Chucura)
Registration
Hut
La Cumbre   Statue of Christ   To Coroico (66km);
Ponds   To La Paz (7km)   Chulumani (81km)

THE CORDILLERAS & YUNGAS

with a guide. Camp out of sight if possible and do not leave anything outside your tent.

Tours

A growing number of La Paz outfits offer organized El Choro treks. Most include meals, guides and camping equipment; some include the services of porters. For suggestions of agencies, see p74 and p350.

Access

Once you find the trailhead, the trail is easy to access and follow. From Villa Fátima in La Paz, catch any Yungas-bound transportation and ask to be dropped at La Cumbre, marked by a statue of Christ, where the trek begins.

The road climbs steeply out of Villa Fátima, and less than an hour out of La Paz at the 4725m crest of the La Paz–Yungas road is La Cumbre. For the best chance of good clear views of the stunning scenery, start as early as possible, before the mist rises out of the Yungas.

You can also take a taxi to the trail (30 minutes). One advantage of this is that they can take you up the first bit to the pass at Abra Chucura, thus avoiding the initial climb if you think it might cause you altitude problems.

The Route

At the **statue of Christ** is a park registration office where you should sign in. Traditionally this is also the place to perform the ritual *challas*, which asks for blessing from the gods and good luck for your journey. In former times it was an Aymará sanctuary, being replaced by the Christ monument in the colonial era. From here, follow the well-defined track to your left for 1km then turn off onto the smaller track that turns right and passes between two small ponds (one often dry). Follow it up the hill until it curves to the left and begins to descend.

At this point follow the light track leading up the gravelly hill to your right and toward an obvious notch in the barren hill before you. This is **Abra Chucura** (4859m), and from here the trail tends downhill all the way to its end at Chairo. At the high point is a pile of stones called **Apacheta Chucura**. For centuries travelers have marked their passing by tossing a stone atop it (preferably one that has been carried from a lower elevation) as an offering to the mountain *apus* (spirits). An hour below Abra Chucura lie the remains of a *tambo* (wayside inn) dating from Inca times.

One hour below the *tambo* is the hamlet of **Estancia Samaña Pampa**, where there's a store selling water, a grassy campsite, a shelter and another registration hut.

A short way further on, basic supplies are available at the village of **Chucura** (Achura, 3600m). Here you pay a toll of B$10 for maintenance of the trail: you will notice the difference it makes as you head on. An hour's walk from here leads to some campsites (B$10 per person), which are found along the river. The sites are nice, but you might wish to push on down the beautifully paved Inca road to **Cha'llapampa** (2825m), a lovely village with a roofed campsite and simple shelters approximately seven hours from the start point. There are toilets, and water is available from a convenient stream below a bridge close to town.

After two hours following beautiful but slippery stretches of pre-Columbian paving, you'll reach a **suspension bridge** across the Río Chucura at **Choro** (2200m). The track continues descending steadily along the true left (west) side of the Río Chucura, where there are some small campsites (B$10 per person) and a store providing drinks and snacks.

From the ridge above Choro, the trail alternately plunges and climbs from sunny hillsides to vegetation-choked valleys, crossing streams and waterfalls. You'll have to ford the **Río Jucumarini**, which can be rather intimidating in the wet season. Further along, the trail crosses the deep gorge of the **Río Coscapa** via the relatively sturdy Puente Colgante suspension bridge.

The trail continues through some tiny hamlets, including **San Francisco** and **Buena Vista**, which are separated by the stiff ascent and descent of the 'Subida del Diablo.' Some five to six hours from Choro is the remarkable **Casa Sandillani** (2050m), a home surrounded by beautifully manicured Japanese gardens with a view. You can camp here and there's also a new community project lodge, **Urpuma Ecoturismo** (☎ 7258-4359; urpuma @yahoo.com; dm B$80, s/d B$100/200); it's best to book ahead. Built from natural resources available in the area, the atmospheric wattle and thatch rooms are comfortable. Rates include breakfast as well as a guided walk, and dinner is also available. Even if you're not staying, you can use the toilets for a nominal fee. There are also several snack and soft-drink stalls, and a clear water supply is provided by a pipe located diagonally opposite the house (to the right, 20m along the main trail).

From Casa Sandillani it's an easy 2½ hours downhill to **Chairo**, where camping is possible in a small, flat, grassed area with no facilities, near the bridge above town.

It's possible to walk the relatively level 12km past the Río Selva Resort or take transportation from Chairo to **Yolosa** (16km) and then catch an onward service

the 7km to **Coroico**. A few private vehicles head to Yolosa and Coroico on most days, but beware of being charged scandalous prices. Don't pay more than B$170 – you could call a cab in Coroico to pick you up for less than that. Infrequent minibuses also run the route.

YOLOSITA

Traveling between La Paz and the Beni – or from anywhere to Coroico – you'll pass through Yolosita, which guards the Coroico road junction. It's nothing more than a police checkpoint with a few dodgy-looking food stalls but if you are traveling between La Paz and the Yungas you'll likely find yourself spending at least an hour here. From the *tranca* (police post) there is a muddy turnoff to Coroico and Yolosa, and minibuses and taxis are sometimes waiting around to take you. If not, try hitching a lift from passing traffic.

YOLOSA

pop 1370 / elevation 1200m

With the construction of the new La Paz–Coroico road, little Yolosa finds itself off the main drag, and with the magnetic pull of Coroico drawing most visitors 20km or so to the north, few travelers bother to visit. While the town itself is of little interest and offers none of the home comforts of Coroico, there are a handful of attractive ecolodges in the surroundings that are a great spot to chill for a few days before attempting El Choro. La Paz-based biking company **Gravity Assisted Mountain Biking** (p74) was, at the time of writing, about to launch a zipline in Yolosa. Check its website www.zipline.com for details.

Sleeping & Eating

La Senda Verde Refugio Natural (☎ 7153-2701; www.sendaverde.com; campsites B$30, s/d/q incl breakfast B$120/200/300; ⊠) This delightful spot is accessed from the Yolosa–La Paz road, a short walk from town. It has a verdant setting on the banks of two rivers and is a great spot to relax. The duplex *cabañas* are excellent, and the camping facilities great. You'll find various friendly rescued animals, a restaurant under a *palapa* (open-sided thatched roundhouse) and a good vibe.

Río Selva Resort (☎ 241-2281, 241-1561; www .rioselva.com.bo, in Spanish; r/ste/apt/cabin B$350/

400/630/700; 🖳 🙎) About 5km from the end of the Choro trek in Pacollo is this posh five-star riverside retreat that can be a welcome deal for larger groups. Peripheral amenities include racquetball courts, a sauna and swimming pool. There's a range of accommodations, from double rooms to cabins sleeping up to six. The owners can arrange transportation from La Paz, but it's much cheaper to head to Coroico or Yolosa and get a taxi from there.

El Jiri Ecolodge (☎ 7155-8215, in La Paz 2-278-8264; www.jiribolivia.com; 2-day/1-night program per person B$468; 🙎) Near Charobamba, across the valley from Coroico, this lodge is a fun spot to stay, with hanging bridges, a zipline tour, a pool and meals under a thatched roof. You're kept busy with walks in Parque Nacional Cotapata and plenty of activities. Ask to see the ruins of an old Jewish settlement nearby. Book ahead.

TAKESI (TAQUESI) TREK

Also known as the Inca Trail, the Takesi trek is one of the most popular and impressive walks in the Andes. The route was used as a highway by the early Aymará, the Inca and the Spanish, and it still serves as a major route to the humid Yungas over a relatively low pass in the Cordillera Real. Nearly half the trail's 45km consists of expertly engineered pre-Inca paving, more like a highway than a walking track. It has been posited that this paved section was part of a long road that linked the La Paz area with the Alto Beni region.

The walk itself is demanding and takes two days, but plan on longer because of transportation uncertainties to and from the trailheads. On the first day you ascend to 4650m, so spend a few days acclimatizing in La Paz before heading off. The trail is hiked by about 5000 people annually, more than half of whom are Bolivians, and suffers from a litter problem due to its growing popularity.

The May to October dry season is best for this trip. In the rainy season the wet and cold, combined with ankle-deep mud, may contribute to a less-than-optimal experience. Since the trail's end is in the Yungas, however, plan on some rain year-round.

THE CORDILLERAS & YUNGAS

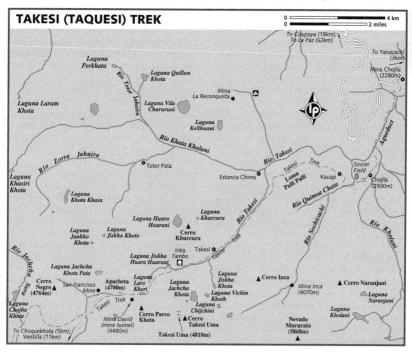

TAKESI (TAQUESI) TREK

The entire route appears on a single 1:50,000 IGM topo sheet: *Chojlla – 6044-IV.* A good source of information is **Fundación Pueblo** (☎ 212-4413; www.fundacionpueblo.org, in Spanish; PO Box 9564, La Paz), an NGO that supports rural development projects that encourage local self-sufficiency. The group has done much work with villagers along the trail to improve facilities. The foundation can organize a package that includes transportation to and from the trailheads, meals, accommodations and a guide for B$500 to B$700 per person.

Access

If you're traveling by public transportation, your first destination will be **Ventilla**. *Micros* leave from La Paz (B$12, three hours) hourly from 7am until noon from the market area above Calle Sagárnaga, at the corner of Calles Rodríguez and Luis Lara. Another option for groups is to charter a taxi (around B$350 for up to four people) to the Choquekhota trailhead. Most La Paz tour agencies (p74) can organize this for you or contact Fundación Pueblo (p127).

You can also take an urban *micro* or *trufi* (collective minibus that follows a set route) from La Paz to Chasquipampa or Ovejuyo, then trek through the beautiful Palca Canyon (and the Valle de las Ánimas if you like; p92) to Palca and then to Ventilla. This will add at least one extra day to the trip, but will be a fitting prelude to the longer trek.

Transportation between Ventilla and the San Francisco mine trailhead is sparse. If you're lucky, you may be able to hitch; otherwise you should probably resign yourself to paying for a taxi, or slogging three hours uphill to the trailhead.

With a fully serviced lodge two-thirds of the way along the route, the hike is easily done with just a daypack, but agencies and Fundación Pueblo in La Paz can arrange guides and mules if you want them.

The Route

About 150m beyond Ventilla, turn left and take the road uphill, following the Río Palca. After climbing for 60 to 90 minutes, you'll reach the village of **Choquekhota**, where the landscape is reminiscent of North Wales. You'll come to the access road to the **San Francisco mine** after a further hour or two of uphill hiking; after crossing a stream, you'll see the signpost indicating the trailhead. The mine route veers left here, but hikers should continue along the signposted track which is where the original pre-Columbian trail begins.

After an hour of climbing you'll begin switchbacking for 30 minutes for the final ascent, partly on superb pre-Inca paving, to the 4700m **Apacheta** (Abra Takesi) pass. There, you'll find the *apacheta* (shrine of stones) and a spectacular view of Nevado Murata (5868m) to the right and the plunging valleys of the Yungas far below. Just beyond the pass you'll see an abandoned **Mina David mine tunnel**; wolfram and tin are mined around here. Entry is not advisable.

From the pass the trail begins to descend into the valley, passing a series of abandoned mining camps and high glacial lakes. If daylight is on your side, look for another lake, **Laguna Jiskha Huara Huarani**, to the left of the trail midway between the pass and Takesi. The trail from here contains some of Bolivia's finest examples of Inca paving. A little later the trail widens to between 6m and 8m and you will reach **Inka Tambo** with five rooms, a good place to spend the night. If you prefer to push on, you'll next reach the ancient-looking thatched village of **Takesi** where there's a hut and campsite; you'll also find meals of potatoes and local trout. It is at this point that you will begin to experience the sudden change to Yungas vegetation.

Beyond Takesi the increasingly muddy trail winds downhill until it crosses a bridge over the **Río Takesi** then follows the beautifully churning river before it moves upslope from the river and makes a long traverse around the **Loma Palli Palli**, where you're protected from steep drop-offs by a pre-Columbian wall. Shortly after passing a particularly impressive *mirador* (lookout), you'll enter the village of **Kacapi**, the heart of the former colonial *estancia* (ranch) that once controlled the entire Takesi valley. Most of the overseers' dwellings have been reclaimed by vegetation, but you can still see the ruins of the Capilla de las Nieves. Kacapi's 10-bed **Albergue Turístico** (dm B$30) and campsite are equipped with solar-powered showers. Basic meals are available as well. From the *apacheta* to this point is approximately six hours' continuous walking, leaving four more hours for the following day.

After Kacapi the track drops sharply to a bridge over the **Río Quimsa Chata** (which suffers varying degrees of damage each rainy season), then climbs past a soccer field on the left to a pass at the hamlet of **Chojlla**. From there the route descends to the final crossing of the Río Takesi via a concrete bridge, marking the end of the pre-Columbian trail. It's then a 1½-hour trudge along an **aqueduct** to the ramshackle mining settlement of **Mina Chojlla** (2280m), where there is a cheap *alojamiento* (basic accommodation).

From Mina Chojlla, crowded buses leave for Yanacachi (B$3, 30 minutes) and La Paz (B$12, four hours) at 5:30am and 1pm daily – buy your ticket on arrival. If you can't endure a night in Mina Chojlla (and few people can), keep about one hour down the road past the headquarters of the hydro-electric power project to the more pleasant village of **Yanacachi**.

YUNGA CRUZ TREK

This is a relatively little-trodden trek between the village of Chuñavi and the Sud Yungas' provincial capital of Chulumani. Declared a 'national monument' in 1992, it preserves good stretches of pre-Hispanic paving and archaeological remains dating from the Tiwanaku and Inca periods.

There are a couple of variations to the standard trek, including a pass over the northern shoulder of Illimani to get you started, as well as an alternative – and considerably more spectacular – route over Cerro Khala Ciudad, which begins beyond Lambate. Some guides even offer the trek backwards, starting at Chulumani, but that's a fairly punishing alternative. Crossing several passes at over 5000m, it's easily the most demanding of the Inca trails and usually takes five or six days. There are no official campsites along the route.

If you are going to attempt this trek you'll need to carry the 1:50,000 topo sheets *Palca – 6044-I, Lambate – 6044-II* and *Chulumani – 6044-III* or, even better, arrange a guide. Many agencies in La Paz offer this trek, with guides, cook and pack animals; see p74 and also p351 for a list of agencies.

Access

There's a good case for hiring a 4WD to take you to the trailhead at Lambate. Otherwise you can go straight to Chuñavi

(five hours) or Lambate (six hours) by *micro* from La Paz, with departures from Calle Venancio Burgoa, near Plaza Líbano, leaving daily at 7am.

The return to La Paz is straightforward: catch one of the many daily buses or *camiones* from the *tranca* in Chulumani.

CHULUMANI

pop 2950 / elevation 1700m

Perched scenically on the side of a hill, this peaceful little town is the capital of the Sud Yungas. The town was founded because of the supposed healing qualities of the mineral streams in the vicinity, but with the fertile soils providing bumper crops of coca (the country's best for chewing), citruses, bananas, coffee and cacao it soon became more important as a trade center for the nearby farming communities. The area is also a paradise for birds and butterflies, with clouds of the latter, and several endemic species of the former. At a tropically warm and often wet altitude, it's a great trekking base camp and a relaxing weekend retreat with a great view. The only time Chulumani breaks its pervasive tranquility is during the week following August 24, when it stages the riotous **Fiesta de San Bartolomé**.

During the 1781 La Paz revolt, rebels escaped to the Yungas and hid out in the valleys around Chulumani. Today the area is home to a large population of African-Bolivians (see the boxed text, p131).

Information

Chulumani's tourist office is in a kiosk on the main plaza, but if you are thinking of exploring the region it is worth seeking out hotel owners such as English-speaking Javier Sarabia at the Country House (p130). There's no ATM in Chulumanni; Banco Unión changes traveler's checks for 5% commission, and Prodem changes US dollars and gives cash advances on credit cards (5% commission). The Cotel office on Plaza Libertad is one of several central phone offices. Internet connections are sporadic; on a good day head to **Enternet** (Sucre s/n).

Sights & Activities

Chulumani sees few visitors, but it is a good base for several worthwhile excursions. An interesting day trip is to the **Apa-Apa Reserva**

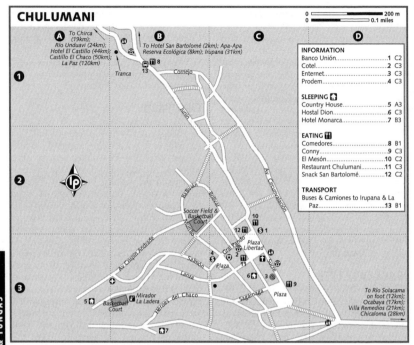

CHULUMANI

INFORMATION	
Banco Unión	1 C2
Cotel	2 C3
Enternet	3 C3
Prodem	4 C3

SLEEPING	
Country House	5 A3
Hostal Dion	6 C3
Hotel Monarca	7 B3

EATING	
Comedores	8 B1
Conny	9 C3
El Mesón	10 C2
Restaurant Chulumani	11 C3
Snack San Bartolomé	12 C2

TRANSPORT	
Buses & Camiones to Irupana & La Paz	13 B1

Ecológica (☎ 213-6106, 7202-1285; apapayungas@ hotmail.com), 8km from town. The private 500-hectare property has dry forest and one of the last remnants of primary cloud forest in the Yungas, and is rich in trees, orchids, butterflies and birds. You can also stay in the beautiful historic hacienda or camp at the well-equipped site above it (opposite). The reserve runs four-hour guided forest walks (B$50 per person with a B$200 minimum) and has a cafe serving meals and home-made ice cream. A taxi from Chulumani to the reserve costs B$15.

There are several lovely walks in the Chulumani area. A butterfly-clouded, five-hour (one-way) downhill hike will take you from Chulumani down to the Río Solacama; you can easily get a bus or *micro* back. In three to four hours you can also walk to Ocabaya, while other walks take you from the higher village of Villa Remedios to the lower one, or from Chicaloma down to Ocabaya. Another beautiful hike is the four-hour walk from Chulumani to Chirca, where there's the church of a revered local virgin.

Sleeping

Apa-Apa Reserva Ecológica (☎ 213-6106, 7202-1285; apapayungas@hotmail.com; r per person B$50, campsites B$70 plus per person per night B$15; ⟁) This beautiful old adobe hacienda makes a good place to stay. It's set in elegant grounds, and the cordial owners maintain the property with care and thought. There's an excellent grassy camping area with palm-thatched tables, barbecues and good bathroom facilities, as well as five rooms, a cafe-restaurant and a lovely pool. It's 8km from Chulumani.

Hostal Dion (☎ 213-6070; Bolívar s/n; r per person B$50, with bathroom B$70) The best of the central options, this is a friendly, clean and well-maintained choice just off the plaza. Rates include a simple breakfast.

Hotel Monarca (☎ 213-6121, in La Paz 2-235-1019; r per person B$60; ⟁) Like most ex-prefectural holiday camps, the Monarca is a bit run-down and lacks character, but it's managed by nice people and is good value. The enormous pool is open to nonguests for B$15.

our pick Country House (Tolopata 13; r per person with bathroom B$70; ⟁) A welcoming home in a relaxing setting 10 minutes west of the plaza.

The rooms, decorated in an attractively rustic style, are spotless, and have hot-water bathrooms and fresh flowers. Great breakfasts, abundant birdlife, a pool table and an extensive video collection are other highlights, as are the delicious home-cooked dinners and relaxing mineral pool. Owner Javier can organize all sorts of local excursions including inner-tubing on local rivers.

Hotel El Castillo (☎ 235-9881; www.hotelcastilloloro .com, in Spanish; r per person with bathroom B$150; 🖳) Located along the Chulumani road (20km beyond Unduavi) at 1934m, this unique riverfront castle is a real surprise for the eyes; it looks very out of place in the Yungas! It functions as a hotel and restaurant, and is only a couple of hours from La Paz. With its swimming pool, waterfalls and subtropical climate, it makes for an appealing weekend getaway.

Hotel San Bartolomé (☎ 213-6114; d with bathroom from B$220; 🖳) This relatively upscale pad is notable for its odd Z-shaped swimming pool. Deals include four-person *cabañas* and all-inclusive weekend packages from B$500 per person. For weekend guests the hotel organizes minibus transportation from La Paz. It's 2km out of town on the road to Irupana.

Eating

Food choices are limited in most cases to *almuerzos* (set lunches) and it's a case of first come first served. After 2pm you'll be hard pressed to find anything decent to eat. For cheap and cheerful fried chicken, **Snack San Bartolomé** on the plaza is a friendly choice. There are also basic *comedores* (dining halls) near the *tranca* (police post).

The best *almuerzos* can be had at **El Mesón** (Plaza Libertad s/n; almuerzo B$10) and **Conny** (Sucre s/n; almuerzo B$10), which has a pleasant dining room with views and is also open in the evenings. Also on the plaza, Restaurant Chulumani has an upstairs dining terrace.

If you are looking for something more adventurous, the Country House (opposite) and Apa-Apa Reserva Ecológica (opposite) do tasty dinners with a few hours' notice.

Getting There & Away

Since the closure of the original La Paz–Coroico road to traffic, the nail-biting route from La Paz to Chulumani, which extends on to Irupana, has claimed the title of 'The World's Most Dangerous Road.' If you can keep your nerves in check, it is actually an exceptionally beautiful route, though it's hard to appreciate when your bus is reversing round a blind, muddy bend in search of a section wide enough to let oncoming traffic past.

Yunga Cruz trekkers finish in Chulumani, and the town is readily accessed from Yanacachi at the end of the Takesi trek. From Yanacachi, walk down to the main road and wait for transportation headed downhill; it's about 1½ hours to Chulumani.

From Villa Fátima in La Paz, around the corner of Calles San Borja and 15 de Abril, different companies depart when full for Chulumani (B$25, four hours) from 8am to 4pm. From Chulumani, La Paz-bound buses wait around the *tranca*. Theoretically, there are several departures before 10am and after 4pm, but in reality services are frequently cancelled due to lack of interest. Buy your ticket in advance; even if your

THE CORDILLERAS & YUNGAS

AFRO-BOLIVIANS

The hill villages of the Chulumani region are home to a high proportion of the country's African-Bolivian people. At a rough estimate, there are some 35,000 Bolivians descended from African slaves who were brought over to work the Potosí silver mines (where an astronomical number of them died). One of the traditional Bolivian dances, the *morenada*, has its roots in a portrayal of an African slave train arriving at the mines.

Slavery in Bolivia was abolished in 1851, and the African-Bolivians of the Yungas live as farmers, growing coca and other local products. Seeing them dressed in typical *cholita* costumes, you might assume total integration, but they are a community somewhat apart; while relations with the Aymará community are friendly, there is little intermarriage. At a political level, their existence as a people has fundamentally been ignored.

In their haunting *saya* music (a hybrid of African, Aymará and Spanish styles) and distinct funerary rites, however, are many echoes from the other side of the Atlantic Ocean.

company doesn't depart it will be valid for one of those that does.

If you're coming from Coroico, get off at Unduavi and wait for another vehicle. It will likely be standing-room only; if a seat is a priority, you'll have to go all the way back to La Paz.

It's also possible to go to Coroico via Coripata; take a La Paz-bound bus and get off at the crossroads just after Puente Villa at Km 93. Here, wait for a bus or *camión* to Coripata and then change again for a lift to Coroico. It's a lo-o-o-ng and dusty but worthwhile trip. An easier option is to hire a taxi; expect to pay B$300 for the trip to Coroico for up to four people.

AROUND CHULUMANI

The area around Chulumani is a beautiful, fertile zone comprised both of patches of forest and of farms producing coca, coffee, bananas and citrus fruits. Some of the villages are remote colonial gems. Another interesting aspect of the region is the presence of a significant population of African-Bolivians (see the boxed text, p131), the descendants of slaves who once were forced to work the Potosí mines.

An intriguing circuit takes you from Chulumani past the **Apa-Apa Reserva Ecológica** (p130) toward the humble fruit-farming hamlets of **Villa Remedios**. There are two hamlets, a higher and a lower one; the latter has a pretty little church. Look out for coca leaves being harvested and dried.

The main road winds its way down to the **Río Solacama**, whose banks are populated by numerous butterflies; it's a lovely spot to bathe on a hot day. Just after the bridge, a left turn heads away from the main road up a steep hill to **Laza**. A *via crucis* (Stations of the Cross) leads up to the pretty square and its church, where there's an appealing dark-wood and gold altarpiece and baldachin. The much-revered statue of Christ, *El Señor de la Exaltación*, is the destination for an important *romería* (pilgrimage-fiesta) on September 14.

The main settlement over this side of the river is **Irupana**, an attractive, sleepy colonial town founded in the 18th century on one of the few bits of flat ground in the area. It became an important fortress, just as the nearby ruins of **Pasto Grande** had once been in Tiwanaku and Inca times.

From Irupana, you can head back to Chulumani a different way, fording the Río Puri and passing through the principal Afro-Bolivian town, dusty **Chicaloma** – known for its annual town festival on May 27, which features lots of traditional *saya* music – before crossing the Río Solacama again. On the way back, you pass through tiny, postcard-pretty **Ocabaya**, which has one of the oldest churches in Bolivia, fronted by a liberty bell and a memorial to two local martyrs in the struggle for *campesino* (subsistence farmer) rights. Locals may well offer food in their homes here.

Javier Sarabia at the Country House in Chulumani (p130) will happily give walking information (even for nonguests) and can help arrange taxi drop-offs or pick-ups.

Whitewater Rafting

The road to Chulumani follows part of another good whitewater river, the **Río Unduavi**. The upper section ranges from essentially unnavigable Class V to Class VI, with steep chutes, powerful currents, large boulder gardens, blind corners and water-falls. Beyond this section it mellows out into some challenging Class II whitewater followed by Class II and III rapids. Access is limited, but the Chulumani road does offer several put-ins and take-outs. The best access points have been left by construction crews who've mined the riverbanks for sand and gravel. A good take-out point is Puente Villa, which is three to four hours below the best put-ins.

Sleeping

As well as a few cheap *alojamientos* (the **Sarita** on the main street is the cleanest), Irupana has a couple of interesting accommodations options. The **Hotel Bougainvillea** (☎ 213-6155; Sucre 243; r per person with bathroom B$70; 🅿) is an attractive, modernized, white-washed building built around a pool. Its rooms are clean and appealing, although management is not overly welcoming.

One of the most memorable places to stay in the Yungas is **Nirvana Inn** (☎ 213-6154; www.posadanirvanainn.cjb.net; cabañas per person B$180; 🅿) in the barrio of Chiriaca at the top of Irupana (go past the soccer field and turn right). It consists of five sublime *cabañas* in an immaculate hillside garden full of orange and mandarin trees with top views over the valley. It's run by considerate hosts, and the rooms are well looked after – comfortable and romantic with a log fire – and there are optional kitchen facilities. There's also a swimming pool and sauna. Breakfast is included, and other meals can be arranged. Staff can also arrange forest walks.

Getting There & Away

Regular buses drive the 31km from Chulumani to Irupana (B$3, one hour) and there are also some direct connections to Irupana from La Paz. *Micros* run to the smaller villages from Chulumani and Irupana.

One of the most comfortable ways to see these places is to hire a taxi from Chulumani (although not in the rainy season, December to February). For the whole circuit, expect to pay around B$200 to B$300 for a day's hire. It's worth getting hold of a driver who can also act as a guide; ask Javier Sarabia at the Country House (p130) in Chulumani for a recommendation.

SORATA

pop 2250 / elevation 2670m

Sorata wins many travelers' votes as the most relaxing spot in Bolivia. This laid-back place preserves a crumbling colonial atmosphere in a spectacular natural setting, perched on a hillside in a valley beneath the towering snow-capped peaks of Illampu and Ancohuma. Though there isn't much to do in town, it's a great spot to just chill for a few days, and a popular base camp for hikers and mountain-bikers.

In colonial days Sorata provided a link to the Alto Beni's goldfields and rubber plantations, and a gateway to the Amazon Basin. In 1791 it was the site of a distinctly unorthodox siege by indigenous leader Andrés Tupac Amaru and his 16,000 soldiers. They constructed dykes above the town, and when these had filled with runoff from the slopes of Illampu, they opened the flood-gates and the town was washed away.

In September 2003, Sorata hit the national headlines. A blockade further up the La Paz road, expression of an overwhelming wave of *campesino* dissatisfaction that eventually led to the downfall of the government, trapped hundreds of Bolivian and foreign tourists in Sorata. In a misplaced show of force, the army busted them out, killing a *campesino* and inducing a riot. Tourism

dropped off in the wake of this and the town is still struggling to recover in the face of competition from the ever-more-popular and more accessible Coroico.

Information

Sunday is market day, and Tuesday, when many businesses are closed, is considered *domingo sorateño* (Sorata's Sunday). There's no tourist information center or ATM.

Buho's Internet & Café (per hr B$12) For slow and expensive internet access; on the south side of the plaza. It also sells a small selection of local arts and crafts.

Prodem (☎ 213-6679; Plaza Enrique Peñaranda 136; ⏰ 2:30-6pm Tue, 8:30am-noon & 2:30-6pm Wed-Fri, 8:30am-4pm Sat, 8:30am-3pm Sun) Changes US dollars and does cash advances.

Sights

There isn't much of specific interest in Sorata itself – its main attractions are its historic ambience and its maze of steep stairways and narrow cobbled lanes. It's worth taking a look at **Casa Günther**, a rambling, historic mansion that now houses the Residencial Sorata (p135). It was built in 1895 as the home of the Richters, a quinine-trading family, and was later taken over by the Günthers, who were involved in rubber extraction until 1955.

The main square, **Plaza General Enrique Peñaranda**, is Sorata's showcase. With the town's best view of the *nevados* (snow-capped mountain peaks), it's graced by towering date palms and immaculate gardens. Upstairs in the town hall on the plaza is the free **Alcaldía Museum** (⏰ 8am-noon & 2-5pm Wed-Mon), containing a number of artifacts from the Inca Marka site near Laguna Chillata, and an exhibit of old festival clothing.

Although it's not the most spectacular of caves, a popular excursion is to the **Gruta de San Pedro** (San Pedro Cave; admission B$5; ⏰ 8am-5pm), 12km from town. The cave is approximately 400m deep with an enclosed lagoon, and though it is no longer possible to swim in it, it can be crossed with pedal boats.

It's a scenic 6km hike to the cave along a dirt road (two hours each way). Taxis will do the return trip for around B$30, including waiting time, or else call the **San Pedro Community** (☎ 238-1695) which manages cave visits and might be able to arrange transportation. The community has also set up two simple *albergues* to overnight in the

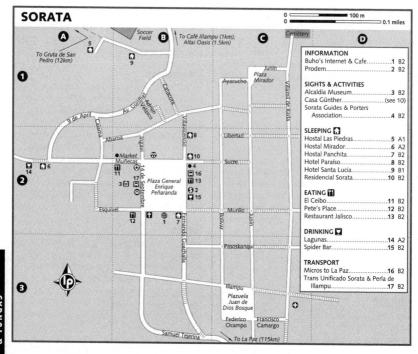

SORATA

INFORMATION
Buho's Internet & Cafe...............1 B2
Prodem...............................2 B2

SIGHTS & ACTIVITIES
Alcaldía Museum....................3 B2
Casa Günther....................(see 10)
Sorata Guides & Porters
    Association.......................4 B2

SLEEPING
Hostal Las Piedras..................5 A1
Hostal Mirador.....................6 A2
Hostal Panchita...................7 B2
Hotel Paraíso......................8 B2
Hotel Santa Lucia.................9 B1
Residencial Sorata................10 B2

EATING
El Ceibo...........................11 B2
Pete's Place......................12 B2
Restaurant Jalisco................13 B2

DRINKING
Lagunas...........................14 A2
Spider Bar........................15 B2

TRANSPORT
Micros to La Paz..................16 B2
Trans Unificado Sorata & Perla de
    Illampu.........................17 B2

community. There are a total of four rooms with a single bed in each and prices are negotiable. Remember that all proceeds go to help the community, so be generous.

Activities
HIKING

Sorata is best known as a convenient base for hikers and climbers pursuing some of Bolivia's finest landscapes. The peak hiking season is May to September.

The most popular walk is the hike to **Laguna Chillata**, a pretty spot with great views of the surrounding sierra and Lake Titicaca. It's a fairly stiff five-hour climb, ascending some 1500m, and, while you can get there and back in a day, it's a pleasant and popular spot to camp. It's worthwhile taking a guide, as it's easy to get lost. If you're going to overnight there, a beast of burden is a sound investment; let the mule do the carrying while you enjoy the views.

An optional third day can be built into this hike. Leaving the tent and your gear at Laguna Chillata (it'll get nicked if you haven't brought a guide, who can detail

someone to watch over it), a steep ascent takes you up to **Laguna Glacial**, a top spot where you can watch big chunks of ice cracking off into the water. It's at 5100m, so take it easy; the altitude can make it a tough climb.

Ambitious adventurers can do the seven-day **El Camino del Oro trek** (p136), an ancient trading route between the Altiplano and the Río Tipuani goldfields. Otherwise there's the challenging **Mapiri trail** (five days; p138) or the Illampu circuit (seven days). The latter was plagued with armed robberies for a while but things seemed to have calmed down since. However, we recommend that you do not attempt this route without a guide.

The ultimate hardcore challenge is the 20-day **Trans Cordillera route**: eight days gets you from Sorata to Lago Sistaña, with possible four-day (to Huayna Potosí) and eight-day (to Illimani) extensions.

Basic information on climbing some of the region's peaks is included under Cordillera Real (p141). For detailed trekking information, Lonely Planet's *Trekking in the Central Andes* pick & mix chapters are available from shop.lonelyplanet.com.

Hikers should carry the *Alpenvereinskarte Cordillera Real Nord* (Illampu) 1:50,000 map, which can be bought at Buho's Internet & Café (p133).

While it's possible to hike independently, it is best to hook up with a guide, mainly because of the need to be aware of local sensibilities and the difficulty of finding passable routes.

The most economical, authorized option is to hire an independent, Spanish-speaking guide from **Sorata Guides & Porters Association** (☎/fax 213-6672; guiasorata@hotmail.com; Sucre 302), which also rents equipment of varying quality and arranges many different treks. Expect to pay around B$200 per day for a guide; it costs around B$40 extra to hire a mule. Cooking equipment is included in these prices, but food is extra. Clients are expected to pay for the guide's food.

MOUNTAIN BIKING

The Sorata area, with its thrillingly steep descents and spectacular mountain scenery, makes it a top two-wheel destination. The Jach'a Avalancha (Grande Avalanche) Mountain Bike race takes place in Sorata each year. This is the biggest downhill race course in South America based on the Mega Avalanche format. It is a 2000m descent using a mass start and draws riders from across Bolivia and the world.

our pick **Andean Epics Ride Company** (☎ 7127-6685; www.andeanepics.com; inside Lagunas) is a professional and enthusiastic set-up that offers a range of great mountain-bike trips for riders of all levels. These range from sedate half-day excursions to awesome multiday adventures in the surrounding sierras. Owner Travis is always building downhill trails and plotting out new routes; one of his specialties is a five-day trip from Sorata to Rurrenabaque, starting with a two-day ride from Sorata to Mapiri via Consata (descending over 4000m from the starting point in the mountains), followed by a three-day boat journey with hikes as side-trips. The trip leaves every Monday from Sorata and costs B$1400. A minimum of four people is required for the longer rides; prices are from B$350 to B$500 per ride. The season is from April to December – it's too muddy at other times, but other rides are available year-round. Full-day downhill trips around Sorata cost around B$500 per person.

Sleeping

Altai Oasis (☎ 7151-9856; www.altaioasis.lobopages .com; campsites B$12, s/d B$70/100, without bathroom B$40/70, cabins for 2-5 people B$300-420; ☒) This really does feel like an oasis, with a lush garden, hammocks, caged macaws, a pretty balcony cafe-restaurant and a range of accommodations options. Welcoming hosts Johny and Roxana run this beautiful riverside retreat, and offer grassy campsites, comfortable rooms, and romantic accommodations in appealingly rustic *cabañas*, each one intricately and fancifully painted. To get there, follow the downhill track past the soccer field to the river, climb back up to the road and turn left before reaching Café Illampu.

Residencial Sorata (☎ 279-3459; r per person B$30-70) On the northeast corner of the plaza, this ultra-characterful colonial-style mansion makes a romantic place to stay. Do your eyes a favor and ask to see the old-style rooms; do your back a favor and ask to stay in one of the new ones (with private bathroom). There's a restaurant, laundry service, wild garden and a friendly welcome. Manager Louis Demers speaks several languages and is a mine of information on local trekking routes.

Hotel Santa Lucia (☎ 213-6686; r per person without/ with bathroom B$40/70) This cheerful, bright yellow place with carpeted rooms and laundry sinks has a friendly owner, Serafín, who'll do his utmost to make your stay comfortable.

Hostal Panchita (☎ 213-4242; s/d B$50/70) Built around a clean and sunny courtyard on the south side of the plaza, the pleasant, atmospheric Panchita has spacious rooms with private or shared bathroom. The management is friendly, there's hot water, and the attached cafe-restaurant does arguably the best pizzas in town.

Hostal Mirador (☎ 289-5008; hostellingbolivia @yahoo.com; Muñecas 400; s/d B$50/80) Sorata's pleasant Hostelling International affiliate has a sunny terrace, a cafe, decent rooms with shared bathroom and lovely views down the valley. HI members get a 10% discount.

Hostal Las Piedras (☎ 7191-6341; Ascarrunz s/n; r per person B$50, s/d with bathroom B$100/140) The most pleasant of Sorata's *hostales*, this spot offers very pretty rooms each named after a precious stone. Attractive wooden furniture and comfy beds with duvets add a homelike feel. Some rooms have great valley views, and the optional breakfast includes home-made wholemeal bread and yoghurt.

Hotel Paraíso (☎ 213-6671; Villavicencio s/n; r per person B$60) This central spot has a bright, flowery patio, a series of roof terraces with nice views and decent rooms with bath-room. There's also a restaurant, which at the time of research opened only on request.

Eating & Drinking

A curiosity of Sorata is that it's bristling with almost identical pizza restaurants, some of which share a kitchen. They are all much-of-a-muchness and prices are similar.

our pick Café Illampu (snacks B$10-20; ☺ closed Tue) A 15-minute down-and-up walk from town, this lovely relaxing spot is en route to the San Pedro cave. Leave it for the return journey, for if you stop here on the way to the cave, you might not make it as the place is exceedingly tranquil (views, garden, llamas), and there's good coffee, sandwiches on homemade bread and great cakes – the Swiss owner is a master baker.

El Ceibo (Muñecas 339; mains B$15-25) This is one of a row of simple Bolivian eateries serving hearty portions of typical Bolivian dishes.

Pete's Place (Esquivel s/n; almuerzo B$15, mains B$15-40) Serves big breakfasts that set you up for a day's hiking, as well as a large selection of well-prepared and presented vegetarian fare, chicken curry and tasty steaks, all in a cheerful, comfortable setting. Owner Pete keeps an extensive library of maps and guidebooks and provides up-to-date trek-king information. It's well worth picking up a copy of his book *Bolivia – Between a Rock and a Hard Place*, a comprehensive synthesis of Bolivian political history.

Altai Oasis (☎ 7151-9856; mains B$20-50) The peaceful balcony restaurant at this loveable retreat (see p135), 15 minutes' walk from town, serves coffee, drinks and a range of vegetarian dishes. There are also T-bone steaks and, for an Eastern European touch, Polish borscht and tasty goulash. It's a great place to just sit with a drink too, with views over the valley and the tinkle of wind chimes.

Restaurant Jalisco (mains B$30-40) On the east side of the plaza, Jalisco delivers an ambitious menu of pizzas, Bolivian choices, pasta and creditable attempts at Mexican food – tacos and burritos.

Drinking & Entertainment

Not a lot goes on in Sorata at night. The Spider Bar on the plaza (its name is taken from a former bar of that name) has a decent drinks selection and outdoor seating, but shuts fairly early. Lagunas has a worldly vibe and offers vegetarian dishes as well as beer, cocktails and homemade liquor.

Getting There & Away

Sorata is a long way from the other Yungas towns, and there's no road connecting it directly with Coroico, so you must go through La Paz.

From La Paz, **Trans Unificado Sorata** (☎ 238-1693) and Perla del Illampu each leave hourly from Manuel Bustillos with Angel Babaia between 4am and 5:30pm (B$15, three hours). From the plaza in Sorata, La Paz–bound *micros* depart when full and *flotas* (long-distance buses) leave on the hour between 4am and 5pm. For Copacabana you must get off at the junction town of Huarina and wait for another, probably packed, bus. Similarly, for Charazani you should change at Achacachi, but you'll need to start out from Sorata very early.

The only road route between Sorata and the lowlands is a rough 4WD track that leads to the gold-mining settlement of Mapiri. It strikes out from Sorata and passes through Quiabaya, Tacacoma and Consata, roughly following the courses of the Ríos Llica, Consata and Mapiri all the way. The biggest drawbacks are the horrendous mud, the road construction and some river crossings that are passable only with a 4WD. *Camionetas* (pickup trucks) leave Sorata sporadically for the grueling journey to Consata (seven hours) and on to the Sorata Limitada mine (10 hours). From Sorata Limitada, you'll find *camionetas* to Mapiri, which is another hour away.

EL CAMINO DEL ORO (GOLD DIGGER'S TRAIL)

For nearly 1000 years this Inca road has been used as a commerce and trade link between the Altiplano and the lowland goldfields. Indeed, the Tipuani and Mapiri valleys were major sources of the gold that once adorned the Inca capital, Cuzco.

Today, however, the fields are worked primarily by bulldozers and dredgers owned by mining cooperatives. They scour and scrape the landscape and dump the detritus, which is picked over by out-of-work Aymará refugees from the highlands. Fortunately, the upper part of the route remains magnificent, and almost everything between Ancoma and Chusi has been left alone, including some wonderfully exhausting Inca staircases and dilapidated ancient highway engineering.

This trek is more challenging than the Takesi and El Choro routes; if you want to get the most from it, plan on six or seven days to walk between Sorata and Llipi, less if you opt for a 4WD to Ancoma. At Llipi, find transportation to Tipuani or Guanay to avoid a walking-pace tour through the worst of the destruction.

Access

Nearly everyone does the route from Sorata down the valley to Tipuani and Guanay, simply because it's generally downhill. If you don't mind a climb, however, you might prefer to do it in reverse, thus leaving the prettiest bits to last. Whatever you choose to do, it is best with a guide.

There are three options for the route between Sorata and Ancoma. First, you can rent a 4WD in Sorata and cut two days off the trek. You'll have to bargain but expect to pay at least B$350. A challenging alternative is the steep route that begins near the cemetery in Sorata. The route roughly follows the Río Challasuyo, passing through the village of Chillkani and winding up on the road just below the Abra Chuchu (4658m) – this is also the access to the Mapiri trail (p138), a four-hour walk from Ancoma. The third option, which is shorter and more scenic, is to follow the route through the village of Lakathiya and over the Abra de Illampu (4741m) to meet up with the road about 1½ hours above Ancoma. Foreigners are charged B$10 per person to camp anywhere in the vicinity of Ancoma or you can ask about lodging in the school room. There is also a B$3 charge for crossing the bridge. Alternatively, continue a few kilometers on to Tushuaia where there is a flat terrace which makes for excellent camping.

The Route

Once you're in **Ancoma**, the route is fairly straightforward. Leave the 4WD track and follow the southern bank of the **Río Quillapituni**

(which eventually becomes the Río Tipuani). At a wide spot called **Llallajta**, 4½ hours from Ancoma, the route crosses a bridge and briefly follows the north bank before re-crossing the river and heading toward Sumata. Another Inca-engineered diversion to the north bank has been destroyed by bridge washouts, forcing a spontaneously constructed, but thankfully brief, detour above the southern bank.

Just past the detour is the village of **Sumata**; just beyond, a trail turns off to the north across the river and heads for **Yani**, which is the start of the Mapiri trail. A short distance further along from the trail junction is **Ocara**. From here, the path goes up the slope – don't follow the river. After 1½ hours you'll reach **Lambromani**, where a local may ask you to pay B$3 per person to pass. You can camp here in the schoolyard.

An hour past Lambromani you'll reach **Wainapata**, where the vegetation grows thicker and more lush. Here, the route splits (to rejoin at Pampa Quillapituni); the upper route is very steep and dangerous, so the lower one is preferable. A short distance along, the lower route passes through an interesting tunnel drilled through the rock. There's a popular myth that it dates from Inca times, but it was actually made with dynamite and likely blasted out early in the 20th century by the Aramayo mining company to improve the access to the Tipuani goldfields. At **Pampa Quillapituni**, 30 minutes beyond, is a favorable campsite. Just east of this, a trail branches off to the right toward Calzada Pass, several days away on the Illampu circuit.

Four hours after crossing the swinging bridge at the **Río Coocó**, you'll reach the little settlement of **Mina Yuna**, where you can pick up basic supplies, and it's possible to camp on the soccer field.

An hour further down is **Chusi**, which is four hours before your first encounter with the road. There's no place to camp here, but you can stay in the school. **Puente Nairapi**, over the Río Grande de Yavia, is a good place for a swim to take the edge off the increasing heat.

Once you reach the road, the scene grows increasingly depressing. For a final look at relatively unaffected landscape, follow the shortcut trail, which begins with a steep **Inca staircase** and winds up at **Baja Llipi** and

THE CORDILLERAS & YUNGAS

the **Puente de Tora** toll bridge (B$2) over the **Río Santa Ana**.

After crossing the bridge, climb up the hill and hope for a *camioneta* or 4WD to take you to **Tipuani** and **Guanay**. *Camionetas* between the Río Santa Ana bridge and **Unutuluni** cost B$5 per person; to continue on to Tipuani or Guanay costs an additional B$15.

You can pick up basic supplies at Ancoma, Wainapata, Mina Yuna, Chusi and Llipi, as well as at all the lower settlements along the road. Spartan accommodations may be found in Unutuluni, Chima (rough-and-ready and not recommended), Tipuani and Guanay, all of which are along the road.

MAPIRI TRAIL

A longer and more adventurous alternative to the El Camino del Oro trek is the six- to seven-day pre-Hispanic Mapiri trail, which was upgraded 100 years ago by the Richter family in Sorata to connect their headquarters with the *cinchona* (quinine) plantations of the upper Amazon Basin.

It's a tough, demanding trek with a lot of physical exertion besides mere walking – expect to clamber over and under logs, hack at vegetation with a machete, get assaulted by insects and destroy formerly decent clothing! That said, it's an amazing experience; the nature is unspoiled, and for the large part you are out on your own miles from any roads or villages.

While the trailhead is technically at the village of Ingenio, you can also begin this unspoiled route by climbing from Sorata over the 4658m Abra Chuchu, then ascending and descending through the open grassy flanks of the Illampu massif to Ingenio. For the next three days it descends along one long ridge through grassland, dense cloud forest and *pampa* to the village of Mapiri. With the Sorata approach, the entire route takes anywhere from six to eight days, depending on the weather, your fitness and whether you reach the trailhead at Ingenio on foot or by motor vehicle.

An excellent side-trip before you get started will take you from Ingenio up to the lovely and medieval, cloud-wrapped village of Yani, where there's a basic *alojamiento*. Bolivia doesn't get much more enigmatic than this and adventurers won't regret a visit.

No maps are available for this route, due to government sensitivity on mining issues, and landslides often cause changes to the paths, which in some parts are heavily overgrown – a machete will be necessary. Therefore, it is strongly recommended to take a guide from Sorata (p135). Guides for this trek charge around B$750 per group, and porters are B$500 each. You'll thank yourself for every kilo you're not carrying if you opt for the porter.

Access

The Mapiri trail begins at the village of **Ingenio**, which has basic *alojamientos*. It can be reached either by 4WD from Sorata (around B$350 for five people, three to four hours) or on foot over Abra Chuchu (4658m). For the latter, start at the cemetery in Sorata and follow the track up past the tiny settlements of Manzanani and Huaca Milluni to the larger village of Chillkani, about three hours beyond Sorata. From there you have five hours of fairly relentless climbing of the semiforested slopes to the Abra Chuchu. You'll meet up with the road twisting 4km below the pass.

Shortly after the crest, take the left turn – the route straight on leads to Ancoma and El Camino del Oro trek (p136) – down toward a small lake. This route will take you over Paso Lechasani (4750m) and down past Mina Suerte to Ingenio and the start of the Mapiri trail at 3550m.

The Route

Past Ingenio you'll cross the **Río Yani**. Here the trail starts downstream, but half an hour later it cuts uphill along a side stream; there's a good campsite where it crosses the stream. The path then twists uphill for 1½ hours over a 4000m pass. In the next two hours you'll cross three more ridges, then descend past **Cueva Cóndor**, a cave that is also a good campsite, to a small lake. From the lake the route ascends to **Paso Apacheta Nacional** (3940m), then twists down **El Tornillo**, a corkscrew-like track that drops 150m. In under an hour you'll cross the **Río Mamarani**, where a good campsite is protected by large rocks.

The next campsite lies three hours further along, beside a stream-crossing at the foot of the next big ascent. At the next stream, 30 minutes later (collect water here!), is another campsite. Here the trail climbs a long staircase, then descends into another valley before climbing to the next pass, **Abra**

Nasacara (4000m). At this stage you're on the ridge that dominates most of the Mapiri trail route, with great views of the Illampu massif. For the next three days, you'll follow this ridge up and down, slowly losing altitude and passing through mostly lush jungle vegetation; fill your water bottles at every opportunity. The first water along this stretch is at **Tolapampa**, which also makes a good campsite.

The next stretch passes through thick forest and may require a bit of bush bashing with a machete; plan on getting good and wet from mud and the soaked vegetation. Six hours beyond Abra Nasacara is a very pleasant ridge-top campsite, **Koka Punku**, with water in a shallow pond 50m away. About three hours later, just before a prominent landslide, watch for the water 3m off the track to the right. Four hours and three crests later is the last permanent water source and campsite at **Lagunillas**. An hour later you'll find good (but dry) campsites on the hill, **Alto Palmar**.

From Alto Palmar, the trail tunnels through dense vegetation along the **Cuesta de Amargura** (Bitterness Ridge). After three hours the jungle gives way to merely thick bush. Six hours later you'll reach **Pararaní** (1900m), where there's water (which needs to be purified) in a small pond near the ruins of an old house. An hour later there's a semi-permanent lake, and just beyond it the trail leaves the dense vegetation and issues onto a grassy ridge flanked by thick forest. It's then 4½ hours to **Incapampa**, with a semi-permanent marsh and a campsite. Along this stretch, wildlife is rife – mainly in the form of bees, ants, ticks, flies and mosquitoes, as well as plenty of butterflies.

About three hours beyond Incapampa you'll reach the hamlet of **San José** (1400m), where there's a campsite and a view over the village of Santiago. Water can sometimes be found 300m down to the right of the route. After an open area that's actually an old cemetery, the left fork provides the faster track to Mapiri.

Four to five hours of walking from San José brings you to **Mapiri**, which is visible 1½ hours before you arrive. Here you'll find several decent *alojamientos* (avoid the Alojamiento Sorata) and motorized canoes that race the 80km downstream to **Guanay** (B\$25, three hours), which will seem like

a city after a week of isolation! Boats leave around 9am, but get there an hour earlier to get a place. Alternatively, catch a *camioneta* along the 4WD track first to Santa Rosa (don't attempt to walk as there are two large river crossings), which has a decent *hostal* with a swimming pool, and then 175km uphill back to Sorata (B\$45, 12 hours).

GUANAY

Isolated Guanay makes a good base for visits to the gold-mining operations along the Ríos Mapiri and Tipuani. If you can excuse the utter rape of the landscape for the sake of gold, chatting with the down-to-earth miners and *barranquilleros* (panners) can make for a particularly interesting experience. This area and points upriver are frontier territory that are reminiscent of the USA's legendary Old West.

A block downhill from the plaza, **Hotel Pahuichi** (r per person B\$30) is fairly primitive but probably offers the best value in town, and it also boasts Guanay's best and most popular restaurant.

A good alternative to Pahuichi (and right next door) is **Hotel Minero** (r per person B\$30).

Getting There & Away

For information on walking routes from Sorata, see El Camino del Oro (p135) and Mapiri trek (opposite) descriptions.

BOAT

Access to the mining areas is by 4WD along the Llipi road, or by motorized dugout canoes up the Río Mapiri. Boats to Mapiri leave daily at 9am (B\$30, four hours) from Puerto Mapiri when the river is high enough. The exhilarating three-hour downstream run back to Guanay costs B\$25. Charter boats take travelers to Rurre, but these are pricey (B\$2500 for a 10- to 15-person boat, 10 hours). Stock up on equipment and food. Some agencies in La Paz offer this trip (p74 and p351 for agency listings).

BUS

The bus offices are all around the plaza, but buses actually depart from a block away toward the river. Four companies offer daily runs to and from La Paz via Caranavi and Yolosita (B\$5, 10 hours). Departures in La Paz are from along Av Las Americas daily at 9am, 10:30am and 1:30pm (noon on

Sunday). For Coroico, get off at Yolosita and catch a lift up the hill.

AUCAPATA & ISKANWAYA
elevation 2850m

The tiny, remote village of **Aucapata** is truly an undiscovered gem. Perched on a ledge, on the shoulder of a dramatic peak, it's a great place to hole up for a couple of days' reading, hiking and relaxing. While most of Aucapata's very few visitors want to see Iskanwaya – somewhat optimistically dubbed 'Bolivia's Machu Picchu' – they may well take one look at the 1500m descent to the ruins (and the corresponding climb back up) and seek out the small Iskanwaya museum in the village itself, which contains artifacts from the site. Admission is free but donations are expected.

The major but near-forgotten ruins of **Iskanwaya**, on the western slopes of the Cordillera Real, sit in a cactus-filled canyon, perched 250m above the Río Llica. Thought to date from between 1145 and 1425, the site is attributed to the Mollu culture.

While Iskanwaya isn't exactly another Machu Picchu, the 13-hectare site is outwardly more impressive than Tiwanaku. This large city-citadel was built on two platforms and flanked by agricultural terraces and networks of irrigation canals. It contains more than 70 buildings, plus delicate walls, narrow streets, small plazas, storerooms, burial sites and niches.

For more information ask around Acuapata for Señor Jorge Albarracín, who is passionate about the area and the Iskanwaya ruins, or Marcelo Calamani, who can guide you to the ruins and speaks a little English. You can get in touch with them on the village telephone (☎ 213-5519). For background reading, *Iskanwaya: La Ciudadela que Sólo Vivía de Noche,* by Hugo Boero Roja (1992), contains photos, maps and diagrams of the site, plus information on nearby villages.

Sleeping & Eating

Hotel Iskanwaya (r per person with bathroom B$35) Aucapata's one smart-looking, little hotel has clean rooms and hot showers. There is no phone, but you can try to reserve a room via the village Entel point (☎ 213-5519).

There's also a small **alojamiento** (r per person B$15) behind the church. For meals

there's only a small eatery on the corner of the plaza where you'll get whatever happens to be available. Be sure to bring small change or you're likely to clean out the town!

Getting There & Away

Aucapata lies about 20km northeast of Quiabaya and 50km northwest of Sorata, but is most easily reached from La Paz. A **Trans Provincia del Norte** (☎ 238-2239) bus departs at 5am from Reyes Cardona in the cemetery district of La Paz every Tuesday and Friday (B$35, 10 hours). You might have better luck getting transportation from more accessible Charazani, or getting off at the *cruce* (turnoff) for Aucapata, but don't bank on it.

There's also rather difficult access from Sorata, which involves a four-day hike via Payayunga. Guides are available from Sorata Guides & Porters (p135). One other access route, which is quite challenging and very interesting, is a little-known trek from the village of Amarete, in the Cordillera Apolobamba. A guide is essential; you may be able to hire one by asking around Amarete, Curva or Charazani. Note that there's no accurate map of the area, and in the rainy season hiking is dangerous on the exposed routes in the region and not recommended.

CARANAVI
elevation 976m

All buses between La Paz and the lowlands pass through uninspiring Caranavi, a bare-brick town midway between Coroico and Guanay that could do with a lick of paint. Travelers love to knock this place, but it doesn't deserve their scorn. If you're passing time here, take a look at the **Untucala suspension bridge**, which spans a crossing used since Inca times.

Caranavi has several inexpensive hotels, all near the highway. **Hotel Landivar** (☎ 823-2052; Calama 15; r per person B$50; ☒) is one of the better ones and has a pleasant pool. More sophisticated is the recommended **Hostal Caturra Inn** (☎ 823-2209; www.hostalcaturra.cjb.net, in Spanish; s/d US$120/180; ☒), which has hot showers, fans, lovely gardens, a good restaurant and a clean pool – a really unexpected treat if you've just climbed out of a dusty bus.

CORDILLERA REAL

Bolivia's Royal Range has more than 600 peaks over 5000m, most of which are relatively accessible and many of which are just a few hours' drive from the nation's capital. They're also still free of the growing bureaucracy attached to climbing and trekking in the Himalayas. The following section is a rundown of the more popular climbs in the Cordillera Real, but it is by no means an exhaustive list. There are many other peaks to entice the experienced climber, and whether you choose one of those described here or one of the lesser known, climbing in the Bolivian Andes is always an adventure.

The best season for climbing in the Cordillera Real is May to September. Note that most of the climbs described here are technical and require climbing experience, a reputable climbing guide and proper technical equipment. You should be fully acclimatized to the altitude before attempting any of these ascents. For information on Bolivian mountaineering, see p54. A good website to consult is www.andeshandbook .org; it offers route information on several of the peaks in the Cordillera Real in Spanish. Or ask at the tourist office in La Paz (p66) for a free copy of *Nuestras Montañas*, written by local mountaineering guides.

Guides & Equipment

By far the easiest way of tackling these mountains is to go on a guided climb. Several La Paz agencies offer trips that include transportation, *refugio* (mountain hut) accommodations, equipment hire and a guide. Some of the same agencies will rent you equipment on its own if you want to tackle the peaks without taking the tour but this option should only be considered by those with extensive mountaineering experience at similar altitudes. Prices start at around B$800 for an ascent of Huayna Potosí, but are significantly higher for the more technical climbs – say, B$3000-plus for Illimani. Several agencies and foreign climbing-tour agents offer packages that combine ascents of several of the Cordillera Real peaks. See p350 for more information. Choose your tour agent carefully; cheaper does not mean better.

You can also contract a guide independently. The **Asociación de Guías de Montaña** (☎ 214-7951; www.agmtb.org; Edificio Doryan, Sagárnaga 189, La Paz) is an association of registered mountain guides. If you are in a group, it's worth paying extra to make sure that there are two guides accompanying you, so that if one member of the group succumbs to altitude sickness the ascent isn't compromised.

HUAYNA POTOSÍ

This is Bolivia's most popular major peak because of its imposing beauty and ease of access, as well as the fact that it's 88m over the magic 6000m figure (but 26ft under the magic 20,000ft figure). There are a number of routes to the top; the one described below is the North Peak route, the most popular with visitors and tour companies. It's appealing because it can be climbed by beginners with a competent guide and technical equipment. Beginners yes, but fit beginners; it's quite steep toward the end and it's a tough climb.

Though some people attempt to climb Huayna Potosí in one day, it is not recommended. It's a 1500m vertical climb from Paso Zongo (the trailhead, and a mountain pass, situated at 4700m) and a 2500m vertical altitude gain from La Paz to the summit. To ascend in one day would pose a great risk of potentially fatal cerebral edema. It's far more sensible to spend a night at the trailhead, head up to the base camp (5200m) the next day, then make your attempt on the summit that next night.

There are two *refugios* in the Paso Zongo area; the better-equipped is **Huayna Potosí Refugio** (☎ in La Paz 2-245-6717; dm low/high season incl breakfast B$50/70). Run by a La Paz tour company, it's a comfortable, heated spot and a fine place to acclimatize – there's pretty walking to be done hereabouts and plenty of advice and good cheer. Reserve ahead. The other, **Refugio San Calixto** (Casa Blanca; dm B$40), is right by the La Paz–Zongo road (buses will let you off outside) and is a simpler, but very hospitable spot. You can also camp here. Transportation to the *refugios*, guides, rations and porters can be arranged through most La Paz tour agencies.

Access

A 4WD from La Paz to the trailhead at Paso Zongo costs around B$500 for up to five people. A taxi should be a bit less with haggling – make sure your driver knows the way. Daily Trans Zongo buses leave at 6am from Plaza Ballivián in El Alto (B$13, two hours).

As Huayna Potosí is so popular, lots of climbers are headed out that way during the climbing season. If you only want a lift, check with specialist climbing agencies. Someone will probably have a 4WD going on the day you want, and you can share costs for the trip.

The Route

From the Refugio Huayna Potosí, cross the dam and follow the aqueduct until you reach the third path on your left signed 'Glacier Huayna Potoś.' Take this path to a glacial stream then through and across the rocks to reach the ridge of a moraine. Near the end of the moraine descend slightly to your right and then ascend the steep scree gullies. At the top, bear left and follow the cairns to reach the **Campo Rocas Glacier** (5200m). There's a hut to sleep in, and dry places to camp. Most tours stop here for the night, before commencing the ascent at around 2am. Other people choose to continue to Campo Argentino.

The glacier is crevassed, especially after July, so rope up while crossing it. Ascend the initial slopes then follow a long, gradually ascending traverse to the right, before turning left and climbing steeply to a flat area between 5500m and 5700m known as **Campo Argentino**. It will take you about four hours to reach this point. Camp on the right of the path, but note that the area further to the right is heavily crevassed, especially later in the season.

The following morning you should leave from here between 4am and 6am. Follow the path/trench out of Campo Argentino, and head uphill to your right until you join a ridge. Turn left here and cross a flat stretch to reach the steep and exposed **Polish Ridge** (named in honor of the Pole who fell off it and died while soloing in 1994). Here you cross a series of rolling glacial hills and crevasses to arrive below the summit face. Either climb straight up the face to the summit or cross along the base of it to join the ridge that rises to the left. This ridge provides thrilling views down the 1000m-high west face. Either route will bring you to the summit in five to seven hours from Campo Argentino.

The descent to Campo Argentino from the summit takes a couple of hours; from there, it's another three hours or so back to the *refugio* at Paso Zongo.

ILLIMANI

Illimani, the 6438m giant overlooking La Paz, was first climbed in 1898 by a party led by WM Conway, a pioneer 19th-century alpinist. Although it's not a difficult climb technically, the combination of altitude and ice conditions warrants serious consideration and caution. Technical equipment is essential above the snow line; caution is especially needed on the exposed section immediately above Nido de Cóndores where several climbers have perished.

Access

The easiest way to reach the first Illimani camp, **Puente Roto**, is via Estancia Unni, a three-hour trip by 4WD from La Paz (about B$850). From there, it's three to four hours' walk to Puente Roto. At **Estancia Unni** you can hire porters and mules for around B$150 to carry your gear to Puente Roto or to the high camp at Nido de Cóndores. It is a wise investment.

A daily 5am bus (B$10) goes from near La Paz's Mercado Rodríguez to the village of **Quilihuaya**, from where you'll have a two-hour slog to Estancia Unni – complete with a 400m elevation gain. Buses return from Quilihuaya to La Paz several days a week at around 8:30am, but if you're relying on public transportation you should carry extra food just in case.

An alternative route to the base camp is via **Cohoni**. Buses and *camiones* leave La Paz for Cohoni (B$30, five hours) in the early afternoon Monday to Saturday from the corner of General Luis Lara and Calle Boquerón. They leave Cohoni to return to La Paz around 8:30am and may take anywhere from five hours to all day depending on which route is followed.

The Route

The normal route to Pico Sur, the highest of Illimani's five summits, is straightforward but heavily crevassed. If you don't have technical glacier experience, hire a competent professional guide.

The route to **Nido de Cóndores**, a rock platform beside the glacier, is a four- to six-hour slog up a rock ridge from Puente Roto. There's no water at Nido de Cóndores, so you'll have to melt snow – bring sufficient stove fuel.

From Nido de Cóndores you need to set off at about 2am. Follow the path in the snow leading uphill from the camp; the path grows narrower and steeper, then flattens out a bit before becoming steeper again. It then crosses a series of crevasses before ascending to the right to reach a level section. From here, aim for the large break in the skyline to the left of the summit, taking care to avoid the two major crevasses, and cross one steep section that is iced over from July onwards. After you pass through the skyline break, turn right and continue up onto the summit ridge. The final three vertical meters involve walking 400m along the ridge at over 6400m elevation.

Plan on six to 10 hours for the climb from Nido de Cóndores to the summit and three to four hours to descend back to camp.

If possible continue down from Nido de Cóndores to Puente Roto on the same day. The 1000m descent is not appreciated after a long day, but your body will thank you the following day and will recover more quickly at the lower altitude. You'll also avoid having to melt snow for a second night.

On the fourth day you can walk from Puente Roto back out to Estancia Unni in about two to three hours.

CONDORIRI MASSIF

The massif known as Condoriri is actually a cluster of 13 peaks ranging in height from 5100m to 5648m. The highest of these is **Cabeza del Cóndor** (Head of the Condor), which has twin winglike ridges flowing from either side of the summit pyramid. Known as Las Alas (The Wings), these ridges cause the peak to resemble a condor lifting its wings on takeoff. According to local legend, the massif is the last refuge of the biggest and most ferocious condors in the Andes, which kidnap children and educate them to become 'man-condors' and then return them to the human population to bring terror and death.

Cabeza del Cóndor is a challenging climb following an exposed ridge, and should be attempted only by experienced climbers. However, a number of other peaks in the Condoriri Massif, including the beautiful Pequeño Alpamayo, can be attempted by beginners with a competent guide.

Access

There is no public transportation from La Paz to Condoriri. A 4WD to the start of the walk-in at the dam at **Laguna Tuni** costs around B$550. If you don't want to use a 4WD transfer, you can trek the 24km from Milluni to the Laguna Tuni dam on the road to Paso Zongo. Take everything you will need with you as there is nowhere to buy provisions once you begin the trek.

It isn't possible to drive beyond the dam because there's a locked gate across the road. Some drivers know a way around it, but if you need to hire pack animals you'll have to do so before you reach the dam. Locals charge B$50 per day for mules, and a bit less for llamas, which can carry less. You also might have to sign into the Parque Nacional Condoriri.

From Laguna Tuni, a rough road circles south around the lake and continues up a drainage trending north. Once you're in this valley, you'll have a view of the Cabeza del Cóndor and Las Alas.

The Route

From the end of the road, follow the obvious paths up along the right side of the valley until you reach a large lake, **Chiar Khota**. Follow the right shore of the lake to arrive at the **base camp**, which is an easy three hours from Laguna Tuni.

Leave base camp at about 8am and follow the path up the north-trending valley through boulders and up the slope of a moraine. Bear to the left here and descend slightly to reach the flat part of the glacier above the seriously crevassed section. You should reach this point in about 1½ hours from base camp.

Here you should rope up and put on crampons. Head left across the glacier before rising to the col (lowest point of the ridge), taking care to avoid the crevasses. Climb to the right up the rock-topped summit **Tarija** (5240m), which affords impressive views of Pequeño Alpamayo, before dropping down a scree and rock slope to rejoin a glacier on the other side. From there, either climb directly up the ridge to the summit or follow a climbing traverse to the left before cutting back to the right and up to the summit. The summit ridge is very exposed.

ANCOHUMA

Ancohuma is the highest peak in the Sorata Massif, towering on the remote northern edge of the Cordillera Real. It was not climbed until 1919 and remains a challenging climb.

For a long time, various sources put Ancohuma at around 7000m, which would have made it higher than Argentina's Aconcagua, but in 2002 an American student lugged GPS equipment to the top and determined that its true height is 6427m, a few meters short of Bolivia's highest mountain, Sajama.

Access

The peak is accessed via Sorata from where it is possible to rent a 4WD for the long traverse to **Cocoyo**. More convenient is hiring a 4WD all the way from La Paz to Cocoyo, but it is also considerably more expensive. If you have a serious amount of gear, you can rent a mule train to carry it from Sorata to base camp, which is in the lake basin east of the peaks at about 4500m. Plan on at least two days for these various transportation arrangements to get you to the lakes. Alternatively, Ancohuma can be climbed from the west, using **Laguna Glacial** as a base camp. Further advice and information is available in Sorata (p134).

The Routes

From the lakes head west up to the glacier following the drainage up through loose moraine. Make camp below the north ridge, the normal route. After a circuitous path through a crevasse field, a steep pitch or two of ice will gain the north ridge. An exposed but fairly easy ridge walk will take you to the summit.

If you have opted for the more easily accessed western route, hike from Sorata to the base camp at Laguna Glacial. From here the route climbs the obvious moraine and then ascends the glacier, over fields of extremely dangerous crevasses to a bivouac at 5800m. It then climbs to the *bergschrund* (crevasse) and across a relatively level ice plateau to the summit pyramid. This is most easily climbed via the north ridge; the first part is quite steep and icy, but then gets easier toward the summit.

CORDILLERA APOLOBAMBA

The remote Cordillera Apolobamba, flush against the Peruvian border north of Lake Titicaca, is becoming a popular hiking, trekking and climbing venue. Mountaineers in particular will find a wonderland of tempting peaks, first ascents and new routes to discover, and the trek from Lagunillas to Agua Blanca – with magnificent Andean landscapes – is one of the most memorable in the country.

While access is improving, it must be emphasized that this is an isolated region, and far from set up for tourism. There are few services, transportation isn't reliable and the people maintain a fragile traditional lifestyle. Comparatively few locals – mostly men – speak more than rudimentary Spanish. Sensitivity to the local sentiments of this highly traditional Aymará- and Quechua-speaking area will help keep its distinctive character intact.

Every town and village in the region holds an annual festival, most of which fall between June and September. The **Fiesta de La Virgen de las Nieves**, one of the best, takes place in Italaque, northeast of Escoma, around August 5. It features a potpourri of traditional Andean dances.

CHARAZANI

pop 605 / elevation 3250m

Charazani is the administrative and commercial center and transportation axis of Bautista Saavedra province, and by far the largest town in the area. You can hike from here to the trailhead for the Lagunillas–Agua Blanca trek. Services in Charazani have increased exponentially in recent years, and several NGOs are working in the area on sustainable development projects, including solar power, textile production and the promotion of responsible tourism. It's a relaxed spot to visit, and weary hikers will enjoy the hot springs.

Two fiestas are held in Charazani; the biggest takes place around July 16 and the smaller one around August 6. There's also a wonderful children's dance festival (around November 16) in honor of the Virgen del Carmen, an invocation of the Virgin Mary.

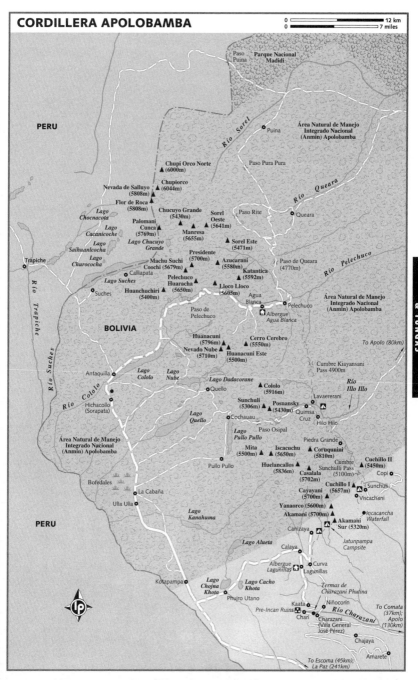

CORDILLERA APOLOBAMBA

0 ————————— 12 km
0 ————————— 7 miles

PERU

Parque Nacional
Madidi

Paso
Puina

Río Sorel

Puina

Área Natural de Manejo
Integrado Nacional
(Anmin) Apolobamba

Paso Pura Pura

Río Queara

Chupi Orco Norte
▲ (6000m)

Chupiorco
▲ (6044m)

Nevada de Salluyo
(5808m)

Queara

Flor de Roca
(5808m)

Chucuyo Grande
(5430m)

Sorel
Oeste
(5641m)

Paso Rite

Lago
Chocnacota

Palomani
Cunca
(5769m)

Manresa
(5655m)

Sorel Este
(5471m)

Lago
Cacanicoche

Lago Chucuyo
Grande

Lago
Saihuanlcocha

Presidente
(5700m)

Azucarani
(5580m)

Paso de Queara
(4770m)

Río Pelechuco

Lago
Churococha

Machu Suchi
Coochi (5679m)

Katantica
▲ (5592m)

Trapiche

Calliapata

Pelechuco
Huaracha
(5650m)

Lloco Lloco
(5605m)

Área Natural de Manejo
Integrado Nacional
(Anmin) Apolobamba

Lago Suches

Huanchuchiri
(5400m)

Agua
Blanca

Suches

Pelechuco

Río Trapiche

Paso de
Pelechuco

Albergue
Agua Blanca

BOLIVIA

Huanacuni
(5796m)

Cerro Cerebro
(5550m)

To Apolo (80km)

Nevado Nube ▲
(5710m)

Huanacuni Este
(5500m)

Cumbre Kiayansani
Pass 4900m

Antaquilla

Lago
Cololo

Lago
Nube

Lago Dadacorane

Cololo
(5916m)

Río
Illo Illo

Río
Cololo

Quello

Lavaererani

Hichacollo
(Sorapata)

Sunchuli
(5306m)

Posnansky
(5430m)

Quimsa
Cruz

Lago
Quello

Cochauau

Hilo Hilo

Lago
Pullo Pullo

Paso Osipal

Piedra Grande

Área Natural de Manejo
Integrado Nacional
(Anmin) Apolobamba

Mita
(5500m)

Iscacuchu
(5650m)

Corquinini
(5810m)

Cumbre
Sunchulli Pass
(5100m)

Cuchillo II
(5450m)

Pullo Pullo

Huelancallos
(5836m)

Casalala
(5702m)

Copi

Bofedales

Cuchillo I
(5657m)

Sunchuli

Cayayani
(5700m)

Viscachani

La Cabaña

Yanaorco (5600m)

Inqacancha
Waterfall

Ulla Ulla

Akamani (5700m)

Akamani
Sur (5320m)

PERU

Cañizaya

Lago Alueta

Calaya

Jatunpampa
Campsite

Albergue
Lagunillas

Curva
Lagunillas

Lago
Kanahuma

Termas de
Charazani Phutina

Kotapampa

Lago
Chojna
Khota

Lago Cacho
Khota

Niñocorin

To Comata
(37km);
Apolo
(130km)

Phujro Utano

Kaata

Pre-Incan Ruins

Río Charazani

Chari

Charazani
(Vila General
José Pérez)

Chajaya

To Escoma (45km);
La Paz (241km)

Amarete

Information

There are telephones at the **Transportes Altiplano** (☎ 213-7439) office on the plaza and in the **alcaldía** (town hall; ☎ 213-7282), a block below the plaza. There is no ATM in town; ask at your hotel for local moneychangers. If you happen to find it open, the public Nawiriywasi Library has books on medicinal plants and the Kallawaya culture, and maps and information for hikers, trekkers and climbers. Market day is Sunday.

Sights & Activities

Along the river, about 10 minutes' walk upstream from town, you'll pass the **Termas de Charazani Phutina** (admission B$5; ☉ 7am-9pm, closed Mon to 2pm for cleaning), a hot-springs complex where you can bathe and enjoy a hot shower. Other natural **thermal baths**, complete with a steaming hot waterfall, can be found a two-hour hike away down the valley from Charazani along the Apolo road alongside the Río Kamata. It's a lovely spot.

The traditional Kallawaya village of **Chari**, 1½ hours' walk from Charazani, is a blend of terraces, flowers and vegetable gardens. A German anthropologist started the Tuwans textile project, which is designed to market the local hand-dyed weavings. The town is also home to a **Kallawaya cultural museum**, a stone and thatch structure with exhibits pertaining to medicinal plants and textile arts. About an hour's walk outside the village are some **pre-Incan ruins**, reached by walking through town and turning left at the enormous boulder that creates a small cave. Follow this path to the cemetery, keep left until you gain the ridge, then continue 200m up to the ruins. Because of local suspicion it's best to advise locals where you're headed before setting off.

Sleeping & Eating

Accommodations are basic no matter where you look. These are relatively comfortable options.

Hotel Charazani (r per person B$20) Just off the plaza on the Curva road, this two-room hotel is on your right. It's fairly basic but offers a fabulous view over the valley, and, crucially, quicker access to *dueña* (proprietor) doña Sofia's fine Bolivian cooking.

Hotel Akhamani (r per person B$20, apt B$40) A block below the plaza, Hotel Akhamani has the highest standards and the widest variety of options, including a four-bed mini-apartment with a private bathroom and small kitchen.

Residencial Inti Wasi (r per person B$25) This place is near the Hotel Akhamani and is arranged around a traditional cobbled courtyard that provides a pleasant atmosphere.

Several *pensiones* around the plaza offer soup, a main course and bad coffee for under B$10. The efficient but quick-tempered doña Sofia (above), serves *almuerzos* at 12:30pm sharp and *cenas* (dinners) at 6pm or 7pm; reserve early, don't arrive late, stay humble and clean your plate. After dark follow your nose just off the plaza to **Tu Esnack Kiosko**, which lives up to its name with greasy, esnackalicious *pollo al broaster* (fried chicken).

Essentials can be purchased at *tiendas* (small, family-run shops) surrounding the plaza. Trekkers, however, are advised to bring their supplies from La Paz.

Getting There & Away

From La Paz (B$25), **Trans Provincia del Norte** (☎ in La Paz 2-238-2239) and the more reliable **Trans Altiplano** (☎ in La Paz 2-238-0859) depart daily at 6am from Calle Reyes Cardona in the cemetery district. The services take six to eight hours and return from Charazani daily at 6pm. Book tickets in advance.

From Charazani, a 4WD route winds down to the Yungas village of Apolo at the edge of the Amazon Basin, where you can stay overnight at the monastery. The route is frequently negotiated by *camiones* during the dry season, but several serious stream crossings and landslide risks mean it's best suited to mountain bikes or foot traffic in the wet.

ÁREA NATURAL DE MANEJO INTEGRADO NACIONAL (ANMIN) APOLOBAMBA

In the late 1990s the Reserva Nacional de Fauna Ulla Ulla was renamed the Área Natural de Manejo Integrado Nacional (Anmin) Apolobamba and was expanded by nearly 300,000 hectares to 484,000 hectares. It now includes the entire Cordillera Apolobamba and most of the renowned Lagunillas to Agua Blanca trek (opposite) along the range's eastern slopes. At its northern end it abuts Parque Nacional Madidi to form one of the western hemisphere's most extensive protected areas.

The original park – a loosely defined vicuña reserve along the Peruvian border – was established in 1972, and was upgraded in 1997 in Unesco's 'Man and Biosphere Reserve Program.' Later that same year the Instituto Nacional de Fomento Lanero (Infol) was created to represent wool producers and was charged with researching, monitoring and preventing habitat degradation of the reserve's camelids. Infol morphed into the Instituto Boliviano de Tecnología Agropecuaria (IBTA), which focuses more on agricultural development and social services.

The modern park is home to several thousand alpacas and vicuñas, and also to Bolivia's densest condor population. In addition to the popular hiking routes, you'll find excellent wild trekking around Lagos Cololo, Nube, Quello, Kanahuma and Pullo Pullo, all of which enjoy snow-covered backdrops and rich waterbird populations, including flamingoes and several species of Andean geese.

Information

A team of park rangers roams between several far-flung Casas de Guardaparques, which are all linked via radio communication but infrequently staffed during the daytime. For pre-departure information contact Servicio Nacional de Áreas Protegidas (SERNAP, p63) in La Paz. In an emergency contact them by radio on frequency 8335 USB.

The village of Curva (3780m) has a few basic stores, and at nearby Lagunillas is the Museo Interpretativo Center, which provides limited local information and an exhibition on the Kallawaya traditions. As part of the same project, Agua Blanca has a small museum and weaving workshop. Curva's main festival is a colorful affair that takes place on June 29.

Sleeping & Eating

Noncampers can normally find accommodations in local homes for B$20 per person *más o menos* (more or less) – just ask around. The biggest *tienda* is in Ulla Ulla. At La Cabaña, 5km from Ulla Ulla village, IBTA has a small hostel where you may be able to stay, but it's suggested that you reserve via SERNAP in La Paz (p63).

The best accommodations in the area are two associated *albergues* at **Lagunillas** (☎ 213-37439; per person B$25) and **Agua Blanca** (☎ 872-0140; per person B$25, with meals B$65). They offer dorm beds, hot showers, kitchen facilities and a fireplace in a modern building. Reserve ahead, or hunt around to find the keeper of the keys. There are ranger stations at Antaquilla, Charazani, Curva, Kotapampa, Pelechuco, Pullo Pullo, Suches and Hichacollo; the last three were designed by a La Paz architect and blend adobe construction, domed thatched roofs and passive solar walls to reflect both modern and traditional styles.

Hikers can camp at any of these sites or stay inside – sufficient space and your Spanish skills permitting.

LAGUNILLAS TO AGUA BLANCA (CURVA TO PELECHUCO) TREK

This fantastic four- to five-day hike (45km) passes through splendid and largely uninhabited wilderness. The track stays mostly above 4000m and includes five high passes. There's arguably no better scenery in the Andes, and along the way you're sure to see llamas and alpacas, as well as more elusive Andean wildlife, such as viscachas, vicuñas, condors and perhaps even a spectacled bear. (The Wildlife Conservation Society runs a bear research center five hours on foot from Pelechuco, where a couple of bears have been tagged and are occasionally observed.)

The trek may be done in either direction, as both ends have relatively reliable – albeit limited – public transportation links with La Paz. Most people do the route from south to north, but starting in Agua Blanca would mean an additional day of downhill walking and could include a grand finale at Charazani's hot springs. The trail is pre-Columbian and was built on a stone platform, with some areas still having cobbled paving up to 2m wide.

It is strongly recommended that you hire a guide and pack animals for the trek – no reliable maps of the region exist. Clients must often carry their own food and stove, and are also often expected to provide meals for their guides, porters and muleteers. Bring enough food for a week, preferably from La Paz, as Curva and Pelechuco have only basics at inflated prices.

Access

Trans Altiplano (☎ in La Paz 2-238-0859) runs daily buses to Lagunillas from La Paz. They leave from Reyes Cardona in the cemetery district in the early hours of the morning. **Trans Norte** (☎ in La Paz 2-238-2239) runs a daily service to Agua Blanca and Pelechuco from El Alto (at the ex-*tranca* Río Seco) at 6am (B$35, 12 hours). The bus may stop en route – depending on the driver's mood – at the market in Huancasaya on the Peruvian border, before continuing to Ulla Ulla, Agua Blanca and Pelechuco. Buses return at odd hours so check the schedules before leaving La Paz, as they change often. At the time of writing, the return from Agua Blanca departed between 3am and 4am. See p146 for services to Charazani.

A more expensive but considerably easier and more comfortable way to go is by 4WD. A vehicle and driver from La Paz to Lagunillas (B$2100, seven hours) or Agua Blanca (B$2500, 10 hours) may be worthwhile because it allows daylight travel through the incomparable scenery. Alternatively, you can pay to leave the logistics to someone else and do the trek with an agency (p74).

The Route

Because most people do the trek from south to north – from Lagunillas (also known as Tilinhuaya) to Agua Blanca – that's how it's described here. If you want to start from **Charazani**, you can either follow the long and winding road for four to five hours or take the 3½- to four-hour shortcut. Cross the river at the thermal baths, then climb the other bank and head back to the road. After about an hour you should follow a path that climbs to a white-and-yellow church on your left. Beyond the church, descend the other side of the hill, to just above the community of **Niñocorín**. After a short distance you'll strike an obvious path; turn left onto it and follow it as it contours through the fields and then descends to cross a river, where it starts the steep climb into Curva.

Most people choose to start in **Lagunillas**, with its pretty lake bristling with waterbirds. The *albergue* here (p147) can arrange beasts of burden and guides. From here, it's a short walk to the village of **Curva**, center of the Kallawaya community. From Curva, head toward the cross on the hill

north of the village and skirt around the right side of the hill. About an hour out of Curva, you'll go across a stream. Continue uphill along the right bank of the stream. At a cultivated patch about 200m before the valley descending from the right flank of the snowy peak, cross the stream to join a well-defined path entering from your left. If you continue along this path, you'll reach an excellent flat, streamside campsite. Alternatively, keep following this trail for another 1½ hours to an ideal campsite at **Jatunpampa** (4200m).

From Jatunpampa, head up the valley and across a small plain to the *col* with a cairn, about two hours along. Known as the **Cumbre Tambillo**, this 4700m pass offers fabulous views of Akamani off to the northwest. One to two hours further along you'll arrive at a good campsite (4100m) near the **Incacancha** (aka Incachani) waterfall.

The following morning's zig-zag ascent of the **Akamani Sacred Hill** looks a bit daunting, but it isn't that bad. Cross the bridge below the waterfall and follow the switchbacks up the scree gully. As you ascend, enjoy distant views of Ancohuma and Illampu. After two hours or so you'll reach **Mil Curvas** (4800m), another high pass.

From the pass, traverse gently uphill to the left until you gain the ridge, which affords great views of the Cordillera Real to the south and Cuchillo II to the north. At this point the obvious trail descends past a small lake before arriving at a larger lake with a good view of Akamani.

Climb up to the next ridge before descending an hour to the small mining settlement of **Viscachani**, where you'll strike the 4WD track toward Hilo Hilo (aka Illo Illo). In another hour this road ascends to the **Cumbre Viscachani** pass (4900m), which also provides superb views of the Cordillera Real to the south and the Sunchulli Valley to the north and west.

At the pass the road drops into the valley; at the point where it bears right, look for a path turning off to the left. This will take you to a point above the **Sunchulli gold mine**. From Sunchulli, follow a contour line above the aqueduct for about an hour, until you see an idyllic campsite (4600m) below Cuchillo I.

The fourth day of the hike is probably the finest, as it includes sections that have been used for centuries by miners and *campesinos*. From the campsite, the road ascends for about two hours via a series of switchbacks to the **Cumbre Sunchulli** (5100m) pass. From the pass, you can scramble up to a cairn above the road for excellent views dominated by **Colocolo** (5916m), the southern Cordillera Apolobamba's highest peak.

Descend along the road for a few minutes, then jog right down a steep but obvious path that crosses a stream opposite the glacier lake below Cuchillo II before descending to the valley floor. If you follow the valley floor, you'll rejoin the road a couple of minutes above the picturesque stone-and-thatch village of **Piedra Grande**, three hours from the pass. Camping is possible here.

Follow the road for about an hour, then join the pre-Hispanic road turning off downhill to your right. After you cross a bridge, you should follow the obvious path to the right, leading you up into the village of **Hilo Hilo** in about an hour. Here you'll find small stores selling the basics and it may even be possible to rent a room for the night.

When leaving Hilo Hilo don't be tempted onto the path to the left, which leads west to Ulla Ulla (although this is also a viable trek). The correct route is to the right, leaving the village above the school between the public facilities and the cemetery. From there, cross the llama pastures until the path becomes clear again. After crossing a bridge (about an hour out of town) and beginning up the **Palca Valley** with a sharp rock peak at its head (if it's too overcast to see the rock, look for several small houses on your left and turn there), you'll stumble onto an ideal campsite set in a bend in the valley, where there are a number of large fallen rocks.

From the campsite, head up the valley for about 1½ hours until you reach a bridge over the stream. At this point the route begins to ascend to the **Cumbre Kiayansani** pass (4900m), which you should reach in another 1½ hours. From the pass, descend past a lake, crossing pastures full of llamas, and follow some pre-Columbian paving as well as stone steps cut into the rock that date from the same period. In less than two hours you'll arrive in **Pelechuco**, a

---

THE KALLAWAYA

Originating in six villages around Curva in the Apolobamba region, the Kallawaya are a group of healers who pass ancient traditions down the generations, usually from father to son. Around a quarter of the inhabitants of these villages become involved in the healing tradition, although there are many more people throughout the Andes that pass themselves off as authentic Kallawaya when they are nothing of the kind.

The origins and age of the Kallawaya tradition are unknown, although some Kallawaya claim to be descended from the vanished people of Tiwanaku. The Kallawaya language, however, which is used exclusively for healing, is derived from Quechua, the language of the Incas. Knowledge and skills are passed down through generations, although it's sometimes possible for aspiring healers to study under acknowledged masters.

The early Kallawaya were known for their wanderings and traveled all over the continent in search of medicinal herbs. The most capable of today's practitioners will have memorized the properties and uses of 600 to 1000 different healing herbs, but their practices also involve magic and charms. They believe that sickness and disease are the result of a displaced or imbalanced *ajallu* (life force). The incantations and amulets are intended to encourage it back into a state of equilibrium within the body.

A hallmark of the Kallawaya is the *alforja* (medicine pouch) which is carried by the men. While women don't become healers, they still play an important part in the gathering of herbs.

In Lagunillas, there's a small exhibition about the Kallawaya in the Museo Interpretativo Center. The Kallawaya's legacy has also been recorded by several anthropologists and medical professionals; German university psychiatrist Ina Rössing has produced an immense four-volume work called *El Mundo de los Kallahuaya* about her ongoing research, and Frenchman Louis Girault has compiled an encyclopedia of herbal remedies employed by the Kallawaya, entitled *Kallahuaya, Curanderos Itinerantes de los Andes*.

quaint colonial village founded by Jesuits in 1560.

There are a couple of simple *alojamientos* in Pelechuco, but a 30-minute walk further, passing two intriguing pre-Columbian settlements, takes you to the mining village of **Agua Blanca**, where there's an *albergue* (p147), for a well-deserved rest.

CORDILLERA QUIMSA CRUZ

The Cordillera Quimsa Cruz, although close to La Paz, is a largely undiscovered wilderness of 5000m-plus peaks, some of which have only been climbed for the first time in the last few years. Basque climbing magazine *Pyrenaica* once labeled it a 'South American Karakoram.' In 1999, near the summit of Santa Veracruz, the Spaniard Javier Sánchez discovered the remains of an 800-year-old ceremonial burial site with ancient artifacts and weavings.

The Quimsa Cruz is not a large range – it's only some 50km from end to end – and the peaks are lower than in other Bolivian ranges. The highest peak, Jacha Cuno Collo, rises to 5800m, and the other glaciated peaks range from 4500m to 5300m. Granite peaks, glaciers and lakeside camping make the Quimsa Cruz an unforgettable, untouristed Andean experience. It lies to the southeast of Illimani, separated from the Cordillera Real by the Río La Paz, and geologically speaking it's actually a southern outlier of that range.

The Quimsa Cruz lies at the northern end of Bolivia's tin belt, and tin reserves have been exploited here since the late 1800s. However, with the replacement of tin by plastics and aluminum, the current market prices mean that it is no longer viable to extract it from such remote sites. The few miners who've stayed on and continue to work some of the mines here either take their chances with cooperatives or are employed as caretakers for mining companies who don't want to abandon their holdings, and are presumably hoping for better days. In any case all the major mining areas in the region – which includes every valley along the western face of the Quimsa Cruz – are still populated.

ACTIVITIES

The Quimsa Cruz offers some of the finest adventure climbing in all of Bolivia, and in every valley mining roads provide access to the impressively glaciated peaks. Although all of the *nevados* of the Quimsa Cruz have now been climbed, there are still plenty of unclimbed routes, and expeditions are likely to have the mountains to themselves. If you have no previous climbing experience you should take a guide from a La Paz agency (p75) who really knows the area.

Trekking is also possible throughout the range, which is covered by IGM mapping (p63). The main route is the two- to three-day **Mina Viloco to Mina Caracoles trek**, which crosses the range from west to east. Of interest along this route is the renowned site of a 1971 airplane crash, which had already been stripped by local miners before rescue teams arrived at the scene two days later! Mina Viloco is 70km southeast of La Paz, and is centered on what was once quite a major tin mine. Mina Caracoles is still worked by cooperatives, and is 13km northwest of Quime.

Staples are available in both Mina Viloco and Quime, but it's still best to carry everything you'll need (food, fuel and other supplies) from La Paz.

GETTING THERE & AWAY

Road access is relatively easy because of the number of mines in the area, and it's possible to drive to within 30 minutes' walk of some glaciers. Others, however, are up to a four-hour hike from the nearest road. The easiest access is provided by **Flota Trans-Inquisivi** (☎ in La Paz 2-228-4050), which leaves daily in the early morning from La Paz's main bus terminal for the eastern side of the range (to Quime, Inquisivi, Cajuata, Circuato, Suri, Mina Caracoles, and, less often, Yacopampa and Frutillani). **Trans Araca** (☎ in La Paz 2-228-4050) serves the communities and mines on the western side of the range from its office on Av Francisco Carvajal, in Barrio Villa Dolores, El Alto. To Mina Viloco, Araca or Cairoma, a bus departs daily at 7am taking seven to 10 hours.

Those with a bit more ready cash can rent a 4WD and driver for the five- to seven-hour journey (expect to pay at least B$1000); any of the services used by mountaineers and trekkers can organize the trip.

THE CORDILLERAS & YUNGAS

Southern Altiplano

The harsh, at times almost primeval geography of the Southern Altiplano will tug at the heartstrings of those with a deep love of bleak and solitary places. Stretching southwards from La Paz, it encompasses majestic volcanic peaks, swathes of treeless wilderness and the white emptiness of the *salares,* eerie salt deserts almost devoid of life.

There's something otherworldly about the area, enhanced by shimmering heat hazes, hardy *kiswara* trees and bizarre rock formations. At night, the starscapes are spectacular, and worth enduring the bitter after-dark temperatures for. It can get seriously cold here; the altitude combined with scouring winds and lack of shelter or vegetation can sometimes make traveling here something of an endurance test.

The region has traditionally lived off mining, backed up by agriculture (corn, potatoes, quinoa) and llama herding. Oruro is a mining city par excellence: gritty, honest and straight-talking, where meat, carbohydrates and hard work rule the day. It's well worth a visit, especially during Carnaval, but many travelers only pass through, heading with bated breath for Uyuni and the surreal landscapes of the southwest. This is the domain of the 4WD, in which people head out on multiday adventures into the rugged remote terrain.

Southeast of Uyuni is Tupiza, where the jagged cactus-studded scenery evokes memories of Sergio Leone films and lone gunslingers on fading horses. It's a great place to jump in the saddle yourself. The western associations are further enhanced by Butch Cassidy and the Sundance Kid, whose last stand took place in the remote village of San Vicente.

SOUTHERN ALTIPLANO

HIGHLIGHTS

- Gorge your senses with the almost extraterrestrial landscapes of **Los Lípez** (see p176 and p177) region in the country's extreme southwest

- Explore the **Parque Nacional Sajama** (p163) with its towering snow-coned volcano, Bolivia's loftiest peak

- Strap on some serious sunglasses and wonder at the salty expanse of the **Salar de Uyuni** (p174)

- Marvel at the stunning costumes of Oruro's boisterous **Carnaval** (see boxed text, p157)

- Whistle the theme from your favorite western as you guide your horse up the narrow gullies around **Tupiza** (p180)

Parque Nacional Sajama ★

★ Oruro

★ Salar de Uyuni

Tupiza ★

Los Lípez ★

■ TELEPHONE CODE: 2	■ POPULATION: 623,800	■ ELEVATION: 3500M TO 6542M

SOUTHERN ALTIPLANO

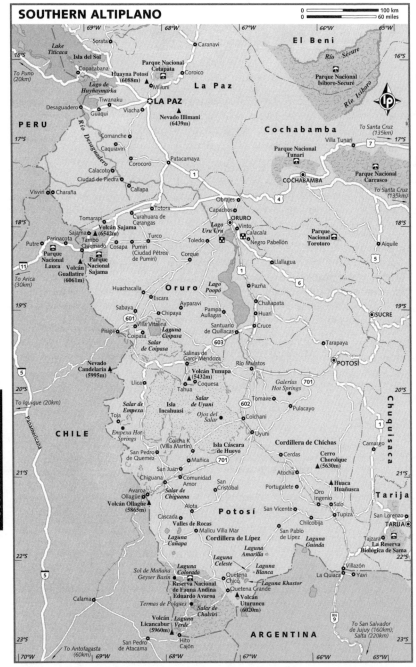

History

The prehistoric Lakes Minchín and Tauca, which once covered most of this highland plateau, evaporated around 10,000 years ago, leaving behind a parched landscape of brackish puddles and salt deserts. Humans haven't left much of a mark on the region; some time in the mid-15th century, the Inca ruler sent his son Tupac Inca Yupanqui southward to conquer all the lands he encountered. Yupanqui and his gang marched on across the wastelands to the northern bank of Chile's Río Maule, where a fierce band of Araucanian people inspired them to stake out the southern boundary of the Inca empire and turn back toward Cuzco.

These days, outside the major towns and cities, most of the people cluster around mining camps. Mining has been fundamental to most of the area, and although many of the major operations closed down in the crisis period of Bolivian mining during the late '80s, miners continue to operate on a local cooperative basis.

Climate

Climatically, the best months to visit are August, September and October, after the worst of the winter chills and before the summer rains. From May to early July, nighttime temperatures combined with stiff winds can lower the wind-chill temperature to -40.5°C. Summer is warmer but, for an arid area, there's quite a lot of rainfall between November and March. At any time of year you'll need protection against sun, wind and cold.

National Parks

Parque Nacional Sajama (p163), Bolivia's first national park, is a region of magnificent peaks, plains and wildlife habitat as well as home to the world's highest forest and some of South America's loftiest hot springs. Even if you're not into superlatives or hardcore mountaineering, an evening dip in the clear springs at the base of Volcán Sajama in the company of a few camelids is worth the trek. The Reserva Nacional de Fauna Andina Eduardo Avaroa (p173) is a highlight of Southwest Circuit tours and the gateway to Chile for those headed for the desert oasis of San Pedro de Atacama.

Getting There & Away

From La Paz, the Southern Altiplano is easily accessed by bus, although off the paved main roads it can be a long and bumpy ride. The route from the central highland cities of Potosí and Sucre is rough on the back, bum and bladder. The overland route from Chile is a scenic mountain traverse on a good road from Arica, and Villazón has an easy border crossing with Argentina.

The train between Oruro and Villazón, which stops in Uyuni and Tupiza, provides a fine overland alternative to grueling bus travel.

ORURO

pop 260,000 / elevation 3706m

By far the largest settlement of the Southern Altiplano, palindromic Oruro is a miners' city with a tough climate. In many ways it's the most Bolivian of Bolivia's nine provincial capitals, an intriguing place where 90% of the inhabitants are of pure indigenous heritage. Locals refer to themselves as *quirquinchos* (armadillos), after the carapaces used in their *charangos* (traditional Bolivian ukulele-type instruments). *Oruneños* are salty, hard-working and upfront people who have had it tough over the years with the decline of Bolivian mining and the extreme climate.

Oruro, whose name means 'where the sun is born,' sits against a range of mineral-rich low hills at the northern end of the salty Lakes Uru Uru and Poopó, linked by river to Titicaca. While many visitors slate Oruro, it's got decent museums and restaurants, and there's plenty to see in the surrounding area. It's also culturally very colorful, with a rich dance and musical heritage that culminates in the riotous Carnaval celebrations, famous throughout South America for the lavish costumes and elaborate traditions on display.

History

Founded in the early 17th century, Oruro owes its existence to the mineral-rich 10-sq-km range of hills rising 350m behind the city. Chock-full of copper, silver and tin, these hills still form the city's economic backbone.

By the 1920s Bolivia's thriving tin-mining industry rested in the hands of three powerful capitalists. The most renowned

ORURO

0   700 m
0   0.4 miles

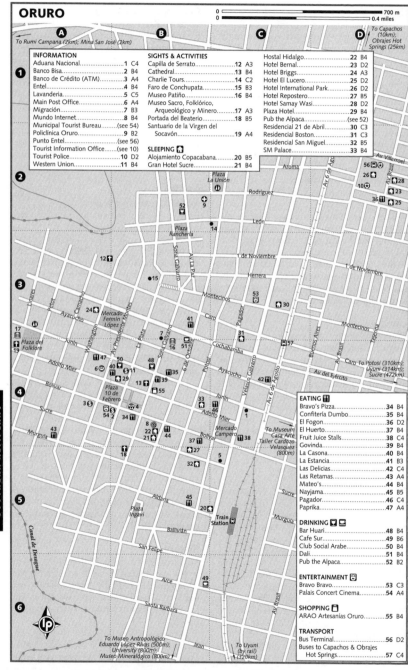

INFORMATION	
Aduana Nacional	1 C4
Banco Bisa	2 B4
Banco de Crédito (ATM)	3 A4
Entel	4 B4
Lavandería	5 C5
Main Post Office	6 A4
Migración	7 B3
Mundo Internet	8 B4
Municipal Tourist Bureau	(see 54)
Policlínica Oruro	9 B2
Punto Entel	(see 56)
Tourist Information Office	(see 10)
Tourist Police	10 D2
Western Union	11 B4

SIGHTS & ACTIVITIES	
Capilla de Serrato	12 A3
Cathedral	13 B4
Charlie Tours	14 C2
Faro de Conchupata	15 B3
Museo Patiño	16 B4
Museo Sacro, Folklórico, Arqueológico y Minero	17 A3
Portada del Beaterio	18 B5
Santuario de la Virgen del Socavón	19 A4

SLEEPING	
Alojamiento Copacabana	20 B5
Gran Hotel Sucre	21 B4

Hostal Hidalgo	22 B4
Hotel Bernal	23 D2
Hotel Briggs	24 A3
Hotel El Lucero	25 D2
Hotel International Park	26 D2
Hotel Repostero	27 B5
Hotel Samay Wasi	28 D2
Plaza Hotel	29 B4
Pub the Alpaca	(see 52)
Residencial 21 de Abril	30 C3
Residencial Boston	31 C3
Residencial San Miguel	32 B5
SM Palace	33 B4

EATING	
Bravo's Pizza	34 B4
Confitería Dumbo	35 B4
El Fogon	36 D2
El Huerto	37 B4
Fruit Juice Stalls	38 C4
Govinda	39 B4
La Casona	40 B4
La Estancia	41 B3
Las Delicias	42 C4
Las Retamas	43 A4
Mateo's	44 B4
Nayjama	45 B5
Pagador	46 C4
Paprika	47 A4

DRINKING	
Bar Huari	48 B4
Cafe Sur	49 B6
Club Social Arabe	50 B4
Dali	51 B4
Pub the Alpaca	52 B2

ENTERTAINMENT	
Bravo Bravo	53 C3
Palais Concert Cinema	54 A4

SHOPPING	
ARAO Artesanías Oruro	55 B4

TRANSPORT	
Bus Terminal	56 D2
Buses to Capachos & Obrajes Hot Springs	57 C4

was Simón Patiño, a mestizo from the Cochabamba valley who became one of the world's wealthiest men. In 1897 Patiño purchased La Salvadora mine near the village of Uncia, east of Oruro, which eventually became the world's most productive tin source. Patiño's fortunes snowballed and by 1924 he had gained control of about 50% of the nation's tin output.

Once secure in his wealth, Patiño emigrated from Bolivia to Britain, where he started buying up European and North American smelters and tin interests. As a consequence, Bolivia found itself exporting both its precious metal and its profits. Public outcry launched a series of labor uprisings, and set the stage for nationalization of the mines in 1952 and the subsequent creation of the government-run Corporación Minera de Bolivia (Comibol).

Decades of government inefficiency, corruption and low world tin prices preceded the push for *capitalización* (a variation on privatization), which eventually brought about the dissolution of Comibol in the mid-1980s. When the last mine had closed in Oruro, it was a hard hit for the city.

The price of tin went up yet again in the early 1990s and a handful of local cooperative mines reopened. Until 2008, tin cost US$19 per pound on the global market and the average monthly salary of a miner was US$3000. In 2008, the price of tin dropped to US$7 per pound, salaries plummeted to US$280, several mines closed down and 1500 miners were out of work. Things have slowly started to look up since, as the Morales government is now seeking investment to reopen some of the mines.

Orureños are extremely proud that Morales is from their province; he was born in Isallavi, a tiny Aymará village on the western side of Lake Poopó, and went to secondary school in Oruro.

Information

EMERGENCY

Tourist police (☎ 528-7774) Round-the-clock operation at the bus terminal; shares the kiosk with the tourist info point and gives out maps.

IMMIGRATION

Migración (☎ 527-0239; S Galvarro, btwn Ayacucho & Cochabamba; ⏰ 8:30am-12:30pm & 2:30-6:30pm Mon-Fri) Extend your stay here (last door on the left).

INTERNET ACCESS

There are plentiful places to get online in Oruro. The going rate is about B$3 per hour although places out of the centre charge only B$1. Many also offer cheap international calls. One of the better connections in town is **Mundo Internet** (Bolívar 573).

LAUNDRY

Lavanderia (Sucre 240, at Pagador) Charges B$10 per kilo for 24-hour service.

MEDICAL SERVICES

Policlínica Oruro (☎ 524-2871; Rodríguez, btwn La Paz & 6 de Octubre) Near Plaza la Unión, this is Oruro's best hospital.

MONEY

There are several banks with ATMs in town (as well as change kiosks at the bus and train stations), which will change several currencies, including euros (at a pretty poor rate). There are several Western Union offices, including one half a block north of the plaza. Banks listed here change cash and traveler's checks (for 4% to 6% commission).

Banco Bisa (Plaza 10 de Febrero) Cashes Amex traveler's checks into bolivianos without commission (for US dollars, there's a US$6 fee).

Banco de Crédito (Plaza 10 de Febrero) ATM issues US dollars or bolivianos.

POST & TELEPHONE

The main post office is just north of Plaza 10 de Febrero. Parcels must first be inspected by the **Aduana Nacional** (Customs; Velasco Galvarro at Junín). The modern Entel office is west of the corner of S Galvarro and Bolívar. There are numerous other telecom centers around town, plus there is also a Punto Entel and a last-minute postal kiosk downstairs at the bus station.

TOURIST INFORMATION

Municipal tourist bureau (☎ 525-0144; Plaza 10 de Febrero; ⏰ 8am-noon & 2:30pm-6:30pm Mon-Fri) On the top floor of Cine Palais Concert, the municipal tourist office isn't really designed for walk-ins but can be helpful and gives out maps. A better map to look for is Plano Turístico (B$10), available in book stores around town.

Tourist information office (Caseta de Información Turística; ☎ 528-7774; bus terminal; ⏰ 24hr) This booth does double duty as the tourist police and the tourist info point, giving out city maps and leaflets. There's another kiosk opposite the train station, only open on weekends.

Dangers & Annoyances

Watch your cash stash, especially around the train and bus stations. Readers have reported groups of young men pretending to help buy tickets or transfer luggage to a bus, and then taking off with backpacks. Carnaval is a godsend for competent pickpockets, bag-slashers and con artists. It is also the time when as a foreigner you are likely to get hit by water bombs and sprayed with water guns and foam (see boxed text, opposite). If you don't want to get soaked, it's wise to wear a poncho. Also, when buying seats for the parade, get a higher seat as you'll be less of a target for water bombs.

Sights

MUSEUMS

The **Museo Sacro, Folklórico, Arqueológico y Minero** (☎ 525-0616; Plaza del Folklore s/n; admission both museums B$10, camera/video use B$3/20; ☷ 9-11:15am & 3:15-5:30pm) is an excellent double museum attached to the Santuario de la Virgen del Socavón. Access is by guided tour only, which descends from the church down to an old mining tunnel with various tools from both the colonial and modern mining eras as well as representations of the devilish El Tío, spirit of the underground. The tour then goes upstairs to the other part of the museum, which has a variety of exhibits, from Wankarani-period stone llama heads to Diablada costumes. Guides are knowledgeable but you should be aware that they don't speak English; however, some exhibits have bilingual explanations.

At the south end of town adjacent to the zoo, the **Museo Antropológico Eduardo López Rivas** (☎ 527-4020; España s/n; admission B$3; ☷ 8am-noon & 2-6pm Mon-Fri, 10am-6pm Sat & Sun) is an anthropological and archaeological museum well worth a visit. The fascinating hodgepodge of exhibits includes mastodons, Carnaval costumes, stone-carved llama heads, mummies from the *chullpares* (funerary towers) that dot the region and skulls exhibiting the horrific cranial deformations once practiced on children. Take any *micro* (minibus) marked 'Sud' from the northwest corner of Plaza 10 de Febrero or opposite the train station, and get off just beyond the old tin-foundry compound.

A university-administered cultural complex, the **Museo Patiño** (☎ 525-4015; S Galvarro 5755; admission B$8; ☷ 8:30-11:30am & 2:30-6pm Mon-Fri, 9am-2:30am Sat) is a former residence of tin baron Simón Patiño inside Casa de la Cultura. Exhibits include his furniture, personal bric-a-brac, fine toys and an ornate Art Nouveau stairway. Visiting exhibitions are featured in the downstairs lobby; the permanent collection is on the upper level. Entry is by guided tour only.

On the university campus south of town, the **Museo Mineralógico** (☎ 526-1250; Ciudad Universitaria; admission B$10; ☷ 8:30am-noon & 2:30-6pm Mon-Fri, weekends by appointment) houses a remarkable collection of more than 5200 minerals, precious stones, fossils and crystals from around the world, housed in wooden cabinets amid a series of stairways, exposed bricks and glass. Hop on minibus 102 or 2 or any *micro* marked 'Sud' or 'Ciudad Universitaria' from opposite the train station or Plaza 10 de Febrero.

Museum Casa Arte Taller Cardozo Velasquez (☎ 527-5245; juegueoruro@hotmail.com; Junín 738; admission B$8; ☷ no specific hours, call ahead) A family of seven artists – Gonzalo (sculptor), his wife María (potter) and their five daughters – open their whimsical little house and art studio to visitors. The tour includes a peek into their workshop, the many nooks and crannies with artsy bric-a-brac and a leafy patio with Gonzalo's fascinating sculptures (check out the one in the middle, devoted to Pachamama). If you're lucky, you may even get a tea made with medicinal herbs from their courtyard garden. On Sunday mornings, the family goes out to the streets to paint with children. Every first Friday of the month, they hold a *k'oa* ceremony, an Andean ritual that pays respect to Pachamama, which you are welcome to join if you announce yourself.

CHURCHES

Just east of the main plaza, the **cathedral** has fine stained-glass above the altar. The adjacent tower was constructed by the Jesuits as part of a church before Oruro was founded. When the Jesuits were expelled, it was designated as the cathedral of the Oruro bishopric. In 1994, the original baroque entrance was moved and reconstructed at the **Santuario de la Virgen del Socavón** (Virgin of the Grotto), which presents a grand city view. It was here that 16th-century miners began worshipping the Virgen de

A DEVIL OF A GOOD TIME

Oruro's **Carnaval** has become Bolivia's most renowned and largest annual celebration. It's a great time to visit, when this somewhat unfashionable mining city becomes the focus of the nation's attention. In a broad sense, these festivities can be described as re-enactments of the triumph of good over evil, but the festival is so interlaced with threads of both Christian and indigenous myths, fables, deities and traditions that it would be inaccurate to oversimplify it in this way.

The origins of a similar festival may be traced back to the medieval kingdom of Aragón, these days part of Spain, although *oruraños* (Oruro locals) maintain that it commemorates an event that occurred during the early days of their own fair city. Legend has it that one night a thief called Chiruchiru was seriously wounded by a traveler he'd attempted to rob. Taking pity on the wrongdoer, the Virgin of Candelaria gently helped him reach his home near the mine at the base of Cerro Pié del Gallo and succored him until he died. When the miners found him there, an image of the Virgin hung over his head. Today, the mine is known as the Socavón de la Virgen (Grotto of the Virgin), and a large church, the Santuario de la Virgen del Socavón (opposite), has been built over it to house the Virgin. The Virgen del Socavón, as she is also now known, is the city's patron. This legend has been combined with the ancient Uru tale of Huari and the struggle of Archangel Michael (San Miguel) against the seven deadly sins into the spectacle that is presented during the Oruro Carnaval.

Ceremonies begin several weeks before Carnaval itself, with a solemn pledge of loyalty to the Virgin in the sanctuary. From this date on, there are various candlelit processions, and dance groups practice boisterously in the city's streets.

As well as traditional Bolivian dance groups, such as the Caporales, Llameradas, Morenadas and Tinkus, Oruro's Carnaval features **La Diablada** (Dance of the Devils). These demonic dancers are dressed in extravagant garb. The design and creation of Diablada costumes has become an art form in Oruro, and several Diablada clubs – consisting of members from all levels of Oruro society – are sponsored by local businesses. There are anywhere between 40 and 300 dancing participants, whose costumes may cost several hundred dollars each.

The main event kicks off on the Saturday before Ash Wednesday with the spectacular *entrada* (entrance procession) led by the brightly costumed San Miguel character. Behind him, dancing and marching, come the famous devils and a host of bears and condors. The chief devil Lucifer wears the most extravagant costume, complete with a velvet cape and an ornate mask. Faithfully at his side are two other devils, including Supay, an Andean god of evil that inhabits the hills and mineshafts. The procession is followed by other dance groups, vehicles adorned with jewels, coins and silverware (in commemoration of the *achura* rites in which the Inca offered their treasures to Inti (the sun) in the festival of Inti Raymi), and the miners offer the year's highest-quality mineral to El Tío, the demonic character who is owner of all underground minerals and precious metals. Behind them follow Inca characters and a group of conquistadores, including Francisco Pizarro and Diego de Almagro.

When the archangel and the devils arrive at the soccer stadium, they engage in a series of dances that tell the story of the ultimate battle between good and evil. After it becomes apparent that good has triumphed over evil, the dancers retire to the Santuario de la Virgen del Socavón at dawn on the Sunday, and a mass is held in honor of the Virgin, who pronounces that good has prevailed.

There's another, less spectacular *entrada* on the Sunday afternoon, and more dance displays on the Monday. The next day, Shrove Tuesday, is marked by family reunions and *cha'lla* libations, in which alcohol is sprinkled over worldly goods to invoke a blessing. The following day people make their way into the surrounding countryside where four rock formations – the Toad, the Viper, the Condor and the Lizard – are also subjected to *cha'lla* as an offering to Pachamama. Plenty of the spirit is sprinkled down the revelers' throats as well.

Thursday is a big party day, with fairground rides and general merriment, and the Saturday sees a final performance of the dance groups in the stadium. On Sunday, the 'burial' of Carnaval is celebrated with a children's procession.

Tickets typically cost between B$80 and B$230 for the seats along Av 6 de Agosto. On the main plaza, prime seats cost between B$320 and $450.

Candelaria, the patron of Oruro miners. The present church, which is a 19th-century reconstruction of the 1781 original, figures prominently in Oruro's Carnaval as the site where good ultimately defeats evil (see boxed text, p157).

Capilla de Serrato, a steep climb from the end of Calle Washington, offers impressive city views. A couple of blocks southeast of the main plaza, it's worth checking out the **Portada del Beaterio**, the facade of a convent church carved with ornate vegetal and bird motifs.

FARO DE CONCHUPATA

On November 17, 1851 Bolivia's red, gold and green flag was first raised at **Faro de Conchupata**: red for the courage of the Bolivian army, gold for the country's mineral wealth and green for its agricultural wealth. The spot is now marked by a platform and column topped by an enormous glass globe, illuminated at night. It provides a fine vista over the town.

MINES

There are numerous mines in the Oruro area, most of which are abandoned or operated by *cooperativos* (small groups of miners who purchase temporary rights). One of the most important is **Mina San José** (☎ 524-7759), which has been in operation for over 450 years. Now run by six cooperatives, they have opened a part of the mine to tourists. The tour lasts about three hours and costs B$50. It's available in Spanish only; English tours are available through Charlie Tours (right) for B$250, with transport and guide. To get there take a yellow *micro* (marked 'D' or 'San José') or the light-blue mini (B$5) from the northwest corner of Plaza 10 de Febrero.

Activities

Rumi Campana (Bell Rock), named after an unusual acoustic phenomenon, is a climber's playground just 2km northwest of town. On weekends you can practice your skills with the friendly local climbing club, **Club de Montañismo Halcones** (cmh_oruro@yahoo .com). There's a range of routes with protection already in place. Try your hand at the challenging overhanging routes of the Angel sector, with the wonderful 7-rated route known as Sueño Lejano. For softer routes, try the Vieja Palestra sector.

Tours

There's a wealth of things to explore in the wild reaches of Oruro department. Tour operators can arrange custom excursions or simpler trips to nearby sites such as Calacala (p162) or the Termas de Obrajes hot springs (p162).

Run by the knowledgeable Juan Carlos Vargas, **Charlie Tours** (☎ 525-2979; charlietours@ yahoo.com; León 501) is a real specialist of the region. In addition to city tours, mine visits and excursions to nearby attractions such as Calacala and Obrajes, they offer trips to places further afield, such as the Chipaya (a day trip costs B$1550 based on two people traveling; a two-day trip costs B$1950), Salar de Coipasa and Sajama.

Highly recommended as a private guide comes **Freddy Barron** (☎ 527-6776, lufba@hotmail .com), especially for trips to Uyuni and the Southwest Circuit. He charges by the kilometer (B$3.20) plus his guide services (B$267 per day). His tours are reportedly very safe, more personalized and generally of higher quality.

Sleeping

Accommodations are often booked solid during Carnaval, when there's also a three-night minimum stay. It's wise to reserve ahead of time or ask the tourist office about rooms in local homes. Expect to pay up to five or six times the normal price for a room.

There are good lodging options by the bus station and less appealing ones by the train station, but by far the most interesting place to be is in the centre. A rather ostentatious five-star hotel is currently in construction on the main square but it will take some time before it opens.

BUDGET

Residencial San Miguel (☎ 527-2132; Sucre 331; s/d B$30/50, with bathroom B$40/60) This is handy for both the train station and the centre, but it's pretty rock-bottom in terms of comfort. Hot water is sporadic, rooms tiny and the cleanliness questionable.

Pub the Alpaca (☎ 527-5715, 523-2707; wcamargo_gallegos@yahoo.com; La Paz 690; r per person B$40) Marked only by a wooden alpaca sign by the door, this is among the best budget options in town. The three simple rooms are cozy, sunny and spacious, plus you've got a shared kitchen and the city's best pub in your front room (p160)! Make sure you email ahead.

Hotel Bernal (☎ 527-9468; Brasil 701; s/d B$40/70, with bathroom B$70/100) Opposite the bus terminal, this is a good-value and friendly place with appealing rooms featuring back-friendly beds, decent hot showers and cable TV. Try to avoid the noisier front rooms. Breakfast is available for B$15.

Residencial 21 de Abril (☎ 527-9205; simon21deabril@bolivia.com; Montecinos 198; s/d B$50/80, d with bathroom B$120) Friendly family-run spot a short walk from the centre with tidy bright rooms, all with TV and hot water available all day. There's a sauna for guests' use.

Alojamiento Copacabana (☎ 525-4184; aloj.copacabana@hotmail.com; V Galvarro 6352; d B$70) A significant step above the row of budget and mostly dire *alojamientos* opposite the train station, this bright, clean and cheerful spot has 19 rooms set around a pleasant inner patio. It's secure and staff are used to dealing with travelers.

Hotel El Lucero (☎ 528-5884; 21 de Enero 106; s/d B$70/110) This recent opening right by the bus terminal, run by the owners of Hotel Bernal, offers a string of pleasant rooms, all sporting private bathrooms and cable TVs.

Residencial Boston (☎ 527-4708; Pagador, btwn Caro & Cochabamba; d B$80, with bathroom B$100) A class above most Oruro *residenciales*, this welcoming place with a freshly painted yellow front is built around a courtyard and cheerfully tiled in blue and yellow. The rooms are darkish (with small bathrooms) but comfortable.

MIDRANGE & TOP END

Hostal Hidalgo (☎ 525-7516; 6 de Octubre 1616; s/d/tr B$50/100/150, with bathroom B$100/180/250) This three-floor place is very central, with spacious rooms, each equipped with a phone and TV, that are a reasonable bet. The cheaper rooms without bathroom have no windows.

Hotel Repostero (☎ /fax 525-8001; Sucre 370; s/d/tr B$100/135/155) This faded but likeable old place has a variety of rooms in two wings, all with hot showers and cable TV. The older section is pretty run-down, with somewhat concave beds. It's worth paying extra to stay in the renovated wing (s/d/tr B$145/150/195) with carpeted rooms.

SM Palace (☎ 527-2121; smpalace@coteor.net.bo; Mier 392; s/d with bathroom B$130/200) This glass-fronted hotel has a dark lobby but pleasant 1970s-style rooms with TV and phone. Book a room with a street view; these offer lovely vistas of the surrounding hills. It's fairly bland but friendly.

Hotel International Park (☎ 527-6227; Bakovic s/n; s/d/tr B$130/230/315) Once a modern hotel of good quality, this high-rise on top of the bus terminal is definitely past its heyday. Rooms are run-down but come with heating and panoramic town vistas; the service is spotty and the restaurant nothing to write home about.

Hotel Samay Wasi (☎ 527-6737; samaywasioruro@hotmail.com; Brasil 232; s/d/tr B$150/210/270; 💻) This attractive European-style hotel by the bus station has rooms with tiled floors, firm beds, decent bathrooms and cable TV. The staff is helpful and the hotel is HI-affiliated so members get a discount (B$20 off per person). Get a room with a patio view.

Plaza Hotel (☎ 525-2561; plazahotelenoruro@yahoo.com; Mier 735; s/d/tr/ste B$200/290/360/360; 💻) Right in the heart of town, along the main plaza, this three-star hotel has eight floors of pleasant and well-maintained rooms with nice city or square vistas. Request a room on a higher floor for better views.

Gran Hotel Sucre (☎ 527-6320; hotel sucreoruro@hotmail.com; Sucre 510; s/d/tr/ste B$200/280/320/380; 💻) This noble and characterful old lodging, although on the dark side, combines modern conveniences with an appealing sense of past grandeur. The rooms have decent hot-water bathrooms, TVs and comfortable beds. An abundant buffet breakfast is included. There's private parking and a laundry service available.

Hotel Briggs (☎ 525-1724; www.s-hotelbriggs.com.bo; Washington 1206; s/d/ste B$280/440/650; 💻) Centrally located across Mercado Fermín López, this is Oruro's most upscale hotel, with spacious spick-and-span rooms of different configurations, some with great city views, some with private terraces and Jacuzzis. All have sizable bathrooms and wi-fi.

Eating

The markets are an interesting eating option; Mercado Campero and Mercado Fermín López have rows of lunch spots as well as drinks stalls serving *mate* (a herbal infusion of coca, chamomile or similar), *api* (a local drink made of maize) and coffee. Local specialties include *thimpu de cordero* (a mutton-and-vegetable concoction smothered with *llajhua*, a hot tomato-based sauce) and *charquekan* (sun-dried llama meat with corn, potatoes, eggs and cheese). On hot days, locals flock to the row of excellent fruit juice stalls on Av Velasco Galvarro opposite the Mercado Campero. Note that most restaurants are closed on Sunday evening, except the fast-food places along the main plaza.

Confitería Dumbo (Junín, near 6 de Octubre; almuerzo B$9; [clock] closed weekends) A decent quick stop for cakes, empanadas, *salteñas* (meat and vegetable pasties), hot drinks and *helados* (ice creams).

Govinda (Junín, btwn 6 de Octubre & S Galvarro; almuerzo B$9-16, mains B$11-13; [clock] closed Sun) Forget you're in Bolivia at this Hare Krishna-devoted restaurant behind a modern glass front where vegetarian meals are fresh, cheap and creative, the decor blue and light, and the music ambient.

El Huerto (Bolívar near Pagador; almuerzo B$10; [clock] closed Sat) Tasty cakes, snacks and cooked-to-order vegetarian lunches are served at this friendly hole-in-the-wall place.

Mateo's (cnr Bolívar & 6 de Octubre; mains B$16-35) This traditional cafe-restaurant, on a busy corner in the heart of town, is popular with families for its range of decent snacks, meals, coffee and cold beer.

Paprika (Junín 821; almuerzo B$15, mains B$18-40) Comparatively formal by Oruro standards, this upstairs restaurant, frequented by business lunches, has good service and decent, if unspectacular, food.

Bravo's Pizza (cnr Bolívar & S Galvarro; pizzas B$19-30, pastas B$28-45) Bright, with big windows overlooking the square and a light ambience, this 2nd-floor eatery has 20 pizza varieties, including a spicy one with dried llama meat, plus hamburgers, sandwiches, burritos and breakfasts (B$20).

La Casona (Montes 5969; pizzas from B$20) Out-of-the-oven *salteñas* by day, quick sandwiches for lunch, and pizza and pasta at dinner keep this little place buzzing, especially at night when it gets really busy and hot, temperature-wise.

La Estancia ([phone] 528-5839; 6 de Octubre 5686; mains B$25-38; [clock] closed Mon for dinner) Grilled meat is the specialty at this family-style restaurant with an Argentine flavor in its two dining rooms and a covered courtyard. Their pork lunch is popular on weekends.

Las Delicias ([phone] 527-7256; 6 de Agosto 1284; almuerzo B$13-25, mains B$28-50) Of several grilled-meat restaurants *(churrasquerías)*, on this long street, this one is the best, with attentive service, sizzling tableside *parrilladas* (plates of mixed grilled meats), great *almuerzos* and a pleasant covered patio.

Nayjama ([phone] 527-7699; Aldana at Pagador; mains B$30-55; [clock] closed Sun for dinner) This appealing three-floor choice serves high-quality traditional Oruro food with a dash of innovation. The servings are huge so ask for half a portion of anything you order. Lamb is the specialty, as is *cabeza*, the sheep's head served with salad and dehydrated potatoes. The English menu is slightly more expensive so ask for the Spanish one.

Las Retamas ([phone] 525-2375; Murguía 930; almuerzo B$30, mains B$34-42; [clock] closed Sun for dinner) One of Oruro's best restaurants, this rustic spot in a cozy series of rooms with leafy views dishes out international meals and Bolivian specialties such as *pacumutu* (grilled beef chunks with veggies on a skewer) and *silpancho* (a thin schnitzel). Their selection of cakes is stellar.

The cheapest *almuerzos* (set lunches) are to be found around the train station and Mercado Campero. **Pagador** (Pagador 1440; almuerzo B$14, mains B$25-45) is a no-frills restaurant deservedly popular with locals who eat in the simple dining room or the covered patio outside. If you want to try *charquekan*, head to one of the eateries around the bus station; **El Fogon** (Brasil 5021; charquekan B$25) is on the glossy side but the best of the bus terminal lot.

Drinking & Entertainment

Pub the Alpaca ([phone] 527-5715; La Paz 690; [clock] 8pm-1am Thu-Sat) A worthwhile option, this Swedish- and Bolivian-run pub is an intimate recently renovated spot set up in a front room. The good-mood feel is helped with good mixed drinks. If the door is locked, just knock or ring the bell.

Bar Huari (Junín 608, cnr S Galvarro) Not much seems to have changed in this traditional bar since the 1930s – locals still while away their evenings playing games and drinking beer in its series of high-ceilinged rooms. There are cheap *almuerzos* (B$10) and dinner mainstays.

Café Sur (Arce, btwn V Galvarro & 6 de Agosto) The most bohemian place in town, with live music on weekends and occasional poetry readings.

Club Social Arabe (Junín 729; ✇ closed Sun) A slice of old-fashioned Oruro, this 2nd-floor spot hosts occasional live music on weekends.

Dali (6 de Octubre & Cochabamba) This stylish and popular cafe is a fun weekend option and a great place for a coffee break during the day.

Bravo Bravo (Montecinos and Pagador) The best karaoke in town is run by the same owners as Bravo's Pizza (opposite).

Palais Concert Cinema (Plaza 10 de Febrero) Housed in an opulent baroque-style colonial-era concert hall, this no-name cinema screens first-run films nightly for B$12 and is the gathering spot for local youngsters.

Shopping

The design, creation and production of artistic Diablada masks and costumes is Oruro's main industry. Av La Paz, between León and Villarroel, is lined with small workshops offering devil masks, headdresses, costumes and other devilish things.

ARAO Artesanías Oruro (☎ 525-0331; www .artesaniasoruro.com; Mier 5999) This place offers the best selection of high-quality, cooperatively produced handicrafts from four communities in the Oruro department, starting at B$70. The naturally dyed wool rugs and wall hangings, shoulder bags and ponchos are especially notable.

Llama and alpaca wool bags and clothing are sold at *artesanías* (stores selling locally handcrafted items) in the center and at the bus terminal, while the cheapest articles are found around the northeast corner of Mercado Campero. Hawkers sell cheap *zampoñas* (pan flutes made of hollow reeds), *charangos* and other indigenous musical instruments near the train station.

Tucked away in the middle row of the Mercado Fermín López is the impressive Mercado Tradicional, which has more dried llama fetuses and flamingo wings than a voodoo master has pins. The affable vendors are more than happy to explain the usage of their wares, but make sure to ask if you want to take a photo.

For herb remedies and witchcraft items, head to Calle Junín between V Galvarro and 6 de Agosto.

Getting There & Away
BUS

All long-distance buses use the **bus terminal** (☎ 527-9535; terminal fee B$1.50), a 15-minute walk or short cab ride northeast of the center. There's a *casa de cambio* (money-changing office) on the upper level, luggage storage on the ground floor (B$5) and a sporadically open tourist info kiosk, which provides maps.

Numerous companies run buses to La Paz (B$20, three hours) every half-hour or so; sit on the right side of the bus for great views of La Paz as you approach. There are also several daily buses to Cochabamba (B$25, four hours), Potosí (B$20, five hours) and Sucre (B$40, eight hours). Several night services depart daily for Uyuni (B$40, eight hours) along a rough, cold route that is often impassable after rains. For Santa Cruz, you must make a connection in Cochabamba; buses depart on Saturdays. There are daily services to Tupiza (B$80 to B$120, 12 hours) and Villazón (B$80 to B$120, 14 hours).

Several daily services ply the route to Arica, Chile (B$100, 10 hours), via Tambo Quemado and Chungará. There are a lot more buses going to Iquique (B$80, eight hours) via the Pisiga border crossing.

TRAIN

Thanks to its mines, Oruro has one of Bolivia's most organized train stations, but only with southbound services to Uyuni and beyond. Since 1996, the railway has been run by the **Empresa Ferroviaria Andina** (FCA; www.fca.com.bo), which operates a relatively tight ship timetable-wise. Buy tickets at least a day ahead from the **station** (☎ 527-4605; ✇ 8:15-11:30am & 2:30-6pm Mon & Thu, 8:15am-6pm Tue & Fri, 8:15am-noon & 2:30-7pm Wed, 8:15-11am & 3-7pm Sun); don't forget your passport. On train days, there's a left-luggage kiosk here.

The principal service runs south to Uyuni and on to Tupiza and Villazón on the Argentine border. It's the most popular way of reaching Uyuni, as it avoids the cold, bumpy journey on the night bus. From Uyuni, there are slow rail services to Chile (see p173).

The *Expreso del Sur* offers reclining seats with plenty of leg room, heaters, videos, a dining car and a choice of *salón* and *ejecutivo* classes. It departs Oruro at 3:30pm Tuesday and Friday to Uyuni (*salón/ejecutivo* B$52/101, seven hours), Tupiza (B$92/202, 13 hours) and Villazón (B$109/236, 16 hours). It returns from Villazón at 3:30pm Wednesday and Saturday.

The *Wara Wara del Sur* runs Wednesday and Sunday at 7pm to Uyuni (*popular/salón/ejecutivo* B$31/40/86, 7½ hours), Tupiza (B$54/69/153, 13½ hours) and Villazón (B$65/86/185, 17 hours). It returns from Villazón at 3:30pm Monday and Thursday.

At the train station, there's also a booth by **Balut** (☎ 7047-8983), a company that offers a bus service to Buenos Aires via Villazón, where you change buses. It runs Monday through Wednesday and Saturday at 7pm (B$750, 36 hours). Reserve at least two days ahead.

Getting Around

Micros (B$0.80 to B$1.50) and minibuses (B$1) connect the city center with outlying areas. Their routes are designated by their letters, colors and signs (and in the case of minibuses, numbers). It's a fairly confusing system so check with the driver before boarding. Note that *micros* and minibuses are small and crowded, so if possible, avoid carrying luggage aboard.

Taxis around the center, including to and from the terminals, cost a non-negotiable B$3. **Radio taxis** (☎ 527-7775) cost around B$4.

AROUND ORURO

There's plenty to see around Oruro, particularly along the road south towards Uyuni, where bleak and epic scenery holds old mines and the remnants of ancient lakeside cultures. These areas can be visited by bus from Oruro or on a tour (see p158).

The **Termas de Obrajes hot springs** (admission B$10), 25km northeast of town, are a popular destination. It's a well-run complex, with a pool and, around the edge, private bathrooms, which you reserve for half an hour and gradually fill up with the magnesium-

rich water. You can buy (but not rent) towels here; make sure you have a swimming costume to enter the public pool. There's an unspectacular restaurant adjacent to a modest hotel. From the corner of Caro and Av 6 de Agosto, catch an Obrajes *micro* (B$5, 30 minutes) from 7:30am to 5pm daily, which also passes the grungier **Capachos hot springs**, 10km east of town. The last *micro* to Oruro departs at 4pm.

The atmospheric **Calacala** (admission B$40) makes a worthwhile trip from Oruro. The site consists of a series of rock paintings of llamas and humans in red and orange tones, presumably dating to the first millennium BC. It's located under an overhang 2.5km beyond the village of Calacala, which is 26km east of Oruro. Stop in the village to locate the guard who has the keys and collects the fee; she can often be found in the small cafe marked by a rusted Pepsi sign. The site itself is a 30-minute walk past the village, near the old brewery. The views from the site of the exceptionally beautiful

---

CHULLPA TOMBS

A *chullpa* is a funerary tower or mausoleum that various Aymará groups built to house the mummified remains of some members of their society, presumably people of high rank or esteem within the community. Oruro province is particularly rich in *chullpas*, especially along the shores of Lago Poopó and around the Sajama area. A *chullpa* was constructed of stone or adobe, and typically had a beehive-shaped opening, which nearly always faced east towards the rising sun. The body was placed in the fetal position along with various possessions. Some communities would ritually open the *chullpas* on feast days and make offerings to the mummified ancestors; the Chipaya (see boxed text, p179) still do. Most of the tombs, however, have been looted, apart from some bones here and there, and the mummies can now be found in museums, such as the Museo Antropológico Eduardo López Rivas in Oruro (p156). The biggest concentration is found along the road from Patacamaya to Chile. There are also between 18 and 25 *chullpas* along the Lauca circuit (see p165).

ANDEAN CAMELIDS

Unlike the Old World, the western hemisphere had few grazing mammals after the Pleistocene era, when mammoths, horses and other large herbivores disappeared from North and South America. For millennia, the Andean people relied on the New World camelids – the wild guanaco and vicuña and the domesticated llama and alpaca – for food and fiber.

Guanaco (*Lama guanicoe*) and vicuña *(Vicugna vicugna)* are relatively rare today but are the likely ancestors of the domesticated llama (*L glama*) and alpaca *(Vicugna pacos)*. In fact they were among few potential New World domestic animals – contrast them with the Old World cattle, horses, sheep, goats, donkeys and pigs that have filled so many vacant niches in the Americas. While the New World camels have lost ground to sheep and cattle in some areas, they are not likely to disappear.

The rust-colored guanaco ranges from sea level up to 4000m or higher. There's only a small population in Bolivia; the animals can be seen in the highland plains of the Reserva Nacional de Fauna Andina Eduardo Avaroa (p173).

The vicuña occupies a much smaller zone, well above 4000m in the highlands from southern Peru to northwestern Argentina. Although not as numerous as the guanaco, it played a critical role in the cultural life of pre-Columbian Peru. Its very fine golden wool was the exclusive property of the Inca emperors.

Strict Inca authority protected the vicuña, but the Spanish invasion destroyed that authority. By the middle of last century, poaching reduced vicuña numbers from two million to perhaps 10,000 and caused it to become endangered. Conservation efforts in Chile's Parque Nacional Lauca and Bolivia's Parque Nacional Apolobamba have been so successful that economic exploitation of the species is now being allowed in some communities.

The Altiplano's indigenous communities still depend on llamas and alpacas for their livelihood. The two species appear very similar but they differ in several important respects. The taller, rangier and hardier llama has relatively coarse wool that is used for blankets, ropes and other household goods. It also works as a pack animal, but thanks to the introduction of the *camión* (flatbed truck), llama trains are increasingly rare in Bolivia.

Llamas can survive and even flourish on relatively poor, dry pastures, whereas the smaller, more delicate alpacas require well-watered grasslands to produce their much finer wool, which has a higher commercial value than that of llamas. Both llama and alpaca meat are consumed by Andean households and are sold in urban markets all over Bolivia.

valley, which provides some of Oruro's water, are spectacular. There's no public transport unless it's the feast day of Señor de la Laguna (Lord of the Lake) on September 14; a taxi there and back will cost you B$120.

PARQUE NACIONAL SAJAMA

Bolivia's first national park occupies 1000 sq km abutting the Chilean border. It was created on November 5, 1945 for the protection of the rare wildlife that inhabits this northern extension of the Atacama Desert. Unfortunately, depredation has already eliminated several species, and only limited numbers of vicuña (whose wool is very prized, at US$500 per kilo), condor, flamingo, rhea and armadillo survive.

The world's highest forest covers the foothills flanking the awe-inspiring **Volcán Sajama**, which at 6542m is Bolivia's highest peak. The forest consists of dwarf *queñua* trees, an endemic and ancient Altiplano species, but while technically a forest, it's a little underwhelming – the 'trees' have the size and appearance of creosote bushes!

The volcano is a popular mountain to climb, especially between May and September; there are also some hikes on its lower slopes. Although it's a relatively straightforward climb, Sajama's altitude and icy conditions make the peak more challenging than it initially appears. Quite a few La Paz agencies offer organized climbs of Sajama; see p350 for a list of recommended tour agencies. Only consider going without a guide if you have experience of high-altitude climbing, but prepare for extremely cold and icy conditions and carry lots of water in a woolen bag (otherwise it will freeze). Do not try to climb the volcano in the rainy season; the electrical storms make this a dangerous time to ascend.

For a relaxing warm soak, there are four lovely 35°C **hot springs** 8km northwest of Sajama village, an easy 45-minute walk; look for the screaming orange house to the left of the road. There's a B$60 admission fee, with use of changing cabins, towels and a box lunch. About 7km (1½ hours) on foot due west of Sajama is an interesting spouting **geyser field**.

Orientation & Information

The best map of the park is the glossy 1:50,000 *Nevado Sajama* published by Walter Guzmán Córdova; it can be found in better La Paz bookstores (p63).

Park admission (B$30, for which you are also provided with a small map) is payable at the Servicio Nacional de Areas Protegidas (SERNAP) headquarters in the sleepy Sajama village (4200m), 18km north of the Arica–La Paz highway. The fee applies to all foreigners, including those just visiting the village. SERNAP will help climbing expeditions organize mules and porters to carry equipment to the base camp; guides cost around B$560 per day, porters about B$140 for the climb. If you're planning to climb the volcano, consider reading Yossi Brain's definitive and carefully researched *Bolivia – A Climbing Guide* (Mountaineers, 1999), which describes several routes clearly and concisely.

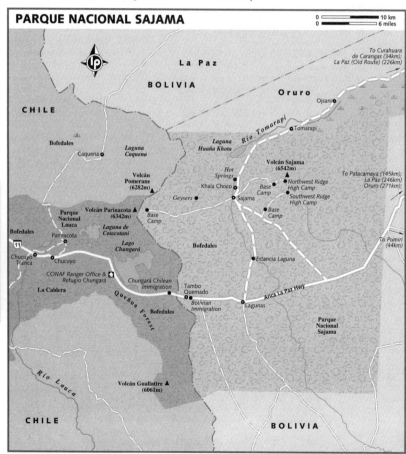

PARQUE NACIONAL SAJAMA

Sleeping & Eating

Camping is fine just about anywhere in this sparsely populated region, so a tent and a good cold-weather sleeping bag are recommended. Otherwise, contact the **tourism office** (☎ 513-5526; SERNAP headquarters) in Sajama village about **homestays** (per person B$35-55) with local families, which are organized on a rotation basis between 22 homes. Most are very modest so, again, you'll need a sleeping bag and many layers of clothing for the typically cold, windy nights. Try to book a room at Hostal Sajama, the best of the homestays, where each room comes with a private bathroom. A couple of restaurants serve breakfast (B$9), lunch (B$14) and dinner (B$14).

Albergue Ecoturístico Tomarapi (☎ in La Paz 2-241-4753; www.boliviamilenaria.com; s/d B$400/550) on the northern border of the park, 12km beyond Sajama, is an enticing community-run 35-bed ecolodge, which offers the area's most comfortable accommodations. It has been widely cited as an ideal model for community involvement in tourism projects, with about 31 families from the nearby village of Caripe working at the lodge on a rotational basis. Occupying a lovely thatched building, styled along traditional local architectural lines, it boasts simple, comfortable rooms with private baths and hot water, a very welcome log fire and excellent food, featuring lots of alpaca meat. Rates include two meals per day. If you have any old clothes you no longer need and wish to donate, leave them here; Bolivia Milenaria gifts clothing to local families each holiday season. A two-day program from La Paz is available for B$1020 per person, including three meals per day, private transportation, a bilingual guide and visits to attractions in Sajama National Park.

Getting There & Away

There is a daily bus from the town of Patacamaya to Sajama village (B$18 to B$25, 1pm, 3½ hours); a return bus departs Sajama village at 6:30am. Patacamaya is easily reached on most buses from La Paz to Cochabamba, Oruro and Arica. La Paz–Arica buses pass through Sajama National Park; the border crossing between Tambo Quemado (Bolivia) and Chungará (Chile) 12km away is straightforward; it's open from 8am till 8pm.

AROUND PARQUE NACIONAL SAJAMA

The area around the Sajama National Park has several attractions worth seeing. These are tricky to visit without your own wheels but can be seen with most of the agencies in La Paz or Oruro. In the scenic village of **Curahuara de Carangas**, the lovely adobe-and-thatch **church** (admission B$15, photos $5) has been dubbed 'the Sistine Chapel of the Altiplano.' While that's rather overblown, the charming little structure does contain a wealth of lovely naive 17th-century frescoes depicting typical mestizo-style themes and Biblical scenes as well as some interesting artifacts in a small room behind the altar. A direct bus from Patacamaya runs regularly (B$10, 2½ hours). There's also a small **hostal** (dm B$15) in the village and a few eateries. If there's nobody at the church, look for the key in the Entel shop.

Located near Parque Nacional Sajama, a new tourist circuit called **Lauca** is slowly attracting visitors. It's organized between three communities – Macaya, Julo and Sacabaya – that are trying to promote the area and boost their income. Highlights include several lagoons with flamingos and about 25 painted *chullpas* erected between 1470 and 1540. The area is difficult to visit independently so your best bet is going with one of the agencies in La Paz, such as Bolivia Milenaria (see p351); the tour can be done in about four hours from Sajama National Park and costs B$425, with jeep transportation, entrance fee and lunch. You can ask to be dropped off in Tambo Quemado, if continuing on to Chile.

SOUTHWESTERN BOLIVIA

The southwest of Bolivia is perhaps its most magical corner, a wilderness of harsh hillscapes, bubbling geysers and psychedelic mineral colors. Although it gets plenty of visitors, in many ways it's still a remote wilderness, with rough dirt roads, scattered mining settlements, quinoa-producing villages and little public transportation.

The main town, Uyuni, is a military outpost with a real frontier feel; at times you expect the harsh temperatures and biting winds to do away with it altogether. It's the launching point for expeditions into the region, from the desolate expanses of the *salares* to the craggy hills of Los Lípez, which rise into the high Andean peaks along the Chilean frontier. Many of these are active volcanoes, and they preside over a surreal landscape of geothermal features and flamingo-filled lakes.

UYUNI

pop 20,000 / elevation 3669m

Seemingly built in defiance of the desert-like landscape, Uyuni stands desolate yet undaunted in Bolivia's southwestern corner. Mention Uyuni to a Bolivian and they will whistle and emphasize '*harto frío*' – extreme cold. Yet despite the icy conditions,

Uyuni's got a cheerful buzz about it. Travelers arrive and eagerly plan a trip around the Southwest Circuit; those who return from the wilderness see Uyuni with new eyes, as a sort of paradise filled with much-missed daily comforts.

Although there's not much to see here, and the wind chill can strip your soul bare as you pace the wide streets, Uyuni's isolated position and outlook elicit an affectionate respect from both Bolivians and foreign travelers.

Founded in 1889 by Bolivian president Aniceto Arce, Uyuni today remains an important military base; tourism and mining are the other major sources of employment in the town.

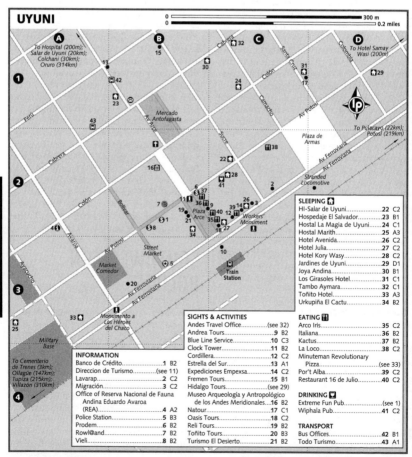

SOUTHERN ALTIPLANO

UYUNI

0 _____ 300 m
0 _____ 0.2 miles

To Hospital (200m); Salar de Uyuni (20km); Colchani (30km); Oruro (314km)

To Hotel Samay Wasi (200m)

Mercado Antofagasta

To Pulacayo (22km); Potosí (219km)

Plaza de Armas

Stranded Locomotive

Plaza Arce

Workers' Monument

Street Market

Market Comedor

Train Station

Monumento a Los Héroes del Chaco

Military Base

To Cementerio de Trenes (3km); Ollagüe (147km); Tupiza (215km); Villazón (310km)

INFORMATION
Banco de Crédito	1	B2
Direccion de Turismo	(see 11)	
Lavarap	2	C2
Migración	3	C2
Office of Reserva Nacional de Fauna Andina Eduardo Avaroa (REA)	4	A2
Police Station	5	B3
Prodem	6	B2
Rowl@nd	7	B2
Vieli	8	B2

SIGHTS & ACTIVITIES
Andes Travel Office	(see 32)	
Andrea Tours	9	B2
Blue Line Service	10	C3
Clock Tower	11	B2
Cordillera	12	C2
Estrella del Sur	13	A1
Expediciones Empexsa	14	C2
Fremen Tours	15	B1
Hidalgo Tours	(see 29)	
Museo Arqueología y Antropológico de los Andes Meridionales	16	B2
Natour	17	C1
Oasis Tours	18	C2
Reli Tours	19	B2
Toñito Tours	20	B3
Turismo El Desierto	21	B2

SLEEPING
HI-Salar de Uyuni	22	C2
Hospedaje El Salvador	23	B1
Hostal La Magia de Uyuni	24	C1
Hostal Marith	25	A3
Hotel Avenida	26	C2
Hotel Julia	27	C2
Hotel Kory Wasy	28	C2
Jardines de Uyuni	29	D1
Joya Andina	30	B1
Los Girasoles Hotel	31	C1
Tambo Aymara	32	C2
Toñito Hotel	33	A3
Urkupiña El Cactu	34	B2

EATING
Arco Iris	35	C2
Italiana	36	B2
Kactus	37	B2
La Loco	38	C2
Minuteman Revolutionary Pizza	(see 33)	
Por't Alba	39	C2
Restaurant 16 de Julio	40	C2

DRINKING
Extreme Fun Pub	(see 1)	
Wiphala Pub	41	C2

TRANSPORT
Bus Offices	42	B1
Todo Turismo	43	A1

Information

IMMIGRATION

Migración (Ferroviaria btwn Arce & Sucre; ⏱ 8:30am-noon & 2:30-6pm Mon-Fri, 8:30am-noon Sat & Sun) Exit stamps cost B$21.

INTERNET ACCESS

There are several internet places in town but most have painfully slow dial-up connections; an hour costs between B$4 and B$5. One of the more reliable and cheaper spots is **Rowl@and** (Potosí, btwn Bolívar & Arce), opposite the ATM. Minuteman Pizza, inside Hotel Toñito, has a wireless signal that's pretty reliable.

LAUNDRY

Most hotels offer some sort of laundry service, costing between B$8 and B$20 per kilo. **Lavarap** (cnr Ferroviaria & Sucre; ⏱ 7am-10pm) charges B$10 per kilo.

MEDICAL SERVICES

Hospital (☎ 693-2025) Along Arce on the edge of town; does good work and accepts most travel insurance.

MONEY

The lone and long-awaited ATM outside the **Banco de Crédito** (Potosí, btwn Arce & Bolívar) is very often out of service, especially on weekends, so bring sufficient amounts of cash. The same bank gives cash advances on credit cards at the best rate, and changes US dollars. **Prodem** (Plaza Arce) and several similar places also change dollars and give cash advances. For travelers checks, head to **Vieli** (Potosí 25), which has a 3% commission. Several places on Potosí between Arce and Bolívar buy Chilean and Argentine pesos.

EMERGENCY

There is quite a bit of petty theft around the bus and train stations.

Police station (cnr Ferroviaria & Bolívar) If you happen to get mugged, head here to fill out a report.

TOURIST INFORMATION

Dirección de Turismo (direccionturismouyuni@hotmail.com; Potosí cnr Arce; ⏱ 8:30am-noon & 2pm-6:30pm Mon-Fri) Inside the clock tower, this tourism office has sporadic hours and, theoretically, distributes information about Uyuni and the rest of Bolivia. Printed materials were being prepared at the time of research.

Office of Reserva Nacional de Fauna Andina Eduardo Avaroa (REA; ☎ /fax 693-2400; www

.bolivia-rea.com; Colón, at Avaroa; ⏱ 8:30am-12:30pm & 2:30-6:30pm Mon-Fri) Somewhat helpful administrative office for the park of the same name. You can buy your park entry (B$30) here if going under your own steam.

Sights & Activities

The **Museo Arqueología y Antropológico de los Andes Meridionales** (Arce at Colón; admission B$5; ⏱ 8:30am-noon & 2-6:30pm Mon-Fri) is a small affair featuring mummies, long skulls, fossils, ceramics and textiles. There are Spanish descriptions of the practices of mummification and cranial deformation.

Uyuni's only other real tourist attraction is the **Cementerio de Trenes** (Train Cemetery), a large collection of historic steam locomotives and rail cars, which are decaying in the yards about 3km southwest of the station along Av Ferroviaria. There have long been plans to turn the collection into a railway museum, but that seems a pipe dream and they'll most likely just keep on rusting. Many tours visit the train cemetery as a first or last stop on the three-day *salar* circuit.

You can hire bikes in Uyuni to explore the town itself at the makeshift **bike rental kiosk** (per 3hr B$25; ⏱ closed Sun) opposite the post office.

The big market day in Uyuni is Thursday when Potosí gets taken over by stalls selling anything from arts and crafts to television sets; Sunday is a smaller market day.

Tours

While you can theoretically visit the Salar de Uyuni and the attractions of the Southwest Circuit independently, it is extremely challenging due to unreliable transport and the remoteness of the area. So the vast majority of people take an organized tour from either Uyuni or Tupiza (p182).

The most popular tour is the three-day circuit taking in the Salar de Uyuni, Laguna Colorada, Sol de Mañana, Laguna Verde and points in between. Check with the agency about reversing the standard circuit, that way, you will arrive at the *salar* early in the morning on the third day, when the lighting is at its best. Expect to pay between B$600 and B$850 for this trip, with six people in the jeep. The main advantages are that the circuit takes in many stunning natural sights and that, because it is so popular, you'll have little trouble finding companions to make up the numbers on a tour. The disadvantage is that it is very much a 'trail' – it's not unusual to see a couple of dozen 4WDs parked up alongside some of the major attractions.

If you have the time and cash, opt for the four-day circuit which is a lot more rewarding. These cost between B$800 and B$1000, and many end up in Tupiza. Possible activities include climbing volcanoes and visiting some off-the-beaten path attractions (p177).

Another option offered by a variety of agencies is to do the three-day circuit and then connect at Laguna Verde with an onward transfer to the pretty town of San Pedro de Atacama in northeast Chile. This is now a popular means of crossing between Bolivia and Chile. When booking, check that the price of the transfer to San Pedro is included.

Shorter visits, basically taking in just the *salar,* cost from B$200 to B$400 for two days and one night. Single-day trips also run (B$150 to B$230), but these have angered the locals around the *salar,* who feel that their community gains nothing from these visits.

Note that during the rainy season, between January and March, some agencies shut down. Those that do operate offer cheaper tours and tend to be more open to negotiation. Ensure the vehicle and driver are reliable, as entering the *salar* during the rains can be downright dangerous.

With the increasing number of people on the standard trail, and a growing number of interesting choices of accommodations around the Salar de Uyuni and Southwest Circuit, it's an appealing prospect to customize your own tour, striking off into lesser-known areas, or incorporating some climbing or walking opportunities. Some agencies are more willing to do this than others; be especially wary when they've got a 'standard' tour to fill and will promise you any route you want just to sign you up!

Accommodations tend to be in basic hostels that are icy at night. If you don't have a warm sleeping bag, make absolutely certain that the agency provides one; no one should make these trips without one. If you're willing to pay a little extra, there are now several more enticing lodging choices around the *salar*; some companies can arrange stays in these (see boxed text, p174).

Food varies in quality and quantity. There have been reports of travelers' vegetarian requests not being heard so make sure you get that in writing. It's always better to sign up with an agency that has a cook onboard, otherwise the driver will double as the cook, which isn't an appealing prospect.

CHOOSING THE SOUTHWEST CIRCUIT AGENCY

Your choice of tour operator is an important one; a well-run trip might well be a highlight of your traveling life, while a surly *salar* disaster could wreck your trip. Uyuni is a far-flung outpost, and tourism is what keeps it viable these days, so it's little wonder that everyone wants a piece of the pie. A mushrooming number of agencies – nearly 80 at last count – offer *salar* tours. While this means you have more choice, the flipside is that there are many dubious operators who have neither the best interests of their customers nor the environment at heart.

Some of the agencies are 'pirate' operations, meaning they hire private jeep owners without any insurance and with poorly kept vehicles, just to make a few bucks. Some agencies are even involved in smuggling cocaine into Chile. Worst of all, there have been a few deadly accidents in the *salar* in the last couple of years, due to often drunk or reckless drivers. So do think twice before trying to bargain down the price and going with the cheapest agency on the block.

The typical tour is in a 4WD of variable health holding up to six passengers, a cook (with some agencies) and a driver/guide who may or may not speak English. Some agencies will try to squeeze in the seventh passenger into the jeep but this is inadvisable for comfort and safety reasons. Also, try to find out who else signed up for the tour; there have been reports of solo travelers being put with a group of people who don't even speak their language, which can turn into a very lonely trip.

Especially significant is the condition of the vehicle. The *salar* is super-tough on cars, so maintenance is crucial. That said, even the most reliable companies have frequent breakdowns; how they deal with them (and you) is the crux of the matter.

Of course, an important criterion for many travelers is price. But, while it's often possible to negotiate a cheaper rate, you're often only cutting off your own options. Due to the competition, the agencies make a very small profit on these tours. So if you manage to chop B$100 off the price, think about where it'll be made up – a seventh person squeezed in next to you perhaps, part of the circuit skipped, or, much simpler, by serving smaller meals. Think carefully about whether you want to wreck a once-in-a-lifetime experience for the sake of a few dollars. The cheapest operators also tend to be those with least knowledge of, and respect for, the unique environment of the southwest.

Trips are cheaper if you form a group of four to six. While agencies will do this for you, in practice it works better if you can do it yourself. This avoids the problem of one company sending you off as a filler for another company's tour (it's common to book with one company but you end up going with another), and means that you can really plan your own custom itinerary around the region, rather than just going with the standard trip. This is highly recommended, as there are many places of interest around the *salar* that are not on the standard trip, and many interesting choices emerging with regard to accommodations. Another benefit is that you avoid the underwhelming experience of seeing one of the world's great wildernesses in a convoy of a couple of dozen 4WDs all on the same route.

Think carefully about what your priorities are – is an English-speaking guide, for example, crucial given that the guide spends most of the time driving, and much of what there is to see is self-explanatory? Also, always check whether things like accommodations and national park entry are included in the price you are quoted.

Note that only larger Uyuni agencies accept credit cards so it's better to show up with enough cash to cover your tour.

Tour Agencies
The agency market in Uyuni is notably volatile, and it's impossible to recommend operators with any confidence. The best option is to get information when you arrive in Uyuni. Travelers who've just returned from a tour are an obvious source. We also

strongly suggest that you speak to several companies after doing some research of your own in town.

The best operators typically have written itineraries outlining meals, accommodations and other trip details. Get any verbally agreed changes written down, as it's a common complaint that agencies don't adhere to promised 'extras.'

Most of the following Uyuni agencies received mixed reports from travelers. We've also noted the upscale operators, which are usually (but not always) a better bet, if you have cash to splash.

Andes Travel Office (☎ 693-2227; tamboaymara@ gmail.com; Tambo Aymara, Calle Camacho s/n) Exclusive private tours with the owner of Tambo Aymara as the guide.

Andrea Tours (☎ 693-2638; andreatours@hotmail .com; Arce 27) Plus another office at Peru 200, behind the bus terminal.

Blue Line Service (☎ 693-3546; blueday_54@hotmail .com; Ferroviaria 3)

Cordillera (☎ 693-3304; cordilleratravel_927@hotmail .com; Ferroviaria 314)

Estrella del Sur (☎ 693-3132; toursestrelladelsur@ hotmail.com; Arce, at bus terminal)

Expediciones Empexsa (☎ 693-2348; expedicion _empexsa@hotmail.com; Ferroviaria s/n)

Fremen Tours (☎ 693-3543; www.andes-amazonia .com; Sucre 325) More upmarket.

Hidalgo Tours (☎ 693-2989; www.salardeuyuni.net; Potosí 113, Hotel Jardines de Uyuni) This upscale agency owns a couple of salt hotels (see boxed text, p174).

Natour (☎ 693-3287; www.uyuni.com.bo/uyuni; Santa Cruz btwn Colón & Potosí) Upscale operator.

Oasis Tours (☎ 693-2308; oasistours2002@yahoo.com; Arce s/n)

Reli Tours (☎ 693-3209; www.relitours.com; Arce 42)

Toñito Tours (☎ 693-2094; www.bolivianexpeditions .com; Ferroviaria 152) More upmarket.

Turismo El Desierto (☎ 693-3087; Arce 42)

Festivals & Events
Uyuni's big **annual festival** falls on July 11 and marks the founding of the town. Celebrations entail parades, speeches, dancing, music and, naturally, lots of drinking.

Sleeping
Uyuni's tourism boom means that new hotels are opening all the time and older midrange properties are getting refurbished to keep up with the competition. The best of the bunch fill up fast in the high season

so reservations are recommended, especially if you're chugging in on a late-night train. Cheap places near the station come in handy as most trains arrive and depart at ungodly night hours. Only better hotels offer heating. In the rainy season, prices are slightly lower and it's not as cold at night. Note that there are water rations in Uyuni year-round.

BUDGET
Hostal Marith (☎ 693-2096, fax 693-2174; Potosí 61; r per person B$30, with bathroom B$50) This quiet no-nonsense cheapie is a backpackers' favorite and hence often full. About 20 rooms are set around a courtyard, which is a good place to meet other travelers. Some rooms are on the dark side, service varies and hot water is sporadic. Breakfast is available for B$12.

Hotel Avenida (☎ 693-2078; Ferroviaria 11; s/d/tr B$30/60/90, with bathroom s/d B$60/120) Near the train station, this place is popular for its clean, renovated rooms, friendly staff, laundry sinks and hot showers (available 7am to 9pm, in theory). If you get off the train and they don't answer the door, it means they're full.

Hospedaje El Salvador (☎ 693-2407; Arce 346; s/d/tr B$40/70/100, with bathroom s/d B$50/90) Convenient if you're arriving by bus late at night, this pleasant spot has friendly service, clean simple rooms with TV and a cafeteria where breakfast is available (B$12 to B$16).

HI-Salar de Uyuni (☎ 693-2228; cnr Potosí & Sucre; dm B$45-50, d with bathroom B$120-150) This HI affiliate offers good beds and all the typical hostel amenities. It's on the dark side and the rooms vary significantly so do check out a few. There is a TV room, a clean shared kitchen, laundry service (B$10 per kilo) and hot water (between 8:30am and 6pm, with a 10-minute daily shower limit). Breakfast is available (B$10 to B$15).

Urkupiña Ei Cactu (☎ 693-2032; Arce 46; r per person B$55) Handy shelter near the train station with hot water and plenty of blankets, it was being refurbished at the time of research, with two new floors going up. There are two chit-chatty parrots in the courtyard but no communal space to meet other travelers (which should be changing after completion of the renovations).

Hotel Julia (☎ /fax 693-2134; juliahotel5@hotmail .com; Ferroviaria, at Arce; s/d B$60/100, with bathroom B$80/150; 💻) Decent central choice if other

hotels are full, with internet room off the lobby (B$5 per hour). It's worth paying more for a room with bathroom, as these have more light.

Hotel Kory Wasy (☎ /fax 693-2670; Potosí 350; r per person B$80) Rooms are poky and dark, all with private bathroom (though some are external to the room). The management is friendly and the prices, including breakfast, low. It was being spruced up at the time of research.

MIDRANGE
Hotel Samay Wasi (☎ 693-3596; samaywasi uyuni@gmail.com; Potosí 965; s/d/q B$260/350/530; 💻) Uyuni's latest hotel sits in a large pink-orange building on the edge of town. Beige-colored rooms arranged around a big patio with a skylight come with feather duvets, extra-large beds, heated floors and hot water 24 hours. There are also 15 rooms with shared bathroom (singles/doubles/triples B$135/200/280), private parking and a sauna (in the works).

Hostal La Magia de Uyuni (☎ /fax 693-2541; www .hostalmagiauyuni.com; Colón 432; s/d/tr B$190/280/415) One of the pioneers of Uyuni hotels, this choice is still a solid one, but past its golden days. Older darkish backpacker rooms downstairs (doubles B$130) are arranged around an indoor courtyard. The newer rooms upstairs are decently well-kept. Three floors were under construction at the time of research, slated to house a set of spacious suites (B$380 to B$445).

Joya Andina (☎ /fax 693-2076; reservasjoyaandina@ hotmail.com; Cabrera 473; s/d/tr B$200/280/400) A good choice if other hotels are booked, this spot is housed in a garish pink building, with 10 somewhat kitschy rooms set around an inner courtyard. The rates are inclusive of breakfast and hot water.

Toñito Hotel (☎ 693-2094; www.bolivian expeditions.com; Ferroviaria 60; old wing s/d/tr B$200/280/420, new wing s/d/tr B$260/400/550; 💻) An appealing choice built around a central courtyard, the Toñito has a set of pleasant rooms with spacious beds and electric showers in the old wing and 33 vibrantly colored doubles with solar showers in the sparkling new section. There's a safe, private garage, laundry service (B$10 per kilo), free wi-fi and Uyuni's best breakfasts and pizzas on the premises. It gets packed with tour groups so book ahead.

Tambo Aymara (☎ /fax 693-2227; www
.tamboaymara.com; Camacho s/n; s/d/tr/ste B$220/350/500/
380) The most stylish option in town, run by
a Bolivian-Belgian couple, this recent opening has an ethnic theme and 14 rooms with
earth tones around a flower-filled patio.
Some rooms are on the dark side but there's
reliable hot water and the service is friendly.

TOP END

Los Girasoles Hotel (☎ /fax 693-3323; girasoleshotel@
hotmail.com; Santa Cruz 155; s/d/tr B$280/480/600) This
spacious and handsome hotel offers helpful
service and attractive rooms with big comfortable beds, TV, cactus-wood paneling and
gas-heated bathrooms. The breakfast buffet
is generous, there's bike rental (B$65 per
hour) and laundry service (B$20 per kilo).

Jardines de Uyuni (☎ 693-2989; www.salardeuyuni
.net; Potosí 113; s/d B$300/495; 🖥 🚿) Built around
a courtyard in a delightful rustic style, this
hotel has adobe walls and beds, wall paintings and a fish pond. A little comfort has
been sacrificed for the ambience – rooms
are darkish and feel a mite overpriced, but
offer heating and reliable hot water. Nonetheless, it's got many attractions, including
a pretty bar area, hammocks, a sauna and
an indoor pool.

Eating & Drinking

For quick eats, cheap meals are on offer
at the market *comedor* (dining hall) and
nearby street food stalls. A fast-food kiosk
next to the clock tower has a few tables
outside and cheap bites (B$8 to B$35)
like sandwiches and hamburgers. Food in
restaurants generally revolves around
pizzas, pastas and tacos, and service is
quite slow in most places. On sunny days
there are outside tables along Arce, a nice
spot to spend an afternoon lounging over
a coffee.

Restaurant 16 de Julio (Arce 35; almuerzo B$18,
mains B$18-45) Right along the main strip, this
is a good place to escape the fellow gringos.
Pleasant and friendly, it has a full spectrum
of international and Bolivian dishes. Expect
to wait a while to get served, especially at
lunchtime when locals flock here.

Italiana (Arce, btwn Potosí & Ferroviaria; mains B$24-
33) Service can be painfully slow at this buzzing place with bamboo decor and plenty of
travelers. The menu features a variety of
Mexican and Italian dishes such as tacos,

enchiladas, pastas, and some vegetarian
options. You can wash your meal down
with a beer or cocktail.

La Loco (Potosí, btwn Sucre & Camacho; snacks B$9,
mains B$25-30; 🕐 4pm-2am, closed in low season) This
friendly French-run restaurant and pub is a
barn-like space that's lit low and furnished
with comfortingly chunky wooden furniture around a log fire. There are plenty of
drinks and a short but classy menu that
offers *croques monsieur* (grilled ham and
cheese sandwiches), crepes and llama steaks
with a gourmet touch.

Por't Alba (Ferroviaria 332; mains B$25-45) A good
place to fill up before the train ride, with
a spacious interior clad in wood and a big
fireplace in the middle. Food choices consist of the usual: pizzas, pastas, hamburgers
and some national dishes.

Wiphala Pub (Potosí 325; mains B$25-50) Named
after the multicolored Aymará flag, this
place has a welcoming feel with its wooden
tables, earthy vibe and board games. It serves
tasty Bolivian dishes, specializing in llama
meat and quinoa, and has quinoa beer.

Arco Iris (☎ 693-3177; Arce 27; pizzas B$30-35)
Something of an Uyuni classic for pizza
and drinks, this place with wooden benches
and ethnic decor is friendly and popular as
a place to socialize and link up with other
travelers.

Kactus (cnr Potosí & Arce; almuerzo B$20, mains B$30-
38) In an upstairs location along Arce, this is
a no-fuss restaurant popular with locals for
its affordable food choices. The service can
be spotty and the menu isn't particularly
exciting, but the food is decent.

Minuteman Revolutionary Pizza (☎ 693-2094;
Ferroviaria 60; personal pizzas B$30-40; 🕐 breakfast &
dinner) This convivial spot, inside the Toñito
Hotel, run by Chris from Boston and his
Bolivian wife Sussy, is a deserved travelers'
favorite with the best pizzas in town, tasty alternatives like salads, pastas and sandwiches
and fantastic desserts. It's also a cozy spot
for a beer or candlelit glass of Tarija wine
or a hearty breakfast (B$20 to B$30) with
all you can drink coffee or tea. If you have
old sunglasses, you can do a good deed –
drop them off here and they'll be donated
to the salt workers in Colchani.

Extreme Fun Pub (☎ 693-2102; Potosí 9; mains
B$35-45) This relaxed spot is a very enticing
place for a tea or coffee, a meal or sociable
cocktail – try a Sexy Llama Bitch (B$20).

It has salt floors, friendly service, a book exchange and beautiful *salar* photos. It's also a good place to learn the classic Bolivian dice games or engage in an extreme challenge drink competition: who will chug down 10 drinks in the shortest time possible.

Getting There & Away

Getting out of isolated Uyuni can be problematic. Buy your bus ticket the day before and your train ticket as far in advance as you can. An airstrip is currently being built by the military air force with money from Venezuela. There's talk of commercial flights with TAM starting up once it's done (rumor has it by the end of 2010).

If you're heading on to Chile, it can be a wise idea to pick up a Bolivian exit stamp at Migración (p167), since the hours of the Bolivian border post at Hito Cajón (just beyond Laguna Verde) are somewhat unreliable. Although it's rarely enforced, you're expected to leave Bolivia within three days of getting the stamp. If you need more time, Migración will give you up to five days, if you ask nicely.

BUS

There's a new bus terminal in the works but it will most likely be a couple of years before it opens. For now, all buses are still leaving from the west end of Av Arce, a couple of minutes' walk from the plaza. There's a choice of companies to most destinations, so ask around to get the best price or service.

Several companies offer daily evening buses to Oruro (B$40, seven hours), where you can change for La Paz. It's a chilly, bone-shaking trip, so you might prefer the train or **Todo Turismo** (☎ 693-3337; www .touringbolivia.com; Cabrera 158, btwn Bolívar & Arce), which runs a heated bus service with friendly staff and an onboard meal. It heads between Uyuni and La Paz (B$230, 10 hours) via Oruro (B$230, seven hours), leaving at 8pm daily, except Wednesday and Sunday. While it's expensive, the advantage of using this service is that you avoid having to deal with freezing Oruro in the middle of the night – travelers have reported being robbed while waiting there for a connection to La Paz. The cheaper option with reliable buses and good drivers is Omar, right next to the post office. They have a daily 8pm bus (B$100 to B$130, 11 hours).

There are several departures around 10am and 7pm for Potosí (B$40, six hours), with connections to Sucre (B$60, nine hours). From there, you can make your way to Tarija. The road to Potosí was being paved at the time of research and should be up and running by the time you read this, reducing travel time by about an hour.

There are daily bus services to Tupiza (B$60, seven to eight hours), leaving around 6am. The same buses continue on to Villazón (B$80, 10 hours), which is the way to go if you're continuing on to Salta, as there are regular buses from there.

There are buses at 3:30am on Monday and Thursday and at 5am on Sunday and Wednesday to Calama (B$100, nine hours) in Chile. You'll have to change buses in Avaroa at the Chilean border; there are sometimes waits of up to two hours.

An alternative route to Chile is with an organized tour, which will leave you in San Pedro de Atacama. Some of the tour companies, including Estrella del Sur (p169) and Cordillera (p169), both with offices in Chile, offer direct jeep transfers to San Pedro, which cost around B$280 per person. The jeeps typically leave at 4pm, there's a sleepover in Villa Mar, and you arrive in San Pedro at noon the next day. From San Pedro, buses to Salta depart three times weekly (Tuesday, Friday and Saturday) at 10:30am.

TRAIN

Uyuni has a modern, well-organized **train station** (☎ 693-2320). Seats often sell out so buy your ticket several days in advance or get an agency to do it for you.

Comfortable *Expreso del Sur* trains ramble to Oruro (*salón/ejecutivo* B$52/101, seven hours) on Wednesday and Saturday at 12:05am (arriving the next morning, on Thursday or Sunday) and southeast to Tupiza (B$41/101, 5½ hours) and Villazón (B$63/152, 8½ hours) on Tuesday and Friday at 10:40pm.

Wara Wara del Sur trains chug out of the station at 1:45am on Monday and Thursday nights for Oruro (*popular/salón/ejecutivo* B$31/40/86, 7½ hours) and on Sunday and Wednesday nights at 2:50am for Tupiza (B$24/33/64, six hours) and Villazón (B$36/48/99, 10 hours). Note that during the rainy season the trains coming from Villazón tend to run late.

Depending on size, you may have to check your backpack/case into the luggage compartment. Look out for snatch thieves on the train just before it pulls out.

On Monday at 3:30am a train trundles west for Avaroa (B$32, five hours) on the Chilean border, where you cross to Ollagüe and may have to wait a few hours to clear Chilean customs. From here, another train continues to Calama (B$91 from Uyuni, six hours from Ollagüe). The whole trip can take up to 24 hours but it's a spectacular, if uncomfortable journey. Taking a bus to Calama is more reliable.

AROUND UYUNI

At the semi-ghost town of **Pulacayo**, 22km northeast of Uyuni, brilliantly colored rocks rise beside the road and a mineral-rich stream reveals streaks of blue, yellow, red and green. The **Pulacayo mines** north of the village, which yielded mainly silver, were first opened in the late 17th century; today, only a few hundred hardy souls remain. There are several kilometers of **mine tunnels** to explore, if you find a local guide. Also worthwhile is the **mill** that spins llama wool into cloth, and the **mansion** of the 22nd president of Bolivia, Aniceto Arce Ruíz. Pulacayo is also home to several decaying **steam locomotives** that were originally imported to transport ore. A bus departs daily at noon (B$5) outside the post office in Uyuni; you can return with one of the buses coming into Uyuni from Potosí.

Right on the edge of the Salar de Uyuni, **Colchani**, 20km north of Uyuni, is the easiest point to access that great salt flat, and the place to go if you just want a glimpse of it without going on a tour. There remain at least 10 billion tons of salt in the Salar de Uyuni, and around Colchani *campesinos* (subsistence farmers) hack it out with picks and shovels and pile it into small conical mounds that characterize the *salar* landscape. Most of the salt is sold to refiners and hauled off by rail, but some is exchanged with local villages for wool, meat and grease. Most tour groups stop at the small **museum** (admission B$5) dealing with the *salar* and the salt trade. Apart from the handful of salt sculptures, it's more of a souvenir stop selling ponchos, hats, gloves and sweaters. Another attraction on the *salar* tourist circuit is just southwest of Colchani, the extraordinary **Cooperativa Rosario workshop**, also called the Bloques de Sal (Salt Blocks). Here, blocks of salt are cut from the *salar* and made into furniture and lively works of art. Colchani is also home to several salt hotels (see boxed text, p174). Some salt workers living in Uyuni commute daily to Colchani in private vehicles or on motorcycles; if you wait at the gas station just outside of town, you may be able to hitch along for a small fee. Otherwise, a return taxi ride will cost around B$200, with a little extra for any wait time.

THE SOUTHWEST CIRCUIT

Bolivia's southwestern corner is an awe-inspiring collection of harsh, diverse landscapes ranging from the blinding white Salar de Uyuni salt flat to the geothermal hotbed of Los Lípez, one of the world's harshest wilderness regions and an important refuge for many Andean wildlife species. The ground here literally boils with minerals, and the spectrum of colors is extraordinary. A circuit from Uyuni takes you through absolutely unforgettable, literally breath-taking landscapes and is the highlight of many people's visit to Bolivia.

Much of the region is nominally protected in the **Reserva Nacional de Fauna Andina Eduardo Avaroa** (REA; www.bolivia-rea.com; admission B$30), which was created in 1973, covers an area of 7150 sq km and receives in excess of 50,000 visitors annually. Its emphasis is on preserving the vicuña and the *yareta* plant, both of which are threatened in Bolivia, as well as other unique ecosystems and endemic species. (Note: there is talk of a steep admission hike.)

Most people visit the region on an organized trip from Uyuni (p167) or Tupiza (p182); see the boxed text, p178 for some alternative things to do. This section is organized to highlight the attractions of the standard three-day circuit, as well as some lesser-visited sights typically visited only on longer tours.

Apart from a couple of Entel points, there are no phones out in the Southwest Circuit. All communication is by radio. Any phone numbers listed in this section are for offices

SALT HOTELS & THE TAYKA CHAIN

There are several hotels around the *salar* (salt pan or salt desert) that are built of salt, of various categories and levels of comfort. These are unique and comfortable places to stay, where nearly everything is constructed of blocks of salt (with a few obvious exceptions). Note that it is illegal to actually construct buildings on the *salar* itself – Playa Blanca salt hotel, a morning stop on many tours, falls into this category due to its sewage system polluting the salt pan. Local environmentalists strongly recommend that you don't give them any business so try to boycott if you can, even if the driver stops the jeep there.

Right on the edge of the salt, the **Hotel Palacio de Sal** (☎ 622-9512; www.palaciodesal.com; s/d B$1190/1400; 🏊) is a luxurious complex built almost completely out of the white condiment, the first such hotel opened in the region. It boasts all sorts of facilities ranging from a pool and sauna to a salt golf course (don't bring your favorite white balls). Breakfast and dinner are included in the rates. The hotel is booked through Hidalgo Tours (p235) in Potosí or at the Jardines de Uyuni hotel (p171); it comes cheaper as part of a package.

Another salty option is **Luna Salada Hotel** (☎ 278-5438; www.lunasaladahotel.com.bo; s/d B$605/780), an award-winning place, 7km from Colchani, with 23 stylish rooms and a panoramic restaurant.

At the time of writing, there were three hotels being constructed on the edge of salt, about 4km from Colchani, and more around the other edges of the *salar* where most agencies spend the first night of the three-day tour. These are typically small, private affairs in local villages such as Quimisa and Candelaria.

At the village of **Coquesa,** under the Tunupa volcano, there is a cozy salt hostel called **Maya** (r per person B$35) run by a local Aymará family. The beds are built on salt blocks, the doors and windows of cactus wood, and the dining room has salt tables with a splendid view over the *salar*. At night, a camp fire and candle lights illuminate the place.

While many of the lodgings around the *salar* are rudimentary, if you want a more upmarket and interesting experience, the **Tayka Hoteles** (☎ 693-2987; www.taykahoteles.com) are a great option that promotes sustainable tourism. The chain is a community-run business project, each of the three properties having been built in small remote communities that were involved in the hotel construction and now manage the hotels. **Hotel de Sal** (s/d/tr US$88/95/115), near the village of Tahua on the foothills of Tunupa volcano, is built entirely of locally extracted salt, apart from the thatched roof and the black stone bathrooms. At the southwestern tip of the *salar*, off the beaten track, **Hotel de Piedra** (s/d/tr US$88/95/115), built of rugged local stone, lies near the village of San Pedro de Quemez, by the burned-down ruins of a pre-Columbian settlement. **Hotel del Desierto** (s/d/tr US$100/110/140) is set in a landscape of stupendous ocher colors near Arbol de Piedra, a short drive from Laguna Colorada. The latest **Hotel de los Volcanes** (s/d/tr B$530/775/985) is set to open by the time this book comes out.

All the Tayka hotels offer plenty of perks, such as comfortable beds with feather duvets, heaters and solar-powered hot water in the rooms, as well as restaurants serving tasty typical meals (like llama steaks with quinoa and dehydrated potatoes). Hotel staff can organize intriguing local excursions to little-known points of interest.

located in Uyuni. Note that the toilet facilities in most stops along the way cost B$5.

SALAR DE UYUNI

One of the globe's most evocative and eerie sights, the world's largest salt flat (12,106 sq km) sits at 3653m. When the surface is dry, the *salar* is a pure white expanse of the greatest nothing imaginable – just the blue sky, the white ground and you. When there's a little water, the surface perfectly reflects the clouds and the blue Altiplano sky, and the horizon disappears. If you're driving across the surface at such times, the effect is positively surreal, and it's hard to believe that you're not actually flying through the clouds.

The Salar de Uyuni is now a center of salt extraction and processing, particularly around the settlement of Colchani (p173). The estimated annual output of the Colchani operation is nearly 20,000 tons, 18,000 tons of which is for human consumption while the rest is for livestock.

Formation

Between 40,000 and 25,000 years ago, Lago Minchín, whose highest level reached 3760m, occupied much of southwestern Bolivia. When it evaporated, the area lay dry for 14,000 years before the appearance of short-lived Lago Tauca, which lasted for only about 1000 years and rose to 3720m. When it dried up, it left two large puddles, Lagos Poopó and Uru Uru, and two major salt concentrations, the Salares de Uyuni and Coipasa.

This part of the Altiplano is drained internally, with no outlet to the sea; the salt deposits are the result of the minerals leached from the mountains and deposited at the lowest available point.

The Standard Circuit
ISLA INCAHUASI

For most Salar de Uyuni tours, the main destination is the spectacular **Isla Incahuasi** (admission B$15), better known as Isla del Pescado, in the heart of the *salar* 80km west of Colchani. This hilly outpost is covered in Trichoreus cactus and surrounded by a flat white sea of hexagonal salt tiles. It was once a remarkably lonely, otherworldly place but since the advent of *salar* tours, it has become overrun with tourists. All the tour groups arrive at the same time, at midday, and swarm over the hiking trails chasing the perfect photo of cacti and salt. This is where most groups have their lunch but there's also a café-restaurant run by La

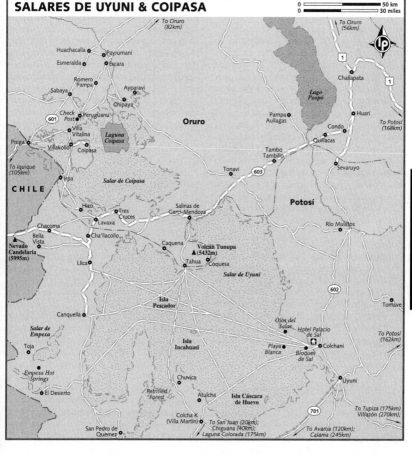

SALARES DE UYUNI & COIPASA

0 —— 50 km
0 —— 30 miles

To Oruro (82km)
To Oruro (56km)

Huachacalla
Payrumani
Esmeralda
Escara
Chaliapata
Romero Pampa
Sabaya
Ayparavi
Chipaya
Lago Poopó
Check Post
Peruguanu
Villa Vitalina
Laguna Coipasa
Oruro
Pampa Aullagas
Huari
Pisiga
Villakollo
Coipasa
Condo
To Potosí (168km)
Quillacas
CHILE
To Iquique (105km)
Irpa
Tambo Tambillo
Tonavi
603
Sevaruyo
Salar de Coipasa
Hizo
Salinas de Garci-Mendoza
Potosí
Tres Cruces
Chacoma
Lavaxa
Río Mulatos
Bella Vista
Cha'llacollo
Nevado Candelaria (5995m)
Caquena
Volcán Tunupa (5432m)
Llica
Tahua
Coquesa
Salar de Uyuni
602
Tomave
Isla Pescador
Canquella
Salar de Empexa
Ojos del Salar
Hotel Palacio de Sal
To Potosí (162km)
Toja
Isla Incahuasi
Playa Blanca
Bloques de Sal
Colchani
Empexa Hot Springs
Chuvica
El Desierto
Petrified Forest
Atulcha
Isla Cáscara de Huevo
Uyuni
Colcha K (Villa Martín)
To Tupiza (175km); Villazón (270km);
701
San Pedro de Quemez
To San Juan (20km); Chiguana (40km); Laguna Colorada (175km)
To Avaroa (120km); Calama (245km)

SOUTHERN ALTIPLANO

Paz-based **Mongo's** (mains B$15-48). Altogether an industrialized tourist experience, it's still a beautiful sight if you forget the crowds.

TUNUPA & COQUESA

A rounded promontory juts into the Salar de Uyuni diagonally opposite Colchani, and on it rises **Volcán Tunupa** (5432m). One legend states that Atahualpa slashed the breast of a woman called Tunupa on its slopes, and the milk that spilled out formed the *salar*. Another story goes that, back in those ancient days, mountains were men and women. Right after giving birth to their baby, Tunupa learned her man was living with another woman. Devastated, she wept and wept, spilling her salty tears over her breast milk, and creating this vast area of sadness and beauty that is now the *salar*.

Altitude aside, this hulking yellow mountain is a relatively easy climb. At the foot of the volcano is the village of **Coquesa** in an area specked with ruined ancient villages and burial grounds. Articles of clothing and artifacts in ceramic, gold and copper have been discovered at some of the sites, indicating the presence of an advanced but little-known culture. Unfortunately, its remoteness has left it vulnerable to amateur treasure hunters who have plundered several items of archaeological value. At **Hospedaje Chatahuana**, you can ask for the keys to the **Museo Coquesa** (admission per 4WD B$20), which has a collection of ceramics and mummies. In Coquesa, you can also arrange a nighttime visit to the nearby **observatory**, to really appreciate the starry skies.

LOS LÍPEZ

Entering the remote and beautiful region of Los Lípez, many tours pass through a military checkpoint at the village of **Colcha K** (*col*-cha *kah*), where there's a pleasant adobe church and a series of fairly rudimentary dormitory accommodations. About 15km further along is the quinoa-growing village of **San Juan** at an elevation of 3660m. It has a lovely adobe church, a population of 1000, and several volcanic-rock tombs and burial *chullpas* in the vicinity. The community-run **Museo Kausay Wasi** (donation B$5) displays regional archaeological finds.

At this point the route turns west and starts across the borax-producing **Salar de Chiguana**, where the landscape opens up

and snowcapped **Ollagüe** (5865m), an active volcano straddling the Chilean border, appears in the distance.

The route then turns south and climbs into high and increasingly wild terrain, past the several mineral-rich lakes filled with flamingos (see boxed text, opposite) and backed by hills resembling spilled chocolate sundaes. After approximately 170km of rough bumping through marvelous landscapes, the road winds down to the much-photographed **Árbol de Piedra** (Stone Tree) in the Desierto Siloli, 18km north of Laguna Colorada.

The next attraction, **Laguna Colorada** is a fiery red lake (4278m) that covers approximately 60 sq km and reaches a depth of just 80cm. The rich red coloration is derived from algae and plankton that thrive in the mineral-rich water, and the shoreline is fringed with brilliant white deposits of sodium, magnesium, borax and gypsum. The lake sediments are also rich in diatoms, tiny microfossils used in the production of fertilizer, paint, toothpaste and plastics, and as a filtering agent for oil, pharmaceuticals, aviation fuel, beer and wine. More apparent are the flamingos that breed here; all three South American species are present (see boxed text, opposite). The clear air is bitterly cold and winter nighttime temperatures can drop below -20°C.

Apart from tour groups, most vehicles along the tracks around Laguna Colorada will be supplying or servicing mining and military camps or the geothermal project 50km south at **Sol de Mañana**. The main interest here is the 4850m-high geyser basin with bubbling mud pots, hellish fumaroles and the thick and nauseating aroma of sulfur fumes. Approach the site cautiously; any damp or cracked earth is potentially dangerous and cave-ins do occur, sometimes causing serious burns.

At the foot of Cerro Polques lies the **Termas de Polques**, a small 29.4°C hot-spring pool, and an absolute paradise after the chilly *salar* nights. Although they're not boiling by any means, they're suitable for bathing, and the mineral-rich waters are thought to relieve the symptoms of arthritis and rheumatism. There's a restaurant here, and changing sheds with toilet facilities.

The stunning blue-green **Laguna Verde** (4400m) is tucked into the southwestern

SOUTHERN ALTIPLANO

corner of Bolivian territory, 52km south of Sol de Mañana. The incredible green color comes from high concentrations of lead, sulfur, arsenic and calcium carbonates. In this exposed position, an icy wind blows almost incessantly, whipping the water into a brilliant green-and-white froth. This surface agitation, combined with the high mineral content, means that it can remain liquid at temperatures as low as -21.2°C.

Behind the lake rises the cone of **Volcán Licancabur** (5960m), whose summit is said to have once sheltered an ancient Inca crypt. Some tours include an ascent of Licancabur (see boxed text, p178), and although it presents no technical difficulties, the wind, temperature, altitude and ball-bearing volcanic pumice underfoot make it quite grueling.

Where the route splits about 20km south of Sol de Mañana, the more scenic left fork climbs up and over a 5000m pass, then up a stark hillside resembling a freshly raked Zen garden dotted with the enormous **Rocas de Dalí**, which appear to have been meticulously placed by the surrealist master Salvador himself.

GETTING THERE & AWAY

Most agencies now offer cross-border connections to San Pedro de Atacama by arrangement with Chilean operators. It's wise to check out of Bolivia at Migración in Uyuni (see p167). The Hito Cajón border post near Laguna Verde is much more reliable than it used to be but has been known to take unpaid leave. Try to be there by 6pm or you may have to wait a long time. There's a B$21 exit tax.

OTHER SOUTHWEST ATTRACTIONS

Some of the tour agencies are increasingly offering alternative tours of the Southwest Circuit. These customized trips are usually pricier than typical three-day jaunts but involve visits to some less-visited attractions in Los Lípez and a real sense of discovery. This region is a land of bizarre lava formations, active volcanoes, abandoned villages, badlands, salt flats, pre-Incan cave cemeteries, lone quinoa fields, flying condors, multicolored lagoons and sulfur lakes. We've listed some of the places where you won't be surrounded by packs of jeeps and other travelers, where the feel of the last frontier is true and real.

Isla Cáscara de Huevo

The small **Eggshell Island** was named for the broken shells of birds' eggs that litter it. It lies near the southern end of the Salar de Uyuni and is visited mainly to see the strange patterns of salt crystallization in the area, some of which resemble roses.

FROZEN FLAMINGOS

Three species of flamingo breed in the bleak high country of southwestern Bolivia, and once you've seen these posers strutting through icy mineral lagoons at 5000m elevation, you'll abandon time-worn associations between flamingos, coconut palms and the steamy tropics. The sight of these pinky-white birds with their black bills and tails adds yet another color to the already spectacular palette hereabouts.

Flamingos have a complicated and sophisticated system for filtering the foodstuffs from highly alkaline brackish lakes. They filter algae and diatoms from the water by sucking in and vigorously expelling water from the bill several times per second. The minute particles are caught on fine hairlike protrusions that line the inside of the mandibles. The suction is created by the thick fleshy tongue, which rests in a groove in the lower mandible and pumps back and forth like a piston.

The Chilean flamingo reaches heights of just over 1m and has a black-tipped white bill, dirty blue legs, red knees and salmon-colored plumage. The James flamingo is the smallest of the three species and has dark-red legs and a yellow-and-black bill. It's locally known as *jututu*. The Andean flamingo is the largest of the three and has pink plumage, yellow legs and a yellow-and-black bill.

Environmentalists have been particularly concerned for the birds in recent years, as tourism has affected the flamingos' breeding. Don't try to creep up to them to get a better photo; above all don't put them to flight or encourage any guide that suggests doing this.

CLIMBING VOLCANOES

There are plenty of opportunities for getting out of the 4WD and doing something active throughout the Southwest Circuit. One of the most popular activities is volcano climbing, with guides easily available in the region's settlements. Most of the climbs are challenging for the altitude rather than being technically difficult. Taking a guide is a good idea and contributes something to the local communities, which are so often bypassed by the Uyuni-based tours. The most frequently climbed is the **Volcán Licancabur** (5960m; see p177); it takes about eight hours to climb to the summit, and two to get down. Several Uyuni and Tupiza agencies are happy to include a guided climb of the volcano in a Southwest Circuit route, adding an extra day to the trip. You can normally find a guide somewhere around Laguna Verde – they tend to charge about US$35 to US$40 for an ascent of the mountain, with a beautiful lagoon at the top, which can be done comfortably (if you handle the altitude) in one day. As the volcano is sacred to the locals, the guides usually perform a ritual for Pachamama, asking the earth goddess her permission to climb.

Nevado Candelaria (5995m), southwest of the Salar de Coipasa, is also an exhilarating climb. The active **Volcán Ollagüe** (5865m) on the Chilean border southwest of San Pedro de Quemez is another interesting option, with spectacular views – you can get pretty close to the summit with a jeep and then hike the 400 remaining meters to the top. Another volcano to climb is the hulking **Tunupa** (5400m), which you can approach from two sides – the village of Coquesa (10 hours there and back, including a visit to the caves with pre-Incan mummies) or the village of Jirira (four hours there and back).

It's also possible to climb **Uturuncu** (6020m), which is an active volcano; jeeps can drive up to just 1km below the summit and you can hike to the top – an easy way to say you've climbed a 6000m-high volcano!

Gruta de las Galaxias

Some agencies now offer a side trip to Aquaquiza, a quinoa-producing village in Nor Lípez where there's a basic **alojamiento** (B$20). The area's attraction lies 8km away, **Gruta de las Galaxias** and **Cueva del Diablo**. Between March and December, a B$10 admission is charged for the complex; otherwise it's free but there's nobody to show you around. Discovered in 2003, Gruta de las Galaxias is a small two-level grotto full of beautiful petrified algae and corrals from the ancient lake. Part of the same complex is Cueva del Diablo, a cave sacred to the locals with a pre-Incan cemetery scattered with small *chullpas*. Note the cross as you enter the cave, marking where a shepherd girl was found mysteriously dead after seeking protection from a storm inside the cave. There's a viewpoint at the top to admire the spectacularly desolate scenery and the petrified cacti.

Salar de Coipasa

This great 2218-sq-km remote salt desert, northwest of the Salar de Uyuni at an elevation of 3786m, was part of the same system of prehistoric lakes as the Salar de Uyuni – a system that covered the area over 10,000 years ago. The 4WD-only road to the Salar de Coipasa is extremely poor and the salt is thin so it's easy to get stuck, especially during the rainy season. If you go, make sure the vehicle and the driver are reliable. The salt-mining village of Coipasa, which (not surprisingly) is constructed mainly of salt, occupies an island in the middle of the *salar*. You can also reach the Salar de Coipasa from Oruro province.

Lagoons

The blue lake of **Laguna Celeste** or, more romantically, 'heaven lake,' is still very much a peripheral trip for most Uyuni agencies, but it's gaining popularity with adventurous travelers as a one-day detour. A local legend suggests the presence of a submerged ruin, possibly a *chullpa*, in the lake. Behind the lake, a road winds its way up Volcán Uturuncu (6020m) to the Uturuncu sulfur mine, in a 5900m pass between the mountain's twin cones. That means it's more than 200m higher than the road over the Khardung La in Ladakh, India, making it quite possibly the highest motorable pass in the world.

In the vast eastern reaches of Sud Lípez are numerous other fascinating mineral-rich lakes that are informally named for their odd coloration and have so far escaped much attention. Various milky-looking lakes are known as **Laguna Blanca**, sulfur-colored lakes are **Laguna Amarilla** and wine-colored ones are known as **Laguna Guinda**. **Laguna Cañapa** and **Laguna Hedionda** are also part of some circuits. You can negotiate to add any of these to a tailored circuit.

Quetena Chico & Around

About 120km northeast of Laguna Verde and 30km southwest of Laguna Celeste is the small mining settlement of Quetena

---

CHIPAYA

Immediately north of the Salar de Coipasa, on the Río Sabaya delta, live the Chipaya people. They occupy two main desert villages (Santa Ana de Chipaya and Ayparavi) of unique circular mud huts known as *khuyas* or *putucus*, which have doors made from cactus wood and always face east. Chipayas are best recognized by their earth-colored clothing and the women's unique hairstyle, which is plaited African-style into 60 small braids. These are, in turn, joined into two large braids and decorated with a *laurake* (barrette) at each temple.

Some researchers believe the Chipaya were the Altiplano's first inhabitants, and that they may in fact be a remnant of the lost Tiwanaku civilization. Much of this speculation is based on the fact that their language is vastly different from both Quechua and Aymará, and is probably a surviving form of Uru.

Chipaya tradition maintains that they came into the world when it was still dark, and that they are descended from the 'Men of Water' – perhaps the Uru. Their religion, which is nature-based, is complex and symbolic, deifying phallic images, stones, rivers, mountains, animal carcasses and ancestors. The village church tower is worshipped as a demon – one of 40 named demons who represent hate, ire, vengeance, gluttony and other deadly sins. These are believed to inhabit the whitewashed mud cones that exist within a 15km radius of the village, where they're appeased with libations, sacrifices and rituals to prevent their evil from invading the village.

The reverent commemoration of dead ancestors culminates on November 2, **Día de los Muertos** (Day of the Dead), when bodies are disinterred from *chullpas* (funerary towers). They're feted with a feast, copious drink and coca leaves, and informed about recent village events and the needs of the living. Those who were chiefs, healers and other luminaries are carried to the church where they're honored with animal sacrifices.

The Lauca River, on which the Chipaya have depended for thousands of years, is not only heavily polluted but has also been drying out due to global warming. A lot of the Chipaya have emigrated to Chile and the ones left in the community are facing extinction. In the main settlement, Santa Ana de Chipaya, the traditional way of life is slowly vanishing. It's rare to see the circular houses, also known as *huayllichas*, and the original dress unless you go to Ayparavi or the rural areas.

Visiting the Chipaya

In general, tourists aren't especially welcome, and are expected to pay a fee for entering the Chipaya 'nation' (visitors have been charged anything from US$50 to US$100 per person; you'll pay a lot less if you don't turn up in a 4WD!). The Chipayas don't like to be photographed but some will do so for a fee (expect to be charged between B$20 and B$100 per photo). There's a simple *alojamiento* in Chipaya village and a small shop. At the time of research, a community lodge was under construction and should be up and running by the time you read this.

From Oruro, buses leave daily for Huachacalla; there you'll have to arrange onward transportation to Chipaya, 30km beyond. From Sabaya, it takes about an hour to get there. Ask for Jaime Soruco, who is the owner of the restaurant and hotel. It costs about B$400 to get there and back, with a wait of two to three hours. Alternatively, you can reach Sabaya or Huachacalla on any bus between Oruro and Iquique along a bumpy road.

In addition, a few tour companies organize visits to the village; check with Charlie Tours (see p158) in Oruro, or Bolivia Milenaria (see p351) in La Paz. Note that visiting the Chipaya in the rainy season is practically impossible, as the roads get washed away.

Chico, which has a few basic services and supplies, a military post and the **Centro de Ecología Ch'aska**, which has an exhibition on the geology and biology of the Los Lípez region, and the lives of the local llama herders. There are also a couple of simple *albergues* (hostels) here.

Southeast of here, 6km away, is the picturesque abandoned village of **Barrancas**, which nestles against a craggy cliff.

To the northeast, and well off the standard circuit (although visited by some of the tours from Tupiza), the village of **San Pablo de Lípez** features the latest Tayka property, **Hotel de los Volcanes** (see boxed text, p174).

Heading back toward Uyuni, the village of **Villa Mar** has an interesting *mercado artesanal* (craft market) that's worth a visit. Stretch your legs by strolling the 4km to some of the area's most spectacular *pinturas rupestres* (rock paintings), with impressive human figures wearing headdresses, and incised animals. There are several simple *albergues* in Mallcu, and also the upmarket **Mallku Cueva Lodge** (☎ 622-9512; www.salardeuyuni.net; s/d B$283/495) run by Hidalgo Tours (p235).

Valles de Rocas & San Cristóbal

In the midst of high, lonesome country stretch several valleys of bizarre eroded rock formations known as **Valles de Rocas**. These strangely shaped badlands are great for a wander and snapping some great photos. From the dusty village of **Alota** nearby, it's a six-hour jostle back to Uyuni through a string of 'authentic villages,' the most picturesque of which, **Culpina K**, has colorful little houses and a cafe.

The mining village of **San Cristóbal** is worth a stop for the lovely 350-year-old church. The entire village, including the church and the cemetery, was moved from its original location next to the mine by the American-Japanese mining project that took over the area digging for lead, zinc and silver. The **Hotel San Cristóbal** (dm B$80, s B$140, d B$210-280) offers electricity, sporadically hot solar-powered showers and a restaurant. There's a 2pm bus from Uyuni and back at 6am the following day (B$15).

TUPIZA

pop 22,300 / elevation 2950m

The pace of things in tranquil Tupiza seems a few beats slower than in other Bolivian towns, which makes it a top spot to hang out in for a while. Set in spectacular countryside, the capital of Sud Chichas lies in the valley of the Río Tupiza, surrounded by rugged scenery – weird eroded rainbow-colored rocks cut by tortuous, gravelly *quebradas* (ravines, usually dry) whose slopes are studded with cactus.

The climate is mild year-round, with most of the rain falling between November and March. From June to August, days are hot, dry and clear, but at nighttime the temperatures can drop to below freezing.

Economically, the town depends on agriculture and mining. A refinery south of town provides employment, and the country's only antimony (a flame-retardant metallic element) smelter operates sporadically.

Tupiza and its surroundings have much to offer the traveler. Explore the surrounding hills and canyons on horseback or on foot, check out where the Butch Cassidy & the Sundance Kid story ended (see boxed text, p187) or just take a few days out to read novels in the pretty central square or by the hotel pool. Tupiza is also an excellent place to embark on a tour of the Southwest Circuit to Uyuni, a four-day route that is attracting growing numbers of travelers.

History

The tribe that originally inhabited the region called themselves Chichas and left archaeological evidence of their existence. Despite this, little is known of their culture or language, and it's assumed they were ethnically separate from the tribes in neighboring areas of southern Bolivia and northern Argentina.

Officially, Tupiza was founded on June 4, 1574, by Captain Luis de Fuentes (who was also the founder of Tarija). From Tupiza's inception through the War of Independence, its Spanish population grew steadily, lured by the favorable climate and suitable agricultural lands. Later, the discovery of minerals attracted even more settlers. More recently, *campesinos* have drifted in from the countryside and many unemployed miners have settled.

Information

INTERNET & TELEPHONE

There are several internet places on the plaza that charge B$3 per hour, as does **Entel** (cnr

Avaroa & Santa Cruz), where you can also make calls. The dial-up connection in Tupiza is painfully slow most of the time.

LAUNDRY
All accommodations can do a load of washing for you. There's a **laundry** (Mon-Sat) on Florida that charges B$10 per kilo.

MAPS
Most agencies distribute small maps of the town and the surroundings.

MONEY
You can change cash or get cash advances at Banco de Crédito or Prodem on the plaza. Another place for cash is the **Latin America**

Cambio (Avaroa 160), which accepts several currencies but not at the best rates. You can change travelers checks here or, for a better deal, at the Hotel Mitru, which charges only 5% commission.

TOURIST INFORMATION
There's no tourist office although there is talk of an info kiosk opening at the bus terminal. The hotels and agencies are your main source of information.

Sights & Activities
Tupiza's main attraction is the surrounding countryside, best seen on foot or horseback. The short hike up **Cerro Corazón de Jesús**, flanked by the Stations of the Cross, is a

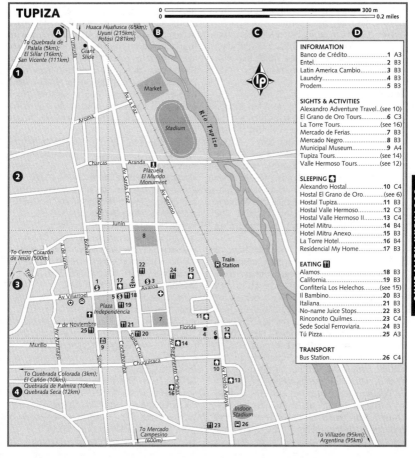

INFORMATION
Banco de Crédito...................1 A3
Entel...................................2 B3
Latin America Cambio.............3 B3
Laundry...............................4 B3
Prodem...............................5 B3

SIGHTS & ACTIVITIES
Alexandro Adventure Travel..(see 10)
El Grano de Oro Tours............6 C3
La Torre Tours.....................(see 16)
Mercado de Ferias.................7 B3
Mercado Negro.....................8 B3
Municipal Museum.................9 A4
Tupiza Tours.......................(see 14)
Valle Hermoso Tours............(see 12)

SLEEPING
Alexandro Hostal..................10 C4
Hostal El Grano de Oro..........(see 6)
Hostal Tupiza......................11 B3
Hostal Valle Hermoso............12 C3
Hostal Valle Hermoso II.........13 C4
Hotel Mitru.........................14 B4
Hotel Mitru Anexo................15 B3
La Torre Hotel.....................16 B4
Residencial My Home............17 B3

EATING
Alamos...............................18 B3
California............................19 B3
Confitería Los Helechos........(see 15)
Il Bambino..........................20 B3
Italiana..............................21 B3
No-name Juice Stops............22 B3
Rinconcito Quilmes...............23 C4
Sede Social Ferroviaria..........24 B3
Tú Pizza.............................25 A3

TRANSPORT
Bus Station.........................26 C4

SOUTHERN ALTIPLANO

pleasant morning or evening outing when the low sun brings out the fiery reds of the surrounding countryside.

The permanent **Mercado Negro**, where you'll encounter a mishmash of consumer goods, occupies an entire block between Santa Cruz and Chichas. Lively **street markets** convene Thursday and Saturday mornings near the train station. A kilometer south of town, the **Mercado Campesino** features more of the same on Monday, Thursday and Saturday. The central **Mercado de Ferias** has lots of produce stalls and *comedores* upstairs.

Tupiza's **municipal museum** (Sucre, near plaza; admission B$10; 🕑 8am-noon & 2-6pm Mon-Fri) houses a mixture of historical and cultural artifacts in two rooms, including an antique cart, old photographs, archaeological relics, pre-Columbian items, cold weapons and historic farming implements.

Nonguests can enjoy Hotel Mitru's solar-heated **swimming pool** for B$20 per half-day; in the high season, it has a snack bar with drinks, sandwiches and pizzas.

Tours

There's an ever-increasing number of operators in Tupiza offering trips through the Southwest Circuit, ending in Uyuni or back in Tupiza (or, in some cases, San Pedro de Atacama in Chile). Tupiza is a great place to do this trip from, as you get to explore the lesser-known wild lands of Sud López as well as seeing the well-established highlights at different times to the large convoys of 4WDs that visit them out of Uyuni. The sunrise over the *salar* on the last morning is one of the highlights.

The downside is that you may have to wait a while in Tupiza to get a group together (although the larger outfits have departures almost daily). Expect to pay between B$1200 and B$1350 per person for the standard four-day trip, based on four people in a jeep during the high season. This price typically includes all meals, basic accommodations, entrance fees and bottled water. Customized trips, many including climbing options, will cost a bit more but they're worth the surcharge.

While most tour operators display enthusiastic comments from satisfied customers, the truth is that standards vary widely. Many people end up choosing the agency based on their accommodations choice, but it's well worth getting out there and chatting to a few different operators. Professionalism, honesty and flexibility are the things to look for, rather than willingness to haggle on the price. The same safety precautions apply as in Uyuni when looking for the right tour operator for you; see p168.

All agencies offer horseback riding; there are jaunts of three, five or seven hours, or even two or four days. Rates range between B$25 and B$30 per hour; longer rides typically include a lunch of delicious *tamales*. Two-day rides cost from B$380 to $480, with a sleepover in basic accommodations in the villages of Espicaya or Quiriza. Also on offer by all the agencies is the triathlon, an active full-day tour of the surrounding area by jeep, horse and mountain bike. These range in price between B$200 and B$300 per person with lunch, based on four people. Jeep tours are also available, priced between B$450 and B$600 per day. All agencies also offer guided treks from B$100 to B$150 for a half-day. Note that in low season, you'll often find the rates negotiable but don't haggle too much, as the quality is also likely to go down.

The following recommended operators, all offer the tours and activities described previously:

Alexandro Adventure Travel (☎ 694-4752; aleadventure4x4@hotmail.com, Arraya s/n) This friendly and experienced agency offers great service, good jeeps and English-speaking guides who are excited to show travelers off-the-beaten path spots (such as the viewpoint and village of Palquiza and a hike inside Canyon del Duende). They specialize in volcano climbs (Tunupa, Uturuncu or Licancabur), usually tacked onto a standard four-day *salar* tour (B$1500 for a five-day trip).

El Grano de Oro Tours (☎ 694-4763; elgranodeorotours@hotmail.com; Arraya 492) This family-run agency offers personal service and good local knowledge. The owner's father has a working farm 12km from Tupiza, where it's possible to arrange a stay for B$40 per night. This is especially great as part of a two-day horseback route. They also offer jeep transfer to Uyuni for B$1500 (for five people).

La Torre Tours (☎ 694-2633; www.latorretours-tupiza .com; Hotel La Torre, Chichas 220) Run by a friendly couple, this agency offers more personalized tours of Tupiza's surroundings and into the *salar*. Their one-day excursions to San Vicente or Huaca Huañusca cost B$1200. Their two-day *salar* trip with an overnight in Colchani costs

B$500 per person. During the dry season, they rent bikes for B$70 per day.

Tupiza Tours (☎ 694-3003, in La Paz 2-224-4282; www.tupizatours.com; Hotel Mitru, Chichas 187) This outfit pioneered many of the Tupiza-area routes now also offered by competitors. While the agency is well-run and has daily departures to the *salar*, there have been mixed reports about the quality of their tours that apparently lack a personal touch (they use 12-person minivans). Their two-day Butch and Sundance tour is popular, with an overnight in the hamlet of Tatasi and a visit to the abandoned mining village of Portugalete; it costs B$600 (based on four people).

Valle Hermoso Tours (☎ 694-2370; www.bolivia .freehosting.net; Hostal Valle Hermoso, Arraya 478) The agency inside Hostal Valle Hermoso gets mixed reviews and the owners tend to be pushy. Their full-day trip to Huaca Huañusca is affordable, at B$600 per jeep. To get to San Vicente, it's B$1500 for a 12-hour day.

Sleeping

You'll often be quoted cheaper rates for rooms in the hope that you'll then take a tour with the hotel's agency. The cheapest options are several basic *residenciales* opposite the train station. At the time of research, Hotel Mitru was about to open a new budget option, **El Refugio del Turista** (☎ 694-4811; Santa Cruz 244; r per person B$40), just five blocks from the train station, with six rooms with shared bath, a kitchen and a big garden for barbecues. A boon: guests can use the swimming pool at Hotel Mitru for free.

Hostal Tupiza (☎ 694-5240; Florida 10; r per person B$25) This recently opened hostel is a family-run affair with small but decent rooms on the 2nd floor, around a courtyard with a giant fig tree. There's use of a communal shower and a shared kitchen.

Residencial My Home (☎ 694-2947; Avaroa 288; r per person B$25-40, with bathroom B$50) A good last resort if all else is booked up, this place is a cheapie option. The no-frills rooms are set around a big concrete courtyard, the more expensive ones are equipped with TV.

Alexandro Hostal (☎ 694-4752; aleadventure4x4@ hotmail.com; Arraya s/n; r per person B$35, with bathroom B$40) Friendly familial spot with only three clean rooms set around a terrace upstairs from the agency, with a fig tree in the middle. Rates include breakfast and use of a shared kitchen, a laundry sink and TV room.

Hostal El Grano de Oro (☎ 694-4763; elgrano deorotours@hotmail.com; Arraya 492; r per person B$40)

This family-run place offers four simple and sunny rooms with large comfortable mattresses, cactus furniture, a shared bathroom with reliable hot water and a welcoming feel. Guests have use of a garden area. Breakfast is available (from B$12) as is massage (B$45 for 45 minutes).

La Torre Hotel (☎ 694-2633; latorrehotel@yahoo .es; Chichas 220; r per person B$40, s/d with bathroom B$60/120) This sound, central choice run by a retired nurse and doctor offers clean rooms with good beds and clean bathrooms (with hot water after a 10-minute wait). Rooms at the front of the rambling house are much lighter but chillier, and have no curtains. Guests have use of a kitchen, a safe, a roof terrace and a TV lounge – a good place to meet other travelers. A small breakfast is included.

Hostal Valle Hermoso (☎ 694-2370; www.bolivia .freehosting.net; Arraya 478 & Arraya 505; r per person B$40, s/d with bathroom B$60/120) Set in two separate buildings a block apart, this is an old-school hostel with a book and money exchange and a roof terrace. The one nearer the bus station is more up-to-date, with rooms featuring more space, light and cable TVs. It's HI-affiliated (members get a 10% discount), clean and convenient, and guests have use of a kitchen. Breakfast is available (B$10 to B$20).

Hotel Mitru Anexo (☎ 694-3002; Avaroa at Serrano; r per person B$40, s/d with bathroom B$70/120) An offshoot of Hotel Mitru, this place offers very good value, with solid rooms sporting cable TV, phone and hot water. The bathrooms are modern, and guests have use of a kitchen and terraces as well as the pool at the Mitru. Convenient if you're arriving at night by train.

Hotel Mitru (☎ 694-3003; www.tupizatours.com; Chichas 187; r per person B$40, s with bathroom B$80-160, d B$140-200, ste B$320; 🏊) The best and most reliable hotel in town, the busy Mitru has been run by the same family for generations and is a relaxing choice built around a swimming pool that's just the ticket after a dusty day out on horseback. There's a variety of rooms in two sections: the older 'garden' part and the newer 'cactus' area; the suites with a fridge and minibar are particularly appealing. Rates include a tasty generous breakfast. You can change money, have your laundry done, and exchange books.

Eating

Tupiza's accommodations are much more inviting than its eateries, but there are a couple of decent places. There's a pretty clear distinction between the tourist restaurants on Chichas and Florida and places frequented by locals. The upstairs section of the central market is the best place to fill up at lunch, for between B$10 and B$15.

For a real morning treat, head for Mercado Negro after 8am, when the renowned Doña Wala starts serving up her fabulous *charque*-filled *tamales* (cornmeal dough filled with jerky; B$1.50) – go early because she always sells out. Her stall is outside the market, just to the right of the entrance. A couple of no-name **juice stops** (Santa Cruz) blend delicious and refreshing juices and milkshakes from such things as carrots and papayas (B$2.50).

Alamos (Avaroa & Santa Cruz; snacks B$4-9, mains B$9-15) A green light outside marks this popular saloon-style spot where locals and tourists mingle in the funky two-floor space with a Mexican vibe and lots of knick-knacks. The menu features mainly meat dishes, like *pique macho* (beef chunks and sausages over french fries with lettuce, tomatoes, onions and spicy *locoto* peppers), and comes in huge tasty portions.

Il Bambino (Florida & Santa Cruz; almuerzo B$12) This friendly corner eatery offers excellent *salteñas* (B$3) in the morning, and is a popular spot with locals for its filling *almuerzos* at high noon.

Confitería Los Helechos (Avaroa s/n; mains B$13-45) Attached to the Mitru Anexo, this spacious spot offers tasty breakfasts, a salad bar, sandwiches, burgers and vegetarian dishes, as well as refreshing juices. The atmosphere is sedate, apart from the TV blasting, and the service on the slow side.

Sede Social Ferroviaria (Avaroa & Chichas; mains B$15-30; ☺ closed Sun) The railway workers' club is a no-frills spot where locals come for the *parilladas* (B$60 for two people). There's sometimes live music on weekends.

Tú Pizza (Plaza Independencia s/n; mains B$16-30) This stylish little eatery on the main plaza has a rustic feel, high ceilings, nice artwork and good service. The food runs the usual gamut of pizzas, pastas and lasagna as well as mains with local goat cheese and quinoa. Try the sweet pizza with chocolate (and *dulce de leche*).

Italiana (Florida near Plaza Independencia; mains B$18-35) This is perhaps the best of several tourist places in Tupiza that all have an almost identical decor and menu. The food options are wide and varied, from thin-crusted pizzas and pastas to finger food, Chinese choices and breakfasts. Good for a glass of wine, cocktail or beer.

California (Plaza Independencia s/n; mains B$23-26) On the main plaza, this pleasant spot clad in cactus wood is a popular choice for a drink, a game of cards or a meal. The vegetarian choices are decent but overpriced; there's also llama steak, burgers, pizzas and beer.

Rinconcito Quilmes (Suipacha 14; almuerzo B$10, mains B$25-30) You'll see few other gringos in this little spot known for cheap filling lunches served in a spacious dining room and a couple of outside tables. It's popular on weekends for its *asados* (barbecues) with quality meat from Argentina.

Getting There & Away

BUS

Note that the upper prices of the range reflect high-season bus costs; travel is cheaper in low season. Several *flota* (long-distance bus company) buses leave the **bus station** (terminal tax B$4) in the morning and evening for Potosí (B$50 to B$100, seven to eight hours); the road to Potosí is being paved so this should reduce travel time by a couple of hours. There are multiple departures daily for Villazón (B$15 to B$25, three hours); once you cross the Argentine border at La Quiaca you can catch a bus to Salta, with five daily departures (US$18). There are evening departures for Tarija (B$60, eight hours), with connections for Villamontes and Santa Cruz. There are several departures to La Paz (B$90 to B$180, 15 hours) in the evening via Oruro (B$70, 11 hours). Buses also leave for Sucre (B$80, 10½ hours) and Cochabamba in the evening (B$100, 18 hours). There are three daily buses to Salta (B$200, 10 hours); the trip sometimes involves a three-hour border wait in La Quiaca. There are regular morning departures for Uyuni (B$50 to B$80, six hours).

TRAIN

Unfortunately, if you travel by train you miss most of the brilliant scenery on the route to Uyuni, so you might consider the less comfortable bus service. The **ticket**

SOUTHERN ALTIPLANO

CROSSING THE BORDER TO ARGENTINA

The Bolivian side of the main border crossing to Argentina is a sprawling, dusty, chaotic sort of place. The frontier and bus station are always busy, for numerous Bolivians work in Argentina. Watch out for the usual scammers who tend to congregate at borders; dodgy banknotes and petty theft are not unknown.

The **Argentine consulate** (☎ 597-2011; Plaza 6 de Agosto 123; ⌚ 10am-1pm Mon-Fri) is on the main square. Numerous *casas de cambio* near the bridge along Av República Argentina offer reasonable rates of exchange for US dollars and Argentine pesos, less for bolivianos. **Banco Mercantil** (JM Deheza 423) changes cash and has an ATM dispensing US dollars and bolivianos. There are several internet places (about B$3 per hour), including **ChatMania** (20 de Mayo 130) and **Punto Entel** (cnr La Paz & 20 de Mayo), which also has telephone cabins.

All northbound buses depart from the **Villazón bus terminal** (fee B$2). All except those bound for Tarija pass through Tupiza (B$15, 2½ hours); it's a beautiful trip, so try to go in the daylight and grab a window seat – at night, it can be a very scary ride. Regular bus services also head to La Paz (B$140 to B$170, 21 hours) via Potosí (B$80 to B$120, 11 hours) and Oruro (B$140 to B$160, 17 hours). Daily evening buses along the rough but amazing route to Tarija (B$40, seven to eight hours) continue to Bermejo (there are four onward departures per day). Argentine bus companies have ticket offices opposite Villazón's terminal, but all Argentine buses leave from the La Quiaca bus terminal. You'll be hassled by ticket sellers for both Argentine and Bolivian bus services; don't be rushed into buying a ticket, as there may be a service leaving sooner. You can easily bargain down the price on longer routes; conversely, the sellers may try and overcharge you on shorter journeys.

The Villazón train station is 1.5km north of the border crossing – a taxi costs B$5. The *Expreso del Sur* departs Wednesday and Saturday at 3:30pm for Tupiza (*salón/ejecutivo* B$22/51, 2¾ hours), Uyuni (B$63/152, 8½ hours) and Oruro (B$109/236, 16½ hours). This is an enjoyable trip with superb scenery for the first few hours. The more crowded and basic *Wara Wara del Sur* departs Monday and Thursday at 3:30pm for Tupiza (*popular/salón/ejecutivo* B$13/17/38, three hours), Uyuni (B$24/48/99, 11 hours) and Oruro (B$30/86/185, 18 hours). It's a good option as far as Tupiza, but after dark it turns tedious.

To just visit La Quiaca briefly, there's no need to visit immigration; just walk straight across the bridge. Crossing the border is usually no problem, but avoid the line of traders getting their goods searched; otherwise it may take you hours to clear customs.

On the north side of the international bridge, **Bolivian customs & immigration** (⌚ 24hr) issues exit and entry stamps (the latter normally only for 30 days) – there is no official charge for these services. Argentine immigration and Argentine customs are open from 7am to 11pm. Formalities are minimal but the wait and exhaustive custom searches can be very long. In addition, those entering Argentina may be held up at several control points further south of the border by more customs searches.

window (☎ 694-2527) at the train station opens irregularly on days when there's a train, so it can be easier to have an agency buy your tickets for a small surcharge.

The *Expreso del Sur* trundles north to Uyuni (*salón/ejecutivo* B$60/101, five hours) and Oruro (B$101/202, 12 hours) at 6:40pm on Wednesday and Saturday. At 3:30am on Tuesday and Friday the *Expreso* speeds south to Villazón (B$22/51, three hours), arriving on Wednesday and Saturday.

The *Wara Wara del Sur*, which is often delayed, leaves at 6:50pm on Monday and Thursday evenings for Uyuni (*popular/salón/ejecutivo* B$24/33/64, six hours) and Oruro (B$54/73/150, 13½ hours), and at 8:40am on Monday and Thursday for Villazón (B$13/17/38, 3½ hours).

AROUND TUPIZA

Much of Tupiza's appeal lies in the surrounding landscape, a visually stunning wilderness of *quebradas*, thirsty riverbeds and thriving cactus that'll have you whistling a Morricone theme tune in no time. It's great hiking country and also perfect for exploration on horseback or 4WD – several

Tupiza operators offer these excursions (see p182).

If you're hiking without a guide, it's not easy to get lost, but take a map anyway – you can get them from various tour agencies. Carry at least 3L of water per day in this dry desert climate. It's wise to wear shoes that can withstand assault by prickly desert vegetation, and to carry a compass or GPS if you're venturing away from the tracks. Flash flooding is also a danger, particularly in the summer months; avoid camping in the *quebradas* or entering the canyons, especially if it looks like rain.

Just northwest of Tupiza is **Quebrada de Palala**, a broad wash lined with some very impressive red formations known as fins. During the rainy season it becomes a tributary of the Río Tupiza, but in the winter months it serves as a highway into the back country and part of the salt route from the Salar de Uyuni to Tarija. Beyond the dramatic red rocks, the wash rises very gently into hills colored greenish-blue and violet by lead and other mineral deposits. To get here, head north on Tupiza's Av La Paz from Plazuela El Mundo past the giant slide; 2km ahead, along the railroad line, you'll see the mouth of the *quebrada*. About 5km further along, the route passes some obvious fin formations and continues up the broad *quebrada* into increasingly lonely country, past scrub brush and cacti stands.

Two canyons, **El Cañón del Duende** and **El Cañón del Inca** are part of most itineraries. The first can be reached from Tupiza on a great half-day stroll; ask any of the agencies for a map and directions. You can also enter the canyon on foot for a scenic twenty-minute hike through its towering red rock formations.

El Sillar (The Saddle), 15km from Tupiza, is where a road straddles a narrow ridge between two peaks and two valleys. Throughout this area, rugged amphitheaters have been gouged out of the mountainsides and eroded into spires that resemble a stone forest. The road continues on to **San Vicente** (right), of Butch and Sundance fame. This entire route is part of a centuries-old trade route. From May to early July you may see a trickle of llama, alpaca and donkey trains (nowadays more likely *camiones*) humping salt blocks 300km from the Salar de Uyuni to trade in Tarija.

Between Tupiza and Quebrada Seca lies **Quebrada Palmira**, a wonderful, normally dry wash flanked by tall and precarious fin formations. The right fork of the wash is rather comically known as **Valle de los Machos** (Valley of Males) or Valle de los Penes (Valley of Penises). The names stem from the clusters of exceptionally phallic pedestal formations.

Another scenic sight near Tupiza is **El Angosto**, a spectacular tunnel of a road carved into the mountain – great for photographs.

Huaca Huañusca & San Vicente

> Kid, the next time I say let's go someplace like Bolivia, let's go someplace like Bolivia!
>
> *Paul Newman, in the film*
> Butch Cassidy & the Sundance Kid

November 4, 1908, Robert LeRoy Parker (Butch Cassidy) and Harry Alonzo Longabaugh (the Sundance Kid) pulled off the last robbery of their careers when they politely and peacefully relieved Carlos Peró of the Aramayo company payroll, which amounted to US$90,000, at the foot of a hill called **Huaca Huañusca** (Dead Cow). The name was apparently applied because of the hill's resemblance to a fallen bovine. From an obvious pass on the ridge, a walking track descends the steep slopes to the west for about 2km to the river, where there's a small meadow, a tiny cave and some rugged rock outcrops where the bandits probably holed up while waiting for the payroll to pass. Several Tupiza agencies offer jeep trips to Huaca Huañusca.

San Vicente is a remote one-mule village that wouldn't even rate a mention were it not the legendary spot where the outlaws met their untimely demise (see boxed text, opposite). The mine in San Vicente is now closed and the place has declined to little more than a ghost town. Most of those remaining are military people, mine security guards and their families. To be honest, even hardcore Butch and Sundance fans are sometimes a little disappointed by the place, a dusty spot with a tiny **museum** (admission B$10) and little tourist infrastructure. The museum is often closed, with the key-holder often difficult to track down. Bring your imagination: you can

THE LAST DAYS OF BUTCH CASSIDY & THE SUNDANCE KID *Anne Meadows & Daniel Buck*

Butch and Sundance (real names Robert LeRoy Parker and Harry Alonzo Longabaugh) came to southern Bolivia in August 1908 and took up residence with the Briton AG Francis, who was transporting a gold dredge on the Río San Juan del Oro. While casing banks to finance their retirement, the outlaws learned of an even sweeter target: a poorly guarded US$480,000 mine-company payroll to be hauled by mule from Tupiza to Quechisla.

On November 3, 1908, manager Carlos Peró picked up a packet of cash from Aramayo, Francke & Compañía in Tupiza and headed north with his 10-year-old son and a servant, but they were discreetly tailed by Butch and Sundance. Peró's party overnighted in Salo, then set off again at dawn. As the trio ascended the hill called Huaca Huañusca, the bandits watched from above with binoculars. In a rugged spot on the far side of the hill, they relieved Peró of a handsome mule and the remittance, which turned out to be a mere US$90,000 – the prized payroll had been slated for shipment the following week.

Dispirited, Butch and Sundance returned to Francis' headquarters at Tomahuaico. The following day, Francis guided them to Estarca, where the three of them spent the night. On the morning of November 6, the bandits bade farewell to Francis and headed west to San Vicente.

Meanwhile, Peró had sounded the alarm, and posses were scouring southern Bolivia. A four-man contingent from Uyuni reached San Vicente that afternoon. Butch and Sundance arrived at dusk, rented a room from Bonifacio Casasola and sent him to fetch supper. The posse came to investigate and had scarcely entered the courtyard when Butch shot and killed a soldier. During the brief gunfight that ensued, Sundance was badly wounded. Realizing that escape was impossible, Butch ended Sundance's misery with a shot between the eyes, then fired a bullet into his own temple.

At the inquest, Carlos Peró identified the corpses as those of the men who had robbed him. Although buried as *desconocidos* (unknowns) in the cemetery, the outlaws fit descriptions of Butch and Sundance, and a mountain of circumstantial evidence points to their having met their doom in San Vicente. For example, Santiago Lowe, Butch's well-known alias, was recently found among the hotel guest list published in the Tupiza newspaper just a few days before the Aramayo holdup, which confirms eyewitness accounts that he was there. Nonetheless, rumors of their return to the USA have made their fate one of the great mysteries of the American West.

In 1991 a team led by forensic anthropologist Clyde Snow attempted to settle the question by excavating the bandits' grave. No one in the village had any knowledge of its location, except one elderly – and as it turned out, imaginative – gentleman, who led them to a specific tombstone. The grave's sole occupant turned out to be a German miner named Gustav Zimmer.

Anne Meadows is the author of Digging Up Butch and Sundance, *University of Nebraska Press, 2003*

still see the adobe house where the bandits holed up and eventually died, the cemetery where they were buried and the sign welcoming visitors to the town: 'Here death's Butch Kasidy Sundance the Kid.'

There's no regular public transportation between Tupiza and San Vicente; occasionally, a *camión* departs for San Vicente early on Thursday morning from Tupiza's Plazuela El Mundo. The easiest way to go is with an agency from Tupiza. While the one-day trips to San Vicente and back are a long, expensive slog, some of the agencies offer a more interesting two-day excursion, taking in Huaca Huañusca en route (see p182).

Central Highlands

The Central Highlands are not only located at the heart of the country, but for many represent the spiritual heart of the nation. Gorgeous whitewashed Sucre, whose elegant patioed houses and noble churches make it the nation's handsomest city, is still the judicial capital of the country. It was here that Bolivian independence was declared in 1825, and it's still known as the 'Cradle of Liberty.'

Potosí, on the other hand, is a powerful symbol of the natural wealth of the country. The Cerro Rico looms over the city; so much silver has been extracted from it over the centuries, it's a wonder it still stands. These days, cooperative miners eke out a living in its cramped tunnels in some of the most appalling working conditions still extant in the 21st century.

At a much lower altitude, Cochabamba is one of Bolivia's most livable cities, with a perfect climate, and surrounded by fertile valleys. It's got a more modern feel, with cinema centers and Americanized chain restaurants popping up, but it still preserves much character, and has excellent restaurants and nightlife.

But it's not all about cities here. Throughout the region, there are lovely, little-known colonial towns gently crumbling with age. It's well worth eschewing the city-to-city mode of travel to give you time to explore them. A more distant past is evoked by the Inca ruins in the Cochabamba valley, but Parque Nacional Torotoro has the last laugh on the age front. A rugged, geologically fascinating wilderness, it's bristling with dinosaur footprints and fossils, some of which date back 300 million years.

HIGHLIGHTS

- Admire the churches of **Potosí** (p227), filled with evocative religious artworks
- Goggle at the colonial beauty of **Sucre** (p210), Bolivia's most attractive city
- Pack on the pounds or party hard in **Cochabamba** (p190), which boasts some of the country's best restaurants and bars
- Home in on remote, wild **Parque Nacional Torotoro** (p207), literal stomping ground of dinosaurs
- Roam the **Cordillera de los Frailes** (p223), home to the intriguing Jalq'a weaving culture

★ Cochabamba

★ Parque Nacional Torotoro

Cordillera de los Frailes ★
★ Sucre

★ Potosí

■ TELEPHONE CODE: 4	■ POPULATION: 3 MILLION	■ ELEVATION 1600M TO 5400M

History

Prior to Spanish domination, the town of Charcas, where Sucre now stands, was the indigenous capital of the valley of Choque-Chaca. It served as the residence of local religious, military and political leaders, and its jurisdiction extended to several thousand inhabitants. When the Spanish arrived, the entire area from Southern Peru to the Río de la Plata in present-day Argentina came to be known as Charcas.

In the early 1530s Francisco Pizarro, the conquistador who felled the Inca empire, sent his brother Gonzalo to the Charcas region to oversee indigenous mining activities that might prove to be valuable to the Spanish realm. He was not interested in the Altiplano, and concentrated on the highlands east of the main Andean cordilleras. As a direct result, in 1538 a new Spanish capital of the Charcas was founded. Following in the conquered population's footsteps, he chose the warm, fertile valley of Choque-Chaca for its site. The city, later to become Sucre, was named La Plata – silver was God in those days.

Whereas previously all territories in the region had been governed from Lima, in 1559 King Felipe II created the Audiencia (Royal Court) of Charcas, with its headquarters in the young city, to help administer the eastern territories. Governmental subdivisions within the district came under the jurisdiction of royal officers known as *corregidores*.

In 1776, a new Viceroyalty was established in what is now Buenos Aires, and the Charcas came under its control. The city became known as Chuquisaca (a Spanish corruption of Choque-Chaca), as there were too many La Platas around for comfort.

The city had received an archbishopric in 1609, according it theological autonomy. That, along with the establishment of the University of San Xavier in 1622 and the 1681 opening of the Academía Carolina law school, fostered continued development of liberal and revolutionary ideas and set the stage for 'the first cry of Independence in the Americas' on May 25, 1809. The mini-revolution set off the alarm throughout Spanish America and, like ninepins, the northwestern South American republics were liberated by the armies of the military genius Simón Bolívar (see boxed text, p214).

After the definitive liberation of Peru at the battles of Junín and Ayacucho, on August 6 and December 9, 1824, Alto Peru, historically tied to the Lima government, was technically free of Spanish rule. In practice, however, it had been administered from Buenos Aires and disputes arose about what to do with the territory.

On February 9, 1825 Bolívar's second-in-command, General Antonio José de Sucre, drafted and delivered a declaration that rejected Buenos Aires authority and suggested that the political future of the region should be determined by the provinces themselves.

Bolívar, unhappy with this unauthorized act of sovereignty, rejected the idea, but de Sucre stood his ground, convinced that there was sufficient separatist sentiment in Alto Peru to back him up. As he expected, the people of the region staunchly refused to wait for a decision from the new congress, which was to be installed in Lima the following year, and also rejected subsequent invitations to join up with the Buenos Aires government.

On August 6, the first anniversary of the Battle of Junín, independence was declared in the Casa de la Libertad at Chuquisaca and the new republic was christened Bolivia, after its liberator. On August 11 the city's name was changed for the final time to Sucre, in honor of the general who'd promoted the independence movement.

Difficult years followed in the young republic, and Bolívar commented on his namesake, 'Hapless Bolivia has had four different leaders in less than two weeks! Only the kingdom of Hell could offer so appalling a picture discrediting humanity!'

For more on the region's fascinating past, see the History sections of Cochabamba (opposite) and Potosí (p229).

Climate

The saying *'Las golondrinas nunca migran de Cochabamba'* (The swallows never migrate from Cochabamba) aptly describes what *cochabambinos* believe is the world's most comfortable climate, with warm, dry, sunny days and cool nights. Sucre residents rightfully maintain that their climate is just as salubrious. The coolest time of year is winter (June to August), with clear skies and mild temperatures, but chilly Potosí is one of Bolivia's few big cities to see snow.

National Parks

The region's protected areas include the remote Parque Nacional Torotoro (p207), peppered with thousands of dinosaur footprints, and Parque Nacional Tunari (p201), easily accessible from the city of Cochabamba.

Getting There & Away

The Central Highlands' major population centers are well served by intercity buses. Getting between towns in the region is a bit more of a challenge if venturing beyond the Potosí-Sucre paved highway; the route between Cochabamba and Sucre is a particularly slow one.

Cochabamba has the busiest airport, while for Potosí you must fly into Sucre, not too far away.

COCHABAMBA

pop 517,000 / elevation 2553m

Busy, buzzy Cochabamba is one of Bolivia's boom cities, and has a distinct, almost Mediterranean vitality that perhaps owes something to its clement climate. While much of the city's population is typically poor, parts of town have a notably prosperous feel. The spacious new-town avenues have a wide choice of restaurants, eagerly grazed by the food-crazy *cochabambinos*, and the bar life is lively, driven by students and young professionals. Despite this, Cochabamba remains a very affordable city, with prices far below those in Sucre or La Paz. You could easily find yourself staying a lot longer than you planned.

The city's name is derived from the Quechua *khocha pampa,* meaning 'swampy plain.' Cochabamba lies in a fertile green bowl, 25km long by 10km wide, set in a landscape of fields and low hills. To the northwest rises Cerro Tunari (5035m), the highest peak in central Bolivia. The area's rich soil yields abundant crops of maize, barley, wheat, alfalfa, and orchard and citrus fruits. Cochabamba is famous for its *chicha,* a fermented corn drink that is the locals' favorite tipple.

History

Cochabamba was founded in January 1574 by Sebastián Barba de Padilla. It was originally named Villa de Oropeza in honor of the Count and Countess of Oropeza, parents of Viceroy Francisco de Toledo, who chartered and promoted its settlement.

During the height of Potosí's silver boom, the Cochabamba Valley developed into the primary source of food for the miners in agriculturally unproductive Potosí. Thanks to its maize and wheat production, Cochabamba came to be the 'breadbasket of Bolivia.' As Potosí's importance declined during the early 18th century, so did Cochabamba's, and grain production in the Chuquisaca (Sucre) area, much closer to Potosí, was sufficient to supply the decreasing demand.

By the mid-19th century, however, the city had reassumed its position as the nation's granary. Elite landowners in the valley grew wealthy and began investing in highland mining ventures. Before long, the Altiplano mines were attracting international capital, and the focus of Bolivian mining shifted from Potosí to southwestern Bolivia. As a result,

Cochabamba thrived and its European-mestizo population gained a reputation for affluence and prosperity.

In 2000, the eyes of the world turned to Cochabamba as its citizens protested against rises in water rates. The World Bank had forced the Bolivian government to sell off its water company to US giant Bechtel in order to provide financing for a tunnel that would bring water from the other side of the mountains. The resultant price rise brought the citizens out in force, with several hundred thousand people taking to the streets in protest and eventually driving Bechtel out. Anti-globalization campaigners around the world saw it as a highly symbolic victory over a multinational that had bullied the Bolivian government with the complicity of the World Bank.

Orientation

Cochabamba is a large, sprawling city, but its business district, centered on the Plaza 14 de Septiembre, is compact. The largest market zones are on, or south of, Av Aroma, sandwiched between Colina San Sebastián and Laguna Alalay. The long-distance bus terminal and most of the intravalley bus terminals are also in this area.

Cochabamba addresses are often measured relative to the crossroads of two main avenues, Heroínas (running east–west) and Ayacucho (north–south). Numbers on streets that cross Heroínas are preceded by 'N' *(norte)* to the north of the avenue and 'S' *(sud;* south) to the south. Those that cross Ayacucho are preceded by 'E' *(este)* to the east or 'O' *(oeste)* to the west – although to avoid confusion, a 'W' is sometimes used instead. The number immediately after the letter tells you how many blocks away from these division streets the address falls.

MAPS

The tourist office gives out a good free city map. See the **Instituto Geográfico Militar** (☎ 425-5563; 16 de Julio S-237) for topo sheets covering Cochabamba department.

Information
BOOKSTORES

There's an alleyway next to the post office on Heroínas that is full of vendors of Spanish-language literature and other books for reasonable and negotiable prices.

Los Amigos del Libro (☎ 425-4114) Stocks the best range of English, French and German paperbacks, plus Bolivian literature and Lonely Planet guides. Several branches including España near Bolívar.
Spitting Llama (☎ 7489-4540; www.thespittingllama .com; España 615) Camping equipment and foreign-language books, including Lonely Planet guidebooks, on sale, plus online store.

CONSULATES

See p331 for details of foreign consulates in Cochabamba.

CULTURAL CENTERS

The following centers sponsor cultural activities and language classes:
Centro Boliviano-Americano (☎ 422-1288; info@ cbacoch.org; 25 de Mayo N-365) Can recommend private language teachers.
Instituto Cultural Boliviano-Alemán (☎ 412-2323; www.icbacbba.com; Lanza 727, btwn La Paz & Chuquisaca) Offers group Spanish lessons.
Volunteer Bolivia (☎ 452-6028; www.volunteer bolivia.org; Ecuador 342) Runs the Café La Republika cultural center and arranges short- and long-term volunteer work, study and homestay programs throughout Bolivia. Also offers language courses.

EMERGENCY
Tourist police (☎ 120, 451-0023; Achá 0-142)

IMMIGRATION
Migración (☎ 453-3331; General Galindo at Torrez; 8:30am-4pm Mon-Fri) For visa and length-of-stay extensions. In the northeast of town a couple of kilometers from the centre. Ignore the queues; they are for a separate department.

INTERNET ACCESS

If you happen to spot a city block that does *not* have an internet place let us know; they are everywhere. Most of them charge B$3 to B$4 per hour.

LAUNDRY

Most hotels offer laundry services, but for commercial laundries try **Brillante** (Ayacucho 923) and **Lavaya** (Salamanca & Antezana).

MEDICAL SERVICES
Ambulance (☎ 181, 424-8381)
Centro Medico Boliviano Belga (☎ 422-9407; Antezana N-455) Private clinic.
Hospital Viedma (☎ 422-0226) Full-service public hospital.

COCHABAMBA

0 — 500 m
0 — 0.3 miles

A

To SERNAP Office (4km)

B

To El Ajuicho (500m)

C

D

Paccieri

7

Plaza Colón

Iglesia del Hospicio

Ecuador

Venezuela

José de la Reza
79

Chuquisaca
73 81

48
54 89
43
80
61
51
45 6
24 67
22 21
78 57
41
84
9 52 53
14 50
70 18
16
23 8 88
29
32 72 55 35

Salamanca
Antezana

España
Baptista
25 de Mayo
Av San Martín

Colombia
Av de las Heroínas
Bolívar
Plaza 14 de Septiembre
3
82
Sucre
46
Pasaje Catedral
Market
Jordán

Enlargement

0 — 500 m
0 — 0.3 miles

Av América
69
59
Av Buenos Aires
33
44 Garden
34
Av Portales
Portales
Park
15
56
Blanco
60
87
Beni
28
Sejas
85
Paseo de la Recoleta
Av Aniceto Padilla
62 86
Av Oblitas
83
Park
Av Uyuni
90
Stadium
Park
Av del Ejército
Park
Av Ramón Rivero
66
Plaza Quintanilla
4
64 75
Av Ballivián
Oruro
Antezana
La Paz
Plaza Constitución
20
49
58
Av Oquendo
Vázquez
42
68
11
93
Chuquisaca
Salamanca
13
2
See Enlargement
Paccieri
Plaza Colón
Venezuela
Ecuador
10
To Apart Hotel Concordia (1km) Migración (2km)
Teleférico (Cable car) Station
Cable car route
25
Rubén Darío
México
39
Mayor Rocha
España
Baptista
Colombia
Av San Martín
Lanza
Av de las Heroínas
37
26
Tarapaca
Junín
Hamiraya
Lanza
92
38
63
36
71
19
Plaza 14 de Septiembre
Market
Acha
Santiváñez
To Escuela Runawasi (4.5km)
Aguirre
25 de Mayo
Calle Arce
Bolívar
Sucre
Jordán
Calama
Ladislao Cabrera
Uruguay
Plaza Busch
65
12
Antezana
Pasteur
A. Melean
Universidad Mayor de San Simón
Julián M. López
Mariano R Terrazas
Av Guillermo Urquidi
J A Méndez
Río Rocha
Av Humboldt
Av Libertador Bolívar
Villarroel
Av Gran Paula
La Paz
José de la Reza
Méndez Arcos
To Quillacollo (15km)
Sipe Sipe (27km)
Plaza San Sebastián
91
40
5
Brasil
Av Aroma
Av República
Av 9 de Abril
Montes
30
Honduras
Punata
Tarata
Cliff
cliff
Heroínas de la Coronilla Monument
Colina San Sebastián
cliff
Former Train Station
31
Pulacayo
Barzola
Totora
Quillacollo
Tapacarí
Guayaramerín
Laguna Alalay
To Airport (3km)
To Mercado de Ganado (3km)
Arani
Liza
Angostura
Chipirin
Riberalta
Moxos
República
Manupiri

CENTRAL HIGHLANDS

INFORMATION
American.....................................1 C2
Argentine Consulate..................2 C3
Banco Unión..............................3 D3
Brazilian Consulate....................4 B2
Brillante.....................................5 B5
Centro Boliviano-Americano......6 D1
Centro Medico Boliviano Belga...7 D1
Efex..8 D3
German Consulate.....................9 D2
Hospital Viedma.....................10 C3
Instituto Cultural
   Boliviano-Alemán (ICBA)......11 B3
Instituto Geográfico Militar
   (IGM)..................................12 C4
Lavaya....................................13 B3
Los Amigos del Libro...............14 D2
Peruvian Consulate.................15 B2
Post Office & Entel.................16 C2
Spitting Llama........................17 C1
Tourist Office.........................18 C3
Tourist Police.........................19 A4
US Consulate..........................20 B3
Volunteer Bolivia....................21 D2

SIGHTS & ACTIVITIES
Bolivia Cultura.......................22 D2
Cathedral...............................23 D3
Convento de Santa Teresa.......24 C2
Cristo de la Concordia.............25 D3
Fremen Tours..........................26 A4
Iglesia & Convento de San
   Francisco.............................27 D2
Iglesia de la Recoleta..............28 B2
Iglesia de Santo Domingo........29 C3
Mercado Cancha Calatayud.....30 B5
Mercado de Ferias...................31 B6
Museo Arqueológico...............32 C3

Museo de Historia Natural
   Alcide d'Orbigny.................33 B1
Palacio Portales......................34 B1

SLEEPING 🛏
City Hotel...............................35 D3
Hostal Colonial.......................36 A4
Hostal Jardín..........................37 A4
Hostal La Fontaine..................38 A4
Hostal México.........................39 A3
Hotel Americana......................40 B5
Hotel Boston...........................41 D2
Hotel Diplomat.......................42 A3
Hotel Gina's...........................43 D1
Hotel Portales.........................44 B1
Monserrat Hotel......................45 D1
Residencial Familiar.................46 D3
Residencial Familiar Anexo.......47 D2

EATING 🍴
Brazilian Coffee Bar.................48 D1
Búfalo's Rodizio......................49 C3
Café Paris...............................50 D2
Casa de Campo..................(see 62)
Co Café Art.............................51 D1
Cristal....................................52 D2
Dumbo...................................53 D2
Dumbo...................................54 D1
Espresso Café Bar...................55 D3
Globo's..................................56 B2
Gopal.....................................57 D2
HWA......................................58 B3
IC Norte.................................59 C1
Kabbab..................................60 B2
La Cantonata..........................61 C1
La Estancia.............................62 B2
La Mora.................................63 A4
Los Castores...........................64 B3

Mosoj Yan..............................65 C4
Páprika...................................66 A2
Picasso...................................67 C2
Savarín...................................68 B3
Sole Mio.................................69 C1
Street Vendors........................70 C3
Sucremanta............................71 A4
Sucremanta............................72 D3
Sucremanta............................73 D1
Super Haas.............................74 D2
Tunari....................................75 B3
Uno's.....................................76 D2

DRINKING 🍸
Black Jack..............................77 D1
Cerebritos..............................78 D2
Dali..79 C1
Prikafé...................................80 D1
Top Chopp.............................81 D1

ENTERTAINMENT 🎭
Cine Astor..............................82 D3
Cine Center............................83 B2
Cine Heroínas.........................84 D2
Deep......................................85 B2
Levoa.....................................86 C2
Lujos Discoteca y Karaoke........87 B2

SHOPPING 🛍
Arte Andino............................88 D3
Asarti.....................................89 D1

TRANSPORT
AeroSur..................................90 A2
Avis Rent-a-Car.................(see 44)
Main Bus Terminal..................91 B5
TAM.......................................92 A4
TAM Mercosur.......................93 B3

MONEY

Moneychangers gather along Av de las Heroínas. Their rates are competitive but they only accept US cash. There are numerous ATMs and cash advances are available at major banks. **Banco Unión** (25 de Mayo & Sucre) has one of several Western Union offices. The best places to change cash or traveller's checks (2% to 3% commission):
American (☎ 422-2307; Baptista S-159)
Efex (☎ 412-8963; Plaza 14 de Septiembre; ☿ 9am-6pm Mon-Fri) Handy location, but doesn't change traveler's checks (despite the sign).

POST & TELEPHONE

The main post and **Entel** (Ayacucho & Heroínas; ☿ 6:30am-10pm) offices are together in a large complex. The postal service from Cochabamba is reliable and the facilities are among the country's finest. Downstairs from the main lobby is an express post office. In the alleyway behind, the customs office is a good place for sending packages; it stamps them so that they won't be opened

later on, and offers a cheaper rate than the post office itself.

You'll have no problem making phone calls. Entel and Punto Viva offices are scattered around the city as well as large numbers of private telephone *cabinas*.

TOURIST INFORMATION

Cochabamba has a superb website for visitors, at www.cochabamba-online.net. This site also has details and information about places of interest, links to flight information, hotel listings, photos and local events.

SERNAP office (Servicio Nacional de Areas Protegidas; ☎ 445-2534; Atahuallpa 2367 ☿ 8:30am-12:30pm & 2:30-6:30pm Mon-Fri) Has limited information about national parks. Private tour companies are usually better equipped to answer questions.

Tourist Office (☎ 425-8030; Plaza 14 de Septiembre; ☿ 8am-noon, 2:30-6:30pm Mon-Fri) Very welcoming, and hands out good city material. There are several information kiosks, which also open Saturday mornings including at the bus station and airport.

CENTRAL HIGHLANDS

Dangers & Annoyances

According to locals the streets south of Avenida Aroma are best avoided and are positively dangerous at night – don't be tempted by the cheaper accommodation in this area. The bus station is around here, so don't be surprised if, when arriving in the early hours of the morning, you are not allowed off the bus until sunrise. Pickpocketing and petty thefts are common in the markets, so don't carry any more than you are likely to need. The Colina San Sebastián is dangerous throughout the day, so it is inadvisable to walk on any part of it at all.

Sights

Cochabamba is Bolivia's biggest market town, and shopping and gastronomy are the city's biggest draws. However, the town is also blessed with a number of attractive churches and a couple of interesting museums. If you are too lazy to walk, take the **tourist bus** (☎ 450-8920; per person B$30) that leaves from Plaza Colón at 10am and 3pm and visits all the city sights.

MARKETS

The main market is the enormous **La Cancha**, which is one of the most crowded, chaotic, claustrophobic and exhilarating spots in the country. Around the markets you'll find just about everything imaginable, including pickpockets.

The largest and most accessible area is **Mercado Cancha Calatayud**, which sprawls across a wide area along Av Aroma and south toward the former railway station. Here is your best opportunity to see local dress, which differs strikingly from that of the Altiplano.

The **Mercado de Ferias** spills out around the old railway station. *Artesanías* (stores selling locally handcrafted items) are concentrated along the alleys near the junction of Tarata and Calle Arce, in the southern end of the market area. The fruit and vegetable section is on the shore of Laguna Alalay in the southeast of town.

The fascinating **Mercado de Ganado** livestock market operates Wednesday and Sunday at the end of Avenida Panaméricana, far to the south of the centre; it's worth taking a taxi out there to see it in operation. As always, it pays to get there early-ish.

MUSEO ARQUEOLÓGICO

The **Museo Arqueológico** (☎ 425-0010; Jordán E-199, cnr Aguirre; admission B$10; ⏰ 8:30am-5:30pm Mon-Fri, 8:30am-2:30pm Sat) has an excellent overview of Bolivia's various indigenous cultures. The collection is split into three sections: the archaeological collection, the ethnographic collection and the paleontological collection. The first deals primarily with indigenous culture from the Cochabamba region. Look out for the Tiwanaku section; their shamans used to snort lines of hallucinogenic powder through elegant bone tubes. The ethnographic collection provides material from Amazonian and Chaco cultures including examples of nonalphabetized writing, which is from the 18th century and was used to bring Christianity to the illiterate Indians. The paleontological collection deals with fossilised remains of the various creatures that once prowled the countryside. There's good information in Spanish, and an English-speaking guide is sometimes around in the afternoons.

PALACIO PORTALES & MUSEO DE HISTORIA NATURAL ALCIDE D'ORBIGNY

The **Palacio Portales** (☎ 424-3137; Potosí 1450; admission incl guide B$10; ⏰ gardens 3-6:30pm Tue-Fri, 9am-noon Sat & Sun, Spanish/English tours every 30min 3:30-6pm Tue-Fri, 9:30-11:30am Sat, 11-11:30am Sun) in the barrio of Queru Queru provides evidence of the extravagance of tin baron Simón Patiño. Patiño's tastes were strongly influenced by European styles and though he never actually occupied this opulent mansion it was stocked with the finest imported materials available at the time – Carrara marble, French wood, Italian tapestries and delicate silks. The European influence is obvious as you venture through the building; the gardens and exterior were inspired by the palace at Versailles, the games room an imitation of Granada's Alhambra, whilst the main hall takes its design from the Vatican City. Construction began in 1915 and was finalized in 1927. Today it is used as an arts and cultural complex and as a teaching center.

Adjacent to the Palacio Portales is the rather more low-key **Museo de Historia Natural Alcide d'Orbigny** (☎ 448-6969; Potosí 1458; admission free but donation welcomed; ⏰ 9am-12:30pm & 3-6:30pm Mon-Fri, 9am-12:30pm Sat), the city's natural history museum. With its creaky wooden floors and array of stuffed birds and mammals this is a good way to kill half an hour while waiting for your Palacio Portales tour to begin. You can also take a look at a small geological collection.

Take *micro E* north from east of Av San Martín.

CONVENTO DE SANTA TERESA

The most interesting building in town is the noble, timeworn **Convento de Santa Teresa** (☎ 422-1252; Baptista & Ecuador; incl guide B$20; ⊙ 9am-12:30pm & 2-6pm Mon-Fri). Visits to this timeless and gracefully decaying complex are by guided tour only and provide a snapshot of the extraordinary lives led by the cloistered nuns that inhabit it (see boxed text, below). You see the peaceful cloister, fine altarpieces and sculptures (from Spanish and Potosí schools), the convent church, and even get to ascend to the roof for a glorious view over the city. The convent was founded in 1760, then destroyed in an earthquake; the new church was built with an excess of ambition, and was too big to be domed. The existing church was built inside it in 1790. There's still a Carmelite community here, but its 12 nuns are

---

THE NUNS OF SANTA TERESA

The Santa Teresa convent in Cochabamba houses what remains of an order of cloistered Carmelite nuns. A strict Catholic order with a strong devotion to the Virgin Mary, the Carmelites are thought to have been founded in the 12th century on Mt Carmel (hence the name). The order believes strongly in the power of contemplative prayer, and shuns the excesses of society.

In recent times, and with local families believing that a daughter in the convent guaranteed the entire family a place in heaven, there was strong pressure on the first daughter of every *cochabambino* family to enter into the convent. Such was the demand to buy some real estate in heaven that there was even a waiting list set up when no vacancies were available. An elderly nun had to pass on before a new young nun was allowed in.

Life inside was tough and a rigid class system operated. Those who paid a considerable dowry (equivalent to over US$150,000 in modern money) earned themselves a *velo negro* (black veil) and a place on the council under the control of the Mother Superior. The council was responsible for all the decisions in the convent. As the elite members of the order, *velo negro* were blessed with a private stone room with a single window (more like a prison cell), where they spent most of their day in prayer, religious study and other acceptable activities such as sewing tapestries.

Each *velo negro* was attended by members of the *velo blanco* (white veil), second-class nuns whose family paid some dowry but could not afford the full cost of a *velo negro*. *Velo blanco* nuns spent part of their day in prayer and the rest in personal service of the *velo negro*. Daughters of poor families who could not afford any kind of dowry became *sin velos* (without veil). These were employed in the roughest chores of the convent, cooking, cleaning and attending to the needs of the *velo blanco*. These nuns slept in communal quarters.

The rules inside the convent were strict. Personal effects were not permitted and communication with other nuns was allowed for only one hour a day – the rest was spent in total silence. Meals were eaten without speaking and contact with the outside world was almost completely prohibited. Once a month each nun was allowed a brief visit from their family, but this took place behind bars and with a black curtain preventing them from seeing and touching each other. Visits were supervised to ensure that no rules were broken and no goods changed hands. The only other contact with the city was through the sale of candles and foodstuffs, which was performed via a revolving door so that the vendor and the client were kept apart. Such transactions were the sole source of income for the nuns who were otherwise completely self-sufficient.

In the 1960s the Vatican declared that such conditions were inhuman and offered all cloistered nuns the world over the opportunity to change to a more modern way of life. Many of the nuns in Santa Teresa rejected the offer, having spent the better part of their life in the convent and knowing no different. Today just 12 nuns remain in Santa Teresa, most of advancing years, and whilst the rules are no longer as strict as they once were, the practices have changed little. These days the cloistered lifestyle is understandably less attractive to young girls in an age where their families permit them to exercise their own free will.

now housed in more comfortable modern quarters next door. It's a fascinating visit; pacing the convent's corridors, you could be in a García Márquez novel.

OTHER CHURCHES

On the arcaded Plaza 14 de Septiembre, the **cathedral** (8am-noon & 5-7pm Mon-Fri, 8am-noon Sat & Sun) is the valley's oldest religious structure, begun in 1571. Later additions and renovations have removed some character, but it preserves a fine eastern portal. Inside it's light and airy, with various mediocre ceiling paintings. There are statues of several saints, a gilded altarpiece and a grotto for the ever-popular Inmaculada (Virgin of the Immaculate Conception).

Constructed in 1581, the **Iglesia & Convento de San Francisco** (25 de Mayo & Bolívar; 7:30-11am) is Cochabamba's second-oldest church. Major revisions and renovation occurred in 1782 and 1925, however, and little of the original structure remains. The attached convent and cloister were added in the 1600s. The cloister was constructed of wood rather than the stone that was customary at the time. The pulpit displays good examples of mestizo design, and there's a fine gold retable.

The rococo **Iglesia de Santo Domingo** (Santivañez & Ayacucho) was founded in 1612 but construction didn't begin until 1778. The intriguing main facade is made of stone, with anthropomorphic columns. The interior, with a much-revered Trinity, is less interesting.

North of the river, the baroque **Iglesia de la Recoleta** was started in 1654. It houses the attractive wooden Cristo de la Recoleta.

CRISTO DE LA CONCORDIA

This immense Christ statue standing atop Cerro de San Pedro behind Cochabamba is the largest of its kind in the world. It's 44cm higher than the famous Cristo Redentor in Rio de Janeiro, which stands 33m high, or 1m for each year of Christ's life. *Cochabambinos* justify the one-upmanship by claiming that Christ actually lived '*33 años y un poquito*' (33 years and a bit).

There's a footpath from the base of the mountain (1250 steps) but several robberies have been reported here and signs along the route warn you of the dangers, not-so-subtly suggesting that you should take the

teleférico (cable car; return B$6; closed Mon). On Sunday you can climb right to the top of the statue (B$2) for a Christ's-eye view of the city.

The closest public transportation access is on *micro A*. Taxis charge B$30 for the round-trip to the top, including a half-hour wait while you look around.

Courses

Cochabamba is a popular place to hole up for a few weeks of Spanish or Quechua lessons. Several cultural centers offer courses for around B$35 per hour (p191).

The **Escuela Runawasí** (/fax 424-8923; www .runawasi.org; Blanco Galindo km 4.5, Villa Juan XXIII) offers a recommended program that involves linguistic and cultural immersion. It also includes a trip to a relaxing Chapare rainforest hideout.

There are plenty of private teachers who offer instruction but not all are experienced. You may have to try several before finding one that brings out the best of your abilities. The Centro Boliviano-Americano (p191) has a list of recommended teachers.

For information about a wide variety of volunteer opportunities, check out the Cochabamba page at www.bolivia-online .net.

Tours

Various agents run a variety of activities, particularly excursions to spots of interest in the province. The following are recommended:

Bolivia Cultura (452-7272; www.boliviacultura.com; España 301) Professional trips to PN Torotoro and other regional attractions.

Fremen Tours (425-9392; www.andes-amazonia .com; Tumusla N-245) Organizes local excursions or high-quality trips to the Chapare, Amazon and Salar de Uyuni.

Villa Etelvina (424-2636; www.villaetelvina.com; Juan de la Rosa 908, Torotoro) A good operator specialising in trips to Torotoro National Park (see p209).

Festivals & Events

A major annual event is the **Heroínas de la Coronilla** (May 27), a solemn commemoration in honor of the women and children who defended the city in the battle of 1812. At the fiesta of **Santa Veracruz Tatala** (May 2), farmers gather at a chapel 7km down the Sucre road to pray for fertility of the soil during the coming season. Their petitions are accompanied by folk music, dancing and lots of merrymaking. The **Fiesta de la Virgen de Urkupiña** (August 15 to 18) is the valley's biggest, with pilgrims converging on the village of Quillacollo, 13km west of Cochabamba.

Sleeping

BUDGET

Don't be tempted by the rock-bottom prices for accommodation in the market areas and around the bus station. It's cheap for a reason, the area is positively dangerous after dark and it is in your best interests to pay a bit more to stay somewhere north of Calle Sucre.

Hostal México (☎ 452-5069; México near Ayacucho; r per person B$20, with bathroom B$25) Very basic but clean and a great central location make this a good choice for those on a very tight budget.

Residencial Familiar (☎ 422-7988; Sucre E-554; r B$30, s/d with bathroom B$50/80) Set in a lovely old building, this recently renovated and recommendable place has plenty of character. It's built around a secluded patio, complete with nude sculpture in the fountain, and is a real haven from the hustle and bustle of the street outside.

Residencial Familiar Anexo (☎ 422-7986; 25 de Mayo N-234; r per person B$35, with bathroom B$60) Similar to Residencial Familiar but with slightly more faded charms and a slightly more central location.

Hostal Colonial (☎ 422-1791; Junín N-134; s/d B$40/70) A traveler's favorite but somewhat over-rated considering the facilities and the other options in the price range. Rooms are a bit run down, the best are upstairs overlooking the leafy courtyard gardens.

Hostal Jardín (☎ 424-7844; Hamiraya N-248; s/d with bathroom B$50/80) In a quiet part of town, this long time favorite is centered around a likably chaotic garden with an enormous starfruit tree. Rooms come with bathroom and hot water.

Apart Hotel Concordia (☎ 422-1518; hotelconcordia@hotmail.com; Arce 690; apt per person B$80; 🖳) This fading but likable place is family run and family oriented. Three- and four-person apartments include a bath, kitchenette (dishes available on request) and phone. Guests have access to the pool and laundry service. It's north of town near the university and accessible on *micro B*.

MIDRANGE

our pick **Hotel Gina's** (☎ 422-2295; www.ginashotel.web.bo; México 346 near España; r per person B$80, with bathroom B$90, ste B$250-280) Above Gina's beauty parlor, this is a modern, bright and freshly furnished hotel. Don't be put off by the girly reception (what is with those lilac hearts?); this is a great place and the suites, equipped with kitchen and living room, are superb value.

Hostal La Fontaine (☎ 425-2838; hostalfontaine@hotmail.com; Hamiraya 181; s/d B$95/160; 🖳) This little hotel offers great value, even if the odd religious paintings adorning the stairwells are slightly unnerving. Rooms are spacious, with cable TV and minibar, and breakfast is included.

City Hotel (☎ 422-2993; www.cityhotelbolivia.com; Jordán E-341; s/d/f B$100/140/180; 🖳) This spotless, friendly and central hotel is an excellent choice. Rooms are bright and well equipped, and the beds are firm and enticing. There's a laundry service, cable TV and breakfast included. It's close to the best value in town.

Hotel Americana (☎ 425-0552; Arce S-788; s/d/ste B$140/240/320) This friendly three-star option is a sound choice. The service is good, and the spotless rooms have plenty of natural light and pleasing facilities, including cable TV. Only the location leaves a little to be desired.

Hotel Boston (☎ 422-4421; hboston@supernet.com.bo; 25 de Mayo N-167; s/d B$145/220) The reliable old Boston has been surpassed in recent years by other hotels in this price category, but still offers a central location, cable TV, breakfast and a warm welcome if other places are booked up.

Monserrat Hotel (☎ 452-1011; www.hotelmonserrat.com; España N-342; s/d B$160/200; 🖳) In a renovated historic building at the heart of the eating and cafe scene. The rooms are elegant and comfortable though some are a bit dark. Great views of the *Cristo* from the 2nd floor.

TOP END

Hotel Diplomat (☎ 425-0687; www.hdiplomat.com; Ballivián 611; s/d with bathroom US$67/77; 🖳) Though the Diplomat, an upmarket business hotel, is clinically efficient in its service, it has a snobbish atmosphere that some might feel verges on the unfriendly. There are great views from some of the well-appointed rooms and it has a good location on Av Ballivián, known as 'El Prado,' a centre for shopping or bar-hopping. Free airport transfer.

Hotel Portales (☎ 428-5444; www.hotel-portales .com; Pando 1271; s/d/ste with bathroom B$550/700/1200; ❂ ▣ ▣) In the wealthy Recoleta district, the Portales is replete with elegant busts and chandeliers. It has fine grounds, but it isn't the five-star establishment it claims to be. The rooms are comfortable enough, and the service is willing, but the restaurant and bar are overpriced. Check the website for discount package deals.

Eating

Cochabambinos pride themselves on being the most food-loving of Bolivians, and there is a dazzling array of local specialties for foodies to try including *lomo borracho* (beef with egg in a beer soup) and *picante de pollo* (chicken in spicy sauce). Ask at the Tourist Office (p193) for their *Cochabamba Gastronòmica* leaflet.

Markets (p194) are cheap but keep an eye on hygiene levels and don't leave your bags unattended.

BOLIVIAN CUISINE

Sucremanta (☎ 422-2839; Ballivián 510; Hamiraya 126; Esteban Arce 340; mains from B$15; ❨ lunch only) A chain of *restaurantes típicos* where you can sample dependable local dishes, including *mondongo* (pork ribs) and *menudito* (pork, chicken and beef stew).

Savarín (☎ 425-7051; Ballivián 626; almuerzo B$20) This popular, well-established barn on Ballivián has a wide streetside terrace where people congregate at lunchime for filling *almuerzos* (set lunches) and, in the evening, for a beer or three.

Tunari (☎ 452-8588; Ballivián 676; mains B$20-45) With the distinction of being the oldest restaurant in the city, this local favorite specializes in the sort of things you either love or hate: grilled kidneys (a patent local hangover cure), tripe and tasty chorizo. But if innards aren't your thing, there are other typical Cochabamba plates.

Casa de Campo (☎ 424-3937; Pasaje Boulevar 618; mains B$25-50) A Cochabamba classic, this loud and cheerful partly open-air restaurant is a traditional spot to meet, eat, and play *cacho* (dice). There's a big range of Bolivian dishes and grilled meats; the food is fine (and piled high on the plates), but the lively, unpretentious atmosphere is better.

INTERNATIONAL CUISINE

Kabbab (☎ 424-9149; Potosí N-1392; mains B$15-25; ❨ dinner only) A thousand-and-one variations on Persian kebabs served in an intimate space adjacent to the Palacio de Portales. Highlights include clay-oven flat bread, Turkish coffee and decent baklava.

Páprika (☎ 425-7035; Ramón Rivero & Lanza; mains B$20-35) One of the 'in' spots, this is a block removed from the roar of Av Ballivián, and is a quiet leafy place popular for its food – both Bolivian and international, including tasty baked potatoes and fondues. After dark it becomes a trendy spot for a late drink and is also a good place to meet up with young Bolivians.

La Mora (Hamiraya, at Heroínas; mains B$20-40) What this place lacks in space it more than makes up for in charisma with hand-written menus and bizarrely painted furniture. The food is excellent and with a distinctly Italian flavor, but don't leave without trying one of the *singani* fruit cocktails.

Picasso (☎ 488-2923; España & Rocha; mains B$20-40) As with many of the places along España, Picasso blurs the boundaries between cafe, restaurant and bar, metamorphosing from one to the next, depending on the time of day. It's worth a look for its informal atmosphere and Mexican food.

HWA (☎ 452-9591; Salamanca 868; mains B$20-40) If you like Asian food then you are in for a treat. Korean and Japanese dishes are on offer and the food is good, even if the surroundings aren't very authentic. It's just past the Plaza Constitucíon.

Sole Mio (☎ 428-3379; América E-826; pizzas B$25-50; ❨ dinner only Mon-Fri, lunch & dinner Sat & Sun) The best pizzas in Cochabamba are to be found here. The owners, encouragingly, are from Napoli and import the ingredients for their robust brick-oven, wood-fired pizzas – thin crust, light on the sauce. Soft opera music, rich Italian wines and excellent service make this a comfortable place to linger a while over a meal. They also serve a range of meat and pasta entrées.

La Estancia (☎ 424-9262; Uyuni E-786, near Plaza Recoleta; mains B$30-50) One of a knot of spacious restaurants just across the river in Recoleta, this Argentine-style grill is a fine place. There are thick, juicy steaks (it's worth upgrading to the Argentine meat), ribs and kidneys, as well as fish and chicken, all sizzled on the blazing grill in the middle. There's also a decent salad bar and very good service.

La Cantonata (☎ 425-9222; España & Rocha; mains B$35-60; ☽ closed Mon) This classy Italian place is one of the city's better places to eat. The cozy interior has a roaring fire, candlelit tables and waistcoated waiters. Pizza and pasta is top notch but pricey.

Búfalo's Rodizio (☎ 425-1597; Torres Sofer, Oquendo N-654; buffet B$40; ☽ lunch only Sun, dinner only Mon) This all-you-can-eat Brazilian-style grill has smart waiters bringing huge hunks of delicious meat to your table faster than you can pick up your fork. There's a large salad bar, but, let's face it, it's designed for the carnivore. It's on the 2nd floor of a shopping arcade; take the lift.

CAFES

Along Calle España, near Ecuador and Venezuela/Major Rocha, you'll find an ever-changing assortment of trendy cafes, whose names seem to change every fortnight or so.

Mosoj Yan (☎ 450-7536; Bolívar at Plaza Busch; almuerzo B$10; ☽ lunch only Mon-Fri) This attractive, light and airy café is a very pleasant spot, and as well as serving delicious desserts, decent coffees and cheap lunches, your bolivianos go to a good cause. It's part of a support centre for street kids who create some of the handicrafts in the store next door. There's a decent book exchange here too.

Espresso Café Bar (☎ 425-6861; Esteban Arce 340) Just behind the cathedral, this wins the 'best coffee in town' award. It's an attractive, traditional-looking place with pleasant staff. It also serves good juices. A word of advice – don't order a 'large' espresso unless caffeine is more of a compulsion than a pleasure.

Café Paris (☎ 450-3561; España cnr Bolívar) Walls lined with Parisian street scenes, newspapers on racks and a variety of crepe for every day of the week. This is a popular, if slightly pricey cafe that will bring out the hidden French person in you.

Co Café Arte (Venezuela, near España; ☽ dinner only) A relaxed cafe with wooden tables and repro art on the walls. The cordial owner does decent coffee, juices and a few snacks.

Brazilian Coffee Bar (Ballivián 55) This Brazilian chain spot does a weird mixture of coffee, sushi and alcohol. The sushi reminds you why the Brazilian's aren't famed for it, but the coffee and booze are passable. It claims to be open 24 hours.

QUICK EATS

There's tasty street food and snacks all over Cochabamba, with the *papas rellenas* (potatoes filled with meat or cheese) at the corner of Achá and Villazón particularly delicious. Great *salteñas* (filled pastry shells) and empanadas are ubiquitous; for the latter, try **Los Castores** (Ballivián 790; empanadas B$2.50), which has a range of delicious fillings both savory and sweet. Locals swear by the *anticuchos* (beef-heart shish kebabs) that sizzle all night at the corner of Av Villaroel and Av América.

The jumbo-size **Dumbo** (☎ 450-1300; Heroínas E-345; ☎ 423-4223; Ballivián 55; mains B$10-40) and **Cristal** (Heroínas E-352; mains B$10-40) serve a range of eats throughout the day, from pancakes to bland but decent burgers and main dishes, and are particularly popular for a late-afternoon *helado* (ice cream) and coffee. A similar place that's a real fun palace for children is **Globo's** (cnr Beni & Santa Cruz; mains B$10-40). Balloons, ice creams, juices and kid-friendly meals – it's got the lot.

VEGETARIAN

Uno's (Heroínas & San Martín; almuerzo B$7; ☽ 8am-1pm Mon-Sat) Tasty and remarkably cheap, with vegetarian buffet fare served on plastic, prison-style trays. They also do good fruit salads and soy burgers, but there's no alcohol served. Blink and you'll miss it, though – there is no sign outside and it's barely larger than a walk-in closet.

Gopal (☎ 423-4082; España N-250; mains B$15-30; ☽ lunch daily, dinner Mon-Fri) Half-decent vegetarian dishes that include soy-based conversions of Bolivian dishes and a few curries. There's another branch at Mayor Rocha 375.

GROCERIES

IC Norte (América at Pando) Well-stocked US-style supermarket with imported and unique export-quality Bolivian products.

Super Haas (Heroínas E-585) Convenient if expensive mini-market with a deli and snack counter.

Drinking

There's plenty of drinking action along El Prado (Avenida Ballivián), where Top Chopp is a typical Bolivian beer hall. Calle España is also fertile territory, with an ever-changing parade of appealing, bohemian cafe-bars.

Black Jack (☎ 425-7467; Plaza Colón 342) Neon lights and loud music. There is a pool table here and cheap *tragos* (alcoholic drinks) for those who like the simpler things in life.

Cerebritos (España N-251; � 8pm-late) A grungy, likable bar with cable drums for tables and loud rock and hip-hop music. The house special is a mixed platter of colorful shooters; local students down them as *cacho* forfeits.

Dali (☎ 422-8216; Plazuela Barba de Padilla, Reza E-242) An interesting and popular *boliche* (nightclub) that successfully mixes alcohol consumption with an appreciation for art. Regular exhibitions and live musical performances make it worth staying a while.

El Ajuicho (Santa Cruz in front of Colegio Anglo-Americano) A grisly *chichería* (bar specializing in chicha) for most of the year, after 10pm on the first Friday of every month it converts into a ritual site for *K'hoa Comunitaria*. Dating from Incan times the ritual gives thanks to Pacha Mama under the direction of an *amauta* (priest), who offers llama fetuses and burns incense in her honor. Note that this is an authentic ritual, not a tourist trap. Visitors are welcomed but are expected to participate actively, chewing coca leaves and drinking *chicha* until well after midnight.

Prikafé (España & Rocha) This cozy corner spot is an intimate, candlelit place popular with romancing couples. It's better for drinks – coffee, wine, cocktails – than the tasty but calorie-laden food.

Entertainment

The huge new multiplex, **Cine Center** (Ramón Rivero s/n) has several screens; more atmospheric are the bright **Cine Heroínas** (Heroínas s/n) and the smaller **Cine Astor** (Sucre & 25 de Mayo). For information about what's on, see the newspaper entertainment listings.

Many of the bars along España and Av Ballivián turn into mini-discos after midnight throughout the week, but at weekends the in-crowd head to the Recoleta and Avenida Pando to trendy places like **Deep** (Pando) and **Levoa** (Paseo de la Recoleta). Expect to pay more than B$30 to get in. Elsewhere popular dancing spots include **Lujo's Discoteca y Karaoke** (Beni E-330; ☼ 8pm-late Wed-Sun), which, when the clientele don't take the music into their own hands, plays salsa and pop.

Shopping

Locally made woollens are available at a few outlets. Try the expensive but reliable **Asarti** (☎ 425-0455; Edificio Colón No 5, Paccieri at 25 de Mayo), which makes export-quality alpaca and the cooperative **Arte Andino** (☎ 450-8367; www.artesandinos.com; Pasaje Catedral s/n). Cheaper alpaca- and llama-wool *chompas* (sweaters) are found in the markets. For inexpensive souvenirs, scour the *artesanía* stalls behind the main post office.

Getting There & Away

AIR

Cochabamba's **Jorge Wilstermann Airport** (CBB; domestic/international departure tax B$14/170) is served daily by **AeroSur** (☎ 440-0912; Villarroel 105) from La Paz, Santa Cruz and Sucre. The flight between La Paz and Cochabamba must be one of the world's most incredible (sit on the left coming from La Paz, the right from Cochabamba), with fabulous views of the dramatic Cordillera Quimsa Cruz, and a (disconcertingly) close-up view of the peak of Illimani. **Aerocon** (☎ 448-7665; office at airport) has a couple of daily flights to Trinidad with onward connections to Riberalta.

TAM (☎ 441-1545; Hamiraya N-122) has a flight to La Paz daily except Wednesday, and flies to Santa Cruz daily from Monday to Wednesday and again on Friday. They also fly to Tarija and Yacuiba via Sucre on Saturdays at 8:30am. **TAM Mercosur** (☎ 452-0118; Plazuela Constitución) connects Cochabamba with Asunción, Buenos Aires and São Paulo via Santa Cruz daily except Sunday, while AeroSur flies three times a week to Miami, also via Santa Cruz.

BUS

Cochabamba's **main bus terminal** (☎ 422-0550; Ayacucho near Aroma; terminal fee B$4) has an information kiosk, a branch of the tourist police, ATMs, luggage storage and a *cambio* (money exchange bureau). Prices given in this section are for standard buses. *Bus cama* (sleeper) service is available on most long-distance routes for about twice the price of those listed here.

There are at least 20 buses daily to La Paz (B$45, seven hours). Most leave between 7am and 9pm. Numerous *flotas* (long-distance bus companies) run daily services to Oruro (B$25, four hours). Most Santa Cruz buses (B$66, 8 to 13 hours) depart before 9am or after 6pm; more expensive ones take the old Chapare road, cheaper ones the new.

Frequent buses leave for Sucre (B$40 to B$80, 10 to 12 hours) between 4:30pm and 6:30pm daily. Some then continue on to Potosí (B$52, 15 hours). *Micros* and buses to Villa Tunari (B$20, three hours) and less frequently to Puerto Villarroel (B$35, seven hours) in the Chapare region leave every hour or so from 8am to 7pm from the corner of Oquendo and República.

Flechabus and Almirante Brown offer a marathon international service to Buenos Aires (B$500, 72 hours) leaving at 5:30am and 6:30pm daily.

Trufis (collective taxis) and *micros* to eastern Cochabamba Valley villages leave from the corner of República and 6 de Agosto. Torotoro *micros* leave on Thursday and Sunday at around 5:45am and Wednesday and Saturday at 6:30pm. To the western part of the valley, services leave from the corner of Ayacucho and Aroma.

Getting Around
TO/FROM THE AIRPORT
Micro B (B$2) shuttles between the airport and the main plaza. Taxis to or from the center cost B$20.

BUS
Convenient, lettered *micros* and *trufis* display their destinations and run to all corners of the city (B$1.50).

CAR
Avis Rent-a-Car (☎ 428-3132; www.avis.com.bo; Pando 1187), next to Hotel Portales, isn't the cheapest, but it's the best. It's also at Jorge Wilstermann Airport.

TAXI
The taxi fare around the centre is B$3 per person. An extra boliviano is charged if you cross the river or go far to the south. For a radio taxi, ring **Cristal** (☎ 428-0880) or **Señor Taxi** (☎ 458-0058).

PARQUE NACIONAL TUNARI
This easily accessible, 3090 sq km park was created in 1962 to protect the forested slopes above Cochabamba, as well as the wild summit of Cerro Tunari. It encompasses a wide diversity of habitats from dry inter-Andean valleys to the more humid and highly endangered *Polylepis* forests of the Cordillera Tunari.

The SERNAP office in Cochabamba (p193) may have simple walking maps of the park, but often finds itself without material.

Cochabamba Area
A good dirt road zigzags its way from the park gate (open until 4pm) up the steep mountain face. About 3km after the gate, you'll reach a **picnic site** with barbecues and a playground. Beyond here is a *sendero ecológico* (nature trail). Don't expect too much in the way of *ecología,* but it's a well-made path that gains altitude rapidly, winding into thickening mature woodland. The views are tremendous, with Cochabamba spread out below, and in the opposite direction, Cerro Tunari and the Cordillera. With an early start and plenty of water, you should be able to make it up to some of the nearer peaks on a long day hike.

Coming from town, take *micro F2* or *trufi 35* from Av San Martín, which will drop you three minutes from the park entrance, a big wooden archway with a fire-risk indicator. You may have to show ID and sign into the park. From the gate, turn right, then turn left after 100m; the road zigzags up past the playground to the lakes.

Cerro Tunari Area
Snow-dusted Cerro Tunari (5035m) is the highest peak in central Bolivia (it's the second peak from the left on the Taquiña beer label). Its flanks are 25km west of Cochabamba along the road to Independencia. This spectacular area offers excellent hiking and camping, but access is less than straightforward. For climbs, pick up the 1:50,000 map *Cordillera de Tunari* (sheet 6342III) from the IGM (p191).

From Quillacollo (p202) it's a complicated four- to five-hour ascent to the summit, with some sections requiring technical equipment. Experienced climbers can manage the round-trip in a long day, but the high-altitude ascent will be more pleasant

AROUND COCHABAMBA

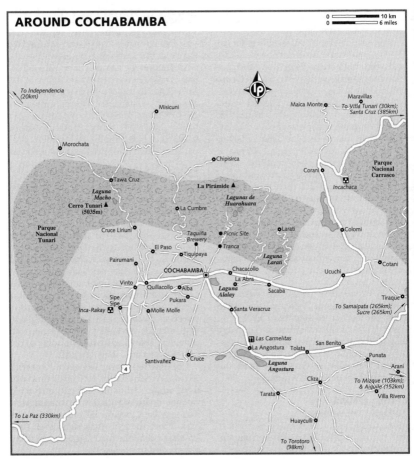

0   10 km
0   6 miles

To Independencia (20km)

Misicuni

Maica Monte

Maravillas

To Villa Tunari (30km); Santa Cruz (385km)

Morochata

Chipisirca

Corani

Parque Nacional Carrasco

Tawa Cruz

La Pirámide ▲

Incachaca

Laguna Macho

Cerro Tunari ▲ (5035m)

Lagunas de Huarahuara

Parque Nacional Tunari

Cruce Liriuni

La Cumbre

Larati

Colomi

Taquiña Brewery

Picnic Site

El Paso

Tranca

Laguna Larati

Pairumani

Tiquipaya

COCHABAMBA

Chacacollo

Ucuchi

Cotani

La Abra

Vinto

Quillacollo

Alba

Laguna Alalay

Sacaba

Sipe Sipe

Pukara

Santa Veracruz

Tiraque

To Samaipata (265km); Sucre (265km)

Inca-Rakay

Molle Molle

4

Santivañez

Cruce

Las Carmelitas

La Angostura

Tolata

San Benito

Punata

Arani

Laguna Angostura

Cliza

To Mizque (103km); & Aiquile (152km)

To La Paz (330km)

Tarata

Villa Rivero

Huayculli

To Torotoro (98km)

if you allow two days and camp overnight. You'll need a guide to find the best route.

An easier route ascends from Estancia Chaqueri or Tawa Cruz, 12km beyond Cruce Liriuni (which has accommodations at the village school) at 4200m. *Micros* and *camiones* (flatbed trucks) toward Morochata leave on Monday, Thursday and Saturday at 7am from three blocks off the main plaza in Quillacollo; they return to Cochabamba in the afternoon on Tuesday, Friday and Sunday. The relatively easy path, which takes around five hours, ascends the north face of the peak.

Another option is Fremen Tours (p196). It leads all-inclusive two-day excursions using the northern route.

COCHABAMBA VALLEY
Quillacollo

Besides Cochabamba itself, Quillacollo (13km west of Cochabamba) is the Cochabamba Valley's most commercially important community, although it has lost much of its independent feel in recent years as Cochabamba's growth has more or less absorbed it as a suburb. Apart from the **Sunday market** and the **pre-Inca burial mound** discovered beneath Plaza Bolívar, the main attraction is in its church, the revered **Virgen de Urkupiña**. Tradition has it that long ago, the Virgin Mary appeared several times to a shepherd girl at the foot of the hill known as Calvario. The visits were later witnessed by the girl's parents and a crowd of villagers when she shouted *'Orkopiña'* (There on the hill!) as the Virgin was seen ascending heavenwards. At the summit of the hill, the townspeople discovered the stone image of the Virgin, which now stands in the church to the right of the altar, surrounded by votive offerings and commemorative plaques giving thanks for blessings received.

One thing to do here is to sample *garapiña,* a deceptively strong blend of *chicha* (fermented corn), cinnamon, coconut and *ayrampo,* which is a local mystery ingredient that colors the drink red.

FESTIVALS & EVENTS

From August 14 to 18 is the **Fiesta de la Virgen de Urkupiña**, which is the biggest annual celebration in Cochabamba department. Folkloric musicians and dancers come from around Bolivia to perform, and the *chicha* flows for three days. It can be a fairly chaotic scene, with more attention paid to hitting the bottle than on reverence. It's also very crowded.

SLEEPING & EATING

At Estancia Marquina, 5km north of Quillacollo, is **Eco-Hotel Planeta de Luz** (☎ 426-1234; www.planetadeluz.com; camping per person B$15, full board s/d B$200/280, 3–4-person cabins/ste B$525; 🔊), a curious place with Gaudíesque architecture, spa treatments, a sauna, wandering domestic animals and a kooky New Age vibe. The variety of different accommodations options is as wide as your imagination, from round huts with circular beds to posh suites.

GETTING THERE & AWAY

Micros and *trufis* to Quillacollo (B$2, 30 minutes) leave frequently from Oquendo, Heroínaś, the corner of Ayacucho and Aroma, and the corner of Circunvalación and América in Cochabamba. In Quillacollo, the *trufi* stop is on Plaza Bolívar.

Sipe Sipe

This quiet and friendly village 27km southwest of Cochabamba is the base for visiting Inca-Rakay, the most easily accessible of the Cochabamba area ruins. If you're in Sipe Sipe on a Sunday between February and May, try to sample the local specialty, a sweet grape liquor known as *guarapo.*

On Wednesday and Saturday, *micros* run directly to Sipe Sipe from the corner of Ayacucho and Aroma in Cochabamba. On other days, take a *micro* from the same spot to Plaza Bolívar in Quillacollo and then a *trufi* or a *micro* to Sipe Sipe.

Inca-Rakay

The ruins of Inca-Rakay, in the Serranía de Tarhuani, are mostly crumbling stone walls these days, and you'll need some imagination to conjure up their former glory. It has been postulated that Inca-Rakay served as an Inca administrative outpost, which oversaw agricultural colonies in the fertile Cochabamba Valley. That seems unlikely, however, given its lofty position and the difficulty of access.

The site includes the remains of several hefty buildings, and a large open plaza overlooking the valley. One odd rock outcrop resembles the head of a condor, with a natural passageway inside leading to the top. Just off the plaza area is a cave that may be explored with a flashlight. Legend has it that this cave is the remnant of another of those apocryphal Inca tunnels – this one linking Inca-Rakay with faraway Cuzco. If you're there on a smog-free day, the plaza affords a spectacular overview of the valley.

The rare Spanish-language book *Inkallajta & Inkaraqay,* by Jesús Lara, contains good site maps and theories about its origins and purposes.

GETTING THERE & AWAY

Inca-Rakay is accessed on foot from Sipe Sipe. Since staying overnight is not a safe option, you must get an early start out of Cochabamba; the trip takes the better part of a day and you'll need time to explore the ruins.

It's a 5km, 2½-hour cross-country (but well-signed) walk up a steep hill from Sipe Sipe to the site. From the southwest corner of Sipe Sipe's main plaza, follow the

---

WARNING

Spending the night in the unattended ruins cannot be recommended. A foreign couple was reportedly killed here while sleeping in their vehicle, and several other readers have reported serious violent incidents while camping here.

road past the secondary school. From there the road narrows into a path and crosses a small ditch. Across the ditch, turn left onto the wider road. Starting several hundred meters up the road from town, follow a water pipeline uphill to the first major ridge; there'll be a large ravine on your left. From there, bear to the right, following the ridge until you see a smaller ravine on the right. At this point you're actually able to see Inca-Rakay atop a reddish hill in the distance, but from so far away it's hard to distinguish.

Cross the small ravine and follow it until you can see a couple of adobe houses on the other side. In front you'll see a little hill with some minor ruins at the top. Climb the hill, cross the large flat area, and then climb up two more false ridges until you see Inca-Rakay.

Tiquipaya

The town of Tiquipaya, whose name means 'Place of Flowers' is located 11km northwest of Cochabamba. It is known for its **Sunday market** and its array of unusual festivals. In late April or early May there's an annual **Chicha Festival**; in July there is a **Potato Festival**; the second week in September sees the **Trout Festival**; around September 24 is the **Flower Festival**; and in the first week of November there's the **Festival de la Wallunk'a**, which attracts colorfully dressed traditional women from around the Cochabamba department.

The classy **Cabañas Tolavi** (☎ 431-6834; www.cabanastolavi.com; s/d/tw with breakfast buffet B$200/280/350, cabañas B$450-650; 🖭) has chalet-style *cabañas* constructed of perfumed wood, which occupy a gardenlike setting among the trees. Nonguests can enjoy German-style meals, including a buffet breakfast. It's 500m downhill from the *trufi* stop in Tiquipaya.

Micros leave half-hourly from the corner of Avs Ladislao Cabrera and Oquendo in Cochabamba. A taxi costs around B$140 if you have enough people to fill it.

Villa Albina

If you haven't already had your fill of Simón Patiño's legacy in Oruro and Cochabamba, in the village of Pairumani you can visit **Villa Albina** (☎ 424-3137; 🕑 3-3:45pm Mon-Fri, 9am-1pm Sat) and tour the home the tin baron

actually occupied. This enormous white mansion, which could have inspired the TV home of the Beverly Hillbillies, was named for his wife. Albina was presumably as fussy as her husband when it came to the finer things in life, and the elegant French decor of the main house and the Carrara-marble mausoleum seem typical of royalty anywhere in the world. There's a formal garden, complete with topiary and the family mausoleum in which the Don and his wife were finally laid to rest.

To reach Pairumani, take *trufi 211Z* or *micro 7* or *38* from Av Aroma in Cochabamba, or from Plaza Bolívar in Quillacollo, and get off at Villa Albina. It's only 18km from Cochabamba, but the trip may take a couple of hours, so you might consider a taxi.

La Angostura

This village stands on the shores of the artificial lake of the same name, and is a popular spot for *cochabambinos* to head to fill up on fish. It's on the route to Tarata, 18km from Cochabamba. There are many places to eat along the lake shore, which feed you up with enormous plates of *trucha* or *pejerrey* (trout or king fish) with rice, salad and potato. There are also places to hire rowboats and kayaks at weekends. From the corner of Barrientos and Manuripi in Cochabamba, take any *micro* toward Tarata or Cliza and get off at the Angostura bridge; if you see the dam on your right, you've gone too far (just). Nearby, on the highway, is the famous open-air **Las Carmelitas**, where Señora Carmen López bakes delicious cheese and onion empanadas (B$3) in a large beehive oven.

Punata

This small market town 50km east of Cochabamba is said to produce Bolivia's finest *chicha*. Tuesday is market day and May 18 is the riotous **town festival**. Access from Cochabamba is via *micros* (B$3.50, one hour), taxis (B$5) and buses (B$4) that depart when full from Plaza Villa Bella at the corner of República (the southern extension of Antezana) and 6 de Agosto from 5am to 8pm.

If you have been hunting for the perfect alpaca sweater, contact the *alcaldía* (town hall) about **Alpaca Works** (☎ 457-7922; www

.geocities.com/alpacaworks/home.html; Bolivia 180), a women's cooperative where you can browse their existing stock or order a customized Western-style sweater.

Tarata & Huayculli

Tarata, 29km southeast of Cochabamba, is one of the region's loveliest towns, a picturesque but decaying beauty that's well worth a visit for its noble buildings, cobbled streets and gorgeous plaza, filled with palm trees and jacarandas. The town's name is derived from the abundant *tara* trees, whose fruit is used in curing leather. Tarata is famous as the birthplace of the mad president General Mariano Melgarejo, who held office from 1866 to 1871 and whose remains now lie in the town church. While the citizens aren't necessarily proud of his achievements, they're pretty proud of producing presidents (populist military leader René Barrientos, who ruled from 1964 to 1969, was also born here), so there's a huge horseback statue of him on the main road.

The enormous neoclassical **Iglesia de San Pedro** was constructed in 1788 and restored between 1983 and 1985; several of the interior panels include mestizo-style details carved in cedar. The 1792 **Franciscan Convent of San José**, which contains lovely colonial furniture and an 8000-volume library, was founded as a missionary training school. It now operates as a museum and contains the ashes of San Severino, Tarata's patron saint, whose feast day is celebrated on the last Sunday in November.

The village also has several other **historic buildings**: the Palacio Consistorial (government palace) of President Melgarejo (built in 1872) and the homes of President Melgarejo, General Don Esteban Arce and General René Barrientos.

Huayculli, 7km from Tarata, is a village of potters and glaziers. The air is thick with the scent of eucalyptus being burned in cylindrical firing kilns. The local style and technique are passed down from generation to generation and remain unique.

From Cochabamba, taxis (B$5, 30 minutes) leave when full and *micros* (B$4, 45 minutes) leave every 15 minutes between 6am and 8pm from Av Barrientos and Manuripi. There are no *micros* to Huayculli, but minibuses running between Tarata and Anzaldo can drop you here.

INCALLAJTA

The nearest thing Bolivia has to Peru's Machu Picchu is the remote and rarely visited site of Incallajta (meaning 'Land of the Inca'), 132km east of Cochabamba on a flat mountain spur above the Río Machajmarka. This was the easternmost outpost of the Inca empire and after Tiwanaku it's the country's most significant archaeological site. The most prominent feature is the immense stone fortification that sprawls across alluvial terraces above the river, but at least 50 other structures are also scattered around the 12-hectare site.

Incallajta was probably founded by Inca Emperor Tupac Yupanqui, the commander who had previously marched into present-day Chile to demarcate the southern limits of the Inca empire. It's estimated that Incallajta was constructed in the 1460s as a measure of protection against attack by the Chiriguanos to the southeast. In 1525, the last year of Emperor Huayna Capac's rule, the outpost was abandoned. This may have been due to a Chiriguano attack, but was more likely the result of increasing Spanish pressure and the unraveling of the empire, which fell seven years later.

The site is on a monumental scale; some researchers believe that, as well as serving a defensive purpose, it was designed as a sort of ceremonial replica of Cuzco, the Inca capital. The site's most significant building, the *kallanka,* measures a colossal 80m by 25m. The roof was supported by immense columns. Outside it is a large boulder, probably a speakers' platform. At the western end of the site is a curious six-sided tower, perhaps used for astronomical observation. On the hilltop, a huge zigzag defensive wall has a baffled defensive entrance.

The ruins were made known to the world in 1914 by Swedish zoologist and ethnologist Ernest Nordenskiöld, who spent a week at the ruins, measuring and mapping them. However, they were largely ignored – except by ruthless treasure hunters – for the next 50 years, until the University of San Simón in Cochabamba launched its investigations.

At Pocona, 17km from the ruins, there's an information centre and a small exhibition of archaeological finds from the site.

Tours

Cochabamba agencies run day-long tours to Incallajta when they have a group large enough to make it worthwhile. Fremen Tours (p196) is recommended. Beware of tours that seem suspiciously cheap or that involve 'trekking.' These generally involve getting a cab to the *cruce* (turnoff) and walking up to the site – you can do that yourself.

Sleeping & Eating

Without your own transportation, visiting Incallajta will prove inconvenient at best. Additionally, if you can't arrange lodging in private homes, you'll probably have to camp for two or three nights, so be sure to take plenty of water, food, warm clothing and camping gear. Camping and basic shelters are available at the Centro de Investigaciones in Pocona.

Getting There & Away

Taxis (B$18, three hours) and *micros* (B$15, five hours) to Pocona leave Cochabamba when full between 5am and 7pm from the corner of República and Manuripi. Get off at the turnoff for the site at Collpa. From here it's an 8km uphill walk. Pocona is a further 9km past Collpa.

TOTORA

Totora, 142km east of Cochabamba, huddles in a valley at the foot of Cerro Sutuchira. It is on the main route between Cochabamba and Sucre, but few travelers ever see it because most buses pass through at night. Nevertheless it is a lovely colonial village, built around a postcard-pretty plaza with colorful buildings and arcades. In May 1998 the town was struck by an earthquake measuring 6.7 on the Richter scale. While there's still plenty of damage visible, much of the town has since been lovingly restored.

The annual **town festival** on February 2 features bullfights. There's a **piano festival** at the end of September, but Totora's most charming and famous festival is that of **San Andrés**. On November 2, giant swings are erected on the streets, and throughout the month young women who are hoping for marriage are swung high on them. They are also believed to be helping the wandering souls, who descended to earth on All Souls' Day, return to heaven.

The **Hotel Municipal** (☎ 413-6464; Plaza Ladislao Cabrera s/n; r per person B$50) is an attractive reconstruction of what was once the town's hospital, and is one of two good hotels in town. It's got spacious, comfortable rooms in an old-fashioned style. There's also a couple of simple *alojamientos* (cheap guesthouses).

Micros (B$10, three hours) destined for Aiquile leave daily for Totora between noon and 5pm from the corner of 6 de Agosto and Barrientes in Cochabamba.

MIZQUE

This pretty colonial village enjoys a lovely pastoral setting on the Río Mizque. Founded as the Villa de Salinas del Río Pisuerga in 1549, it soon came to be known as the Ciudad de las 500 Quitasoles (City of 500 Parasols), after the sun shields used by the locals. It makes a great escape from the cities and main tourist sights, and the few visitors who pass through on trips between Sucre and Cochabamba are impressed by the beauty of the Mizque and Tucuna Valleys, where flocks of macaws squawk and frolic in the early morning.

Sights & Activities

The lovely, restored **Iglesia Matríz**, which was slightly damaged in a 1998 earthquake, once served as the seat of the Santa Cruz bishopric (until the seat was shifted to Arani in 1767). There's also a small archaeological and historical **museum**. Monday is **market day**.

With the help of Peace Corps volunteers, the *alcaldía* (on the north side of the plaza) organizes **self-guided hiking circuits** and **guided trips** to several local sites of natural and historic interest. Moises Cardozo at the Entel office or Restaurant Plaza will arrange an interesting visit to his **apiary** just outside of town.

Besides its cheese and honey, Mizque is best known for its **Fería de la Fruta** (April 19), which coincides with the *chirimoya* (custard apple) harvest and **Semana Santa**. From September 8 to 14, Mizque holds the lively **Fiesta del Señor de Burgos**, which features much revelry and bull- and cockfighting.

Sleeping & Eating

Residencial Mizque (☎ 434-2039; r per person B$25) Set amid gardens, this clean place is the easiest to find if you arrive at night – look for the Prodem sign.

Hotel Bolivia (☎ 434-2158; r per person B$20, with bathroom B$40) Next to the *campesino* (subsistence farmer) market on the road to the river, Hotel Bolivia has firm beds and is probably the nicest place in town.

Hostal Graciela (☎ 413-5616; r per person with bathroom B$40) A good option with rooms that have decks; it's affiliated with the also recommended Restaurant Plaza.

Mizque has several cheap Taquiña-sponsored *alojamientos* that serve typical Bolivian meals. They're all within a block of the plaza. Alternatively, you can eat at the street stalls beside the church.

Getting There & Away

Three daily *micros* (B$15, four hours) leave Cochabamba from the corner of Avs 6 de Agosto and República at noon, 2pm and 6pm; from Mizque they depart for Cochabamba at 8am, 10am and noon and for Aiquile at 3pm daily. Occasional *micros* travel between here and Totora – 31km on a rough road.

AIQUILE

Aiquile, was decimated by the same 1998 earthquake that damaged Totora and is known for some of Bolivia's finest *charangos* (traditional Bolivian ukulele-type instrument). In late November it holds the **Feria del Charango**. Every Sunday is a busy market day.

The small **Museo del Charango** (admission B$10) holds a collection of the instruments, including the ones that won prizes at the festival, and also has some archaeological pieces. The **cathedral** is quite spectacular, with a free-form central building flanked by two free-standing towers.

Accommodations are available at the pleasant **Hostal Campero** (r per person B$25) and the basic **Hotel Los Escudos** (r per person B$35), which both serve simple meals. The Campero is in an old colonial building surrounding a pleasant courtyard, and the personable owner likes to chat with guests. The cost of accommodations rises during the *charango* festival. If you are desperate, a series of dodgy-looking 24-hour fried-chicken places line up on the northern edge of town.

Aiquile lies on the main route between Cochabamba and Sucre, but most intercity buses pass in the wee hours of the night

when this already soporific settlement is sound asleep. Buses to Aiquile (B$15) depart daily between noon and 5pm from Av 6 de Agosto between Barrientos and República in Cochabamba.

It's about 90 minutes between Aiquile and Mizque. There are a couple of *micros* a day, or you can readily thumb a ride on passing *camiones,* but be prepared for a real dust bath.

PARQUE NACIONAL TOROTORO

One of Bolivia's most memorable national parks, Torotoro at times can seem like a practical demonstration of geology on an awe-inspiring scale. Beds of sedimentary mudstone, sandstone and limestone, bristling with marine fossils and – from drier periods – dinosaur footprints, have been muscled and twisted into the sharp, inhospitable hillscapes of the Serranía de Huayllas and Serranía de Cóndor Khaka. In places, the immensity of geological time is showcased, with exposed layers revealing fossils below a hundred meters or more of sedimentary strata.

Amidst it all, the characterful, impoverished colonial village of Torotoro itself (2720m) is one of the region's most remote settlements (although road access is steadily improving).

Information & Registration

Information about the park is sometimes available from the SERNAP office in Cochabamba (p193), but don't bank on it. You may have more luck at one of the tour companies or online at www.torotoro-bolivia .com (in Spanish). On the main street in the village of Torotoro, the **tourist office** (Charcas s/n; ☯ daily) is housed in the entrance of the *alcaldía*. This is where you contract guides and register for your visit to the park (B$20). Hang on to your ticket at all times as it will be inspected by park rangers.

On the main street in Torotoro, there's an **Entel office** (☎ 413-5736), which also has internet access.

GUIDES

In order to protect the park's geological wonders, it is compulsory to take a guide on any excursion outside the village. The best place to find a guide is at the park office – ask for '*un guía confiable*' (a reliable guide), as your visit will be greatly enhanced. Be aware that your guide is very unlikely to speak English.

The going rate for a guide is around B$45 for a half-day excursion for up to four people, more for a visit to the Gruta de Umajalanta. For dinosaur footprints, it can be very helpful if the guide has a brush (otherwise buy one) to whisk the dust out of the hollows. If you are going to the cave, the guide should have head-lanterns and rope.

Dinosaur Tracks

Most visitors to Torotoro come for the paleontology. The village, which sits in a wide section of a 20km-long valley at a 2600m elevation, is flanked by enormous, inclined mudstone rock formations, bearing bipedal and quadrupedal dinosaur tracks from the Cretaceous period (spanning 145 million to 65 million years ago).

There are numerous tracks (huellas) all over the place, and much work remains to be done on their interpretation. Many different dinosaur species are represented, both herbivorous and carnivorous.

The closest tracks are just at the entrance to the village, on the other side of the river. Above the water but below the road are the area's largest tracks, made by an enormous quadruped dinosaur (diplodocus or similar), and they measure 35cm wide, 50cm long and 20cm deep. Near here, just above the road, the angled plane of rock reveals a multitude of different tracks, including a long set of a heavy quadrupedal dinosaur that some have posited are those of the armadillo-like anklyosaurus.

Along the route to Umajalanta cave, the flat area known as the Carreras Pampa site has several excellent sets of footprints (on both sides of the path). These were made by three-toed bipedal dinosaurs, both herbivores (with rounded toes) and carnivores (pointed toes, sometimes with the claw visible).

All the tracks in the Torotoro area were made in soft mud, which then solidified into mudstone. They were later lifted and tilted by tectonic forces. For that reason, many of the tracks appear to lead uphill. Many local guides, however, believe that the footprints were made in lava as the dinosaurs fled a volcanic eruption.

Sea Fossils

In a small side gully, an hour's walk southwest of Torotoro, on the Cerro de las Siete Vueltas (Mountain of Seven Turns – so called because the trail twists seven times before reaching the peak), is a major sea-fossil deposit. At the base of the ravine you may see petrified shark teeth, while higher up, the limestone and sedimentary layers are set with fossils of ancient trilobites, echinoderms, gastropods, arthropods, cephalopods and brachiopods. The site is thought to date back about 350 million years. There's another major sea-fossil site in the **Quebrada Thajo Khasa**, southeast of Torotoro.

Pachamama Wasi

This amazing and beautiful **house-museum** (Sucre s/n; admission B$5) is the quirky home of a man who has spent years of his life pacing the cerros (hills) with a rockhound's eye. The house is like a botanic garden, but made of stones: fossils, geological quirks and unusually shaped rocks form a unique, soothing ensemble. It's uphill from the main street but only open when the owner or his family are at home.

Cañón de Torotoro & El Vergel

Three kilometers from Torotoro, the ground suddenly drops away into an immense and spectacularly beautiful canyon, over 250m deep. From the mirador (viewpoint) at the top, you can gaze along it, watching vultures wheeling. The cliffside here is also home to the rare paraba frente roja (Red-fronted macaw; p316), which you have a good chance of seeing, or at least hearing.

From here, following the diminishing canyon along to the left, you come to a flight of 800 stairs that lead down to El Vergel (also called Huacasenq'a, meaning 'cow's nostrils' in Quechua), which always has water and is filled with incongruous moss, vines and other tropical vegetation. At the bottom a crystal-clear river tumbles down through cascades and waterfalls, forming idyllic swimming pools.

Batea Q'ocha Rock Paintings

Above the third bend of the Río Torotoro, 1.5km downstream from the village, are several panels of ancient rock paintings collectively called Batea Q'ocha because the pools below them resemble troughs for pounding laundry. The paintings were executed in red pigments and depict anthropomorphic and geometric designs as well as fanciful representations of serpents, turtles and other creatures.

Gruta de Umajalanta

The Río Umajalanta, which disappears beneath a layer of limestone approximately 22m thick, has formed the impressive Umajalanta Cavern, of which 4.5km of passages have been explored.

The exciting descent is moderately physical, and you must expect to get both wet and dirty; there are several parts where you must crawl and wriggle to get through, and a couple of short roped descents. Make sure you have good nonslip shoes on.

Inside are some spectacular stalagmite and stalactite formations, as well as a resident population of vampire bats who have produced an impressively large pile of steaming dung over the years.

You eventually descend to an underground lake and river, which is populated by small, white, completely blind catfish. The ascent from here is fairly easy, as it takes a more direct route.

The 8km one-way walk to the cavern entrance takes two hours from the village, with plenty of dinosaur footprints to inspect on the way.

There are numerous other caverns in the area, many of which are virtually unexplored.

Llama Chaqui

A challenging 19km hike around the Cerro Huayllas Orkho from Torotoro will take you to the ruins known as the Llama Chaqui (Foot of the Llama). The multilevel complex, which dates from Inca times, rambles over distinctive terraces and includes a maze of rectangular and semicircular walls, plus a fairly well-preserved watchtower. Given its strategic vantage point, it probably served as a military fortification, and may have been somehow related to Incallajta (p205), further north.

Tours

Villa Etelvina are experts in the Torotoro area, and passionate about the national park and the local community. They arrange comfortable 4WD transfers from Cochabamba, and put visitors up in their excellent lodge (below) in Torotoro village. A few Cochabamba agencies (p196) run trips, including visits to the major sights. One of the best is Bolivia Cultura (p196).

Festivals & Events

From July 24 to 27, the village stages the **Fiesta del Señor Santiago**, which features sheep sacrifices, dynamite explosions, colorful costumes, much *chicha* and some light *tinku* (traditional Bolivian fighting; see boxed text, p237). This is an interesting time to visit – and there's much more public transportation than usual – but the natural attractions are very crowded.

Sleeping & Eating

There are several downmarket *residenciales* (simple accommodations) in Torotoro, but few that are much more than huts with signs. One that's substantially better is **Hostal Las Hermanas** (Cochabamba; r B$40), which is simple but clean and comfortable, with hot water; it's on the street that enters the village, on the left.

Villa Etelvina (☎ 7073-7807; www.villaetelvina .com; Sucre s/n; r per person B$120, 4-person bungalow B$400) The best option in town, this is a comfortable and welcoming oasis. As well as having extremely comfortable and stylish accommodation, they put on some of the most delicious home cooking you're likely to find on your travels in Bolivia. Vegetarian fare is available on request, and is particularly good. The owners can organise transfers from Cochabamba, tours in the area and mountain-bike descents as part of the trip. Book ahead, as they need notice to be able to accompany guests.

If you wish to camp, locals will expect you to pay. It's important to set a mutually agreeable price and pay only the family in control of the land.

Getting There & Away

Parque Nacional Torotoro is 135km southeast of Cochabamba in Potosí department. The road has been improved in recent years, and works are continuing, but more than half the distance is still a mud road and access in the rainy season (November to February) can be problematic. Flying can be the best way to arrive.

AIR
No air services are scheduled to Torotoro, but you can charter a plane for around B$1000 for up to five passengers one-way. It takes 30 minutes. Call pilot **Eugenio Arbinsona** (☎ 422-7042, 424-6289) for details.

BUS & CAMIÓN
Buses (B$25, six hours) depart Cochabamba on Wednesday and Saturday at 6:30pm, and Thursday and Sunday at 5:45am from the corner of Avs República and 6 de Agosto. They return on Monday, Tuesday, Friday and Saturday at 6am from near the plaza in Torotoro.

Camiones ply the same route during the dry season, leaving at around the same time. It's cheap (B$15) but not very comfortable unless you get a seat in the cab (B$20).

CAR & MOTORCYCLE
By far the most comfortable terrestrial way to get to Torotoro is by 4WD or motorbike. Tour agencies (see p209) arrange transfers from Cochabamba; the journey takes around five hours.

You can rent 4WDs in Cochabamba (p201). Fill the tank in Cochabamba, as there's no petrol in Torotoro itself. To reach Torotoro, head out on the old Santa Cruz road. Once you see the signs advertising La Angostura, take the uphill right turn that follows the lake above the village. If you reach the Angostura dam on your right, you have gone too far by a couple of hundred meters.

Follow this road via Caluyo until you reach the town of Tarata (35km from the La Angostura turnoff). Cross one bridge, then take a right turn immediately before a second bridge. About 500m along this road, you need to cut across the riverbed to your left; on the other side, a good cobblestone road starts and soon reaches the potters' village of Huayculli. Continue on this road past the town of Anzaldo; this is the last possible refueling place. About 10km beyond here, you turn left onto a dirt road; this is signposted, but easy to miss. This spectacular road descends into a river valley, and finally makes a precipitous switchback ascent to Torotoro itself.

MOUNTAIN BICYCLE
Villa Etelvina (see p209) offers an exciting option to ride a good part of the journey by mountain bike. While not quite as heart-in-mouth as the more famous Coroico descent (see boxed text, p121), it's a memorable downhill run through spectacular scenery, and with almost no traffic. The bikes are in good condition and much care is taken.

SUCRE
pop 215,800 / elevation 2750m
Proud, genteel Sucre is Bolivia's most beautiful city, and the symbolic heart of the nation. It was here that independence was proclaimed, and while La Paz is now the seat of government and treasury, Sucre is recognized in the constitution as the nation's capital. A glorious ensemble of whitewashed buildings sheltering pretty patios, it's a spruce place that preserves a wealth of colonial architecture. Sensibly, there are strict controls on development (don't even think about painting your house black!), which have kept Sucre as a real showpiece of Bolivia. It was declared a Unesco World Heritage site in 1991. See p188 for an overview of Sucre's history.

Set in a valley surrounded by low mountains, Sucre enjoys a mild and comfortable climate. It's still a center of learning, and both the city and its university enjoy reputations as focal points of progressive thought within the country.

With a selection of excellent accommodations, a wealth of churches and museums, and plenty to see and do in the surrounding area, it's no surprise that visitors end up spending much longer in Sucre than they bargained on.

Orientation
Sucre is compact and laid out in an easily negotiated grid pattern. Tourist offices give out a good town map and better hotels and tour agencies include maps on the back of their brochures. The **Instituto Geográfico Militar** (☎ 645-5514; Arce 172) has topographic maps of Chuquisaca department.

Information
CULTURAL CENTERS
There's a monthly brochure detailing Sucre's cultural events; look for it at tourist offices or in bars and restaurants.
Alliance Française (☎ 645-3599; www.afbolivia.org; Arce 35) French-language library, foreign films and La Taverne restaurant (p220).

Casa de la Cultura (☎ 645-1083; Argentina 65) Hosts art and *artesanía* exhibitions as well as music recitals and the public library.

Centro Boliviano-Americano (☎ 644-1608; www .cba.com.bo; Calvo 301) English-language library. Referrals for private Spanish-language teachers and homestay courses.

Instituto Cultural Boliviano Alemán (☎ 645-2091; www.icba-sucre.edu.bo; Avaroa 326) German-language library, listings of rooms for rent, Kulturcafé Berlin (p220). Also offers Spanish lessons (see p217).

Orígenes Bolivianos (Azurduy 473; ⏲ 7-11pm Tue-Sat) Runs a highly entertaining Bolivian folklore show including dances, music and costumes from across Bolivia. Tickets available in advance from Candelaria Tours (p218).

IMMIGRATION

Migración (☎ 645-3647; Bustillos 284; ⏲ 8:30am-4:30pm Mon-Fri) A no-fuss place to extend visas and lengths of stay.

LAUNDRY

Lavandería Laverap (☎ 644-2598; Bolívar 617; ⏲ 8:30am-8pm Mon-Sat) Full-service laundry in 90 minutes.

Lavandería LG (☎ 642-1243; Loa 407; per kg B$12; ⏲ Mon-Sun) Delivers to hotels.

Limpecable (Pérez 331, in Supermercado SAS (p221); per kg B$12; ⏲ daily)

MEDICAL SERVICES

Hospital Santa Bárbara (☎ 646-0133; Ayacucho cnr René Moreno)

MONEY

There are numerous ATMs around the city center but not at the bus station or at the airport. Many businesses display 'Compro Dólares' signs, but they only change cash. Street moneychangers, who operate outside the market along Av Hernando Siles, are handy on weekends when banks are closed but check rates beforehand.

INTERNET ACCESS, POST & TELEPHONE

The tranquil **main post office** (cnr Estudiantes & Junín) has an *aduana* (customs) office downstairs for *encomiendas* (parcels). It doesn't close for lunch and is open late. There are numerous Entel and Punto Viva telecoms centers around, charging competitive rates for international calls, and most also have internet access for B$3 to B$4 per hour.

TOURIST INFORMATION

In addition to the following, at the airport and bus terminal there are tourist offices, which are actually often the most useful.

Municipal Tourist Office (☎ 643-5240; Argentina 65) First floor of the Casa de la Cultura; staff can provide information on the city.

Oficina Universitaria de Turismo (☎ 644-7644; Estudiantes 49; ⏲ 8-11am & 3-5pm Mon-Fri) Information office run by university students, sometimes offering guides for city tours.

Regional Tourist Office (☎ 645-5983; Dalence 1) Up the stairs behind the Prefectura building. Can help with information about the Chuquisaca region.

Dangers & Annoyances

Sucre has long enjoyed a reputation as one of Bolivia's safest towns, but occasionally visitors are harassed by bogus police or 'fake tourists.' If you have a problem, report it to the **tourist police** (☎ 648-0467; Plazuela Zudáñez).

Sights

Sucre boasts several impressive museums and colonial churches, as well as the shiny new Parque Cretácico for dinosaur lovers. For the best view in town, inquire about climbing the cupula at the national police office inside the **Prefectura de Chuquisaca** (State Government Building), next to the cathedral. Note the murals depicting the struggle for Bolivian independence as you go upstairs.

CASA DE LA LIBERTAD

For a dose of Bolivian history, it's hard to beat this **museum** (☎ 645-4200; www.casadelalibertad .org.bo; Plaza 25 de Mayo 11; admission incl optional guided tour B$15; ⏲ 9am-noon & 2:30-7pm Tue-Sat, 9am-noon Sun) where the Bolivian declaration of independence was signed on August 6, 1825. It has been designated as a national memorial, and is the symbolic heart of the nation.

The first score of Bolivian congresses were held in the Salón de la Independencia, originally a Jesuit chapel. Doctoral candidates were also examined here. Behind the pulpit hang portraits of Simón Bolívar, Hugo Ballivián and Antonio José de Sucre. Bolívar claimed that this portrait, by Peruvian artist José Gil de Castro, was the most lifelike representation ever done of him.

SUCRE

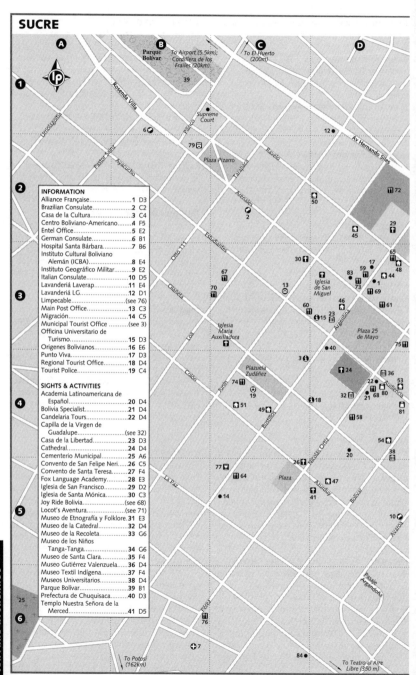

INFORMATION

Alliance Française	**1** D3
Brazilian Consulate	**2** C2
Casa de la Cultura	**3** C4
Centro Boliviano-Americano	**4** F5
Entel Office	**5** E2
German Consulate	**6** B1
Hospital Santa Bárbara	**7** B6
Instituto Cultural Boliviano Alemán (ICBA)	**8** E4
Instituto Geográfico Militar	**9** E2
Italian Consulate	**10** D5
Lavanderiá Laverap	**11** E4
Lavanderiá LG	**12** D1
Limpecable	(see 76)
Main Post Office	**13** C3
Migración	**14** C5
Municipal Tourist Office	(see 3)
Officina Universitario de Turismo	**15** D3
Origenes Bolivianos	**16** E6
Punto Viva	**17** D3
Regional Tourist Office	**18** D4
Tourist Police	**19** C4

SIGHTS & ACTIVITIES

Academia Latinoamericana de Español	**20** D4
Bolivia Specialist	**21** D4
Candelaria Tours	**22** D4
Capilla de la Virgen de Guadalupe	(see 32)
Casa de la Libertad	**23** D3
Cathedral	**24** D4
Cementerio Municipal	**25** A6
Convento de San Felipe Neri	**26** C5
Convento de Santa Teresa	**27** F4
Fox Language Academy	**28** E3
Iglesia de San Francisco	**29** D2
Iglesia de Santa Mónica	**30** C3
Joy Ride Bolivia	(see 68)
Locot's Aventura	(see 71)
Museo de Etnografía y Folklore	**31** E3
Museo de la Catedral	**32** D4
Museo de la Recoleta	**33** G6
Museo de los Niños Tanga-Tanga	**34** G6
Museo de Santa Clara	**35** F4
Museo Gutiérrez Valenzuela	**36** D4
Museo Textil Indígena	**37** F4
Museos Universitarios	**38** D4
Parque Bolívar	**39** B1
Prefectura de Chuquisaca	**40** D3
Templo Nuestra Señora de la Merced	**41** D5

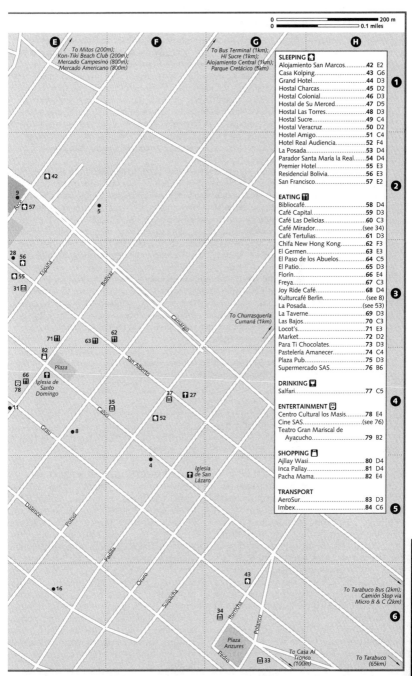

SLEEPING 🛏
Alojamiento San Marcos..........**42** E2
Casa Kolping..........................**43** G6
Grand Hotel...........................**44** D3
Hostal Charcas.......................**45** D2
Hostal Colonial.......................**46** D3
Hostal de Su Merced................**47** D5
Hostal Las Torres....................**48** D3
Hostal Sucre..........................**49** C4
Hostal Veracruz......................**50** D2
Hostel Amigo.........................**51** C4
Hotel Real Audiencia................**52** F4
La Posada..............................**53** D4
Parador Santa María la Real.....**54** D4
Premier Hotel.........................**55** E3
Residencial Bolivia..................**56** E3
San Francisco.........................**57** E2

EATING 🍴
Bibliocafé.............................**58** D4
Café Capital...........................**59** D3
Café Las Delicias.....................**60** C3
Café Mirador.......................(see 34)
Café Tertulias.........................**61** D3
Chifa New Hong Kong.............**62** F3
El Germen.............................**63** E3
El Paso de los Abuelos.............**64** C5
El Patio.................................**65** D3
Florín...................................**66** E4
Freya...................................**67** C3
Joy Ride Café.........................**68** D4
Kulturcafé Berlin...................(see 8)
La Posada...........................(see 53)
La Taverne............................**69** D3
Las Bajos..............................**70** C3
Locot's.................................**71** E3
Market.................................**72** D2
Para Ti Chocolates..................**73** D3
Pastelería Amanecer...............**74** C4
Plaza Pub..............................**75** D3
Supermercado SAS..................**76** B6

DRINKING 🍷
Salfari..................................**77** C5

ENTERTAINMENT 🎭
Centro Cultural los Masis...........**78** E4
Cine SAS............................(see 76)
Teatro Gran Mariscal de
 Ayacucho...........................**79** B2

SHOPPING 🛍
Ajllay Wasi............................**80** D4
Inca Pallay............................**81** D4
Pacha Mama..........................**82** E4

TRANSPORT
AeroSur................................**83** D3
Imbex..................................**84** C6

THE LIBERATOR – SIMÓN BOLÍVAR

Born of Basque parents in Caracas in 1783, Bolívar, greatest of the Libertadores (the liberators) of South America, was sent to Spain and France as a 15-year-old to be educated. The works of Rousseau and Voltaire imbued in the young man notions of progressive liberalism that would shape his entire life and the destiny of a continent.

Bolívar married a Spaniard in 1802, but she succumbed to yellow fever in Caracas shortly afterwards. Although he had many lovers, he could never again marry. The death of his wife marked a drastic shift in Bolívar's destiny. He returned to France, where he met with the leaders of the French Revolution and then traveled to the USA to take a close look at the new order after the American Revolution. By the time he returned to Caracas in 1807, he was full of revolutionary theories and experiences taken from these two successful examples. It didn't take him long to join the clandestine pro-independence circles.

Spain at the time was in a terrible mess. Napoleon had taken advantage of the weakness of Carlos IV, beset by family strife, to put his own brother, a notorious drunkard, on the Spanish throne. In 1808 Spain revolted; French troops were sent in, which started the Guerra de la Independencia (Peninsular War). Fighting desperately for their own freedom, they were in no state to effectively counter any independence movements on the other side of the Atlantic.

At the time, disillusionment with Spanish rule was close to breaking into open revolt. On April 19, 1810 the Junta Suprema was installed in Caracas, and on July 5, 1811 the Congress declared independence. This turned out to be the beginning of a long and bitter war, most of which was to be orchestrated by Bolívar.

His military career began with the Venezuelan independence movement, of which he soon took command. Battle followed battle with astonishing frequency until 1824. Of those battles personally directed by Bolívar, the independence forces won 35, including a few key ones: the Battle of Boyacá (August 7, 1819), which secured the independence of Colombia; the Battle of Carabobo (June 24, 1821), which brought freedom to Venezuela; and the Battle of Pichincha (May 24, 1822), which led to the liberation of Ecuador.

In September 1822 the Argentine liberator General José de San Martín, who had occupied Lima, abandoned the city to the Spanish, and Bolívar took over the task of winning in Peru. On August 6, 1824 his army was victorious at the Battle of Junín, and on December 9, 1824 General

The charter of independence takes pride of place, mounted on a granite plinth. A fine inlaid wooden ceiling and elaborate choir stalls are also noteworthy.

MUSEO TEXTIL INDÍGENA

This superb **museum of indigenous arts** (☎ 645-3841; www.bolivianet.com/asur; San Alberto 413; admission B$16; ☯ 9:30am-noon & 2:30-6pm Mon-Fri) is a must for anyone interested in the indigenous groups of the Sucre area, focusing particularly on the woven textiles of the Jalq'a and Candelaria (Tarabuco) cultures. It's a fascinating display, and has an interesting subtext: the rediscovery of forgotten ancestral weaving practices has contributed to increased community pride and revitalization.

Information in English is available, and you can observe the weavers at their patient work. The contiguous store markets ceramics and weavings, but it's a more satisfying experience to buy them direct from the villages where they are made (see Candelaria, p223, Tarabuco, p222, and boxed text, p224).

MUSEO DE ETNOGRAFÍA Y FOLKLORE

Known locally as **Musef** (☎ 645-5293; www.musef.org.bo; España 74; ☯ 9:30am-12:30pm & 2:30-6:30pm Mon-Fri, 9:30am-12:30pm Sat) and housed in the impressive former Banco Nacional building, this new museum brings together a series of fascinating displays that vividly illustrate the great diversity of Bolivia's ethnic cultures. On the ground floor is a professionally presented display of masks with over 50 original examples, some of which you wouldn't want to bump into in a dark alleyway. The other permanent display deals with the Uru-Chipaya culture, with reconstructions of village life and exhibitions of artifacts used in their daily life.

Antonio José de Sucre inflicted a final defeat at the Battle of Ayacucho. Peru, which included Alto Perú, had been liberated and the war was over. On August 6, 1825, the first anniversary of the Battle of Junín, Bolivia declared independence from Peru at Chuquisaca (Sucre), and the new republic was christened 'Bolivia,' after the liberator.

But, as Bolívar well knew, freedom means just that and, although he had grand dreams for a unified state in the north of South America, they would prove difficult to realize. 'I fear peace more than war,' he wrote perceptively in a letter.

Establishing Gran Colombia (which comprised modern-day Venezuela, Colombia, Panamá and Ecuador) was easy, but holding it together as president was impossible for Bolívar. Clinging stubbornly to his dream of the union, although it was rapidly slipping from his hands, he lost influence, and his glory and charisma faded. He then tried to set up a dictatorship, saying 'Our America can only be ruled through a well-managed, shrewd despotism;' he still saw himself (perhaps correctly) as the best steward of the young nations. After surviving an assassination attempt in Bogotá, he resigned in 1830, disillusioned, and in poor health. Almost at once, his Gran Colombia dissolved.

Venezuela seceded in 1830, approved a new congress and banned Bolívar from his homeland. A month later, Antonio José de Sucre, Bolívar's closest friend, was assassinated in Colombia. These two news items reached Bolívar just as he was about to sail for France. Depressed and ill, he accepted the invitation of a Spaniard, Joaquín de Mier, to stay in his home in Santa Marta, Colombia.

Bolívar died on December 17, 1830, of pulmonary tuberculosis. A priest, a doctor and a few officers were by his bed, but none of these were close friends. Joaquín de Mier donated one of his shirts to dress the body, as there had been none among Bolívar's humble belongings. Perhaps the most important figure in the history of the South American continent had died. 'There have been three great fools in history: Jesus, Don Quixote and I.' So he summed up his own life shortly before his death.

That Bolívar died lonely and abandoned is scarcely believable when you see the extent to which he is idolized in South America today. He is a symbol of South American freedom and, crucially, a symbol free of party-political connotations. Today, the Libertador is a hero once more.

One of the final remarks in Bolívar's diary reads, 'My name now belongs to history. It will do me justice.' It has.

PARQUE CRETÁCICO (CAL ORCK'O)

It seems that 65 million years ago the site of Sucre's Fancesa (Fabrica Nacional de Cemento SA) cement quarry, 5km north of the centre, was the place to be for large, scaly types. When the grounds were being cleared in 1994, plant employees uncovered a nearly vertical mudstone face bearing around 5000 tracks of at least eight different species of dinosaur – the largest collection of dinosaur footprints in the world.

Though you can see some of the prints from outside, entering the family-friendly **Cretaceous Park** (www.parquecretacicosucre .com; admission B$30, ☷ 7am-7pm Mon-Fri, 10am-3pm Sat & Sun) gives a better panorama. This slick theme park has a number of life-size models of dinosaurs, as well as an audiovisual display, optional guided tours and a restaurant. From the terrace, you can examine the tracks on the rock face opposite with binoculars, though the ex-posed prints are increasingly eroded with every passing winter.

A Dino Bus to the park leaves daily from in front of the Cathedral at 9:30am, noon and 2:30pm. Alternatively you can take a taxi (around B$30), but you may have to walk uphill from the entrance to the Fancesa quarry unless your driver can convince the guard to let you past.

CATEDRAL

Sucre's **cathedral** (☎ 645-2257; Plaza 25 de Mayo) dates from the middle of the 16th century and is a harmonious blend of Renaissance architecture with later baroque additions. It's a noble structure, with a bell tower that is a local landmark. Inside, the white single-naved space has a series of oil paintings of the apostles, as well as an ornate altarpiece and pulpit. The cathedral opens on Sundays; otherwise you can enter as part of the Museo de la Catedral visit (p216).

MUSEO DE LA CATEDRAL & CAPILLA DE LA VIRGEN DE GUADALUPE

Next door to the cathedral this **museum** (Nicolás Ortiz 31; admission B$20; ☉ 10am-noon & 3-5pm Mon-Fri, 10am-noon Sat) holds one of Bolivia's best collections of religious relics. There are four sections, ritually unlocked as your visit progresses. In the entry room is a series of fine religious paintings from the colonial era. Next, a chapel has relics of saints, and fine gold and silver chalices. The highlight, however, comes in the **Capilla de la Virgen de Guadalupe**, which was completed in 1625. Encased in the altar is a painting of the Virgin, the city's patron. She was originally painted by Fray Diego de Ocaña in 1601, but the work was subsequently coated with highlights of gold and silver and adorned in robes encrusted with diamonds, amethysts, pearls, rubies and emeralds donated by wealthy colonial parishioners. The jewels alone are worth millions of dollars, making it the richest virgin in the Americas.

TEMPLO NUESTRA SEÑORA DE LA MERCED

Contrary to its ordinary exterior, this **church** (☎ 645-1483; Pérez 1; admission B$5; ☉ 10am-noon & 3-5pm Mon-Fri) is blessed with the most beautiful interior of any church in Sucre and possibly in Bolivia. Because the order of La Merced left Sucre for Cuzco in 1826, taking its records with it, the church's founding date is uncertain, but it's believed to be sometime in the 1540s.

The baroque-style altar and carved mestizo pulpit are decorated with filigree and gold inlay. Several paintings by the esteemed artist Melchor Pérez de Holguín are on display – notably *El Nacimiento de Jesús, El Nacimiento de María* and a self-portrait of the artist rising from the depths of Purgatory. The views from the bell tower are splendid.

MUSEO DE LA RECOLETA

Overlooking the city of Sucre from the top of Calle Polanco, **La Recoleta** (☎ 645-1987; Plaza Pedro Anzures; admission B$10; ☉ 9-11:30am & 2:30-4:30pm Mon-Fri, 3-5pm Sat) was established by the Franciscan Order in 1601. It has served not only as a convent and museum but also as a barracks and prison. The highlight is the church choir and its magnificent wooden carvings dating back to the 1870s, each one

intricate and unique, representing the martyrs who were crucified in 1595 in Nagasaki. The museum is worthwhile for its anonymous sculptures and paintings from the 16th to 20th centuries, including numerous interpretations of St Francis of Assisi.

Outside are courtyard gardens brimming with color and the renowned *Cedro Milenario* (Ancient Cedar), a huge tree that is the one of the few survivors of the cedars that were once abundant around Sucre.

MUSEO DE LOS NIÑOS TANGA-TANGA

On the same square as La Recoleta, and set in a beautiful building, this excellent interactive children's **museum** (☎ 644-0299; Plaza Pedro Anzures; adult/child B$8/5; ☉ 9am-noon & 2:30-6pm Tue-Sun) focuses on renewable energy sources. Highlights include the botanical gardens and explanations of Bolivian ecology. The attached Café Mirador is a great place to relax while enjoying the best view in town. The adjacent Ananay handicrafts store sells unique high-quality *artesanías,* including especially cute children's clothing.

CONVENTO DE SAN FELIPE NERI

The view from the bell tower and tiled rooftop of the **San Felipe Neri convent** (☎ 645-4333; Ortíz 165, entry via the school; admission B$10; ☉ 4-6pm Mon-Sat) more than explains Sucre's nickname of the 'White City of the Americas.'

In the days when the building served as a monastery (it is now a parochial school), asceticism didn't prevent the monks from appreciating the view while meditating; you can still see the stone seats on the roof terraces. The church was originally constructed of stone but was later covered with a layer of stucco. Poinsettias and roses fill the courtyard, an interesting painting of the Last Supper hangs at the entrance, and the stairwell is lined with paintings that prepared the monks for confession.

MUSEO DE SANTA CLARA

Located in the Santa Clara Convent, this **museum of religious art** (☎ 645-2295; Calvo 212; admission B$10; ☉ 9am-noon & 3-6pm Mon-Fri, 9am-noon Sat), founded in 1639, contains several works by Bolivian master Melchor Pérez de Holguín and his Italian instructor, Bernardo de Bitti. In 1985 it was robbed, and several paintings and gold ornaments were taken. One of the canvases, however, was apparently deemed too large to carry away, so the thieves sliced a big chunk out of the middle and left the rest hanging. The painting has been restored but you can still see evidence of the damage. Guides may also demonstrate the still-functional pipe organ, which was fabricated in 1664.

OTHER CHURCHES

Sucre has an astonishing number of handsome churches, but if you are short on time the following are worth a look.

The brilliant white **Convento de Santa Teresa** (☎ 645-2661; San Alberto; 10am-noon) belongs to an order of cloistered nuns. They sell homemade candied oranges, apples, figs and limes daily by way of a miniature revolving door. The adjacent **Callejón de Santa Teresa**, a lantern-lit alleyway, was once partially paved with cow knee bones laid out in the shape of a cross, a local good luck symbol known as *tabas*. The alley was considered to be a haunted place, inhabited by a variety of local ghouls including a baby with a moustache and teeth, and the cow knees were thought to be the most reliable way of protecting passers-by. In the 1960s it was repaved with its current cobbles.

The **Iglesia de San Francisco** (☎ 645-1853; Ravelo 1 at Arce; 7-9am & 4-7pm Mon-Fri) was established in 1538 soon after the founding of the city, but was turned over to the military in 1809. The soldiers weren't big on maintenance and it fell into disrepair before eventually being reconsecrated in 1925. Its most interesting features are its *mudéjar* (Moorish) paneled ceiling and the Campana de la Libertad, Bolivia's Liberty Bell, which called patriots to revolution in 1825.

The **Iglesia de Santa Mónica** (Junín 601 at Arenales) was begun in 1574 and was originally intended to serve as a monastery for the Ermitañas de San Agustín. However the order ran into financial difficulties in the early 1590s, resulting in its conversion into a Jesuit school. The interior is adorned with *mestizo* carvings and the courtyard is one of the city's finest. The church now serves as a civic auditorium and is only open to the public during special events.

MUSEOS UNIVERSITARIOS & MUSEO GUTIÉRREZ VALENZUELA

The **Museos Universitarios** (☎ 645-3285; Bolívar 698; admission B$15; 8:30am-noon & 2:30-6pm Mon-

Fri, 9am-noon & 3-6pm Sat) are three separate halls housing colonial relics, anthropological artifacts and modern art. In the southeast corner of the main plaza, the university also runs the **Museo Gutiérrez Valenzuela** (☎ 645-3828; Plaza 25 de Mayo; admission B$8; 8:30am-noon & 2-6pm Mon-Fri), an old aristocrat's house with 19th-century decor and a small natural history museum.

CEMENTERIO MUNICIPAL

The enthusiasm surrounding Sucre's **cemetery** (8:30am-noon & 2-5:30pm) seems disproportionate to what's there. There are some arches carved from poplar trees, as well as picturesque palm trees and the mausoleums of wealthy colonial families. At weekends it's jam-packed with families. You can walk the eight blocks from the plaza south along Junín, or take a taxi or *micro A*.

PARQUE BOLÍVAR

A short walk north of the plaza, the elongated **Parque Bolívar** is sandwiched between two avenues flanked with *ceibo* trees and overlooked by handsomely imposing government buildings. It's a pleasant place for a quiet stroll, and its strongly European style is highlighted by the presence of a miniature replica of the Eiffel Tower, remarkably built by the same hand as the larger original in 1906. The French influence is further seen in an archway that looks suspiciously like the Arc de Triomphe.

Courses

Sucre is a popular place to learn Spanish. The **Instituto Cultural Boliviano Alemán** (☎ 645-2091; www.icba-sucre.edu.bo; Avaroa 326) offers recommended Spanish lessons with homestay options; they also run Quechua classes. The **Academia Latinoamericana de Español** (☎ 646-0537; www.latinoschools.com; Dalence 109) has a comprehensive program featuring cultural classes and homestay options. **Fox Language Academy** (☎ 644-0688; www.foxacademysucre.com; San Alberto 30) runs volunteer schemes and learning Spanish or Quechua there subsidizes English classes for underprivileged local kids.

Tours & Activities

While Sucre traditionally has been visited for its sublime colonial architecture and wealth of museums, there's an increasing amount on offer in the surrounding area, whether you are interested in indigenous culture or adrenaline-fuelled adventure.

There are numerous agencies in town, and nearly all offer trips to Tarabuco (p222; around B$35 per person) for the Sunday market; many hotels and *hostales* can also arrange this trip. Many also offer day-trips to the Cordillera de los Frailes (p223), but you will contribute more to the local communities by going for longer (see boxed text, p224).

Operators include the following:

Bolivia Specialist (☎ 643-7389; www.boliviaspecialist .com; Ortiz 30) Organizes tours all over Bolivia as well as in the local region. If the office is closed, ask at Florín.

Candelaria Tours (☎ 646-1661; www.candelariatours .com; Audiencia 1) Intelligent and reliable agency running many types of trips. Particularly recommendable for trips to Tarabuco and Candelaria.

Joy Ride Bolivia (☎ 642-5544; www.joyridebol.com; Ortiz 14) Popular hikes, bikes and horses, with groups leaving almost daily. Also offers paragliding; both tandem jumps and courses. Bookings and inquiries at the cafe of the same name (p220).

Locot's Aventura (☎ 691-5958; Bolívar 465) Hiking, biking, horse-riding and paragliding. Again, based at the bar-restaurant of the same name (p220)

Festivals & Events

On the weekend closest to September 8, people from all over the country flock to join local *campesinos* in a celebration of the **Fiesta de la Virgen de Guadalupe** with songs, traditional dances and poetry recitations. The following day, they dress in colorful costumes and parade around the main plaza carrying religious images and silver arches. On November 2 **Todos Santos** is celebrated with much fervor.

Sleeping

Accommodations in Sucre are among the country's most expensive, but, on the upside, most of the choices are in typical, attractive whitewashed colonial buildings built around a pretty central courtyard. For an authentic Bolivian experience ask at Candelaria Tours (above) about homestay options from B$85 per night (minimum five nights).

BUDGET

The cheaper places are clustered near the market and along Calles Ravelo and San Alberto.

Alojamiento San Marcos (☎ 646-2087; Arce 233; r per person B$30) This place gets a good rap from travelers, who appreciate its friendly owners and clean, quiet rooms as well as kitchen and laundry access. Currently all rooms are with shared bathrooms but a new block with private bathrooms was under construction at the time of writing.

Hostel Amigo (☎ 646-1706; www.hostelsucre .com; Colón 125; dm B$30, s/d B$35/40, with bathroom B$70/80; ☐) Making a name for itself as a backpacker haven the Amigo Hostel is well-equipped with kitchen, TV room and barbecue terrace. A basic breakfast is included in the price and there is a laundry service if you are too lazy to wash your own clothes. Spanish lessons are also offered.

Hostal Charcas (☎ 645-3972; Ravelo 62; s/d B$40/60, with bathroom B$60/100) In a central location right opposite the market, this is a travelers' favorite. Laundry service, 24-hour hot water and simple but clean and attractive rooms, with or without bath, mean it's a reliable bet and more than the sum of its parts. Breakfast is available.

Residencial Bolivia (☎ 645-4346; San Alberto 42; s/d B$40/60, with bathroom B$80/120) Good location with rooms set around a triple courtyard. Some rooms are markedly nicer than others; ask to see a selection before making your choice if you want value for money.

HI Sucre (☎ 644-0471; www.hostellingbolivia .org; Loayza 119; dm B$40, s/d B$50/80, with bathroom B$90/150; ☐) Set in a building with attractive original features, Sucre's HI hostel is one of Bolivia's few purpose-built hostels and thus has excellent amenities. It's clean and friendly and has a shared kitchen and even some private rooms with spa baths and cable TV. It is very handy for the bus station too (from the terminal, cross the street, head left, then take the first right).

Hostal Veracruz (☎ 645-1560; Ravelo 158; s/d B$45/70; ☐) A central choice and consistently popular, this has a fair variety of rooms, some nice and sunny, some a little echoey from the central vestibule. Breakfast and laundry are available.

San Francisco (☎ 645-2117; Arce 191; s/d B$60/120) With a stunning entry hall and eye-catchingly ornamental staircase, this place belongs in a higher price range, but while the rooms don't quite live up to the initial impression, you won't feel you've wasted your bolivianos.

MIDRANGE & TOP END

Grand Hotel (☎ 645-2461; Arce 61; s/d B$100/140) With a central location, excellent staff and tastefully decorated rooms, this really is a grand hotel and a deserved favorite among travelers of all budgets. There's a popular restaurant here, a beautiful, plant-filled courtyard, and some of the spacious rooms have their own separate lounge area.

Hostal Las Torres (☎ 644-2888; www.lastorreshostal .com; San Alberto 19; s/d B$110/170) Light and pleasant, this attractive hotel is entered down a little alleyway. The rooms have comfy beds with cutesy frilly coverings, cable TV and good bathrooms. Breakfast is included and served in an elegant dining room.

Hostal Sucre (☎ 646-1928; Bustillos 113; s/d with bathroom B$135/180; 🖥) Another HI affiliate, this pleasant, typically white hotel has a particularly beautiful double courtyard, complete with well and fountain. Rooms, with attractive, if faded, old furniture, don't quite live up to it, being a little dingy, but they are acceptable. Breakfast is served in an antique dining room.

our pick **Casa Al Tronco** (☎ 642-3195; Topater 57; r B$140) A real home from home, this new charming guesthouse in the Recoleta district has just three rooms so book in advance. Glorious views of the city from two terraces, use of a kitchen and a welcoming reception might make you stay longer than planned. Stay longer than five nights and there is a price reduction.

Casa Kolping (☎ 642-3812; www.grupo-casas -kolping.net; Pasaje Iturricha 265; s/d B$175/225; 🖥) High on a hill by Plaza Pedro Anzures, with great views over town, this excellent hotel caters mostly for conferences but is an appealing place to stay. As well as efficient service and a good restaurant, it boasts clean, well-equipped rooms – on the smallish side but very comfortable. It's also a good place for the kids, with family apartments, plenty of space and a ping-pong table.

Premier Hotel (☎ 645-3510; premierhotel@ hotmail.com; San Alberto 43; s/d/ste B$210/275/350; 🖥) A handsome modern option catering for the local business-traveler market, this has a central courtyard and is sparklingly clean, with leather armchairs, and rooms with inviting beds and minibars. It's in the heart of town but pretty quiet.

Hostal Colonial (☎ 644-0309; www.hostal colonial-bo.com; Plaza 25 de Mayo 3; s/d/tr/ste B$210/280/ 350/490) A handsome colonial edifice that exudes a restrained stylishness befitting its location among the plaza's noble buildings. However, despite the welcoming fireplace in the foyer, the rooms are disappointingly bare and somewhat overpriced.

Hostal de Su Merced (☎ 645-1355; www .boliviaweb.com/companies/sumerced; Azurduy 16; s/d B$240/360) In true Sucre style, this charming and beautiful hotel is decorated with antiques and paintings, with rooms set around an intimate, tiled courtyard. Room No 7 is particularly nice and the view from the rooftop terrace is stunning. The helpful staff are English-speaking and there's also a restaurant.

La Posada (☎ 646-0101; www.laposadahostal.com; Audiencia 92; s/d B$250/350; 🖥) This comfortable and classy place has spacious, uncluttered rooms with a very appealing colonial ambience and wooden trimmings. There are views over town, a stylish and intimate feel, and a good family suite. The courtyard restaurant is also a recommendable spot. Excellent service adds to the package.

Hotel Real Audiencia (☎ 643-1712; www .hotelrealaudiencia.net; Potosí 142; s/d/ste B$300/380/450; 🖥 🐾) This welcoming place in an appealing part of Sucre has a mixture of the old and new. It's attractively set out, with a pool area and Mediterranean-style balustrades. Rooms are spacious and have cable TV, but the 'executive' suites in a more modern wing are significantly better, with beautiful furniture and a minibar for not much more cash.

Parador Santa María la Real (☎ 643-9592; www .parador.com.bo; Bolívar 625; s/d B$400/450, ste B$500-650; 🖥) Swish, stylish and refined, this five-star hotel takes Sucre's 'top place to stay' mantle. Magnificently elegant, it boasts an arcaded courtyard, antique furniture, a spa bath with a view, and a curious historical underground section.

Eating

Sucre has a pleasant variety of quality restaurants and is a great place to spend time lolling around cafes while observing Bolivian university life.

RESTAURANTS

Freya (☎ 642-1928; Loa 751; almuerzo B$15; 🕙 noon-2pm Mon-Sat) Part of the Freya Gym this likable place serves up tasty vegetarian *almuerzos* though the choice is very limited.

Las Bajos (☎ 645-2531; Loa 759; mains B$15-35) One of the oldest and most typical of the *choricerías* (restaurant specializing in chorizo) in Sucre, though it's not just sausage on the menu. The owner is a Beatles fanatic and downstairs is a miniature recreation of Liverpool's Cavern Club, the walls adorned with posters, album covers and other Fab Four memorabilia.

Florín (☎ 645-2902; Bolívar 567; mains B$15-35) Rapidly turning into the place to be seen in Sucre, this atmospheric bar-restaurant serves a mixture of typical Bolivian food and international dishes, including a 'Full English' breakfast. Popular with locals and gringos alike, who line up along the enormous 13m-long bar (surely the biggest in Bolivia?) at night during the two-for-one happy hour.

Locot's (☎ 691-5958; Bolívar 465; mains B$15-40; 🕒 7am-late; 🖳) Relaxed and attractive, this bar-restaurant is in an interesting old building, with candlelit tables and original art on the walls. It offers a limited choice of Bolivian, Mexican and intenational food, including vegetarian, and a gringo-friendly vibe.

Chifa New Hong Kong (☎ 644-1776; San Alberto 242; mains B$20-35) Great value authentic Chinese food with huge portions. Watch your head on the ceiling upstairs though!

Joy Ride Café (☎ 642-5544; Ortiz 14; mains B$20-40; 🕒 7:30am-2am Mon-Fri, 9am-2am Sat & Sun) 'Probably the Best Bar in Town,' or so the promotion will have you believe, this wildly popular gringo-tastic cafe, restaurant and bar has everything, from dawn espressos to midnight vodkas, nightly movies to weekend dancing on tables. It's spacious, friendly, well-run and the food is great too.

La Taverne (☎ 7288-1863; Arce 35; mains B$20-40) With a quiet sophisticated atmosphere, the restaurant of the Alliance Française (p210) is a delight to visit. The short, select menu has a French touch and there are excellent daily specials. There's live music every Friday night and film screenings several times a week.

El Germen (☎ 646-2810; San Alberto 237; mains B$25-40) This simply decorated, service-with-a-smile spot is a favorite for its tasty vegetarian dishes; they also do decent goulash and roast meat, as well as cracking curries and tempting cakes. There's a book exchange too.

El Huerto (☎ 645-1538; Cabrera 86; mains B$25-40) Set in a lovely secluded garden, this is a favorite spot for Sucre's people in the know. It's got the atmosphere of a classy lawn party, with sunshades and grass underfoot; there's great service and stylishly presented traditional plates (especially the chorizo) that don't come much better anywhere in the country.

Plaza Pub (☎ 644-7610; Plaza 25 de Mayo 34; mains B$30-50) Filling, mostly meat-based meals are a little pricey, but this is also a great place for a drink, with the outdoor balconies perfect for people-watching on a lazy Sunday afternoon.

La Posada (☎ 646-0101; Audiencia 92; mains B$30-60; 🕒 closed Sun dinner) This comfortable hotel (p219) also has one of Sucre's most appealing spots for a meal or a drink, offering elegant indoor and outdoor seating around its stone-flagged courtyard. There are tasty fish and meat dishes, pastas and salads, set meals, and good-natured service.

Churrasquería Cumaná (☎ 643-2273; Plaza Cumaná, Barrio Petrolero; mains B$40-60; 🕒 dinner only Tue-Thu, 11:30am-10:30pm Fri-Sun) A Sucre secret, this carnivore's delight is in the Barrio Petrolero, a cab ride from the center. The full portions of exquisitely grilled meat can comfortably feed two; the courtyard is also a pleasant place to drink wine or cocktails.

CAFES

Kulturcafé Berlin (Avaroa 334; mains B$12-30; 🕒 closed Sun; 🖳) This dark and atmospheric spot is affiliated with the ICBA (p191), and offers German-language newspapers and magazines, a book exchange and filling dishes; try the *papas rellenas* (spicy filled potatoes). It's also a fine spot for an evening beer, with some German choices.

Bibliocafé (☎ 644-7544; Ortiz 80; mains B$15-25; 🕒 closed Mon) With two adjacent locations, this has something for everyone; one side is dark and cozy, the other a little smarter. There's good service, a menu of pasta and Mexican-Bolivian food, and also drinks until late in a cheerful and unpretentious atmosphere, plus regular live music.

Café Capital (Arce 13; mains B$15-25; 🕒 dinner only) Currently Sucre's in place with the trendy student crowd.

Café Las Delicias (Estudiantes 50; mains B$15-25; 🕒 4-7pm Mon-Sat) Specialty cakes and pastries from the Chiquitania region of

Bolivia including the delicious *masaco* (bananas with cheese).

Café Tertulias (☎ 642-0390; Plaza 25 de Mayo; mains B$15-25) An intimate bohemian hangout for chats over coffee, beer or food, which is principally pizza, salads and pasta.

QUICK EATS

Pastelería Amanecer (off Junín btwn Colón & Olañeta) Tucked away in a dead-end alley behind the police station, this petite, four-table, nonprofit bakery has delightful homemade goodies, breakfast, coffee and fresh juices. Proceeds benefit local children's projects.

Good *salteñerías* (bakeries that specialize in *salteñas*) include **El Patio** (San Alberto 18; ☪ 10am-12:30pm) and **El Paso de los Abuelos** (Bustillos 224); get there early as they sell out fast. Thanks to Sucre's status as Bolivia's chocolate capital, there are plenty of stores that cater to sweet tooths. The best is **Para Ti Chocolates** (☎ 645-5689; Arenales 7), where tasty bonbons are only the tip of the iceberg.

GROCERIES

The central **market** (☪ 7am-7:30pm Mon-Sat, Sun breakfast only) is home to some gastronomic highlights. Don't miss the fresh juices and fruit salads – they are among the best in the country. The vendors and their blenders always come up with something indescribably delicious – try *jugo de tumbo* (unripe passion-fruit juice). **Supermercado SAS** (Pérez 331; ☪ 8am-10pm daily) is a reliable place for basic necessities.

Drinking

Places mentioned in the Eating section, such as Joy Ride, Locot's, Bibliocafé and Florín, are popular spots for a drink, and get pretty lively.

Salfari (☎ 644-5002; Bustillos 237; ☪ 8pm-3am) This little gem of a pub has friendly service, a loyal local crowd, and lively games of poker and *cacho* usually going on. Try their tasty but potent homemade fruit liqueurs.

For *discotecas* (weekends only) you'll need to head north of the center, it's easiest by taxi. **Mitos** (Cerro s/n; women/men B$5/10) is a spacious basement spot a 15-minute walk from the centre. It really fills up around 1am and plays well-loved local and international hits. Nearby **Kon-Tiki Beach Club** (Junín 71; women/men B$5/10) is popular with students and plays a mixture of rock and pop.

Entertainment

The **Centro Cultural los Masis** (☎ 645-3403; Bolívar 561; ☪ 10am-noon & 3:30-9pm Mon-Fri) hosts concerts and other cultural events. It also has a small museum of local musical instruments and offers Quechua classes.

Southeast of the center, the Teatro al Aire Libre is a wonderful outdoor venue for musical and other performances. **Teatro Gran Mariscal de Ayacucho** (Plaza Pizarro), is an opulent old opera house. The tourist office and the Casa de la Cultura (p211) both distribute a monthly calendar of events. **Cine SAS** (Pérez 331) has three screens showing the latest Hollywood releases.

Shopping

The best place to learn about traditional local weavings is the Museo Textil-Indígena (p214), but to buy them you are best off going direct to the villages (see p222 and p223). Prices are steep by Bolivian standards, but the items are high quality.

A trip to the **Mercado Americano**, around the junction of Mujía and Reyes, will keep clothes-junkies busy for hours, while nearby on Aguirre, the **Mercado Campesino** is a fascinating traditional food market with a really authentic feel.

Inca Pallay (☎ 646-1936; incapallay@entelnet.bo; cnr Grau & Bolívar) This weavers and artisans cooperative has an impressive array of high-quality handmade crafts, not all from the Sucre area. Prices are high, but this is the store that returns the highest percentage to the weavers themselves. You can sometimes see weavers at work in the patio.

Pacha Mama (Calvo 91 cnr Bolívar) A new store offering the biggest and best selection of local *artesanías* in town. Aymará owner Sayda Quispe offers some of his own jewelry and clothing designs, and it's also a sales point for Lonely Planet books.

Ajllay Wasi (Audiencia 19) A complete selection of quality textiles from different weaving centers. Weavers take their crafts to the shop personally so they receive a bigger chunk of the profits. An explanation of the design of your textile is provided with every purchase.

Getting There & Away

AIR

The domestic departure tax is B$11. **AeroSur** (☎ 646-2141; Arenales 31) has a daily 11:30am flight to La Paz and numerous departures to Santa Cruz with onward connections. **TAM** (☎ 645-1310; airport) flies on Monday, Wednesday and Friday to La Paz and Santa Cruz, with an additional La Paz departure on Sunday. It also has a 10am Saturday flight to Tarija. **Juana Azurduy airport** (☎ 645-4445) is frequently shut in bad weather, so check with the airline before heading out there.

BUS & SHARED TAXI
The **bus terminal** (☎ 644-1292) is a 15-minute walk uphill from the centre, and most easily accessed by *micros A* or *3* from along Calle España, or by taxi (as the *micros* are too crowded for lots of luggage). Unless you're headed for Potosí, it's wise to book long-distance buses a day in advance, in order to reserve a good seat. There's a terminal tax of B$3; services include a good information kiosk but no ATM. To save the trip to the bus station many central travel agents also sell tickets on selected services for a small commission.

Several daily buses run to Cochabamba (B$80, 12 hours), all departing between 6pm and 8pm. El Dorado runs a luxury bus on this route but frequent thefts have been reported on this service. There are also afternoon (4pm to 6pm) services to Santa Cruz (B$70 to B$120, 15 to 20 hours), mostly via the rough but scenic Samaipata route.

Lots of *flotas* have morning and evening departures for La Paz (B$70 to B$120, 14 to 16 hours) via Oruro (B$50 to B$70, 10 hours). You'll have no problem finding a *flota* for Potosí (B$20, three hours) with countless departures between 7am and 6pm. Alternatively, take a shared taxi (B$30 for up to four people, 2½ hours), which is quicker and comfier, to Potosí. Most hotels can help arrange shared taxis. Try **Turismo Global** (☎ 642-5125), **Cielito Lindo** (☎ 644-1014) or **Infinito del Sur** (☎ 642-2277). Expect speed. If you are headed to Tarija, Villazón or Uyuni, you'll have more luck going to Potosí. Andesbus and Emperador alternate for the daily service to Camiri (B$90, 14 hours), a beautiful trip.

TRAIN
A spectacular train (in reality it's more like a tram!) service from Sucre to Potosí leaves from El Tejar siding near the cemetery at 8am Monday, Wednesday and Friday for the scenic six-hour journey (one way B$40), returning from Potosí at 8am on Tuesday, Thursday and Saturday. The service is frequently suspended. Call ☎ 7287-6280 for the latest schedules.

Getting Around
TO/FROM THE AIRPORT
The airport, 9km northwest of town, is accessed by *micros 1* or *F* (allow an hour to be safe) from Av Hernando Siles, by the *banderita blanca* taxi *trufi* from Av España, or by taxi (fixed tariff B$25).

BICYCLE
Several places rent bikes, including Locot's Aventura (p218).

BUS & MICRO
Lots of buses and *micros* (B$2) ply circuitous routes around the city's one-way streets, and all seem to congregate at or near the market between runs. They're usually crowded, but fortunately Sucre is a town of short distances. The most useful routes are *micros 7*, *C* and *G* that climb the steep Av Grau hill to the Recoleta, and *micro A*, which serves the main bus terminal.

RENTAL CAR
Imbex (☎ 646-1222; Serrano 165) has 4WDs from B$300 a day.

TAXI
Taxis between any two points around the center, including the bus terminal, charge B$4 per person, a bit more after midnight. Avoid overcharging by booking through the kiosk on the plaza in front of Café Tertulias, which has fixed rates and reliable drivers.

TARABUCO
elevation 3200m

This small, predominantly indigenous village, 65km southeast of Sucre, is famous for its textiles, among the most renowned in all of Bolivia. To travelers though, Tarabuco is best known for its Sunday market, a popular day-trip from Sucre, and for its March Pujllay celebrations.

Tarabuco's colorful, sprawling **Sunday market**, which features high-quality *artesanías* (pullovers, *charangos,* coca pouches, ponchos and weavings that feature geometric and zoomorphic designs), is one of

Bolivia's most popular. By any standards, it's pretty touristy, which has meant the inevitable arrival of higher prices and lots of articles from well outside the local area. While there is some very high-quality work here, there's also a lot of generic stuff, and few bargains to be had.

On market days, the **Centro Artesanal Inca Pallay** (Murillo 25) sells an array of local weavings and serves meals in its tourist-friendly restaurant. Several places put on exhibitions of *pujllay* dancing (see below) while the market is on, for a small charge.

Festivals & Events

On March 12, 1816, Tarabuco was the site of the Battle of Jumbati, in which the villagers defended themselves under the leadership of a woman, Doña Juana Azurduy de Padilla, and liberated the town from Spanish forces. In commemoration of the event the village stages **Pujllay** ('play' in Quechua) on the third Sunday in March, when over 60 surrounding communities turn up in local costume. The celebration begins with a Quechua mass and procession followed by the **Pukara** ceremony, a Bolivian version of Thanksgiving. Folkloric dancers and musicians perform throughout the two-day weekend fiesta. It's one of Bolivia's largest festivals, and is great fun.

Sleeping & Eating

During Pujllay, accommodations fill up quickly – so you may want to hedge your bets and carry camping gear. The nicest digs are at **Centro Ecológico Juvenil** (☎ 644-0471; r per person B$60), which is signposted from the plaza. The Centro is a member of Hostelling International and has brand spanking new rooms arranged around a little courtyard. They can also arrange meals if you are peckish.

The plaza and nearby streets have a handful of basic restaurants. Meals of chorizo, soup and *charquekan* (dried llama meat served with potatoes and corn) are available from street stalls during market hours. The best place to eat though is at Mallki, just off the plaza, where much better fare is served in an attractive, sunny courtyard.

Getting There & Away

The easiest way to get to Tarabuco is by charter bus (B$35 round-trip, two hours each way) from Sucre, which leaves from outside Hostal Charcas on Ravelo around 8:30am. Tickets must be bought in advance from bigger hotels or any travel agent. From Tarabuco, the buses return to Sucre anytime between 1pm and 3pm.

Alternatively, *micros* (B$10, two hours) leave when full from Av de las Américas in Sucre on Sunday between 6:30am and 9:30am. Either walk from the center or take *micros B* or *C*. Returns to Sucre leave between 11am and 3:30pm.

CANDELARIA

The Tarabuco Sunday market (opposite) is fairly touristy these days, so to get a better idea of the regional culture and textiles you could visit the appealingly rustic indigenous village of Candelaria, which produces many of the finest hand-weavings – blankets, rugs, ponchos and bags – of the local style. There's a very traditional way of life here, and it's far removed from the bustle of Sucre or Tarabuco. The community has established a weaving association, which owns a **museum** (admission B$5) and textile store that explain the intricate weavings with displays depicting their culture rendered in vividly coloured yarns. The store contains a large selection of the same high quality weaving found in Sucre but at lower prices, with 100% of the profits going back into the small fair-trade association.

Some Sucre operators run tours leaving for Candelaria on Saturday, staying the night and proceeding to Tarabuco's market on Sunday morning. Candelaria Tours (p218) runs a highly recommended one, overnighting in a beautiful colonial hacienda. The weaving association can also arrange stays in private homes.

There are buses from Sucre to Candelaria at 4pm on Tuesday, Thursday and Saturday. They are run by Flota Charcas and leave from the clock-tower on Av Mendoza (the ring road). Several *camiones* pass through Candelaria daily, heading for Sucre.

CORDILLERA DE LOS FRAILES

The imposing serrated ridge forming Sucre's backdrop creates a formidable barrier between the departments of Chuquisaca and Potosí. It's home to the Jalq'a people, and offers a rich selection of scenery, activities and intriguing options for getting to know the Jalq'a culture.

CENTRAL HIGHLANDS

THE JALQ'A COMMUNITIES

The Cordillera de los Frailes is the home of the Quechua-speaking Jalq'a people, of whom there are some 10,000 in the area around Potolo and Maragua. They have traditionally made a living from farming potatoes, wheat and barley, and herding sheep and goats. The weaving of elaborately patterned *aqsus* (an apron-like skirt) is an important craft tradition, and these Escher-like red-and-black garments are instantly recognizable, being patterned with inventive depictions of *khurus* – strange, demon-like figures.

In 2001 the Jalq'a decided that they wanted to embrace tourism, but in a sustainable form that would benefit the community without destroying its traditions. They have developed a series of accommodations, cultural centers and guiding services, all involving maximal community participation. The villages receive 100% of profits.

To date, tailored accommodations and restaurant services have been set up in the villages of Maragua and Potolo. Sets of attractive thatched *cabañas* have been constructed using traditional methods and materials; they boast comfortable beds, hot water and attractive wooden furniture, and are decorated with local textiles. These cost B$60 per person per night; for B$100 per person, meals and cultural displays are included. The villages also have good camping areas. In Chaunaca, there's also a camping area, and six beds set up in the information center, but no restaurant service.

These are well-placed for a three-day circuit of the area, starting in Chataquila, heading to the rock paintings, and sleeping in Chaunaca. The next day you could head to Maragua (three hours), from where it's a spectacular six- to seven-hour walk – via *chullpa* (funerary towers) and with a short diversion to see the dinosaur footprints at Niñu Mayu – to Potolo.

On the way, you will eat traditional Bolivian *campesino* meals – such as *kala purca,* a maize soup cooked by immersing hot stones in it. Cultural activities that can be organized include demonstrations of *pujllay* dancing or traditional medicine. Weaving workshops can be found in all the villages mentioned, as well as some others, while Chaunaca has an interpretation center, and Potolo a museum of indigenous healing. Maragua has an agricultural museum in the pipeline. Note that the Jalq'a aren't fond of being photographed.

You can reach the area independently and organize guides, or take a pre-organized tour from Sucre. While many agencies offer day-trips to villages in the area, a longer trip that gives more back to the locals is recommended. There's a list of recommended Sucre agencies on p218.

To book the Maragua *cabañas,* call ☎ 644-5341. For Potolo call ☎ 693-8204. Alternatively ask at the Museo Textil Indígena (p214) in Sucre.

Orientation

A highly recommended three- or four-day circuit taking in several Cordillera highlights and the villages at the heart of the community tourism project begins at Chataquila, on the ridge above Punilla, 25km northwest of Sucre. From here (with an optional side trip to the abstract red, white and black man-animal rock paintings at Incamachay and Pumamachay) you descend to Chaunaca, then head to the Cráter de Maragua, before heading up to the village of Potolo, from where there's daily transportation back to Sucre. (For more on these places, see Hiking, below.) You can do this circuit just on foot or combine hiking and public transportation. It's also a very enjoyable region to explore by bike – you can rent one in Sucre (p222).

MAPS

There are numerous walking routes through the Cordillera de los Frailes, some of which are marked on the 1:50,000 topo sheets *Sucre,* sheet 6536IV, and *Estancia Chaunaca,* sheet 6537III (see p210).

Hiking

The best way to see this region is on foot. While hiking between the major villages is easy, a guide is highly recommended to increase your enjoyment of the region and communicate with the Quechua-speaking *campesinos.* A guide will also help to avoid misunderstandings, minimize your impact and help you get a better feeling for the local culture. It's easy to find a guide in any of the villages, or you could arrange one from Sucre. From Sucre, if you call the

CORDILLERA DE LOS FRAILES

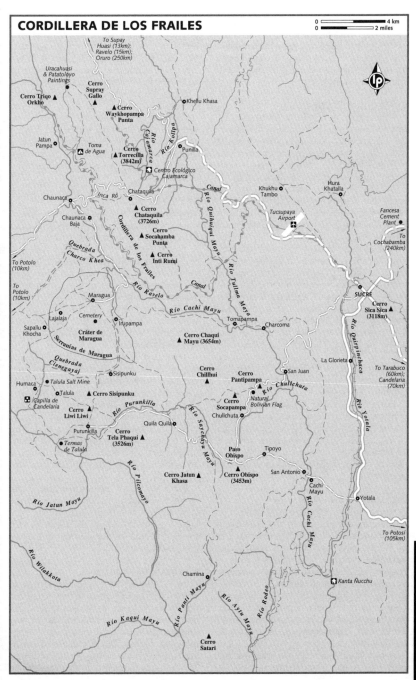

Maragua Entel (☎ 693-8088) a couple of days in advance, you can arrange for a guide to come to the city and meet you, to do the complete trip with you. Guides charge around B$150 a day for up to four people, plus costs (food, transportation etc).

CHATAQUILA TO CHAUNACA
On the rocky ridge top at **Chataquila** is a lovely stone chapel dedicated to the Virgen de Chataquila, a Virgin-shaped stone dressed in a gown and placed on the altar.

From Chataquila look around on the south side of the road for an obvious notch in the rock, which leads into a lovely pre-Hispanic route that descends steeply for 6km (three hours) to the village of **Chaunaca**, 39km from Sucre. Lots of good paved sections remain and it's easy to follow.

Chaunaca is home to a school, tiny church, and an interpretation and information centre on the Jalq'a region. Beds are available in the information centre, but you'll have to find your own food. There's also a campsite, and the renovated colonial hacienda, **Samay Huasi** (☎ 645-4129; 29avila@cotes.net.bo; r per person B$280), which offers pricy but high-quality accommodation. The price includes three meals a day, and transportation can be arranged for a small fee. Slightly higher prices may apply if there are fewer than three people – ring to check.

From Chaunaca you have the option of continuing west 13km direct to Potolo, or taking the very rewarding detour south via Maragua and Humaca. The latter will add an extra day to your hike but takes in some sites of real geological and paleontological interest.

INCAMACHAY & PUMAMACHAY
A worthwhile side trip from Chataquila or Chaunaca (above) leads to two fascinating sets of ancient rock paintings estimated to be at least 2500 years old. At the first major curve on the road west of Chataquila, a rugged track heads north along the ridge. For much of its length the route is flanked by rugged rock formations, but it's relatively easy going until you've almost reached the paintings, where you face a bit of a scramble. The first set, **Pumamachay**, lies well ensconced inside a rock cleft between two stone slabs. The pictographs here depict humans and geometric shapes in monochrome black. A

more impressive panel, **Incamachay**, is 15 minutes further along beneath a rock overhang that contains anthropomorphic, zoomorphic and geometric motifs painted in red and white. Guides at the entrance charge B$10. You will need one to find the paintings.

From Incamachay, you can continue downhill for a couple of hours until you strike the road at the **Tomo de Agua** aqueduct, where there's drinking water and a good campsite. From there take the road 6km to the Chataquila–Chaunaca road, where you can either ascend to Chataquila or descend to Chaunaca.

CRÁTER DE MARAGUA
This unearthly natural formation, sometimes called the Ombligo de Chuquisaca (Chuquisaca's Belly Button), features surreal settlements scattered across a 8km-wide red-and-violet crater floor, and bizarre slopes that culminate in the gracefully symmetrical pale green arches of the Serranías de Maragua. It's one of the most visually striking places in Bolivia. There's plenty to see: waterfalls, caves and a picturesque cemetery in the middle of the crater that dates from pre-Hispanic times.

The village of **Maragua** is an active weaving centre. The weavers have set up a store, and will take visitors into their homes to show them the creation of the textiles. Maragua has a store, three *cabañas* (see boxed text, p224) and a campsite. A kilometer from the village, in **Irupampa**, the villagers started up a lovely little **hostel** (r per person B$15), with running water, a cold shower next door and an appealing little garden. You can also camp here.

Maragua is an easy three-hour walk along the road from Chaunaca. For the lazy, a direct bus from Sucre to Maragua leaves on Sunday at 9am from Yuraj Yuraj, the roundabout on the road out of the city toward the airport.

MARAGUA TO POTOLO
From Maragua, it's a spectacular walk to Potolo. You can get there in five hours, but there's plenty to see on the way to slow you down. In the area around **Humaca** you will find *chullpa* (funerary towers) and a paleontological deposit where embedded fossils are clearly visible in the rocks. Additionally dinosaur footprints at **Niñu Mayu** can be

visited if you are prepared to add an extra hour or so to your hike. All of these can be found most easily with a local guide. Ask around in the villages and negotiate a price that is fair to the community.

Another side trip from Humaca could take you to the **Termas de Talula**, 5km away. You'll need to ford the Río Pilcomayo twice. The Talula hot springs issue into rock pools that have temperatures up to 46°C. Camping is possible anywhere in the vicinity.

From Talula it's 500m to the constricted passage that conducts the Río Pilcomayo between the steep walls of the Punkurani gorge. When the river is low, you can cross over to the Potosí shore and see the many rock-painting sites above the opposite bank.

POTOLO

The village of **Potolo**, end point of the hike, has some typically stunning weaving going on in the workshops, and also has a museum of traditional medicine, which demonstrates vernacular healing practices and other aspects of the culture. There are three *cabañas* here (see boxed text, p224), a store and a campsite.

Infrequent buses from Sucre via Chataquila and Chaunaca leave from Yuraj Yuraj, the roundabout on the road out of the city towards the airport. Take urban bus 1 or F from the corner of Hernando Siles and Loa to get there. They return to Sucre from Potolo when full.

SUPAY HUASI

Among the most interesting rock paintings in the Cordillera de los Frailes are those at Supay Huasi (House of the Devil). These unusual images in ocher, white and yellow include several animals, an ocher-colored 40cm man wearing a sun-like headdress, and several faded geometric figures and designs.

The paintings are south of Maragua – it's a longish day walk there and back. They are almost impossible to find without a local guide.

QUILA QUILA

Another worthwhile destination on the circuit is the beautiful village of Quila Quila, three hours south of Maragua by foot. It's a formerly deserted village of largely mud buildings that is being slowly repopulated. The tower of the elegant colonial church dominates the skyline and adjacent to it are

buried the remains of the revered 18th-century indigenous leader Tomás Katari who was murdered at the chapel in Chataquila in 1781. In 1777 Katari walked to Buenos Aires to confront colonial leaders and claim rights for the Aymará and had returned triumphantly with a document signed by the viceroy ceding to his demands and recognizing him as cacique. Upon his return to Bolivia he was imprisoned, sparking a widespread uprising that eventually led to his death. A kilometer away are the Marca Runi monoliths with pictographs. The area is rich in pre-Columbian archaeological artifacts.

Daily *camiones* to Talula via Quila Quila (B$5, three to four hours) depart at 6:30am from Sucre's Barrio Aranjuez, returning the afternoon of the same day. In recent times some visitors have reported an unpleasant reception by villagers and it is strongly recommended that you check the current situation before setting out, and go with a guide.

Tours

Several Sucre travel agencies (see p218) offer quick jaunts into the Cordillera – for example, a two-day circuit from Chataquila to Incamachay and Chaunaca. It's important to go with a responsible operator committed to giving something to the region – day-trips aren't a great idea. See boxed text on p224 for opportunities to interact more with the Jalq'a culture.

POTOSÍ

pop 149,200 / elevation 4070m

> I am rich Potosí,
> The treasure of the world…
> And the envy of kings.

The conquistadors never found El Dorado, the legendary city of gold, but they did get their hands on Potosí and its Cerro Rico, a 'Rich Hill' full of silver. This quote, from the city's first coat of arms, sums it up. The city was founded in 1545 as soon as the ore was discovered, and pretty soon the silver extracted here was bankrolling the Spanish empire.

Potosí's story is wholly tied to its silver. During the boom years, when the metal must have seemed inexhaustible, it became the largest and wealthiest city of the Americas. Even today, something very lucrative is

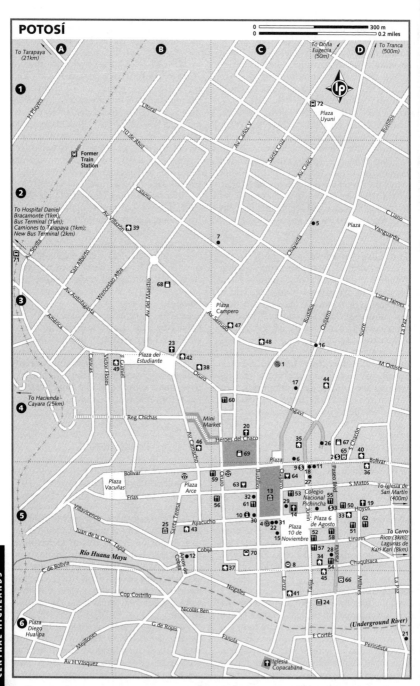

POTOSÍ

INFORMATION			
Acces Computer	1 C4	Museo & Convento de Santa	
Banco de Crédito (ATM)	2 D4	Teresa	25 B5
Banco Mercantil	3 D5	Pasaje de Siete Vueltas	26 D4
Café Internet Candelaria	4 C5	Portón Mestizo	27 C5
Instituto Geográfico Militar	5 D2	Potosí Specialist	28 D5
Janus Limpieza	6 C4	Silver Tours	29 C5
Migración	7 C2	Sin Fronteras	30 C5
Post Office	8 C5	South American Tours	31 C5
Prodem	9 C5	Sumaj Tours	(see 42)
Secretaria de Turismo	10 C5	Torre de la Compañía de	
Tourist Police	(see 10)	Jesús	(see 10)
		Turismo Claudia	32 C5
SIGHTS & ACTIVITIES		Victoria Tours	(see 37)
Altiplano Tours	(see 4)		
Andes Salt Expeditions	11 D5	**SLEEPING**	
Arcos de Cobija	12 B5	Hostal Colonial	33 D5
Casa de las Tres Portadas	(see 36)	Hostal Compañía de Jesús	34 D5
Casa Nacional de Moneda	13 C5	Hostal Felimar	35 C4
Cathedral	14 C5	Hostal Las Tres Portadas	36 D5
El Cabildo	15 C5	Hostal María Victoria	37 C5
Esquina de las Cuatro Portadas	16 D3	Hostal San José	38 B4
Greengo Tours	17 C4	Hotel Cima Argentum	39 B2
Hidalgo Tours	18 C5	Hotel Coloso Potosí	40 D4
Iglesia de la Merced	19 D5	Hotel El Turista	41 C6
Iglesia de San Lorenzo de		Hotel Jerusalén	42 B4
Carangas	20 C4	Hotel Santa Teresa	43 B5
Ingenio San Marcos	21 D6	Koala Den	44 D4
Koala Tours	22 C5	La Casona Hostal	45 D6
La Capilla de Nuestra Señora de		Macuquina Dora Hotel	46 B4
Jerusalén	23 B3	Residencial 10 de	
Marco Polo Tours	(see 32)	Noviembre	47 C3
Museo & Convento de San		Residencial Felcar	48 C3
Francisco	24 D6	Residencial Sumaj	49 B4

EATING			
4060	50 D5		
Café Cultural Kaypichu	51 D5		
Café de la Merced	(see 19)		
Cafe de la Plata	52 D5		
Chaplin Café	53 C5		
Cherry's Salon de Té	54 D5		
Confitería Capricornio	55 D5		
El Fogón	56 C5		
El Mesón	57 D5		
La Salteña	58 D5		
Malpartida	59 C5		
Manzana Mágica	60 C4		
Pizzería El Mana	61 C5		
Potocchi	62 D5		

DRINKING			
La Casona Pub	63 C5		
Sumaj Orcko	64 C5		

ENTERTAINMENT			
Cine Universitario	65 D4		
Multicine Universal	66 D6		

SHOPPING			
Arte Nativo	67 D4		
Artesanías Palomita's	68 B3		
Market	69 C4		

TRANSPORT			
Aerosur	70 C5		
Buses to Uyuni	71 A3		
Micros to Sucre	72 D1		

said to *vale un Potosí* (be worth a Potosí). Then, once the silver more or less dried up, decline and poverty were the hard facts. The ore has been extracted by miners in some of the most abysmal conditions imaginable – a visit to see today's miners at work provokes disbelief at just how appalling the job is. But the rest of Potosí – its grand churches, ornate colonial architecture and down-to-earth, friendly inhabitants – is a real delight.

History

No one is certain how much silver has been extracted from Cerro Rico over its four centuries of productivity, but a popular boast was that the Spanish could have constructed a silver bridge to Spain and still had silver left to carry across it. The Spanish monarchy, mortgaged to the hilt by foreign bankers, came to rely completely on the yearly treasure fleets, which brought the Potosí silver. On the rare occasions when they were intercepted by storms or pirates, it was a national disaster.

Although the tale of Potosí's origins probably takes a few liberties with the facts, it's a good story. It begins in 1544 when a local Inca, Diego Huallpa, searching for an escaped llama, stopped to build a fire at the foot of the mountain known in Quechua as 'Potojsi' (meaning 'thunder' or 'explosion,' although it might also have stemmed from *potoj,* 'the springs'). The fire grew so hot that the very earth beneath it started to melt, and shiny liquid oozed from the ground.

Diego immediately realized he had run across a commodity for which the Spanish conquerors had an insatiable appetite. Perhaps he also remembered the Inca legend associated with the mountain, in which Inca Huayna Capac had been instructed by a booming voice not to dig in the hill of Potojsi, but to leave the metal alone, because it was intended for others.

Whatever the truth of this, the Spanish eventually learned of the enormous wealth buried in the mountain of Potojsi and determined that it warranted immediate attention. On April 1 (according to some sources, April 10), 1545, the Villa Imperial de Carlos V was founded at the foot of Cerro Rico and large-scale excavation began. In the time it takes to say 'Get down there and dig,' thousands of indigenous slaves were pressed into service and the first of the silver was already headed for Spain.

The work was dangerous, however, and so many workers died of accidents and silicosis pneumonia that the Spanish imported millions of African slaves to augment the labor force. The descendants of the very few to survive mainly live in the Yungas (see boxed text, p131).

In order to increase productivity, the Viceroy of Toledo instituted, in 1572, the Ley de la Mita, which required all indigenous and African slaves over age 18 to work in shifts of 12 hours. They would remain underground without seeing daylight for four months at a time, eating, sleeping and working in the mines. When they emerged from a 'shift,' their eyes were covered to prevent damage in the bright sunlight.

Naturally these miners, who came to be known as *mitayos*, didn't last long. Heavy losses were also incurred among those who worked in the *ingenios* (smelting mills), as the silver-smelting process involved contact with deadly mercury. In all, it's estimated that over the three centuries of colonial rule (1545 to 1825) as many as eight million Africans and indigenous Bolivians died from the appalling conditions.

In 1672 a mint was established to coin the silver, reservoirs were constructed to provide water for the growing population, and exotic European consumer goods found their way up the llama trails from Arica and Callao. Amid the mania, more than 80 churches were constructed, and Potosí's population grew to nearly 200,000, making it one of the largest cities in the world. One politician of the period put it succinctly: 'Potosí was raised in the pandemonium of greed at the foot of riches discovered by accident.'

As with most boom towns, Potosí's glory was not to last. The mines' output began to decline in the early 19th century, and the city was looted in the independence struggles in Alto Perú. The population dropped to less than 10,000, and the mid-19th century drop in silver prices dealt a blow from which Potosí has never completely recovered.

In the present century only the demand for tin has rescued Potosí from obscurity and brought a slow but steady recovery. Zinc and lead have now taken over from tin as Bolivia's major metallic exports. Silver

extraction continues only on a small scale, but reminders of the city's grand colonial past are still evident.

Most of the operations in Cerro Rico today are in the control of miner-owned cooperatives, which operate under conditions that have changed shamefully little from the colonial period. There's little prospect of change in sight, as the miners barely extract enough ore to keep them in bread. The dream of the lucky strike (there are still a few) keeps them going, although the number of miners is steadily dwindling over the years.

In 1987 Unesco named Potosí a World Heritage Site in recognition of its rich and tragic history and its wealth of colonial architecture.

Orientation

Most things are in easy walking distance, except the mines and the bus station. The lack of oxygen can be disorienting, so take it easy if you are arriving from the lower areas.

MAPS

The tourist office periodically gives out a city map; many of the tour agencies also include a useful map on the reverse of their brochure. **Instituto Geográfico Militar** (IGM; Chayanta at 10 de Abril) sells topo sheets of all areas of Potosí department.

Information
EMERGENCY

Tourist police (☎ 622-7477; Ayacucho & Bustillos) Helpful; on the ground floor of the Torre de la Compañía de Jesús building, together with the tourist office. They also run a kiosk on Pasaje Boulevar, on the corner with Hoyos.

IMMIGRATION

Migración (☎ 622-5989; Calama 188) For visa extensions.

INTERNET ACCESS

There are numerous places to get online, mostly charging between B$2 and B$4 per hour, including **Café Internet Candelaria** (Ayacucho 5), where the first 15 minutes is free with breakfast, and the speedy **Acces Computer** (Bustillos 869).

LAUNDRY

Most hotels can organize laundry services for their guests. Failing that, try **Janus Limpieza** (Bolívar 773; per kg B$10; ☯ closed Sun).

MEDICAL SERVICES

If you need an English-speaking doctor, visit the **Hospital Daniel Bracamonte** (☎ 624-4960; Italia s/n).

MONEY

ATMs are common in the center of town. Lots of businesses along Bolívar, Sucre and in the market change US dollars at reasonable rates; stalls along Héroes del Chaco also change euros, and Chilean and Argentine pesos. Cash advances are available at **Banco de Crédito** (Bolívar & Sucre), **Banco Mercantil** (Paseo Blvd 9) and **Prodem** (cnr Bolívar & Junín), which also change US dollars.

POST & TELEPHONE

The central **post office** (Lanza & Chuquisaca) is close to the main square. There are lots of cheap international telecom centers.

TOURIST INFORMATION

Secretaria de Turismo (☎ 622-7477; Ayacucho near Bustillos; 8:30am-noon & 2-6pm) Located up the stairs in the beautiful Torre de la Compañía de Jesús. Quite helpful: making a big effort to improve the standard of Potosí's services.

Sights & Activities

Such was the wealth of colonial Potosí that more than 80 churches were constructed here. But if it's a glimpse of hell you're after, see p234.

CASA NACIONAL DE MONEDA

The **National Mint** (☎ 622-2777; Ayacucho at Bustillos; admission B$20 for mandatory 2-3hr guided tour; 9am-noon & 2:30-6:30pm Tue-Sat, 9am-noon Sun, English tours depart at 9am, 10:30am, 2:30pm & 4:30pm) is Potosí's star attraction and one of South America's finest museums. Potosí's first mint was constructed on the present site of the Casa de Justicia in 1572 under orders from the Viceroy of Toledo. This, its replacement, is a vast and strikingly beautiful building that takes up a whole city block. It was built between 1753 and 1773 to control the minting of colonial coins; legend has it that when the king of Spain saw the bill for its construction, he exclaimed 'that building must be made of silver' (expletive presumably deleted). These coins, which bore the mint mark 'P,' were known as *potosís*.

The building has walls that are more than a meter thick, and it has not only functioned as a mint but also done spells as a prison, a fortress and, during the Chaco War, as the headquarters of the Bolivian army. As visitors are ushered into a courtyard from the entrance, they're greeted by the sight of a stone fountain and a mask of Bacchus, hung there in 1865 by Frenchman Eugenio Martin Moulon for reasons known only to him. In fact, this aberration looks more like an escapee from a children's fun fair, but it has become a town icon (known as the *mascarón*).

Apart from the beauty of the building itself, there's a host of historical treasures. They include a fine selection of religious paintings from the Potosí school, culminating in *La Virgen del Cerro*, a famous anonymous work from the 18th century, as well as the immense assemblies of mule-driven wooden cogs that served to beat the silver to the width required for the coining. These were replaced by steam-powered machines in the 19th century. The last coins were minted here in 1953.

The guided tour is long, and the temperatures inside the building are chilly, so rug up. Although there are English and French tours available on request, the quality of the Spanish one is much higher and the visit more comprehensive, so it's well worth doing even if your levels are fairly limited.

CATHEDRAL

Construction of **La Catedral** (Plaza 10 de Noviembre) was initiated in 1564 and finally completed around 1600. The original building lasted until the early 19th century, when it mostly collapsed. Most of what is now visible is the neoclassical construction, and the building's elegant lines represent one of Bolivia's best exemplars of that style. The interior décor represents some of the finest in Potosí but it's currently closed for a facelift. You can visit the **bell tower** (admission B$7; 11am-12:30pm & 2:30-6pm Mon-Fri) for nice views of the city.

CALLE QUIJARRO & ESQUINA DE LAS CUATRO PORTADAS

North of the Iglesia de San Agustín, **Calle Quijarro** narrows as it winds between a wealth of colonial buildings, many with doorways graced by old family crests. It's thought that the bends in Calle Quijarro were an intentional attempt to inhibit the cold winds that would otherwise whistle through and chill everything in their path. This concept is carried to extremes on the **Pasaje de Siete Vueltas** (Passage of Seven Turns), which is an extension of Calle Ingavi, east of Junín. During colonial times Calle Quijarro was the street of potters, but it's now known for its hat makers. One millinery worth visiting is that of **Don Antonio Villa Chavarría** (Quijarro 41). The intersection of Calles Quijarro and Modesto Omiste, further north, has been dubbed the **Esquina de las Cuatro Portadas** because of its four decorative colonial doorways.

MUSEO & CONVENTO DE SAN FRANCISCO

The **San Francisco Convent** (☎ 622-2539; Tarija & Nogales; admission B$15, photo B$10, camera B$20; ☼ 9am-noon & 2:30-6:30pm Mon-Fri) was founded in 1547 by Fray Gaspar de Valverde, making it the oldest monastery in Bolivia. Owing to its inadequate size, it was demolished in 1707 and reconstructed over the following 19 years. A gold-covered altar from this building is now housed in the Casa Nacional de la Moneda. The statue of Christ that graces the present altar features hair that is said to grow miraculously.

The museum has examples of religious art, including various paintings from the Potosí School, such as *The Erection of the Cross* by Melchor Pérez de Holguín, various mid-19th-century works by Juan de la Cruz Tapia, and 25 scenes from the life of St Francis of Assisi.

The highlight of the obligatory tour (ask for an English-speaking guide), which has no real schedule and lasts about 1½ hours, comes at the end, when you're ushered up the tower and onto the roof for a grand view of Potosí. You also visit the catacombs, which have a smattering of human bones and a subterranean river running nearby.

MUSEO & CONVENTO DE SANTA TERESA

The fascinating **Santa Teresa Convent** (Santa Teresa at Ayacucho; admission by guided tour B$21, photo permit B$10; ☼ 9am-12:30pm & 2:30-6:30pm Mon-Sat, 9am-11am & 3-5pm Sun, last tours 11am & 5pm Mon-Sat) was founded in 1685 and is still home to a small community of Carmelite nuns. One of them is an architect, and has directed a superb restoration project that has converted part of the sizable building into a museum.

The excellent guided tour (in Spanish and English) explains how girls of 15 from wealthy families entered the convent, getting their last glimpse of parents and loved ones at the door. Entry was a privilege, paid for with a sizable dowry; a good portion of these offerings are on display in the form of religious artwork.

There are numerous fine pieces, including a superb Madonna by Castilian sculptor Alonso Cano, several canvases by Melchor Pérez de Holguín, Bolivia's most famous painter, and a room of painted wooden Christs. Some of the artworks verge on the macabre, as does the skull sitting in a bowl of dust in the middle of the dining room, and a display of wire whisks that some of the nuns used for self-flagellation.

As impressive as the works of art on show is the building itself, with two pretty cloisters housing numerous cacti and a venerable apple tree, and the glimpse into a cloistered world that only really changed character in the 1960s, with the reforms of the Second Vatican Council.

The guided tour lasts almost two hours; note that some of the rooms are particularly chilly. There's also a cafe and store, where you can buy almond and peanut sweets made by the nuns.

TORRE DE LA COMPAÑÍA DE JESÚS

The ornate and beautiful bell tower, on what remains of the **former Jesuit church** (Ayacucho near Bustillos; mirador admission B$10; ☼ 8am-noon & 2-6pm Mon-Fri, 8am-noon Sat), was completed in 1707 after the collapse of the original church. Both the tower and the doorway are adorned with examples of Mestizo baroque ornamentation. The tourist office is in the same building.

CHURCHES

The rather ordinary-looking **Iglesia de San Martín** (☎ 622-3682; Hoyos near Almagro; admission B$15; ☼ 7-11am & 3-6pm Mon-Fri, 7am-noon Sat) was built in the 1600s and is today run by the French Redemptionist Fathers. Inside is an art museum, with at least 30 paintings beneath the choir depicting the Virgin Mary and the 12 Apostles. The Virgin on the altarpiece wears clothing woven from silver threads. However, San Martín is outside the center and is sometimes closed, so phone before traipsing out here.

La Capilla de Nuestra Señora de Jerusalén is a little-known Potosí gem. Originally built as a humble chapel in honor of the Virgen de Candelaria, it was rebuilt more lavishly in the 18th century. It houses a fine gilt baroque *retablo* (portable boxes with depictions of religious and historical events) – the Virgin has pride of place – and a magnificent series of paintings of Biblical scenes by anonymous artists of the Potosí school. The impressive pulpit has small paintings by Melchor Pérez de Holguín. It is currently only open for mass.

The ornate Mestizo baroque portal of **Iglesia de San Lorenzo de Carangas** (Héroes del Chaco at Bustillos; ☼ 10am-noon Mon-Sat) is probably one of the most photographed subjects in Bolivia. It was carved in stone by master indigenous artisans in the 16th century, but the main structure wasn't completed until the bell towers were added in 1744. Inside are two Holguín paintings and handcrafted silverwork on the altar. The church was renovated in 1987.

Constructed between 1555 and 1687, restored **Iglesia de la Merced** (Hoyos at Millares; admission B$10; ☼ 11am-12:30pm, 2-6pm Mon-Fri, 11am-12:30pm Sat) has a carved pulpit, a gorgeous wooden ceiling and a beautiful 18th-century silver arch over the altarpiece. It houses a lovely small museum and you can visit the catacombs and the bell tower.

HISTORIC BUILDINGS

Potosí's elaborate colonial architecture merits a stroll around the narrow streets to take in the ornate doorways and facades, as well as the covered wooden balconies that overhang the streets. Architecturally notable homes and monuments include **El Cabildo** (Old Town Hall; Plaza 10 de Noviembre), the pretty **Casa de las Tres Portadas** (Bolívar 1052) and the **Arcos de Cobija** (Arches of Cobija) on the street of the same name.

On Calle Junín, between Matos and Bolívar, is an especially lovely and elaborate **portón mestizo** doorway, flanked by twisted columns. It once graced the home of the Marqués de Otavi, but now ushers patrons into the Banco Nacional.

LOS INGENIOS

On the banks *(la ribera)* of the Río Huana Mayu, in the upper Potosí barrios of Cantumarca and San Antonio, are some fine ruined examples of the *ingenios* (smelters). These were formerly used to extract silver from the ore hauled out of Cerro Rico. There were originally 82 *ingenios* along 15km of the stream. Some remaining ones date back to the 1570s and were in use until the mid-1800s.

Each *ingenio* consists of a floor penetrated by shallow wells *(buitrones)* where the ore was mixed with mercury and salt. The ore was then ground by millstones that were powered by water that was impounded in the 32 artificial Lagunas de Kari Kari (p241).

The **Ingenio San Marcos** (San Marcos Smelter; La Paz near Periodista) is the most interesting and has a good **restaurant** (La Paz 1565; www.hca-potosi.com/sanmarcos). Most tours of the Cerro Rico mines include a stop at a working *ingenio* as part of the trip.

COOPERATIVE MINES

A visit to the cooperative mines will almost surely be one of the most memorable experiences you'll have in Bolivia, providing an opportunity to witness working conditions that are among the most grueling imaginable. We urge you not to underestimate the dangers involved in going into the mines and to consider the voyeuristic factor involved in seeing other people's suffering. You may be left stunned and/or ill (see boxed text, p235).

Dozens of Potosí operators (p235) offer guided tours through the mines. The best tour guides tend to be ex-miners, who know the conditions and are friendly with the men at work. The safety standards are hit-and-miss; you really are going down at your own risk.

Mine visits aren't easy, and the low ceilings and steep, muddy passageways are best visited in your worst clothes. You'll feel both cold and hot at times, there will likely be a bit of crawling through narrow shafts and the altitude can be extremely taxing. On some tours, you'll end up walking 3km or 4km inside the mountain. You'll be exposed to noxious chemicals and gases, including silica dust (the cause of silicosis), arsenic gas and acetylene vapors, as well as asbestos deposits. Anyone with doubts or medical problems should avoid these tours. The plus side is that you can speak with the friendly miners, who will share their insights and opinions about their difficult lot. The miners are proud of their work in such tough conditions, and generally happy for visitors to observe their toil.

Tours begin with a visit to the miners' market, where miners stock up on acetylene rocks, dynamite, cigarettes and other essentials. In the past, gifts weren't expected, but with the growing number of tourists, you'd be very unpopular if you didn't supply a handful of coca leaves and a few cigarettes – luxuries for which the miners' meager earnings are scarcely sufficient. Photography is permitted. The tours then generally visit an *ingenio* (see p233), before heading up to the Cerro Rico itself. There's often a demonstration of a dynamite explosion; the force is like a hammer blow to the chest even at some distance. This can be potentially dangerous and is detrimental to the environment so we urge you to request a tour without dynamite explosion when signing up.

Tours run in the morning or afternoon and last from four to five hours. The standard

---

THE JOB FROM HELL

In the cooperative mines on Cerro Rico, all work is done with mostly primitive tools, and underground temperatures vary from below freezing – the altitude is over 4200m – to a stifling 115°F on the 4th and 5th levels. Miners, exposed to all sorts of noxious chemicals and gases, normally die of silicosis pneumonia within 10 to 15 years of entering the mines.

Women are admitted to many cooperative mines but only five are allowed to be in the mine's interior at any one time. That's because quite a few miners hang on to the tradition that women underground invite bad luck, and in many cases, the taboo applies only to miners' wives, whose presence in the mines would invite jealousy from Pachamama. At any rate, lots of Quechua women are consigned to stay right outside the mines picking through the tailings, gleaning small amounts of minerals that may have been missed.

Since cooperative mines are owned by the miners themselves, they must produce to make their meager living. The majority of the work is done by hand with explosives and tools they must purchase themselves, including the acetylene lamps used to detect pockets of deadly carbon monoxide gas.

Miners prepare for their workday by socializing and chewing coca for several hours, beginning work at about 10am. They work until lunch at 2pm, when they rest and chew more coca. For those who don't spend the night working, the day usually ends at 7pm. On the weekend, each miner (or a group of miners) sells his week's production to the buyer for as high a price as he can negotiate.

When miners first enter the mine, they offer propitiation at the shrine of the miners' god Tata Kaj'chu, whom they hope will afford them protection in the harsh underground world. Deeper in the mine, visitors will undoubtedly see a devilish figure occupying a small niche somewhere along the passageways. As most of the miners believe in a god in heaven, they deduce that there must also be a devil beneath the earth in a place where it's hot and uncomfortable. Since hell (according to the traditional description of the place) must not be far from the environment in which they work, they reason that the devil himself must own the minerals they're dynamiting and digging out of the earth. In order to appease this character, whom they call Tío (Uncle) or Supay – never Diablo – they set up a little ceramic figurine in a place of honor.

On Friday nights a *cha'lla* (offering) is made to invoke his goodwill and protection. A little alcohol is poured on the ground before the statue, lighted cigarettes are placed in his mouth and coca leaves are laid out within easy reach. Then, as in most Bolivian celebrations, the miners smoke, chew coca and proceed to drink themselves unconscious. While this is all taken very seriously, it also provides a bit of diversion from an extremely harsh existence. It's interesting that offerings to Jesus Christ are only made at the point where the miners can first see the outside daylight.

In most cooperative operations there is a minimal medical plan in case of accident or silicosis (which is inevitable after seven to 10 years working underground) and a pension of about US$15 a month for those so incapacitated. Once a miner has lost 50% of his lung capacity to silicosis, he may retire, if he so wishes. In case of death, a miner's widow and children collect this pension.

charge is between B$80 and B$100 per person; slightly lower rates may be available during the low season. This price includes a guide, transportation from town and equipment (jackets, helmets, boots and lamps). Wear sturdy clothing and carry plenty of water and a handkerchief/headscarf to filter some of the noxious substances you'll encounter. There is less activity in the mines on Sundays.

Tours

In addition to mine tours, there are a variety of guided tours offered by the agencies, including a three-hour city tour (B$60 to B$100) of the museums and monuments. Other popular options include Tarapaya (see p242; B$70 to B$100); guided trekking trips around the Lagunas de Kari Kari (see p241; B$160 to B$280) and tours of colonial haciendas around Potosí (B$300 for a full day). Agencies, offering all of these, include the following:

Altiplano Tours (☎ 622-5353; Ayacucho 19) At the end of their mine tours, you can try some of the work yourself. They offer *tinku* excursions.

Andes Salt Expeditions (☎ 622-5175; www .bolivia-travel.com.bo; Bolívar at Junín) The agency's founder and ex-miner Raul Braulio Mamani worked as the guide for *The Devil's Miner* documentary; 15% of the profits go to the miners' on-site health facility.

Greengo Tours (☎ 623-1362; www.greengotours.com .bo; Quijarro 42) This agency has been getting good reader reviews about its mine tours. The owner is actively fighting to cease dynamite explosions as part of the tours.

Hidalgo Tours (☎ 622-9512; www.salardeuyuni.net; Bolívar at Junín) One of the best upmarket options.

Koala Tours (☎ 622-4708; ktourspotosi@hotmail.com; Ayacucho 3) Runs some of the best mine tours, with ex-miners as guides (Efrain Mamani is highly recommended); 15% of the profits go to the mining community. They also offer guided mountain biking to Tarapaya (B$150), *tinku* excursions (a four-day trip costs B$800) and a nine-day trek along the ancient llama caravan route to Cochabamba.

Marco Polo Tours (☎ 623-1385; marcopoloagency@ hotmail.com; Bustillos 1036) Boss Wily of this reader-recommended agency is a former miner who speaks good English. The visit is to the Qory Mayu cooperative mine; 10% of the profits go to the cooperative for social help.

Potosí Specialist (☎ 622-5320; jhonnybolivia@ hotmail.com; Padilla 12) Friendly agency run by knowledgeable Jhonny Montes who offers reliable service. An interesting option is a full-day tour to Hacienda Cayara, with a sampling of Andean agricultural work (B$160 with breakfast & lunch.

WARNING!

The cooperatives are not museums but working mines that are fairly nightmarish places. Anyone planning to take a tour needs to realize that there are risks involved (see p234). People with medical problems – especially claustrophobia, asthma and other respiratory conditions – should avoid these tours. While medical experts including the NHS note that limited exposure from a few hours' tour is extremely unlikely to cause any lasting health impacts, if you have any concerns whatsoever about exposure to asbestos or silica dust, you should not enter the mines. Accidents can also happen – explosions, falling rocks, runaway trolleys, etc. For these reasons, all tour companies make visitors sign a disclaimer absolving them completely from any responsibility for injury, illness or death – if your tour operator does not, choose another. Visiting the mines is a serious decision. If you're undeterred, you'll have an eye-opening and unforgettable experience.

Silver Tours (☎ 622-3600; silvertoursreservas@hotmail .com; Quijarro 12) All the standard tours around Potosí (15% of mine tour profits go to the mining community), adventure tours to the *salares*(salt flats) and transfers for San Pedro de Atacama.

Sin Fronteras (☎ /fax 622-4058; www.organizacion sinfronteras.com; Bustillos 1092) Not really designed for walk-ins, these are mostly private tours that are pricier but of a higher quality. Worth booking in advance.

South American Tours (☎ 622-8919; osmedtur@ hotmail.com; Ayacucho 11) Visits the mine San Miguel la Poderosa, in addition to offering the standard tours.

Turismo Claudia (☎ 622-5000; jacky_gc@yahoo.com; Bustillos 1078) Small group tours available in English and French to the mines as well as further afield, such as to Salar de Uyuni.

Victoria Tours (☎ /fax 622-2132; Chuquisaca 148) Budget agency running all of the tours previously mentioned. It's located at Hostal María Victoria.

Festivals & Events
FIESTA DEL ESPÍRITU

Potosí's most unusual event happens on the last three Saturdays of June and the first Saturday of August. It's dedicated to Pachamama, the earth mother, whom the miners regard as the mother of all Bolivians.

Campesinos bring their finest llamas to the base of Cerro Rico to sell to the miners for sacrifice. The ritual is conducted to a meticulous schedule. At 10am, one miner from each mine purchases a llama, and their families gather for the celebrations. At 11am, everyone moves to the entrances of their respective mines. The miners chew coca and drink alcohol from 11am to precisely 11:45am, when they prepare the llama for Pachamama by tying its feet and offering it coca and alcohol. At noon, the llama meets its maker. As its throat is slit, the miners petition Pachamama for luck, protection and an abundance of minerals. The blood of the llama is splashed around the mouth of the mine to ensure Pachamama's attention, cooperation and blessing.

For the next three hours, the men chew coca and drink while the women prepare a plate of grilled llama. The meat is served traditionally with potatoes baked along with *habas* (fava beans) and oca in a small adobe oven. When the oven reaches the right temperature, it is smashed in on the food, which is baked beneath the hot shards. The stomach, feet and head of the llama are buried in a 3m hole as a further offering to Pachamama, then the music and dancing begin. In the evening, celebrants are taken home in transportation provided by the miner who bought his mine's llama.

FIESTA DE SAN BARTOLOMÉ (CHU'TILLOS)
This rollicking celebration takes place on the final weekend of August or the first weekend of September and is marked by processions, student exhibitions, traditional costumes and folk dancing from all over the continent. In recent years it has even extended overseas and featured musical groups and dance troupes from as far away as China and the USA. Given all the practicing during the week leading up to the festival, you'd be forgiven for assuming it actually started a week early. Booking accommodations for this period is essential.

EXALTACIÓN DE LA SANTA VERA CRUZ
This festival, which falls on September 14, honors Santo Cristo de la Vera Cruz. Activities occur around the church of San Lorenzo and the railway station. Silver cutlery features prominently, as do parades, dueling

brass bands, dancing, costumed children and, of course, lots of alcohol.

Sleeping
Usually only the top-end hotels have heating, and there may be blanket shortages in the cheapies, so you'll want a sleeping bag.

BUDGET
Residencial Felcar (☎ 622-4966; Serrudo 345; s/d B$25/50, with bathroom & breakfast B$70/140) This friendly place makes a sound option with its clean, simple rooms (you'll want a sleeping bag in the cheaper ones). Newer rooms with bathrooms are attractive, with typical Latin American furniture, TVs and heaters. There are reliable hot showers throughout and a nice terrace. On Sunday, they offer a traditional lunch of barbecued llama for B$15.

Residencial 10 de Noviembre (☎ 622-3253; Serrudo 181; r per person B$30, s/d with bathroom B$50/90) Run by the Cerro de Plata tour agency, it's a recently renovated spot in a tall white building with fresh paint outside and in. Rooms are perfectly decent, with reliable hot water, and there's a pleasant covered terrace.

Residencial Sumaj (☎ 622-3336; hoteljer@ entelnet.bo; Gumiel 12; s/d/tr B$30/60/90) This long-time budget standby has small rooms with shared bathroom. It's only worth staying on the top floor, which is lit by skylights; those downstairs are dreadfully dingy. There's an adequate kitchen for guests, but you have to pay B$15 per day for the privilege. The shared showers are hot, and there's a 10% discount for HI members.

Koala Den (☎ 622-6467; ktourspotosi@hotmail.com; Junín 56; dm B$35-50, d with bathroom B$130-150) The colorful and clean Koala is a favorite for its traveler-friendly facilities and backpacker-social vibe. The dorms and rooms are cozy, with bedspreads that have designs ranging from Dr Seuss to Garfield. Amenities include a kitchen, a TV room with a DVD collection, book exchange, free internet access, 24-hour hot showers, heating from 6pm, and a pleasant lounge area. A small continental breakfast is included.

Hostal María Victoria (☎ 622-2132; Chuquisaca 148; s/d B$40/70, with bathroom B$70/90) This attractive hostel occupies an old colonial home at the end of a quiet lane. The rooms surround a classic whitewashed and tree-shaded courtyard; there's also a roof terrace with

TINKU – THE ART OF RITUAL MAYHEM

Native to the northern part of Potosí department, *tinku* fighting, which takes place on May 3, ranks as one of the few Bolivian traditions that has yet to be commercialized. This bizarre practice lies deeply rooted in indigenous tradition and is thus often misunderstood by outsiders, who can make little sense of the violent and often grisly spectacle.

Tinku may be best interpreted as a type of ritualized means of discharging tensions between different indigenous communities. Fights between *campesinos* are very rare in these communities in daily life. Festivities begin with singing and dancing, but participants eventually drink themselves into a stupor. As a result, celebrations may well erupt into drunken mayhem and frequently violence, as alcohol-charged emotions are unleashed in hostile encounters.

A *tinku* usually lasts two or three days, when men and women in brightly colored traditional dress hike in from surrounding communities. The hats worn by the men strongly resemble those originally worn by the Spanish conquistadores, but are topped, Robin Hood style, with one long, fluorescent feather.

On the first evening, the communities parade through town to the accompaniment of *charangos* and *zampoñas* (a type of pan pipe). Periodically, the revelers halt and form two concentric circles, with women on the inside and the men in the outer circle. The women begin singing a typically repetitious and cacophonous chant while the men run in a circle around them. Suddenly, everyone stops and launches into a powerful stomping dance. Each group is headed by at least one person – usually a man – who uses a whip to urge on any man whom he perceives isn't keeping up with the rhythm and the pace.

This routine may seem harmless enough, except that alcohol plays a significant and controlling role. Most people carry bottles filled with *puro* (rubbing alcohol), which is the drink of choice, if the intent is to quickly become totally plastered. By nightfall, each participating community retreats to a designated house to drink *chicha* until they pass out.

This excessive imbibing inevitably results in social disorder, and by the second day the drunk participants tend to grow increasingly aggressive. As they roam the streets, they encounter people from other communities with whom they may have some quarrel, either real or imagined. Common complaints include anything from land disputes to extramarital affairs to the theft of farm animals, and may well result in a challenge to fight.

The situation rapidly progresses past yelling and cursing to pushing and shoving, before it turns into rather mystical – almost choreographed – warfare. Seemingly rhythmically, men strike each other's heads and upper bodies with extended arms (in fact, this has been immortalized in the *tinku* dance, which is frequently performed during Carnaval *entradas* – entrance processions – especially in highly traditional Oruro). To augment the hand-to-hand combat, the fighters may also throw rocks at their opponents, occasionally causing serious injury or death. Any fatalities, however, are resignedly considered a blood offering to Pachamama in lieu of a llama sacrifice for the same purpose.

The best known and arguably most violent *tinku* takes place in the village of Macha during the first couple of weeks of May, while the villages of Ocurí and Toracarí, among others, also host *tinkus*.

As you'd imagine, few foreigners aspire to witness this private and often violent tradition, which categoricallly cannot be thought of as a tourist attraction, and many people who have attended insist they'd never do it again. For the terminally curious, however, Koala Tours and Altiplano Tours in Potosí conduct culturally sensitive – and patently less-than-comfortable – visits to several of the main *tinku* festivities. Note, however, that if you do go it will be at your own risk. Keep a safe distance from the participants and always remain on the side of the street to avoid being trapped in the crowd. When walking around the village, maintain a low profile, speak in soft tones and ignore any taunting cries of 'gringo.' Also, bear in mind that these traditional people most definitely do not want hordes of foreign tourists gawking at them and snapping photos; avoid photographing individuals without their express permission and do not dance or parade with the groups unless you receive a clear invitation to do so.

views. A small breakfast is included and there's a tour agency on site. Note there's an eight-minute shower limit.

La Casona Hostal (☎ 623-0523; www.hotelpotosi .com; Chuquisaca 460; s/d/tr B$45/70/105, with bathroom B$81/122/183) A restored 18th-century colonial house at the centre of town, with rooms set around a yellow atrium. Recently opened, it's a great spot to meet other travelers. There's a money exchange, a shared kitchen, a small cinema (B$3 per film) and internet terminals (B$2). The eight-person dorm costs just B$30 and breakfast is included.

Hostel Compañía de Jesús (☎ 622-3173; Chuquisaca 445; s/d/tr B$50/80/110, with bathroom B$70/110/140) For sparkling clean rooms, firm mattresses, lots of blankets and a friendly atmosphere, stay in this old but freshly painted Carmelite monastery with a leafy courtyard and two patios. It's a lovely building, but not for people who feel the cold too much. Rooms are spacious and come with TVs and breakfast; room No 18 is especially nice.

Hostal San José (☎ 622-4394; Oruro 171; s/d B$60/120, with bathroom B$160) This cheap place has a cheery welcome and decent location; a second floor was going up at research time. Cheaper rooms are pokey with low ceilings so it's worth paying the extra for a better room: more warmth, an electric socket and a bigger bed with a less lumpy mattress.

Hostal Felimar (☎ /fax 622-4357; Junín 14; s/d B$50/80, s/d/tr/ste with bathroom B$90/130/160/220) This pleasant and centrally located hostel has some low-ceilinged rooms and some nicer upstairs rooms with balconies affording views over the colonial street below. A small breakfast is included and there's a great suite on the top floor.

MIDRANGE

Hotel El Turista (☎ 622-2492; hotelturistapotosi@ hotmail.com; Lanza 19; s B$140, d B$200-220, tr/ste B$280/300; 🖳) This recently revamped hotel offers spacious and fairly comfortable rooms with heating, electric showers, TVs and superb views from the top floor. It's pretty good value, with an airy feel, nice wooden floors and vibrantly colored patio. Room No 34 has the best view; a junior suite has a nice alcove overlooking the street.

Hotel Jerusalén (☎ 622-4633; hoteljer@entelnet .bo; Oruro 143; s/d/tr B$150/250/330; 🖳) Popular

with visiting groups, this relaxed hotel is a dependable choice. Nobody would really claim that it's great value for money, but comfort counts; the staff can arrange all sorts of tours, and the rooms have quality gas showers and cable TV.

Macuquina Dora Hotel (☎ 623-0257; www .macuquinadorahotel.com; Camacho 243; s/d/tr B$160/260/340; 🖳) This pleasant if slightly faded modern hotel is in a handy central location. There's cordial service, and clean, attractive heated rooms with heart-shaped cushions on the frilly beds. The front rooms (Nos 301 to 303) have miles more light and space than the others; try to bag one. There's also a sauna, restaurant and roof terrace.

Hostal Las Tres Portadas (☎ 623-1558; www .tresportadas.com; Bolívar 1092; s B$200, d B$300-350, ste B$500; 🖳) Situated in one of Potosí's most characterful buildings and based around two pretty patios, this blue-colored hotel is well run and adequately heated. The rooms all have comfortable beds and come with minibar and excellent bathroom. The family suite is particularly appealing, but some of the ground floor rooms might be a little dark for some tastes and not all have showers. Ask to see a couple of rooms.

Hotel Santa Teresa (☎ 622-5270; www.hotel santateresa.com.bo; Ayacucho 43; s/d/tr B$220/380/ 480; 🖳) This well-appointed hotel is by the convent of the same name, in a quiet part of central Potosí. Built around a whitewashed courtyard, it has smallish but pleasant rooms; the upstairs units have more light. The restaurant, Rosicler, is one of the city's best, a somewhat formal dining experience that can be enjoyed in your room with less fuss.

TOP END

Hostal Colonial (☎ 622-4809; www.hostalcolonial potosi.bo.vg; Hoyos 8; s/d/tr/ste B$280/360/400/480; 🖳) In a well-kept colonial building near the main plaza, this warm, whitewashed retreat has smallish rooms with windows onto a central courtyard; all have minibars and cable TV, and some have bathtubs. It's a longstanding favorite with midrange travelers, but perhaps feels in need of a little facelift. Nevertheless, it still boasts very helpful English-speaking staff and a great location.

Hotel Cima Argentum (☎ 622-9538; www.hca -potosi.com; Villazón 239; s/d B$310/350, ste B$440- 470; 🖳) This professionally run place with a light-flooded patio is a handsome, somewhat formal choice with decent facilities, including safes and minibars in every room, and off-street parking. The suites are a good choice for families, and all the rooms have good bathrooms, heating and wi-fi. The international restaurant offers room service.

Hotel Coloso Potosí (☎ 622-2627; www.potosihotel.com; Bolívar 965; s/d B$495/636, ste B$707-884; 🖥 🖳) Potosí's latest and only five-star opening, it has all the perks of a luxury hotel – spick-and-span rooms with minibars, heating and wi-fi – but suffers from a stuffy formal atmosphere. There's a pool, a restaurant, a sauna and room service. Some rooms come with great city views.

Eating

There are several appealing restaurants in Potosí: good spots to ward off the nighttime chill with a hearty meal.

RESTAURANTS

Doña Eugenia (☎ 626-2247; cnr Santa Cruz & Ortega; dishes B$10-40; 🕓 9:30am-12:30pm, closed Wed) Potosí residents swear by this convivial local restaurant at the northern end of town. Head there early (around 10am is best) to make sure you get some of the legendary *kala purca* (thick maize soup with a hot rock in it). Other specialties include a hearty pork stew *(fricasé)* only served on Sunday.

Pizzeria El Mana (☎ 623-0881; Bustillos 1080; almuerzo B$12) You can't beat this family-style locals' favorite right opposite Casa de Moneda for its great-value lunches. The blue-painted spot is simple both in decor and cuisine. At night, they serve pizzas only (B$12 to B$21).

Manzana Mágica (☎ 7183-6312; Oruro 239; mains B$12-20; 🕓 8:30am-3pm & 5:30-10pm Mon-Sat) This is a worthwhile, strictly vegetarian spot known for its breakfast – muesli, juice, eggs and brown bread, and tasty soy steaks. Lunch is ultra-healthy and à la carte dinners are assertively spiced and portions are big.

Potocchi (☎ 622-2759; Millares 13; mains B$18-25) This pleasant family-run place has a rustic vibe and serves llama steak and quinoa soup as the specialties, and plenty of vegetarian choices. It hosts an acoustic *peña* (folk music performance; cover B$15) nightly during the high season; on Wednesday and Friday otherwise.

4060 (☎ 622-2623; Hoyos 1; mains B$18-60; 🕓 4pm-midnight) This spacious contemporary café-bar has earned plenty of plaudits for its pizzas, burgers and Mexican food (and paella, if you order it in advance) and as a sociable spot for a drink. There's a good beer selection.

El Mesón (☎ 622-3087; cnr Tarija & Linares; mains B$25-38) The air at this vaulted restaurant on a corner of the plaza is heavy with smells of warm garlic. The elaborate menu is somewhat French, with food (steak, pasta, salads) that is a tad overpriced but nonetheless excellent. The attractive ambience adds to the experience.

El Fogón (☎ 622-4969; Oruro & Frías; almuerzo B$30, mains B$30-45; 🕓 noon-11pm) This spacious, brightly lit central restaurant is popular with travelers for its range of international and Bolivian food, including llama steaks. In truth, it's not what it was – portions aren't huge, and the service leaves much to be desired.

CAFES

Confitería Capricornio (Paseo Blvd 11; mains B$6-17; 🕓 9am-10pm) Packed with students in the evening, this quick-bite eatery with a funky old-school vibe serves soup, fast food, pizza, sandwiches, spaghetti, coffee and juices.

Chaplin Café (Matos near Quijarro; meals B$10-20; 🕓 7am-noon & 4-10:30pm) Friendly and comfortable, this place serves mostly Bolivian fare with a few international, including Mexican, dishes. They do decent breakfasts too.

Cherry's Salon de Té (☎ 622-5320; Padilla 8; mains B$12-25; 🕓 8am-10pm) Open all afternoon, this cafe makes a nice but very slow pit stop while you're out exploring the town. The apple strudel, chocolate cake and lemon meringue pie are superb. They also serve light meals and breakfasts.

Café de la Merced (Iglesia de la Merced, Hoyos s/n; light meals B$15; 🕓 11am-12:30pm & 2-6pm) You couldn't ask for a better location than this rooftop cafe: atop the Iglesia de la Merced, right by the bells, with stellar city views. They serve very tasty juices, adequate coffee, delicious cakes and light meals; you may have to wait for a table though, as it's a small space.

Café de la Plata (☎ 622-6085; Plaza 10 de Noviembre; mains B$15-30; 🕓 9:30am-11pm) This handsome place is cozy and chic in a restored sort of way, and a good place to hang out.

There are rich espressos, magazines to read and wine served by the glass. Pastas, cakes, salads, sandwiches; it's all pretty tasty.

Café Cultural Kaypichu (☎ 623-0611; Millares 14; mains B$17-30; 7:30am-2pm & 5-11pm Tue-Sun) A peaceful and relaxed mainly vegetarian spot, good at any time of day, starting with healthy breakfasts (10 different varieties), and heading through sandwiches to pasta and pizza dinners, and regular nighttime entertainment of folk music on weekends.

Stalls in the market *comedor* (dining hall) serve inexpensive breakfasts of bread, pastries and coffee. Downstairs there are some excellent juice stands.

Most Bolivians acknowledge, when pushed, that Potosí does the best *salteñas* – juicy, spicy and oh-so-tasty. Go no further than **La Salteña** (Padilla 6) or **Malpartida** (Bolívar 644), where one of these delicious items goes for B$3.50. Cheese or meat empanadas are sold around the market until early afternoon, and in the evening, street vendors sell cornmeal and cheese *humitas*.

Drinking

The atmospheric **La Casona Pub** (☎ 622-2954; Frías 41; 6pm-midnight Mon-Sat) is tucked away in the historic 1775 home of the royal envoy sent to administer the mint. It's a memorable, friendly watering hole with pub grub. On Friday it stages live music performances. **Sumaj Orcko** (☎ 622-3703; Quijarro 46; 10am-10pm) is a popular restaurant with a low-lit, comfortable bar on the corner.

Entertainment

The Potocchi cafe-restaurant (p239) hosts acoustic *peñas*.

Potosí has two cinemas, the **Multicine Universal** (☎ 622-6133; Padilla 31) and the **Cine Universitario** (☎ 622-3049; Bolívar 893), which both screen relatively recent releases; both charge B$10 per screening.

Real Potosí, the local soccer team, is one of Bolivia's best, and play at the town stadium. When they make the Libertadores Cup, a South American club championship, even the best Brazilian sides dread drawing them and having to play at this altitude!

Shopping

Favored Potosí souvenirs include silver and tin articles available in stands near the market entrance on Calle Oruro; many of them were produced in the village of Caiza, 80km south of Potosí, which now has its own co-op store featuring naturally dyed wool items. Here, small dangly earrings, hoop earrings, spoons and platters cost between B$8 and B$35.

A recommended store is **Arte Nativo** (☎ 622-5640; Sucre 30), selling ecologically sound, indigenous handiwork and so improving the economic condition of rural women who weave with the naturally dyed wool of sheep, llamas and alpacas. **Artesanías Palomita's** (Museo Etno-Indumentario; ☎ 622-3258; Serrudo 148-152; 9am-noon & 3-6pm Mon-Fri, 9am-noon Sat) is half-shop, half-museum and has costumes and weavings from each of the 16 provinces of Potosí department.

Getting There & Away

AIR

Potosí boasts the world's highest commercial airport, Aeropuerto Capitán Rojas. In the early 1990s the runway was extended to 4000m to accommodate larger planes. **AeroSur** (☎ 622-8988; Cobija 25) had flights for a while, but no more.

BUS & SHARED TAXI

All road routes into Potosí are quite scenic, and arriving by day will always present a dramatic introduction to the city. The **bus terminal** (☎ 624-3361) is about 15 minutes on foot downhill (1km) from the center, and *micros* and minibuses (B$1) run every minute or two. The more inviting new terminal is currently under construction on the northwestern edge of town, in the barrio of Las Lecherías, but the opening date is not yet set. Note that the higher prices refer to holiday season.

Numerous *flotas* offer a daily overnight service to La Paz (B$40 to B$60, eight hours) via Oruro (B$25, five hours) departing around 8pm; you can also opt for a *bus cama* (B$60 to B$80).

Buses leave for Tupiza (B$60 to B$100, seven hours) and Villazón (B$60 to B$100, nine hours) daily in the evening. Buses to Tarija (B$50 to B$70, 12 hours) run twice, early in the morning and in the evening; *bus cama* is available (B$70 to B$100). There are numerous nighttime services to Cochabamba (B$40 to B$60, eight hours).

Quite a few *flotas* leave for Sucre (B$20, three hours) between 7am and 5pm. Alternatively, you can take a shared taxi (B$30 for up to four people, 2½ hours), which is quicker and comfier, to Potosí. Most hotels can help arrange shared taxis, which run till midnight daily. Try **Cielito Express** (☎ 624-6040), **Infinito** (☎ 624-5040), **Correcaminos** (☎ 624-3383) or **Expreso Potosí** (☎ 624-6600). Expect high velocity.

If you prefer to take the least expensive route, *micros* (B$15 to B$20, five hours) leave from the *tranca* 500m north of Plaza Uyuni all day when full.

Buses to Uyuni (B$30 to B$40, six hours) depart three times daily (11am, noon and 6:30pm) from just below the railway line, higher up on Av Antofagasta with Av Tinkuy. The rugged route is quite spectacular.

Getting Around

Micros and minibuses (B$1) shuttle between the center and the Cerro Rico mines, as well as the bus terminal. Taxis charge B$4 per person around the center and to the bus terminal.

AROUND POTOSÍ

The **Lagunas de Kari Kari** are artificial lakes constructed in the late 16th and early 17th centuries by 20,000 indigenous slaves to provide water for the city and for hydropower to run the city's 82 *ingenios*. Of the 32 original lakes, only 25 remain and all have been abandoned – except by waterfowl, which appreciate the incongruous surface water in this otherwise stark region.

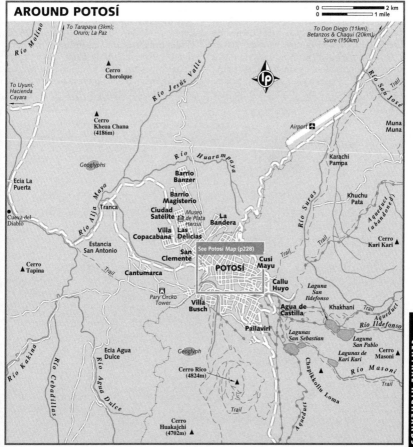

AROUND POTOSÍ

The easiest way to visit Lagunas de Kari Kari is with a Potosí tour agency (p235). If you prefer to strike out on your own, carry food, water and warm clothing. In a long day, you can have a good look around the *lagunas* and the fringes of the Cordillera de Kari Kari, but it may also be rewarding to camp overnight in the mountains. Access is fairly easy, with public transport from Potosí. Inquire with one of the agencies in town and make sure you get a good map of the area. The Cordillera de Kari Kari is included on the IGM topo sheet *Potosí (East)* – sheet 6435 (p230).

For a peaceful retreat or some comfortable hill walking, visit **Hacienda Cayara**, which lies 25km down the valley northwest of Potosí. Set amid lovely hills at 3550m, this beautiful working farm produces vegetables and milk for the city. It dates back to colonial times and these days, it's owned by the English Aitken family, who converted it into a hostel in 1992. The hostel is like a museum: an opulent colonial mansion furnished with original paintings and period furniture. Guests have the use of the fire-place and extensive library, which includes works dating from the 17th century. For bookings (B$180 per person with breakfast) and how to get here, contact **Señora María Luisa Serrano** (☎ /fax 622-6380; www.cayara.com.bo; lunch & dinner B$50, tea B$20).

Belief in the curative powers of **Tarapaya** (3600m), the most frequently visited **hot-springs** area around Potosí, dates back to Inca times. It even served as the holiday destination for Inca Huayna Capac, who would come all the way from Cuzco (now in Peru) to bathe. The most interesting sight is the 30°C **Ojo del Inca**, a perfectly round, green lake in a low volcanic crater, 100m in diameter. Along the river below the crater are several *balnearios* (resorts) with medicinal thermal pools utilizing water from the lake. *Remolinos* (whirlpools) make bathing here a hazardous affair. *Camiones* leave for Tarapaya (B$4, 30 minutes) from Plaza Chuquimia near the bus terminal in Potosí roughly every half hour from 7am to 7pm. Taxis cost about B$50 for up to four people. The last *micro* from Tarapaya back to Potosi leaves between 5pm and 6pm.

South Central Bolivia & The Chaco

Famed for its dances, wines and an almost Mediterranean character, the isolated department of Tarija is a Bolivia that not many travelers know. It shows the country in a guise of tranquility, with steely blue skies stretching above the gnarled vines that braid the windswept, dry land.

The culture here gravitates towards neighboring Argentina and dreams of being closer to faraway Andalucía. The references to the region's resemblance to the south of Spain were started by Tarija's founder, Luis de Fuentes, who was seemingly anxious to lend a bit of home to a foreign land. He thus named the river flowing past the city of Tarija the Guadalquivir (after Andalucía's biggest river), and left the *chapacos* – as *tarijeños* (Tarija locals) are otherwise known – with a lilting dialect of European Spanish.

Tarija's far eastern regions are full of petroleum-rich scrublands, backed by stark highlands and surrounded by the red earth of the Gran Chaco. This is where you'll find Bolivia's hottest town – Villamontes can reach up to 120°F in the relentless summer sun. Further down, reaching as far south as you can go before you hit the Argentine border, lie the lush sugarcane-producing valleys and oil-pumping veins that feed the prosperous town of Bermejo.

HIGHLIGHTS

- Taste the world's highest-grown wines in **Tarija** (p245)
- Get revolutionary on the **Camino del Ché** in Camiri (p259)
- Hike the fascinating Inca Trail in the **Reserva Biológica Cordillera de Sama** (p254) and discover wildlife on the way
- Discover spectacular Chaco wildlife in the **Parque Nacional y Área Natural de Manejo Integrado Aguaragüe** (p258) and the **Reserva Privada de Patrimonio Natural de Corbalán** (p259) and **Reserva Nacional de Flora y Fauna Tariquía** (p255)
- Get down and party Tarija-style at the **Fiesta de San Roque** (p248)

■ TELEPHONE CODE: 4   ■ POPULATION: 391,200   ■ ELEVATION: 380M TO 2200M

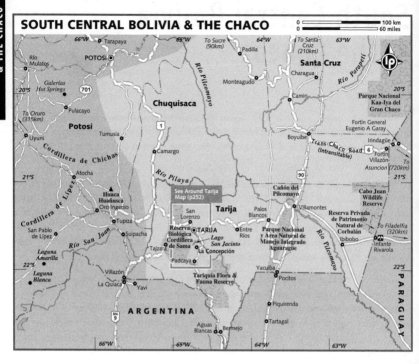

SOUTH CENTRAL BOLIVIA & THE CHACO

History

Prior to the 1932–35 Chaco War, Bolivia had long claimed rights to the Chaco, an inhospitable region beneath which rich oilfields were mooted to lie. The disputed area of about 240,680 sq km stretched northeast of the Paraguay and Pilcomayo Rivers in Paraguay, and included the 168,765-sq-km chunk of Argentina north of the Río Bermejo. With political turmoil in Paraguay causing a distraction, and economic hardship in Bolivia providing a stimulus, the Bolivians saw their opportunity and began to slowly advance into Paraguayan territory.

After losing the War of the Pacific in 1884, Bolivia was desperate to have the Chaco as an outlet to the Atlantic via the Río Paraguay. Hoping that physical possession would be interpreted as official sovereignty, the Bolivian army set up a fort at Piquirenda on the Río Pilcomayo. Bolivia then refused to relinquish rights to Fuerte Vanguardia, its only port on the Paraguay river (and not in Bolivian territory). In 1928 Paraguay responded by sending its army to seize the fort, and although things got

heated, both sides maintained a conciliatory attitude, hoping that a peaceful solution might be possible.

Things, however, didn't go as planned. During settlement talks in Washington and under orders from President Daniel Salamanca, the Bolivian army tried to seize land without authorization, triggering full-scale warfare. Bolivia was widely seen as the aggressor in diplomatic circles and its case generated little support. The hot, dry climate made access to fresh water a decisive factor in the war, with capturing and keeping access to wells a key strategy. Conditions were miserable, soldiers were ill-equipped and disease was rife, and as a result casualties on both sides were heavy.

As the war progressed the Bolivians were driven back beyond their current borders, though they continued to fight, with their most successful battle in the town of Villamontes in 1934. Though no decisive victory was reached in the war, both nations had grown weary of fighting and peace negotiations held four years later awarded most of the disputed territory to Paraguay. To this day, no oil has ever been found in the Paraguayan Chaco, though prospectors are still searching.

Climate

This is the area of Bolivia where you most feel the country's proximity to the equator and its distance from the sea. Tarija's Mediterranean climate quickly disappears as soon as you head downhill, replaced by scorching aridity and a merciless sun. The dry season in the region lasts from April to November.

National Parks & Reserves

Remote, wild and off the beaten track, South Central Bolivia's parks and reserves are perfect for hardcore adventure seekers. Infrastructure is almost nonexistent, but a visit to any of the reserves will make a lasting impression. Those covered in this chapter include the Reserva Biológica Cordillera de Sama (p254), Reserva Nacional de Flora y Fauna Tariquía (p255), Parque Nacional y Área Natural de Manejo Integrado Aguaragüe (p258) and the Reserva Privada de Patrimonio Natural de Corbalán (p259).

Getting There & Around

Most people visit Bolivia's far south on the way to or from somewhere else. Overland connections from Argentina and Paraguay and other regions within Bolivia involve long bus rides. Tarija has the biggest airport in the area and scheduled flights to La Paz, Sucre and other major towns go several times a week.

Public transportation runs frequently between towns, but you'll need a 4WD to get almost anywhere else. Few roads are paved so prepare yourself for hauls that take longer than they should.

SOUTH CENTRAL BOLIVIA

The region's capital is a quiet provincial town, with few visitors and some quality Argentine-style meat houses. The mild climate has attracted a few foreign settlers in the recent years, and tourist facilities and activities are beginning to develop. The wine country surrounding the city of Tarija offers some good tasting opportunities.

Despite the fact that the Bolivians from bigger cities regard South Central Bolivia as a half-civilized backwater, and that 'chapaco' is the butt of tasteless jokes told in La Paz, Tarija is a pleasant place to stop off on your way to Argentina.

TARIJA

pop 132,000 / elevation 1905m

This little city is as laid-back as they get, with palm-lined squares, sizzling Argentine barbecues, sprawling bar and cafe terraces, and tight streets with narrow pavements. Nothing much happens in Tarija, but the city has some interesting colonial architecture and grows on those who stay a while taking in the atmosphere. If you have time, go around some of the surrounding wineries and try the Bolivian *vino* or the throatheating *singani* (distilled grape spirit).

History

Tarija was founded as La Villa de San Bernardo de Tarixa, by Don Luis de Fuentes y Vargas on July 4, 1574, under the orders of Viceroy Don Francisco de Toledo. In 1810 the region declared independence from Spanish rule. Although the breakaways weren't taken seriously by the Spanish, the situation did erupt into armed warfare on April 15, 1817. At the Batalla de la Tablada, the *chapacos* won a major victory over the Spanish forces. In the early 19th century, Tarija actively supported Bolivia's struggle for independence. Although Argentina wanted to annex the agriculturally favorable area, Tarija opted to join the Bolivian Republic when it was established in 1825.

Orientation

Street numbers are preceded by an O (*oeste* – west) for those addresses west of Calle Colón and an E (*este* – east) for those east of Colón; addresses north of Av Victor Paz Estenssoro (Av Las Américas) take an N.

Information

Between 1pm and 4pm Tarija becomes a virtual ghost town. Conduct all your business in the morning or you'll have to wait until after the siesta.

EMERGENCY

Hospital San Juan de Dios (☎ 664-5555; Santa Cruz s/n)
Police (☎ 664-2222; cnr Campero & 15 de Abril)

TARIJA

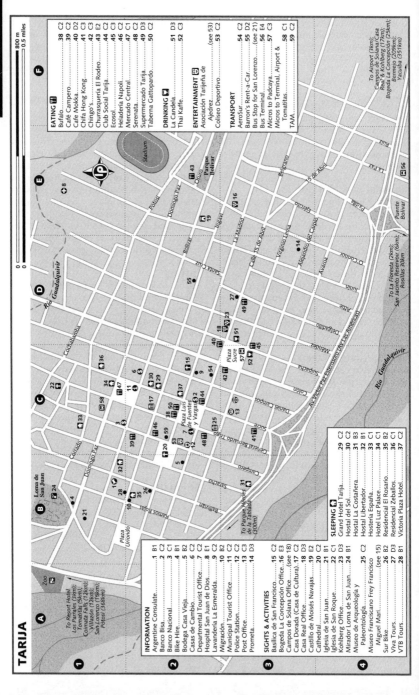

INFORMATION
Argentine Consulate.....................1 B1
Banco Bisa...................................2 C2
Banco Nacional............................3 C1
Bike Hire....................................4 B1
Bodega Casa Vieja.......................5 B2
Casas de Cambio.........................6 C2
Departmental Tourist Office.........7 C2
Hospital San Juan de Dios............8 E1
Lavandería La Esmeralda..............9 C2
Migración..................................10 B2
Municipal Tourist Office..............11 C2
Police Station............................12 C3
Post Office.................................13 C3
Prometa....................................14 D3

SIGHTS & ACTIVITIES
Basílica de San Francisco............15 C2
Bogeda La Concepción Office......16 E3
Campos de Solana Office........(see 18)
Casa Dorada (Casa de Cultura)....17 C2
Casa Real Office.........................18 D3
Castillo de Moisés Navajas..........19 E2
Cathedral...................................20 B1
Iglesia de San Juan.....................21 B1
Iglesia de San Roque..................22 C1
Kohlberg Office..........................23 D3
Mirador Loma de San Juan..........24 B1
Museo de Arqueología y
  Paleontología...........................25 C2
Museo Franciscano Frey Francisco
  Miguel Marí........................(see 15)
Sur Bike....................................26 B2
Viva Tours.................................27 D3
VTB Tours..................................28 B1

SLEEPING
Grand Hotel Tarija.....................29 C2
Hostal del Sol............................30 D3
Hostal La Costañera....................31 B3
Hostal Libertador.......................32 B1
Hostería España.........................33 C1
Hotel Luz Palace........................34 C1
Residencial El Rosario..................35 B2
Residencial Zeballos...................36 C1
Victoria Plaza Hotel....................37 C2

EATING
Bufalo......................................38 C2
Café Campero............................39 C2
Café Mokka...............................40 D2
Chifa Hong Kong.......................41 C3
Chingo's...................................42 C3
Churrasquería El Rodeo...............43 E2
Club Social Tarija.......................44 C2
Ecosol......................................45 C3
Heladería Napoli........................46 C2
Mercado Central........................47 C1
Serenata....................................48 C2
Supermercado Tarija..................49 D3
Taberna Gattopardo...................50 C2

DRINKING
La Candela.................................51 D3
Thai Kaffe.................................52 C3

ENTERTAINMENT
Asociación Tarijeña de
  Ajedrez..............................(see 53)
Coliseo Deportivo......................53 C2

TRANSPORT
AeroSur....................................54 C2
Barron's Rent-a-Car....................55 D2
Bus Stop for San Lorenzo.......(see 21)
Bus Terminal.............................56 E4
Micros to Padcaya......................57 C3
Micros to Terminal, Airport &
  Tomatitas.................................58 C1
TAM...59 C2

IMMIGRATION
Migración (☎ 664-3594; Ingavi 789) For entry/exit stamps or to extend your stay.

TELEPHONE & INTERNET ACCESS
Internet places are ten a penny and usually have phone cabins incorporated as well. Try along Bolívar for decent connections (per hour B$3 to B$4).

LAUNDRY
Out of hours at the lavandería, ask at larger hotels which charge B$2 to B$3 per item.
Lavandería La Esmeralda (☎ 664-2043; La Madrid 0-157; ☺ 8:30am-12:30pm & 3-7:30pm Mon-Fri, 8am-1pm Sat) Does a quick machine wash and dry service for B$12 per kilo.

MONEY
There are numerous ATMs around the plaza. **Casas de cambio** (Bolívar) change US dollars and Argentine pesos. Banco Bisa and Banco Nacional, both on Sucre, will change traveler's checks.

POST OFFICE
Post office (cnr Sucre & Lema)

TOURIST INFORMATION
The municipality has a helpful tourist website: www.tarija.bo, in Spanish. There is also a tourist booth at the **bus terminal** (☎ 666-7701) which is open when the main offices are closed.
Departmental tourist office (☎ 663-1100; cnr 15 de Abril & Trigo; ☺ 8:30am-noon & 3-6pm Mon-Fri) Distributes basic town maps and is reasonably helpful with queries regarding sites within and around town.
Municipal tourist office (☎ 663-3581; cnr Bolívar & Sucre; ☺ 8:30am-noon & 3-6pm Mon-Fri) Not much material or information, but friendly staff.

Sights
You can see everything Tarija has to offer in an afternoon. Wandering around the squares and checking out the remaining colonial atmosphere are the main attractions.

MUSEO DE ARQUEOLOGÍA Y PALEONTOLOGÍA
The free university-run **Archaeology & Paleontology Museum** (cnr Lema & Trigo; ☺ 8am-noon & 3-6pm Mon-Sat) provides a good oveview of the prehistoric creatures and the early peoples that once inhabited the Tarija area.

Downstairs you'll see the well-preserved remains of several animals: *megatherium,* a giant ground sloth which was the size of an elephant; *glyptodon,* a prehistoric armadillo-like creature about the size of a Volkswagen Beetle; *lestodon,* another ground sloth which resembled a giant-clawed aardvark; *scelidotherium,* a small ground sloth; *smilodon,* the saber-toothed tiger; and *Cuvierionius tarijensi,* a fossil elephant discovered by the great French zoologist Cuvier close to the city.

Displays are accompanied by artistic representations of how the animals appeared in the flesh. The archaeological section displays ancient tools, weapons, copper items, textiles and pottery from all over southern Bolivia.

The rooms upstairs focus on history, geology and anthropology, containing displays of old household implements, weapons, ceramics and various prehistoric hunting tools, including a formidable cudgel known as a *rompecabezas* (head-breaker). Look for the desiccated, mummified corpse of an adult human from the Pampagrande area that has shrunk via natural processes to measure just 35cm long.

CASA DORADA (CASA DE LA CULTURA)
The **Gilded House** (☎ 664-4606; Ingavi 0-370; ☺ 8am-noon & 2:30-6:30pm Mon-Fri) dates back to 1930, when it was one of several properties owned by the wealthy Tarija landowner Moisés Navajas (often described as Bolivia's Teddy Roosevelt) and his wife, Esperanza Morales. The building appears imposing and impressive on tourist brochures, but in reality the exterior is sloppily splashed with gold and silver paint, and the roof is topped with a row of liberating angels.

The ground floor is painted a scintillating shade of purple and the frescoes could have been the work of precocious preschoolers. There's also a winning kitsch collection of lamps: rose lamps, peacock lamps, morning glory lamps and, of course, crystal chandeliers that sprout light bulbs. Perhaps the most worthwhile relic is the *funola,* an early type of player piano that produced music by forcing air through a strip of perforated paper. The building now belongs to the university and houses the Casa de la Cultura. Brief guided tours are sometimes offered for a small donation.

CHURCHES

Architecturally, Tarija's most unusual church and major landmark is the bright, white 1887 **Iglesia de San Roque**. Dedicated to the city's patron saint, the church sits on the hill at the end of General Bernardo Trigo, lording it over the town. Its balcony once served as a lookout post.

The rather dull-looking **cathedral** (cnr Campero & La Madrid) contains the remains of prominent *chapacos,* including Tarija's founder, Don Luis de Fuentes y Vargas. It was constructed in 1611 and has some interesting stained glass depicting harvest scenes.

The **Basílica de San Francisco** (cnr Campos & La Madrid) was founded in 1606 and is now a national monument. The 16th-century convent library and archives, which may conjure up images from *The Name of the Rose,* can be used only by researchers who have been granted permission by the Franciscan order. Inside the basilica, the free **Museo Franciscano Frey Francisco Miguel Mari** (8am-6pm Mon-Fri) displays ecumenical paintings, sculptures and artifacts.

The **Iglesia de San Juan,** at the top of Bolívar, was constructed in 1632. Here the Spanish signed their surrender to the liberation army after the Batalla de la Tablada. The garden serves as a *mirador* (lookout) of Tarija and its dramatic backdrop of brown mountains.

MIRADOR LOMA DE SAN JUAN

This park area above the tree-covered slopes of the **Loma de San Juan** provides a grand city view and is a favorite with smooching students. Climb uphill to the end of Calle Bolívar, then turn right behind the hill and follow the footpath up the slope that faces away from the city.

CASTILLO DE MOISÉS NAVAJAS

The exterior of this oddly prominent and deteriorating **private mansion** (Castillo de Beatriz; Bolívar E-644) is worth a look for its garish blue-and-white striped 'bananas in pyjamas' extravagance. It's still inhabited but is occasionally open for informal tours – check at the tourist office.

Tours

For wine tours and adventurous ecotrips to Tarija's hinterlands – including four nearby national reserves – it's tough to beat **Viva Tours** (/fax 663-8325; cnr 15 de Abril & Delgadillo), which charges between B$80 and B$150 per person for half or full-day tours. **VTB Tours** (664-3372; Ingavi 0-784) also runs trips to most sites of interest around the city and the region. For quality biking and hiking with a knowledgeable guide in the surrounding hills and stunning countryside, try **Sur Bike** (7619-4200), which comes highly recommended by readers.

Festivals & Events

Tarija is one of Bolivia's most festive towns, especially around **Carnaval** (see the boxed text, opposite). If you're in town during the last week of March, check out the **Fiesta de Leche y Queso** outside of town in Rosillas.

APRIL

In keeping with its gaucho heritage, Tarija stages an annual rodeo in Parque Héroes de la Tablada, beginning on the departmental holiday. **Rodeo Chapaco** (April 15-21) includes all the standard cowboy events. Take *micro C* from the center.

AUGUST

Tarija's well-known **Fiesta de San Roque** (August 16) gives thanks to the saint whose appearance supposedly marked the end of the plague and leprosy in the area. The main celebration, however, doesn't begin until the first Sunday of September and then continues for eight days. It features traditional musical performances and a colorful Chuncho (an indigenous tribe) procession in which the participants wear 'cover-all' clothes traditionally worn by lepers. A statue of the saint is carried, his clothes being changed daily during the festival, and believers line the streets asking him to cure their family's ills.

OCTOBER

The annual **Fiesta de las Flores** (2nd Sunday in October) is a religious celebration dedicated to the Virgin of Rosario. It begins with a procession, which sets off from the Iglesia de San Juan. Along the route, spectators shower participants with petals. The highlight of the day is a colorful fair and bazaar in which the faithful spend lavishly for the benefit of the Church.

Ask around about the **arts fair** in October and about the **Serrano Ham & Cheese Festival**.

HOW TO PARTY CHAPACO-STYLE

Tarija is Bolivia's music and dance region, famous for its unique traditions and loud, colorful festivals, especially during Carnaval, when all *chapacos* (Tarija locals) come out to dance, sing and party the days away. If you find yourself in the region during a fiesta, here's what to expect.

The folk music of Tarija features unusual woodwind instruments, such as the *erque* and *quenilla*, the *caña* and the *camacheña*. The song that accompanies the music is called a *copla* – a direct import from Spain – with comic verses, sung in a duet, and the dance that tops it all off is the traditional Chuncho. Dancers wear colorful outfits, feathered headgear and masks, symbolizing the Chiriguano tribes and their long-term resistance of the conquerors.

Tarija's **Carnaval** is one of the most animated in Bolivia and brilliant fun. To launch the festivities, two Thursdays before Carnaval, Tarija celebrates the **Fiesta de Compadres**. This unique fiesta, celebrated the following Thursday, is Tarija's largest pre-Carnaval festival. It's assumed that the celebration, originating in the village of Pola de Siero, in the northern Spanish region of Asturias, was inspired by the wives of Spanish colonial authorities and soldiers, who saw to it that social customs and morals were strictly followed. It was eventually adopted by the local indigenous population and is now celebrated by the entire community with music, dancing and special basket tableaux constructed of bread known as *bollus preñaus*. There are flowers, fruits, tubers, small cakes and other gifts, all passed between female friends and relatives.

Throughout the Carnaval season, the streets fill with dancing, original *chapaco* (local Tarijan) music and colorfully costumed country folk who turn up in town for the event. There's a Grand Ball in the main plaza after the celebration and the entire town comes out for the dancing and performances by folkloric groups, bands and orchestras. Beware: water balloons figure prominently in the festivities.

On the Sunday after Carnaval, the barrio near the cemetery enacts a 'funeral' in which the devil is burned and buried in preparation for Lent. Paid mourners lend the ritual a morose air – although we suspect they're actually lamenting that they must remain vice free for the 40 days until Easter.

Sleeping

BUDGET

Residencial El Rosario (☎ 664-2942; Ingavi 777; s/d B$35/70, s with bathroom B$70) It's rare to find a budget place that is so well-tended, with freshly painted and clean, though rather small, rooms looking onto a quiet patio. There are reliable gas-heated showers, laundry sinks and a common cable TV room.

Hostería España (☎ 664-1790; Corrado 0-546; s/d B$40/80, with bathroom B$60/120) A decent budget option, though the slightly overpriced rooms are pretty cold in winter. The hot showers and a pleasant flowery patio keep it popular with long-term university student residents and there is plenty of tourist information at reception.

Residencial Zeballos (☎ 664-2068; Sucre N-966; s/d B$40/80, with bathroom B$80/140) Superficially the most attractive budget option, with dozens of potted plants and climbers giving the place a fresh, spring feel. However, make sure you see the room before you commit: the basement ones are grim and dark, so go for something upstairs.

MIDRANGE & TOP END

Hostal Libertador (☎ 664-4580; Bolívar 0-649; s/d with bathroom B$100/180) This central and welcoming place has dated en suite rooms with phones and cable TV. No fan or air-conditioning provided.

Grand Hotel Tarija (☎ 664-2684; Sucre N-770; s/d with bathroom B$160/300) One of the town oldies that's busy for lunch when locals flood in to the hotel restaurant. The spacious, ocher-colored rooms are comfortable and central, though some are ageing gracefully. Don't go for the patio-facing rooms or you'll have to have your curtains drawn all day.

Victoria Plaza Hotel (☎ 664-2600; hot_vi@entelnet .bo; cnr La Madrid & Sucre; s/d with bathrooms B$170/250; 💻) A charming, four-star place just off the main plaza, with lovely 1950s rooms decked with gleaming wooden floors, comfy beds and retro furnishing. All rooms are en suite (though the bathrooms are a bit dated) and have cable TV. A stylish café-bar, La Bella Epoca, is downstairs.

Hotel Luz Palace (☎ 664-2741; Sucre N-921; s/d B$180/250) Recently refurbished, this huge colonial hotel offers great value with its modern, spacious rooms. Breakfast is included in the price and the tourist agency downstairs will help you plan your trip.

Hostal La Costanera (☎ 664-2851; cnr Estenssoro & Saracho; s/d with bathroom B$180/280; 🖳 ⛄) Rooms here are elegant and decorated in caramels and sandy shades, with spacious bathrooms and great showers. There are phones, mini-bar, heaters (upon request) and parking, plus the staff is super friendly. Full buffet breakfast included. Lower rates may be negotiated for longer stays or in the low season.

Hostal del Sol (☎ 666-5259; www.hoteldelsoltarija .com; Sucre N-782; s/d with bathroom B$220/300; 🖳 ⛄) Among the nicest in town, Hostal del Sol has coffee-colored walls, flat screen TVs, marble floors and a bright, modern design all round. Friendly service, good breakfasts and free internet make this a great place to stay.

Resort Hotel Los Parrales (☎ 664-8444; www .losparraleshotel.com; Urbanización Carmen de Aranjuez; s/d B$805/980; 🖳 ⛄ 🏊) In a relaxed setting 3.5km from the center, Tarija's only five-star option offers you a complimentary cocktail when you arrive and has a spa, a giant Jacuzzi, and a lovely open-air dining area overlooking the countryside. The rooms are colonial-style luxury, with very comfy beds. Significant discounts (up to 45%) are available for stays of more than one night during the low season.

Eating

RESTAURANTS

Club Social Tarija (☎ 664-2108; 15 de Abril E-271; almuerzo B$15 ☽ lunch only Mon-Fri) Old-fashioned *almuerzos* are the favorite of the loyal crowd of monthly meal-plan subscribers.

Serenata (Trigo; almuerzo B$15) This *palapa*-roofed restaurant is an atmospheric place to enjoy a great value *almuerzo*, which includes a salad bar and a drink.

Chingo's (☎ 663-2222; Plaza Sucre; meals B$20-45) Juicy steaks are the name of the game at Chingo's, specializing in hefty Argentine beef *parrillada* (barbecued or grilled) with all the standard trimmings – rice, salad and potatoes. Pizzas and chicken dishes are also available for a similar price. Delivery to hotels is for a nominal fee.

Bufalo (☎ 665-0000; Plaza Luis de Fuentes y Vargas; mains B$26-55) Bufalo's ranch house setting is a clue to their meat-based menu, but this place also injects a portion of creativity into its dishes that takes it beyond the realm of the 'ordinary *churrasquería*'. Try for example *medallones de lomito con salsa de mariscos* (beef medallions in seafood sauce); if meat isn´t your thing, there is a wide selection of pizza, chicken and fish dishes to choose from.

Taberna Gattopardo (☎ 663-0656; Plaza Luis de Fuentes y Vargas; mains B$26-58) This welcoming European-run tavern is one of Tarija's most popular hangouts. There are good espressos and cappuccinos in the morning, well-prepared salads, burgers and *ceviche* (Peruvian citrus-marinated fish dish) at midday, and chicken fillets and fondue bourguignon in the evening.

La Floresta (☎ 664-2894; Carretera a San Jacinto, Barrio Germán Busch; buffet lunch B$30-40) A great place for pitchers of fresh lemonade and all-you-can-eat buffets of pork, chicken and salads, served in a lovely, leafy garden with a large swimming pool. Local families stream in on weekends when the atmosphere is particularly lively. It's a bit out of town, so get a taxi here – the staff will call one for the return journey.

Churrasquería El Rodeo (☎ 663-1696; Oruro E-749; mains B$35-45) With Argentina so close, it's not surprising that big slabs of red meat are popular in Tarija, and that is all that you get here. This sparkling and classy choice also has a salad bar.

Chifa Hong Kong (☎ 663-7076; Sucre N-235; mains B$40) Adjacent to a busy Chinese store, this place offers good food, cheap cocktails, huge lunches and an extensive Chinese menu, and its all priced the same to make it easier to calculate your bill! Delivery to hotels is also available.

QUICK EATS

Mercado Central (Sucre & Domingo Paz) At the northeast corner of the market, street vendors sell snacks and pastries unavailable in other parts of Bolivia, including delicious crêpe-like *panqueques*. Breakfast is served out the back, other cheap meals are upstairs, and you'll find fresh juices are in the produce section. Don't miss the huge bakery and sweets section off Bolívar.

Café Campero (Campero near Bolívar; mains B$10-30; ☽ dinner only Tue-Sun) Dive into the fabulous range of breads, cakes and pastries, including French-style baguettes, chocolate cake and *cuñapes* (cassava and cheese rolls). If you prefer to have yours to go, pop into the Palacio de las Masas next door, which is open in the morning.

Café Mokka (☎ 665-0505; Plaza Sucre; mains B$16-38) A stylish place with a pavement terrace overlooking the square, they serve not-amazing coffee, decent cocktails and good, light grub. Tables are decorated with weird arrangements of peanuts and coffee beans.

Heladería Napoli (Campero N-630; per kilo B$36) Serves simply divine scoops of ice cream until 8pm.

GROCERIES
Ecosol (Plaza Sucre) Pick up organic and ecofriendly foodstuffs from this interesting little corner shop.

Supermercado Tarija (cnr 15 de Abril & Delgadillo) Tarija's best supermarket is well-stocked with imported foodstuffs and a good wine selection.

Drinking & Entertainment
Tarija´s bar and café scene is vibrant, and many of the popular lunch spots during the day metamorphose into drinking dens after dark. Plaza Sucre is the hub of the activity for the younger generation.

La Candela (☎ 664-9191; Plaza Sucre; ✆ 9am-midnight Mon-Fri, 9am-2am Sat & Sun) French-owned, this thriving little bar-cafe, has a bohemian atmosphere, a great snack menu and live music at weekends.

Thai Kaffe (Plaza Sucre; ✆ 9am-midnight Mon-Fri, 10am-2am Sat & Sun) Popular with trendy twenty-somethings who gossip over a milkshake in the afternoon and gulp *singanis* in the evenings.

Keep an eye out for flyers advertising *peñas* (folk-music programs), usually held at restaurants on weekends. Entertaining basketball, *futsal* (five-a-side soccer) and volleyball games are played at the **Coliseo Deportivo** (Campero). After 6pm, chessheads can pick up a game next door at the **Asociación Tarijeña de Ajedrez** (Campero), where you can play for free if you respect club rules: no smoking and quiet, please.

Getting There & Away
AIR
The **Oriel Lea Plaza Airport** (☎ 664-2195) is 3km east of town off Av Victor Paz Estenssoro. **TAM** (☎ 664-2734; La Madrid 0-470) has Monday and Friday flights to Santa Cruz (B$558) and flights to La Paz (B$783) via Sucre (B$477) departing on Tuesday, Wednesday, Friday and Sunday. The short hop to Yacuiba (B$308) leaves on Wednesday and Saturday. **AeroSur** (☎ 901-1015555; 15 de Abril) flies three times a week to La Paz (B$850) and daily to Santa Cruz (B$661).

BUS
The **bus terminal** (☎ 663-6508) is at the east end of town, a 20-minute walk from the center along Av Victor Paz Estenssoro. Annoyingly, if you are looking for a quick getaway, almost all services leave in the afternoon between 4:30pm and 8:30pm, so you'll have to wait until then. Several *flotas* (long-distance bus companies) run buses to Potosí (B$70, 12 to 15 hours), continuing on to Oruro (B$90, 20 hours), Cochabamba (B$100, 26 hours) and Sucre (B$90, 18 hours). Services to Yacuiba (B$40, nine hours) leave between 6:30pm and 7:30pm. SAMA run a 7am service to Oruro and Expreso Tarija an 8am service to La Paz, but if you want to travel on either of these morning buses then you should buy your ticket in advance. Services to Santa Cruz (B$100, 24 hours) pass through Villamontes (B$50, seven hours) from where there are connections to Asunción, but frustratingly they pass through in the early hours of the morning and you'll have to wait almost 20 hours for your onward ride. The roads to Yacuiba and Villamontes pass through some fabulous scenery, especially the stretch between Entre Ríos and Palos Blancos, and through the Pilcomayo Gorge.

Getting Around
TO/FROM THE AIRPORT
Syndicate taxis from the airport to the center cost around B$20, but if you walk 100m past the airport gate (visible from outside the terminal), you'll pay as little as B$12 per person for a normal taxi. Otherwise, cross the main road and take a passing *micro A* or *trufi*, which passes by the bus terminal and the Mercado Central.

BUS
City *micros* and *trufis* cost B$2.50 per ride. Routes are clearly marked on the front windows of the vehicles.

AROUND TARIJA

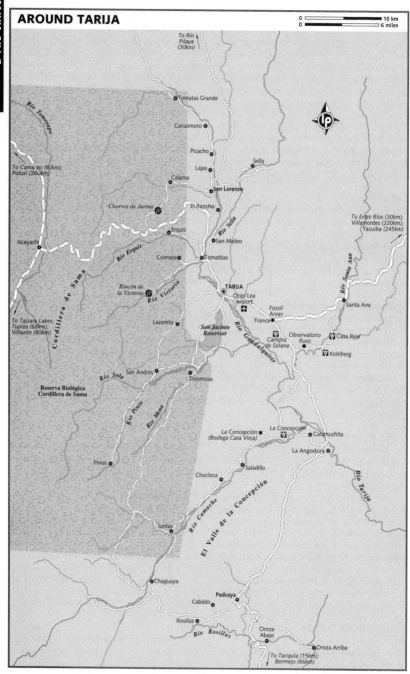

TARIJA ON THE GRAPEVINE

The Tarija region claims to be home to the 'world´s highest wines'. The grapevines, first brought to the region by 17th-century missionaries, grow at a staggering 1900m and 2100m and are only 22 degrees south of the equator. They ripen quicker than their sea-level cousins and the wine is given a head start in the maturing process, making rich reserves easier to produce. The grapes grown here are a mix of Muscat of Alexandria and Californian, but with a taste all their own.

Most bodegas also produce *singani*, a distilled grape spirit (40%) of varying quality. *Mi Socio*, the cheapest and harshest, is marked by a blue-label; the red-label *Special de Oro* is of medium price and quality; the best, *Coleción Privada*, a flowery, fresh, fragrant spirit, has a black label. The cheaper types are usually drunk mixed with soda and lemon. Bodega La Concepción produces the region's best *singani*.

To visit the wineries and sample the wines, inquire at the individual offices in Tarija. All offices sell bottles at factory prices (B$15 to B$100). Taxis to Concepción leave when full (B$5, 20 minutes) from the corner of Corrado and Trigo. Alternatively, both Viva Tours and VTB Tours (p248) offer excellent half-day and day-long wine tasting tours. Local wineries include:

Bodega La Concepción (☎ 664-5040; www.bodegaslaconcepcion.com, in Spanish; office O'Connor N-642, Tarija) The region's best winery promotes its vintages as the 'world's highest wines.' It's found 25km south of Tarija, just before the village of Concepción.

Bodega Casa Vieja (☎ 666-2605; www.lacasavieja.info, in Spanish; office 15 de Abril & Saracho, Tarija) Home to the best *patero* (foot-stamped) wine, this atmospheric winery has a lovely restaurant (lunch only B$25). It's in the village of Concepción, about 30km from Tarija.

Campos de Solana/Casa Real (☎ 664-8481; www.csolana.com, in Spanish; office 15 de Abril E-259, Tarija) Modern winery with big vaults of wine, in Santa Ana, 17km southwest of Tarija.

Kohlberg (☎ 663-6366; www.bodegaskohlberg.com, in Spanish; office 15 de Abril E-275, Tarija) The area's oldest winery and also the most popular.

CAR & BIKE HIRE
Barron's Rent-a-Car (☎ 663-6853; Ingavi E-339)
Bike Hire (☎ 664-2392; cnr San Juán & Domingo Paz) From B$50 per day, with guides available.

TAXI
Although you can walk just about anywhere in Tarija (including the airport), taxis cost B$5/8 per person for day/night trips around the center, including the bus terminal. For a radio taxi, ring **4 de Julio** (☎ 664-6555/7676) or **Radio Taxi Tarija** (☎ 664-7700).

SAN JACINTO RESERVOIR
If you're hot in Tarija and after some aquatic refreshment, go to the 1700-hectare reservoir, 6km southwest of town. There's a tourist complex with little *cabañas* (cabins), a restaurant serving *dorado* (a delicious local fish) and a place to rent canoes or, if you feel the need for speed, jet-skis. Those who prefer more tranquil ways to enjoy themselves will delight in the nice walks along the shore and surrounding ridges. Though billed as one of the region's biggest attractions, its not, but it does make for a pleasant day-trip and is popular with

chapacos on Sunday afternoons. *Trufis* run to San Jacinto (B$2.50, 10 minutes) every 20 minutes from the corner of Ingavi and Campos (outside the Palacio de la Justicia) in Tarija.

SAN LORENZO
pop 21,400
San Lorenzo, 15km north of Tarija along the Tupiza road, is a quaint colonial village with cobbled streets, carved balconies, a church built in 1709 and a flowery plaza. It's best known, however, as the home of one José Eustaquio 'Moto' Méndez, the hero of the Batalla de la Tablada, whose home now houses the **Museo Moto Méndez** (admission free; 9am-12:30pm & 3-5pm Mon-Sat, 10am-noon Sun). His personal belongings have been left exactly as they were when he died. Méndez left everything he owned to the people of Tarija. The popular **Fiesta de San Lorenzo** takes place here on August 10 and features *chapaco* musical instruments and dancing.

After seeing the museum, head 2km north to the **Capilla de Lajas**, a delicate chapel of exquisite proportions and a fine example of colonial architecture. It was once the

Méndez family chapel and remains in private ownership. Just to the north is the former home of **Jaime Paz Zamora**, with an adjacent billboard paying homage to the ex-president.

Micros and *trufis* (B$3, 30 minutes) leave from the corner of Domingo Paz and Saracho in Tarija approximately every 20 minutes during the day.

EL VALLE DE LA CONCEPCIÓN

The Concepción Valley, or simply 'El Valle,' is the heart of Bolivian wine (see the boxed text p253) and *singani* production. La Concepción still bears many picturesque colonial elements and the plaza sports some lovely endemic flowering ceibo trees. To visit the valley's wineries, contact Viva Tours or VTB Tours (p248) or the winery offices in Tarija (see boxed text p253). The **Fiesta de la Uva** (Grape Festival) is held here for three days in March, corresponding with the grape harvest.

El Valle lies off the route toward Bermejo; take the right fork at the *tranca* east of Tarija. Taxis leave when full (B$5, 20 minutes) from the corner of Corrado and Trigo.

PADCAYA & CHAGUAYA

Visiting Padcaya, south of Tarija, brings full meaning to the old saying that 'it's better to travel than to arrive,' the route twisting its way through 45km of lovely mountainous desert with green river valleys. The town itself has a few old colonial buildings and is located in an area rich in fossils, meaning you are more likely to bump into a paleontologist than another tourist.

If you're up for something totally off the wall, check out the annual **Fiesta de Leche y Queso** in **Rosillas** (population 1000), west of Padcaya. This festival of milk and cheese takes place during the last week of March and celebrates the vital contributions of local cows.

Chaguaya, 68km south of Tarija, is home to the pilgrimage shrine Santuario de la Virgen de Chaguaya. The **Fiesta de la Virgen de Chaguaya** begins on August 15; celebrations follow on the subsequent Sunday. Alcohol is forbidden at this time. Pilgrims from all over Bolivia arrive during the following month, some making the trip on foot (including an annual procession from Tarija).

Micros (B$7, 90 minutes) from Tarija to Padcaya depart every 20 minutes from the Parada del Chaco in Tarija. Less frequent services run to Chaguaya from the same place, leaving mid-afternoon.

RESERVA BIOLÓGICA CORDILLERA DE SAMA

The **Sama Biological Reserve** protects representative samples of both the Altiplano and the inter-Andean valley ecosystems. In the highland portion of the reserve (3400m above sea level), one can visit the Tajzara lakes, an important site for aquatic birds. Temperatures in the highlands stay quite chilly year-round but are slightly more comfortable in the drier winter months (May to August). The best time to visit the lower elevations is in the summer, when it's warm enough to swim.

The reserve is jointly administered by **Servicio Nacional de Áreas Protegidas** (SERNAP; Map pp68-9; see pp62-3) in La Paz and **Prometa** (Map p246; ☎ 663-3873; www.elgranchaco.com/prometa; Carpio E-659, Tarija). Check their website or the Tarija office for latest ecotouristic developments.

Tajzara Section

The area known as Tajzara lies high on the cold and windy *puna* (high open grasslands) of western Tarija department. Here, several shallow flamingo-filled lagoons appear like jewels in the harsh Altiplano, vegetated only by *thola* (a small desert bush of the Altiplano) and *paja brava* (spiky grass of the high Altiplano). Tarija's New Agers consider Tajzara to be a natural power site whilst the locals claim that the lakes are haunted by nocturnal spirit voices, and woe betide anybody that stays out after dark. The night air does produce some eerie voice-like cries, but unimaginative people ascribe the phenomenon to winds rushing through the *thola*.

Along the eastern shores of the lagoons, the wind has heaped up large *arenales* (sand dunes). An interesting climb takes you to the symmetrical peak of **Muyuloma**, which rises about 1000m above the plain. The summit affords views across the lagoons and beyond to the endless expanses of the southern Altiplano. The return climb takes the better part of a day.

Near the Tajzara visitors' center, Prometa has an **albergue** (r per person under/over 25 yr B$70/100) with hot showers, a communal kitchen and an observatory where birdwatchers are able to spot the 45 resident species including three of the world´s six flamingo species, and horned and giant coots. Hikers can spend a very enjoyable six to eight hours on the wonderful **Inca Trail** as it descends 2000m to the valley below. With luck, you may see vicuñas, condors or mysterious petroglyphs of unknown origin. Arrive the night before you intend to hike and bring food supplies with you.

Inter-Andean Valleys

During the summertime, there are several places in the valley to go swimming in the rivers, including Tomatitas, Coimata and Chorros de Jurina.

Tomatitas, with its natural swimming holes, three lovely rivers (the Sella, Guadalquivir and Erquis) and happy little eateries, is popular with day-trippers from Tarija. The best swimming is immediately below the footbridge, where there's also a park with a campground and barbecue sites. From here you can walk or hitch the 9km to **Coimata**. From Tarija, turn left off the main San Lorenzo road. After less than 1km, you'll pass a cemetery on the left, which is full of flowers and brightly colored crosses. Just beyond it, bear right towards Coimata. Once there, turn left at the soccer field and continue to the end of the road. Here you'll find a small cascade of water and a **swimming hole** that makes a great escape, as lots of Tarijeño families can attest. There's also a choice of small restaurants serving *misquinchitos* and *doraditos* (fried local fish with white corn), as well as *cangrejitos* (small freshwater crabs). From this point, you can follow a walking track 40 minutes upstream to the base of the two-tiered **Coimata Falls**, which has a total drop of about 60m.

Another swimming hole and waterfall are found at **Rincón de la Victoria**, 6km southwest of Tomatitas in a green plantation-like setting. Instead of bearing right beyond the colorful cemetery, as you would for Coimata, follow the route to the left. From the fork, it's 5km to Rincón de la Victoria.

The twin 40m waterfalls at **Chorros de Jurina,** 26km from Tarija, also make an agreeable destination for a day trip. Set in a beautiful but unusual landscape, one waterfall cascades over white stone while the other pours over black stone. In late winter, however, they may diminish to a mere trickle or even be dry.

The route from Tarija to Jurina passes through some impressive rural landscapes. From near the flowery plaza in San Lorenzo, follow the Jurina road, which turns off beside the Casa de Moto Méndez. After 6km, you'll pass a school on the left. Turn left 200m beyond the school and follow that road another 2.5km to the waterfalls. From the end of the road, it's a five-minute walk to the base of either waterfall. The one on the left is reached by following the river upstream; for the other, follow the track that leads from behind a small house.

Getting There & Away

From Tarija, Viva Tours (p248) organizes overnight trips to several areas of Sama. Buses to Villazón depart between 8pm and 9pm and pass through Tajzara approximately five hours later. The Tajzara visitors' center is a 20-minute walk from the road. Contact Prometa (opposite) about other transportation options including guided tours.

Micros to Tomatitas leave every 20 minutes from the corner of Av Domingo Paz and Saracho in Tarija (B$1.50), some continuing on to Jurina (B$5) via San Lorenzo. Get off near the school and then walk the rest of the way. For Coimata, similarly frequent departures leave from the corner of Campesino and Comercio (B$3), in Tarija.

RESERVA NACIONAL DE FLORA Y FAUNA TARIQUÍA

The lovely and little-known 247,000-hectare **Tariquía Flora & Fauna Reserve** (created in 1989) protects a large portion of cloud-forest and a smaller area of *Polylepis* woodland on the eastern slopes of the department of Tarija's mountains. Ranging in altitude from 400m to 1500m, it houses rare animals such as the spectacled bear, as well as hundreds of bird species including the threatened rufous-throated dipper and the spectacular military macaw.

The only way to see this largely wild reserve is on foot, but hiking can be challenging in this remote area and is best done with a guide. The best time to visit Tariquía is during the dry winter months (May to September) when the climate is mild and river crossings are possible.

Prometa (p254) operates seven camps in Tariquía, including a simple **albergue** (r per person B$100-150) with free camping and cooking facilities – the Tariquía Community Center in the heart of the reserve. From the road it's a two-day hike to the center, but allow six days to fully explore the area on foot. You'll need to bring camping gear. Transportation may be organized through Prometa, which runs day trips and can also organize volunteer work.

THE CHACO

Flat and sparsely populated, the Chaco is a vast expanse of thorn scrub where dispersed ranchers, isolated indigenous villages and Mennonite communities farm plots of land – it's also dotted by police and military troops, guarding their posts. This silent, flat land covers most of southeastern Bolivia and western Paraguay and stretches into neighboring Argentina.

Wildlife abounds in the undisturbed wilderness of the Chaco. With humans a relatively rare species, animals are bolder and more visible here than in the Amazon and this is one of the best places in South America to see large mammals like the tapir, jaguar and puma. Plant life amazes with a series of bizarre (and often spiny) adaptations to the xeric environment. Apart from being prickled by various species of cacti, you'll be surprised by brilliant flowering bushes and trees, such as the yellow *carnival* bush; the white-and-yellow *huevo* (egg) tree; the pink or white thorny bottle tree, locally known as the *toboroche* or *palo borracho* (drunken tree); and the red-flowering, hard *quebracho* (axe-breaker) tree, whose wood, too heavy to float, is one of the Chaco's main exports.

YACUIBA

pop 83,500 / elevation 625m

There's only one reason to visit Yacuiba – and it's to cross the border into Argentina, or indeed into Bolivia. Tiny **Pocitos**, 5km south, is the easternmost Bolivia-Argentina border crossing. Most people won't even spend the night here, but if you're unfortunate enough to be stranded in this border town, you can explore the town's abundance of old, dysfunctional, com-

mercial goods, and join the Yacuibans in shopping sprees.

The town's name is Guaraní for 'watering hole of the turkeys', referring to the turkey-like Chaco Chachalaca, a bird endemic to the Chaco who´s ear-splitting morning choruses are one of the trademark sounds of the region.

Information

Yacuiba's main north-south street is flanked by several *casas de cambio*, which only deal in cash. Calculate the amount you're to receive before leaving the window and beware of fake US bills. Pickpocketing and petty theft have been reported, especially in crowded shopping areas. An online web portal provides information about the town for locals and visitors – www.yacuiba.com, in Spanish.

Sleeping & Eating

The only thing Yacuiba has going for it is that there are lots of hotels. It gets seriously hot here, so if you are staying for any length of time its worth splashing out for air-conditioning.

Gran Residencial Victoria (☎ 682-3752; San Martín 639; r per person B$25, with bathroom & cable TV B$70; 🖳) Hyperbolic name? Well yes, but this is the best of the motley selection of *residenciales* in front of the bus terminal, useful if you have an early bus to catch or indeed a late one and are looking for somewhere to rest your head for a few hours. Even the cheap rooms have air-con.

Hotel Valentín (☎ 682-2645; San Martín 1153; s/d with bathroom B$150/250; 🖳) A box-like building but rooms are nice, with all mod cons, as you'd expect for the price. Breakfast is included and served in the attached restaurant.

Hotel Paris (☎ 682-2182; Comercio at Campero; s/d with bathroom B$180/225; 🖳) Two blocks from the plaza this is an upmarket hotel decked out in hardwoods which give it a classical feel. All rooms have TV and air-conditioning and there's a pleasant courtyard restaurant for meals.

El Asador (Plaza Principal; mains B$30-60) For a taste of Argentina north of the border try the huge racks of meat at El Asador, recognised locally as the best *churrasquería* in town. There are pastas and salad on the buffet, and portions are huge – ask for a half-portion if you are on your own.

Getting There & Around

Yacuiba´s bus terminal is about 10 blocks from the plaza on Avenida San Martín. Buses for Tarija (B$40 to B$60, 12 hours) leave before 9am and after 6pm. Numerous *flotas* leave every evening for Santa Cruz (B$60, 15 hours) via Villamontes and Camiri. Beware of over-charging by ticket vendors for their 'commission' – just pay the price written on your ticket. There is a B$2 fee payable on boarding the bus, for the use of the terminal.

Yacuiba's **railway station** (☎ 682-2308) ticket window opens in the morning on the day of departure; line up early. A reasonably quick and comfortable *Ferrobus* service runs to Santa Cruz (B$120 to B$135, 11 hours) via Villamontes (B$50 to B$60, two hours) on Monday and Friday at 6pm. Flights to Tarija depart with TAM on Thursday and Sunday (B$308) if there is enough demand, from where there are onward connections to major cities.

VILLAMONTES

pop 23,800 / elevation 383m

As the temperature soars and the hot, dry winds coat everything with a thick layer of dust, you can see the pride rising in the residents of Villamontes almost as fast as the mercury, for this is officially Bolivia's hottest town. Despite the heat, this is a welcoming place, and the majority indigenous Guaraní population means that lovely woven baskets and furniture made from natural Chaco materials can be found at the town's market. Villamontes is famous for its fish restaurants which line the main road to Yacuiba, and the best time to visit is during the annual August **fishing festival** on the Río Pilcomayo. There isn't much to do in town, but this is the main connection town for bus services into Paraguay.

History

During Inca times, Guaraní tribes emigrated here from present-day Paraguay. Their descendants now make up most of the town's indigenous population. Villamontes remained a lonely outpost until it emerged as a strategic Chaco War stronghold. The Paraguayans considered Villamontes their key to undisputed victory over the Bolivian resistance, but the Bolivian army saw its most significant victory here in the 1934 Battle of Villamontes. In more modern times the town has seen a second Paraguayan invasion, this time of migrants looking for work in the nearby oil and gas fields.

Sleeping & Eating

Residencial El Pescadito (☎ 672-2896; r per person B$40, with bathroom B$60; 🛏) Budget option on the main road, close to the bus offices for departures to Paraguay. Basic but ideal if you want to catch the early morning connections across the border.

Hotel Villamontes (☎ 684-2297; Oruro 672; s/d B$60/100, with bathroom B$80/150; 🛏) A decent value central option just around the corner from the new market. All rooms have cable TV and air-conditioning, though not necessarily a bathroom.

CROSSING THE BORDER TO ARGENTINA

The two main border crossings to Argentina are at Yacuiba and Bermejo, the former being the most accessible from Santa Cruz and the latter from Tarija. *Casas de cambio* (exchange houses) are abundant in both border towns. It is in your best interest to get rid of your extra bolivianos before crossing the border – rates in Argentina are not favorable. Note that Argentina is always one hour ahead of Bolivia.

Shared taxis (B$10) shuttle between the terminal at Yacuiba and Argentine immigration at Pocitos. After crossing the border on foot, onward bus services to Tartagal and Embarcación leave every couple of hours, where you can make connections to Salta, Jujuy and Buenos Aires.

Crossing to Argentina from Bermejo is slightly more complicated as the border is only open from 8am to 5pm. *Chalanas* (ferries) over the river (B$3) leave every few minutes. Be sure to pick up an exit stamp before crossing.

Bermejo's bus terminal is eight blocks southeast of the main plaza. Hourly buses connect Bermejo and Tarija (B$20, three hours) along a fully asphalted road. From Agua Blanca, Argentine buses to Orán (US$2, one hour) depart hourly from the terminal opposite the immigration office. From Orán, you can connect to Argentina's Salta, Jujuy and Tucumán.

Hotel El Rancho (☎ 684-2049; Av Méndez Arcos; s/d B$280/330; ❄) Upmarket hotel opposite the railway station, with bungalows that come with TVs and much-needed air-conditioning. A pleasant restaurant sits by the side.

Villamontes is famous for its fish restaurants, shack-like structures lining the main road to Yacuiba, which serve freshly-caught *surubí* amongst other local scalies. There are a couple of good *churrasquerías* near the recently remodelled plaza, the best of the bunch being El Arriero, half a block along Villaroel.

Getting There & Away

Buses run several times daily to Yacuiba, Tarija, Camiri and Santa Cruz. However, the main reason for stopping in Villamontes is to catch a bus connection to Paraguay via the Trans-Chaco road without heading north to Santa Cruz. Several companies pass through between 1am and 3am, but quality of service varies considerably. The best company is **Yacyreta** (☎ 7717-4744), which has a comfortable *cama* service to Asunción (B$220, 15 hours). All companies have their offices on the main road close to the local landmark 'El Pescadito' statue – you should buy your ticket in advance.

By train, Villamontes is two hours north of Yacuiba and eight hours south of Santa Cruz. The train to Yacuiba passes through on Thursday and Sunday at 3:05am, and the return to Santa Cruz on Monday and Friday at 8pm. Taxis (per person day/night B$3/5) frequent the railway station, on the same street as the bus station, 2km north of town.

PARQUE NACIONAL Y ÁREA NATURAL DE MANEJO INTEGRADO AGUARAGÜE

The long and narrow 108,000-hectare Aguaragüe National Park takes in much of the mountains of **Serranía de Aguaragüe**, which divides the vast Gran Chaco and the highlands of the department of Tarija. Plum in the region known for being the hottest in Bolivia, it is best visited in the cooler, winter months (May to October).

Although it lacks visitor facilities, the **Cañón del Pilcomayo** is easily accessible from Villamontes. The name of the park comes from Guaraní, meaning 'the lair of the jaguar,' because the range is famous for being home to this lovely, spotty (and scary) cat. Foxes, tapir, anteater, assorted parrots, numerous plant species and 70% of the region's potable water sources can also be found here. Viva Tours (p248) conducts guided hikes and visits.

Cañón del Pilcomayo

In the beautiful Pilcomayo Canyon at **El Chorro Grande** waterfall, fish are prevented from swimming further upstream. Abundant *surubí, sábalo* and *dorado* are easily caught, making the area a favorite with anglers from all over the country. The predatory *dorado* is prized by game fishermen

---

CROSSING THE BORDER INTO PARAGUAY

Crossing the border into Paraguay has never been easier. The infamous Trans-Chaco Road is paved along its entire length on the Paraguay side, though it takes a slight detour away from the original Trans-Chaco at La Patria, crossing into Bolivia at the military checkpoint of Infante Rivarola. Several bus services from Santa Cruz via Villamontes now run this route to Asunción on a daily basis.

Bolivian customs formalities take place at Ibibobo. You will need to present your passport and visa first to a military representative and then walk 100 yards or so to get your stamp at customs. Buses typically pass here around 4-5am, so don´t expect a tranquil night´s sleep. From here the Paraguayan border point, Infante Rivarola, is another hour or so away, but Paraguayan customs formalities are not carried out until you are well beyond here, at the impressive new *aduanas* building in Mariscal Estigarribia. Buses typically arrive there around 7-8am.

This is a notorious smuggling route so expect to be lined up with your bags as customs officials and sniffer dogs rifle through your private possessions. Once you are given the 'Ok' to proceed, you get your entry stamp from the small immigration office just outside the main compound. There is a service station here which sells food if you're peckish and, provided you are not carrying anything you shouldn´t be, it is as simple as that!

because of its legendary fight; it's particularly interesting because it has an odd hinge at the front of its jawbone that allows its mouth to open wide horizontally.

There are great views from the restaurants 7km to 10km west of town where you can sample local fish dishes.

To reach the gorge, take any Tarija-bound transportation, or taxi to the *tranca*, and hitch or walk from there (as usual, weekends are the best time to hitchhike). Where the road forks, bear right and continue another 2km to the mouth of the gorge.

RESERVA PRIVADA DE PATRIMONIO NATURAL DE CORBALÁN

This private 4500-acre reserve on the Paraguayan border was established in 1996 to protect a choice piece of Gran Chaco. Jaguar, puma, tapir, giant anteater and giant armadillo are found here, though you'll more likely see Azara's fox, three-banded armadillo, and birds such as the blue-fronted amazon parrot and chaco chachalaca. The only access route is the poor road from Villamontes, which takes at least four hours with a good vehicle. If you plan to visit, accommodation is limited to a simple park rangers' camp, and you'll need to bring your own food, water and other supplies. The only commercial access is with Viva Tours (p248) and Prometa (p254).

CAMIRI

pop 35,000 / elevation 825m

The most southerly point on the vaguely defined 'Camino del Ché', which ends in Vallegrande (p283), the real revolutionary growth of the cobble-stoned streets of Camiri occurred in the 1990s, when the town became the center for the production of petroleum and gas for the national oil company, YPFB (known more simply as 'Yacimientos'). The town is so proud of its oily role that it bills itself as the Capital Petrolífero de Bolivia (Oil Capital of Bolivia).

Information

There are several banks with ATMs along Oruro just off the plaza. A crazy proliferation of telephone and internet places are found on the streets around the plaza. The **post office** (Santa Cruz) is a relic from the days

when people had a lot more time than they do now. There is no official tourist information office, but local resident **doña Karen** (☎ 7262-0027) gives information by phone.

Sights & Activities

Camiri was the site where the French intellectual Regis Debray and Argentine artist Ciro Bustos, members of Ché Guevara's guerilla group, where held and tortured following their capture. Debray spilled the beans on Guevara's operation and Bustos sketched the group members for his captors. The site of their imprisonment was the **Cuartel-Museo** (☷ 9am-noon & 2-6pm Mon-Fri), the local military barracks. Bustos's original images are displayed in the Cuartel's 'Casino', the site where, bizarrely-enough, Debray was married, receiving a two-hour 'permission' for his nuptials before returning to his cell. The two were tried and found guilty (what a surprise!) in the local library.

Camiri is damn proud of its **YPFB plant**. There's no formal tour, but if you're keen to visit (weirdo!), get up at the crack of dawn and roll up at 8am and they might let you look around. Don't miss the **Petrolero (Oil Worker) monument** in the middle of Av Petrolero.

Sleeping

All the places listed below are within two blocks of the main plaza.

Residencial Marieta (☎ 952-2264; Petrolero 15; s/d B$35/60) A great little budget option with a weird kind of retro appeal. Friendly owners, a vine-covered patio and strange 'semi-private' bathrooms shared between two rooms and independently accessed from each, just add to the charm. Spacious, comfortable, and when did you last see a TV like that?

Hotel Premier (☎ 952-2204; Busch 60; s/d with bathroom B$80/120) A block from the plaza, this is a nice, modern hotel with small rooms, each with cable TV, and hot shower. Particularly nice are the bright and spacious upstairs rooms that open onto a leafy patio.

Hotel JR (☎ 952-2200; Sánchez 247; s/d with bathroom B$165/245; ✷) If you fancy hanging out with oil barons, check out the friendly JR, possibly named after the *Dallas* soap character. All rooms have telephones, heating and cable TV, and there's a bright sitting area with fine views. The hotel restaurant Cupesi is considered by many the best in town.

Eating

Tasty breakfasts can be had near the **market** (cnr Bolívar & Comercio), where street vendors sell hot drinks, *licuados* (fruit shakes made with either milk or water), bread and basic Bolivian grub. The streets around the plaza have clusters of unappealing greasy junk food and chicken joints, but for a decent meal, your choices are limited.

Club Social (cnr Plaza Principal & Oruro; almuerzo B\$12) A cheap, filling and decent *almuerzo*.

Membiray (Plaza Principal; mains B\$15-40) A new restaurant trying to introduce Chinese and vegetarian dishes to the conservative town residents. Portions are large, well-cooked and the surroundings are pleasant – though there is nothing Oriental about them.

Cupesi (Sánchez 247; mains B\$30-60) Under the Hotel JR, this is arguably the best food in town. The extensive menu contains meat, chicken and fish dishes which are not cheap, but if you are in town for more than a few days it's worth the extra bolivianos to avoid succumbing to a monotonous diet of junk food.

Getting There & Away

There's no central bus terminal in town – most buses leave from their respective company offices near the corner of Bolívar and Cochabamba. Numerous *flotas* leave every two hours or so to Santa Cruz (B\$60, five hours). Buses for Yacuiba via Villamontes (where you should change for connections to Tarija or Paraguay) leave at 9am, 2pm and 5pm (B\$35, four hours). Andesbus and Emperador alternate for a daily 1pm service to Sucre (B\$90, 14 hours).

Santa Cruz & Gran Chiquitania

The Bolivian Oriente is not what you generally see in Bolivian tourist brochures. This tropical region, the country's most prosperous, has a palpable desire to differentiate itself from Bolivia's renowned highland image. It has an odd mixture of conservatism, cosmopolitanism and provincialism, with a business head and a multicultural population. The region's agriculture boom in recent years brought about a rise in income and a standard of life that isn't matched by any other Bolivian province.

Following Evo Morales' proposed changes to the Bolivian constitution, the Oriente appealed strongly for local autonomy, but a national referendum backed the president and the region has been forced to search for more diplomatic avenues to get its way.

Despite the fact that Santa Cruz is Bolivia's most populous city, it still has a small-town atmosphere, peppered with international restaurants, trendy youth, and Japanese, German, Italian, Eastern European, Arabic, Indian Sikh and German-Canadian Mennonite communities. From here you can visit the charming Jesuit mission towns, which contain the country's loveliest and most fascinating examples of Jesuit architecture. Pre-Inca ruins hide near the small town of Samaipata, and there are miles of trekking and tons of wildlife at the little-disturbed Parque Nacional Amboró. Revolutionaries can check out where Ché Guevara met his maker at the northern end of the work-in-progress Ché Trail in La Higuera and Vallegrande. If you want a look into a part of Bolivia that defies the stereotype, this is the place to be.

SANTA CRUZ & GRAN CHIQUITANIA

HIGHLIGHTS

- Check out the international cuisine of **Santa Cruz** (p269) and wander around the city's streets
- Trek the still-untouched wilderness and spot rare wildlife at **Parque Nacional & Área de Uso Múltiple Amboró** (p276)
- Explore the pre-Inca ruins in **Samaipata** (p278) and relax in this lovely village
- Get revolutionary on the **Ché Trail** in Vallegrande (p283) and La Higuera (p285)
- Admire the restored architecture around the wonderful **Jesuit missions circuit** (p287)

- TELEPHONE CODE: 3
- POPULATION: 2.03 MILLION
- ELEVATION: 0M TO 1300M

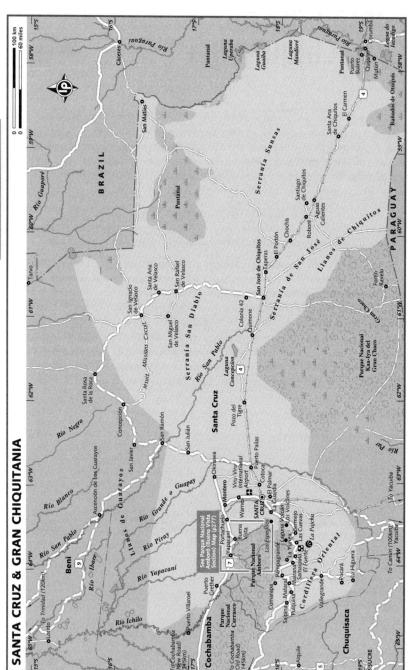

Climate

The Oriente's climate is tropical, but because it occupies the transition zone between the Amazon rainforest, the highlands and the dry Chaco plains, Santa Cruz enjoys more sun and less stifling temperatures than the humid Amazon Basin. Winter rainfalls mean little more than 10-minute downpours, but a single summer deluge can last for days. At times during winter, *surazos* (chilly winds) blow in from Patagonia and the Argentine pampas and the temperature plummets.

National Parks

Parque Nacional Amboró (p276) is an unquestionable highlight of the region. The remote Parque Nacional Kaa-Iya del Gran Chaco is Latin America's largest park but is largely inaccessible.

Getting There & Away

Santa Cruz is the country's most connected city. Many flights from Europe and neighboring countries come direct to Santa Cruz and are worth considering if you're arriving from sea level and don't want to spend days acclimatizing in La Paz. Direct flights depart daily for Buenos Aires, Miami, São Paulo and Rio de Janeiro.

Trains trundle south to Argentina and east to the Brazilian Pantanal, and there are long-distance buses running along paved roads to the west and south, as well as frequent domestic flights.

SANTA CRUZ

pop 1.54 million / elevation 417m

Santa Cruz may surprise you with its small-town feeling, lack of high-rise blocks and a lightly buzzing, relaxed tropical atmosphere. Bolivia's largest city oozes modernity yet clings stubbornly to tradition. The city center is vibrant and thriving, its narrow streets crowded with suited businessmen sipping *chicha* (fermented corn) at street stalls, whilst taxis jostle with horses and carts for pole position at traffic lights. Locals still lounge on the main square listening to *camba* (Eastern Lowlands) music, restaurants close for siesta and little stores line the porch-fronted houses selling cheap local products.

This is not the Bolivia that you see in pictures, but this is the place with the largest population diversity in the country – from the overall-wearing Mennonites strolling the streets past local Goth kids, to a Japanese community, Altiplano (High Plateau) immigrants, Cuban doctors, Brazilian immigrants, bearded Russians and fashionable *cruceños* (Santa Cruz locals) turning sharp corners in their SUVs.

The *cruceños* are an independent lot who feel little affinity for their government in La Paz and are well aware of their stock value as the country's trade and transport center. Support for President Morales is thin on the ground here and *cruceños* voiced their overwhelming desire for the region's autonomy in 2006. Though they lost that battle following a national referendum, calls for independence continue to be the main source of inspiration for the city's graffiti artists and the matter is far from settled.

It's worth spending a few days here, wandering the streets, eating at the many international restaurants and checking out the rich kids' play area, Equipetrol, where nightlife is rife with naughtiness. Alternatively, simply chill out at the town square.

History

Santa Cruz de la Sierra was founded in 1561 by Ñuflo de Chavez, a Spaniard who hailed from present-day Paraguay. The town originated 220km east of its current location, but in 1621, by order of the King of Spain, it moved to its present position, 50km east of the Cordillera Oriental foothills. The original location had proved too vulnerable to attack from local tribes. Ñuflo himself was killed in 1568 at the hands of the mestizo Itatine tribe made up of indigenous and Spanish settlers.

The city's main aim was to supply the rest of the colony with products such as rice, cotton, sugar and fruit. Its prosperity lasted until the late 1800s, when transportation routes opened up between La Paz and the Peruvian coast, making imported goods cheaper than those hauled from Santa Cruz over mule trails.

During the period leading up to Bolivia's independence in 1825, the eastern regions of the Spanish colonies were largely ignored. Although agriculture was thriving around Santa Cruz, the Spanish remained intent upon extracting every scrap of mineral wealth that could be squeezed from the rich and more hospitable highlands.

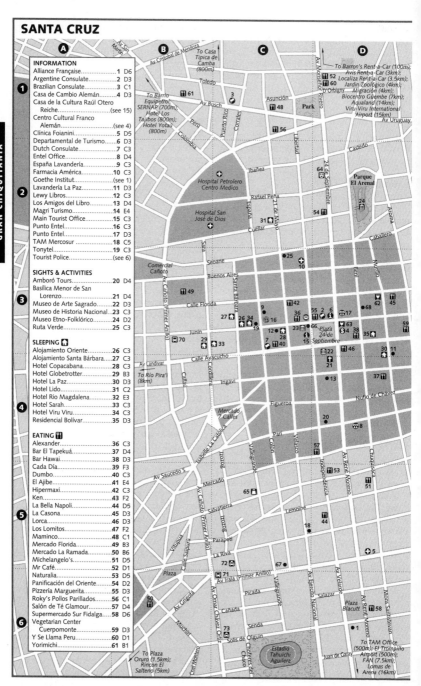

SANTA CRUZ

INFORMATION
Alliance Française....................**1** D6
Argentine Consulate................**2** D3
Brazilian Consulate..................**3** C1
Casa de Cambio Alemán..........**4** D3
Casa de la Cultura Raúl Otero
  Reiche...............................(see 15)
Centro Cultural Franco
  Alemán..............................(see 4)
Clínica Foianini.......................**5** D5
Departamental de Turismo......**6** D3
Dutch Consulate......................**7** C3
Entel Office.............................**8** C3
España Lavandería...................**9** C3
Farmacia América....................**10** C3
Goethe Institut.......................(see 1)
Lavandería La Paz....................**11** D3
Lewy Libros.............................**12** C3
Los Amigos del Libro...............**13** D4
Magri Turismo.........................**14** E4
Main Tourist Office..................**15** D3
Punto Entel.............................**16** C3
Punto Entel.............................**17** D3
TAM Mercosur **18** C5
Tonytel..................................**19** C3
Tourist Police..........................(see 6)

SIGHTS & ACTIVITIES
Amboró Tours.........................**20** D4
Basílica Menor de San
  Lorenzo...............................**21** D4
Museo de Arte Sagrado...........**22** D3
Museo de Historia Nacional....**23** C3
Museo Etno-Folklórico............**24** D2
Ruta Verde.............................**25** C3

SLEEPING
Alojamiento Oriente................**26** C3
Alojamiento Santa Bárbara.....**27** C3
Hotel Copacabana...................**28** C3
Hotel Globetrotter...................**29** B3
Hotel La Paz...........................**30** D3
Hotel Lido..............................**31** C2
Hotel Río Magdalena...............**32** E3
Hotel Sarah............................**33** C3
Hotel Viru Viru........................**34** C3
Residencial Bolívar..................**35** D3

EATING
Alexander...............................**36** C3
Bar El Tapekuá........................**37** D4
Bar Hawai...............................**38** D3
Cada Día.................................**39** F3
Dumbo...................................**40** C3
El Ajibe..................................**41** E4
Hipermaxi...............................**42** C3
Ken..**43** F2
La Bella Napoli........................**44** D5
La Casona...............................**45** D3
Lorca.....................................**46** D3
Los Lomitos............................**47** F2
Maminco.................................**48** C1
Mercado Florida......................**49** B3
Mercado La Ramada................**50** B6
Michelangelo's.........................**51** D5
Mr Café..................................**52** D1
Naturalia................................**53** D5
Panificación del Oriente...........**54** D2
Pizzería Marguerita.................**55** D3
Roky's Pollos Parillados...........**56** C1
Salón de Té Glamour...............**57** D3
Supermercado Sur Fidalga.......**58** D6
Vegetarian Center
  Cuerpomonte......................**59** D3
Y Se Llama Peru......................**60** D1
Yorimichi...............................**61** B1

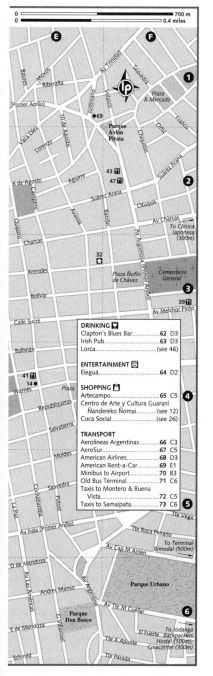

DRINKING 🍷
Clapton's Blues Bar................62 D3
Irish Pub..............................63 D3
Lorca.................................(see 46)

ENTERTAINMENT 🎭
Eleguá................................64 D2

SHOPPING 🛍
Artecampo...........................65 C5
Centro de Arte y Cultura Guaraní
Ñandereko Ñomai...........(see 12)
Coca Social.......................(see 26)

TRANSPORT
Aerolíneas Argentinas 66 C3
AeroSur..............................67 C3
American Airlines................68 D3
American Rent-a-Car...........69 E1
Minibus to Airport...............70 B3
Old Bus Terminal................71 C6
Taxis to Montero & Buena
Vista................................72 C5
Taxis to Samaipata............73 C6

In 1954 a highway linking Santa Cruz with other major centers was completed, and the city sprang back from its 100-year economic lull. The completion of the railway line to Brazil in the mid-1950s opened trade routes to the east, after which time tropical agriculture boomed and the city grew as prosperously as crops such as oranges, sugar cane, bananas and coffee. It has continued to grow to the present day.

Orientation

Roughly oval in shape, Santa Cruz is laid out in *anillos* (rings), which form concentric circles around the city center, and *radiales* (spokes) that connect the rings. Radial 1, the road to Viru-Viru airport, runs roughly north–south; the *radiales* progress clockwise up to Radial 27.

Most commercial enterprises, hotels and restaurants lie within the *primer* (first) *anillo,* which is centered on the Plaza 24 de Septiembre. The street of the same name becomes Av Monseñor Rivero, a stretch full of restaurants, cafes and bars. The bimodal terminal (bus and railway station) is within the third *anillo* but is still only a half-hour walk east from the center. The second to seventh *anillos* are mainly residential and industrial.

Within the *primer anillo*, Junín is the street with most banks, ATMs and internet cafes, and Av René Moreno has loads of souvenir stores. To the northwest of the center, Av San Martin, otherwise known as Barrio Equipetrol, has tons of bars and clubs.

MAPS

The best city map, *Multiplano Santa Cruz City Guide,* covers the first to fourth *anillos* and is available free from the tourist office. A similar map is in the free Check-In magazine distributed by the Departamental tourist office.

Information
BOOKSTORES

Near the plaza, **Los Amigos del Libro** (☎ 336-0709; Ingavi 114) and **Lewy Libros** (☎ 332-7937; lewylibros@cotas.com.bo; Junín 229) have limited selections of foreign-language books for sale or trade.

International periodicals are sold at street kiosks around the plaza.

CULTURAL CENTERS

Casa de la Cultura Raúl Otero Reiche (west side of Plaza 24 de Septiembre) Hosts free music and modern art exhibitions plus theater performances; also home to the city tourist office.

Centro Boliviano Americano (CBA; ☎ 342-2299; Potosí 78) Has an English-language library.

Centro Cultural Franco Alemán (Plaza 24 de Septiembre; ☼ 9am-noon & 3-8pm Mon-Fri) Houses the Alliance Française (☎ 333-3392) and Goethe Institut (☎ 332-9906; icbasc@sccbs-bo.com), and offers courses in French, German, Spanish and Portuguese. Facilities include a trilingual multimedia library, the outdoor Kulture Café and an art exhibition gallery; it also sponsors lectures and screens foreign films.

EMERGENCY

Private ambulance (Clínica Foianini; ☎ 336-2211, 7162-7647)

Tourist police (☎ 322-5016; north side of Plaza 24 de Septiembre)

IMMIGRATION

Migración (☎ 333-2136; ☼ 8:30am-4:30pm Mon-Fri) is north of the center, opposite the zoo entrance. Visa extensions are available here. There's an office at the **train station** (☼ supposedly 10am-noon & 1:30-7pm), which is more convenient but which is reportedly plagued by phony officials. The most reliable office is at the airport.

INTERNET ACCESS

There are numerous internet places on Junín including **Punto Entel** (Junín 140; per hr B$3; ☼ 8am-11pm) and you will have no problem getting online.

LAUNDRY

Central, efficient wash-and-dry places offer same-day service (with drop-off before noon) for around B$12 per kilo:

España Lavandería (España 160)

Lavandería La Paz (La Paz 42)

MEDICAL SERVICES

Clínica Foianini (☎ 336-2211; Irala 468) Hospital used by embassies, but be aware that some travelers have reported unnecessary tests and being required to stay for longer than is strictly necessary.

Clínica Japonesa (☎ 346-2038) On the third *anillo*, east side; recommended for inexpensive and professional medical treatment.

Farmacia América (☎ 337-1094; Libertad 333) The best pharmacy, efficient and inexpensive.

MONEY

Cash advances are available at most major banks, and ATMs line Junín and most major intersections. The easiest place to change cash or traveler's checks (2% to 3% commission) is **Casa de Cambio Alemán** (east side of Plaza 24 de Septiembre). Street moneychangers shout '*¡Dolares!*' in your face on the main plaza, but make sure you know the value of what you are changing. **Magri Turismo** (☎ 334-4559; cnr Warnes & Potosí) is the American Express agent but doesn't cash traveler's checks.

TELEPHONE

Fun can be had using public telephone boxes, which come in a variety of shapes – anything from toucans to jaguars suspended mid-growl. Better rates are found at phone centers, such as the main **Entel office** (Warnes 82), and internet telecom stores along Bolívar that offer cheap international calls. The **Punto Entel** (Junín 284) office near the plaza has landlines. Local cell-phone rates are very cheap and chips already charged with credit can be bought at Tonytel on Junín.

TOURIST INFORMATION

Online information about the city of Santa Cruz and the main attractions of the Oriente region can be found at www.destinosantacruz.com and www.santacruz-online.net.

Departamental de Turismo (☎ 333-3248; Palacio Prefectural, north side of Plaza 24 de Septiembre)

Fundación Amigos de la Naturaleza (FAN; ☎ 355-6800; www.fan-bo.org; Km 7.5, Carretera a Samaipata) Though no longer in charge of the parks, FAN is still the best contact for Amboró and Noel Kempff Mercado National Parks information. West of town (minibus 44) off the old Cochabamba road.

Main tourist office (☎ 334-5500; Ground fl, Casa de la Cultura, west side of Plaza 24 de Septiembre)

SERNAP (☎ 335-2325; www.sernap.gov.bo in Spanish; Calle 9 Oeste, Barrio Equipetrol) For information on national parks.

Dangers & Annoyances

Beware of bogus immigration officials and carefully check the credentials of anyone who demands to see your passport or other ID. No real police officer will ever ask to see your documents in the street; be especially wary of 'civilian' police who will most certainly turn out to be frauds. If you're suspicious, insist that they accompany you to the police station, where things can legitimately be sorted out. Readers have reported several violent robberies in broad daylight during the week at Río Piray; it's best only to venture out there on weekends, when there's safety in numbers.

Sights & Activities

Santa Cruz is not the richest town when it comes to sightseeing. You'll probably spend most of your time here strolling around and sipping coffee in one of the city's many cafes.

PLAZA 24 DE SEPTIEMBRE & MUSEO DE HISTORIA NACIONAL

The city's main plaza serves as a lush tropical space where you'll see locals lounging on benches and strolling, *camba* bands banging out their tropical rhythms and families bringing their kids to play. Once there were resident jaywalking sloths here, but they were relocated to the zoo in an effort to protect them from electrocution and increasing traffic hazards in the city center.

A block away along Junín is the little **Museo de Historia Nacional** (8am-noon & 3:30-6pm Mon-Fri) which houses a permanent display of Chiquitania art and photographic exhibits explaining the customs of this little-known indigenous group.

BASÍLICA MENOR DE SAN LORENZO & MUSEO DE LA CATEDRAL

Although the original cathedral on Plaza 24 de Septiembre was founded in 1605, the present structure dates from 1845 and wasn't consecrated until 1915. Inside, the decorative woodwork on the ceiling and silver plating around the altar are worth a look. There are good views of the city from the **belltower** (admission B$3; 10am-noon & 4-6pm Tue, Thu, Sat & Sun).

The cathedral's air-conditioned **Museo de Arte Sagrado** (admission B$10; 8:30am-noon & 2:30-6pm Tue, Thu & Sun) has a collection of religious icons and artifacts but very little typical religious art. Most interesting are the many gold and silver relics from the Jesuit Guarayos missions.

PARQUE EL ARENAL & MUSEO ETNO-FOLKLÓRICO

Locals relax around the lagoon at Parque El Arenal, but it's best not to dawdle here at night. On an island in the lagoon, a bas-relief mural by renowned Bolivian artist Lorgio Vaca depicts historic and modern-day aspects of Santa Cruz. Located at the park entrance on Beni and 6 de Agosto is the **Ethno-Folkloric Museum** (342-9939; admission free; 8am-noon & 2:30-6:30pm Mon-Fri), which has a small collection of traditional art and artifacts from several *camba* cultures including Guaraní, Mojeño, Ayoreo and Chiquitano.

JARDÍN ZOOLÓGICO & MUSEO GUARANÍ

Santa Cruz' **zoo** (342-9939; adult/child B$10/5; 9am-6:30pm) has a collection of native birds, mammals and reptiles kept in pleasingly humane conditions, although the llamas are a bit overdressed for the climate. If you're not into going to the jungle, this is a good place to see spectacular species such as tapirs, pumas, jaguars and spectacled bears. Keep your eyes open for free-ranging sloths and squirrel monkeys in the trees. Around the corner from the zoo entrance is the entry to the **Guaraní Museum** (admission B$5; 8am-4pm Mon-Fri), a small but fascinating and professionally presented exhibition of Guaraní culture. Look for the animal masks and *tinajas* (huge clay pots) used for making *chicha*. You'll need to knock on the gate for entry.

Take *micro 55* from Calle Vallegrande, 76 from Calle Santa Bárbara or anything marked 'Zoológico.' Taxis for up to four people cost around B$15 from the center.

BIOCENTRO GÜEMBE

A great place for a day out of Santa Cruz, **Güembe** (370-0541; www.biocentroguembe.com; Km 7, Camino Porongo, Zona Los Batos; admission adult/child B$160/80) has a butterfly farm, orchid exhibitions, 10 natural pools, fishing and trekking in the surrounding forest. There's a restaurant with international cuisine, so you won't go hungry, and cabins if you wish to stay the night. The best way to get here is by taxi from Santa Cruz; expect to pay around B$30.

PARQUE AVION PIRATA

On the *primer anillo*, this small plaza has a huge airplane as its centerpiece. According to local legend the plane belonged to drug smugglers who, after entering into difficulties, touched down at its current location only to be raided by police. The police decided to leave the plane there as a reminder to other would-be *narcotrafficantes*. It's not true of course, but it's a nice story!

AQUALAND

For a real splash, dive into this **water park** (☎ 385-2500; half day B$35-50, full day B$50-70; ✆ 10am-6pm Thu-Sun May-Sep) near the airport, north of the city center. The best way to get here is by taxi (around B$30).

LOMAS DE ARENA

Located 16km south of the city, this small nature reserve is famed for its gorgeous sand dunes – a geological mystery, given that the sand apparently originates from Argentina and no other sand dunes have formed anywhere in the area. This is a great spot for birdwatchers, with temporary pools filling with migrant birds from September to November and February to March. The relict Chiquitania forest in the area is home to vocal titi monkeys and toucans. A taxi will take you to the entrance to the park (around B$20 from the city center), but if you wish to explore further you'll either have to walk or you'll need a 4WD vehicle. Bird Bolivia (see below) runs recommended day-trips to the park. If you wish to stay there is an excellent hotel, **Sol y Arena** (☎ 322-1375; cabins for 4 people B$420), which is close to the park entrance.

Tours

Numerous companies offer organized tours, but it's hard to vouch for quality, particularly for those with cheap rates. Recommended agencies:

Amboró Tours (☎ 314-5858; www.amborotours.com; Pari 81) Trips to Amboró and Noel Kempff Mercado national parks and Jesuit missions.

Bird Bolivia (☎ 358-2674; www.birdbolivia.com) Professional birding and wildlife tours with expert guides for those with a special interest in nature.

Ruta Verde (☎ 339-6470; www.rutaverdebolivia.com; 21 de Mayo 332) Great for local information and tours to the Pantanal, Jesuit missions, Amboró and Noel Kempff Mercado national parks, plus Amazon riverboat trips and more.

Festivals & Events

If you're in Santa Cruz during **Carnaval**, you should most certainly head for the paintball-plagued streets and join in the collective chaos. Carnaval occurs annually

in February or March, one week before Lent begins.

International Theater Festival Theater groups from all over the world perform in venues around the city. Held from April 14 to 24 (odd-numbered years only), it's a great time to be in Santa Cruz.

International Festival of Baroque Music A 10-day festival, held from the end of April to the beginning of May, with concerts in Santa Cruz and the Jesuit mission towns.

International Festival of Cheese & Wine A relatively new festival, held in August, where locals showcase their best offerings. Great opportunity to taste Bolivian wine from Tarija.

ExpoCruz (www.fexpocruz.com.bo) Every year in mid- to late September, Santa Cruz hosts this enormous two-week fair where you can buy anything from a toothbrush or clothing to a new house, a combine harvester or a 20-ton truck.

Sleeping

BUDGET

Alojamiento Santa Bárbara (☎ 332-1817; Santa Bárbara 151; s/d B$35/50) This is a low-key place with a courtyard and bare rooms with hospital-like beds. It's much loved by backpackers and young Bolivians for being cheap and central.

Alojamiento Oriente (☎ 332-1976; Junín 362; s/d B$35/60, with bathroom B$60/90; ✆) A bit run-down and with peeling walls, but given its central location and the fact that floor fans come as standard even in the cheapest rooms, this is a good budget option.

Hotel Rio Magdalena (☎ 339-3011; Arenales 653; dm B$50, s/d B$110/120; ✆ ✆) Former Peace Corps hangout, this is a top-notch midrange option with comfortable rooms, an inviting pool and a roof terrace with glorious views of the city.

Jodanga Backpackers Hostel (☎ 312-0033; www .jodanga.com; El Fuerte 1380 696; dm B$65-75, d B$140, d with bathroom B$200; ✆ ✆) The 'in' place for Santa Cruz backpackers, this superbly equipped hostel has a pool, jacuzzi, pool table, free internet and seriously groovy, air-conditioned rooms, as well as a party atmosphere inspired by its own bar. They also organize great value Spanish classes.

our pick **Hotel Sarah** (☎ 332-2425; Sara 85; s/d B$70/120; ✆) Arguably the best option in this price range, this brand-new hotel boasts a great location and spotless rooms with cable TV. Walls are adorned with jungle scenes to prepare you for any Amazonian adventures that may lie ahead.

Residencial Bolívar (☎ 334-2500; Sucre 131; s/d B$75/130) Leafy tropical patios, a toucan snoozing on a branch and clean, if small, rooms. You can laze in the hammocks or read in the courtyard. Breakfast is included and Spanish lessons available for guests.

MIDRANGE

Santa Cruz has a growing number of mid-range hotels, all with private bathrooms and reasonable prices.

Hotel Copacabana (☎ 336-2770; Junín 217; without air-con s/d B$139/196, with air-con s/d B$213/251) A strange sort of retro Buddhist joint that will appeal to some but be a turn-off for others. Dated, wood-paneled rooms with modern bathrooms and cable TV compound the mixed messages that this place sends. Breakfast included and 10% discount for HI members.

Hotel Globetrotter (☎ 337-2754; Sara 49; s/d B$160/200; 🖂) Lovely traditional Santa Cruz house converted into a hotel, with a long courtyard laden with plants and rooms with cable TV. The friendly multilingual owner is a well of local information who can book plane tickets and help with your itinerary. Breakfast, though included, isn't a standout and is best avoided.

Hotel La Paz (☎ 333-1728; La Paz 69; s/d B$160/250; 🖂 🖥) Decent value for comfortable suite-like double rooms arranged around a leafy courtyard. Single rooms are quite a bit smaller, but they will upgrade you to a suite for an extra B$40.

Hotel Viru Viru (☎ 333-5298; www.viruviru .com; Junín 338; s/d B$210/280; 🖂 🖥 🖳) Great for stifling hot Santa Cruz days, Viru Viru has a pool in the center to cool off in. The rooms and rates are decent, with good beds, breakfasts, TVs and free internet access for guests, and the location is great.

Hotel Lido (☎ 336-3555; www.lido-hotel.com; 21 de Mayo 527; s/d B$240/310; 🖂 🖥) A nice but relatively simple upmarket choice in the center, above a Chinese restaurant, the Lido has comfortable rooms with TVs, and access to laundry facilities. There's also a weight-lifting gym on the ground floor.

TOP END

Santa Cruz' five-star hotels are away from the center and are more like resorts than hotels. Many were built during the oil boom, but things went pear-shaped in the mid-1990s when the casinos were closed due to political wrangling.

Hotel Los Tajibos (☎ 342-1000, 800-10-2210; www .lostajiboshotel.com; San Martín 455, Barrio Equipetrol; s/d/ ste B$1200/1300/1500; 🖂 🖥 🖳) If you stay at Los Tajibos you won't want to go out to see the city. There's a nightclub to go wild in and a health club to recover in, while muscle flexing can go on at the racquetball courts, followed by a massage or relaxing in the lush tropical gardens. Weekend package rates (from B$500 per person) are often available.

Hotel Yotaú (☎ 336-7799; San Martín 7, Barrio Equipetrol; s/d B$1500/1700; 🖂 🖥 🖳) This beautiful tropical-style high-rise has fitness facilities and a sauna, as well as executive and family rooms for up to six people (B$2200). Lunches and dinners cost B$60 each.

Eating

RESTAURANTS

The international population has rolled up its sleeves and opened some fine restaurants, so what the city lacks in sightseeing it makes up in gastronomic offerings.

Alexander (☎ 312-8888; Junín; mains B$10-30) This is a haven for delicious breakfasts and good coffee. Part of a chain, Alexander is excellent for sampling local Madidi coffee and any range of breakfasts, including *huevos rancheros* (spicy scrambled eggs) and gigantic fruit salads served with yoghurt and honey.

Vegetarian Center Cuerpomonte (☎ 337-1797; Aroma 54; buffet per kg B$15; 🕑 9am-7pm Mon-Sat) Basic and simple, this place has a buffet selection, including quinoa cake, mashed sweet potato, salad bar goodies, veggie soups and lots of other nice wholesome things to keep your body healthy.

Los Lomitos (☎ 332-8696; Uruguay 758; mains B$15-70) Argentinian-style *churrasqueria* (grilled meat restaurant): if you are a beef fanatic then look no further. Famed for its excellent-value tender cuts, the portions for two will feed four normal-sized people. Delivery to your hotel available.

Ken (☎ 333-3728; Uruguay 730; mains B$20-35; 🕑 closed Wed) Everybody's favorite Japanese eatery. The *yaki udon* (stir-fried noodles) is massive, laden with chicken and cashews, and there's a great choice of daily dishes to be savored. Just check out all the folk from the Japanese community licking their whiskers in satisfaction.

El Aljibe (☎ 335-2277; Ñuflo de Chavez; mains B$25-40) An atmospheric little restaurant specializing in *comida tipica* (typical food), which is increasingly difficult to find in cosmopolitan Santa Cruz.

Cada Día (Melchor Pinto; mains B$25-40) Chinese-owned, this is one of the city's most popular vegetarian restaurants, with delicious tofu and gluten dishes that really do taste just like meat.

Pizzería Marguerita (☎ 337-0285; north side of Plaza 24 de Septiembre; mains B$25-50) Long known for its high-quality pizza, pasta and salads, and always popular with foreigners, this well-located place is good for a casual meal.

Casa Típica de Camba (☎ 342-7864; www .casadelcamba.com; Mendoza 539; mains B$25-55) You are likely to end up at this lively, sprawling landmark if you ask Bolivian friends where to find the 'most typical' *cruceños/camba* experience. Juicy meat comes sizzling off the grill while live crooners holler traditional tunes and straw-hatted waiters attend to your every need. Take *micro 35* or *75* from the center.

La Bella Napoli (☎ 332-5402; Independencía 635; pizzas & mains B$30-50; ☽ 6pm-midnight Tue-Sun) In a rustic barn six blocks south of the plaza, this place serves fine pizza and pasta dishes – including ravioli, cannelloni and lasagna – on chunky hardwood tables, some outside on a vine-covered patio.

La Casona (☎ 337-8495; www.bistrolacasona.com; Arenales 222; mains B$35-80; ☽ closed Sun) One of Santa Cruz' best places to eat, this German-run splash of California gourmet has seating in a shady courtyard or inside amid the colorful indigenous art that adorns the walls. The food is diverse, with a variety of salads, German dishes, or pasta in a spicy, palate-biting *arrabiatta* (spicy tomato sauce).

Yorimichi (☎ 334-7717; Busch 548; mains B$36-70; ☽ 11:30am-2:30pm & 6-11pm) A swish Japanese restaurant with bamboo screens separating eating spaces and traditional music tinkling from the speakers, this is the place to come for brilliant sushi, sashimi, tempura and heart-warming sips of sake. It's a favorite of upmarket *cruceños*.

Lorca (☎ 334-0562; Moreno 20; mains B$40-60; ☽ 8am-late) Arguably the city center's trendiest restaurant, bar, theater and general hangout, Lorca play with several world cuisines, and its llama steak, dribbled with a

blue-cheese sauce, is top class. If you are feeling more adventurous, try *cola de lagarto* (alligator tail).

Y Se Llama Peru (☎ 335-4969; Monseñor Rivero; mains B$45-90) Adventurous seafood restaurant with a huge variety of imaginative fish and shellfish dishes. Try the *Picante de Mariscos* if you like your shellfish to come with a nip.

Maminco (☎ 337-1911; Busch 150; mains B$45-130) Grill restaurant with a rustic *quincho* (open-air grill) atmosphere, this place specializes in duck, which it has been preparing on the premises since the early 1980s. If you work up a thirst in the process try the juice wagon in front for great-value tropical drinks.

Michelangelo's (☎ 334-8403; Chuquisaca 502; mains B$50-80) Located in a classy house, complete with fireplaces and marble floors, this is a good choice for a romantic evening or a little Italian self-indulgence.

CAFES

Av Monseñor Rivero is lined with snazzy cafes and coffee shops that seem to get trendier, or at least more expensive, the further along that you walk.

Mr Café (Monseñor Rivero 260; snacks B$20-40) Sandwiches, juices, cakes, light meals and ice cream to complement its rich espressos all make this place a favorite local hangout.

Bar El Tapekuá (☎ 334-5905; cnr La Paz & Ballivián; ☽ from 7:30pm Wed-Sat) This casual yet upscale Swiss and Bolivian-owned place serves good, earthy food and has live music most nights (B$15 to B$20 cover).

QUICK EATS

As Bolivia's most modern, hustle-and-bustle town, Santa Cruz also boasts more junk food outlets than you can shake a happy meal at. For the highest concentration of fast-food places head south of the center to Plaza Blacutt. It's surrounded by cheap burger and chicken joints and all you can eat dives such as El Bibosi, where you can get a fill-your-boots lunch for B$15.

Panificación del Oriente (☎ 336-7258; 24 de Septiembre 501; pastries from B$3) If the smell of freshly-baked bread doesn't drive you crazy then take your pick from the mouthwatering variety of cakes, buns, pastries and tarts on offer.

Salón de Té Glamour (☎ 333-6633; Independencia 479; tea B$5) So what is so glamorous about a cup of tea you may ask? Well nothing really, but this minimalist, super-clean tearoom does its best to introduce you to the world of flavors that tealike drinks can provide, with herbal infusions, *mates*, coffees and sticky cakes on offer. Have a quick look at the teapot collection too – bizarre!

Bar Hawai (cnr Sucre & Beni; mains B$20) An expansive cross between an ice-cream joint and a fast-food eatery, this spot is popular for sundaes, cakes, light meals and good coffee. A reasonably priced buffet lunch is served in the garden.

Roky's Pollos Parrillados (☎ 333-8886; Cañoto 50; chicken B$20-30) If you have a soft spot for fried poultry then try Roky's charcoal-grilled roosters. There's free home delivery if you are too lazy to walk.

Dumbo (☎ 336-7077; Ayacucho 247; ice creams B$5-15, mains B$20-50) Dumbo serves gourmet frozen yogurt in the usual flavors plus *maracuya* (passion fruit), papaya, *guayaba* (guava), almond, tangerine and so on. One thing you can say about the meals here is that you get a lot of food for your money.

GROCERIES

For simple, cheap eats, try Mercado La Ramada but consider hygiene levels carefully before indulging. Mercado Florida is wall-to-wall blender stalls serving exquisite juices and fruit salads for B$5.

For a good variety of (relatively expensive) fixings to prepare meals yourself, try minimart **Hipermaxi** (cnr 21 de Mayo & Florida). **Supermercado Sur Fidalga** (east Plaza Blacutt) is the best stocked, cheapest option for groceries. **Naturalia** (☎ 333-4374; Independencia 452) organic grocery store has a wide selection of locally produced healthy goodies and a small cafe to try them in.

Drinking

The hippest nightspots are along Av San Martin, between the second and third *anillos* in Barrio Equipetrol, a B$7 to $B10 taxi ride from the center. Hot spots change frequently so it's best to dress to impress, cruise the *piranhar* (strip; literally 'to go piranha fishing') and see what catches your fancy. Cover charges run from B$20 to B$70 and drinks are expensive; most places start selling drinks between 6pm and 9pm but don't warm up until 11pm; they then continue until sunrise.

If you don't want to pay entry fees to the discos, at weekends a young beach crowd gathers with their cars at Río Pira'i, banging out unbelievably loud music from their gigantic car-boot speakers, while drinking beer, dancing and chatting till late. The area is potentially unsafe at other times though. Near the university, Av Busch is lined with places catering to more serious, mostly male drinkers with less ready cash.

Irish Pub (☎ 333-8118; east side Plaza 24 de Septiembre) A travelers' second home in Santa Cruz, this place has pricey beers, delicious soups and comfort food, plus tasty local specialties. It serves breakfast, lunch and dinner, though most people while the hours away drinking beer, relaxing and watching the goings-on in the plaza below.

Lorca (☎ 334-0562; Moreno 20; admission for live music B$20; ☯ 8am-late) Meeting place of the city's arty crowd and those loving diversity, Lorca is one of the most innovative and happening places in town. It's perfect for chilled *caipirinha* and *mojito* cocktails while you enjoy the live music. Before the music starts, short films are screened and there is an art gallery in the back, right next to the little theater.

Clapton's Blues Bar (cnr Murillo & Arenales; admission B$20; ☯ Sat & Sun) A tiny, dark jazz-and-blues bar with local bands playing to a sparse drinking audience till very late. There can be good jazz here (and very bad rock), so check what's playing by asking at the bar.

Entertainment

Santa Cruz has a number of discos and karaoke bars, which reflects the city's young, liberal and cosmopolitan character. The bars and clubs close and open monthly, so ask around for what's hot. For movie schedules and other venues, see the daily newspapers *El Mundo* and *El Deber*.

Cinecenter (☎ free phone 900-770077; second anillo; cinema admission B$30-50) Modern mall with food court, trendy shops and a 12-screen US-style cinema that shows all the latest Hollywood releases. This place has rapidly become the place to be seen in Santa Cruz, to the detriment of a number of smaller cinemas and art-houses that have closed as a result.

Eleguá (Libertad) During the week this is a Cuban cultural-center-cum-bar-cum-dance-school (it depends which day you visit!). At weekends it metamorphoses into a groovy Latino disco where you can swing your thing to the latest samba sounds.

El Rincón Salteño (☎ 353-6335; 26 de Enero at Charagua; ⏰ from 10pm Fri, Sat & Sun) Traditional *peñas* (folk-music programs) are scarce in modern Santa Cruz, but this is an excellent choice. Positioned on the second *anillo*, there's a great variety of musical styles, from Argentine guitarists to Cuban village drummers, local singers and dancers in costume.

Shopping

Wood carvings made from the tropical hardwoods *morado* and the more expensive *guayacán* (from B$150 for a nice piece) are unique to the Santa Cruz area. Relief carvings on *tari* nuts are also interesting and make nice portable souvenirs. Locals also make beautiful macramé *llicas* (root-fiber bags).

Av René Moreno is a good place for souvenir shopping. Be aware that prices are much higher here than in La Paz for llama and alpaca wool goods. Paseo Artesanal La Recova, a block north from the plaza along Libertad is packed with little stores selling both authentic and fabricated handicrafts at reasonable prices.

Artecampo (☎ 334-1843; Salvatierra 407) The best place to find fine *artesanías* (locally handcrafted items), this store provides an outlet for the work of 1000 rural *cruceña* women and their families. The truly inspired and innovative pieces include leatherwork, hammocks, weavings, handmade paper, greeting cards and lovely natural-material lamp shades.

Centro de Arte y Cultura Guaraní Ñandereko Ñomai (☎ 337-6285; Junín 229; ⏰ 9am-12:30pm & 3-7pm) You'll find lovely wooden carvings and textiles from Guaraní villages here, all created by indigenous families who benefit directly from the sales. It's only small but worth a visit.

Coca Social (Junín) All manner of coca produce is on sale at this fascinating little store, the likes of which you won't find in your home town.

Getting There & Away

AIR

Viru-Viru international airport (VVI; ☎ 338-5000), 15km north of the center, handles domestic and international flights.

TAM (☎ 353-2639) flies direct to La Paz daily. It also runs popular direct flights to Puerto Suárez on Tuesday and Saturday, and on Sunday there are flights to Riberalta and Tarija via Yacuiba. **AeroSur** (☎ 336-4446; Irala at Colón) has daily services to Cochabamba, La Paz and Sucre, as well as several other Bolivian cities, plus services to Asunción on Monday, Wednesday, Friday and Sunday. **TAM Mercosur** (☎ 339-1999; La Riva & Velasco) flies to Asunción Tuesday, Thursday, Saturday and Sunday, with connections to Buenos Aires, Santiago de Chile and several Brazilian cities. **Aerocon** (☎ 351-1200; El Trompillo Airport) flies several times daily to Trinidad with onward connections to Cobija and Riberalta from El Trompillo airport just south of the center.

American Airlines (☎ 334-1314; Beni 167) flies direct daily to Miami in the morning, with a second evening flight from Thursday to Sunday. **Aerolíneas Argentinas** (☎ 333-9776; Junín 22) flies several times a week to Buenos Aires.

BUS, MICRO & SHARED TAXI

The full-service **bimodal terminal** (☎ 334-0772; terminal fee B$3), the combined long-distance bus and train station, is 1.5km east of the center, just before the third *anillo* at the end of Av Brasil. The main part of the terminal is for *flotas* (long-distance buses) and the train; on the other side of the tunnel is the *micro* (minibus) terminal for regional services. Taking a series of connecting *micros* or taxis can be a faster, if more complicated way, of reaching your destination, rather than waiting all day for an evening *flota*.

There are plenty of daily services to Cochabamba (B$30, eight to 10 hours), from where there are connections to La Paz, Oruro, Sucre, Potosí and Tarija. Cosmos has two direct daily services to La Paz (B$130, 15 to 23 hours) at 5pm and 5:30pm. Several companies offer daily evening services to Sucre (B$80, 15 to 25 hours), connecting to Potosí. Most services to Camiri (B$30, five to six hours) and Yacuiba (B$50, 10 hours) depart in the late afternoon. Buses to Vallegrande (B$35, six to seven hours) leave in the morning and afternoon. A number of buses leave every evening to Trinidad (B$50 to B$120, at least nine hours) and beyond. The trip frequently gets rough in the rainy season and it's worth paying a bit extra for a *bus cama* (bed bus).

To the Jesuit missions and Chiquitania, *flotas* leave in the morning and early evening (7pm to 9pm) to San Xavier (B$40, five hours) and Concepción (B$40, six hours). Departures at 8pm go on to San Ignacio de Velasco (B$50, 10 hours). *Micros* run throughout the day, every two hours or so, but only go as far as Concepción (B$35, five hours).

International routes have offices at the left-hand end of the main terminal as you enter. Daily services connect Santa Cruz with Buenos Aires (B$500, 36 hours), whilst Yacyreta run the most comfortable service to Asunción, Paraguay (B$320, 24 hours).

Smaller *micros* and *trufis* (collective taxis or minibuses that follow a set route) to Viru-Viru airport, Montero (with connections to Buena Vista and Villa Tunari), Samaipata and other communities in Santa Cruz department leave regularly from outside the old bus terminal and less regularly from the *micro* platforms at the bimodal terminal. To Buena Vista (B$20, two hours), they wait on Izozog (Isoso), near the old bus terminal. To Samaipata (B$25, three hours), *trufis* leave on the opposite side of Av Cañoto, about two blocks from the old bus terminal.

TRAIN
Trains depart from the bimodal terminal bound for Quijarro (see the boxed text, p292) and Yacuiba. For access to the platform you need to buy a platform ticket and show your passport to the platform guard.

The rail service to Yacuiba (p256) on the Argentine border, via Villamontes (p257; the connection point for buses to Paraguay), is a reasonably quick and comfortable *Ferrobus* (passenger rail bus; *semi-cama/cama* B$120/135, 11 hours), which departs at 6pm on Thursday and Sunday, returning on Friday and Monday at 6pm.

Getting Around
TO/FROM THE AIRPORT
Handy minibuses leave Viru-Viru for the center (B$3, 30 minutes) when flights arrive. Minibuses to the airport leave every 20 minutes starting at 5:30am from Av Cañoto at stops along the first *anillo*. Taxis for up to four people cost B$50.

TO/FROM THE BUS & TRAIN STATION
The bimodal bus-train station is beyond easy walking distance, but you can get to the center in about 10 minutes on *micro 12*. Expect to pay B$5 to B$7 per person for a taxi.

BUS
Santa Cruz' system of city *micros* (B$1.50) connects the transportation terminals and all the *anillos* with the center. *Micros 17* and *18* circulate around the first *anillo*. To reach Av San Martin in Barrio Equipetrol, take *micro 23* from anywhere on Vallegrande. A *Guia de Micros* documenting all the city routes is available from bookstores and kiosks (B$25 to B$50).

CAR
Most rent-a-car companies also have offices at the airport.

American Rent-a-Car (☎ 334-1235; Justiniano 28 at Uruguay)

Avis Rent-a-Car (☎ 343-3939; Km 3.5, Carretera al Norte)

Barron's Rent-a-Car (☎ 333-8823; www.rentacarbolivia.com; Cristóbal de Mendoza 286

Localiza Rent-a-Car (☎ 343-3939; Km 3.5, Banzer)

TAXI
Taxis are very cheap but there is no rigid price structure. Typically the price is higher if you are in a group, are carrying lots of luggage or wish to travel after 10pm, and drivers will quote a fee that they consider fair for the journey. If you think it is too much refuse and try the next one: there are plenty to choose from. Typically a trip for one person within the first *anillo* during the day is about B$5, rising to B$7 if you stray to the second *anillo*. Agree your price in advance to avoid arguments.

BUENA VISTA
pop 13,300

Despite the presence of two hulking cell-phone masts overlooking the plaza, Buena Vista is a nice little town two hours (103km) northwest of Santa Cruz, serving as an ideal staging point for trips into Parque Nacional Amboró's forested lowland section. Though most foreigners prefer Samaipata (p278) for national park exploration, Buena Vista has some of the best places to view wildlife, observe birds and see local traditions.

Information
There is no tourist office at the time of writing. For information on Parque Nacional Amboró, visit **SERNAP** (Servicio National de Areas Protegidas; ☎ 932-2055; www.sernap.gov.bo in Spanish; ☺ 7am-7pm), a block south of the plaza, where you can pick up an entry permit and

inquire about current park regulations and accommodations options.

There's no bank or ATM here, so bring cash from elsewhere. If you are desperate, a **Moneygram office** (🕒 8:30am-noon & 2:30-6pm Mon-Fri, 8:30am-noon Sat) on the street corner two blocks north of the plaza can wire money from abroad. An acceptable internet connection is available at **Punto Viva** (per hr B$4; 🕒 8am-10pm) on the northwest corner of the plaza.

English-speaking **Amboró Tours** (☎ 314-5858; www.amborotours.com; Pari 81) in Santa Cruz runs adventurous trips to the northern section of the park, starting at B$400 per person per day for two people, including transportation, a guide and food. They no longer have an office in Buena Vista.

Sights & Activities
IGLESIA DE LOS SANTOS DESPOSORIOS
Buena Vista's Jesuit mission was founded in 1694 as the fifth mission in the Viceroyalty of Peru, but in its current form dates from 1767. When the Jesuits were expelled from Bolivia later that year, the administration of the church passed to the bishop of Santa Cruz. Although the building is deteriorating, it has a lovely classic form, but you'd have to be a brave soul to scale the precarious ladder to the bell tower for views of the plaza.

RÍO SURUTÚ, SANTA BÁRBARA & EL CAIRO
Río Surutú is a popular excursion for locals, and there's a pleasant sandy beach ideal for picnics, swimming and camping during the dry season. From Buena Vista it's an easy 3km walk to the river bend nearest town. The opposite bank is the boundary of Parque Nacional Amboró.

A good longer option is the six-hour **circuit walk** through the community of Santa Bárbara and partially forested tropical plantation country. From Buena Vista, follow the unpaved road to Santa Bárbara and ask for the track that leads to an idyllic river beach on the Río Ucurutú. After a picnic and a dip, you can return to Buena Vista via the Huaytú road.

An even better swimming hole is at **El Cairo**, which is an hour's walk from town. To get there, head downhill from the plaza past the alcaldia (town hall) and follow the unpaved

road as it curves to the right. About 2km from town, take the left fork and cross over a bridge. After passing El Cairo, on your right, keep going until you reach the river.

Festivals & Events
The local fiesta, **Día de los Santos Desposorios** (November 26), features bullfights, food stalls and general merrymaking. Culinary festivals include: the **Chocolate Festival** (last Sunday in January), the **Coffee Festival** (third Sunday in April) and the **Rice Festival** (early May) after the harvest.

Sleeping
La Casona (☎ 932-2083; western cnr of plaza; r per person B$30) This is a colorful place on the plaza, with a friendly owner and a nice patio with sagging hammocks. The rooms are decked out in pastel shades, have good beds and a floor fan. Spotlessly clean shared bathrooms only.

Residencial Nadia (☎ 932-2049; Sevilla 186; r per person B$70) Just off the main square, the spacious rooms at this family home surround a patio. There are firm beds and the owner is a good source of park information. All rooms have fans.

Buena Vista Hotel (☎ 339-1080; www.buena vistahotel.com.bo; r per person B$100-150; 🔀 🖳 🖳) A glorious range of suites, cabins and rooms set in gorgeous gardens around a refreshing pool. There is something for everyone in this, the best hotel within walking distance of the center; restaurant is top class too.

Hotel Flora & Fauna (☎ 710-43706; amboro adventures@hotmail.com; r per person all-inclusive B$350) British ornithologist/entomologist Robin Clarke runs this modern, utilitarian collection of cabins. Pluses include wildlife-viewing platforms, an extensive book exchange and guided walks (for guests only) from B$70. Access is by car/moto-taxi (B$25/15) from Buena Vista. Book in advance.

Amboró Eco-Resort (☎ 932-2048, in Santa Cruz 3-342-2372; s/d/ste B$600/700/1000; 🔀 🖳) A 20-minute walk outside of town, this resort is surrounded by its own tropical forest, complete with walking paths and fenced-in forest animals. Amenities include a swim-up bar in the pool, a sauna and a disco. It's not the world's quietest place, but it's fun if you're with children. The resort also operates Mataracú Tent Camp (p276).

Eating

A few places are dotted around the plaza, serving a similar uninspiring selection of deep-fried meat and chicken with rice and salad. None are particularly appetizing or cheap, and given the proximity to the national park the fact that they also serve wild game means that any responsible traveler should treat them with suspicion. Beware too of 'special tropical juices' served in some of these places; the only special thing about them is the inflated price. Patujú on the south side of the plaza sells homemade jams, honeys and *comida tipica* to take away or eat in.

Pensión Gladibal (1 block north of plaza; almuerzo B$12) Cheap and cheerful with wholesome, home-cooked food in spotless surroundings.

La Plaza (☎ 932-2079; north side of plaza; mains B$35-70) By far the best eating in town, La Plaza serves a variety of beef, fish and chicken dishes in rustic ranch house style surroundings. This is a good place to pig out if you are back from roughing it in the park.

Shopping

On the west side of the plaza, **El Tojo** sells lamp shades, handbags, boxes and panama hats made from *jipijapa* (the fronds of the cyclanthaceae fan palm); the use of these fronds for making *artesanías* is specific to Buena Vista. Up the street, the recommended Artecampo store also sells *jipijapa* products, plus other local creations.

Getting There & Away

From Santa Cruz, shared taxis (☎ 356-7084; per person B$20) leave for Yapacaní from the *micro* side of the bimodal terminal and behind the old long-distance bus terminal. Make it clear that you want to get off at Buena Vista.

AMBORÓ COMMUNITY PROJECTS

The location of Parque Nacional Amboró is a mixed blessing; although it's conveniently accessible to visitors, it also lies practically within spitting distance of Santa Cruz and squarely between the old and new Cochabamba–Santa Cruz highways. Considering that even the remote parks of the Amazon Basin are coming under threat, Amboró feels 'people pressure' more than most.

When Parque Nacional Amboró was created in 1973, its charter included a clause forbidding settlement and resource exploitation. Unfortunately for naturalists and conservationists, hunters, loggers and *campesino* (subsistence farmer) settlers continued to pour in – many of them displaced from the Chapare region by the US Drug Enforcement Agency. By 1996, with conflicts increasing over the park, it was redesignated as the Área de Uso Múltiple Amboró, which effectively opened it up for settlement.

This reducing of the park's protection status necessitated a change in tactics by local NGOs and conservation groups keen to avoid the complete destruction of the natural treasures of the region, but also fully aware of the needs of the human population. As a result, a number of responsible and sustainable 'community projects' have sprung up in the area, using tourism as a means of generating income for locals without them having to exploit their natural resources. The following are some of the more interesting of these projects:

Candelaria Ecoalbergue (☎ 7600-7785; r per person B$150) In the community of Candelaria 3km south of Buena Vista, this place manages comfortable four-person cabins and offers forest walks in the surrounding area. Perhaps more interesting is the opportunity to observe local craftsmen practicing the arts of weaving *jipijapa* and whittling *tacuara* (bamboo) into all manner of useful objects.

Hacienda El Cafetal (☎ 935-2067; www.anditradecoffee.com; s/d B$150/220, ste B$330, cabañas B$580; ❌ ❍) Set up to support Bolivian coffee growers and their families; the accommodations are good, with stylish, self-catering *cabañas* (cabins) and suites, all with good views. You can go around the plantations and see how coffee is produced, taste different types of the strong black stuff, and then, caffeine-pumped, ride horses and go bird-watching.

Refugio Volcánes (☎ 337-2042; www.refugiovolcanes.net; r per person all inclusive B$500) Ecofriendly *cabañas* with hot showers in the breathtaking Los Volcánes region 4km off the Santa Cruz–Samaipata road at Bermejo. Transportation from the road is offered, as well as guided hikes through the wonderfully wild landscapes.

To return to Santa Cruz, wait for a shared taxi coming from Yapacaní, which will cruise around the plaza in search of passengers with its horn blaring, or ask at one of the taxi offices on the main plaza.

Getting Around
Car taxis and moto-taxis (B$2) wait at one corner of the plaza; there's also another taxi stand along the road to Santa Bárbara for Hotel Flora & Fauna.

PARQUE NACIONAL & ÁREA DE USO MÚLTIPLE AMBORÓ
This 430,000-hectare park lies in a unique geographical position at the confluence of three distinct ecosystems: the Amazon Basin, the northern Chaco and the Andes.

The park was originally created in 1973 as the Reserva de Vida Silvestre Germán Busch, with an area of 180,000 hectares. In 1984, due to the efforts of British zoologist Robin Clarke and Bolivian biologist Noel Kempff Mercado, it was given national-park status and in 1990 was expanded to 630,000 hectares. In late 1995, however, amid controversy surrounding *campesino* colonization inside park boundaries, it was pared down to its current size.

The park's range of habitats means that both highland and lowland species are found here. Mammals include elusive spectacled bears, jaguars, tapirs, peccaries and various monkeys, while more than 800 species of birds have been documented. The park is the stronghold of the endangered horned curassow, known as the unicorn bird (see the boxed text, p316).

Buena Vista Section
Access to the eastern part of the reserve requires crossing over the Río Surutú, either in a vehicle or on foot. Depending on the rainfall and weather, the river may be anywhere from knee- to waist-deep. Inexperienced hikers should not attempt any of the treks in the park without a guide.

RÍO MACUÑUCU
The Río Macuñucu route is the most popular into the Área de Uso Múltiple Amboró and begins at **Las Cruces**, 35km southeast of Buena Vista (taxi B$30). From there it's 7km to the Río Surutú, which you must drive or wade across; just beyond

the opposite bank you'll reach **Villa Amboró**. Villagers may charge an entrance fee to any tourist who passes their community en route to Macuñucu, regardless of whether you intend to stay there or not – avoid unpleasantness and pay.

From here a popular trek runs to the banks of the **Río Macuñucu** and follows its course through thick forest. After four hours or so you pass through a narrow canyon, which confines hikers to the river, and a little later you'll reach a large rock overhang accommodating up to 10 campers. Beyond here the trek becomes increasingly difficult and terrain more rugged as you head towards some beautiful waterfalls and a second camp site. Take a guide if you are considering doing the full hike.

RÍO ISAMA & CERRO AMBORÓ
The Río Isama route turns off at the village of **Espejitos**, 28km southeast of Buena Vista, and provides access to the base of 1300m Cerro Amboró, the bulbous peak for which the park is named. It's possible to climb to the summit, but it is a difficult trek and a guide is essential.

MATARACÚ
From near Yapacaní, on the main Cochabamba road, a 4WD track heads south across the Río Yapacaní into the northern reaches of the Área de Uso Múltiple Amboró and, after a rough 18km, rolls up to Amboró Eco-Resort's **Mataracú Tent Camp** (☎ 932-2048, in Santa Cruz 3-342-2372; r per person with breakfast & lunch B$700), which has palm huts capped by thatched roofs, and *cabañas* on stilts. There is also the community-run **Posada Ecologica** (☎ 716-74582; dm B$35, d B$50), which offers all-you-can-eat meals (breakfast/lunch B$10/15) and can be booked through any agency in Buena Vista. This is the only SERNAP *cabaña* accessible by motor vehicle; however, crossing the Río Yapacaní may be a problem except in the driest part of the year.

Samaipata Area
Samaipata sits just outside the southern boundary of the Área de Uso Múltiple Amboró and provides the best access point for the Andean section of the park. There's no real infrastructure, or public facilities, in this area.

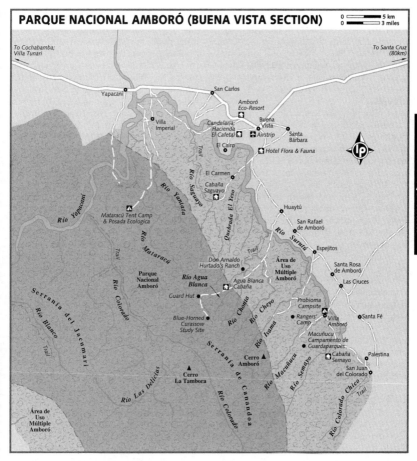

PARQUE NACIONAL AMBORÓ (BUENA VISTA SECTION)

The best guides to the region are available in Samaipata. The road uphill from there ends at a small cabin, and from there it's a four-hour walk to a camping spot near the boundary between the primary forest, giant ferns and Andean cloud forest. From this point, you can continue an hour further into the park.

Mairana Area

From Mairana, it's 7km uphill along a walking track (or take a taxi) to **La Yunga**, where there's a community-run guest hut and a FAN office. It's in a particularly lush region of the Área de Uso Múltiple Amboró, surrounded by tree ferns and other cloudforest vegetation. From La Yunga, a 16km

forest traverse connects with the main road near Samaipata.

To enter the park here, visit the guard post at the south end of the soccer field in La Yunga. Access to Mairana is by *micro* or *taxi* from Samaipata.

Comarapa Area

Northwest of Comarapa, 4km toward Cochabamba, is a little-used entrance to the Área de Uso Múltiple Amboró. After the road crosses a pass between a hill and a ridge with a telephone tower, look for the minor road turning off to the northeast at the settlement of **Khara Huasi**. This road leads uphill to verdant stands of cloud forest, which blanket the peaks.

Other worthwhile visits in this area include the 36-sided **Pukara de Tuquipaya**, a set of pre-Inca ruins on the summit of **Cerro Comanwara**, 1.5km outside of Comarapa; and the colonial village of **Pulquina Arriba**, several kilometers east of Comarapa.

Sleeping

Inside the park are five wilderness *cabañas* (around B$30 per person per day). For bookings and information, contact SERNAP (p273). The *cabañas* are very basic, so you'll need your own sleeping bag. The most popular and accessible *cabaña* is the one on the Río Macuñucu. It's 4km upstream, and has a sleeping loft and rudimentary cooking facilities. Other *cabañas* can be found on the lower Río Semayo, above the Río Mataracú, on the Río Agua Blanca and on the lower Río Saguayo.

Situated at Villa Amboró, near the mouth of the Macuñucu, the nongovernment organization (NGO) **Probioma** (☎ 343-1332; www.probioma.org.bo; Córdoba 7 Este No 29, Santa Cruz) helped start a community-run campsite with clean showers, toilets and some hiking trails. Local Spanish-speaking guides can provide info and the community can organize meals and arrange horse-riding. A two-day stay, including guides, horses, camping gear and meals, costs around B$250 per person.

Getting There & Away

By far the easiest and safest way to visit the park is by guided tour with one of the recommended tour agencies in Santa Cruz. To do it yourself, a *micro* heads south from Buena Vista through Huaytú, San Rafael de Amboró, Espejitos, Santa Rosa de Amboró, Santa Fé and Las Cruces. This boundary provides access to several rough routes and tracks that lead southwest into the interior, following tributaries of the Río Surutú. To really probe into the park though you will need a 4WD vehicle and a good deal of previous experience in jungle trekking. Note that all access to the park along this road will require a crossing of the Río Surutú.

SANTA CRUZ TO SAMAIPATA

The spectacular route from Santa Cruz to Samaipata passes a number of attractions that are worth a brief stop. Any *micro* or *trufi* running this route pass by the places of interest mentioned in this section.

Los Espejillos Community Project (admission B$5) has several waterfalls and natural swimming pools, with lovely, clean and refreshing water sparkling over the polished black rock that characterizes the area. It stands across the Río Pira'i 18km north of the highway. Get off just beyond San José and walk or hitch north along the 4WD track, following the signposts. Basic accommodation is available at the Tacuaracú community (per person B$20) which oversees the project.

Bermejo, 85km southwest of Santa Cruz, is marked by a hulking slab of red rock known as **Cueva de los Monos**, which is flaking and chipping into nascent natural arches. A great place to stay here is the immensely popular organic farm **Ginger's Paradise** (www.gingersparadise.com; r per person half-board/full-board B$80/100) with access from the main road across a rickety drawbridge.

Laguna Volcán is an intriguing crater lake 6km up the hill north of Bermejo. A lovely **walking track** climbs from the lake to the crater rim; it begins at the point directly across the lake from the end of the road. The beautiful nearby region known as **Los Volcánes** (see the boxed text, p275) features an otherworldly landscape of tropical sugarloaf hills.

A turn off to the community of Bella Vista, 100km from Santa Cruz on the Samaipata road leads to the **Codo de los Andes**. In this dramatically beautiful area famed for its giant ferns and monkey-tail cacti, there is great trekking to be had, as well as an excellent community-run **lodge** (☎ 944-6293; www.andeselbow.com; per person B$90, incl meals B$120).

Just 20km short of Samaipata lies **Las Cuevas** (admission B$10). If you walk upstream on a clear path away from the road, you'll reach two lovely waterfalls that spill into eminently swimmable lagoons bordered by sandy beaches. About 100m beyond here is a third waterfall, the biggest of the set. You can also camp here for a small fee.

SAMAIPATA

pop 9700 / elevation 1650m

Samaipata has developed into one of the top gringo-trail spots over the last few years. This sleepy village in the foothills of the Cordillera Oriental is brimming with foreign-run, stylish hostels and restaurants.

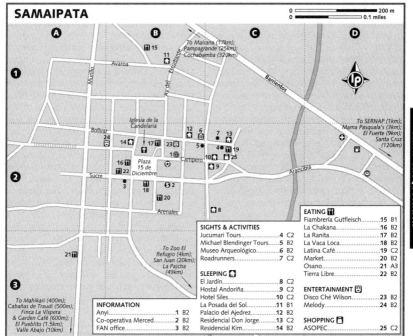

SAMAIPATA

SIGHTS & ACTIVITIES
Jucumari Tours.....................4 C2
Michael Blendinger Tours.....5 B2
Museo Arqueológico............6 B2
Roadrunners.........................7 C2

SLEEPING
El Jardín...............................8 C2
Hostal Andoriña...................9 C2
Hotel Siles..........................10 C2
La Posada del Sol...............11 B1
Palacio del Ajedrez............12 B2
Residencial Don Jorge........13 C2
Residencial Kim..................14 B2

INFORMATION
Anyi....................................1 B2
Co-operativa Merced...........2 B2
FAN office...........................3 B2

EATING
Fiambrería Gutfleisch.........15 B1
La Chakana........................16 B2
La Ranita............................17 B2
La Vaca Loca.....................18 B2
Latina Café........................19 C2
Market...............................20 B2
Osano................................21 A3
Tierra Libre........................22 B2

ENTERTAINMENT
Disco Ché Wilson...............23 B2
Melody...............................24 B2

SHOPPING
ASOPEC.............................25 C2

Visitors flock to see the pre-Inca site of El Fuerte, some in search of a dose of the ancient site's supposed mystical energy, whilst increasingly it is the main jumping-off point for forays to Parque Nacional Amboró (p276). But it's not just foreigners who come up here; Samaipata is a popular weekend destination for *cruceños* too. The Quechua name, meaning 'Rest in the Highlands,' could hardly be more appropriate.

Information
There are no banks or ATMs in Samaipata so it's best to bring cash. Alternatively you can draw cash on a credit card with your passport from the **Co-operativa Merced** just off the main plaza on Calle Sucre.

There is no official tourist office, though many of the tour companies and hostels can help you with information about the local sites. For reliably unbiased advice you may want to check out Samaipata's excellent tourist websites (www.samaipata.info, www.samaipataturistica.com and www.municipiosamaipata.com). **SERNAP** (www.sernap.gov.bo in Spanish) has an office 1km outside

of town on the road to Santa Cruz. The **FAN office** (Sucre & Murillo) can arrange trips to the community of La Yunga at the edge of the park, though it is open only sporadically.

The best internet connection is at **Anyi** (Campero; per hr b$4), one block east of the plaza.

Sights
EL FUERTE
The mystical site of El Fuerte exudes such pulling power that visitors from all over the world make their way to Samaipata just to climb the hill and see the remains of this pre-Inca site.

Designated in 1998 as a Unesco World Heritage site, **El Fuerte** (admission per person B$50, guides per group B$55; 9am-5pm) occupies a hilltop about 10km from the village and offers breathtaking views across the rugged transition zone between the Andes and low-lying areas further east. There are two observation towers that allow visitors to view the ruins from above. Allow at least two hours to fully explore the complex, and take sunscreen and a hat with you. There is a kiosk with food and water next to the ticket office.

First occupied by diverse ethnic groups as early as 2000BC, it wasn't until 1470 that the Incas, the most famous tenants, first arrived. By the time the Spanish arrived and looted the site in the 1600s it was already deserted. The purpose of El Fuerte has long been debated, and there are several theories. The conquistadors, in a distinctly combative frame of mind, assumed the site had been used for defense, hence its Spanish name, 'the fort'. In 1832 French naturalist Alcides d'Orbigny proclaimed that the pools and parallel canals had been used for washing gold. In 1936 German anthropologist Leo Pucher described it as an ancient temple to the serpent and the jaguar; his theory, incorporating worship of the sun and moon, is now the most accepted. Recently the place has gained a New Age following; some have claimed that it was a take-off and landing ramp for ancient spacecraft.

There are no standing buildings, but the remains of 500 dwellings have been discovered in the immediate vicinity and ongoing excavation reveals more every day. The main site, which is almost certainly of religious significance, is a 100m-long stone slab with a variety of sculpted features: seats, tables, a conference circle, troughs, tanks, conduits and *hornecinos* (niches), which are believed to have held idols. A total of seven steps leading up to the main temple represent the seven phases of the moon. Zoomorphic designs on the slab include raised reliefs of pumas and jaguars (representing power) and numerous serpents (representing fertility). *Chicha* and blood were poured into the snake designs as an offering to Pachamama. Sadly, these designs are unprotected from the elements and erosion is making them harder to discern with every passing year.

About 300m down an obscure track behind the main ruin is **Chincana**, a sinister hole in the ground that appears all the more menacing by the concealing vegetation and sloping ground around it. It's almost certainly natural, but three theories have emerged about how it might have been used: that it served as a water-storage cistern; that

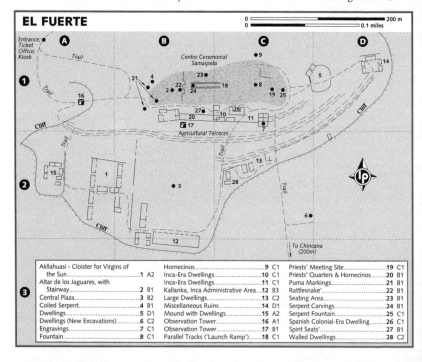

Akllahuasi - Cloister for Virgins of the Sun...**1** A2	Hornecinos...**9** C1	Priests' Meeting Site.......................**19** C1
Altar de los Jaguares, with Stairway.......................................**2** B1	Inca-Era Dwellings........................**10** C1	Priests' Quarters & Hornecinos........**20** B1
	Inca-Era Dwellings........................**11** C1	Puma Markings..............................**21** B1
Central Plaza.....................................**3** B2	Kallanka, Inca Administrative Area...**12** B3	Rattlesnake'....................................**22** B1
Coiled Serpent..................................**4** B1	Large Dwellings.............................**13** C2	Seating Area...................................**23** B1
Dwellings...**5** D1	Miscellaneous Ruins......................**14** D1	Serpent Carvings............................**24** B1
Dwellings (New Excavations).............**6** C2	Mound with Dwellings...................**15** A2	Serpent Fountain............................**25** C1
Engravings..**7** C1	Observation Tower.........................**16** A1	Spanish Colonial-Era Dwelling.........**26** C1
Fountain..**8** C1	Observation Tower.........................**17** B1	Spirit Seats'....................................**27** B1
	Parallel Tracks ('Launch Ramp')......**18** C1	Walled Dwellings............................**28** C2

it functioned as an escape-proof prison; and that it was part of a subterranean communication system between the main ruin and its immediate surroundings.

On the approach to the site look out for **La Cabeza del Inca**, apparently a natural rock formation that bears a startling resemblance to the head of an Inca Warrior, so much so that many insist it is a man-made project that was abandoned halfway through. Watch too for condors soaring on thermals overhead.

Taxis for the round-trip, including a two-hour stop at the ruins, charge B$70 for up to four people from Samaipata. Better yet, taxi up and walk back down. Gluttons for punishment who prefer to walk up should follow the main highway back toward Santa Cruz for 3.5km and turn right at the sign pointing uphill. From here it's a scenic 5km to the summit. Guided tours from Samaipata start from about B$90 per person.

MUSEO ARQUEOLÓGICO

Samaipata's small **archaeological museum** (Bolívar; admission B$5; 8:30am-12:30pm & 2:30-6:30pm) makes an interesting visit, but offers little explanation of El Fuerte. It does have a few Tiwanaku artifacts and some local pottery. If you buy your admission to the ruins here you get into the museum for free.

ZOO EL REFUGIO

This charming and responsible little **zoo** (944-6169; admission B$20; 8am-6pm) is actually a refuge for rescued animals. The zoo accepts volunteers who can lodge for free in exchange for their labor, and there is an attractive wooded camping area if you fancy spending a night among the animals. Horses are available for hire for B$25 per hour.

Tours

Several agencies organize trips to nearby attractions and almost every hotel runs its own tours. Local taxi syndicates also run transport to many of the local attractions and rates are very reasonable, though not up for negotiation.

Amboró Tours (p268) is the most established of the Santa Cruz based agencies, but the Samaipata office is open sporadically. Biologist-run **Michael Blendinger Tours** (944-6227; www.discoveringbolivia.com; Bolívar) is best for orchid, birding and full-moon

tours in English and German. **Jucumari Tours** (7262-7202; Bolívar) is an excellent locally run agency; in addition to the local attractions it offers packages to the Ruta del Ché and Mission circuits. Visit Olaf and Frank at German- and English-speaking **Roadrunners** (944-6294; www.the-roadrunners.info; Bolívar) for self-guided hikes with GPS, and guided hikes to Amboró's waterfalls, cloud forests and El Fuerte.

Sleeping

You're spoiled for choice when it comes to accommodation in Samaipata. From basic dorms to lush campsites, rustic hostels and organic farms, it's all here. Excellent digs can be found in central hostels from around B$30-50 per person. For cabins outside town ask at Blendinger tours for a series of options to fit all budgets.

El Jardín (camping/r per person B$10/30) Hippy-style hangout squirreled away down an unlit dirt track in the southeast corner of town. Chilled music, basic digs and a relaxed scene for those who like to take it easy.

Mama Pasquala's (camping/r per person B$20/40) Basic camping and simple cabins are available in this beautiful valley near some great swimming holes. It's 500m upstream from the river crossing en route to El Fuerte.

Finca La Víspera (944-6082; www.lavispera .org; camping with/without own tent B$30/40, cabins per person B$95-190) This relaxing organic farm and retreat is a lovely place on the 'outskirts' of Samaipata. The owners rent horses (B$50 per hour) and organize adventurous trips throughout the region. The attractive rooms with communal kitchens, and four self-contained guesthouses (for two to 12 people) enjoy commanding views across the valley. Campsite includes hot showers and kitchen facilities. It's an easy 15-minute walk southwest of the plaza.

Residencial Kim (944-6161; r per person B$40) Perhaps the best thing about this family-run budget hostel is the flowery courtyard adorned with jungle murals and masks. Rooms themselves are nothing to write home about; however it's a decent central option a stone's throw from the plaza.

Residencial Don Jorge (944-6086; Bolívar 20; s/d B$40/90) Minimalist whitewashed rooms with private bathroom, set around the standard shady courtyard liberally scattered with hanging oropendola nests. Just a short stagger across the road from the Latino Café.

Hotel Siles (☎ 944-6093; Campero; r per person B$40, with bathroom B$50) This neat and tidy little hostel even throws in a basic breakfast for the price. Rooms are simple but well-kept and there is even the use of a communal kitchen for those who prefer to cook for themselves.

our pick La Posada del Sol (☎ 7211-0628; www .laposadadelsol.net; Zona Barrio Nuevo; r per person B$50) Hotel quality, hostel prices, this is easily the best value in town. Modern, tastefully furnished en-suite rooms, some with kitchens, set around attractive gardens, with spectacular views, and the best breakfasts in Bolivia (also available for nonguests). Owners Trent and Rosario have thought of everything, with a colossal DVD collection, a cozy fireplace, guided tours and even professional Spanish classes for those who are thinking of hanging around for a while. Located a few blocks north of the plaza.

Palacio del Ajedrez (☎ 944-6196; Bolívar; r per person B$50, s/d B$80/120; 🏊) Home of the chess club that has created Bolivia's national chess champions. The rooms are reminiscent of student halls, with modern furniture in oranges and blues, and there's a small swimming pool for guests to enjoy.

Cabañas de Traudi (☎ 944-6094; www.traudi.com; r per person B$70, cabañas per person B$50-105; 🏊) Across from the Finca La Víspera retreat, this amenable Austrian-run spread has ample manicured grounds and horses for rent. It's set up as a family-oriented recreation center with table tennis, tennis and equipment for other activities. The swimming pool is open to nonguests for B$15 per person.

Hostal Andoriña (☎ 944-6333; www.andorina samaipata.com; Campero; s/d B$70/90d with bathroom B$110) Cluttered but characterful, the house and rooms are painted in earthy colors, the beds are comfy and the breakfasts (included in the price) big and healthy. There's a communal room downstairs, with a roaring fire in winter and a *mirador* (lookout) on the top with great views of the valley, plus a decent movie collection to while away rainy days.

Eating

RESTAURANTS

La Chakana (☎ 944-6146; www.chakanatours .com; west side of plaza; mains B$15-30) Small and cozy, the long-established Chakana serves reasonably priced breakfasts, sandwiches, vegetarian meals, excellent pizzas, home-made sweets, cocktails and European specialties. There is a ton of information for tourists here, plus a new tour company to help you plan your trips.

La Vaca Loca (south side of plaza; mains B$20-30; 🕙 Wed-Sun) This is where Samaipatans go for ice cream, devoured either on the small porch overlooking the square or in the back garden. It's a popular hangout for lunch and dinner too.

Tierra Libre (☎ 7602-2729; Sucre 70; mains B$20-35) Top-notch dishes from around the globe are served in a bohemian setting at this new place that's rapidly gained a following among backpackers for its ample and affordable eats. Veggie meals and exotic Indian concoctions are among the treats on offer and you shouldn't miss the succulent *lomito* (steak sandwich) or tasty Lake Titicaca trout.

Latina Café (☎ 944-6153; Bolívar 3; mains B$20-40; 🕙 dinner Mon-Fri, lunch & dinner Sat & Sun) Samaipata's most popular bar-restaurant (and rightly so), this place serves the best food in town: juicy steaks, saucy pastas, vegetarian delights and gorgeous brownies. The lighting is intimate and the sunsets beautiful. For a real treat try the steak in coca sauce. Happy hour is from 6pm to 7pm.

Garden Café (☎ /fax 944-6082; Finca La Víspera; B$25-40) You can gaze at La Víspera's organic garden from its sunny, alfresco cafe and see kitchen staff running up and down to pick your salad fresh from the ground. There are good breakfasts and lunches, and special dietary needs are catered for on request.

QUICK EATS

La Ranita (☎ 944-6390; Estudiante; snacks B$10-30) Inventive breakfast combos and fresh bread and pastries are on offer in this superb, French-style tea house.

Fiambrería Gutfleisch (snacks B$10; 🕙 7am-5pm Mon-Fri) You'll find some of Bolivia's best cheeses, salamis and cold cuts at this factory during the week, and at the market (8am to 4pm) on weekends. Knock on the door for entry.

Osano (🕙 lunch Tue-Sun) Along the road to Finca La Víspera, this Japanese religious sect sells organic vegetables fertilized with divine light. For under B$7 you can be blessed with the 'energy' of the Mahikari Luz Divina – go on, don't be shy.

Entertainment

A slice of Santa Cruz teenage nightlife is transported to Samaipata each weekend and revived at the popular **Disco Ché Wilson** (Bolívar). Alternatively try Melody, a block northwest from the plaza, which has regular live shows. At least once a month there is a live open-air disco at El Jardín, where rock and salsa play to a mixed, and largely inebriated, crowd.

Shopping

Saturday and Sunday are market days. **ASOPEC** (Asociación de Productoras Ecológicas; 8am-noon & 2-6pm) offers *artesanías*, produced and sold by Bolivian women from local communities, with all proceeds going to the makers. Wool, ceramics, soap, candles and even ice cream are on offer.

Getting There & Around

Sindicato El Fuerte (in Santa Cruz 359-8958, in Samaipata 944-6336) run four-passenger services between Santa Cruz and Samaipata (per person week days/weekends B$25/30, three hours). From Santa Cruz, services leave from Calle Aruma near Grigota when full. From Sampaipata, services depart from the main plaza.

Micros leave from near the plaza daily around 4:30am and between noon and 5pm on Sunday.

Finding a lift west to Vallegrande or Cochabamba is a bit trickier. For Vallegrande, buses pass the gas station on the main road at 11am, 4pm, 7pm and 9pm and typically have seats, while for Cochabamba services on the old road leave Mairana around 3pm on Tuesday, Friday and Sunday. To take the new road to Cochabamba it's easiest to just head back to Santa Cruz and catch a *flota* there.

AROUND SAMAIPATA
La Pajcha & El Nido de los Condores

A series of three beautiful waterfalls on a turbid mountain river, which plunge 45m into a dreamy tropical lagoon. **La Pajcha** has a sandy beach for swimming and some inviting campsites. It's 42km (one to two hours by car) south of Samaipata, toward San Juan where there is a turn-off that leads 7km to the falls. The site is privately owned and visitors are charged B$10 to visit and swim here. The easiest way to get here is in a shared taxi from the plaza in Samaipata (B$250, two hours).

El Nido de los Condores (Condor Nest) is the end point of a hugely popular eight-hour hike that begins from the trailhead near La Pajcha. Here, as you might expect, you will find more than 25 condor nests perched precariously on the hillside and have the opportunity to admire these glorious birds at close quarters as they soar on thermals over the valley below. The site has been dubbed the best condor-watching place in South America.

El Pueblito

A beautiful place for a day trip is the resort of **El Pueblito** (944-6386, www.elpueblitoresort.com; r per person B$210;) located just outside Samaipata on the road to Valle Abajo. Arranged like a little village complete with its own church and plaza, the resort has a swimming pool, *artesanía* shops and even a little farm, all set on a hillside with marvelous views of Samaipata in the valley below. There are cabins here and a four-star hotel in a homely, country-house style, as well as an excellent restaurant-bar called El Cabildo.

VALLEGRANDE
pop 16,800 / elevation 2100m

Vallegrande's claim to fame is that it was the spot where Ché Guevara's emaciated corpse was exhibited before its burial (see p285), and it is the main base for the **Ché Trail**, a community-based tourism project. The route traces Ché's final movements on foot, mule, bicycle and boat, with basic, rustic accommodations at encampments and with local families.

Visit the **Ché museum** (admission B$10; 9am-noon & 3-5pm Mon-Fri), which features objects and artifacts that belonged to Ché's guerrilla group on the 2nd floor and a small archaeological museum on the ground floor.

Most visitors to the town are passing through on a Ché pilgrimage, but Vallegrande is also a nice spot to relax and walk in the hills. It's a quiet little town set in the Andean foothills and enjoys a lovely temperate climate.

Information

A tourist office next to the museum on the east side of the plaza provides information on the Ché Trail as well as offering guided tours with local Ché expert Gonzalo Flores Guzmán (☎ 7318-6354). Tours start from B$150 per person for a group of four, or B$450 for a single person for a full day. An interesting aspect of the tour is the chance to chat with people who actually met Ché and gain a first-hand account of events.

Sights

HOSPITAL SEÑOR DE LA MALTA

After Ché Guevara's execution in La Higuera, south of Vallegrande, his body was brought to the now-dilapidated hospital laundry here. The hospital still functions, but the laundry itself has now been cordoned off as a pilgrimage site, where graffiti pays homage to this controversial figure. To get here, head one block south of the plaza along Escalante, and then five blocks east along Malta.

EL MAUSOLEO DEL CHÉ

In 1997, nearly 30 years after Ché's death, one of the soldiers who carried out the burial revealed that his body lay beneath Vallegrande's airstrip. The Bolivian and Cuban governments called for his exhumation and Ché was officially reburied in Santa Clara, Cuba on October 17, 1997. The spot where he was originally buried is marked by a mausoleum adorned with the typical smiling image of Ché that beams out across the valley. The interior can only be visited by guided tour, but the building is clearly visible from the bus station.

Festivals & Events

The weekly *feria* (market) is held every Sunday. Around February 23 the town marks its anniversary with various sporting and cultural events. Since the bodies of Ché and several of his comrades were recovered from the airport in 1997, the town has celebrated an annual **Ché Guevara festival** in October, featuring folk art and cultural activities.

Sleeping & Eating

Vallegrande has a fair number of basic, budget hostelries, so while you're unlikely to be without a bed, you are likely to be without a private bathroom.

Hostal Juanita (☎ 942-2231; Manuel María Caballero 123; r per person B$30) This is a clean, family-run hotel just two blocks from the main square.

La Posada del Guerrlillero (☎ 942-2739; Malta 120; r per person B$30) Aimed squarely at Ché pilgrims (let's face it, you wouldn't be here if you weren't one), this is the best budget option in town. Rooms are simple, but proximity to the delicious home-cooked food in the restaurant below is worth the fee alone. Tourist information and a book exchange are provided too.

Café Galeria de Arte Santa Clara (cnr Plaza 26 de Enero & Florida; snacks B$10-20) Come here for good coffee and snacks.

El Mirador (☎ 942-2341; El Pichacu; mains B$40) Literally the top spot in town, with excellent views, and good fish and meat dishes, this restaurant is run by the German man who took the famous photo of dead Ché.

Other budget options in the street around the plaza all charge around B$25 for very similar rooms with shared bathroom. The better options include **Alojamiento Teresita** (☎ 924-2151; Escalante/Mendoza 107) and **Hotel Copacabana** (☎ 942-2014; Escalante/Mendoza 100).

Getting There & Away

From Plaza Oruro in Santa Cruz, buses and taxis leave for Vallegrande (B$35 to B$60, seven hours) between 10am and 2pm. A *flota* leaves from the bimodal terminal at 6pm. From Samaipata, taxis and *micros* run every two hours or so along the spine-shakingly bouncy road (four hours). Taxis to La Higuera (B$200 – try haggling) via Pucará depart from the market, two blocks east of the main plaza along Sucre.

Vallegrande's new bus terminal 1km north of the center looks impressive, but very few services actually run from there. There are *micros* to Santa Cruz every two hours from 9am to 1pm, and 6pm to 10pm, and a 6pm service to Cochabamba. Taxis to Samaipata and Santa Cruz leave when full, though it is frequently a very long wait.

PUCARÁ

Pucará features on many of the Ché tours, largely because it helps break up the uncomfortably bumpy journey from Vallegrande. Though it has no direct link to Ché, the town itself is pleasant enough and typical of the Bolivian valley towns that dot the region.

From here it is a further 15km along a dusty track to La Higuera. The route is now traversable by ordinary vehicles, but it makes for a pleasant walk if the weather is being kind. Along the route, signposts point out Ché-related sites of historic interest, the most notable being the long cliff, the Quebrada del Churo, where he was captured.

LA HIGUERA

The isolated town of La Higuera is where Ché Guevara was held prisoner following his capture. An oversized bust of the revo-

lutionary lords over the dusty **Plaza del Ché**, while the **Boina del Ché** monument is a replica of the famous star design that once adorned his beret. There's also a **mausoleum**, with the tombstones of Ché and his revolutionary comrades (though Ché himself was never buried here), which you can visit if you get the key from the caretaker – ask for his whereabouts in the village. The schoolroom –

HASTA SIEMPRE, COMANDANTE

As you travel around Bolivia, the iconic image of Ché – the revolutionary with a popularity status reached only by rock stars, and remembered in Cuban songs such as 'Hasta siempre Comandante' (Forever with You, Commander) – will be staring at you from various walls, paintings, posters and carvings. Bolivia is where Ché went to his death and where his image is being fervently resurrected.

Fresh from revolutionary success in Cuba (and frustrating failure in the Congo), Ernesto 'Ché' Guevara de la Serna was in search of a new project when he heard about the oppression of the working classes by dictator René Barrientos Ortuño's military government in Bolivia. Strategically located at the heart of South America, Bolivia seemed like the perfect place from which to launch the socialist revolution on the continent. Though Fidel Castro had required him to sign a letter of resignation upon leaving Cuba, thereby publically distancing the Cuban government from Guevara's activities, the two remained in close contact throughout the Bolivian escapade.

Ché's Bolivian base was established in 1966 at the farm Ñancahuazú, 250km southwest of Santa Cruz. Initially his corevolutionaries had no idea who he was, and only when his trademark beard began to grow back (he had shaved it off to arrive incognito in Bolivia) did they realize that they were in the presence of a living legend. Ché hoped to convince the *campesinos* (subsistence farmers) that they were oppressed, and to inspire them to social rebellion, but was surprised to be met only with suspicion. In fact a cunning move by Ortuño to grant *campesinos* rights to their land had guaranteed their support and all but doomed Ché's revolution to failure before it had even begun.

Bolivian Diary was written by Ché during the final months of his life. Originally planned as a first-hand documentation of the revolution, it reads as a somewhat leisurely adventure. Despite occasional minor setbacks Ché considered things to be moving along nicely and in his last entry on 7 October 1967, 11 months after his arrival in Bolivia, he writes that the plan was proceeding 'without complications.'

The following day he was captured near La Higuera by CIA-trained Bolivian troops under the command of Capitán Gary Prado Salgrado, receiving bullet wounds to the legs, neck and shoulder. He was taken to a schoolroom in La Higuera and, just after noon on 9 October, he was executed by a flurry of bullets to the back of the neck from Salgrado's gun. The finishing touch was a final shot through the heart by Colonel Andrés Selnich, Salgrado's immediate superior. Once the deed was done the assassins were said to be perturbed by the open eyes and peaceful smile on the dead revolutionary's face.

The body was flown to Vallegrande, where it was displayed in the hospital laundry room to prove to the whole world that 'El Ché' was finally dead. Local women noted an uncanny resemblance to the Catholic Christ and took locks of his hair as mementos, while the untimely deaths of many of those involved in his capture and assassination has led to widespread belief in the 'Curse of Ché,' a sort of Tutankhamen-style beyond-the-grave retribution.

Almost 40 years later the socialist revolution finally arrived in Bolivia, via the ballot and not the bullet, with the election of Evo Morales Ayma. The country that executed Ché now embraces him as a hero, and celebrates his time in Bolivia with the establishment of the Ché Trail, a community-based tourism project that traces his last movements. Somewhat vaguely defined, the trail begins in distant Camiri (the southernmost point), though its quite a trek on to the sites of real interest which are clustered in the area immediately around Vallegrande.

now the local clinic – where Ché was kept before being executed is just off the plaza: it's the yellow building with a solar panel on the roof.

Especially for Ché tourists, **La Casa del Telegrafista** (www.lacasadeltelegrafista.com; r per person B$50) offers vegetarian lunches and rustic rooms in the historic house that was used by Ché's unit to send and receive messages from the outside world. You can also stay in the school for B$10 per person, but note that it's very basic and there's no shower.

GRAN CHIQUITANIA

The Gran Chiquitania is the area to the east of Santa Cruz where the hostile, thorny Chaco and the low, tropical savannas of the Amazon Basin have a stand-off. Watched by the foothills of the Cordillera Oriental to the west, the Llanos de Guarayos to the north and the international boundaries of Paraguay and Brazil to the south and east, these two vastly different landscapes stand together, never making peace.

The flat landscapes of the Chiquitania are broken and divided by long, low ridges and odd monolithic mountains. Much of the territory lies soaking under vast marshes, part of the magnificent Pantanal region. Bisected by the railway line; it's also the area of Jesuit mission towns, with their wide-roofed churches and fascinating history.

The region takes its name from the indigenous Chiquitanos, one of several tribes that inhabit the area. The name Chiquitanos (meaning 'little people') was coined by the Spanish who were surprised by the low doorways to their dwellings.

History

In the days before eastern Bolivia was surveyed, the Jesuits established an autonomous religious state in Paraguay in 1609. From there they fanned outwards, founding missions in neighboring Argentina, Brazil and Bolivia and venturing into territories previously unexplored by other Europeans.

Keen to coexist with the numerous indigenous tribes of the region, the Jesuits established what they considered an ideal community hierarchy: each settlement, known as a *reducción*, was headed by two or three Jesuit priests, and a self-directed

military unit was attached to each one. For a time the Jesuit armies were the strongest and best trained on the continent. This makeshift military force served as a shield for the area from both the Portuguese in Brazil and the Spanish to the west, an autonomous theocracy.

Politically, the *reducciónes* were under the nominal control of the *audiencia* (judicial district) of Chacras, and ecclesiastically under the bishop of Santa Cruz, though their relative isolation meant that the *reducciónes* basically ran themselves. Internally, the settlements were jointly administered by a few priests and a council of eight indigenous representatives of the specific tribes who met daily to monitor community progress. Though the indigenous population was supposedly free to choose whether it lived within the missionary communities, the reality was that those who chose not to were forced to live under the harsh *encomienda* (Spanish feudal system) or, worse still, in outright slavery.

The Jesuit settlements reached their peak under the untiring Swiss priest Father Martin Schmidt, who not only built the missions at San Xavier, Concepción and San Rafael de Velasco, but also designed many of the altars, created the musical instruments, acted as the chief composer for the *reducciónes* and published a Spanish–Chiquitano dictionary. He was later expelled from the region and died in Europe in 1772.

By the mid-1700s, political strife in Europe had escalated into a power struggle between the Catholic Church and the governments of France, Spain and Portugal. When the Spanish realized the extent of Jesuit wealth and influence they decided to act. In 1767, swept up in a whirlwind of political babble and religious dogma, the missions were disbanded, and King Carlos III signed the Order of Expulsion, which evicted the Jesuits from the continent. In the wake of the Jesuit departure the settlements fell into decline, their amazing churches standing as mute testimony to their sudden achievements.

Information

For online information about the Gran Chiquitania region and the mission circuits, see www.destinochiquitos.com and www.chiquitania.com.

JESUIT MISSIONS CIRCUIT

The seven-town region of Las Misiones Jesuíticas hides some of Bolivia's richest cultural and historic accomplishments. To travel through the entire circuit takes five or six days, but for those with an interest in architecture or history, it's a rewarding excursion.

Forgotten by the world for more than two centuries, the region and its history captivated the world's imagination when the 1986 Palm d'Or winner *The Mission* spectacularly replayed the last days of the Jesuit priests in the region (with Robert de Niro at the helm). The growing interest in the unique synthesis of Jesuit and native Chiquitano culture in the South American interior resulted in Unesco declaring the region a World Heritage site in 1991. Thanks to 25 years of painstaking restoration work, directed by the late architect Hans Roth, the centuries-old mission churches have been restored to their original splendor.

GETTING THERE AND AWAY

If you wish to travel the mission circuit on public transport, the bus schedules synchronize better going counterclockwise: that is starting the circuit at San José de Chiquitos (p290). Travelling the opposite way, unsynchronized and irregular bus schedules make for a frustrating journey. A much less time-consuming way of doing it is by taking a guided tour from Santa Cruz (p268), which costs around US$450 for a four-day package taking in all the major towns.

San Javier

pop 11,300

The first (or last, depending on which way you travel) settlement on the circuit, San Xavier, founded in 1691, is the oldest mission town in the region. It's also a favorite holiday destination for wealthy *cruceño* families. Swiss priest Martin Schmidt arrived in 1730 and founded the region's first music school and a workshop to produce violins, harps and harpsichords. He also designed the present church, which was constructed between 1749 and 1752. It sits on a lovely forested ridge with a great view over the surrounding low hills and countryside. Restoration work was completed in 1992 to beautiful effect, and the newly restored building manages to appear pleasantly old and authentic.

San Xavier has some inviting **hot springs** 13km northwest of town along a rough road (B$150 return in a taxi). A further 5km along is a natural pool and waterfall, **Los Tumbos de Suruquizo**, where you can enjoy a refreshing swim.

SLEEPING & EATING

Alojamientos San Roque (☎ 963-5154; r per person B$25) Quite basic and a little pokey, this hostel is on the main road and offers budget rooms for those travelers who don't mind sharing a bathroom.

Residencial de Chiquitano (☎ 963-5072; r per person B$60) A little way up from the bus stop is this clean, bright hostel on two floors. Ask for a room with views of the surrounding hills.

Cabañas Totaitú (☎ 963-5171; r per person B$80-150; 🛒) This four-star dairy farm, 4km northwest of town, is probably the mission circuit's loveliest place to stay, with a pool, golf course and tennis courts. You can go on lovely walks or rent mountain bikes and horses and to explore the area.

El Ganadero (☎ 963-5240; mains B$15-20) has half-decent meals and a good value *almuerzo* (B$17). If it doesn't tickle your fancy try the similar **Pascana** (☎ 963-5017; mains B$15-20) next door.

GETTING THERE & AWAY

All Santa Cruz–Concepción buses (six hours) pass through San Xavier, stopping on the main road a short walk from the main plaza. Connections to Concepción pass through every three hours or so from midday to midnight. Buses for San Ignacio de Velasco pass through between 3pm and 4pm. For the return to Santa Cruz you can avoid the often overcrowded buses by taking a taxi; these leave when full. Listen for them honking for passengers along the main road.

Concepción

pop 14,500

Sleepy 'Conce' is a dusty village with a friendly, quiet atmosphere in the midst of an agricultural and cattle-ranching area. It stands 182km west of San Ignacio de Velasco and is the center for all the mission restoration projects. The elaborately restored 1709 **Catedral de Concepción** (open for mass only), sitting on the east of the plaza, has an overhanging roof supported by 121 huge tree-trunk columns and a similar bell tower. It is decorated with golden baroque designs depicting flowers, angels and the Holy Virgin. The decor gives some idea of the former opulence of the village.

Architectural aficionados should visit the **restoration workshops** (10:30am-3:30pm) behind the mission, where many of the fine replicas and restored artworks are crafted. More intricate restoration work is performed in the **Museo Misional** (south side of plaza; admission B$8; 8am-noon & 2-6pm Tue-Sat, 10am-noon Sun), which, apart from being the birthplace of the former Bolivian president Hugo Suárez, also has scale models of all the churches on the mission circuit.

SLEEPING & EATING

Alojamiento Tarija (964-3020; r per person B$30, with bathroom B$50) A block south of the plaza, it's little more than a bed in a room but it makes up for the unappealing decor with a warm welcome, and if you are on a tight budget it's the cheapest in town.

ourpick Hotel Oasis Chiquitano (964-3223; r per person B$70, d with air-con B$180;) Beautifully maintained with sparkling, stylish rooms and an orchid garden. This is the best value hotel in town and the price includes access to the Oasis Chiquitano pool complex (admission for nonguests B$15) next door.

Gran Hotel Concepción (964-3031; west side of plaza; s/d B$200/320;) The most upscale place to lay your head is this charming, unapologetically Jesuit-styled hotel with a pool, a quiet patio with a lush, pretty garden, and intricately carved wooden pillars. There is no air-con, but the laundry comes in handy if you are finishing the dusty mission circuit.

Graffito's (south side of plaza; mains B$7-12) The only place open on a Sunday for food, it serves a basic menu of junk food including burgers and *lomito*.

El Buen Gusto (964-3117; north side of plaza; almuerzo B$20) Good value *almuerzos* with salad bar are served here, all enjoyed on the leafy, quiet patio.

GETTING THERE & AWAY

Buses from Santa Cruz to Concepción run every three hours from 7:30am till 8pm via San Xavier. If you are thinking of visiting Concepción and San Ignacio de Velasco on the same day, you need to leave Santa Cruz early. The San Ignacio bus from Santa Cruz (11 hours) passes through Concepción around 5pm and 2am, stopping on the main road 1km from the plaza. Sardine-can *micros* leave for San Xavier (one hour) and Santa Cruz (six hours) approximately every three hours from 7am to 11pm.

San Ignacio de Velasco

pop 41,400

The first mission church at San Ignacio de Velasco, founded in 1748, was once the largest and most elaborate of all the mission churches. It was demolished in the 1950s and replaced by a modern abomination. Realizing they'd made a hash of it, the architects razed the replacement and designed a reasonable facsimile of the original structure. The new version retains a beautiful altar and wooden pillars from the original church and overlooks an extensive and well-pruned plaza. Several attractive, large wooden crosses (a trademark of Jesuit mission towns and villages) stand at intersections just off the plaza.

Only 700m north of the church is the imposing **Laguna Guapomó**, where you can swim or rent a boat and putter around.

INFORMATION

The Casa de la Cultura on the southwest corner of the plaza houses a small **tourist office** (8am-noon & 2:30-6:30pm Mon-Fri).

FESTIVALS & EVENTS

There's a big party celebrating the **election of Miss Litoral** during the last weekend in March. San Ignacio fetes its patron saint every July 31. Every summer, the Chiquitania hosts the **International Festival of Baroque Music** (see p268), which runs for several weeks and centers on San Ignacio de Velasco.

SLEEPING

San Ignacio de Velasco is the commercial heart of the mission district, so there's a good choice of accommodations.

Casa Suiza (7630-6798; r per person B$35) The helpful proprietor here speaks German and Spanish, has a wonderful library and can organize horseback riding, fishing trips and visits to surrounding haciendas. Paying B$15 extra gets you a fantastic homemade breakfast. Casa Suiza is located seven blocks west of the plaza.

Hotel Palace (☎ 962-2063; west side of plaza; r per person B$50) Palace is overdoing it a bit, but for budget travelers this simple hotel in the shadow of the church couldn't be better placed. Rooms are en suite and lack much in the way of imagination but this is a cheap central option.

Hotel Misión (☎ 962-2333; www.hotel-lamision .com; east side of plaza; s/d B$318/424; 🏊) For a bit of luxury, neocolonial style, try this place with stylish rooms, a little pool and opulent suites. There's also a good upmarket restaurant serving an eclectic choice of dishes. Check out the wooden pillars in front, one is beautifully carved with the image of a group of Bolivian musicians.

EATING

Unfortunately, eating options are pretty poor here and on Sunday everything is closed; eat at your hotel if you can. If you are on a budget try the following, all on the plaza.

Bar-Restaurant Renacer Princezinha (south side of plaza; mains B$15-30) Fortunately, the name of this place isn't the only mouthful on offer here. Basic, filling fare will help you fuel your mission tour, and why not finish off with an ice cream at the Heladería San Ignacio next door?

Restaurant Venecia (southwest corner of plaza; almuerzo B$20) Ignore the name, no pizza or pasta here, just an affordable *almuerzo* with a menu that changes daily.

Club Social (west side of plaza; mains B$30-50) Arguably the best in town, at least at weekends when they serve up juicy *churrasco* (steak) for all and sundry. A la carte menu during the week.

GETTING THERE & AWAY

Micros leave from their respective offices scattered inconveniently around the market district, a B$5 moto-taxi ride from the center. Cover your luggage to prevent it from arriving with a thick coating of red dust.

A midday service with 131 del Este runs to Santa Cruz (11 hours) via San Xavier and Concepción. Several companies run an overly complicated timetable to San José via either San Miguel or Santa Ana (sometimes depending on the day of departure!) with most services leaving in the early hours of the morning. It can be extremely frustrating if you intend to stop off briefly at San Miguel or Santa Ana en route – necessitating an overnight stay. Departure times change constantly and it is worth inquiring locally about your onward trip on arrival.

San Miguel de Velasco
pop 10,300

Sleepy San Miguel hides in the scrub, 38km from San Ignacio. Its **church** was founded in 1721 and is, according to the late Hans Roth, the most accurately restored of all the Bolivian Jesuit missions. Its spiral pillars, carved wooden altar with a flying San Miguel, extravagant golden pulpit, religious artwork, toylike bell tower and elaborately painted facade are simply superb.

Although not designed by Martin Schmidt, the church does reflect his influence and is generally considered the most beautiful of Bolivia's Jesuit missions. A unique feature of San Miguel is the presence of no fewer than seven bells in the bell tower. When rung in combination they transmit a complicated code language to the populace. The largest bell rung in tandem with two others signals the departure of a dignitary, rung alone it's the baptism of a child, while a special bell calls the faithful to prayer. You might want to pray that you never hear the smallest bell in tandem with a medium-sized bell; it means a child has died.

SLEEPING & EATING

Alojamiento Pardo (☎ 962-4209; Sucre; r per person B$50) Just off the plaza, this is a simple but spartan option.

Alojamiento Altiplano (☎ 962-4241; Belisario; r per person B$50) A decent option that has comfortable rooms.

If you'd prefer to camp, speak with the nuns at the church, who can direct you to a suitable site.

GETTING THERE & AWAY

A complicated system of *micros* run the circuit between San Miguel, San Ignacio de Velasco and San Rafael de Velasco, with departures sometimes running clockwise and sometimes counterclockwise (according to the day, rain, driver's fancy etc). Typically they leave in the early morning with an occasional additional service early afternoon, but timetables change constantly and locals recommend that you inquire about your onward travel on arrival.

Santa Ana de Velasco

The mission at this tiny Chiquitano village, 24km north of San Rafael de Velasco, was established in 1755. The **church**, with its earthen floor and palm-frond roof, is more rustic than the others and recalls the first churches constructed by the Jesuit missionaries upon their arrival. In fact the building itself is post-Jesuit, but the interior contains exquisite religious carvings and paintings.

Given its age, the original structure was in remarkable condition and the church has been recently restored. During renovations a diatonic harp, more than 1.5m tall, was found; it's displayed in the church and is a lovely complement to the local children's music practice.

San Rafael de Velasco

pop 5000

San Rafael de Velasco, 132km north of San José de Chiquitos, was founded in 1696. Its **church** was constructed between 1743 and 1747, the first of the mission churches to be completed in Bolivia. In the 1970s and 1980s the building was restored, along with the churches in Concepción and San José de Chiquitos.

The interior is particularly beautiful, and the original paintings and woodwork remain intact. The pulpit is covered with a layer of lustrous mica, the ceiling is made of reeds and the spiral pillars were carved from *cuchi* (ironwood) logs. It's the only mission church to retain the original style, with cane sheathing. Most interesting are the lovely music-theme paintings in praise of God along the entrance wall, which include depictions of a harp, flute, bassoon, horn and maracas.

At the corner of the main road and the street running south from the church, the **Casa de Huéspedes San Rafael** (☎ 962-4018; r per person B$30) has basic rooms with shared bathroom, good enough for a night's stay. On the main road itself, **Alojamiento Paradita** (☎ 962-4008; r per person B$30) is along similar lines but also has a basic *comedor* (dining hall).

The best place to wait for rides south to San José de Chiquitos (five to six hours) or north to Santa Ana, San Miguel or San Ignacio is on the main road in front of Alojamiento San Rafael. In the morning, buses run in both directions. Ask at the small **tourist office** (☎ 962-4022) in the municipal building for the latest timetables. To reach Santa Ana with your own vehicle, use the right fork north of town.

San José de Chiquitos

pop 17,000

An atmospheric place, San José de Chiquitos has the appeal of an old Western film set. The frontier town, complete with dusty streets straight out of *High Noon* and footpaths shaded by pillar-supported roofs, is flanked on the south by a low escarpment and on the north by flat, soggy forest. With an enormous and handsome plaza flanked by *toboroche* (thorny bottle) trees, the most accessible Jesuit mission town is also arguably the nicest.

The Jesuits arrived sometime in the mid-1740s, and began construction of the magnificent town church in 1750.

INFORMATION

There is no ATM in town but local banks will give cash advances on Visa and MasterCard. A useful **tourist information office** (☎ 972-2084) in the Alcaldía on the corner of the plaza has information about all the missions.

SIGHTS & ACTIVITIES
Jesuit Mission Church

San José has the only stone Jesuit mission church and merits a visit even if you miss all the others. Although the main altar is nearly identical to those in other nearby missions and has vague similarities to churches in Poland and Belgium, the reason behind its unusual exterior design remains unclear.

The church compound consists of four principal buildings arranged around the courtyard and occupying an entire city block. The bell tower was finished in 1748, the *funerario* (death chapel) is dated 1752 and the *parroquio* (living area) was completed in 1754. It is believed, however, that only the facades were finished before the Jesuits were expelled in 1767. All construction work was done by the Chiquitano people under Jesuit direction.

The restoration of the church was nearing completion at the time of writing. Work has been going on for over a decade with some delay caused by the unexpected discovery of 1008 sq meters of glorious frescoes depicting the history of the town from the Jesuit era to the Spanish colonization.

Santa Cruz la Vieja Walk

Just south of town, an **archway** supported by *bañistas* (literally 'bathers', in this case women protecting their modesty with towels) indicates your entry into the **Zona Balnéaria** where there are a number of open-air swimming options.

A few kilometers further along is the **Parque Histórico Santa Cruz la Vieja** (admission B$10) site of the original city of Santa Cruz de la Sierra. The only thing left behind of the old city is an abandoned guardhouse. Just beyond here is a statue of town founder Ñuflo de Chavez next to a reconstructed *choza* – a typical Chiquitano dwelling with the characteristic low doorway used for defensive purposes. Excavations taking place at the time of writing were believed to be uncovering the original church.

Uphill from here there is a trek to the **Cataratas del Suton** waterfall and a stunning viewpoint, though it is easy to get lost and a guide is recommended. Ask at the tourist office.

SLEEPING

Hotel El Patriarca (☎ 972-2233; main plaza; s/d B$60-70/100; ❄) A standard but clean hotel that represents good value for money.

Hotel Turubó (☎ 972-2230; main plaza; s B$60-100, d B$80-120; ❄) This is the most attractive place to stay in town. More expensive rooms have air-con.

EATING

El Cubanito (☎ 7766-6981; main plaza; mains B$20-40) A mishmash of decorative styles give this restaurant a somewhat unfinished look, but smiling straw-hatted waiters serving pastas and meats more than make up for it. Located next to Hotel Turubó.

Sabor y Artes (☎ 7210-1666; off the main plaza; mains B$25-40) There's a distinctly French ambience here, though the menu is Italian with mainly pizza and pasta. The paintings and *artesanías* that adorn the place are all for sale. Owner Pierre is a mine of local tourist information.

GETTING THERE & AWAY

The route between San Ignacio and San José (via San Rafael de Velasco and San Miguel de Velasco) suffers from a confused, irregular and frequently changing timetable. Check locally for the latest departure times. Buses from Santa Cruz depart daily from the bimodal terminal between 4pm and 6pm (B$50 to B$80), though the road is in a terrible state.

Easily the easiest and most comfortable way to travel between San José and Santa Cruz or Quijarro is by train (p292). You'll need to show your passport on purchasing your ticket and again to access the platform.

FAR EASTERN BOLIVIA

Between San José de Chiquitos and Roboré the railway line passes through a bizarre and beautiful wilderness region of hills and monoliths. Further east, along the Brazilian border, much of the landscape lies soaking beneath the wildlife-rich swamplands of the Pantanal.

Roboré & Santiago de Chiquitos

There isn't much fun to be had in militarized Roboré, but the landscape surrounding the town is spectacular and it's the access town to Santiago de Chiquitos, a lovely Jesuit mission village.

SIGHTS & ACTIVITIES

A pleasant day trip from Roboré will take you to **El Balneario**, a mountain stream with a waterfall and natural swimming hole. It's a two-hour walk each way from town; you'll need a local guide who knows the right paths in order to find it.

Set in the hills, the Jesuit mission at **Santiago de Chiquitos**, 20km from Roboré, provides a welcome break from the tropical heat of the lowlands. Its church is well worth a look, and there are some great excursions from Santiago, such as **El Mirador**, a 15-minute walk from the village, with dizzy views of the Tucavaca valley. The round-trip taxi fare from Roboré is B$100 for up to four people.

The 40°C (105°F) thermal baths at **Aguas Calientes**, 31km east of Roboré, are popular with Bolivian visitors who believe in their curative powers. Taxis charge B$100 for up to four passengers and though the train stops here it does so in the middle of the night. There is nowhere to stay but it makes for a great day trip.

TRANS-CHIQUITANO TRAIN

No longer the harrowing journey that earned this route the nickname 'Death Train,' the route from Santa Cruz to Quijarro via San José de Chiquitos and Roboré (for Santiago de Chiquitos) is now plied by three different types of train. It's a glorious journey through forest, scrub and Pantanal teaming with wildlife, though you might be advised to take mosquito repellent. Most operate *cama* and *semi-cama* classes with comfortable reclining seats, but note that there are no departures from Santa Cruz on Sunday.

The slowest and most frequent is the *Tren Regional*. It departs Santa Cruz Monday to Saturday at noon, passing through San José de Chiquitos (6:43pm; semi-cama/cama B\$19/53), Roboré (11:36pm; B\$27/77) and arriving at Quijarro (7:10am; B\$52/115) the following day. The return departs Quijarro at 12:45pm, passing through Roboré (7:50pm), San José de Chiquitos (1:23am) and arrives at Santa Cruz at 9:25am.

Next in line in terms of quality is the *Expreso Oriental* which operates a single comfortable Super Pullman class. It departs Santa Cruz on Monday, Wednesday and Friday at 4:30pm, passing through San José de Chiquitos (10:20pm; B\$58), Roboré (2:28am; B\$85) and arriving at Quijarro (8:45am; B\$127) the following day. The return departs Quijarro on Tuesday, Thursday and Sunday at 4:30pm, passing through Roboré (10:11pm), San José de Chiquitos (2:21am) and arrives at Santa Cruz at 8:40am.

The fastest and priciest is the *Ferrobus*. It departs Santa Cruz on Tuesday, Thursday and Saturday at 7pm, passing through San José de Chiquitos (12:09am; semi-cama/cama B\$175/205), Roboré (3:23am; B\$199/288) and arriving at Quijarro (8:40am; B\$222/257) the following day. The return departs Quijarro on Monday, Wednesday and Friday at 7pm, passing through Roboré (11:56pm), San José de Chiquitos (3:10am) and arrives at Santa Cruz at 8:50am.

There is rarely a problem getting a seat from Santa Cruz or Quijarro, but if joining the service midway along the line then tickets are best bought in advance – only a limited number of seats are allotted for these stations. Hot and cold food and drinks are available during daylight hours, and a constant stream of vendors pass through the carriages selling all manner of goods.

SLEEPING & EATING

Eating options in both towns are restricted to fried chicken and pizza joints that do little to inspire the gourmet visitor.

Hotel Pacheco (☎ 974-2074; 6 de Agosto; d B\$50, with bathroom B\$80) A decent, conveniently located option in Roboré with simple but bright and clean rooms.

Hotel Beulá (☎ 313-6274; s/d B\$180/250) On the plaza in Santiago de Chiquitos, the stylish Beulá has big breakfasts and dinners (B\$30 to B\$55), but they need to be arranged in advance. You can also hire local guides here.

GETTING THERE & AWAY

Flota Trans Carretón leaves Santa Cruz daily at 5pm, but due to the poor condition of the roads the easiest and most comfortable way to arrive is by train (see the boxed text, above).

QUIJARRO

pop 12,900

The eastern terminus of the railway line has its home in Quijarro, a muddy collection of shacks and the border crossing point between Bolivia and the city of Corumbá, Brazil (see the boxed text, opposite). On a hill in the distance you will glimpse a wonderful preview of Corumbá, the gateway to the Brazilian Pantanal, a Unesco-recognized ecoregion.

Sights & Activities

Hotels in Quijarro can organize boat tours through the wetlands of the **Bolivian Pantanal**, an alternative to the well-visited Brazilian side. A comfortable three-day excursion, including transportation, food and accommodations (on the boat) should cost around B\$900 per person.

Sleeping & Eating

There are *alojamientos* (basic accommodations) on the left as you exit from the railway station. Better options are below.

Hotel Bilbosi (☎ 978-2113; Luis Salazar de la Vega; s/d B\$70/120; 🖵) This friendly hotel is two blocks from the railway station and has clean rooms with air-con.

CROSSING THE BORDER TO BRAZIL

The main border crossing to Brazil is at Quijarro at the end of the train line, with a second, minor crossing at San Matías, the access point to the northern Brazilian Pantanal.

You'll more than likely arrive in Quijarro by train between 7am and 9am to be greeted by a line of taxi drivers offering to take you the 2km to the border (B$5). **Customs offices** (◷ 8am-noon & 2-5:30pm) are on opposing sides of the bridge. Bolivian officials have been known to unofficially charge for the exit stamp, but stand your ground politely. Crossing this border you are generally asked to show a yellow-fever vaccination certificate. No exceptions are granted and you will be whisked off to a vaccination clinic if you fail to produce it. On the Brazilian side of the border yellow *canarinho* (city buses) will take you into Corumbá (R$1.70). Brazilian entry stamps are given at the border or at the Polícia Federal at the *rodoviária* (haw-doo-*vyahr*-ya; bus terminal); it's open until 5pm. Get your stamp as soon as possible to avoid later problems and make sure you have the necessary visas if you require them.

For a slightly more adventurous border crossing try San Matías. In the dry season, a Trans-Bolivia bus leaves from Santa Cruz to Cáceres in Brazil (30 hours), via San Matías (26 hours). Brazilian entry or exit stamps should be picked up from the Polícia Federal office at Rua Antônio João 160 in Cáceres; get your exit and entry stamps for Bolivia in Santa Cruz (p266).

El Pantanal Hotel-Resort (☎ 978-2020; www .elpantanalhotel.com; s/d B$560/750; ⊠ ☎) This five-star place is in the beautiful Arroyo Concepción, 12km from Puerto Suárez and 7km from Corumbá. It offers wide-ranging luxury, 600 hectares of grounds and several restaurants, as well as a number of touristic packages exploring the Pantanal.

Both these hotels have good restaurants. Alternatively, lots of inexpensive places are lined up along the street perpendicular to the railway station entrance.

Getting There & Away

Train services cross the Chiquitania en route from Quijarro to Santa Cruz, arriving at the border town between 7am and 9am each day. The ticket office opens around 7am and tickets sell out fast, so don't hang around. For train departure information, see the boxed text (opposite). The bus station is two blocks from the train station. Services to Santa Cruz (B$120; 16 hours) via San José (B$60; seven hours) leave at 4pm.

Amazon Basin

The Amazon Basin is one of Bolivia's largest and most mesmerizing regions. The rainforest is raucous with wildlife and spending a few days roaming the sweaty jungle is an experience you're unlikely to forget. This is where you'll find the deep and mysterious lushness that has drawn adventurers and explorers since the beginning of time. And it's not only the forests that are enchanting: it's also the richness of the indigenous cultures, traditions and languages that exist throughout the region.

While Brazilian rainforests continue to suffer heavy depredation, the Amazon forests of northern Bolivia remain relatively intact; unfortunately, though, the region continues to face the serious problems of road construction and highland immigration that have led to an upsurge in logging and slash-and-burn agriculture.

Mossy hills peak around the town of Rurrenabaque, most people's first point of entry into the region and the main base camp from where to visit the fascinating Parque Nacional Madidi. This is home to a growing ethno-ecotourism industry that looks to help local communities. The village of San Ignacio de Moxos has a kicking July fiesta where indigenous traditions, mixed with a strong Jesuit missionary influence, are vigorously celebrated. Trinidad, the region's biggest settlement and an active cattle ranching center, is a transit point toward Santa Cruz.

All of the Amazon Basin's main rivers are Amazon tributaries that would be considered great rivers in their own right in any smaller country. You can indulge in long journeys down these jungle waterways, using hotel-like riverboats, cargo boats, canoes or barges.

HIGHLIGHTS

- Glide down the long **Río Mamoré** (p314) on a boat trip between Trinidad and Guayaramerín
- Take part in responsible tourism, discover the rainforest and peek into the life of a local community on a tour from **Rurrenabaque** (p306)
- Party with the locals at the Amazon's best village fiesta in **San Ignacio de Moxos** (p310)
- Discover the little-explored forests of **Parque Nacional Noel Kempff Mercado** (p318) and see fascinating wildlife and landscapes
- Dive into the rainforest at the community-run Chalalán Ecolodge, deep inside **Parque Nacional Madidi** (p308)

■ TELEPHONE CODE: 3	■ POPULATION: 650,000	■ ELEVATION: 0M TO 200M

History

The Bolivian Amazon has always oozed mystery. The Incas believed that a powerful civilization lived in the great rainforest, and tried to conquer the area in the 15th century. The indigenous peoples of the western Bolivian Amazon, mainly the Moxos tribe, are said to have posed such a mighty resistance to the invading army that, once they realized they were unable to beat them, the Incas asked for an alliance and settled among the Moxos.

The tale of the Incas' experience fired the imagination of the Spanish conquerors a century later – they too were chasing a legend in search of a rich and powerful civilization in the depths of the Amazonian forest. The name of the kingdom was El Dorado (the Golden One) or Paitití (the Land of the Celestial Jaguar), thought to have existed east of the Andean Cordillera, near the source of the Río Paraguay. The Spanish spent the entire 16th century trying to find the elusive kingdom, but, unfamiliar with the rainforest environment, found nothing but death and disease. By the 17th century they moved their search elsewhere.

Though the Spanish were disappointed with their search in the Moxos region, the Jesuits saw their opportunity to 'spread the word' to the highly spiritual *moxeños*. The tough missionaries were the first Europeans to significantly venture into the lowlands. They founded their first mission at Loreto, in the Moxos region, in 1675. While they imposed Christianity and European ways, the Jesuits also recognized the indigenous peoples' expertise in woodwork, which eventually produced the brilliant carvings now characteristic of the missions. They imported herds of cattle and horses to some of their remote outposts, and the descendants of these herds still thrive throughout most of the department.

After the expulsion of the Jesuits in 1767, the Franciscan and Dominican missionaries, as well as the opportunistic settlers who followed, brought slavery and disease. Otherwise, the vast, steamy forests and plains of northern Bolivia saw little activity for decades.

Climate

The seasons are less pronounced here than in other parts of Bolivia, and temperatures are high year-round. During the wet season (November to April) there are unrelenting downpours and the streets may fill with mud and the sound of croaking frogs. The dry season (May to October) also sees a good measure of precipitation, and if you're unlucky you may experience the unpredictable *surazo*, a cold wind blowing from Patagonia and the Argentine pampas. This produces a dramatic drop in temperature and frost even in the hottest parts of the jungle.

National Parks & Reserves

The Bolivian Amazon is blessed with some of the most biodiverse habitats on earth, and the country's best-known national parks and reserves. For birdwatchers, monkey lovers and jaguar seekers, this region is heaven. You can choose between the jungles and wild rivers of Parque Nacional Madidi (p308), the less-frequented, wildlife-rich Reserva Biosférica del Beni (p309) and the virtually unexplored 'lost world' of Parque Nacional Noel Kempff Mercado (p318). **Conservation International** (www.conservation.org) is attempting to raise awareness of the need for protection of the headwaters of several major Amazon tributaries with their ambitious Vilcabamba-Amboró Conservation Corridor initiative.

Getting There & Around

Rurrenabaque is the Amazon's most popular settlement. Flying is the best way of getting here, though many choose to take the tedious and uncomfortable bus ride from La Paz to save money. Buses going back to La Paz from Rurrenabaque are less crowded – many people decide to wing it (or take a faster 4WD) after surviving the initial bus ride.

Transportes Aéreos Militares (TAM) and Amaszonas fly daily between La Paz and Rurrenabaque. Their low-flying planes afford great glimpses of Lake Titicaca after take-off before squeezing past Chacaltaya and soaring over the Yungas. You can see the landscape change from desolate, rugged highlands to lush, forested lowlands. And the grass landing strip in Rurrenabaque is worthy of more than one post-trip tale.

Generally, 4WDs are necessary to reach most off-road spots, but there are regular bus services between major towns. Boat travel is big here, especially in the rainy season, when it is usually the only real option. Riverboat travel isn't for everyone:

THE AMAZON BASIN

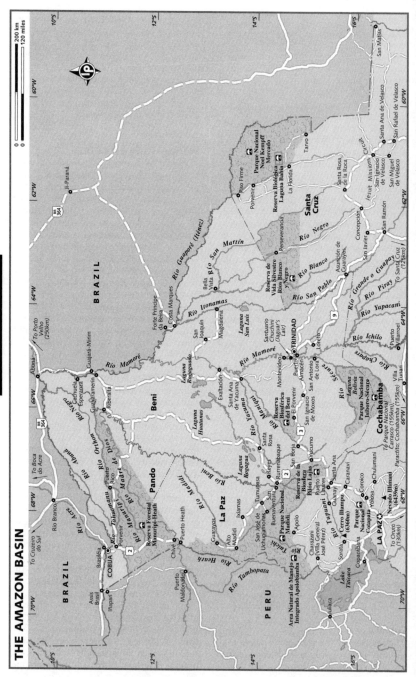

it's relaxing but slow going and there are no real schedules. While the scenery can be mesmerizing, it changes little, so you'll want to bring a couple of books along. Passenger comfort is the last thing cargo-boat builders have in mind, but Bolivian accommodations standards are still superior to those on the Brazilian 'cattle boats' that ply the Amazon proper.

CHAPARE REGION

The Chapare stretches out beyond the last peaks of the Andes into the dramatically different landscape of the upper Amazon Basin, where lush, moist rainforest replaces the dry, barren mountains. The contrast is breathtaking on the spectacular road between Cochabamba and Villa Tunari, where twists around the high peaks and mountain lakes drop steeply into deep, steaming tropical valleys.

The Chapare region is heavily populated with highland *campesinos* (subsistence farmers) who emigrated here in the 1970s and started growing the controversial coca leaf, turning the region into Bolivia's main source of coca grown for the manufacture of cocaine (as opposed to Yungas coca, which makes up the bulk of what Bolivians themselves chew, make into tea etc). Subsequent attempts by the US Drug Enforcement Agency (DEA) to eradicate coca have made the region unstable, with frequent messy confrontations between *cocaleros* (coca growers), the DEA and the Bolivian government. The Bolivian media frequently expose cases of human-rights abuse and disregard for property. A former coca farmer himself, President Evo Morales has worked hard to protect the rights of those involved in the legal production of the plant while simultaneously targeting cocaine production and smuggling.

VILLA TUNARI

pop 2510 / elevation 300m
Strung out along the Cochabamba–Santa Cruz highway, Villa Tunari is a pleasant spot to relax, hike and swim in cool rivers, and is a relatively tame introduction to the wilder Amazon. Whether you are coming from the frozen highlands, or heading toward them, the hot, steamy, jungle air will make you grateful for the proximity of 'Las Pozas,' a series of natural swimming holes. With visitor numbers increasing, the town is developing into something of a tourist trap and your bolivianos won't go as far here as they do further north in the Amazon.

Information

There's no ATM here yet, so bring cash with you or get advances at Prodem bank on the main road. Some hotels may change cash. There are several telecom and internet places along the highway.

Sights & Activities

Swimming holes, or *pozas*, are the main source of fun in Villa Tunari. In addition to Hotel de Selva El Puente's Las Pozas (p299), there are several free *pozas* in town along the Río San Mateo. Great opportunities for **fishing**, **kayaking** and **whitewater rafting** abound in the surrounding rivers, but ask around to see what's safe before heading out into the forest on your own.

A good, independent **hike** will take you to the friendly village of **Majo Pampa**. Follow the route toward Hotel de Selva El Puente and turn right onto the walking track about 150m before the hotel. After crossing the Arroyo Valería, it's 8km to the village.

PARQUE MACHÍA

This 36-hectare **wildlife refuge** (Inti Wara Yassi; ☎ 413-6572; www.intiwarayassi.org; admission B$6, photo/video permit B$15/20; ☺ closed Mon) houses over 200 free-ranging, poached or injured animals and other abused critters. An international crew of volunteers tends to the animals' every need, but no attempts are made to reintroduce them into the wild (the animals, not the volunteers!). It's a relaxing place to **camp** (r per person B$10) and wander through the forest, taking in the sights, sounds and tranquility.

Tours for prospective volunteers are conducted daily at 10am. Volunteers must stay for a minimum of 15 days and can choose between rustic camping and the hostel, both of which cost B$1400 for the first two weeks, including food.

ORQUIDARIO VILLA TUNARI

Lovingly tended by a group of German botanists, Villa Tunari's beautiful **orchid nursery** (☺ closed Mon) is home to more than

AMAZON BASIN

70 species of tropical orchids. There's also a small **museum** that is worth visiting, El Bosque restaurant and a couple of *cabañas* (cabins) available for rent. It's just north of the highway, 2km west of town near the *tranca* (police post).

Tours

Villa Tunari is the main focus for Cochabamba-based **Fremen Tours** (p196), which arranges all-inclusive tours, accommodations, river trips and other activities at out-of-the-way sites. It also offers live-

---

SACRED COCA?

Erythroxylum coca is the scientific name for coca, a plant of the family Erythroxylaceae, native to northwestern South America. A small tree growing to a height of seven to 10 feet, the species is identified by its long, opaque, green leaves and small clusters of yellowish-white flowers, which mature into red berries. In Bolivia the plant grows primarily in the Yungas (p119), north of La Paz, and in the Chapare region of the Amazon.

But, unless you are a botanist, or have a strange taste in garden plants, you are likely to have heard of coca for other reasons – prince among them being its role in the production of the narcotic cocaine. To make the drug, leaves are dried, soaked in kerosene and mashed into a pasty pulp. Then they are treated with hydrochloric and sulfuric acids until they form a foul-smelling brown base. Further treatment with petrol and other chemicals creates cocaine.

For most Bolivians, however, the expensive white powder snorted by party-goers worldwide has nothing to do with their sacred plant, and they resent the suggestion that they should be held responsible for anyone else's misuse of it. President Evo Morales, a former *cocalero* (coca grower) himself, has vowed to continue to fight the war against narcotrafficking, but not at the expense of the country's coca industry – according to his government, the two are very different animals. During his address to the UN on the issue in 2006, Morales held up a coca leaf to demonstrate that the leaf and cocaine are not the same (p28).

So what else is coca used for?

Coca has formed a part of the religious rituals of the inhabitants of the Altiplano since the pre-Inca period and plays a fundamental part in offerings to the Gods *Apus* (mountains), *Inti* (sun) and *Pachamama* (earth). It is drunk as a tea (*mate de coca*) or chewed to combat altitude sickness or overcome fatigue and hunger. To *picchar* (to chew coca, from the Aymará) involves masticating a pile of leaves stored as a ball in the cheek. The ball is added to continuously and saliva passed over the mass has a mild stimulant and anesthetic effect on the user. Furthermore chewing coca also serves as a powerful symbol of religious and cultural identity.

During the conquest the Spanish rulers were somewhat perturbed by the religious connotations that came with the consumption of the leaf by the local population. Seeing it as a potential obstacle to their evangelization of the masses, they were, however, aware that consumption greatly increased output by the labor force. It was a double-edged sword which led King Philip II to permit its use as 'essential to the well-being of the Indians' but to discourage its association with religious practices.

Outside Bolivia, most people know that cocaine was the original active ingredient in Coca-Cola, but few realize that the plant is still involved in the manufacture of the fizzy drink. Medical company Stepan is one of the very few to possess a license permitting it to possess the plant and its derivatives in the US, and it imports 100 tonnes of dried leaf annually, some of it for the manufacture of medicines, some of it for the production of a cocaine-free derivative used by Coca-Cola as a flavoring agent.

The appearance of the leaf in Europe pre-dates Coca-Cola, though, and it was first imported in the 16th century. Its usage didn't become popular until the mid-19th century with the invention of cocaine and only later the production of pure cocaine.

But regardless of attitudes in Bolivia, those of the outside world remain, for the most part, unchanged. If you buy or use coca leaves in Bolivia do not be tempted to try to take any home. As far as most countries are concerned, possession of the leaf itself or the narcotic are one and the same. You face being charged with possession of a Class A drug for having a single petiole in your pocket. Don´t risk it!

aboard riverboat cruises around Trinidad and adventure tours in Parque Nacional Isiboro-Sécure.

Festivals & Events

The festival of **San Antonio**, the town's patron saint, is celebrated in the first week of June. And for delicious and unique Amazonian fish dishes, be in town the first week of August for the **Feria Regional del Pescado**.

Sleeping

BUDGET

Villa Tunari has a huge selection of largely uninviting budget options, all of which are much of a muchness and charge around B$25/40 per person for rooms with shared/private bathrooms. However, note that many do not provide a fan, and you will need one. Those listed below are the ones that stand out.

Alojamiento San Mateo (on unnamed road opposite Parque Machía; r per person B$20, with bathroom B$25) OK if you're on a really tight budget but are looking for tranquil surroundings that cost as little as possible. The wooded gardens and river views here fit the bill. The rooms won't win any awards, but what do you expect for this price?

Hotel San Antonio (☎ 413-6543; Plaza Principal; r per person B$40, with bathroom B$50; ☒) Despite a location on the main square, this budget place goes for an Amazonian-lodge feel and nearly achieves it. Rooms are basic but tidy, and those with shared bathrooms do not have fans. You can, however, cool off in the pool.

Hotel Los Cocos (☎ 413-6578; r per person B$40, with bathroom B$60; ☒) Villa Tunari's top budget option, with well-tended rooms, modern bathrooms and a glorious pool to cool off in. Owner Ray Charles Paz is helpful, friendly and fortunately doesn't own a piano!

MIDRANGE & TOP END

Hotel San Martín (☎ 413-6512; s/d with bathroom B$120/200; ☒) This welcoming place has a gorgeous garden with a pool. It's on the southern side of the main road leading into town.

Los Tucanes (☎ 413-6506; cabins per person B$120, minimum four people, s/d with bathroom B$200/280; ☒ ☒) Luxurious *cabañas* with good beds, elegant decor and a pool to lounge around. Each room is individually decorated with its own unique wall painting and it's a great spot for total vacation surrender. It's at the

Santa Cruz entrance to town opposite the turn off for Hotel El Puente.

Hotel de Selva El Puente (☎ 458-0085; Integración; s/d/tr with bathroom B$150/220/360; ☒) This gorgeous place is set in 22 hectares of rainforest 4km outside Villa Tunari, near the Ríos San Mateo and Espíritu Santo confluence. Handsome stone cabins gravitate around a courtyard and hammocks on the top floor. The big attractions here are 'Las Pozas,' 14 idyllic natural swimming holes (B$10 for non guests) deep in the forest. The hotel is run by Fremen Tours (p196). Moto-taxis will take you here from the center for B$7.

Hotel/Restaurant Las Palmas (☎ 413-6501; s/d with bathroom B$200/320; ☒ ☒) This is another tropical hotel with a refreshing swimming pool and enormous, tiled rooms. Cheaper rooms with fans are available but the family *cabañas* are a better bet for big groups. The open-air restaurant serves well-prepared locally caught fish and there are superb views of the river and surrounding hills.

Eating

With the influx of tourists over recent years, several reasonable restaurants have sprung up around town. A rank of food stalls along the highway sells inexpensive tropical fare, but check hygiene levels before you buy.

Encuentro Sur (Beni; mains B$18-30) Great value on regional and local dishes, plus a wide selection of pastas; it's a block from the bridge over the Río Espírito Santo.

Restaurant San Silvestre (main road next to Las Palmas; mains B$25-50) If the jars of pickled snakes (not for consumption!) and animal skins hanging off the walls don't deter you, dig in to these huge portions big enough for two. Try the gargantuan *pique macho* (beef, sausage and chips dish) to really pig out.

Getting There & Away

Most (but not all!) buses between Cochabamba and Santa Cruz pass through Villa Tunari, though not all at convenient times. Those that leave in the morning are the best bet.

Getting a taxi from Santa Cruz is much faster than the bus, but means several changes – this typically involving hopping out of one taxi and straight into the next. From the old bus terminal take a taxi to Yapacani (B$20, two hours), from there go to Bulo-Bulo (B$11, one hour), then on to

AMAZON BASIN

Ivargazama (B$12, one hour), then another to Shinahota (B$10, 45 minutes) and finally one to Villa Tunari (B$5, 30 minutes). It sounds more complicated than it really is and is a good way of avoiding waiting around for a bus. Taxis from Cochabamba leave from the corner of Avs Oquendo and República throughout the day when full (B$40, three hours).

PARQUE NACIONAL CARRASCO

Created in 1988, this 622,600-hectare park has some of Bolivia's most easily explored cloud forest. It skirts a large portion of the road between Cochabamba and Villa Tunari, and also includes a big lowland area of the Chapare region. The rainforest hides a vast variety of mammal species, together with a rainbow of birds, crawling reptiles, amphibians, fish and insects.

The easiest way to visit is with Fremen Tours (p196). Tour programs include the **Cavernas del Repechón** (Caves of the Night Birds), where you'll see the weird, nocturnal *guáchero* (oilbird) and six bat species. Access is from the village of Paractito, 8km west of Villa Tunari. This half-day excursion involves a short slog through the rainforest and a zippy crossing of the **Río San Mateo** in a cable-car contraption.

Another interesting option is the Conservation International-backed **Camino en las Nubes** (Walk in the Clouds) project, a three-day trek through the park's cloud forests, descending with local guides from 4000m to 300m along the old Cochabamba–Chapare road. For details, contact Fremen Tours (p196).

PUERTO VILLARROEL

pop 1780

This muddy, tropical port on the Río Ichilo is a small settlement with tin-roofed houses raised off the ground to defend them from the mud and wet-season floods. The population here is composed almost entirely of indigenous Yuqui and colonizing Quechua groups. The town has tried hard to promote tourism in recent years without having much success, as there isn't much to actually see – unless you're excited by a military installation, a petroleum plant and a loosely defined port area. However, if you fancy gliding down the river toward Trinidad (p312), then a good place to start would be Puerto Villarroel, a vital transportation terminal and gateway to the Amazon lowlands. For a quick look at the rainforests, it makes an easy two-day round-trip from Cochabamba. Bring lots of insect repellent and wear strong old shoes with lots of tread. Even in the dry season things can get muddy.

Sights & Activities

Two types of boat run between Puerto Villarroel and Trinidad. The small family-run cargo boats that putter up and down the Ríos Ichilo and Mamoré normally only travel by day and reach Trinidad in around six days. Larger commercial crafts travel day and night and do the run in three or four days.

In Puerto Villarroel, the Capitanía del Puerto and other related portside offices can provide sketchy departure information on cargo transporters. Unless military exercises or labor strikes shut down cargo services, you shouldn't have more than a three- or four-day wait. Note that when the river is low you will have much more difficulty finding a boat.

The average fare to Trinidad on either type of boat is B$150 to B$200, including food (it's still wise to carry emergency rations), a bit less without meals. The quality of food varies from boat to boat, but overall the shipboard diet consists of fish, dried meat, *masaco* (mashed yucca or plantain) and fruit; avoid endangered turtle eggs if they're offered. You might want to bring some snacks to help supplement your diet. Few boats along the Ichilo have cabins. Most passengers sleep in hammocks slung out in the main lounge. A mosquito net is a wise investment.

If you are not up to the odyssey of a multi-day river cruise, ask around at the port for owners of *lanchas* (small boats). For a negotiable fee they can organize day-long fishing or camping trips to nearby river beaches, as well as visits to nearby indigenous settlements. In the spirit of responsible tourism offer to pay what you consider a fair price; a gift of diesel is always welcome.

Sleeping & Eating

Accommodation options are extremely basic, with a bunch of run-down *residenciales* (simple accommodations) clustered around the central plaza; they charge around B$20 per person. Those who are using river transportation will normally be permitted to sleep on the boat.

Half a dozen restaurant shacks opposite the port captain's office serve up fish and chicken dishes. For good empanadas, snacks, hot drinks and fresh juices, try the market on the main street.

Getting There & Away

Micros (small buses or minibuses) from Cochabamba to Puerto Villarroel, marked 'Chapare' (B$25, seven hours), leave from the corner of Avs 9 de Abril and Oquendo, near Laguna Alalay. The first one sets off around 6:30am, and subsequent buses depart when full. The first *micro* back to Cochabamba leaves around 7am from the bus stop on the main street. *Camiones* (flat-bed trucks) leave from the same place at any hour of the day, especially when there are boats in port. Note that transportation between Cochabamba and Santa Cruz doesn't stop at Puerto Villarroel.

WESTERN BOLIVIAN AMAZON

This is the Amazon as it's meant to be. Rich with wildlife, flora and indigenous culture, you may never want to leave. In the midst of the tropical lushness is the lovely town of Rurrenabaque, a major gringo trail hangout. Pampas, jungle and ethno-ecotourism options are innumerable here, but vary significantly in quality and price. Parque Nacional Madidi, one of South America's and the world's most precious wilderness gems, sits on Rurrenabaque's doorstep.

For some background reading, pick up *Phoenix: Exploration Fawcett* (2001), by early explorer Percy Harrison Fawcett, or *Back from Tuichi* (1993; also published as *Jungle: A Harrowing True Story of Survival*), about the 1981 rescue of Israeli Yossi Ghinsberg, whose expedition was lost in the rainforest and rescued by locals.

RURRENABAQUE

pop 14,000

The relaxing 'Rurre,' (pronounced zussay, as the town is endearingly known), has a fabulous setting. Sliced by the deep Río

Beni and surrounded by mossy green hills, the town's mesmerizing sunsets turn the sky a burned orange, and a dense fog sneaks down the river among the lush, moist trees. Once darkness falls, the surrounding rainforest comes alive, and croaks, barks, buzzes and roars can be heard from a distance.

Rurre is a major traveler base. Backpackers fill the streets, and restaurants, cafes and hotels cater mainly to Western tastes. Some travelers spend their days relaxing in the ubiquitous hammocks, but the majority go off on riverboat adventures into the rainforest.

The area's original people, the Tacana, were one of the few lowland tribes that resisted Christianity. They are responsible for the name 'Beni,' which means 'wind,' as well as the curious name of 'Rurrenabaque,' which is derived from 'Arroyo Inambaque,' the Hispanicized version of the Tacana name 'Suse-Inambaque,' the 'Ravine of Ducks.'

Information

BOOKSTORES

Most of the popular hotels and bars have book exchanges. Café Piraña (p305) has a fantastic library with an extensive range of books on ecological topics.

IMMIGRATION

Extend your stay by visiting **Migración** (8:30am-4:30pm Mon-Fri) on Aniceto Arce between Busch and Bolívar.

INTERNET ACCESS

Access is pricey in Rurre (B$8 per hour) and sometimes slow. Try **Internet** (Comercio; 9am-10pm).

LAUNDRY

Laundry Service Rurrenabaque (Comercio) and **Number One** (Avaroa), just around the corner, promise a same-day machine-wash-and-dry service (B$12 per kilo).

MONEY

There's no ATM here, so beware. You can get cash advances at **Prodem Bank** (Avaroa; 8am-6pm Mon-Fri, 8am-2pm Sat), but only on Visa and MasterCard (including Visa debit cards). It also does Western Union transfers and changes cash. Tours can usually be paid for

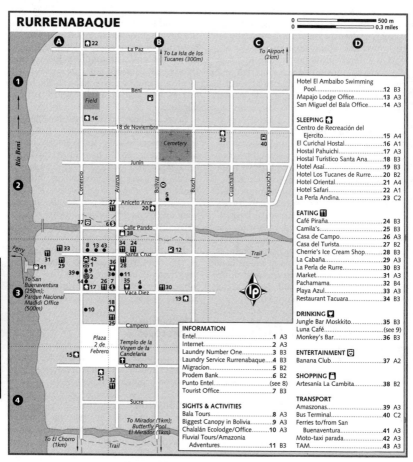

RURRENABAQUE

0 ———— 500 m
0 ———— 0.3 miles

Hotel El Ambaibo Swimming
Pool...**12** B3
Mapajo Lodge Office..................**13** A3
San Miguel del Bala Office........**14** A3

SLEEPING
Centro de Recreación del
Ejercito.......................................**15** A4
El Curichal Hostal..........................**16** A1
Hostal Pahuichi.............................**17** A3
Hostal Turístico Santa Ana........**18** B3
Hotel Asaí...**19** B3
Hotel Los Tucanes de Rurre.....**20** B2
Hotel Oriental...............................**21** A4
Hotel Safari....................................**22** A1
La Perla Andina............................**23** C2

EATING
Café Piraña.....................................**24** B3
Camila's...**25** B3
Casa de Campo.............................**26** A3
Casa del Turista.............................**27** B2
Cherrie's Ice Cream Shop..........**28** B3
La Cabaña..**29** A3
La Perla de Rurre.........................**30** B3
Market..**31** A3
Pachamama.....................................**32** B4
Playa Azul.......................................**33** A3
Restaurant Tacuara......................**34** B3

DRINKING
Jungle Bar Mosskkito...................**35** B3
Luna Café.....................................(see 9)
Monkey's Bar.................................**36** B3

ENTERTAINMENT
Banana Club...................................**37** A2

SHOPPING
Artesanía La Cambita...................**38** B2

TRANSPORT
Amazonas..**39** A3
Bus Terminal...................................**40** C2
Ferries to/from San
Buenaventura............................**41** A3
Moto-taxi parada..........................**42** A3
TAM...**43** A3

INFORMATION
Entel..**1** A3
Internet...**2** A3
Laundry Number One....................**3** B3
Laundry Service Rurrenabaque.....**4** B3
Migracion...**5** B2
Prodem Bank....................................**6** B2
Punto Entel.................................(see 8)
Tourist Office...................................**7** B3

SIGHTS & ACTIVITIES
Bala Tours..**8** A3
Biggest Canopy in Bolivia...........**9** A3
Chalalán Ecolodge/Office.........**10** A3
Fluvial Tours/Amazonia
Adventures..............................**11** B3

AMAZON BASIN

with credit cards, and some bars, agencies and hotels may be willing to facilitate cash advances. Jungle Bar Moskkito (p305) changes cash at decent rates.

TELEPHONE
Punto Entel (☎ 892-8726; Comercio & Santa Cruz; ⏱ 7am-10pm) Cheaper for calls than the main Entel office on Comercio.

TOURIST INFORMATION
The municipal **tourist office** (cnr Vaca Diez & Avaroa; ⏱ 8am-noon & 2:30-6pm Mon-Sat) is happy to answer questions but short on material. SERNAP's main **Parque Nacional Madidi office** (☎ 892-2540) is across the river in San Buenaventura.

Sights & Activities
Rurrenabaque's appeal is in its surrounding natural beauty. It's easy to pass a day or three here while waiting to join a tour. Behind town is a low but steep mirador that affords a view across the seemingly endless Beni lowlands; it's reached by climbing up the track at the southern end of Bolívar. Near here is the Butterfly Pool El Mirador, a fabulous spot where you can swim and sigh over the beautiful views of the Beni lowlands. If you prefer a tiled, chlorinated pool, the Olympic-sized *piscina* at the otherwise overpriced Hotel El Ambaibo on Santa Cruz is open to nonguests for B$20.

Another nice excursion is **El Chorro**, an idyllic waterfall and pool 1km upstream;

you can only reach it by boat so inquire at the harbor. On a rock roughly opposite El Chorro is an ancient **serpentine engraving**, which was intended as a warning to travelers: whenever the water reached serpent level, the Beni was considered unnavigable.

Tours
JUNGLE & PAMPAS
Jungle and pampas tours are Rurrenabaque's bread and butter, and operators mushroom at incredible speed. Familiarize yourself with what to expect from a responsible tour operator and choose your guides with care. Not all provide the same level of service and cheaper does not mean better. For more on jungle and pampas tours, see p304.

Most agencies have offices on Avaroa. The following agencies have received positive reports:

Bala Tours (☎ 892-2527; www.balatours.com; Santa Cruz at Comercio) Has its own jungle camp, Caracoles, and a comfortable pampas lodge on Río Yacumo.

Fluvial Tours/Amazonia Adventures (☎ 892-2372; Avaroa s/n) This is Rurrenabaque's longest-running agency.

OTHER TOURS
See pp306–7 for information on community ecotourism options around Rurrenabaque.

Sleeping
The sleeping scene in Rurrenabaque is ruled by one thing: the hammock. The sagging sack can be the sole factor in deciding whether a business does well here or not, so expect hammocks and enjoy the mandatory laziness.

BUDGET
La Perla Andina (☎ 7283-5792; 18 de Noviembre s/n; r per person B$15) A block from the bus station, this bottom-end budget option is useful if you're looking to catch an early bus. No private bathrooms, but it's clean and they've made an effort at prettifying the rooms despite the price.

Hotel Pahuichi (☎ 892-2558; Comercio; r per person B$30, with bathroom B$70) A Jekyll and Hyde hotel, the older rooms with shared bathroom are cheap, uninspiring and only for those with a close eye on their budget. Newer rooms with private bathrooms are tasteful, well decorated and worth every boliviano.

ourpick Hostal El Curichal (☎ 892-2647; elcurichal @hotmail.com; Comercio 1490; s/d B$30/50, r with bathroom B$70) A recommended place with clean,

comfortable rooms that come with hot showers and walls adorned with jungle murals. There is a barbecue terrace and kitchen available for guests and several hammocks swinging seductively in the shade.

Hostal Turístico Santa Ana (☎ 892-2614; Avaroa nr Vaca Diez; s/d B$35/60, with bathroom B$70/80) Decent value, though some of the rooms with shared bathrooms are dingy and claustrophobic. Like with most places there is the obligatory hammock garden.

Centro de Recreación del Ejército (☎ 892-2375; Plaza 2 de Febrero; s/d B$40/60) If only all army barracks were like this they might not have so much trouble in getting people to sign up! It's a strange concept, almost an officers club, but it's essentially a good, modern, budget hotel with a river terrace and a Chinese restaurant. Just remember to salute if somebody calls your name!

Hotel Los Tucanes de Rurre (☎ 892-2039; www .hotel-tucanes.com; Bolívar at Aniceto Arce; s/d B$50/70, with bathroom B$60/90) This big, thatched-roof house offers a sprawling garden, a roof terrace and sweeping views over the river. There are hammocks swinging on the patio and the clean and simple rooms are painted in gentle colors. Breakfast is included.

Hotel Asaí (☎ 892-2439; Vaca Diez nr Busch; s/d with bathroom B$50/80) All rooms here have their own bathroom and encircle a shaded courtyard. Rooms are bright white – that's walls, floor and furniture – and bathrooms are much bigger than they need to be. There are several obligatory hammocks under a *palapa* (palm-thatched umbrella).

Hotel Oriental (☎ 892-2401; Plaza 2 de Febrero; s/d with bathroom B$70/90) If you meet people who are staying at the Oriental, right on the plaza, they'll invariably be raving about what an excellent place it is – and it really is. Comfy rooms, great showers, garden hammocks for snoozing and big breakfasts are included in the price.

MIDRANGE & TOP END
Hotel Safari (☎ /fax 892-2210; Comercio; s/d with bathroom B$220/300; ⚲) Rurre's poshest option sits by the riverfront, away from the town center. It's a quiet, Korean-run place with simple but comfortable rooms with fans. Amenities, catering to tour groups, include a restaurant and karaoke bar.

La Isla de los Tucanes (☎ 892-2127; Bolívar; www .islatucanes.com; cabins with bathroom B$550-900;

🌐 📷) An ecological cabin complex in the north of town with thatched Amazonian bungalows designed to make you feel further away from the town center than you really are. With pool tables, an international restaurant and several swimming pools there is no real reason to leave – unless of course you are going into the jungle proper.

JUNGLE & PAMPAS TOURS: TREAD LIGHTLY & CHOOSE RESPONSIBLY

Tourism around Rurrenabaque has taken off to an extent that would have been unimaginable a decade ago, thanks to the attractive rainforest and pampas, which support Amazonian wildlife in relatively large numbers. But, as with most development, there are drawbacks, and in this case, it's the plethora of tour operators who are often much less responsible than they ought to be.

'Ecofriendly' operators of pampas and jungle tours are also cropping up on every corner of Rurrenabaque's streets. Many undercut the official prices and, despite claiming to be ecofriendly, don't respect the environment they work in. Inorganic waste is often left at campsites, animals are handled and disturbed, and travelers' safety is often compromised, with inexperienced guides not knowing what to do in an emergency. This is largely a result of over-demanding budget travelers expecting low prices and high delivery: perceiving the large number of operators as fair game for bartering, they beat the operators' prices down to the minimum and demand guarantees of spotting wildlife.

Bear in mind that spotting caimans, anacondas, piranhas and other Amazonian animals is a privilege, not a right. Operators and guides should not promise animal sightings (this encourages their unethical capture), go looking for wildlife or, under any circumstances, feed or handle any animals. One reader wrote in with this report: 'Ecofriendly-wise, our operators were pretty awful – grabbing hold of anacondas when they found them and capturing baby caimans to show us. We heard that one adult caiman was captured and bit its own tail off in a panic.'

Choose your operator carefully. Talk to other travelers and keep in mind the basic standards that guides should adhere to, and, most importantly, be responsible in your own expectations. Better still, opt for one of the community-run ecotourism ventures, which, although more expensive, are definitely more worthwhile and aim to help sustain communities and preserve the richness of the rainforests for the generations to come.

Shop around to get an idea of official prices. Any agency undercutting rates should be regarded with caution. Only SERNAP-authorized operators are allowed to enter Parque Nacional Madidi and foreigners must be accompanied by a local guide. Note that to get the most out of these tours, at least a minimal knowledge of Spanish is required.

Jungle Tours

The Bolivian rainforest is full of more interesting and unusual things than you could ever imagine. Local guides, most of whom have grown up in the area, are knowledgeable about the fauna, flora and forest lore; they can explain animals' habits and habitats and demonstrate the uses of some of the thousands of plant species, including the forest's natural remedies for colds, fever, cuts, insect bites (which come in handy!) and other ailments. Note that you are likely to see a lot more plants than animals.

Most trips are by canoe upstream along the Río Beni, and some continue up the Río Tuichi, camping and taking shore and jungle walks along the way, with plenty of swimming opportunities and hammock time. Accommodations are generally in agencies' private camps.

Rain, mud and *mariguí* (sandflies) make the wet season (especially January to March) unpleasant for jungle tours, but some agencies have camps set up for wildlife watching at this time.

Pampas Tours

It's easier to see wildlife in the wetland savannas northeast of town, but the sun is more oppressive, and the bugs can be worse, especially in the rainy season. Bring binoculars, a good flashlight, extra batteries and plenty of strong anti-bug juice. Highlights include playful pink river dolphins, horseback riding and night-time canoe trips to spot caiman.

Eating

Rurre's eating options are numerous and varied, from good meals from the market and quick chicken to fresh river fish and decent international cooking. Several fish restaurants line the riverfront: candlelit La Cabaña and Playa Azul grill or fry up the catch of the day for around B$20 to B$30. In addition to the Beni standard, *masaco*, try the excellent *pescado hecho en taquara* (fish baked in a special local pan) or *pescado en dunucuabi* (fish wrapped in a rainforest leaf and baked over a wood fire).

Cherrie's Ice Cream Shop (Santa Cruz nr Avaroa; ice cream B$3.50-15) Sometimes you just need one, don't you? This little kiosk has a variety of flavors, plus inventive sundaes and milkshakes to whet your appetite.

Camila's (Avaroa at Campero; breakfast B$10-15, mains B$25-45) Camila's gets more popular by the year with the best-value breakfasts in town. The walls are plastered with photos of happy punters and jungle murals, and oropendolanest lampshades complete the effect. There is a nightly bottled beer happy hour.

Casa de Campo (☎ 7199-3336; Vaca Diez at Avaroa; breakfast B$18-25) Healthy food is the name of the game here, with all-day breakfasts, homemade pastries, vegetarian dishes, soups, salads, you name it. The friendly owner is keen to make her guests happy, but her breakfast is the priciest in town.

Restaurant Tacuara (Santa Cruz at Avaroa; mains B$18-35) This open-air eatery with shaded sidewalk seating has an ambitious menu, covering breakfast to dinner. It's friendly and popular, especially for its lasagna. The Mexican dishes won't have you tossing your *sombrero* into the air, but the sandwiches are huge.

Pachamama (☎ 892-2620; Avaroa; mains B$20-30; ⓨ lunch & dinner only, closed Sun) Set in an old house, this is a restaurant-cum-cultural center where there is always something going on. There is a lounging area on the ground floor, and two movie rooms (B$20 per film) and a billiard table upstairs. There's also a book and music exchange and frequent art classes and shows. The food is good and you can even have a barbecue with your friends in the garden.

Casa del Turista (Avaroa nr Aniceto Arce; mains B$20-40) As interesting for its rickety bamboo structure as for the menu of Italian, Mexican and Bolivian dishes that it serves up. It feels a bit like the House that Jack Built, so be careful on the staircase after indulging in the exotic frozen cocktails during the nightly happy hour.

Café Piraña (Santa Cruz nr Avaroa s/n; mains B$25-40) This Piraña has bite, with a great chill-out area, delicious vegetarian and meat dishes, yummy breakfasts, lovely fresh juices, a library and film screenings every night in the back garden.

La Perla de Rurre (Bolívar at Vaca Diez; mains B$30-45) Everyone in Rurre will tell you that this is their favorite restaurant and 'The Pearl' does indeed serve up some mean fresh fish and chicken dishes. The surroundings are simple but the service is excellent.

Drinking & Entertainment

Rurre is a lively town and there are several bars and discos.

Banana Club (Comercio; admission B$12 incl 1 drink) If you want to try salsa dancing or Bolivianstyle grooving, this slightly sleazy club has Cuban doctors shaking their booties, locals getting drunk and gringos joining in.

Luna Café (Comercio nr Santa Cruz) Another *palapa*-roofed bar-restaurant (mains B$20-B$35), this is a mellow place with a chilled atmosphere that is equally as welcoming for a tasty lunch as it is for ice cold beers in the evening. Film buffs will love the open-air cinema in the back (B$15 per person).

Jungle Bar Moskkito (☎ 892-0267; www.moskkito.com; Vaca Diez) Peruvian-run, English is spoken here. There's a positive vibe, cheery service and the foliage that hangs from the roof makes you feel like you are in the jungle, whether there are 'moskkitos' or not. Throw some darts, shoot some pool and choose your own music – the extensive menu of CDs is played by request. Happy hour runs from 7pm to 9pm on selected cocktails.

Monkey's Bar (www.monkeysrestobar.blogspot.com; Avaroa nr Santa Cruz) An imitation of the successful Moskkito bar, it's very much along the same lines with a bouncing atmosphere, good pizza and great cocktails. Try the *Anaconda en el Río*.

Shopping

The cheap clothing stalls near the market and on Comercio are a good place to pick up *hamacas* (hammocks; single/double B$50/100) and finely woven cotton and synthetic *mosquiteros* (mosquito nets; from

B$50). **Artesanías La Cambita** (Avaroa) has a good selection of local handicrafts.

Getting There & Away

AIR

Rurre's humble airport is a grassy landing strip a few kilometers north of town. The brief flight to La Paz is an affordable way of avoiding the arduous 24-hour bus journey to the capital. Flights sell out fast but are frequently cancelled during inclement weather. You will be refunded only 70% of the ticket value if your flight is cancelled and you're not prepared to wait around for the next one. If you're stuck, try using the Reyes airport, an hour northeast by bus or shared taxi.

TAM (☎ 892-2398; Santa Cruz) flies between La Paz and Rurre (B$480, one hour) at least once a day, with additional services during peak periods. Flights are occasionally diverted to Reyes in the rainy season.

Amaszonas (☎ 892-2472; Comercio nr Santa Cruz) has four daily flights to La Paz (B$525).

Reconfirm your ticket the day before your flight otherwise you may find yourself without a seat. It also flies daily to Trinidad (B$525) via San Borja and to Santa Cruz (B$1059), though the latter flight (via La Paz and Trinidad) takes eight hours, so you might find it easier flying to La Paz and then catching a direct AeroSur flight to Santa Cruz. Irritatingly, if you wish to fly to Riberalta or Guayaramerín, you need to return to La Paz.

BOAT

Thanks to the Guayaramerín road, there's little cargo transportation down the Río Beni to Riberalta these days and there's no traffic at all during periods of low water. You'll need a dose of luck to find something and will have to negotiate what you consider a fair price for the trip, which may take as long as 10 days.

BUS & JEEP

The **bus terminal** is a good 20-minute walk northeast of the center. Minibuses and

---

COMMUNITY-BASED ECOTOURISM

Providing a model for responsible, sustainable ecotourism in Bolivia, the community projects around Rurrenabaque preach a respect for culture, environment and wildlife; and benefit local communities rather than private operators. You can choose from one-day tours to longer stays, incorporating walks in the rainforest with visits to indigenous communities, where you can peek into local lifestyles and traditions. Make sure you don't give sweets or presents to children, no matter how cute they look, as this builds unrealistic expectations. Whether choosing a brief or longer visit, you're bound to have a great experience. Conveniently, the booking offices for all of these community lodges are located in Rurrenabaque.

Chalalán Ecolodge (Map p302; ☎ 892-2419, in La Paz 2-223-1145; www.chalalan.com; Comercio nr Campero, Rurrenabaque) is Bolivia's leading community-based ecotourism project. Set up in the early 1990s by the inhabitants of remote San José de Uchupiamonas, it has become a lifeline for villagers, and has so far generated money for a school and a small clinic. Built entirely from natural rainforest materials by the enthusiastic San José youth, the lodge's simple and elegant huts surround the idyllic oxbow lake, Laguna Chalalán. Chalalán is Parque Nacional Madidi's only formal visitor accommodations and it provides the opportunity to amble through relatively untouched rainforest and appreciate the richness of life. While the flora and fauna are lovely, it's the sounds that provide the magic here: the incredible dawn bird chorus, the evening frog symphony, the collective whine of zillions of insects, the roar of bucketing tropical rainstorms and, in the early morning, the thunderlike chorus of every howler monkey within a 100km radius.

Your trip (once you're in Rurre) starts with a six-hour canoe ride upstream on the misty Río Beni, and moves onto the smaller tributary, Río Tuichi. Once you're at Chalalán, you can go on long daytime treks or on nocturnal walks. Boat excursions on the lake are a delight and you can see different types of monkey who come to feed and drink water. Swimming in the lake among docile caimans is a must, especially at dusk when the light is heavenly. On nights prior to departures from the lodge, the guides throw parties, with windpipe playing, coca chewing and general merriment. The village of San José is another three hours upstream by boat, and if you wish to visit it from Chalalán, though you'll need to arrange it in advance, it's especially shared taxis to Reyes (B$15, 30 minutes) leave when full from the corner of Santa Cruz and Comercio. Several daily services make the daunting trip from Rurrenabaque to La Paz (B$90, 18 to 24 hours), via Yolosita (B$75, 14 to 20 hours), the hop-off point for Coroico. If you find the narrow, twisting Andean roads and sheer drops a harrowing experience on a bus, another option is to bus it as far as Caranavi (p140) and take a shared taxi from there, the rest of the trip being the most scary, or picturesque, depending on your point of view. The route to Trinidad (normal/sleeper B$120/150, 17 to 30 hours) via Yucumo, San Borja and San Ignacio de Moxos remains one of the worst in the country and is typically closed during the rainy season. Buses now run year-round to Riberalta (B$100, 17 to 40 hours) and Guayaramerín (B$120, 18 hours to three days), but you need a healthy dose of stamina, insect repellent and food if you're going to attempt it in the wet season.

Getting Around

TAM and Amazonas *micros* (B$5, 10 minutes) shuttle between the airport and airline offices in town; the quicker and breezier moto-taxis require that you carry all your luggage on your back. Moto-taxis around town cost B$3 per ride; there is a convenient *parada* at the corner of Comercio and Santa Cruz. The ferry across to San Buenaventura leaves from the port area every 20 minutes (B$1) or so from 6am to midnight, though services are less frequent after 6pm.

SAN BUENAVENTURA

Sleepy San Buenaventura sits across the Río Beni, watching all the busy goings-on in Rurre, content with its own slower pace.

If you're looking for fine Beni leather goods, visit the store of well-known leather artisan Manuel Pinto on the main street, but avoid purchasing anything made from wild rainforest species. The **Centro Cultural Tacana** (☎ 892-2394; west side of plaza; admission B$5; ☺ Sun-Thu) has a handicrafts store and

rewarding during the week-long fiesta for the local patron saint around May 1. For a high-season stay in a simple, comfortable lodge, you'll pay US$320 per person (all-inclusive) for three nights and four days; there are longer options too. Rates include transfers to and from the airport (if you're coming from La Paz), one night in Rurre, three great meals per day, a well-trained English-speaking guide, excursions, canoe trips on the lake, plus local taxes and a community levy.

Mapajo Lodge (Map p302; ☎ 892-2317; www.mapajo.com; Santa Cruz btwn Comercio & Avaroa, Rurrenabaque), an outstanding example of community-run, responsible tourism, offers all-inclusive overnight visits to the Mosetén-Chimane community of Asuncíon, three hours upriver from Rurre inside the Reserva de la Biosfera Pilón Lajas. The project takes in six traditional communities of Tacana, Chimane and Mosetén peoples. Since lumbering was stopped in 1998, the ecosystem is relatively intact and wildlife is quickly returning. The visits include bow-and-arrow fishing, rainforest hiking and unchoreographed community visits. The cost is around B$500 per person per day. The individual *cabañas* are comfy, the hosts are friendly and the food is good and plentiful. Guides mostly speak Spanish. The project's profits finance community health and education projects.

San Miguel del Bala (Map p302; ☎ 892-2394; www.sanmigueldelbala.com; Comercio btwn Vaca Diez & Santa Cruz, Rurrenabaque) is a glorious community ecolodge in its own patch of paradise right on Madidi's doorstep, 40 minutes upstream by boat from Rurre. Accommodations are in cabins with mahogany wood floors, separate bathrooms and beds covered by silky mosquito nets. There are several guided walks, including a visit to the San Miguel community. This Tacana community consists of around 230 inhabitants who'll be happy to show you their traditional agricultural methods or weaving and wood-carving. Guests can also chill in hammocks in the communal hut. What the guides lack in English, they make up for with their enthusiasm and knowledge. If you go for the three-days/two-nights arrangement, you can have a day's visit into Parque Nacional Madidi. The price (B$450 per person per day) includes transportation, accommodations, food and guided tours.

If you need more adrenaline, then try the unambiguously named **Biggest Canopy in Bolivia** (☎ 7655-1553; Comercio next to Café Luna; per person B$180), a community-run forest canopy zipline in nearby Villa Alcira. It´s only for those with a head for heights and a strong stomach.

celebrates the Tacana people's unique cosmovision. SERNAP's **Parque Nacional Madidi headquarters** (☎ 892-2540) and a tourist information office, staffed by agencies authorized to conduct tours in the park, provide visitor information.

PARQUE NACIONAL MADIDI

The Río Madidi watershed is one of South America's most intact ecosystems. Most of it is protected by the 1.8 million-hectare Parque Nacional Madidi, which takes in a range of wildlife habitats, from the steaming lowland rainforests to 5500m Andean peaks. This little-trodden utopia is home to an astonishing variety of Amazonian wildlife: 44% of all New World mammal species, 38% of tropical amphibian species, almost 1000 kinds of bird and more protected species than any park in the world.

The populated portions of the park along the Río Tuichi have been accorded a special Unesco designation permitting indigenous inhabitants to utilize traditional forest resources, but the park has also been considered for oil exploration and as a site for a major hydroelectric scheme in the past. In addition, illicit logging has affected several areas around the park perimeter and there's been talk of a new road between Apolo and Ixiamas that would effectively bisect the park. Though the hydroelectric scheme has been abandoned, the debate continues over whether road building and oil exploration will take place, and many suspect that illegal loggers will use the opportunity to benefit from these projects.

It is difficult to visit the park independently, but if you wish to do so the B$95 admission fee is payable at the SERNAP office in San Buenaventura – you must be accompanied by an authorized guide. By far the easiest way to arrange access is by visiting one of the community projects (see boxed text on pp306–7).

SAN BORJA

San Borja is pretty much just a bus- and truck-stop destination, though you may find yourself stuck here waiting for transportation to Trinidad during the rainy season. The town's prosperity is illustrated in the palatial homes rising up on the block behind the church. A long day's walk along the relatively little-traveled road west of town will take you through a wetlands area where you can see numerous waterbirds.

Sleeping

San Borja's hotels specialize in hard mattresses and turquoise walls. Listed are two that try to break the mold.

Hotel San Borja (☎ 848-3133; s/d with bathroom B$40/80) Higher-end rooms cater to the choosier visitor; cheaper ones fall into the turquoise trap but provide a crash-pad for the night. Note that there is a 6am gospel wakeup call courtesy of the nearby Catholic church.

Hostal Jatata (☎ 895-3212; r per person with bathroom B$85) Two blocks off the plaza, pick of the bunch Jatata offers good, comfy rooms and a lovely patio with drooping hammocks. There is a *palapa* roof and a half-decent restaurant.

Getting There & Away

The San Borja to Trinidad road is notoriously bad and can be closed for long periods during the wet season. It's frustrating for anybody wanting to travel between Rurrenabaque and Trinidad, and even more so when buses that set out from Rurre bound for Trinidad announce, after a little local consultation at San Borja, that they can go no further. In theory, more services to Trinidad depart from San Borja than from Rurre, so you may find yourself here whether you like it or not, either looking for a connection, or simply stranded and waiting.

In the dry season buses pull out several times daily from the bus terminal (3km south of the plaza; B$4 by moto-taxi) for the Reserva Biosférica del Beni (B$20, 1½ hours), San Ignacio de Moxos (B$40, five hours), Trinidad (B$50, eight to 12 hours) and Santa Cruz (B$100, 20 to 24 hours). During the wet season the trip to Trinidad is sometimes attempted by privately owned 4WD vehicles (B$100) commissioned by the bus companies, though whether they depart or not depends on the whim of the driver. There are frequent *micro* services to Rurrenabaque (B$30, five to eight hours), which depart when full.

If you're Trinidad-bound, note that the Río Mamoré *balsa* (raft) crossings close at 6pm, and you need five to six hours to reach them from San Borja. There are no accommodations on either side of the crossing, so give yourself plenty of time. Watch for pink river dolphins at river crossings.

Amaszonas (☎ 895-3185; Bolívar 157) has daily round-trip flights between La Paz, San Borja and Trinidad. **TAM** (☎ 895-3609) sometimes makes a surprise landing, but doesn't have any regularly scheduled flights.

RESERVA BIOSFÉRICA DEL BENI

Created by Conservation International in 1982 as a loosely protected natural area, the 334,200-hectare Beni Biosphere Reserve was recognized by Unesco in 1986 as a 'Man & the Biosphere Reserve,' and received official recognition the following year through a pioneering debt swap agreement with the Bolivian government.

The adjacent **Reserva Forestal Chimane**, a 1.15-million-hectare buffer zone and indigenous reserve, has been set aside for sustainable subsistence use by the 1200 Chimane people living there. The combined areas are home to at least 500 bird species as well as more than 100 mammals and myriad reptiles, amphibians and insects.

The Chimane reserve was threatened in 1990 when the government decided to open the area to loggers. Seven hundred Chimanes and representatives of other tribes staged a march from Trinidad to La Paz in protest of the decision that would amount to the wholesale destruction of their land. Logging concessions were changed but not altogether revoked, and the problems continue.

Information

The reserve is administered by SERNAP in La Paz (see p63) in conjunction with a local committee of representatives. Admission to the biosphere reserve is B$35 per person. Horse rentals are available for B$70 per eight-hour day.

When to Visit

The best months to visit the reserve are June and July, when there's little rain and the days are clear; bring warm clothing to protect against the occasional *surazo*. During the rainy season, days are hot, wet, muggy and miserable with mosquitoes, so bring plenty of repellent.

Tours

The reserve headquarters, El Porvenir, is in the *cerrado* (savanna) and quite a distance from the rainforest. The station organizes everything in the reserve: accommodations,

food, guides and horseback riding. The best way to observe wildlife is to hire a guide at the station and go for a hike, though the heat might be easier to take if you hire a horse.

El Porvenir station offers several tours: a four-hour canoe trip to see the black caimans in **Laguna Normandia** (per person B$70); a four-hour **cerrado hike** (per person B$100) to the monkey-rich rainforest islands; and a full-day **Las Torres tour** (per person with food B$200) on horseback to three wildlife-viewing towers where you can observe both *cerrado* and rainforest ecosystems, and fish for piranhas for dinner. If you're a bird fanatic, take the **Loro tour** (per person US$11) on foot or horseback to see the colorful spectacle of macaws and parakeets coming to roost – or you can check them out in the palms at El Porvenir, where they provide a raucous 6am wakeup call.

To go into the rainforest beyond Laguna Normandia, you'll need to organize a tour from El Porvenir. It's a four-hour walk from the lake to the edge of the secondary-growth rainforest. A further four hours' walk takes you into the primary forest. Along the way, a 6m viewing tower provides a vista over an island of rainforest, and a 4m tower along the Río Curiraba provides views over the forest and savanna in the remotest parts of the reserve.

Perhaps the most interesting option is the four-day **Tur Monitoreo** (per person without/with food B$600/700), during which visitors accompany park rangers on their wildlife monitoring rounds into the reserve's furthest reaches to search for monkeys, macaws and pink river dolphins. You will need your own camping gear for this and, of course, plenty of insect repellent.

Laguna Normandia

This savanna lake, an hour's walk from El Porvenir, is the reserve's most popular destination. The sight of the world's largest population of crawling, rare black caimans – there are at least 400 of them – is truly astounding. The reptiles are the descendants of specimens originally destined to become unwilling members of the fashion industry, by providing shoe and bag material for a leather company. When the caiman breeder's business failed, the animals were left behind, and sadly the majority perished

AMAZON BASIN

from neglect, crowding and hunger. The survivors were rescued by Bolivian authorities and airlifted to safety.

Fortunately, caimans have little interest in humans, so it's generally safe to observe them at close range while rowboating around with a guide. If you find them too scary to get up close and personal, climb the 11m **viewing tower**.

Totaizal & Reserva Forestal Chimane

A stone's throw from the road and a 40-minute walk from El Porvenir is Totaizal. This friendly and well-organized village of 140 people lies hidden in the forest of the Chimane reserve. The Chimane, traditionally a nomadic forest tribe, have in recent times faced expulsion from their ancestral lands by lumber companies and highland settlers. Skilled hunters, the Chimane people have a fascinating way of fishing, using natural poisons to kill their prey. They are also highly adept at collecting wild honey and avoiding ballistic bees. People living in the settlement of **Cero Ocho**, a four-hour walk from Totaizal, trudge into the village to sell bananas, while others provide guiding services for visitors. You can visit the village of Totaizal, but you'll have to make prior arrangements through El Porvenir.

Sleeping & Eating

Accommodations at El Porvenir are in airy bunk-bed rooms that cost B$100 per person (price includes three simple meals). Amenities include a library, a researchers' workshop, an interpretive center and a small cultural and biological museum. There's plenty of potable water but you'll want to bring snacks and refreshments as there's nothing available for miles around.

Getting There & Away

El Porvenir is 200m off the highway, 90 minutes east of San Borja, and is accessible via any *movilidad* (anything that moves) between Trinidad and San Borja or Rurrenabaque – ask your driver to drop you at the entrance. In the dry season Trinidad-bound buses mainly pass in the morning between 9am and 11am, those for San Borja usually in the late afternoon between 4pm and 7pm. Otherwise there's surprisingly little traffic. Note that this route is in a dismal state and often closed during the rainy season, so check

the weather forecast before setting out to avoid getting stranded.

SAN IGNACIO DE MOXOS

San Ignacio de Moxos is a friendly, tranquil indigenous Moxos village, 92km west of Trinidad, that dedicates itself to agriculture and oozes an ambience quite distinct from any other Bolivian town. The people speak an indigenous dialect known locally as Ignaciano, and their lifestyle, traditions and food are unique in the country. The best time to visit San Ignacio is during the annual festival on July 30 and 31. This is when the villagers let their hair down and get their feather headgear up, and don't stop drinking, dancing and letting off fireworks for three days (see opposite).

The village was founded as San Ignacio de Loyola by the Jesuits in 1689. In 1749 it suffered pestilence and had to be shifted to its present location on healthier ground.

Sights & Activities

In the main plaza is a **monument** to Chirípieru, El Machetero Ignaciano, with his crown of feathers and formidable-looking hatchet, a look that's recreated extensively during the village festival. The **church** (☯ 8am-7pm) on the plaza was restored and rebuilt from 1995 to 2003 and adopts the familiar Jesuit style with a wide roof supported by wooden columns, though they are noticeably smooth and without decoration in this example. If you get a small group together, one of the church workers will take you around for a small fee.

At the **museum** (admission B$5) in the Casa Belén, near the northwest corner of the plaza, you'll see elements of both the Ignaciano and Moxos cultures, including the *bajones,* the immense flutes introduced by the Jesuits.

North of town at the large **Laguna Isirere**, you can go fishing and swimming, observe the profuse bird life and watch the gorgeous sunset. A statue on the shores depicts the local legend about the formation of the lake. A young boy named Isidoro was paddling in a small pool when he was swallowed up by the waters, the work of the mischievous water spirit *Jichi* who needed a human sacrifice in order to turn the pool into the lake it is today. It's accessible on a 30-minute walk or by hitchhiking from town.

The greater area also boasts a number of obscure – and hard-to-reach – places of interest: the **Lomas de Museruna**, several **archaeological ruins**, and the ruins of the **missions** San José and San Luis Gonzaga.

Sleeping & Eating

Note that prices double during the fiesta, but visitors can camp at established sites just outside town during the festivities. There are numerous accommodations options on the plaza itself.

Residencial 31 de Julio (r per person B$30) A block off the plaza, this friendly place maintains clean and basic rooms.

Plaza Hotel (☎ 482-2032; r per person B$50, with bathroom B$70) On the plaza, a cheery option with bright, spacious doubles with fans.

Residencial Don Joaquín (☎ 482-8012; Montes; r per person B$50, with bathroom B$80) At the corner of the plaza near the church, it offers a nice patio and clean, simple rooms.

Doña Anita (☎ 482-2043; Ballivián; mains B$10) The *doña* is famed for her icy fruit juices and massive burgers topped with cheese, egg and tomato.

Pescadería Don Francisco (Montes; mains B$30-40) A couple of blocks east of the plaza, this is a great fish restaurant where you can enjoy the catch of the day.

Getting There & Away

San Ignacio is located smack-bang in the middle of the notoriously poor Trinidad–San Borja road which is impassable following periods of rain. By far the easiest access is from Trinidad, with *camionetas* (open-backed 4WDs) running when full from the *paradas* at Santa Cruz y Mamoré and 1 de Mayo near Velarde. San Borja-bound bus

---

WHEN THE VILLAGE GOES WILD

Annually, 2pm on July 30 marks the first day of celebrations of the huge Fiesta del Santo Patrono de Moxos, held in honor of San Ignacio, the sacred protector of the Moxos. This is one of the best festivals in the Amazon and if you're in Bolivia during this time, you'd be crazy to miss it.

Strictly speaking, the festival begins on July 22 and gets off to a strange start. The small statue of Santiago from the church is paraded and worshipped each evening until July 25 (Día de la Fiesta de Santiago), after which point the same statue is then worshipped as an image of San Ignacio for the rest of the *fiesta*! During this time each family in the village brings an image of San Ignacio to the church and places it there in his honor. These solemn processions continue for another four days before the real festivities begin.

On July 30, a procession leaves from the church incorporating *macheteros* (local youths dressed in white with remarkable radial headdresses traditionally made from macaw feathers), *achus* (village elders with wooden masks and hats bearing fireworks) and musicians beating out the tunes of the unique Moxos music – using drums, enormous bamboo pan-pipes and flutes. One by one the procession visits every house in the village, returning the images of San Ignacio that had been deposited in the church and receiving food and drink in return. The winding route ends at the church, where they attend Mass, its close signifying the end of formalities and the beginning of festivities.

The evening of the first day of fiesta starts with huge fireworks let off by two rich local families outside the church, who 'compete' with each other through the lavishness of their displays. Then it's over to the *achus,* men and women wearing large, high-topped leather hats with firecrackers fizzling on the top, who run through the crowd, while everyone shrieks and runs away from them, laughing and screaming – children have a particularly good time. Fresh river fish is eaten in abundance, plenty of drinking takes place (as you'll see by the number of booze-casualties sleeping in the streets) and local *artesanía* (locally handcrafted items) is displayed around the village.

On the morning of the second day another Mass is held. The small statue of San Ignacio is returned to the church and a larger statue of the same saint is extracted for the first time to lead a second procession, one that is this time accompanied by local politicians, religious authorities, invited dignitaries and others worthy of a bigger statue. Once the formalities are dispensed with, it's party time again. The second and third days are filled with bull-teasing, when the (drunk) locals attempt to get the bulls' attention, and lots of dancing. A few days later, San Ignacio goes back to its quiet life, only to go wild again the following year.

services pass through San Ignacio in the early afternoon (four hours). From March to October, it's four hours from Trinidad to San Ignacio, including the *balsa* crossing of the Río Mamoré, but this route is often closed during the rainy season. If you're making your own way note that the *balsa* closes at 6pm (it may stay open later at times of heavy traffic) and there are no accommodations on either side, so check the timing before setting out.

From San Borja, buses pull out several times daily from the bus terminal in the dry season and arrive in San Ignacio five hours later. In the wet season 4WD vehicles contracted by the bus services occasionally run, but their departures depend on the whim of the drivers and are frequently canceled.

During intense periods of rain and during the festival, flights to Trinidad may be offered. The tiny airport is at the top end of Av Aeropuerto and you'll have to ask around for information.

There are sporadic departures to Rurrenabaque during the dry season, but it's easier to catch a lift to San Borja and take one of the frequent *micros* from there.

EASTERN BOLIVIAN AMAZON

The eastern side of the Amazon hides the spectacular Parque Nacional Noel Kempff Mercado, still considered one of Bolivia's least accessible parks and ironically easier to get to from Brazil. Trinidad, the Bolivian Amazon's main population center, is still very much a frontier settlement, though it's also an access point for dozens of smaller communities, wild rivers and remote jungle reserves.

TRINIDAD

pop 86,500 / elevation 235m

Trinidad is the place you'll come to if you're after a trip down the long and deep Río Mamoré, or on your way between Santa Cruz and Rurrenabaque. It's a modern town that is growing rapidly; its most notable feature is the massive, green, tropical main square (Trinidad is only 14 degrees south of the equator), once home to a population of friendly sloths.

The city of La Santísima Trinidad (the Most Holy Trinity) was founded in 1686 by Padre Cipriano Barace as the second Jesuit mission in the flatlands of the southern Beni. It was originally constructed on the banks of the Río Mamoré, 14km from its present location, but floods and pestilence along the riverbanks necessitated relocation. In 1769 it was moved to the Arroyo de San Juan, which now divides the city in two.

Information

Trinidad's helpful municipal **tourist office** (☎ 462-4831; Joaquín de la Sierra at La Paz; ☒ 8:30am-12:30pm & 2:30-6pm Mon-Fri) is tucked away inside the Prefectura – go into the courtyard via the gate next to the main entrance and ask for directions. Several Enlace ATMs near the main plaza accept international cards – this is a good spot to get some cash before heading out to the ATM-less San Ignacio de Moxos and Rurrenabaque. Moneychangers gather on Av 6 de Agosto between Suárez and Av 18 de Noviembre.

Telephone cabins and internet access (B$4 per hour) are on almost every block, with a notable concentration along 6 de Agosto near the plaza. **Lavandería Pro-Vida** (☎ 462-0626; Sattori at Suárez; ☒ 8am-noon & 2-7pm Mon-Sat) charges B$10 to B$30 per dozen stinky items, depending on whether you want your clothes ironed or not. The provincial **immigration office** (Busch) is on the 2nd floor of the FELCC building at the corner of the plaza and can grant visa extensions.

Sights & Activities

Trinidad's loveliest feature is **Plaza Gral José Ballivián**, with its tall, tropical trees, lush gardens and community atmosphere. You can spend a pleasant evening eating ice cream and watching hundreds of motorbikes orbiting around the square with more urgency than would seem necessary. In the past, the traffic was refereed by a police officer who sat in a big wooden chair and conjured up red, yellow and green traffic lights by touching an electric wire against one of three nails. On the south side of the plaza, the **cathedral**, built on the site of an earlier Jesuit church, is an unimpressive building that doesn't even have its own bells – the on-the-hour bell ringing is played off a tape.

The Spanish-funded **ethno-archaeological museum** (admission B$5; ☽ 8am–noon & 3-6pm) at the university, 1.5km north of town, exhibits artifacts from the Trinidad region, including traditional instruments and tribal costumes.

Festivals & Events

The town's mid-June **founding fiesta** is a big, loud, drunken party at the Plaza de la Tradición, and features the climbing of greased poles for prizes and a *hocheadas de toros* (teasing of bulls).

Tours

Several agencies run tours into the city's hinterlands. **Turismo Moxos** (☎ 462-1141; turmoxos@entelnet.bo; 6 de Agosto 114) organizes three-day cruises on the Río Ibare, visits to Sirionó villages, four-day canoe safaris into the jungle and one-day horseback trips into remote areas.

Fremen Tours (www.andes-amazonia.com) specializes in all-inclusive river cruises on its posh hotel-boat *Flotel Reina de Enin*, which departs from Trinidad. Cabins include private bathrooms and there's an excellent

dining room and bar. It also owns the houseboat *Ebrio*, with four berths and hammock space, which does the run down into Parque Nacional Isiboro-Sécure. Trips should be booked through the offices in Cochabamba (p196).

Sleeping

BUDGET

Residencial Patujú (☎ 462-1963; Villavicencio 473; s/d B$50/100) A nice, homey, budget option with a bright, but cool courtyard. Unlike most other rooms in *residenciales*, these have cable TV; inexplicably, those with private bathroom cost the same as those with shared bathroom – make sure you let them know which you want.

Residencial Santa Cruz (☎ 462-0711; Santa Cruz 537; s B$60, with bathroom s/d B$80/140) A budget place that makes a real effort to cheer up its rooms with colorful decor, hand-painted wall hangings and bright bedclothes. Rooms on the 1st floor are airier (and slightly pricier). All rooms have cable TV.

Hotel Copacabana (☎ 462-2811; Villavicencio 627; s/d with fan & bathroom B$80/140, with air-con & bathroom

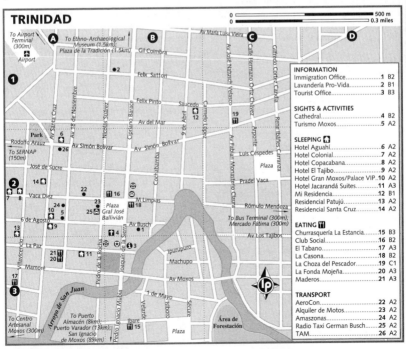

TRINIDAD

0   500 m
0   0.3 miles

INFORMATION
Immigration Office...................1 B2
Lavandería Pro-Vida................2 B1
Tourist Office.........................3 B3

SIGHTS & ACTIVITIES
Cathedral.............................4 B2
Turismo Moxos.....................5 A2

SLEEPING 🏠
Hotel Aguahí.........................6 A2
Hotel Colonial........................7 A2
Hotel Copacabana...................8 A2
Hotel El Tajibo........................9 A2
Hotel Gran Moxos/Palace VIP..10 A2
Hotel Jacarandá Suites............11 A3
Mi Residencia........................12 B1
Residencial Patujú..................13 A2
Residencial Santa Cruz............14 A2

EATING 🍴
Churrasquería La Estancia........15 B3
Club Social...........................16 B2
El Tabano.............................17 A3
La Casona............................18 A3
La Choza del Pescador............19 C1
La Fonda Mojeña....................20 A3
Maderos...............................21 A3

TRANSPORT
AeroCon..............................22 A2
Alquiler de Motos...................23 A2
Amaszonas...........................24 A2
Radio Taxi German Busch.......25 A2
TAM...................................26 A2

DOWN THE LAZY RIVER

River trips from Trinidad will carry you to the heart of the Bolivian Amazon along the Río Mamoré, where you'll experience the mystique and solitude for which the rainforests are renowned. For optimum enjoyment, visit during the dry season, which lasts roughly from May or June until some time in October.

Although the scenery along the northern rivers changes little, the diversity of plant and animal species along the shore picks up any slack in the pace of the journey. The longer your trip, the deeper you'll gaze into the forest darkness and the more closely you'll scan the riverbanks for signs of movement. Free of the pressures and demands of active travel, you'll have time to relax and savor the passing scene.

In general, the riverboat food is pretty good, but meals consist mainly of *masaco* (mashed yucca or plantains, served with *charque* (dried meat), rice, noodles, thin soup and bananas in every conceivable form. After a couple of days you'll probably start dreaming of pizza, so bring along some treats to supplement the daily fare. It's also wise to carry your own water or some form of water purification.

Be sure to discuss sleeping arrangements with the captain before setting out. Passengers must usually bring their own hammocks (available in Trinidad), but you may be allowed to sleep on deck or on the roof of the boat. You'll also need a sleeping bag or a blanket, especially in winter, when jungle nights can be surprisingly chilly. If you're fortunate enough to be on a boat that travels through the night, a mosquito net isn't necessary, but on boats that tie up at night, passengers without a mosquito net will find the experience ranges from utterly miserable to unbearable. See Getting There & Away (opposite) for information on how to arrange a boat trip. For a more lush, hotel-boat river trip, see p313.

B$140/210; 🌀) This is a friendly place with tiled, hospital-like rooms, some with air-conditioning. Ask for a room overlooking the street if you want some fresh air.

MIDRANGE
Hostal El Tajibo (☎ 462-2324; Santa Cruz 423 & 6 de Agosto; s/d with fan & bathroom B$100/150, with air-con & bathroom B$200/250; 🌀) Trinidad's best-value budget option, this hotel has attractive, almost stylish rooms and comfortable beds. Some rooms have balconies overlooking the street and breakfast is included with air-con rooms.

Hotel Colonial (☎ 462-2864; Vaca Diez 76; s/d with fan & bathroom B$100/150, with air-con & bathroom B$200/250; 🌀) If El Tajibo is full, the same owners run the carbon-copy Colonial a couple of blocks further on from the plaza. It's almost identical, from the decor right down to the price.

Hotel Gran Moxos/Palace VIP (☎ 462-8777; www .hotelmoxos.com.bo; 6 de Agosto 146; s/d with bathroom B$130/240; 🌀) Despite the shabby-looking reception, this isn't a bad hotel, though an attack of the hyperboles was obviously involved in its naming. Rooms are carpeted, comfortable and characterless, with breakfast included and served in the cafe downstairs.

TOP END
Mi Residencia (☎ 462-1543; fax 462-2464; Felix Pinto 555; s/d with bathroom B$260/370; 🌀 💻 🍷) A flashy entrance through a wooden gate takes you into the smooth, glass-fronted reception here. The large rooms are decked out in loud, kitsch designs, and each has a TV and fridge. The hotel is a 10-minute walk from the main plaza.

Hotel Aguahí (☎ 462-5569; Bolívar at Santa Cruz; s/d with bathroom B$320/440; 🌀 🍷 💻) The rooms are large, the beds comfortable and there is a large, figure-of-eight pool in the spacious, tropical garden.

Hotel Jacarandá Suites (☎ 462-2446; La Paz nr Pedro de la Rocha; s/d with bathroom B$360/510; 🌀 💻 🍷) Trinidad's best hotel, this is a modern, smart place with an upscale clientele. All rooms are mini-suites with air-conditioning, some of which have small balconies overlooking the leafy courtyard. Enjoy a cocktail in the Tropical Bar or cool off in the pool.

Eating & Drinking
For a city of its size, Trinidad disappoints with the quality of its restaurants and, despite being in the heart of Beni cattle country, it can be surprisingly difficult to get a decent steak.

Club Social (Suárez; almuerzo & dinner B$20) Right on the plaza, in a shady, breezy courtyard, the lovely social club is a local family favorite. The generous two-course menus include soup, meat, rice and veg, plus a drink.

El Tabano (Villavicencio nr Mamoré; mains B$25-40) With cool beers and cocktails served in the courtyard, this bar-pub is a popular place with Trinidad's young crowd on account of its lively atmosphere and excellent food.

La Fonda Mojeña (18 de Noviembre; mains B$25-40) Typical food is the order of the day at this little restaurant famous for its local specialities.

La Casona (east side of Plaza Gral José Ballivián; almuerzo B$25, mains B$40-90) Trinidad's most famous restaurant unfortunately doesn't live up to the hype. Give the overpriced à la carte meals a miss and stick to the lunchtime *almuerzo*.

Churrasquería La Estancia (Ibare nr Velarde; B$40-120) Ask anybody in Trinidad where to get a good bit of beef and you will be sent here. With its palm roof and coal fire barbecue hamming up the ranch-house setting, the succulent and juicy cuts will make you wonder how other restaurants even dare to call themselves *churrasquerías*.

ourpick Maderos (La Paz nr 18 de Noviembre; mains B$45-50; dinner only, closed Mon) If you're a Mexican food fanatic you'll have been scouring the continent for a place like this. Top-class burritos and all the rest are served in this *palapa*-roofed hangout. Key to its success is that it gives you the ingredients and lets you fold up your own *fajitas*.

La Choza del Pescador (Bolívar at Velasco; mains B$45-50) There's not much on the menu here, just fish cooked in about five different ways, but if you are feeling fishy then this is a good place to drop anchor.

Shopping

Local Beni crafts, including weavings, woodwork and ceramics, are sold at the **Centro Artesanal Moxos** (462-2751; Bopi s/n), southwest of town. Look out for the *pifano*, an indigenous flute made from the wing bone of the Jabiru stork using a technique over 1000 years old – it's the staple instrument of the unique Moxos music.

Getting There & Away

AIR

Departing air travelers must pay B$7 for use of the airport. **Amaszonas** (462 2426; 18

de Noviembre 267) shuttles daily between La Paz and San Borja. **AeroCon** (462-4442; Vaca Diez nr 18 de Noviembre) handles several daily flights to Santa Cruz, Riberalta and Cobija. **TAM** (462-2363; Bolívar at Santa Cruz) has a couple of flights a week to Cochabamba and La Paz.

BOAT

If you're looking for river transportation north along the Mamoré to Guayaramerín, or south along the Mamoré and Ichilo to Puerto Villarroel, inquire at the *Capitanía*, in Puerto Almacén, 8km southwest of town. The Guayaramerín run takes up to a week (larger boats do it in three to four days) and costs around B$250 including food, B$200 without. To Puerto Villarroel, smaller boats take five days and cost about B$100 including meals.

For a plusher river affair, get on Fremen Tours' posh hotel-boat *Flotel Reina de Enin* (p313).

BUS & CAMIONETA

The rambling bus terminal is a 10-minute walk east of the center. Several *flotas* (long-distance bus companies) depart nightly between 6pm and 10pm for Santa Cruz (normal/*bus cama* B$50/80, eight to 10 hours). A number of companies theoretically serve Rurrenabaque (B$70, 12 hours) daily via San Borja, though from November to May these services are typically suspended. There are also daily dry-season departures to Riberalta, Guayaramerín and Cobija.

Camionetas run to San Ignacio de Moxos (three to four hours) when full from *paradas* at Santa Cruz and Mamoré and 1 de Mayo near Velarde. Bus services occasionally run from the terminal around 9am but departures are increasingly sporadic.

Getting Around

TO/FROM THE AIRPORT

Taxis to and from the airport charge around B$15, but if you don't have much luggage, moto-taxis are cheaper (B$10) – you'll be surprised how much luggage they can accommodate with a bit of creativity.

MOTORCYCLE

Motorbikes are a great way to while the day away – for B$12 per hour or B$80 for a full day you can rent a bike and join the general public in whizzing around the square.

AMAZON BASIN

Pick one up from **Alquiler de Motos** (Main Plaza; ⏱ 8am-6pm), or alternatively strike a private deal with a moto-taxi driver (though you can expect to be followed!). You'll need a regular driver's license from home.

TAXI

Moto-taxis around town cost B$3, while increasingly scarce car taxis charge B$10. For rides to outlying areas, phone **Radio Taxi German Busch** (☎ 462-0008), or look for one

---

NATIONAL TREASURES: BOLIVIA'S RARE ENDEMIC BIRDS

With over 1200 bird species inhabiting the country, Bolivia is a birdwatcher's paradise. But it's not just the sheer quantity of species that makes Bolivia such an attractive destination for bird lovers; it is the quality of the birds you can see.

Asociacíon Armonía, the Bolivian Birdlife International Partner, has developed a series of community-based conservation programs designed to protect the country's most threatened birds, principally by creating a feeling of pride among the locals.

The gorgeous Blue-throated Macaw (Ara glaucogularis), endemic to the unique Beni savannas, numbers, according to the most optimistic of estimates, just 250 individuals. Known to the Bolivians as Barba Azul (Blue Beard), this charismatic bird has become a flagship species for Armonía, which runs a superb, community-orientated conservation program aimed squarely at making sure the bird is around for future generations to appreciate.

Threats to the species are numerous, but one of the most unusual is indiscriminate killing for the sole purpose of harvesting the tail feathers. This practice affects all macaws, but because of the species' similarity to the common Blue and Yellow Macaw (Ara ararauna) and a lack of public awareness of its plight, this species has suffered at the hands of hunters who collect the tail plumes to adorn ceremonial headdresses for regional celebrations like the famous Moxos festival.

Armonia's response has been rapid, effective and ingenious. It has worked on an extensive public education campaign designed to teach locals how to distinguish between the two similar blue macaws that occur in the area and, crucially, to instill a sense of pride in the citizens of Beni for their emblematic bird. An agreement with local indigenous leaders not to hunt live macaws, but to instead fabricate artificial feathers for headdresses has not only been a huge success, but has led to the creation of a small and very lucrative local manufacturing industry. Perhaps most important of all has been the purchase of a small reserve dedicated to the conservation of the bird, which Armonía hopes to develop for ecotourism, bringing much-needed foreign income to the area.

The endangered Red-fronted Macaw (Ara rubrogenys) known locally as Paraba frente roja reflects its Bolivian specialty status in its red, green and yellow plumage – the colors of the national flag. Found only in dry inter-Andean valleys in the Vallegrande area, this handsome bird has a world population of just 1000. Thanks to an extensive public awareness campaign, Armonía was able to raise the funds to purchase a small reserve dedicated to the conservation of the bird, and with the construction of a superb and comfortable **lodge** (B$490 full board) they are now encouraging tourism as a means of sustainably supporting the reserve.

Equally endangered, the bizarre Horned Currasow (Pauxi unicornis), has been styled the 'Unicorn Bird' by the popular press on account of the weird, bony growth on its forehead. The species stronghold is in Amboró, but with a world population estimated to be as low as 1000, and a dependence on dense, undisturbed humid forest, it is in imminent danger of extinction. A rustic, community-operated **eco-lodge** (B$280 full board), supported by Armonía, has been set up in an effort to conserve the bird.

Strangely beautiful, the Palkachupa (Phibalura boliviana), is endemic to the Apolo region of the Bolivian Yungas. It was considered extinct for 98 years until its remarkable rediscovery in 2000. Though the entire global range of this species is within Parque Nacional Madidi, it occurs within the zone designated a 'management area' where loosely controlled agricultural activity is permitted. With a world population of fewer than 200, the species is far from safe.

Visit the **Armonía office** (☎ 356-8808; www.armonia-bo.org; Lomas de Arenas 400; ⏱ 8:30am-12:30pm & 2:30-6pm Mon-Fri) in Santa Cruz for more information about its conservation programs and details on visiting the lodges mentioned above. For guided birding tours contact **Bird Bolivia** (p268).

THE AMAZONIAN EL DORADO

In the Llanos de Moxos, between San Ignacio de Moxos and Loreto, the heavily forested landscape is crossed with more than 100km of canals and causeways and dotted with hundreds of *lomas* (artificial mounds), embankments and fanciful prehistoric earthworks depicting people and animals. One anthropomorphic figure measures over 2km from head to toe – a rainforest variation on Peru's famed Nazca Lines. The original purpose of the earthworks was probably to permit cultivation in a seasonally flooded area, but inside the mounds were buried figurines, pottery, ceramic stamps, human remains and even tools made from stone imported into the region.

The discovery of the *lomas* has caused scientists to look at the Beni region with entirely new eyes: what was previously considered to be a wilderness never touched by humans, save for a few dispersed tribes who inhabited the region, is now thought to have been an area where a vast, advanced civilization farmed, worked and lived in a highly structured society with sophisticated cities.

It is believed that the ceramic mounds came from the large numbers of people who lived on them and who ate and drank from pots, which were then destroyed and buried to improve soil stability. Archaeologists say that the sheer amount of pots indicates the complexity of this lost society. In *1491: New Revelations of the Americas Before Columbus* (Knopf, 2005) Charles C Mann writes following the archaeologist Clark Erickson of the University of Pennsylvania:

> [...] beginning as much as three thousand years ago, this long-ago society...created one of the largest, strangest, and most ecologically rich artificial environments on the planet. These people built up the mounds for homes and farms, constructed the causeways and canals for transportation and communication, created the fish weirs to feed themselves, and burned the savannas to keep them clear of invading trees. A thousand years ago their society was at its height. Their villages and towns were spacious, formal and guarded by moats and palisades. In Erickson's hypothetical reconstruction, as many as a million people may have walked the causeways of eastern Bolivia in their long cotton tunics, heavy ornaments dangling from their wrists.

Some believe that the prehistoric structures of the Beni were constructed by the Paititi tribe 5500 years ago, and that this ancient Beni civilization was the source of the popular Spanish legends of the rainforest El Dorado known as Gran Paititi. Archaeologists continue their research into this fascinating part of history, but one thing is for sure: once you know what lies here in terms of world history, you'll never look at the forests of the Beni in the same way again.

---

on the plaza. Bank on around B$30 per hour for up to four people, including waiting time.

PUERTOS ALMACÉN & VARADOR

Puerto Almacén is best known for its line-up of rickety fish restaurants, which provide interesting lunch options – **Don Pedrito** (mains B$40) is about the best. The only other reason to come here is to inquire about possibilities for river trips at the *Capitanía*. Continuing on 5km, Puerto Varador offers pink river dolphins in small Mamoré tributaries and more fish restaurants.

Moto-taxis from Trinidad to either port cost from B$10 to B$15 per round-trip; car taxis are B$20 each way. All transportation to San Ignacio de Moxos also passes both Puerto Almacén and Puerto Varador. For information on boat travel from either port, see p315.

SANTUARIO CHUCHINI

The Santuario Chuchini (Jaguar's Lair), 14km northwest of Trinidad, is one of the few easily accessible Paititi sites. This **wildlife sanctuary** sits on an 8-hectare *loma* (artificial mound), one of many dotted throughout the surrounding forest. From the camp, you can take short walks in the rainforest to lagoons with caimans, other larger animals and profuse bird life.

The camp has shady, covered picnic sites, trees, children's swings and a variety of native plants, birds and animals. There's also an **archaeological museum** displaying articles excavated from the *loma*, including bizarre statues as well as a piece that appears to be a female figure wearing a bikini (it's actually thought to be an identification of and homage to specific body areas rather than an article of clothing).

For a day visit, including admission, a three-hour cruise and a meal, the price is B$425; to stay overnight it's B$850. Package tours booked in Trinidad may work out a bit cheaper. Further information is available from **Lorena or Efrém Hinojoso** (☎ 462-1968), or travel agencies in Trinidad.

Unless you organize a tour, which will include transportation, you'll have to negotiate with a moto-taxi driver. The road isn't great, so you'll have to be very persuasive and expect to be charged a bit more than usual. It's also a good destination for those who've rented motorbikes. If you're not staying, exotic dishes are available in the restaurant; the food is great but pricey.

RESERVA DE VIDA SILVESTRE RÍOS BLANCO Y NEGRO

This 1.4-million-hectare reserve, created in 1990, occupies the heart of Bolivia's largest wilderness area and contains vast tracts of undisturbed rainforest and *cerrado* with myriad species of plants and animals. These include giant anteaters, peccaries, tapirs, jaguars, bush dogs, marmosets, river otters, capuchin monkeys, caimans, squirrel monkeys, deer and capybaras. The diverse bird life includes curassows, six varieties of macaw and hundreds of other bird species.

The area's only settlement, the privately owned *estancia* (ranch), **Perseverancia**, is 350km north of Santa Cruz. It started as a rubber production center in the 1920s, working until the last *seringueros* (rubber tappers) left in 1972. When the airstrip was completed, professional hunters went after river otters and large cats. By 1986 the *estancia* had again been abandoned, and it remained so until tourism – albeit scanty – began to be promoted in 1989.

In the mid-1990s Moira logging concerns began encroaching on the eastern portion of the reserve and USAID recommended that loggers clear a section of the forest rather than cut selective trees. Things have calmed down in recent years, though it is the difficulty of access to most of the park that has been the reason for this, rather than a more effective program of protection.

Getting There & Away

The privately owned *estancia* Perseverancia is most easily accessed by a 1½-hour charter flight from El Trompillo airport in

Santa Cruz. For those with a solid backside there's a 100km 4WD track between Asunción de Guarayos and Perseverancia that's passable year-round – with considerable perseverance. Currently no tour companies run trips to the park.

PARQUE NACIONAL NOEL KEMPFF MERCADO

The wonderfully remote Noel Kempff Mercado National Park is a real Amazonian highlight and one of South America's most spectacular parks. It is home to a broad spectrum of Amazonian flora and fauna and has a wide range of dwindling habitats, from open *cerrado* to dense rainforest, lending it world-class ecological significance and making it a fabulous place to explore.

There is an abundance of animals that can be spotted here. The rivers hide alligators, caimans, pink river dolphins and rare giant otters, and peccaries, jaguars, tapirs and spider monkeys come to the riverbanks to drink in the evenings. Among the globally threatened mammals that you may dream of seeing are bush dogs and short-eared dogs.

Birdwatchers are in for a serious treat. You might glimpse any of these: the rusty-necked piculet, Zimmer's tody tyrant, collared crescent-chest, ocellated crake, rufous-winged antshrike, rufous-sided pygmy tyrant, campo miner, yellow-billed blue finch, black and tawny seed-eater and a host of others.

The park lies in the northernmost reaches of Santa Cruz department, between the banks of the Ríos Verde, Guaporé (Río Iténez on Bolivian maps) and Paraguá. It encompasses more than 1.5 million hectares of the most dramatic scenery in northern Bolivia, including rivers, rainforests, waterfalls, plateaus and rugged 500m escarpments.

History

Originally known as Parque Nacional Huanchaca, this lovely park was created in 1979 to protect the wildlife of the Serranía de Huanchaca. Many of the people living around the fringes are descended from rubber tappers who arrived here during the 1940s. When synthetic rubber was developed, their jobs disappeared and they turned to hunting, agriculture, logging and the illegal pet trade.

The park's name was officially changed to its current one in 1988, in honor of its de facto founder, the distinguished Bolivian naturalist Noel Kempff Mercado, who had originally lobbied for the creation of the park, but was murdered by renegades at a remote park airstrip east of the Meseta de Huanchaca on September 5, 1986. The pilot Juan Cochamanidis and guide Franklin Parada also lost their lives. In 2000, the park was inscribed by Unesco as a World Heritage Site.

When to Go

There's no wrong season to visit the park. The wet season is great for river travel, especially if you want to boat up to the two big waterfalls. The wettest months are from December to March. The dry season is obviously better for vehicles, but in the late winter months, smoke from forest burning can obliterate the scenery, especially from mid-August to October. March to June is pleasant and not overly hot or rainy, and from October to December the spring blooms add another fabulous dimension.

Information

The park is administered by SERNAP in La Paz (p63). Every prospective visitor to the park must first visit a park information office in either Santa Cruz (p266) or **San Ignacio de Velasco** (☎ 392-2747; Bolívar 87); this is in order to ensure that park personnel will

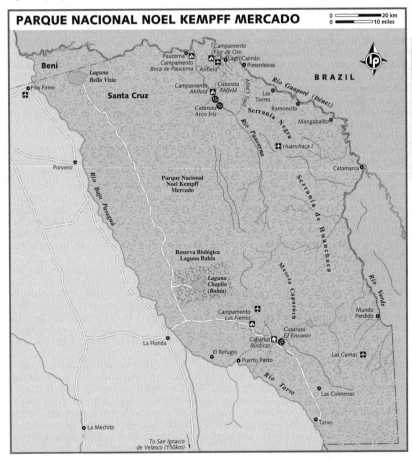

PARQUE NACIONAL NOEL KEMPFF MERCADO

0 ———— 20 km
0 ———— 10 miles

Beni

Laguna Bella Silva

Piso Firme

Santa Cruz

Porvenir

Río Bajo Paraguá

Parque Nacional Noel Kempff Mercado

Reserva Biológica Laguna Bahía

Laguna Chaplin (Bahía)

La Florida

Campamento Los Fierros

El Refugio

Puerto Pasto

La Mechita

To San Ignacio de Velasco (150km)

Paucerna
Campamento Boca de Paucerna
Airfield
Campamento Flor de Oro
Lago Caimán
Pimenteiras

Campamento Ahlfeld
Catarata Ahlfeld
Ahlfeld's Trail
Las Torres
Río Guaporé (Iténez)

Catarata Arco Iris
Serranía Negra
Ramoncito
Mangabalito

BRAZIL

Río Paucerna
Huanchaca I

Catamarca

Serranía de Huanchaca

Río Verde

Meseta Caparúch

Mundo Perdido

Catarata El Encanto
Cabañas Rústicas
Las Gamas

Río Tarvo
Las Colmenas

Tarvo

AMAZON BASIN

be available to accompany travelers on their visit. Visit www.parquenoelkempff.com for an excellent overview of what makes the park so special and for details about the park's ongoing, award-winning Climate Action carbon sequestration program.

Unless you go it alone, the only way to visit the park is by organizing a tour with one of the Santa Cruz–based tour companies (p268).

Dangers & Annoyances

Predictably, you'll need to guard yourself against the park's most populous and varied creatures: *bichos* (insects). During rainy periods, the mosquitoes are fierce and voracious and tiny *garrapatillas* (ticks) can be especially annoying. In the wet season, be particularly wary of blood-sucking sandflies, which carry leishmaniasis. These flies are a real pest at some campsites, particularly in the high forest around the Huanchaca I laboratory ruins.

Between September and December there's a phenomenal bee hatch-out, when the bees seek out human campsites for salt. At such times it's not unusual to have as many as 10,000 bees hanging around a single site so, if you're allergic, avoid the park during these months. The best way to avoid attracting such numbers is to change campsites daily.

Leafcutter ants can also be problematic and although their 6in-wide forest highways – jammed with lines of leaf-bearing workers – can be fascinating to watch, they also often attack the rip-stop nylon of tents. They line their nests with the leaves, which produce fungus for food, and by confusing nylon for leaves the ants do double damage: they can destroy your tent in less than an hour – even while you're sleeping in it – and lose their precious food by lining their nests with plastic. So, don't set up camp anywhere near an ant trail. And if that isn't enough, termites have a taste for backpacks that have been left lying on the ground.

Fire is also a concern. The main natural fire season in the park is from July to November and, since the savanna doesn't burn every year, the amount of dead vegetation is substantial. Never cook or even camp in grassland habitat, no matter how flat and inviting, and never leave a cooking fire unattended, even in the forest.

The park's surface water, which can be scarce between August and November, is delicious and safe to drink, but it's still wise to purify it.

La Florida

Community-run La Florida is the headquarters for budget travelers and the only access point to the park's interior. Note that services here are very basic. There are two *albergues* (basic guesthouses) with shared rooms, no shower and no drinking water. At the time of writing one of the hostels had been left roofless for some time following a storm. Check on local conditions before setting out.

Camping is restricted to designated sites. Wildlife is abundant around the river: you're likely to see river otters, howler monkeys, black caimans and dozens of bird species.

To enter the park you can hike 40km through the forest along the old logging road, rent a mountain bike or hire a 4WD taxi (B$700; April to December only). The community also offers trained local guides who charge around B$150 per day. If you decide to hike, allow two days and carry plenty of water.

Campamento Los Fierros

Los Fierros is a good staging point for jaunts around the southern end of the park, lying in the high Amazonian forest, 2km from the ecological habitat known as 'seasonally inundated termite savanna' (that is, plains dotted with termite mounds). Nearby hikes include trips to **Laguna Chaplin** and **Catarata El Encanto** and steep climbs up onto the wild **Huanchaca Plateau**.

There's superb birdwatching along the forested roads near Los Fierros, and a nearby creek for cooling off in or watching fish-eating bats at night. An early morning visit to the termite savanna will frequently yield glimpses of rare wildlife: maned wolves, crab-eating foxes and even the odd jaguar.

At the time of writing, the accommodations at Los Fierros were in bad condition and accessible only on foot and during the dry season, though work was beginning to improve access. If you arrange your trip in advance, somebody from the community will come to meet you, but you will need to carry and prepare all your own food and drinking water. There are no cooking facilities and no showers for visitors. Prices for camping and guides are negotiated locally.

CATARATA EL ENCANTO

The spectacular 150m **waterfall** that spills off the Serranía de Huanchaca is the main objective of most visitors to Los Fierros, making for an enchanting three-day hike. With a mountain bike, it's a long and tiring day trip; with a vehicle, it can be done in a day, with lots of time for stops along the way.

The excursion begins along the 4WD track that heads east from Los Fierros. Along the way you'll pass through high Amazonian forest, seasonally inundated termite savanna and the threatened *cerrado*.

Once you've crossed the savanna area, continue until you reach a fork in the road; take the left fork. This abandoned logging road passes through some attractive forest, and you're almost guaranteed to see – or at least hear – spider monkeys.

Eventually you'll reach a brook with potable water. Here the logging road ends and you follow a trail running alongside the stream to the foot of the waterfall. Camping is allowed along the stream below the trailhead, but not along the trails to the waterfall. In the evening ask your guide to take you to the *salitrales* (natural salt licks), which attract tapirs, peccaries and other large mammals.

SERRANÍA DE HUANCHACA (LA SUBIDA DE LAS PELADAS)

This excursion begins the same as the trip to Catarata El Encanto but, while crossing the seasonally inundated termite savanna, you'll see a small track that turns left (northeast) off the road and leads through the *cerrado* and forest to the foot of the escarpment. From here it's a steep 500m climb up a footpath that crosses three bald hills known as **Las Peladas**. On the way you'll pass through dry forest on the lower slopes, and *cerrado* and bamboo groves on the upper slopes. Once at the top you're ushered onto a spectacular grassy plain dotted with unusual rock outcrops that lend it the name **Campo Rupestre** (Rocky Landscape). There are also plenty of islands of gallery forest with some excellent campsites.

On a clear day you can see the Amazon forests, termite savannas, Laguna Chaplin and the gallery forests of the Río Bajo Paraguá from the escarpment. It's also a good vantage point to watch hawks and vultures riding the thermals and flocks of blue and yellow macaws migrating between their nesting sites in the highland palm groves and their feeding grounds in the forests below.

On the plateau you can hike for two or three days north to a spectacular unnamed **waterfall** or south to the escarpment overlooking the Catarata El Encanto. Along the way watch for the endangered *gama* (white-tailed deer), which has its last stronghold here. You'll also pass numerous **crystalline ponds** that make for refreshing swimming holes; at least one species of fish here is found nowhere else on earth. Although it may nip at your legs, it's not dangerous.

Those with adequate financial resources can fly into one of two remote airstrips at the abandoned drug-processing laboratories **Huanchaca I** and **Las Gamas**, beautiful places at the southern end of the escarpment. The former lies on the northern end of the plateau amid *cerrado* savanna dotted with islands of Amazonian forest. From there it's a short day hike to the upper reaches of the **Río Paucerna**, which is a fast-running blackwater river. Strong swimmers will be OK, but drag yourself out before you reach the **Arco Irís waterfall**!

Flor de Oro

Here you'll find examples of periodically inundated savanna, degraded *cerrado* and riverine flooded forests, all of which afford superb birdwatching opportunities. More than 300 bird species have been recorded here, and sightings of pink river dolphins are almost guaranteed. It's a 30-minute motorboat ride or a four-hour hike upstream to **Lago Caimán**, predictably a superb spot to see caimans. The lagoon is the trailhead for **Allie's Trail**, which climbs up through dry forest to the **Mirador de los Monos** for great scenery along the edges of the escarpment.

Two spectacular **waterfalls** tumble down the Río Paucerna above the Campamento Boca de Paucerna ranger station. From December to late June, the boat trip from Flor de Oro to the rustic **Campamento Ahlfeld** takes about five hours each way, depending on water levels. From the *campamento* (camping grounds) it's an easy 30-minute walk to the spectacular 35m **Catarata Ahlfeld** and its lovely swimming hole. The more adventurous can hike four hours beyond to the fabulous **Catarata Arco Iris**.

Accessed via private-contracted flights that arrive at the airstrip, visits are currently permitted only when accompanied by a tour company. The once-excellent accommodation facilities have deteriorated considerably, but work to improve them was scheduled to begin at the time of writing. Check the current situation before setting out.

Getting There & Away
AIR

The easiest – and most expensive – way into the park is by contracting a private *aerotaxi*. Round-trip charter flights for up to five passengers from Santa Cruz cost US$1200 to Los Fierros (two hours) and US$1300 to Flor de Oro (2¾ hours) and are the major costs of package tours.

BOAT

From the pleasant little Bolivian village of Piso Firme (which has several humble *alojamientos* and restaurants as well as a small store selling staples), there's an infrequent barge service upriver to Pimenteiras, Brazil (12 hours). From there it's a 30-minute boat ride upstream to Flor de Oro. Otherwise you'll have to negotiate a rented motorboat (up to US$200 one way) or, failing that, swim! There's also a fair amount of Brazilian cargo transportation along the Ríos Mamoré and Guaporé between Guajará-Mirim and Costa Marques, in the Brazilian state of Rondônia. If coming from Brazil, there's no immigration officer in the park, so you'll have to return to Brazil afterwards or make a beeline for immigration in Santa Cruz.

BUS & CAMIÓN

It is not generally advisable to visit the park on your own unless you are familiar with the area, since many underestimate the tough conditions and poor state of accommodations. Setting out on public transportation, you begin an odyssey that may or may not get you to where you want to go – eventually…maybe.

When the roads are driest (normally from June to November), **Trans-Bolivia** (☎ 336-3866; Arana 332, Santa Cruz) buses depart Santa Cruz every Thursday at 7pm, passing Concepción, San Ignacio de Velasco and La Mechita en route to Piso Firme (B$112, 18 hours). For La Florida, get off at La Mechita, a wide spot in the road 55km west. This is a popular route so book well in advance.

If you're traveling this route, it's wise to speak with the SERNAP office in San Ignacio to see if a 4WD taxi can meet you in La Mechita. Alternatively, you can try to hitch a ride with the park rangers or a passing logging truck.

Another option is to take any bus between Santa Cruz and San Ignacio de Velasco and get off at Santa Rosa de la Roca. After you've secured a good supply of food and drink, find the restaurant El Carretero, five minutes' walk from Santa Rosa de la Roca along the road toward San Ignacio, and look for a *camión* headed north toward La Mechita. If you're unsuccessful, you can always stay overnight in Santa Rosa, which has several *alojamientos*.

At La Mechita you'll find a couple of *alojamientos* but, with luck, your *camión* may be passing La Florida turnoff, 20km away, where it's possible to camp. From the turnoff you'll probably have to walk the remaining 35km to La Florida. After 34km from the turnoff, turn right and continue the last kilometer into the village. It's possible to camp here. On the next day, register at the park rangers' office and embark on the 40km hike to Los Fierros.

CAR

It's not generally advisable to visit the park on your own unless you're familiar with the area, since many underestimate the tough conditions. Regardless, you will need to rent a 4WD (US$75 to US$100 per day) in Santa Cruz. From Santa Cruz it takes at least 14 hours to reach Los Fierros, so most people take two days for the trip, spending the night in Concepción en route.

TO BRAZIL

A more radical alternative is the Brazilian connection to Flor de Oro. After picking up a visa in Santa Cruz, take a bus to San Matías (on the Brazilian border) and then on to Cáceres, four hours into Brazil. From there catch another bus to Vilhena (with a federal police post for entrance stamps) in the southern part of Rondônia state. From there daily buses leave for the village of Pimenteiras, 25 minutes by boat downstream from Flor de Oro. Alternatively, from San Ignacio de Velasco (exit stamps sporadically available), you can catch a direct Trans Joao bus into Brazil via San Vincente to La Cerda (B$120, 10 hours) and change buses for Vilhena (B$70, 4½ hours). If stuck overnight, Vilhena has a couple of basic places to spend the night near the *rodoviária* (bus terminal).

THE NORTHERN FRONTIER

The isolated, once-untouched rainforests of northern Bolivia's frontier attract only the intrepid, the renegade and the loggers. Fire, chainsaws and cattle are guzzling the wilderness at increasing speed, but the rare visitor in search of the unexplored and untamed will have their sense of adventure tickled. Facilities are scarce and travel is slow: perfect for those who really want to evade the gringo trail.

GUAYARAMERÍN

pop 36,000 / elevation 130m
Knocking on Brazil's back door, Guayaramerín is twinned with the Brazilian town of Guajará-Mirim on the other side of the Río Mamoré. This lively town thrives on all kinds of trade (legal and illegal) with Brazil, and its streets are full of dusty motorcycle tracks and markets heaving with synthetic garments. It is now the northern terminus for river transportation along the Río Mamoré.

Information

There is a slow internet connection at **Masas** (per hr B$5) just off the plaza. A block east of the plaza, the relatively efficient **Brazilian consulate** (☎ 855-3766; Beni & 24 de Septiembre; ☯9am-5pm Mon-Fri) issues visas in three days. Moneychangers hanging around the port area deal in US dollars, Brazilian *reais* and bolivianos. Prodem on the corner of the plaza can give you cash advances on Visa and MasterCard.

Tours

Mary's Tours (☎ 855-3882; Oruro) conducts five-hour city tours of Guayaramerín and Guajará-Mirim, as well as La Ruta de la Goma

(The Rubber Trail) to Cachuela Esperanza. You can also arrange one-day cruises on the Río Yata or fishing trips to Rosario del Yata, plus they can help organize flights.

Sleeping

Hotel Litoral (☎ 855-3895; 25 de Mayo; s/d B$20/30, r with bathroom B$70) Relax in the clean rooms of this budget place, or chill out in front of Brazilian soaps in its courtyard snack bar.

Hotel Rio-Mar (☎ 855-3900; 25 de Mayo 611; s/d with fan & bathroom B$60/120, d with air-con & bathroom B$150; ⚛) The best of the cluster of hotels on this corner, with spacious, often air-conditioned rooms and some suites with ample living area. Reasonable value, though be sure to avoid the windowless rooms.

Hotel Balneario San Carlos (☎ 855-3555; San Carlos & 6 de Agosto; s/d with bathroom B$150/220; ⚛ ⚛) The choice for anyone here on business, this hotel has a restaurant, redundant sauna, pool room and 24-hour hot water.

Eating & Drinking

Heladería Pato Roca (Central Plaza; ice cream B$5-20) Renowned for its mountainous fruit and ice cream creations.

Snack Bar Antonella (Central Plaza; mains B$12-20) Pleasant place for a beer and a snack as you watch the world go round the plaza.

Churrasquería Patujú (6 de Agosto s/n; mains B$20-30) This place serves up tasty, good-value steak-oriented meals. The best place for a decent feed in the town center.

Churrasquería Sujal (mains B$25-35) This out-of-town steakhouse is a nice, quiet place, most readily accessible by moto-taxi (B$15).

Shopping

Thanks to its designation as a duty-free zone (authorities couldn't fight the illicit trade, so they decided to sanction it), Guayaramerín is a shopper's mecca. There's nothing of exceptional interest, but there are lots of brand-name knock-off shoes and clothes, and fake brand-name electronic goods. For *artesanía*, visit Caritas, near the airfield, which sells locally produced wooden carvings for reasonable prices.

Getting There & Away

AIR

The airport is on the edge of town and the airline offices are on the nearby 16 de Julio, near the corner of 25 de Mayo. **AeroCon** (☎ 855-5025)

AMAZON BASIN

runs daily flights to Trinidad with onward connections to other cities. **TAM** (☎ 855-3924) flies daily to La Paz (B$949) and Trinidad (B$535), and daily except Monday and Saturday to Cochabamba (B$879). It also flies to Santa Cruz (B$956) on Wednesday, Thursday and Sunday. Flights to Cobija via Riberalta (B$500 to B$600) are by private rental *avionetta* (light aircraft) and must be full to depart. Call **Avionetta Ariel** (☎ 852-3774) or **El Capitán** (☎ 7686-2742) at least a day in advance.

BOAT

Cargo boats up the Río Mamoré to Trinidad (around B$200 with food) leave irregularly and take six days. Ask at the port captain's office opposite the immigration office for information. For details, see p314. For information on crossing to Brazil, see p327.

BUS, CAMIÓN & TAXI

The bus terminal is on the south end of town, beyond the market. Buses run to Riberalta (B$20, three hours) several times daily. Foolhardy **Vaca Diez** departs daily in the morning for Rurrenabaque (B$120, 14 to 36 hours) and La Paz (B$170, 30 to 60 hours) via Santa Rosa and Reyes. Do not contemplate either journey if there is even a hint of rain or else be prepared to help pull the bus out of muddy holes every couple of hours. There are daily buses to Cobija (B$70, 16 hours) and Trinidad (B$140, 22 hours). Be aware that if enough tickets aren't sold, any of these runs may be summarily canceled. Flying to either destination is your best option and you will not regret the extra expense. Shared taxis to Riberalta (B$40, two hours) leave from the terminal when they have four passengers.

Getting Around

Guayaramerín is small enough to walk just about anywhere. Moto-taxis and auto rickshaws charge B$5 to anywhere in town. To explore the area, you can rent motorbikes from the plaza for B$15 per hour or negotiate all-day rentals – figure B$70 for 24 hours.

RIBERALTA

pop 100,000 / elevation 115m

Despite being a major town in Bolivia's northern frontier region, Riberalta has very little going for it, unless you count the exciting fact that this is one of the world's top Brazil nut production sites. A crumbly place, it is pleasant enough, even if the only thing to do is watch the orange sunsets and circling motorbikes as you enjoy a beer on the plaza. According to locals of both sexes, *las Riberalteñas* are the most beautiful women in all of Bolivia – but they would say that, wouldn't they.

Information

Banco Ganadero on the plaza has an ATM. If it's not working you can get cash advances and change US dollars at **Prodem** (☎ 857-2212; Suárez 1880). The post office and Entel are near the main plaza and there is an **internet cafe** (per hr B$6) on the plaza itself. The town's municipal water supply is contaminated, so stick to bottled or thoroughly purified water.

Sights & Activities

In the paralyzing heat of the day, strenuous activity is suspended and you'll find yourself clambering into the nearest hammock. Cool down in the Club Náutico's sparkling **riverside pool** (two blocks north of the plaza; B$10), a favorite local activity.

Riberalta's **cathedral** is a wonderful structure in classic Missionary style, wide and elegant, built using red brick and cedar. It sits on the main square in the same spot as the old, less grandiose church and it cost over half a million US dollars to build.

Parque Mirador La Costañera, on Riberalta's river bluff, overlooks a broad, sweeping curve of the Río Beni and affords the standard Amazonian view over water and rainforest.

At **Puerto Beni-Mamoré**, within walking distance of the center, you can watch the hand-carving and construction of small boats and dugouts by skilled artisans. Two kilometers east of the plaza along Ejército Nacional, you can visit an **old rubber plantation**, watch coffee beans being roasted and visit a **carpentry workshop**.

Tumichucuá is a small resort about 5km outside town toward 'El Triángulo' (the road junction to Cobija). There is a lake here for swimming and a forested island with walking trails, plus basic cabins if you want to stay the night. Nobody is really sure exactly how far from Riberalta it is, as according to local legend the lake moves at night, sometimes coming to rest closer to the town, sometimes further away.

Sleeping

Riberalta doesn't see that many visitors so hotel prices are high and you should not expect value for money.

Residencial Los Reyes (☎ 852-2628; s/d B$20/30) Close to the airport, this is a basic choice with a lovely, cool, garden courtyard. Iced water and hot coffee are always available.

Residencial Las Palmeras (☎ 852-5323; Suárez; s B$135, with air-con s/d B$195/235; ✷) Salmon pinks shimmer in this quiet, family home-cum-B&B, 15 minutes' walk from the center. The rooms are cozy and have their own bathrooms. Rates include breakfast.

Hotel Colonial (☎ 852-8212; Baptista; s/d B$180/250; ✷) Riberalta's most expensive hotel is a renovated colonial home dotted with antique furniture and backed by a delightfully fresh garden where you can relax in a hammock. Unfortunately, the rooms themselves lack the same charm and some are just musty and old. Choose carefully.

Eating

Riberalta's specialty is its famous *nuez del Brasil* (Brazil nuts), which are roasted in sugar and cinnamon and sold at the bus terminals and airport for B$10 per packet. The classic Riberalta breakfast of *api* (a syrupy beverage made from sweet purple corn, lemon, cinnamon and lots of white sugar), juice and empanadas is sold in the market.

Club Social El Progreso (Dr Martínez; almuerzo B$15) This place serves inexpensive *almuerzos*, good filtered coffee, drinks and fine desserts.

Horno Camba (Dr Martínez; mains B$25-35) The best of the restaurants on the plaza serving fish, chicken and Beni beef. What's more, the sidewalk seating provides a front-row view of the nightly Kawasaki derby.

Tropical (nr airport; mains B$90-150) This is Riberalta's most upscale restaurant, leading the residents to nickname it *Tropicarísimo* (very expensive…). Gargantuan portions of meat, chicken and fish accompanied by salad, rice and fried manioc feed two or three normal-sized people, though the profusion of animal skins and stuffed wildlife hanging off the walls and ceiling might put you off.

Getting There & Away

AIR

The airport is a 15-minute stroll south of the main plaza. Departing flights are subject to an airport tax of B$7. Flights to Cobija and Guayaramerín are by *avionetta* and must be full to depart. Call **Avionetta Ariel** (☎ 852-3774) or **El Capitán** (☎ 7686-2742) at least a day in advance.

AeroCon (☎ 852-2870; north side of plaza) flies to Trinidad four times a day (three flights leaving before noon), with connections to La Paz, Santa Cruz and Cochabamba. **TAM** (☎ 852-2646) flies from La Paz to Riberalta and continues to Guayaramerín on Monday, Thursday and Saturday, returning the day after.

BOAT

The Río Beni passes through countless twisting kilometers of virgin rainforest and provides Bolivia's longest single-river trip. Unfortunately, boats upriver to Rurrenabaque are now rare and, in any case, they normally only run during the wet season (November to mid-April). For information on departures ask at the Capitanía del Puerto at the northern end of town between Calles Ballivián and Sánchez. Budget B$150 to B$250 (including meals and hammock space) for the five- to eight-day trip. Lucky Peru-bound travelers may also find cargo boats to the frontier at Puerto Heath, which has onward boats to Puerto Maldonado.

BUS & CAMIÓN

The bus terminal is 3km east of the center, along the Guayaramerín road. The road from Riberalta to Guayaramerín is a high-speed gravel track, and taxis (B$40, 1½ hours) ply the route, leaving when full from the bus terminal. Buses (B$20, 2½ hours) are cheaper but slower – they depart in the morning.

All *flotas* between Guayaramerín and Cobija (B$120, 12 hours), and the horrendously uncomfortable route via Rurrenabaque (B$170, 17 to 40 hours) to La Paz (B$280, 35 to 60 hours), stop at Riberalta. Several *flotas* also go to Trinidad (B$280, 17 hours) daily, though the road may be closed during the wet season – it's easier to fly.

Getting Around

Moto-taxis (day/night B$3.50/5) will take you anywhere. With a driver's license from home, you can rent motorbikes (B$15/80 per hour/per day) from *taxistas* (taxi drivers) at the corner of Nicolás Suárez and Gabriel René Moreno.

AMAZON BASIN

RIBERALTA TO COBIJA

The much-improved road between Riberalta and Cobija connects the once-isolated Pando department with the rest of the country. Unfortunately, better access means more logging and the region has now been opened up to indiscriminate exploitation of its natural resources with large tracts of virgin rainforest being cleared at a frightening rate.

The journey requires two major *balsa* crossings, the first at Peña Amarilla, two hours outside Riberalta crossing the **Río Beni**. On the western bank, you can find stands selling empanadas and other snacks.

The most interesting crossing on the trip, however, traverses the **Río Madre de Dios**. From the eastern port, the 45-minute crossing begins with a 500m cruise along a backwater tributary onto the great river itself. Along the way listen for the intriguing jungle chorus that characterizes this part of the country.

The crossing of the **Río Orthon**, at Puerto Rico, is by bridge. From Puerto Rico to Cobija, development has been particularly rampant. The scene is one of charred giants, a forest of stumps and smouldering bush; when something is burning, the sun is like an egg yolk through the dense smoke.

COBIJA

pop 32,000 / elevation 140m

Capital of the Pando and Bolivia's wettest (1770mm of precipitation annually) and most humid spot, Cobija sits on a sharp bend of the Río Acre. Cobija means 'covering' and, with a climate that makes you feel as though you're being smothered with a soggy blanket, it certainly lives up to its name.

Cobija was founded in 1906 under the name 'Bahía,' and in the 1940s it boomed as a rubber-producing center. The town's fortunes dwindled with the shriveling of that industry and it has been reduced to little more than a forgotten village, albeit with a Japanese-funded hospital and a high-tech Brazil nut processing plant.

Information

The **Brazilian consulate** (☎ 842-2110; ☷ 8:30am-12:30pm Mon-Fri) is behind the Alcaldía on Cornejo. **Bolivian immigration** (☷ 9am-5pm Mon-Fri) is in the Prefectural building on the main plaza, with another branch at the airport.

In addition to giving cash advances on Visa and MasterCard and changing US dollars, **Prodem** (☎ 842-2800; Plaza Principal 186) has an ATM; there are a bunch of other ATMs around the plaza. The post office is also on the plaza and a number of telephone places are nearby. Internet use is expensive (B$8 per hour) and to connect you'll need to head to Calle Mercado, predictably located next to the market.

Sights & Activities

The town rambles over a series of hills, giving it a certain desultory charm. If you spend a day here, take a look at the remaining **tropical wooden buildings** in the center, and the lovely avenues of royal palms around the plaza. The **cathedral** has a series of naive paintings from the life of Christ.

The Pando's biggest annual bash, the **Feria de Muestras** (August 18 to 27), features local artisans and is held at the extreme western end of town, near the Río Acre.

A small **Natural History Museum** (6 de Febrero; ☷ 8am-noon & 2-6pm Mon-Fri) is filled with the usual collection of pickled animal bits.

Sleeping & Eating

Most of the best places to eat are along Molina, but none are up to much and prices are fairly high.

Hostería Sucre (☎ 842-3944; Sucre 56 nr Suárez; s/d B$60/80) A block and a half from the plaza, this is a supremely friendly family-run place with clean, airy rooms, all with cable TV, bathroom and ceiling fan. Coffee and cold water are available all day. It represents the best value at the lower end of the price scale.

Hotel Nanijo's (☎ 842-2230; 6 de Agosto 147; s/d B$150/260; ☷ ☷) A large, modern hotel with the best facilities in town. All rooms have tiled floors and cable TV and the courtyard splash pool is very welcome in the sticky climate.

Panadería la Oriental (Molina; snacks B$10-20) Cakes, bread and buns are on offer at this authentic Chinese bakery.

Hong Kong (Molina; mains B$20-40) Next door to the bakery, with standard Chinese fare in the usual big portions.

Esquina de la Abuela (Molina nr Sucre; mains B$40-45) This is Cobija's nicest eatery with alfresco tables and fresh, well-cooked chicken and meat dishes served under a gigantic *palapa* wigwam.

CROSSING THE BORDER INTO BRAZIL

Crossing to Brazil from the northern Bolivian towns of Cobija and Guayaramerín involves crossings of the Ríos Acre and Mamoré respectively.

Popping into the Brazilian town of Guajará-Mirim for the day from Bolivian Guayaramerín is really easy. Day visits are encouraged, and you don't even need a visa. *Lanchas* (B$10) across the river leave from the port every half an hour from 6am to 6pm, and sporadically through the night. To travel further into Brazil or to enter Bolivia, you'll have to complete border formalities. The **immigration offices** (🕑 8am-8pm) are in the respective port areas.

It's a long, hot slog across the bridge from Cobija to Brasiléia. Entry/exit stamps are available at immigration in Cobija and from Brasiléia's Polícia Federal. With some negotiation, taxis will take you to the Polícia Federal in Brasiléia, wait while you clear immigration, then take you on to the center or to the bus terminal. Alternatively, take the *lancha* (B$5) across the Río Acre; from there it's another 1.5km to the **Polícia Federal** (🕑 8am-noon & 2-5pm).

Although officials don't always check, technically everyone needs to have a yellow-fever vaccination certificate to enter Brazil. If you don't have one, head for the convenient and relatively sanitary clinic at the port on the Brazilian side. For more information, check out Lonely Planet's *Brazil*.

Getting There & Away

AIR

Flights arrive and depart from Aeropuerto Anibal Arab (CIJ), five kilometers from the center at the top end of Av 9 de Febrero. The airline offices are located at the junction of Molina and Beni just off the main square, with the exception of **AeroCon** (☎ 842-4575; 16 de Julio). **TAM** (☎ 842-4145) flies directly to La Paz on Monday, Wednesday, Thursday and Friday morning. **AeroSur** (☎ 842-3132) has a direct flight to Santa Cruz on Monday, Wednesday and Saturday. All companies fly daily to Trinidad for onward connections. Flights to Guayaramerín via Riberalta are in *avionettas*; ask at the airport or call (☎ 7621-0035).

BUS & CAMIÓN

There is no bus terminal in Cobija, but buses pull into their respective offices on Av 9 de Febrero out towards the airport. Services to Riberalta and Guayaramerín (12 to 16 hours) depart daily between 5am and 8am. There is one tortuous service to La Paz via Rurrenabaque run by **La Yungueña**, but if you are really smart, you'll take a flight.

Getting Around

Moto-taxis charge a set B$4 to anywhere in town, B$10 to the airport. Taxis charge B$20 to the international airport. A cheaper option is to hop on *Micro A* (B$2.50), which shuttles between the airport and the market.

AMAZON BASIN

Directory

CONTENTS

Accommodations	328
Activities	329
Business Hours	330
Children	330
Climate Charts	330
Customs Regulations	331
Dangers & Annoyances	331
Discount Cards	331
Embassies & Consulates	331
Festivals & Events	332
Food	333
Gay & Lesbian Travelers	333
Holidays	333
Insurance	334
Internet Access	334
Legal Matters	334
Maps	334
Money	334
Photography & Video	336
Post	336
Shopping	336
Solo Travelers	337
Telephone	337
Time	339
Toilets	339
Tourist Information	339
Travelers With Disabilities	339
Visas	339
Women Travelers	340
Work & Volunteering	341

ACCOMMODATIONS

Bolivian accommodations are among South America's cheapest, though price and value are hardly uniform. Be aware that with the exception of the international hotel chains, the star ratings for hotels are not based on the recognized international rating system.

The Bolivian hotel-rating system divides accommodations into *posadas, alojamientos, residenciales, casas de huéspedes, hostales* and *hoteles*. This subjective zero- to five-star rating system reflects the price scale and, to some extent, the quality. (Note that *hostales* are not necessarily hostels as you might normally think; some are in fact upmarket hotels.) Rock-bottom places are usually found around the bus and train stations.

Prices in this book reflect high-season rates (late May to early September). Room availability is only a problem during fiestas (especially Carnaval in Oruro), when prices double, and at popular weekend getaways.

The accommodations sections in this book are organized into budget, midrange and top-end categories. Budget typically means less than B$80 per person per night with a shared bathroom (exceptions are noted). Midrange is usually between B$80 and B$220 per person (mostly with private bathroom and breakfast). The top-end tag is applied to places charging more than B$220 per person; some can fetch upwards of B$700 per night. In La Paz prices are higher (midrange is considered anything between B$90 and B$280 per person). We've noted which accommodations include bathrooms in the quoted price.

Always ask to see a couple of rooms before committing.

Camping

Bolivia offers excellent camping, especially along trekking routes and in remote mountain areas. Gear (of varying quality) is easily rented in La Paz and at popular trekking base camps like Sorata. There are few organized campsites, but you can pitch a tent almost anywhere outside population centers, although it's always a good idea to ask for permission if possible. Remember that highland nights are often freezing. Theft

---

BOOK ACCOMMODATIONS ONLINE

For more accommodations reviews and recommendations by Lonely Planet authors, check out www.lonelyplanet.com/hotels. You'll find the true, insider lowdown on the best places to stay. Reviews are thorough and independent. Best of all, you can book online.

and assaults have been reported in some areas – always inquire locally about security before heading off to set up camp.

Hostels
Hostelling International (HI; www.hostellingbolivia.org) is affiliated with a network of 16 accommodations in different parts of Bolivia. A typical of other 'hosteling' networks, members range from two-star hotels to camping places, but few offer traditional amenities like dorm beds or shared kitchens. HI membership cards may be for sale at the flagship hostel in Sucre (p218), although rumor has it that some HI locations are yet to learn about offering the 10% discount to members.

For affordable accommodations, check out www.boliviahostels.com.

Hostales & Hotels
Bolivia has pleasant midrange places and five-star luxury resorts, although these are generally limited to the larger cities and popular vacation and weekend resort destinations. Standard hotel amenities include breakfast, private bathrooms with 24/7 hot showers (gas- or electric-heated), phones and color TV, usually with cable. Where they exist, luxury accommodations are quite a bargain (compared to their international counterparts).

Posadas, Alojamientos, Residenciales & Casas de Huéspedes
Quality varies little at the bottom of the range, except at the worst *posadas* (B$8 to B$15 per person) where shared facilities can be smelly, showers scarce and hot water unheard of. Most *alojamientos* (B$15 to B$35 per person) have communal bathrooms with electric showers (to avoid electric shock, don't touch the shower while the water is running and wear rubber sandals). Most travelers end up at *residenciales*, which charge B$60 to B$140 for a double with private bathroom, about 30% less without. *Casas de huéspedes* (family-run guesthouses) sometimes offer a more midrange, B&B-like atmosphere.

Warning: several readers have alerted us to improper use of propane heaters in Bolivia. These are sometimes offered in cheaper accommodations but are not meant to be used in enclosed spaces so refrain from using them if supplied.

ACTIVITIES
Want to get the heart pumping and the lungs gasping? Bolivia offers a smorgasbord of activities for the adventure-seeker: from mountaineering to horseback riding, single-track mountain-bike rides to climbing. Hiking and trekking are arguably the most rewarding Bolivian activities; the country

rivals Nepal in trekking potential, and awesome climbing opportunities abound. There's also fantastic river rafting.

Those who simply prefer something a bit more chilled out can head off for pleasant jungle strolls or countryside meanders. Fauna and flora fanatics rejoice – Bolivia abounds with rarely visited, world-class, wildlife-watching destinations. Alternatively, you can absorb archaeological sites, slide across the salt plains in a 4WD, soak in a hot spring or visit vineyards. For more, see the Outdoors chapter, p54.

BUSINESS HOURS

Usual business hours are listed inside the front cover. Exceptions to these have been noted in individual listings in this book. Few businesses open before 9am, though markets stir as early as 6am and some are open on Sunday mornings. Banks are open between 9am and 4pm on weekdays (Banco de Crédito is open till 6pm); in smaller towns, they close for lunch. Cities virtually shut down between noon and 3pm, except markets and restaurants serving lunch-hour crowds. Hours between eateries vary – this book indicates where restaurants and cafes are open for breakfast, lunch and/or dinner. If you have urgent business to attend to, don't wait until the weekend as most offices will be closed.

CHILDREN

Few foreigners visit Bolivia with children, but those who do are usually treated with great kindness; Bolivians love babies and having children in tow will do wonders in breaking down cultural barriers.

Civilian airlines allow children under the age of 12 to fly at a reduced rate (currently 67% of the full fare); children below the age of two pay only 10% of the adult fare. On long-distance buses, those who occupy a seat will normally have to pay the full fare. Most hotels have family rooms with three or four beds. Restaurants rarely advertise children's portions, but will often offer a child-sized serving at a lower price, or will allow two kids to share an adult meal.

Safety seats, diaper-changing facilities and child-care services are only available in the finest hotels. Breastfeeding in public is widespread. Formula milk is available in modern supermarkets in big cities, as are disposable diapers.

There is a fantastic children's museum in Sucre (p216) and a water park in Santa Cruz (p268), but most Bolivians spend Sunday afternoons picnicking with the family in parks and zoos or strolling the traffic-less Prados of La Paz and Cochabamba.

For more information, advice and anecdotes, see Lonely Planet's *Travel with Children*.

CLIMATE CHARTS

The following climate charts provide an indication of temperature and rainfall around the country. Note that for La Paz, the airport (where temperature rates are recorded) is 400m higher than the city center, so official temperature recordings are around 40°F (5°C) cooler than those experienced on the street. For more on Bolivia's climate and the best times to visit, see p13.

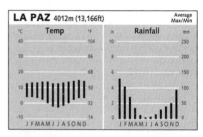

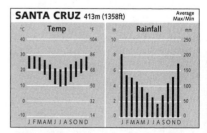

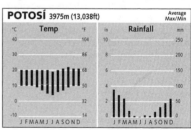

CUSTOMS REGULATIONS

When entering Bolivia you can bring in most articles duty-free provided you can convince customs that they are for personal use. There's also a loosely enforced duty-free allowance of 200 cigarettes and 1L of alcohol per person.

DANGERS & ANNOYANCES

Crime against tourists is on the icrease in Bolivia, especially in La Paz and, to a lesser extent, Cochabamba, Copacabana and Oruro. Scams are commonplace and fake police, false tourist police and 'helpful' tourists are on the rise. Be aware, too, of circulating counterfeit banknotes. See p67 for a detailed run-down of *en vogue* cons.

There is a strong tradition of social protest in Bolivia: demonstrations are a regular occurrence and this can affect travelers. While generally peaceful, they can turn threatening in nature at times: agitated protestors throw stones and rocks and police occasionally use force and tear gas to disperse crowds. *Bloqueos* (roadblocks) and strikes by transportation workers often lead to long delays. Be careful using taxis during transportation strikes – you may end up at the receiving end of a rock, which people pelt at those who are not in sympathy with them.

The rainy season means flooding, landslides and road washouts, which in turn means more delays. Getting stuck overnight behind a landslide can happen; you'll be a happier camper with ample food, drink and warm clothes on hand.

Note that the mine tours in Potosí (p234) and the 4x4 excursions around Salar de Uyuni (p167) have become so hugely popular that agencies are willing to forgo safety. Make sure you do your research before signing up for the tour.

GOVERNMENT TRAVEL ADVICE

The following government websites offer travel advisories and information on current hot spots.

Australian Department of Foreign Affairs (www.smarttraveller.gov.au)
British Foreign Office (www.fco.gov.uk)
Canadian Department of Foreign Affairs (www.dfait-maeci.gc.ca)
US State Department (www.travel.state.gov)

DISCOUNT CARDS

The **International Student Travel Confederation** (ISTC; www.istc.org) is an international network of specialist student travel organizations. It's also the body behind the International Student Identity Card (ISIC), which gives carriers discounts on a few services in Bolivia. La Paz–based **et-n-ic** (☎ 2-246-3782; Illampu 863) sells cards.

EMBASSIES & CONSULATES

It's important to realize what your own embassy can and can't do for you. Generally speaking, your embassy won't be much help in emergencies if the trouble you're in is remotely your own fault. Remember that while in Bolivia you are bound by Bolivian laws. Your embassy will not be sympathetic if you end up in jail after committing a crime locally, even if such actions are legal in your own country.

In genuine emergencies you might get some assistance, but only if other channels have been exhausted. For example, if you need to get home urgently, a free ticket home is exceedingly unlikely – the embassy would expect you to have insurance. If you have all your money and documents stolen, embassy staff might assist with getting a new passport, but a loan for onward travel is out of the question.

For a full list of foreign diplomatic representation in Bolivia, see www.embassies abroad.com/embassies-in/Bolivia.

Argentina La Paz (Map pp62-3; ☎ 2-241-7737, fax 2-242-2727; Aspiazu 497); Cochabamba (Map p192; ☎ 4-425-5859, fax 4-422-9347; Federico Blanco 929); Villazón (☎ 2-596-5253; Saavedra 311); Santa Cruz (Map pp264-5; ☎ 3-334-7133, fax 3-334-8200; Junín 22); Tarija (Map p246; ☎ 4-664-4273; Bolívar 696)
Australia La Paz (Map pp62-3; ☎ 2-211-5655, 242-2957; Aspiazu 416)
Brazil La Paz (☎ 2-216-6400, fax 2-244-0043; www .brasil.org.bo; Arce, Edificio Multicentro); Cochabamba (Map p192; ☎ 4-425-5860, fax 4-411-7084; Avenida Oquendo N-1080); Guayaramerín (☎ 3-855-3766, fax 3-855-4695; 24 de Septiembre 28); Santa Cruz (Map pp264-5; ☎ 3-334-4400, fax 3-335-0488; Germán Busch 330); Sucre (Map pp212-3; ☎ 4-645-2661; Arenales 212)
Canada La Paz (Map pp62-3; ☎ 2-241-5141, fax 2-241-4453; 2nd fl, Victor Sanjinés 2678)
Chile La Paz (☎ 2-279-7331, fax 2-212-6491; www.cgchilelapaz.com.bo; Calle 14 N 8024, Calacoto); Santa Cruz (☎ 3-343-4272; www.consulado-chile.scz.com; 9th fl, Edificio Torre Equipetrol)

Ecuador La Paz (☎ 2-278-4422, fax 2-277-1043; Calle 10 8054, Calacoto); Sucre (☎ 4-646-0622, Los Ceibos 2, Barrio Tucsupaya)

France La Paz (☎ 2-214-9900; www.ambafrance-bo.org; Fernando Siles 5390 at Calle 8, Obrajes)

Germany La Paz (Map pp62-3; ☎ 2-244-0066, fax 2-244-1441; Arce 2395); Cochabamba (Map p192; ☎ 4-425-4024, fax 4-425-4023; 6th fl, Edificio La Promontora, cnr España & Heroínas); Sucre (Map pp212-3; ☎ 4-645-2091; Rosenda Villa 54)

Italy La Paz (Map pp62-3; ☎ 2-278-8506, fax 2-278-8178; www.amblapaz.esteri.it; Calle 5 458, Obrajes); Santa Cruz (☎ 3-353-1796; 1st fl, Edificio Honnen, Av El Trompillo); Sucre (Map pp212-3; ☎ 4-645-1514; Avaroa 546)

Netherlands La Paz (Map pp62-3; ☎ 2-244-4040, fax 2-244-3804; www.mfa.nl/lap-es; 7th fl, Edificio Hilda, 6 de Agosto 2455); Cochabamba (☎ 4-423-0888, fax 4-453-4560; 5th fl, Torre SOFER, Av Oquendo 654); Santa Cruz (☎ 3-335-4498, fax 3-333-4474; Ayacucho 284)

Paraguay La Paz (Map pp62-3; ☎ 2-243-3176; Edificio Illimani, Pedro Salazar 351)

Peru La Paz (Map pp62-3; ☎ 2-244-0631; fax 2-244-4199; www.conperlapaz.org; Edificio Hilda, Av 6 de Agosto 2455); Cochabamba (Map p192; ☎ 4-448-6556; Edificio Continental, Pedro Blanco Nte-1344); Santa Cruz (☎ 3-341-9091; Viador Pinto 84)

Spain La Paz (☎ 2-243-3518, fax 2-243-2752; Av 6 de Agosto 2827); Santa Cruz (☎ 3-332-8921; Santiesteban 237); Santa Cruz (☎ 3-312-1349, fax 2-312-1368; Av Cañoto cnr with Peru)

UK La Paz (Map pp62-3; ☎ 2-243-3424, fax 2-243-1073; www.ukinbolivia.fco.gov.uk/en; Arce 2732); Santa Cruz (☎ 3-353-5035; Santa Cruz International School; Km 7.5)

USA La Paz (Map pp62-3; ☎ 2-216-8000; http://lapaz .usembassy.gov; Arce 2780); Santa Cruz (☎ 3-351-3477; Av Roque Aguilera 146)

FESTIVALS & EVENTS

Bolivians love to party, and celebrations and rituals are integral to their culture. Fiestas are invariably of religious or political origin, and typically include lots of music, drinking, eating, dancing, processions, rituals and general unrestrained behavior. Sometimes water balloons (gringos are sought-after targets; see p157) and fireworks (all too often at eye-level) figure prominently. On major holidays and festive occasions, banks, offices and other services are closed, and public transportation is often bursting at the seams; book ahead.

August and February are important months for Pachamama, the Earth Mother, especially in traditional communities, with ceremonies and rituals taking place in her honor. Occasionally, you might witness a *cha'lla* (ritual blessing), including the burning of *mesa blanca* (literally 'white table') offerings and incense.

The following is a snapshot of nationwide festivals and events. See the destination chapters for city- and town-specific festivals or events that are held around Bolivia; dates are subject to change.

JANUARY

Día de los Reyes Magos 'Kings' Day' (Epiphany) is celebrated on January 6 as the day the three wise kings visited the baby Jesus after his birth. The largest celebrations are in Reyes (Beni), Sucre, Tarija, and rural villages in the departments of Oruro, Cochabamba and Potosí.

Alasitas Taking place in La Paz and Copacabana on January 24 and for two weeks after, this giant fair celebrates Ekeko, the Aymará god of abundance, with stalls and street vendors selling miniatures of items people are longing for (tiny houses, cars, banknotes etc).

FEBRUARY/MARCH

Fiesta de La Virgen de Candelaria This week-long festival is held during the first week of February in Aiquile (Cochabamba); Samaipata (Santa Cruz); Angostura (Tarija) and Cha'llapampa (Oruro). The biggest celebration, which kicks off on February 2, is at Copacabana in the department of La Paz.

Carnaval Celebrations are held nationwide the week before Lent. Oruro is known for the most colorful Carnaval fiesta; Santa Cruz, Sucre and Tarija follow suit.

MARCH/APRIL

Semana Santa One of the most impressive of the nationwide Holy Week activities is the Good Friday fiesta in Copacabana, when hundreds of pilgrims arrive on foot from La Paz.

Phujllay Celebrated in Tarabuco on the second Sunday in March, hordes of indigenous people gather to celebrate the 1816 victory of local armies over Spanish troops with ritual dancing, song, music and chicha drinking.

MAY

Fiesta de la Cruz The Festival of the Cross (May 3) commemorates the cross on which Christ was crucified (or the Southern Cross, in pagan circles). The greatest revelry takes place in Tarija for two weeks. The fiesta is also big in Vallegrande (Santa Cruz), Cochabamba and Copacabana. Tinku ritual combats take place in rural communities around Potosí.

Día de la Madre Mother's Day celebrations (May 27) are held nationwide. In Cochabamba the festivities are known as Heroínas de la Coronilla in honor of the women and children who defended their cities and homes in the battle of 1812.

JUNE

Willkakuti On June 21, the Aymará celebrate the winter solstice – the return of the new sun – and their New Year. The biggest ceremony takes place overnight in Tiwanaku.

San Juan This Christian holiday is held nationwide (June 24), with bonfires, fireworks and traditional burning of wood. The largest bash takes place in Santa Cruz.

JULY

Virgen del Carmen On July 16, many towns around Bolivia celebrate their patron saint with processions and dancing. The bash takes place in La Paz, Cochabamba, Oruro, the Yungas and Sucre.

AUGUST

Independence Day Fiesta Held August 6, this highly charged anniversary provides inspiration for excessive raging nationwide. The largest celebration is held at Copacabana.

OCTOBER

Virgen del Rosario This celebration is held on different days during the first week of the month and in different locations, including Warnes (Santa Cruz); Tarata, Morochata and Quillacollo (Cochabamba); Tarabuco (Chuquisaca); Viacha (La Paz) and Potosí.

NOVEMBER

Día de Todos los Santos All Saints' Day (November 1) sees nationwide cemetery visits, with much mourning and celebrating, and colorful decoration of graves.

DECEMBER

Christmas Celebrated throughout Bolivia from midnight December 24, some of the most unique festivities take place in San Ignacio de Moxos (Beni), Tarija and Sucre.

FOOD

It might not have the reputation for the spices of Asia, the panache of French cuisine, or the profile of Italian food, but Bolivian food is equally delicious. The more you learn about Bolivian cuisine, the more you'll appreciate it. This includes knowing how to consume dishes (heartily, and often with condiments), when to consume them (there are special dishes for specific festivals) and where to consume them (don't miss the regional or local specialties). Bolivian dishes are satisfying and filling, made of fresh ingredients and served in generous helpings. See the Food & Drink chapter (p42) for more information.

The eating recommendations provided in this book for larger cities are often broken down by style of eatery. For those who aren't shy to try, the best-value meals are found at midday (*almuerzos*, set lunches, are a great option) in and around markets (often under B$10) and at no-frills restaurants (usually between B$15 and B$30). At nicer restaurants, four courses run from B$20 to B$40. A meal at one of the best cosmopolitan restaurants with internationally trained chefs starts at around B$70 a head with wine.

Formal tipping is haphazard except in the nicer restaurants. Elsewhere, locals leave coins amounting to a maximum of 10% of the total in recognition of good service.

GAY & LESBIAN TRAVELERS

Homosexuality is legal in Bolivia but still not widely accepted. In 2004, parliament attempted (unsuccessfully) to introduce Law 810, allowing homosexual couples to marry and foster children.

Gay bars and venues are limited to the larger cities, especially Santa Cruz and La Paz, but these are still somewhat clandestine affairs. As for hotels, sharing a room is no problem – but discretion is still in order.

Gay rights lobby groups are active in La Paz (MGLP Libertad), Cochabamba (Dignidad) and most visibly in progressive Santa Cruz, which held Bolivia's first Gay Pride march in 2001. La Paz is known for La Familia Galán, the capital's most fabulous group of cross-dressing queens who aim to educate Bolivians around issues of sexuality and gender through theater performances. The feminist activist group Mujeres Creando is based in La Paz and promotes the rights of oppressed groups.

HOLIDAYS
Public Holidays

Public holidays vary from province to province. The following is a list of the main national and provincial public holidays; for precise dates (which vary from year to year), check locally.

Nuevo Año (New Year's Day) January 1
Carnaval February/March
Semana Santa (Easter Week) March/April
Día del Trabajo (Labor Day) May 1
Corpus Christi May/June
Día de la Independencia (Independence Day) August 6
Día de Colón (Columbus Day) October 12
Día de los Muertos (All Souls' Day) November 2
Navidad (Christmas) December 25

DIRECTORY

Departmental Holidays

Not about to be outdone by their neighbors, each department has its own holiday.

Beni November 18
Chuquisaca May 25
Cochabamba September 14
La Paz July 16
Oruro February 10
Pando & Santa Cruz September 24
Potosí November 10
Tarija April 15

INSURANCE

A good travel-insurance policy to cover theft, loss and medical mishaps is important. Nothing is guaranteed to ruin your holiday plans quicker than an accident or having that brand new digital camera stolen.

There is a wide variety of policies available: shop around and scrutinize the fine print. Some policies specifically exclude 'dangerous activities,' which can include skiing, motorcycling, mountain biking, even trekking. Check that the policy covers ambulances and emergency airlift evacuations. For more on health insurance, see p352.

INTERNET ACCESS

Nearly every corner of Bolivia has a cyber cafe. Rates run from B$1 to B$12 per hour. In smaller towns, expect to pay more – check the local Entel offices and be ready for slow dial-up connections.

If you're traveling with a notebook or hand-held computer, be aware that your modem may not work once you leave your home country. The safest option is to buy a reputable 'global' modem before you leave home, or buy a local PC-card modem if you're spending an extended time in Bolivia. For more information on traveling with a portable computer, see www.teleadapt.com.

For a list of useful Bolivia-savvy websites, see 'Internet Resources,' p16.

LEGAL MATTERS

Bolivia may be the land of cocaine, but you'd be a fool to seek the 'Bolivian experience.' Refined cocaine is highly illegal in Bolivia – the standard sentence for possession of cocaine in Bolivia is eight years – so it's clearly best left alone. The big guys get away with processing and exporting because they're able to bribe their way around the regulations. Backpackers and coca farmers become statistics to wave at foreign governments as proof, if you will, that Bolivia is doing something about the drug problem. It's unwise to carry drugs of any kind, as the consequences are just too costly.

Foreign embassies should be contacted immediately, but note, they don't have the power to resolve the legalities (or illegalities) of the situation.

Be aware that more recently incidences of fake police have been on the rise; see p331.

MAPS

Maps are available in La Paz, Cochabamba and Santa Cruz through Los Amigos del Libro and some bookstores. Government 1:50,000 topographical and specialty sheets are available from the Instituto Geográfico Militar (IGM), with offices in La Paz (p63) and in most other major cities.

The superb *New Map of the Cordillera Real,* published by O'Brien Cartographics, is available at various gringo hangouts and the postcard kiosks within La Paz post offices. O'Brien also publishes the *Travel Map of Bolivia,* which is one of the best country maps. Walter Guzmán Córdova also produces a range of colored contour maps. Freddy Ortiz' widely available, inexpensive *Journey Routes* map series covers the major tourist regions including La Paz and Lake Titicaca; *Bolivia Highlights* is the best general map in the series. **South American Explorers** (www.saexplorers.org) has maps of major cities.

An excellent general map of Bolivia is published by Nelles; Berndston & Bernsdton does a slightly less detailed one. The perfect map of the country for cyclists (because it's plastic and waterproof) is published by World Mapping Project.

International sources for hard-to-find maps include the US-based **Maplink** (www.maplink.com) and **Omnimap** (www.omnimap.com), and the UK-based **Stanfords** (www.stanfords.co.uk). In Germany, try **Deutscher Alpenverein** (www.alpenverein.de), which publishes its own series of climbing maps.

MONEY

ATMs

Sizeable towns have *cajeros automáticos* (ATMs) – usually Banco Nacional de Bolivia, Banco Bisa, Banco Mercantil Santa Cruz and Banco Unión. They dispense bolivianos in 50 and 100 notes (sometimes US dollars as well) on Visa, MasterCard, Plus and Cirrus cards; note that in the past, many Europeans have reported trouble using their cards. In smaller towns, the local bank Prodem is a good option for cash advances on Visa and MasterCard (3% to 6% commission charged) and many branches are meant to be open on Saturday mornings; the hours and machines are unreliable. Don't rely on ATMs; always carry some cash with you, especially if venturing into rural areas.

Change

Finding change for bills larger than B$10 is a national pastime, as change for larger notes is scarce outside big cities. When exchanging money or making big purchases, request the *cambio* (change) in small denominations. If you can stand the queues, most banks will break large bills. Also, check any larger bills for damage as you may not be able to change them if they're torn or taped together.

Credit Cards & Cash Advances

Brand-name plastic, such as Visa, Master-Card and (less often) American Express, may be used in larger cities at the better hotels, restaurants and tour agencies. Cash advances (according to your limit at home) are available on Visa (and less often on MasterCard), with no commission, from most major bank branches. In smaller towns, the local Prodem bank is your best bet for Visa and MasterCard advances (it charges a 3% to 6% commission). Some travel agencies in towns without ATMs will provide cash advances for clients for 3% to 6% commission.

Currency

Bolivia's unit of currency is the boliviano (B$), which is divided into 100 centavos. Bolivianos come in 10, 20, 50, 100 and 200 denomination notes, with coins worth 1, 2 and 5 bolivianos as well as 10, 20 and 50 centavos. Often called pesos (the currency was changed from pesos to bolivianos in 1987), bolivianos are extremely difficult to unload outside the country.

Exchanging Money

Visitors fare best with US dollars (travelers have reported that it's difficult to change euros). Currency may be exchanged at *casas de cambio* (exchange bureaux) and at some banks in larger cities. You can often change money in travel agencies, hotels and sometimes in stores selling touristy items. *Cambistas* (street moneychangers) operate in most cities but only change cash dollars, paying roughly the same as *casas de cambio*. They're convenient after hours, but guard against rip-offs and counterfeit notes. The rate for cash doesn't vary much from place to place, and there is no black-market rate. Currencies of neighboring countries may be exchanged in border areas and at *casas de cambio* in La Paz. Beware, too, mangled notes: unless both halves of a repaired banknote bear identical serial numbers, the note is worthless. Also note that US$100 bills of the CB-B2 series are not accepted anywhere, neither are US$50 bills of the AB-B2 series.

International Transfers

The fastest way to have money transferred from abroad is with **Western Union** (www.westernunion.com). A newer, alternative option is through **Money Gram** (www.moneygram.com), which has offices in all major cities – watch the hefty fees, though. Your bank can also wire money to a cooperating Bolivian bank; it may take a couple of business days.

Traveler's Checks

Changing traveler's checks in smaller towns is often impossible. You'll usually be charged a commission of up to 6% (slightly lower in La Paz) or a flat fee of US$6. American Express is the most widely accepted brand, though with persistence you should be able to change other major brands. Make sure you bring your passport when changing traveler's checks.

A NOTE ABOUT PRICES

Prices in this guidebook are generally listed in bolivianos. However, many higher-end hotels will only quote prices in US dollars; likewise for many travel agencies and tour operators. Therefore, prices in this book are listed in bolivianos, except in cases where a business quotes its costs in US dollars. Both currencies have experienced fluctuations in recent years, so expect many figures to be different from what may be printed in the book.

PHOTOGRAPHY & VIDEO

Bolivian landscapes swallow film, so don't be caught without a healthy supply. Keep in mind, however, that the combination of high-altitude ultraviolet rays and light reflected off snow or water will conspire to fool both your eye and your light meter.

A polarizing filter is essential when photographing the Altiplano, and will help to reveal the dramatic effects of the exaggerated UV element at high altitude. In the lowlands, conditions include dim light, humidity, haze and leafy interference. For optimum shots you need either fast film or a tripod for long exposures.

La Paz is generally the best place to pick up film and for repairs; see p86. As always, avoid exposing your equipment to sand and water.

Photographing People

While some Bolivians are willing photo subjects, others may be superstitious about your camera, suspicious of your motives or interested in payment. Many children will ask for payment, often after you've taken their photo. It's best to err on not taking such shots in the first place – be sensitive to the wishes of locals. Ask permission to photograph if a candid shot can't be made; if permission is denied, you should neither insist nor snap a picture.

POST

Even the smallest towns have post offices – some are signposted 'Ecobol' (Empresa Correos de Bolivia). From major towns, the post is generally reliable (although often involving long delays), but when posting anything important, it's better to pay extra to have it registered or send it by courier. **DHL** (www.dhl.com.bo) is the most reliable courier company with international service.

Parcels

To mail an international parcel in La Paz, take it downstairs in the Central Post Office (p66; the stairs are halfway along the ground floor and to the right). You may be charged a small fee to have the belongings wrapped or your box officially labeled. You'll need two copies of your passport – one will be included in your package. Complete the necessary forms (at the time of research these included a customs declaration form and list of contents, known as a CN-23:

Declaración de Aduana and CP-71 Boletín de Expedición). Take your parcel to the office marked 'Encomiendas.' If your package is less than 2kg it's easier to send by regular mail. Pay the cost of postage and complete the CN-23. A 1kg parcel to the USA will cost B$150 by air and B$238 by faster courier service.

In some cities, you might have your parcels checked by customs at the post office; in cities without inhouse customs agents, you may have to trek across town to the *aduana* (customs office). A parcel's chances of arriving at its destination are inversely proportional to its declared value, and to the number of 'inspections' to which it is subjected.

Postal Rates

Airmail *postales* (postcards) or letters weighing up to 20g cost around B$7.50 to the USA, B$9 to Europe and B$10.50 to the rest of the world. Relatively reliable express-mail service is available for rates similar to those charged by private international couriers.

Receiving Mail

Reliable free *lista de correos (poste restante)* is available in larger cities. Mail should be addressed to you c/o Lista de Correos (Poste Restante), Correo Central, La Paz (or whatever city), Bolivia. Using only a first initial and capitalizing your entire LAST NAME will help avoid confusion. Mail is often sorted into foreign and Bolivian stacks, so those with Latin surnames should check the local stack as well as checking for your first name. La Paz holds *poste restante* for two months. You will need your passport to collect the mail.

SHOPPING

Each town or region has its own specialty *artesanía*. For traditional musical instruments, head for Tarija or Calle Sagárnaga in La Paz (although the latter will be overpriced). For weavings, the Cordillera Apolobamba or the environs of Sucre are your best bet. Ceramics are a specialty around Cochabamba and crafts in tropical woods are sold in the lowlands around Santa Cruz, Trinidad and the Amazon Basin.

You'll find a range of reasonably priced artwork from all over the country in La Paz and Copacabana, but prices are generally lower at the point of original production.

TOP BOLIVIAN SOUVENIRS

- *Chulla* – this traditional hat has got 'I've been to South America' written all over it.
- Irupana chocolate – buy top-quality, organic chocolate for US$0.15 per bar (p86)?
- Wall hanging – the best hail from the Jalq'a region around Sucre (p223).
- Bowler hat – these go for only B$40 in the section of market along Max Paredes, La Paz.
- Ekeko figure – this little lucky man of abundance (see boxed text, p77) may look after you, whether a silver trinket or larger ornament.
- *Sampaña* or *charango* – take a stroll and a strum in Sagárnaga for some top-quality musical instruments (see p38 and p86).
- Alpaca and llama designer wear – go animal and kit yourself out in some stunning international fashions with a local touch (p86).
- Wine – connoisseurs rate La Concepción as up there with the world's best (p253).

All sorts of clothing are available in llama and alpaca wool; wool from vicuñas is the finest and most expensive. Some pieces are hand-dyed and woven or knitted while others are mass-produced by machine.

Many articles are made by cooperatives or profit companies with ecofriendly and culturally responsible practices. See shopping in La Paz (p85) for more.

SOLO TRAVELERS

As always when traveling, safety is in numbers; solo travelers should remain alert when traveling, especially at night. On the whole, however, the benefits of solo travel can be huge, as being alone often opens up many doors to meeting local people as well as other travelers.

On the well-trodden gringo circuit, solo travelers should have little trouble meeting up with others. Some hostels and hotels have notice boards for those wanting to form groups to do activities. In places like Uyuni, it's relatively easy to meet other travelers around town to make up the numbers.

Hostel prices are often based on a per-person rate, although more upmarket hotels have separate prices for single and double, with the latter being more economical.

The recent increase in tourism to Bolivia has meant that locals are becoming more accustomed to seeing Western travelers, including unaccompanied women. This has significantly reduced the incidence of sexual harassment and the concept of the 'loose gringa,' but in some places you may still face unwanted attention.

If you are traveling without a male companion and/or alone, it's wise to avoid testosterone-filled domains such as bars, sports matches, mines and construction sites. It's generally safe to catch a lift on a *camión* (flatbed truck) if you see lots of other people waiting; don't get on board if anything seems fishy. Women should never hitchhike alone. Especially in urban areas and at night, women – even in groups – should be careful, and avoid isolation. Hiking alone is discouraged under any circumstances. See also Women Travelers, p340.

TELEPHONE

Numerous carriers – such as Entel, Viva, Boliviatel, Cotel and Tigo – offer local and long-distance rates on both landlines and cellular phones. Bolivia's first company, Empresa Nacional de Telecomunicaciones (Entel), is still the most prevalent in smaller towns but other companies are making an entrance. Local calls cost just a few bolivianos from these offices. *Puntos,* run by all of the above companies, are small, privately run outposts offering similar services and are open late. Alternatively, street kiosks are often equipped with telephones that charge B$1 for brief local calls.

In some tiny villages you'll find cardphone telephone boxes – phones take both magnetic and computer chip varieties. Both card types *(tarjetas)* come in denominations of B$10, B$20, B$50 and B$100. Touts in fluorescent jackets with cellular phones chained to themselves offer calls for B$1 per minute.

Cellular SIM cards are cheap (starting at B$40, inclusive of B$20–B$30 credit) and available from larger carrier outlets as well as small private phone shops. If you buy from a private outlet, activate the number and check that the phone works before purchasing. Make sure your phone has tri-band network capabilities (similar to the US system). To top up your call amount, buy cards (ask for *crédito*, ie credit) from the numerous *puntos* in any city or town.

Phone Codes

The boxed text below has detailed instructions on making calls.

In this book, when the given phone number is in another city or town (eg some rural hotels have La Paz reservation numbers), the single-digit telephone code is provided along with the number.

International Calls

Bolivia's country code is ☎ 591. The international direct-dialing access code is 00.

DIALING IN TO THE TELEPHONE NETWORK

Even Bolivians struggle with their own telephone network, thanks to the recent changes in the system. With patience, dialing is easy once you get your head – and ears – around it. The following should help you tap into the network.

Numbers for *líneas fijas* (landlines) have seven digits; cellular numbers have eight digits.

Numerous telecommunications carriers include, among others, Entel, Cotel, Tigo, Boliviatel and Viva. Each carrier has an individual code between 010 and 021.

Each department (region) has its own single-digit area code which must be used when dialing from another region or to another city, regardless of whether it's the same area code as the one you're in. The department codes are: (2) La Paz, Oruro, Potosí; (3) Santa Cruz, Beni, Pando; (4) Cochabamba, Chuquisaca, Tarija.

Public phone booths and phone boxes

Dialing landlines from public phone booths is easy; ask the cashier for advice. To make a call to another landline within the same city, simply dial the seven-digit number. If you're calling another region, dial 0 plus the single-digit area code followed by the seven-digit number, eg 02-123-4567. If calling a cell phone, ask the cashier for instructions; most *puntos* have different phones for calls to cellulars and landlines, so you may have to swap cabins if calling both.

Private landlines

If dialing from landline to landline within the same city, dial the seven-digit number. If dialing another region or city, enter 0 + 2-digit carrier code (between 10 and 21) + single-digit area code, followed by the seven-digit number.

Cellular phones

Cellular to cellular calls within the same city are simple – just dial the eight-digit number. A recorded message (in Spanish) may prompt you for a carrier number, indicating that the person is either not within the same city or region (or has a SIM card from another region), in which case you must then redial using a 0 + 2-digit carrier number plus the eight-digit cellular number.

For cellular to landline calls within the same city, in most cases, you must dial the single-digit area code, and then the seven-digit number.

For cellular to landline calls to another region, in most cases, you must dial a 0 + 2-digit carrier code, followed by the single-digit area code, and then the seven-digit number, eg if dialing Sucre from La Paz, dial 0 + 10 (or any one of the carrier codes – 10 is Entel's network carrier) + 4 (Sucre's area code) + the seven-digit number.

International calls

For international calls, you must first dial 00 followed by a country code, area code (without the first 0) and the telephone number.

Calls from telephone offices are getting cheaper all the time, especially now that there's competition between the carriers – they can vary between B$1.50 and B$8 per minute.

In La Paz the cheapest of cheap calls can be made from international calling centers around Calle Sagárnaga for around B$2 per minute.

Some Entel offices accept reverse-charge (collect) calls; others will give you the office's number and let you be called back. For reverse-charge calls from a private line, ring an international operator: for the **USA** (AT&T toll-free ☎ 800-10-1110; MCI ☎ 800-10-2222), **Canada** (Teleglobe ☎ 800-10-0101) or **UK** (BT ☎ 800-10-0044) – be aware that these calls can be bank-breakers.

INTERNET CALLS
Much cheaper Net2Phone internet call centers, charging as little as B$0.20 a minute to a fixed line in the USA or Spain, exist in major cities, but connections can be shaky. Most internet places have Skype installed, which you can use at no extra cost, just paying for the time online.

TIME
Bolivian time is four hours behind Greenwich Mean Time (GMT), and an hour ahead of the US Eastern Standard Time. When it's noon in La Paz, it's 4pm in London, 11am in New York, 8am in San Francisco, 4am the following day in Auckland and 2am the following day in Sydney.

TOILETS
Toilet humor becomes the norm in Bolivia. First and foremost, you'll have to learn to live with the fact that facilities are nonexistent on nearly all buses (except for a few of the luxury ones). Smelly, poorly maintained *baños públicos* abound and charge around B$1 in populated areas and B$5 in the wilderness, like around the Salar de Uyuni. Carry toilet paper with you wherever you go, at all times! Toilet paper isn't flushed down any Bolivian toilet – use the wastebaskets provided. In an emergency, you can always follow the locals' lead and drop your drawers whenever and wherever you feel the need. Some of the most popular spots seem to be below '*No Orinar*' (Don't Urinate) signs threatening *multas* (fines)

equal to the average Bolivian monthly wage. Use the facilities at your hotel before heading out.

TOURIST INFORMATION
Despite the fact that tourism has taken off in recent years, the Bolivian tourist industry is still in its formative stages, and government tourist offices still concentrate more on statistics and bureaucratic spending than on promotion of the country's attractions or imposing safety regulations. Most real development and promotion has been courtesy of the private sector, which is the chief source of brochures and promotional programs.

There are offices covering the *prefectura* (department) and *alcaldía* (local municipality) of a particular city. The major cities, such as Santa Cruz and La Paz, have offices for both, although the different tourism bodies range from helpful to useless. Most municipal offices can provide street plans and answer specific questions about local transportation and attractions. The most worthwhile are those in La Paz, Santa Cruz and Oruro, while those in other major cities seem to be considerably less useful. Note that the posted opening hours are not always followed. There are no tourist offices abroad. Servicio Nacional de Áreas Protegidas (SERNAP) is the best source of information about Bolivia's national parks. For a list of the most valuable certified tour operators in Bolivia, visit www.canotur-bolivia.com (in Spanish).

TRAVELERS WITH DISABILITIES
The sad fact is that Bolivia's infrastructure is ill-equipped for travelers with disabilities. You will, however, see locals overcoming myriad obstacles and challenges while making their daily rounds. If you encounter difficulties yourself, you'll likely find locals willing to go out of their way to lend a hand. For general information, visit the **Global Access – Disabled Travel Network** (www.globalaccessnews.com).

VISAS
Passports must be valid for six months beyond the date of entry. Entry or exit stamps are free, and attempts at charging should be met with polite refusal; ask for a receipt if the issue is pressed. Personal

documents – passports and visas – must be carried at all times, especially in lowland regions. It's safest to carry photocopies rather than originals.

Bolivian visa requirements can be arbitrarily changed and interpreted. Regulations, including entry stays, are likely to change. Each Bolivian consulate and border crossing may have its own entry procedures and idiosyncrasies.

In 2007, as an act of reciprocity, the Morales government introduced visas for US citizens visiting Bolivia (a 90-day visa valid for five years costs US$135). At the time of writing, it was possible to obtain the visa upon arrival in Bolivia; check with the **Bolivian embassy** (☎ 202-483-4410, 202-328-3712; www.bolivia-usa.org, in Spanish; 3014 Massachusetts Ave NW, Washington, DC) before traveling.

Citizens of most South American and Western European countries can get a tourist card on entry for stays up to 90 days (depending on the nationality). Citizens of Canada, Australia, New Zealand and Japan are granted 30 days, while citizens of Israel are granted 90 days. This is subject to change; always check with your consulate prior to entry. If you want to stay longer, you have to extend your tourist card (easily accomplished at the immigration office in any major city with a letter requesting the extension; it's free for some nationalities – for others, it costs B$198 per 30-day extension). The maximum time travelers are permitted to stay in the country is 180 days in one year. Alternatively, you can apply for a visa. Visas are issued by Bolivian consular representatives, including those in neighboring South American countries. Costs vary according to the consulate and the nationality of the applicant but hover around B$2500.

Overstayers can be fined B$14 per day (or more, depending on the nationality) – payable at the immigration office or airport – and may face ribbons of red tape at the border or airport when leaving the country.

In addition to a valid passport and visa, citizens of many Communist, African, Middle Eastern and Asian countries require 'official permission' from the Bolivian Ministry of Foreign Affairs before a visa will be issued.

More about up-to-date visa information can be found at www.lonelyplanet.com.

Vaccination Certificates

US citizens applying for a tourist visa to visit Bolivia need a yellow-fever vaccination certificate, as does anyone coming from a yellow-fever-infected area. Many neighboring countries, including Brazil, require anyone entering from Bolivia to have proof of a yellow-fever vaccination. If necessary, a jab can often be administered at the border but it is preferable to take care of this at home. For more on yellow fever, see p356.

WOMEN TRAVELERS

Women's rights in Bolivia are nearing modern standards and cities are more liberal than country regions. But despite the importance of women in Bolivian society and the elevation of females in public life (including a female president and women mayors), the machismo mind-set still pervades in Bolivia. As a female traveling alone, the mere fact that you appear to be unmarried and far from your home and family may cause you to appear suspiciously disreputable.

Bear in mind that modesty is expected of women in much of Spanish-speaking Latin America. Local women who wear Western dress in the warmer and lower areas tend to show more flesh than elsewhere in the country. That said, as a foreigner, avoid testing the system alone in a bar in a mini-skirt. Conservative dress and confidence without arrogance are a must for gringas, more to be respectful than anything else. Men are generally more forward and flirtatious in the lowlands, where the latino culture is more prevalent, than in the Altiplano where indigenous cultures prevail. The best advice is to watch the standards of well-dressed Bolivian women in any particular area and follow their example.

As a safety measure for a woman traveler, try to avoid arriving at a place at night. If you need to take a taxi at night, it's preferable to call for a radio taxi than to flag one down in the street. Note that during the period leading up to Carnaval and during the festivities, a woman traveling solo can be a popular target for water bombs, which can feel like quite a harassment or at least an annoyance.

See also Solo Travelers on p337.

WORK & VOLUNTEERING

There are hundreds of voluntary and nongovernmental organizations (NGOs) working in Bolivia, but travelers looking for paid work on the spot shouldn't hold their breath.

For paid work, qualified English teachers can try the professionally run **Centro Boliviano-Americano** (CBA; ☎ 243-0107; www.cba.edu.bo; Parque Zenón Iturralde 121) in La Paz; there are also offices in other cities. New, unqualified teachers must forfeit two months' salary in return for their training. Better paying are private school positions teaching math, science or social studies. Accredited teachers can expect to earn up to US$500 per month for a full-time position.

Unpaid work is available in several places, and in others, you pay for the privilege of working on a project. (Be aware that some profit organizations offer 'internship' or 'volunteer' opportunities, when in reality it's unpaid work in exchange for free trips or activities.)

There are a few options to do genuine volunteer work. Government-sponsored organizations or NGOs such as the Peace Corps offer longer-term programs (usually two years) for which you receive an allowance, predeparture briefings and ongoing organizational support; church-affiliated or religious organizations offer short-term opportunities, often on a group basis; and smaller volunteer organizations (often profit-based) offer independent travelers the opportunity to work on community projects. These usually have a two- or four-week minimum for which you pay.

Some popular volunteer options include:

Animales S.O.S. (☎ 2-230-8080; www.animalessos.org; Av Chacaltaya 1759, La Paz) An animal welfare group caring for mistreated or abused stray animals.

Parque Machía (☎ 4-413-6572; www.intiwarayassi.org; Parque Machía, Villa Tunari, Chapare) Volunteer-run wild animal refuge; as previous experience of working with animals is needed, but the minimum commitment is 15 days. See p297.

Sustainable Bolivia (☎ 4-423-3786; www.sustainablebolivia.org; Julio Arauco Prado 230, Cochabamba) Cochabamba-based nonprofit organization with a variety of volunteering programs, both short- and long-term, through 22 local organizations.

Volunteer Bolivia (Map p192; ☎ 4-452-6028; www.volunteerbolivia.org; Ecuador 0342, Cochabamba) Arranges short- and long-term volunteer work, study and homestay programs throughout Bolivia.

For longer-term volunteering assignments, you're better off contacting international NGOs in your country or region, including **Peace Corps** (www.peacecorps.gov) in the USA and **Centre d'Étude et de Coopération Internationale** (CECI; www.ceci.ca) in Canada.

Interested wannabe volunteers and workers can make a start by looking up the following websites of profit and not-for-profit organizations and NGOs.

- www.amizade.org
- www.earthwatch.org
- www.globalcrossroad.com
- www.gvi.co.uk
- www.i-to-i.com
- www.realgap.co.uk
- www.projects-abroad.co.uk
- www.transitionsabroad.com
- www.unv.org
- www.vivabolivia.org/bcmission
- www.volunteerabroad.com
- www.volunteeradventures.com
- www.whybolivia.org
- www.worldvolunteerweb.org

Transportation

CONTENTS

Getting There & Away	**342**
Entering the Country	342
Air	342
Land & River	345
Getting Around	**346**
Air	346
Bicycle	347
Boat	347
Bus	347
Car & Motorcycle	348
Hitchhiking	349
Local Transportation	349
Train	350
Tours	350

TRANSPORTATION

GETTING THERE & AWAY

A landlocked country, Bolivia has numerous entry/exit points. Some are easier and more accessible than others; the more remote borders are recommended for intrepid travelers only – those with time and lust for unpredictable adventure.

Flights, tours and rail tickets can be booked online at www.lonelyplanet.com/bookings.

ENTERING THE COUNTRY

If you have your documents in order and you are willing to answer a few questions about the aim of your visit, entry into Bolivia should be a breeze. If crossing at a smaller border post, you might well be asked to pay an 'exit fee.' Unless otherwise noted in the text, these fees are strictly unofficial. Note that Bolivian border times can be unreliable at best; always check with a *migración* office in the nearest major town. Also, if you plan to cross the border outside the stated hours, or at a point where there is no border post, you can usually do so by obtaining an exit/ entry stamp from the nearest *migración* office on departure/arrival.

AIR

There are only a few airlines offering direct flights to Bolivia, so airfares are as high as the altitude. There are direct services to most major South American cities; the flights to/from Chile and Peru are the cheapest. Santa Cruz is an increasingly popular entry point from Western European hubs. Due to altitude-related costs, flying into La Paz is more expensive than into Santa Cruz. High season for most fares is from early June to late August, and mid-December to mid-February.

Airports & Airlines

Bolivia's principal international airports are La Paz's **El Alto** (LPB; ☎ 2-215-7300), formerly known as John F Kennedy Memorial, and Santa Cruz's **Viru-Viru International** (VVI; ☎ 3-338-5000).

Bolivia's national carrier, Lloyd Aéro Boliviano, became defunct in February 2008. **AeroSur** (☎ 3-336-7400; www.aerosur.com) is now the main domestic airline, and offers regular flights to seven destinations in Bolivia as well as international flights to Miami, Madrid, Cusco, Buenos Aires and more. **Transporte Aéreo Boliviano** (☎ 2-268-1111; www.tam.bo), better known as TAM, offers flights to and from smaller towns within Bolivia, although it is known for its cancelations and delays. **Amaszonas** (☎ 2-222-0848; www.amaszonas.com) flies small planes from La Paz to Rurrenabaque, Trinidad, Santa Cruz and other lowland destinations. The small airline **AeroCon** (www.aerocon.bo) connects the country's major cities as well as some more remote corners. **BOA** (www.boa.bo), a new airline, was starting to fly between major cities at the time of research; however, it was unfortunately not particularly reliable yet.

DEPARTURE TAX

The international departure tax, payable in cash only at the airport, is US$25 (US$31 if you stayed in Bolivia for more than three months). Be aware that there's also a 15% tax on international airfares purchased in Bolivia.

CLIMATE CHANGE & TRAVEL

Climate change is a serious threat to the ecosystems that humans rely upon, and air travel is the fastest-growing contributor to the problem. Lonely Planet regards travel, overall, as a global benefit, but believes we all have a responsibility to limit our personal impact on global warming.

Flying & Climate Change

Pretty much every form of motor travel generates CO_2 (the main cause of human-induced climate change) but planes are far and away the worst offenders, not just because of the sheer distances they allow us to travel, but because they release greenhouse gases high into the atmosphere. The statistics are frightening: two people taking a return flight between Europe and the US will contribute as much to climate change as does an average household's entire gas and electricity consumption over a whole year.

Carbon Offset Schemes

Climatecare.org and other websites use 'carbon calculators' that allow jetsetters to offset the greenhouse gases they are responsible for with contributions to energy-saving projects and other climate-friendly initiatives in the developing world – including projects in India, Honduras, Kazakhstan and Uganda.

Lonely Planet, together with Rough Guides and other concerned partners in the travel industry, supports the carbon offset scheme run by climatecare.org. Lonely Planet offsets all of its staff and author travel.

For more information check out our website: lonelyplanet.com.

AIRLINES FLYING TO/FROM BOLIVIA

Airlines with international flights and offices in La Paz include the following:

Aerolíneas Argentinas (airline code AR; ☎ 3-333-9776; www.aerolineas.com.ar)

AeroSur (airline code 5L; ☎ 3-336-7400; www.aerosur.com)

American Airlines (airline code AA; ☎ 2-334-1314; www.aa.com)

Grupo Taca (airline code TA; ☎ 800-10-TACA; www.taca.com)

Lan Airlines (airline code LA; ☎ 800-100-521; www.lan.com)

TAM Mercosur (airline code PZ; ☎ 2-244-3442; www.tam.com.br)

Varig-Gol Airlines (airline code G3; ☎ 800-100-121; www.voegol.com.br)

Tickets

The world aviation market has never been so competitive, making air travel better value than ever. Research your options carefully to get yourself the best possible deal. Online ticket sales work well if you are doing a simple one-way or return trip on specified dates. However, the whiz-bang online fare generators are in no way a substitute for a knowledgeable travel agent. Please note that ticket prices in this chapter do not include any taxes or fuel levies, which are liable to significantly increase air travel costs.

INTERCONTINENTAL (RTW) TICKETS

Round-the-world (RTW) tickets can be real bargains if you are coming to South America from the other side of the world. They are generally put together by the airline alliances, and give you a limited period (usually a year) in which to circumnavigate the globe.

An alternative type of RTW ticket is one put together by a travel agent. These tickets are more expensive than airline RTW fares, but you choose your itinerary. Travel agents, by combining tickets from two low-cost airlines, can also offer multiple destination fares that are cheaper than a RTW ticket, and allow for two stops on the way to and from South America.

THINGS CHANGE...

The information in this chapter is particularly vulnerable to change. Check directly with the airline or a travel agent to make sure you understand how a fare (and ticket you may buy) works and be aware of the security requirements for international travel. Shop carefully. The details given in this chapter should be regarded as pointers and are not a substitute for your own careful, up-to-date research.

Some online ticket sites for intercontinental tickets:

Airbrokers International (www.airbrokers.com) A US company specializing in cheap RTW tickets.

Oneworld (www.oneworld.com) Airline alliance of 10 major airlines.

Roundtheworldflights.com (www.roundtheworldflights.com) An excellent site that allows you to build your own trip from the UK.

Star Alliance (www.staralliance.com) Another airline alliance.

Australia & New Zealand

Travel between Australasia and South America ain't cheap, so it makes sense to think in terms of a RTW ticket, or a ticket via Buenos Aires or Santiago. Round-trip fares from Sydney to La Paz via Auckland and Santiago start at around A$2500/3000 in low/high season. Fares via the USA are considerably more expensive, starting at around A$3200 return in the low season. RTW tickets including La Paz start at about A$3300. The most direct routes are from Sydney to Santiago on LAN/Qantas or to Buenos Aires with Qantas/LAN and Aerolíneas Argentinas. The best RTW ticket is probably from the Oneworld Alliance, which has two different options: one restricted by the number of continents you visit, the other restricted by mileage. Fares start at around A$3400. The Oneworld Visit South America Airpass (offered by LAN and Oneworld partner airlines) starts at US$102 per coupon.

Destination Holidays (☎ 03-9725-4655, 800-337-050; www.south-america.com.au) and **South American Travel Centre** (☎ 03-9642-5353; www.satc.com.au) specialize in Latin American travel (the latter does tailor-made tours only).

Continental Europe

The best places in Europe for cheap airfares are student travel agencies (you don't have to be a student to use them). If airfares are expensive where you live, try contacting a London agent. The cheapest flights from Europe are typically charters, usually with fixed outward and return flight dates.

Some fares include a stopover in the USA. Note that passengers through New York (JFK) or Miami must pass through US immigration procedures, even if they won't be visiting the USA. That means you'll either need to have a US visa or be eligible for the Visa Waiver Program, which is open to Australians, New Zealanders and most Western Europeans, unless they're traveling on a nonaccredited airline (which includes most Latin American airlines).

South America

AeroSur connects La Paz to Rio de Janeiro, Buenos Aires, Cuzco and Lima several times a week. Aerolíneas Argentinas flies daily between Santa Cruz and Buenos Aires and Varig-Gol Airlines flies between Santa Cruz and Rio de Janeiro (among other destinations). AeroSur has four weekly flights between La Paz and Miami.

LanChile connects La Paz with Santiago daily except Thursday; there are connecting flights to Iquique four times a week (Monday, Wednesday, Friday and Sunday). Brazilian-owned TAM Mercosur connects Asuncíon with Santa Cruz. LanPeru flies to Cuzco (often via Lima) from La Paz daily, except Wednesday and Sunday. AeroSur has direct flights to Cusco on Thursday and Sunday.

The UK

Discount air travel is big business in London. Advertisements for many agencies appear in the travel pages of the weekend broadsheet newspapers, in *Time Out*, the *Evening Standard* and in the free magazine *TNT*.

AeroSur offers the only direct flights to La Paz from Europe, three times weekly from Madrid – fares start at US$1300. From London, all flights go via the US or other South American countries. Expect to pay from around £400 one-way in the low season. RTW tickets from London that take in South America (Santiago and Rio de Janeiro) start from around £1400.

London-based South American specialists include **Journey Latin America** (JLA; ☎ 020-8747-3108; www.journeylatinamerica.co.uk), **South American Experience** (☎ 0845-277-3366; www.southamericanexperience.co.uk) and **Austral Tours** (☎ 020-7233-5384; www.latinamerica.co.uk).

The USA & Canada

Inexpensive tickets from North American gateways (Miami is cheapest) usually have restrictions. Often there's a two-week advance-purchase requirement, and usually you must stay at least one week and no more than three months (prices often double for longer periods). For an idea of what's available, peruse the Sunday travel sections of major newspapers and free alternative weeklies.

Look for agencies specializing in South America, such as **eXito** (☎ 800-655-4053; www .exitotravel.com), which has an expert staff and is superb for anyone traveling with special interests.

Most flights from Canada involve connecting via a US gateway such as Miami or Los Angeles.

LAND & RIVER
Bus
Depending on which country you enter from, some agency-booked, intercountry buses might carry you for the complete route; at other times you'll change into an associated bus company once you cross the border. If going with local buses, you'll usually need to catch onward buses once you've made your border crossing.

Car & Motorcycle
You can enter Bolivia by road from any of the neighboring countries. The routes from Brazil and Chile are poor, and those from Paraguay should be considered only with a 4WD. The routes from Argentina and Peru pose no significant problems.

Foreigners entering Bolivia from another country need a *hoja de ruta* (circulation card), available from the Servicio Nacional de Tránsito/Aduana at the frontier. This document must be presented and stamped at all police posts – variously known as *trancas, tránsitos* or *controles* – which are spaced along highways and just outside major cities. *Peajes* (tolls) are often charged at these checkpoints and vehicles may be searched for contraband.

For details about driving in Bolivia, see p348.

Argentina
Two major overland crossings between Argentina and Bolivia include: **Villazón/ La Quiaca** (🕑 7am-11pm) and **Yacuiba/Pocitos** (🕑 7am-4pm).

You can arrive or depart Villazón by train from Oruro or Tupiza. See boxed text, p185, for timetable information and border-crossing information.

The Yacuiba-Pocitos crossing (for more details see boxed text, p257) is 5km from Yacuiba in the Chaco, reached by taxi (B$10 per person) and crossed on foot. Buses

further into Argentina go every couple of hours.

The minor border crossing at **Bermejo/ Agua Blanca** (🕑 8am-5pm) south of Tarija is at an international bridge that goes onto a highway further into Argentina. For more details, see boxed text, p257.

Brazil
Note: Proof of yellow-fever vaccination is needed when crossing into Brazil.

Bolivia can be reached or departed via the Quijarro/Corumbá crossing. On arrival in Brazil, taxis shuttle passengers to the Brazilian border town of Corumbá, 2km away. You can change dollars or bolivianos into *reais* (pronounced hay-ice) on the Bolivian side, but the boliviano rate is poor. Note that there's no Brazilian consulate in Quijarro, so if you need a visa, get it in Santa Cruz. From Corumbá there are good bus connections into southern Brazil, but no passenger trains. See p293 for more details on getting to and from Quijarro.

Frequent motorboats (B$10) provide a novel water entry/exit via Río Mamoré at **Guayaramerín/Guajará-Mirim** (🕑 8am-8pm). There are no restrictions entering Guajará-Mirim for a quick visit, but if you intend to travel further into Brazil, you must pick up an entry/exit stamp. For departure stamps from Bolivia, head to the Policía Federal in **Bolivian immigration** (🕑 8am-8pm) by the dock. For more information, see p323 and boxed text, p327.

Alternative ferry options facilitate short hops across borders in the Amazon Basin at far flung locales such as Parque Nacional Noel Kempff Mercado and Pimienteras, Brazil, and Cobija and Brasiléia, Brazil; see boxed text, p327.

Chile
Note that meat, fruit and food produce (including coca leaves) cannot be carried from Bolivia into Chile and will be confiscated at the border. The most popular route between Chile and Bolivia is via bus from La Paz to Arica through the border at **Chungará/Tambo Quemado** (🕑 8am-8pm; see p165). A convenient alternative for those doing the 4WD Southwest Circuit tour is to get dropped off on the last day at **Hito Cajón** (🕑 8am-11pm, although it's wise to be there before 6pm) and head to San Pedro, Chile, from where you can pick up

TRANSPORTATION

buses (note the latter cannot be done in the reverse order). Note there's a one-hour trip between the Bolivian border and San Pedro, for which it's better to arrange transportation in advance, in case taxis aren't waiting. For more, see p177. Alternatively, there is a lesser used road route between Oruro and Iquique with a border at **Pisiga/Colchane** (☾ 8am-8pm); p161 for bus details.

A crossing can be done via train or road from Uyuni to Calama (p172), whose border crossing is **Ollagüe-Avaroa** (☾ 8am-8pm).

Paraguay

The easiest route between Paraguay and Bolivia is to cross from Pedro Juan Caballero (in Asunción, Paraguay) to Ponta Porã (Brazil), and then travel by bus or train to Corumbá (Brazil) and Quijarro (Bolivia).

The three-day overland Trans-Chaco bus trip (see boxed text, p258) between Santa Cruz, Bolivia and Asunción, Paraguay, now has a daily bus service during the dry season, but it's still not a breeze. Note that Bolivian customs formalities take place at Ibibobo, where your passport will be checked, about an hour before the Paraguayan checkpoint of Infante Rivarola; the immigration and customs are down the road at Mariscal Estigarribia. This is a notorious smuggling route so expect to be lined up with your bags as customs officials and sniffer dogs rifle through your possessions.

For the adventurous, river transportation between Asunción, Paraguay, and Bolivia (via Corumbá, Brazil) is likely to involve a series of short journeys and informal arrangements with individual boat captains. From Asunción, there's a regular, albeit leisurely, river service to Concepción (Paraguay). Beyond Concepción is where the informal boat arrangements begin. You'll probably wind up doing it in two stages: Concepción to Bahía Negra (northern Paraguay), then Bahía Negra to Corumbá.

Peru

Bolivia is normally reached overland from Peru via Lake Titicaca. If you've got time, the border crossing at **Kasani-Yunguyo** (☾ 8am-6pm) via Copacabana (p107) is more appealing than the faster, less secure and least interesting crossing at **Desaguadero** (☾ 9am-9pm); see p115 for more information.

If departing Bolivia direct from La Paz, the easiest way is to catch an agency bus to Puno (Peru); the bus breaks in Copacabana and again for immigration formalities in Yunguyo. Similar buses go direct to Cuzco. A cheaper way from Copacabana is via minibus from Plaza Sucre to the Kasani-Yunguyo border (B\$3, 15 minutes); there's onward transportation to the border at Yunguyo (five minutes), and on to Puno.

Crillon Tours (☎ 2-233-7533; www.titicaca.com; Camacho 1223, La Paz) sells tickets for all-inclusive bus/hydrofoil tours between La Paz and Puno.

GETTING AROUND

Bolivia boasts an extensive transportation system that covers most parts of the country in varying degrees of comfort and ease. Locals are creative in the ways they get from one place to another, taking a variety of *movilidades* (anything that moves!) including buses, trucks and boats. Interruptions to travel plans are usually not caused by lack of transportation, but by protests in the form of road blockades, floods, damaged roads (especially in the lowlands during rainy season) and, in the Amazon, low river levels. In the major tourist destinations, regular bus transportation usually ensures efficient travel.

AIR

Air travel in Bolivia is inexpensive and it's the quickest and most reliable means of reaching out-of-the-way places. It's also the only means of transportation that isn't washed out during the wet season. Although weather-related disruptions definitely occur, planes eventually get through even during summer flooding in northern Bolivia.

Airlines in Bolivia

Bolivia's major ariline, **AeroSur** (www.aerosur .com), as well as smaller airlines such as **Amaszonas** (www.amaszonas.com) and **AeroCon** (www.aerocon.bo), connect the country's major cities and remote corners. They all charge similar fares and allow 15kg of luggage, ecluding 3kg of carry-on luggage.

The military airline, **Transportes Aéreos Militares** (TAM; Map pp68-9; ☎ 2-268-1101, 277-5222; www.tam.bo; Montes 738), operates domestic flights in smaller planes that fly closer to the landscape. Prices are as much as 20% lower than other airlines and reservations can be made in every town with a travel agency that has an online booking system; note that schedules can change without notice. They are strict with the 15kg baggage limit; each additional kilo costs around B$3.50, depending on the length of the flight.

Departure Tax
AASANA (Administración de Aeropuertos y Servicios Auxiliares a la Navegación Aérea), the government agency responsible for airports and air traffic, charges a B$11 to B$16 domestic departure tax, which is payable at its desk after check-in. International departure tax is US$25. Some airports also levy a municipal tax of up to B$7.

BICYCLE
For cyclists who can cope with the challenges of cold winds, poor road conditions, high altitude and steep terrain, Bolivia is a paradise. Traffic isn't a serious problem, but intimidating buses and *camiones* (flatbed trucks) may leave cyclists lost in clouds of dust or embedded in mud. However, finding supplies may prove difficult, so cyclists in remote areas must carry ample food and water. Given these challenges, many prefer to leave the work to a tour company.

Bolivia has its fair share of inexpensive bikes – mostly supermarket beaters from China. However, quality new wheels are few and far between. Your best bet for purchasing a used, touring-worthy stead is through agencies in La Paz. Try Gravity Assisted Mountain Biking (p74) for spare parts and help with repairs. Bringing your own bicycle into the country is generally hassle-free. If you're considering any biking in Bolivia, make sure you purchase a comprehensive travel insurance policy. For information on mountain biking, see p57.

BOAT
Ferry
The only public ferry service in Bolivia operates between San Pedro and San Pablo, across the narrow Estrecho de Tiquina (Straits of Tiquina; p116) on Lake Titicaca. To visit any of Lake Titicaca's Bolivian islands, you can travel by launch or rowboat. To the Huyñaymarka islands in the lake's southernmost extension, boats and

tours are available in Huatajata (p115). To visit Isla del Sol, you can take a tour, hire a launch or catch a scheduled service in Copacabana, or look for a lift in Yampupata or the villages en route. Cruises by motorboat or hydrofoil are provided by a couple of well-established tour companies; see boxed text, p99.

River Boat
There's no scheduled passenger service on the Amazon, so travelers almost invariably wind up on some sort of cargo vessel. The most popular routes are from Puerto Villarroel to Trinidad (p300) and Trinidad to Guayaramerín (p315). There are also much less frequented routes from Rurrenabaque or Puerto Heath to Riberalta (p325).

BUS
Buses and their various iterations are the most popular form of Bolivian transportation. It's cheap and relatively safe but also quite uncomfortable or nerve-wracking at times. Long-distance bus lines in Bolivia are called *flotas,* large buses are known as *buses,* three-quarter (usually older) ones are called *micros* and minibuses are just that. If looking for a bus terminal, ask for *la terminal terrestre* or *la terminal de buses*. Each terminal charges a small fee of a couple of bolivianos, which you pay to an agent upon boarding or when purchasing the ticket at the counter.

It's a lot safer to travel (and the views are better) during the day. Drunken driving is illegal, but bus drivers have been known to sip the hard stuff on long nighttime hauls. There have been numerous reports of items disappearing from buses' internal overhead compartments. Hold on tight to your day packs and bags if they are with you in the bus. Backpacks and bags are generally safe when stored in the baggage compartment but try to watch as your luggage is loaded – there have been instances of 'lost' or 'disappeared' bags. You will be given a baggage tag, which you must show when reclaiming your bag.

Except on the most popular runs, most companies' buses inexplicably depart at roughly the same time, regardless of the number of competitors. Between any two cities, you should have no trouble finding at least one daily bus. On the most popular

TRANSPORTATION

routes you can choose between dozens of daily departures.

It's always a good idea to check the vehicles of several companies before purchasing your ticket – some buses are ramshackle affairs with broken windows, cracked windshields, and worn tires; it's better to stay away from these and look for a better vehicle, even if it means paying a little more. Don't save on safety.

When traveling in the highlands, especially at night, make sure you have a sleeping bag or a blanket handy. There's often no heating and the temperatures are freezing. On longer bus journeys, make sure you have plenty of water and snacks, as these may not be available en route.

Avoid sitting at the back of the bus – you'll feel the bumpy roads more severely and your bladder won't be happy.

Don't count on arriving at your destination at a said time; journey times are completely unpredictable in Bolivia, especially during the rainy season.

Classes & Costs

The only choices you'll have to make are on major, long-haul routes, where the better companies offer *coche* (or *'bus'*) *cama* (sleeper) service for around double the *común* or normal going rate. The VCR on the newest buses will be in better shape than the reclining seats, heaters *may* function and toilets (yes, toilets) *may* work.

Prices vary according to the different standards of buses (from the more luxurious *bus cama* service to the ancient Bluebird-style buses) and the length of trip (whether overnight or short day-hop). An overnight trip from La Paz to Cochabamba costs between B$45 and B$90 and from La Paz to Potosí between B$52 and B$80.

Reservations

To be safe, reserve bus tickets at least several hours in advance. For the lowest fare, purchase immediately after the driver starts the engine. Many buses depart in the afternoon or evening and arrive at their destination in the wee hours of the morning. On most major routes there are also daytime departures.

CAR & MOTORCYCLE

The advantages of a private vehicle include schedule flexibility, access to remote areas and the chance to seize photo opportunities.

More Bolivian roads are gradually being paved (most recently, that between La Paz and Potosí) but others are in varying stages of decay, so high-speed travel is impossible (unless, of course, you're a Bolivian bus driver) and inadvisable.

The undaunted should prepare their expeditions carefully. Bear in mind that spare parts are a rare commodity outside cities. A high-clearance 4WD vehicle is essential for off-road travel. You'll need tools, spare tires, a puncture repair kit, extra gas and fluids, and as many spare parts as possible. For emergencies, carry camping equipment and plenty of rations. You'll also need a good travel insurance policy purchased back home. If you do decide to get insurance in Bolivia, this broker is the best go-to point for information about various insurance companies and what they offer: **Consultores de Seguros** (☎ 800-102-266; www.consegsa.com).

Low-grade (85-octane) gasoline and diesel fuel are available at *surtidores* in all cities and major towns. Gas costs around B$3.74 per liter, more in remote areas.

In lowland areas, where temperatures are hot and roads are scarce, motorbikes are popular for zipping around the plazas, as well as exploring areas not served by public transportation. They can be rented for around B$80 to B$100 per day from moto-taxi stands. Gringo-run agencies offering motorcycle tours through the rugged highland are popping up like mushrooms in the larger cities. Bear in mind that many travel insurance policies will not cover you for injuries arising from motorbike accidents.

For details on bringing your own vehicle into Bolivia, see p345.

Driver's License

Most Bolivian car-rental agencies will accept your home driver's license, but if you're doing a lot of driving, it's wise to back it up with an International Driver's License. Bolivia doesn't require special motorcycle licenses, but neighboring countries do. For motorcycle and moped rentals, all that is normally required is a passport.

Private Drivers

Hiring a driver can be a more comfortable and efficient alternative to being squashed in a bus on bad roads for long periods. Alternatively, many people just want transportation to trailheads or base camps rather than a tour.

Examples of one-way transportation prices from La Paz with a *chofer* (private driver), regardless of the number of passengers (six to eight maximum), include the following: Refugio Huayna Potosí US$50 to US$60; Estancia Una or Pinaya (for Illimani climb) US$120 to US$140; Curva/Lagunillas (for the Cordillera Apolobamba trek) US$200 to US$350; Chuñavi or Lambate (for the Yunga Cruz trek) US$120 to US$150; Sajama US$200 to US$240; and Rurrenabaque US$300 to US$350. Private Salar de Uyuni and Southwest Circuit tours cost from US$170 per day.

Several La Paz drivers are recommended for their value and reliable cars (for up to eight people); most speak basic English – see the following list. Also recommended are the English-speaking drivers and well-maintained 4WDs of **Climbing South America** (☎ 2-215-2232; www.climbingsouthamerica.com). A modern minibus is also available for hire from **Juliette Narcy** (☎ 2-246-2410, 7259-7761).

Carlos Aguilar (☎ 7152-5897) Has two 4WDs and charges rock-bottom prices.

Egberto Mamani (☎ 7912-5085) Excellent driver with a 2000 Nissan Patrol jeep; charges US$110 for all trips (plus gasoline).

Juan Carlos Mujiano Centellas (☎ 2-273-0382, 7011-6081) Offers transportation in a 4WD (for four people only) or a 14-seater minibus.

Oscar L Vera Coca (☎ 2-223-0453, 7156-1283) Has a reliable 4WD.

Ramiro Ancasi (☎ 2-283-1363, 7129-1880) Offers experienced driving in well-maintained 4WDs.

Rubén Luna (☎ 7301-1196) Pleasant driver-guide who charges slightly higher prices but has reliable cars.

Rental

Few travelers in Bolivia rent self-driven vehicles. Only the most reputable agencies service vehicles regularly, and insurance bought from rental agencies may cover only accidental damage – breakdowns may be considered the renter's problem.

You must be over 25 years, have a driver's license from your home country, have a major credit card or cash deposit (typically around US$1000) and accident insurance. You'll be charged a daily rate and a per-kilometer rate (some agencies allow a set number of free kilometers). They'll also want you to leave your passport as a deposit.

Costs vary widely but the average daily rate for a small Suzuki car starts at around US$50, plus an additional US$0.35 per kilometer. For the least expensive 4WD, companies charge around US$65 per day plus US$0.37 per kilometer. Weekly rates (with up to 1000km free) start at around US$350 for a compact and US$470 for the cheapest 4WD.

For listings of better-known agencies, see Getting Around in the major cities.

Road Rules

Traffic regulations aren't that different from those in North America or Europe. Speed limits are infrequently posted, but in most cases the state of the road will prevent you from exceeding them anyway.

Bolivians keep to the right. When two cars approach an uncontrolled intersection from different directions, the driver who honks (or gets there first) tends to have right of way if passing straight through – but be aware, this can be a bit hit and miss. In La Paz, those going up the hill have right of way at an intersection. When two vehicles meet on a narrow mountain road, the downhill vehicle must reverse until there's room for the other to pass.

HITCHHIKING

Thanks to relatively easy access to *camiones* and a profusion of buses, hitchhiking isn't really necessary or popular in Bolivia. Still, it's not unknown and drivers of *movilidades* – *coches* (cars), *camionetas* (pickup trucks), NGO vehicles, gas trucks and other vehicles – are usually happy to pick up passengers when they have room. Always ask the price, if any, before climbing aboard, even for short distances; if they do charge, it should amount to about half the bus fare for the equivalent distance.

Please note that hitchhiking is never entirely safe in any country. If you decide to hitchhike, you should understand that you are taking a small but potentially serious risk. Travel in pairs and let someone know where you're planning to go.

LOCAL TRANSPORTATION
Camión

Prior to the current expansive bus network, *camiones* were often the only way for travelers to venture off the beaten track.

These days, in the more populated areas, you might consider a *camión* trip more for the novelty than necessity; it is how many *campesinos* (subsistence farmers) choose to travel. *Camiones* generally cost around 50% of the bus fare. You'll need time and a strong constitution; travel can be excruciatingly slow and rough, depending on the cargo and number of passengers. A major plus is the raw experience, including the best views of the countryside.

On any *camión* trip, especially in the highlands, day or night, be sure to take plenty of warm clothing as night temperatures can plunge below freezing; at best they can be chilly.

Micros, Minibuses & Trufis

Micros (half-size buses) are used in larger cities and serve as Bolivia's least expensive form of public transportation. They follow set routes, and the route numbers or letters are usually marked on a placard behind the windshield. This is often backed by a description of the route, including the streets that are followed to reach the end of the line. They can be hailed anywhere along their routes. When you want to disembark, move toward the front and tell the driver or assistant where you want them to stop.

Minibuses and *trufis* (which may be cars, vans or minibuses), also known as *colectivos*, are prevalent in the larger towns and cities, and follow set routes that are numbered and described on placards. They are always cheaper than taxis and nearly as convenient. As with *micros*, you can board or alight anywhere along their route.

Taxis

Urban taxis are relatively inexpensive. Few are equipped with meters but in most cities and towns there are standard per-person fares for short hauls. In some places taxis are collective and behave more like *trufis,* charging a set rate per person. However, if you have three or four people all headed for the same place, you may be able to negotiate a reduced rate for the entire group.

Radio taxis, on the other hand, always charge a set rate for up to four people; if you squeeze in five people, the fare increases by a small margin. When using taxis, try to have enough change to cover the fare; drivers often like to plead a lack of change in the hope that you'll give them the benefit of the difference. As a general rule, taxi drivers aren't tipped, but if an individual goes beyond the call of duty, a tip of a couple of bolivianos wouldn't be amiss.

In larger cities, especially at night if traveling solo, it's advisable to go for a radio taxi instead of hailing one in the street; have your hotel or restaurant call for one.

TRAIN

Since privatization in the mid-1990s, passenger rail services have been cut back. The western network operated by the **Empresa Ferroviaria Andina** (FCA; www.fca.com.bo) runs from Oruro to Villazón on the Argentine border (p161); a branch line runs southwest from Uyuni to Avaroa (on the Chilean border).

The east is operated by **Ferroviaria Oriental** (www.ferroviariaoriental.com), which has a line from Santa Cruz to the Brazilian frontier at Quijarro, where you cross to the Pantanal (see boxed text, p292). An infrequently used service goes south from Santa Cruz to Yacuiba on the Argentine border (p273).

Reservations

Even in major towns along the routes, tickets can be reserved only on the day of departure. At smaller stations tickets may not be available until the train has arrived. Larger intermediate stations are allotted only a few seat reservations, and tickets go on sale quite literally whenever employees decide to open up. The best info is usually available from the *jefe de la estación* (station master).

When buying tickets, make sure you have a passport for each person for whom you're buying a ticket. This is a remnant from the days when ticket scalping was profitable.

TOURS

Many organized tours run out of La Paz or towns closest to the attractions that you wish to visit. Tours are a convenient way to visit a site when you are short on time or motivation; they are frequently the easiest way to visit remote areas. They can also be relatively cheap, depending on the number of people in your group and the mode of transportation.

There are scores of outfits offering trekking, mountain-climbing and rainforest-adventure packages around Bolivia. For climbing in the Cordilleras, operators offer customized expeditions. They can arrange anything from just a guide and transportation right up to equipment, porters and even a cook. Some also rent trekking equipment.

For biking companies, see p74. The following is a list of recommended agencies around the country.

Adventure Climbing & Trekking of South America (☎ 2-241-4197; newhorizons20@hotmail.com; Jaimes Freyre 2950, Sopocachi, La Paz) Carlos Escobar is a UIAGM/UIAA certified international mountain guide (who climbed Mt Everest) and runs serious climbing expeditions to Illampu, Huayna Potosí and others.

Akapana Tours (☎ 2-242-0013; www.akapanatours .com; Piso 11-D, Edificio Melissa, Av Sanchez Lima 2512, Sopocachi, La Paz) German-run agency that offers a variety of personalized tours all over Bolivia with a focus on adventure, culture, trekking and climbing. They specialize in off-the-beaten-path destinations such as Cordillera Apolobamba, Cordillera Quimsa Cruz and Torototo.

America Tours (Map pp68-9; ☎ 2-237-4204; www .america-ecotours.com; Avenida 16 de Julio 1490 No 9, La Paz) Warmly recommended English-speaking agency that organizes trips to anywhere in the country. Specializes in new routes and community-based ecotourism in such places as Parque Nacional Madidi, Parque Nacional Sajama, Rurrenabaque and Salar de Uyuni.

Andean Summits (☎ 2-242-2106; www.andean summits.com; Muñoz Cornejo 1009, Sopocachi, La Paz) Mountaineering, trekking and 4WD tours all over Bolivia, plus adventure tours, bird-watching excursions and archaeology trips, as well as kayaking and sailing.

Bolivian Journeys (☎ 2-235-7848; www.bolivian journeys.org; Sagárnaga 363, La Paz) Specialists in climbing, mountaineering and trekking, they organize guided climbs to Huayna Potosí. Equipment rental is available; maps and gas for MSR stoves are for sale.

Bolivia Milenaria (☎ 2-291-1275; www.millen ariantours.com; Avenida Sanchez Lima 2193, Sopocachi, La Paz) This agency manages Tomarapi in Sajama and offers cultural tours around Bolivia.

Bolivia Specialist (Map pp212-3; ☎ 4-643-7389 www. boliviaspecialist.com; Calle Nicolás Ortíz 30, Sucre) The Dutch owner Dirko and his English-speaking Bolivian staff are real experts on Bolivia, and very friendly and knowledgeable about all corners of the country.

Calacoto Tours (Map p76; ☎ 2-211-2524; www .calacototours.com, in Spanish; Calle 13 8009 with Sanchez Bustamante, La Paz). Specializes in horseback-riding trail rides in the Valle de las Animas and Muela del Diablo, and also offers tours to Lake Titicaca and the islands, Coroico and other nearby attractions.

Candelaria Tours (Map pp212-3; ☎ 4-646-0289; www.candelariatours.com; Audiencia 1, Sucre) One of the most established and professional travel agencies in Sucre offering a variety of tours around Bolivia. They also have participatory programs where visitors can work with indigenous communities, especially with textiles. Arranges travel and accommodations. Fluent in English.

Crillon Tours (☎ 2-233-7533; www.titicaca.com; Camacho 1223, La Paz) An upmarket option offering a range of tours, including the hydrofoil services in Lake Titicaca. They also offer luxury lodgings on the lake.

Forest Tours (☎ 3-337-2042; www.forestbolivia.com; Junín & 21 de Mayo, Galería Casco Viejo, Office 115, Santa Cruz) English-speaking and extremely helpful, offering tours in the Santa Cruz region and elsewhere, including Samaipata, the Ché Trail, and Amboró and Noel Kempff national parks.

Fremen Tours Bolivia (☎ 2-244-0242; www.andes -amazonia.com; Oficina 6-C, Edificio V Centenario, Avenida 6 de Agosto with J J Perez, La Paz) Upmarket agency with offices in Cochabamba, Santa Cruz and Trinidad. Specializes in adventure trips in the Amazon and Chapare.

Inca Land Tours (☎ 2-231-6760; www.incalandtours .com; Sagárnaga 213 No 10, La Paz) Established Peruvian budget operation running tours out of Rurrenabaque and Coroico; it arranges its own charter flights to Rurre and will book tickets in advance with TAM and Amazonas – at a premium.

Magri Turismo (Map pp68-9; ☎ 2-244-2727; www .magriturismo.com; Capitan Ravelo 2101, La Paz) Established agency and American Express representative offering tours to the eastern, southern and La Paz regions of Bolivia including adventure and climbing activities.

Michael Blendinger Tours (Map p279; ☎ /fax 3-944-6227; www.discoveringbolivia.com; Bolívar s/n, Samaipata) Based in Samaipata, biologist Michael Blendinger specializes in tours to the southern Amboró and surrounding region. Also does birding tours as well as trips along the Ché Trail and all around Bolivia. English and German spoken.

Topas Bolivia (☎ 2-211-1082; www .topas.bo; Carlos Bravo 299, La Paz) A joint venture between Topas Denmark and Akhamani Trekking, this English-speaking adventure travel agency is run by experienced people and offers high-quality tours all around Bolivia, with a special focus on trekking and climbing.

Travel Tracks (☎ 2-231-6934; www.travel-tracks.com; Sagárnaga 213 & Sagárnaga 366, La Paz) This English-speaking agency is an excellent choice for guided hikes as well as customized trips. There's free internet for customers and a book exchange.

Turisbus (Map pp68-9; ☎ 2-245-1341; www.turisbus .com; Hotel Rosario, Illampu 702, La Paz) Upmarket agency specializing in Lake Titicaca tours, as well as culture and nature trips all around Bolivia.

TRANSPORTATION

Health

CONTENTS

Before You Go	**352**
H1N1	352
Insurance	352
Medical Checklist	352
Online Resources	353
Further Reading	353
In Transit	**353**
Deep Vein Thrombosis	353
Jet Lag & Motion Sickness	354
In Bolivia	**354**
Availability & Cost of Healthcare	354
Infectious Diseases	354
Travelers' Diarrhea	358
Environmental Hazards	358
Traveling with Children	359
Women's Health	360

Prevention is the key to staying healthy while traveling in Bolivia, as in other countries. Travelers who receive the recommended vaccinations (see box, opposite) and follow a few basic common-sense precautions usually come away with nothing more unpleasant than a little diarrhea.

BEFORE YOU GO

Since most vaccines don't produce immunity until at least two weeks after they're given, visit a physician four to eight weeks before departure. Ask your doctor for an International Certificate of Vaccination, containing a list of your vaccinations. This is mandatory for countries such as Bolivia, Brazil and Venezuela, which may require proof of yellow fever vaccination on entry, but it's a good idea to carry it wherever you travel.

Bring medications in their original containers, clearly labeled, and a signed, dated letter from your physician describing all medical conditions. If carrying syringes or needles, have a physician's letter stating their medical necessity.

H1N1

The H1N1 virus (commonly referred to as 'swine flu') was given a 'Phase 6' rating by the World Health Organization in June 2009. This means that the virus is now considered to be a global pandemic. Like most countries, Bolivia has been affected. As of October 2009, the virus was widespread geographically in Bolivia but the number of cases was relatively low, as was the severity of these cases.

At press time, airport staff in some countries were screening arriving passengers for symptoms of H1N1 flu. Check with the embassy of the country you're visiting to see if they have imposed any travel restrictions. It's best not to travel if you have flu-like symptoms of any sort.

For the latest information, check with the **World Health Organization** (www.who.int).

INSURANCE

If your health insurance does not cover you for medical expenses abroad, consider supplemental insurance. Check the Bookings & Services section of the website of **Lonely Planet** (www.lonelyplanet.com/travel_services) for more information. Find out in advance if your insurance plan will make payments directly to providers or reimburse you later for overseas health expenditures. Most private-practice providers in Bolivia expect cash payment and should provide receipts for your insurance company claims and reimbursement. Credit cards are usually not accepted for medical services.

MEDICAL CHECKLIST

- antibiotics
- antidiarrheal drugs (eg loperamide)
- acetaminophen (Tylenol) or aspirin
- anti-inflammatory drugs (eg ibuprofen)
- antihistamines (for hay fever and allergic reactions)
- antibacterial ointment (eg Bactroban) for cuts and abrasions
- steroid cream or cortisone (for poison ivy and other allergic rashes)
- bandages, gauze, gauze rolls
- adhesive or paper tape
- scissors, safety pins, tweezers

RECOMMENDED VACCINATIONS

The only required vaccine for Bolivia is yellow fever, and that's only if you're arriving in Bolivia from a yellow-fever-infected country in Africa or the Americas. However, a number of other vaccines are recommended:

Vaccine	Recommended for	Dosage	Side effects
Chickenpox	Travelers who have never had chickenpox	Two doses one month apart	Fever; mild case of chickenpox
Hepatitis A	All travelers	One dose before trip; booster six to 12 months	Soreness at injection site, headaches, body aches
Hepatitis B	Long-term travelers in close contact with the local population	Three doses over a six-month period	Soreness at injection site, low-grade fever
Measles	Travelers born after 1956 who have had only one measles vaccination	One dose	Fever, rash, joint pains, allergic reactions
Rabies	Travelers who may have contact with animals and may not have access to medical care	Three doses over a three- to four-week period	Soreness at injection site, headaches, body aches
Tetanus/diphtheria	All travelers who haven't had a booster within 10 years	One dose lasts 10 years	Soreness at injection site
Typhoid	All travelers	Four capsules by mouth, one taken every other day	Abdominal pain, nausea, rash
Yellow fever	Travelers to Beni, Cochabamba, Santa Cruz, La Paz, possibly other areas	One dose lasts 10 years	Headaches, body aches; severe reactions are rare

- thermometer
- pocket knife
- DEET-containing insect repellent for the skin
- permethrin-containing insect spray for clothing, tents and bed nets
- sun block
- oral rehydration salts
- iodine tablets (for water purification)
- syringes and sterile needles
- acetazolamide (eg Diamox) for altitude sickness

ONLINE RESOURCES

There is a wealth of travel health advice on the internet. For further information, the **Lonely Planet website** (www.lonelyplanet.com) is a good place to start. The **World Health Organization** (www.who.int/ith) annually publishes *International Travel and Health,* which is revised annually and is available online at no cost. Another website of general interest is **MD Travel Health** (www.mdtravelhealth.com), which provides complete travel health recommendations for every country and is updated daily.

Consult your government's travel health website before departure:

Australia (www.smartraveller.gov.au/tips/travelwell .html)

Canada (www.hc-sc.gc.ca/english/index.html)

UK (www.direct.gov.uk/en/TravelAndTransport/index .htm)

US (www.cdc.gov/travel)

FURTHER READING

For further information see *Healthy Travel Central & South America,* also from Lonely Planet. If you are traveling with children, Lonely Planet's *Travel with Children* might well be useful. The *ABC of Healthy Travel,* by E Walker et al, is another very valuable resource.

IN TRANSIT

DEEP VEIN THROMBOSIS

Blood clots may form in the legs (deep vein thrombosis) during plane flights, chiefly because of prolonged immobility. The longer the flight, the greater the risk. Though most blood clots are reabsorbed uneventfully, some may break off and travel through the blood vessels to the lungs, where they could cause life-threatening complications.

The chief symptom of deep vein thrombosis is swelling or pain of the foot, ankle or calf, usually but not always on just one side. When a blood clot travels to the lungs, it may cause chest pain and difficulty breathing. Travelers with any of these symptoms should immediately seek medical attention.

To prevent deep vein thrombosis on long flights, walk about the cabin, perform isometric compressions of the leg muscles (ie contract the leg muscles while sitting), drink plenty of fluids, and avoid alcohol.

JET LAG & MOTION SICKNESS

Jet lag is common when crossing more than five time zones, leading to insomnia, fatigue, malaise or nausea. To avoid jet lag try drinking plenty of fluids (nonalcoholic) and eating light meals. On arrival get exposure to natural sunlight and readjust your schedule (for meals, sleep, etc) as soon as possible.

Antihistamines such as dimenhydrinate (Dramamine) and meclizine (Antivert, Bonine) are usually the first choice for treating motion sickness. Their main side effect is drowsiness. A herbal alternative is ginger.

IN BOLIVIA

AVAILABILITY & COST OF HEALTHCARE

Good medical care is available in the larger cities, but may be difficult to find in rural areas. Many doctors and hospitals expect payment in cash, regardless of whether you have travel health insurance. For a medical emergency in La Paz, call **SAMI ambulance** (☎ 2-279-9911) or go directly to the **Clinica del Sur emergency room** (☎ 2-278-4001/02/03; cnr Hernando Siles & Calle 7, Obrajes). In Cochabamba, call the **Medicar Emergency Ambulance Service** (☎ 4-453-3222) or go to the emergency room of **Centro Medico Boliviano Belga** (☎ 4-422-9407, 425-0928, 423-1403; Antezana, btwn Venezuela & Paccieri N-0455). In Santa Cruz, go to the emergency room of **Clinica Angel Foianini** (☎ 3-336-2211, 336-6001/02/03/04; Irala 468). A taxi may get you to the emergency room faster than an ambulance. For a list of reputable medical and dental contacts in La Paz, see also p65.

If you are unlucky enough to develop a life-threatening medical problem, you'll probably want to be evacuated to a country that is able to provide state-of-the-art medical care. Since this may cost tens of thousands of dollars, be sure you have insurance to cover this before you depart.

Bolivian pharmacies offer most of the medications available in other countries. In general it's safer to buy pharmaceuticals made by international manufacturers rather than local companies; buy the brand name prescribed by your doctor, not the generic brand drugs that may be offered at lower prices. These medications may be out of date or have no quality control from the manufacturer. For a list of pharmacies, see the US Embassy website (http://bolivia.usembassy .gov/uploads/images/eOd9_kCdEz0Za _pollKATw/PHYSICIANSLIST1.pdf).

INFECTIOUS DISEASES
Cholera

Cholera is an intestinal infection acquired through ingestion of contaminated food or water. The main symptom is profuse, watery diarrhea, which may be so severe that it causes life-threatening dehydration. The key treatment is drinking oral rehydration solution. Antibiotics are also given, usually tetracycline or doxycycline, though quinolone antibiotics such as ciprofloxacin and levofloxacin are also effective.

Cholera sometimes occurs in Bolivia, but it's rare among travelers. A cholera vaccine is no longer required. There are effective vaccines, but they're not available in many countries and are only recommended for those at particularly high risk.

Dengue Fever

Dengue fever is a viral infection found throughout South America. Dengue is transmitted by Aedes mosquitoes, which bite preferentially during the daytime and are usually found close to human habitations, often indoors. They breed in artificial water containers, such as jars, barrels, cans, cisterns, metal drums, plastic containers and discarded tires. As a result, dengue is especially common in densely populated, urban environments.

Dengue causes flu-like symptoms, including fever, muscle aches, joint pains, headaches, nausea and vomiting, often followed by a rash. The body aches may be quite uncomfortable, but most cases resolve uneventfully in a few days. Severe cases usually occur in children under age 15 who are experiencing their second dengue infection.

There is no specific antiviral treatment for dengue fever except to take analgesics such as acetaminophen/paracetamol (Tylenol) and drink plenty of fluids. Severe cases of the disease may require hospitalization for administration of intravenous fluids and supportive care. There is no vaccine. The cornerstone of prevention is to take adequate insect protection measures (p359).

In winter 2009, there was a major outbreak of dengue fever that turned into a countrywide health emergency. This usually happens during the rainy season in the areas below 2800m, so make sure you read the travel advisories.

Hepatitis A

Hepatitis A is the second most common travel-related infection (after travelers' diarrhea). It's a viral infection of the liver that is usually acquired by ingestion of contaminated water, food or ice, or by direct contact with infected persons. The illness occurs throughout the world, but the incidence is higher in developing nations. Symptoms may include fever, malaise, jaundice, nausea, vomiting and abdominal pain. Most cases resolve without complications, though hepatitis A occasionally causes severe liver damage. There is no treatment.

The vaccine for hepatitis A is extremely safe and effective. A booster six to 12 months later lasts for at least 10 years. It is encouraged for Bolivia. A vaccine has not been established for pregnant women or children under two years – instead, they should be given a gammaglobulin injection.

Hepatitis B

Like hepatitis A, hepatitis B is a liver infection that occurs worldwide but is more common in developing nations. Unlike hepatitis A, the disease is usually acquired by sexual contact or by exposure to infected blood, generally through blood transfusions or contaminated needles. The vaccine is recommended only for long-term travelers (on the road more than six months) who expect to live in rural areas or have close physical contact with the local population. Additionally, the vaccine is recommended for anyone who anticipates sexual contact with the local inhabitants or a possible need for medical, dental or other treatments while abroad, especially if a need for transfusions or injections is expected.

The hepatitis B vaccine is safe and highly effective. However, a total of three injections are necessary to establish full immunity. Several countries added the hepatitis B vaccine to the list of routine childhood immunizations in the 1980s, so many young adults are already protected.

Malaria

Malaria occurs in every South American country except Chile, Uruguay and the Falkland Islands. It's transmitted by mosquito bites, usually between dusk and dawn. The main symptom is high spiking fevers, which may be accompanied by chills, sweats, headache, body aches, weakness, vomiting or diarrhea. Severe cases may involve the central nervous system and lead to seizures, confusion, coma and death.

Taking malaria pills is strongly recommended for areas below 2500m (8202ft) in the departments of Beni, Santa Cruz and Pando, where the risk is highest. Falciparum malaria, which is the most dangerous kind, occurs in Beni and Pando. Malaria is not present in the cities of these departments currently.

There is a choice of three malaria pills, all of which work about equally well. Mefloquine (Lariam) is taken once weekly in a dosage of 250mg, starting one to two weeks before arrival, and continuing through the trip and for four weeks after return. The problem is that a certain percentage of people (the number is controversial) develop neuropsychiatric side effects, which may range from mild to severe. Stomachache and diarrhea are also common. Atovaquone/proguanil (Malarone) is taken once daily with food, starting two days before arrival and continuing daily until seven days after departure. Side effects are typically mild. Doxycycline is relatively inexpensive and easy to obtain, but it is taken daily and can cause an exaggerated sunburn reaction.

HEALTH

For longer trips it's probably worth trying mefloquine; for shorter trips, Malarone will be the drug of choice for most people.

Protecting yourself against mosquito bites is just as important as taking malaria pills (for recommendations see p359), since none of the pills are 100% effective.

If you may not have access to medical care while traveling, you should bring along additional pills for emergency self-treatment, which you should take if you can't reach a doctor and you develop symptoms that suggest malaria, such as high spiking fevers. One option is to take four tablets of Malarone once daily for three days. However, Malarone should not be used for treatment if you're already taking it for prevention. An alternative is to take 650mg quinine three times daily and 100mg doxycycline twice daily for one week. If you start self-medication, see a doctor at the earliest possible opportunity.

If you develop a fever after returning home, see a physician, as malaria symptoms may not occur for months.

Plague

Small outbreaks of the plague sometimes occur in Bolivia, most recently in the town of San Pedro (in the department of La Paz) in the mid-1990s. The plague is usually transmitted to humans by the bite of rodent fleas, typically when rodents die off. Symptoms include fever, chills, muscle aches and malaise, associated with the development of an acutely swollen, exquisitely painful lymph node, known as a bubo, most often in the groin. Most travelers are at extremely low risk for this disease. However, if you might have contact with rodents or their fleas, you should bring along a bottle of doxycycline, to be taken prophylactically during periods of exposure. Those less than eight years old or allergic to doxycycline should take trimethoprim-sulfamethoxazole instead. In addition, you should avoid areas containing rodent burrows or nests, never handle sick or dead animals, and follow the guidelines in this chapter for protecting yourself from insect bites (p359).

Rabies

Rabies is a viral infection of the brain and spinal cord that is almost always fatal. The rabies virus is carried in the saliva of infected animals and is typically transmitted through an animal bite, though contamination of any break in the skin with infected saliva may result in rabies. Rabies occurs in all South American countries. In Bolivia most cases are related to dog bites. Risk is greatest in the southeastern part of the country.

The rabies vaccine is safe, but a full series requires three injections and is quite expensive. Those at high risk for rabies, such as animal handlers and spelunkers (cave explorers), should certainly get the vaccine. In addition, those at lower risk for animal bites should consider asking for the vaccine if they might be traveling to remote areas and might not have access to appropriate medical care if needed. The treatment for a possibly rabid bite consists of the rabies vaccine with rabies-immune globulin. It's effective, but must be given promptly. Most travelers don't need the rabies vaccine.

All animal bites and scratches must be promptly and thoroughly cleansed with large amounts of soap and water; contact health authorities to determine whether further treatment is necessary (p359).

Typhoid Fever

Typhoid fever is caused by the ingestion of food or water contaminated by a species of salmonella known as salmonella typhi. Fever occurs in virtually all cases. Other symptoms may include headache, malaise, muscle aches, dizziness, loss of appetite, nausea and abdominal pain. Either diarrhea or constipation may occur. Possible complications include intestinal perforation, intestinal bleeding, confusion, delirium or (rarely) coma.

A typhoid vaccine is a good idea. It's usually given orally, but is also available as an injection. Neither vaccine is approved for use in children under age two.

It is not a good idea to self-treat for typhoid fever as the symptoms may be indistinguishable from malaria. If you show symptoms for either, see a doctor immediately – treatment is likely to be a quinolone antibiotic such as ciprofloxacin (Cipro) or levofloxacin (Levaquin).

Yellow Fever

Yellow fever is a life-threatening viral infection transmitted by mosquitoes in forested areas. The illness begins with flu-like symptoms, such as fever, chills, headache, muscle aches, backache, loss of appetite, nausea and vomiting. These symptoms usually subside in a few days, but one person in six enters a second, toxic phase characterized by recurrent fever, vomiting, listlessness, jaundice, kidney failure and hemorrhage, leading to death in up to half of the cases. At the present time, there is no treatment except for supportive and palliative care.

Yellow-fever vaccine is strongly recommended for all those visiting areas where yellow fever occurs, which at time of publication included the departments of Beni, Cochabamba, Santa Cruz and La Paz. For the latest information on which areas in Bolivia are reporting yellow fever, go to the 'Blue Sheet' on the website of **Centers for Disease Control & Protection** (CDC; www.cdc.gov/travel/blusheet.htm).

Proof of vaccination is required from all travelers arriving from a yellow-fever-infected country in Africa or the Americas.

The yellow-fever vaccine is given only in approved yellow fever vaccination centers, which provide validated International Certificates of Vaccination (yellow booklets). The vaccine should be given at least 10 days before any potential exposure to yellow fever, and remains effective for approximately 10 years. Reactions to the vaccine are generally mild and may include headaches, muscle aches, low-grade fevers or discomfort at the injection site. Severe, life-threatening reactions have been described but are extremely rare. In general the risk of becoming ill from the vaccine is far less than the risk of becoming ill from yellow fever, and you're strongly encouraged to get the vaccine.

Taking measures to protect yourself from mosquito bites (p359) is an essential part of preventing yellow fever.

Other Infections
BARTONELLOSIS
Bartonellosis (Oroya fever) is carried by sandflies in the arid river valleys on the western slopes of the Andes in Peru, Bolivia, Colombia and Ecuador between the altitudes of 800m (2625ft) and 3000m (9843ft). (Curiously, it's not found anywhere else in the world.) The chief symptoms are fever and severe body pains. Complications may include marked anemia, enlargement of the liver and spleen, and sometimes death. The drug of choice is chloramphenicol, though doxycycline is also effective.

BOLIVIAN HEMORRHAGIC FEVER
Bolivian hemorrhagic fever has been reported from the Beni Department in the northeastern part of the country. The causative organism, known as Machupo virus, is probably acquired by exposure to rodents.

CHAGAS' DISEASE
Chagas' disease is a parasitic infection that is transmitted by triatomine insects (reduviid bugs), which inhabit crevices in the walls and roofs of substandard housing in South and Central America. In Bolivia most cases occur in temperate areas, especially in the departments of Cochabamba, Chuquisaca and Tarija. The triatomine insect lays its feces on human skin as it bites, usually at night. A person becomes infected when he or she unknowingly rubs the feces into the bite wound or sore. Chagas' disease is extremely rare in travelers. However, always protect yourself with a bed net and a good insecticide if in mud, adobe or thatched houses. Do not accept blood transfusions if in these areas – local incidence of the disease is high.

HIV/AIDS
HIV/AIDS has been reported from all South American countries. Be sure to use condoms for all sexual encounters.

LEISHMANIASIS
Leishmaniasis occurs in the mountains and jungles of all South American countries except for Chile and Uruguay. The infection is transmitted by sandflies, which are about one-third the size of mosquitoes. In Bolivia, risk is greatest in the forested foothill regions east of the Andean Cordillera. Most cases of leishmaniasis are limited to the skin, causing slowly growing ulcers over exposed parts of the body. The more severe type, which disseminates to the bone marrow, liver and spleen, occurs only in the Yungas. Leishmaniasis may be particularly severe in those with HIV. There is no vaccine. To protect yourself from sandflies, follow the same precautions as for mosquitoes (p359), except that netting must be finer-mesh (at least 18 holes to the linear inch).

HEALTH

HEALTH

TYPHUS

Typhus may be transmitted by lice in mountainous areas near La Paz.

TRAVELERS' DIARRHEA

To prevent diarrhea, avoid tap water unless it has been boiled, filtered or chemically disinfected (with iodine tablets); only eat fresh fruits or vegetables if peeled or cooked; be wary of dairy products that might contain unpasteurized milk; and be highly selective when eating food from street vendors.

If you develop diarrhea, be sure to drink plenty of fluids, preferably an oral rehydration solution containing lots of salt and sugar. A few loose stools don't require treatment but if you start having more than four or five stools a day you should start taking an antibiotic (usually a quinolone drug) and an antidiarrheal agent (such as loperamide). If diarrhea is bloody, or persists for more than 72 hours or is accompanied by fever, shaking chills or severe abdominal pain, you should seek medical attention.

ENVIRONMENTAL HAZARDS
Altitude Sickness

Altitude sickness may develop in those who ascend rapidly to altitudes greater than 2500m (8100ft). In Bolivia this includes La Paz (altitude 4000m). Being physically fit offers no protection. Those who have experienced altitude sickness in the past are prone to future episodes. The risk increases with faster ascents, higher altitudes and greater exertion. Symptoms may include headaches, nausea, vomiting, dizziness, malaise, insomnia and loss of appetite. Severe cases may be further complicated by fluid in the lungs (high-altitude pulmonary edema) or swelling of the brain (high-altitude cerebral edema).

The best treatment for altitude sickness is descent. If you are exhibiting symptoms, do not ascend. If symptoms are severe or persistent, descend immediately.

To protect yourself against altitude sickness, take 125mg or 250mg acetazolamide (Diamox) twice or three times daily, starting 24 hours before ascent and continuing for 48 hours after arrival at altitude. Possible side effects include increased urinary volume, numbness, tingling, nausea, drowsiness, myopia and temporary impotence.

Acetazolamide should not be given to pregnant women or anyone with a history of sulfa allergy.

For those who cannot tolerate acetazolamide, the next best option is 4mg dexamethasone taken four times daily, best with medical supervision. Unlike acetazolamide, dexamethasone must be tapered gradually on arrival at altitude if taken for longer than 10 days, since there is a risk that altitude sickness will occur as the dosage is reduced. Dexamethasone is a steroid, so it should not be given to diabetics or anyone for whom steroids are contraindicated. A natural alternative is gingko, which helps some people.

When traveling to high altitudes, it's also important to avoid overexertion, eat light meals and abstain from alcohol.

If your symptoms are more than mild or don't resolve promptly, see a doctor immediately. Altitude sickness should be taken very seriously; it can be life-threatening when severe.

Animal Bites

Do not attempt to pet, handle or feed any animal, with the exception of domestic animals known to be free of any infectious disease. Most animal injuries are directly related to a person's attempt to touch or feed an animal.

Any bite or scratch by a mammal, including bats, should be promptly and thoroughly cleansed with large amounts of soap and water, followed by application of an antiseptic such as iodine or alcohol. The local health authorities should be contacted immediately for possible post-exposure rabies treatment, whether or not you've been immunized against rabies. It may also be advisable to start an antibiotic, since wounds caused by animal bites and scratches frequently become infected. Or use one of the newer quinolones, such

FOLK MEDICINE	
Problem	**Treatment**
Altitude sickness	Ginkgo; coca leaf tea
Jet lag	Melatonin
Motion sickness	Ginger
Mosquito-bite prevention	Oil of eucalyptus; coconut oil

as levofloxacin (Levaquin), which many travelers carry in case of diarrhea.

Snakes and leeches are a hazard in some areas of South America. In Bolivia there are two species of poisonous snakes: pit vipers (rattlesnakes) and coral snakes. These are found chiefly in sugar and banana plantations, and in the dry, hilly regions. In the event of a venomous snake bite, place the victim at rest, keep the bitten area immobilized and move the victim to the nearest medical facility immediately. Tourniquets are no longer recommended.

Insect Bites & Stings

To prevent mosquito bites, wear long sleeves, long pants, hats and shoes (rather than sandals). Bring along a good insect repellent, preferably one containing DEET, which should be applied to exposed skin and clothing, but not to eyes, mouth, cuts, wounds or irritated skin. Products containing lower concentrations of DEET are as effective, but for shorter periods of time. In general, adults and children over 12 should use preparations containing 25% to 35% DEET, which usually lasts about six hours. Children between two and 12 years of age should use preparations containing no more than 10% DEET, applied sparingly, which will usually last about three hours. Neurologic toxicity has been reported from DEET, especially in children, but appears to be extremely uncommon and generally related to overuse. DEET-containing compounds should not be used on children under age two.

Insect repellents containing certain botanical products, including oil of eucalyptus and soybean oil, are effective but last only 1½ to two hours. DEET-containing repellents are preferable for areas where there is a high risk of malaria or yellow fever. Products based on citronella are not effective.

For additional protection you can apply permethrin to clothing, shoes, tents and bed nets. Permethrin treatments are safe and remain effective for at least two weeks, even when items are laundered. Permethrin should not be applied directly to skin.

Don't sleep with the window open unless there is a screen. If sleeping outdoors or in accommodations that allow entry of mosquitoes, use a fine-mesh bed net, preferably treated with permethrin, with edges tucked in under the mattress. If the sleeping area is not protected, use a mosquito coil, which will fill the room with insecticide through the night. Repellent-impregnated wristbands are not effective.

Sunburn & Heat Exhaustion

To protect yourself from excessive sun exposure, stay out of the midday sun, wear sunglasses and a wide-brimmed sun hat, and apply sunscreen with SPF 15 or higher, with both UVA and UVB protection. Sunscreen should be generously applied to all exposed parts of the body approximately 30 minutes before sun exposure and should be reapplied after swimming or vigorous activity. Travelers should also drink plenty of fluids and avoid strenuous exercise in high temperatures.

Water

Tap water in Bolivia is not safe to drink. Vigorous boiling for one minute is the most effective means of water purification. At altitudes greater than 2000m (6500ft), boil for three minutes.

Another option is to disinfect water with iodine pills such as Globaline, Potable-Aqua and Coghlan's, available at most pharmacies. Instructions are enclosed and should be carefully followed. Or you can add 2% tincture of iodine to one quart or liter of water (five drops to clear water, 10 drops to cloudy water) and let it stand for 30 minutes. If the water is cold, longer times may be required. The taste of iodinated water may be improved by adding vitamin C (ascorbic acid). Iodinated water should not be consumed for more than a few weeks. Pregnant women, those with a history of thyroid disease and those allergic to iodine should not drink iodinated water.

A number of water filters are on the market. Those with smaller pores (reverse osmosis filters) provide the broadest protection, but they are relatively large and are readily plugged by debris. Those with larger pores (microstrainer filters) are ineffective against viruses, although they remove other organisms. Manufacturers' instructions must be carefully followed.

TRAVELING WITH CHILDREN

When traveling with young children, be particularly careful about what you allow them to eat and drink, because diarrhea can be especially dangerous in this age group and because the vaccines for hepatitis A and typhoid fever are not approved for use in children under two years.

Since there's little information concerning the medical consequences of taking children to high altitudes, it's probably safer not to do so. Also, children under nine months should not be brought to areas where yellow fever occurs, since the vaccine is not safe in this age group.

The main malaria medications, Lariam and Malarone, may be given to children, but insect repellents must be applied in lower concentrations.

WOMEN'S HEALTH

There are English-speaking obstetricians in Bolivia, listed on the **US Embassy website** (http://bolivia.usembassy.gov). However, medical facilities will probably not be comparable to those in your home country, so it's safer to avoid travel to Bolivia late in pregnancy.

If pregnant, avoid travel to high altitudes, where lower oxygen levels can slow fetal growth, especially after the 32nd week. Also, it's safer not to visit areas where yellow fever occurs, since the vaccine is not safe during pregnancy.

If taking malaria pills, mefloquine (Lariam) is the safest during pregnancy.

Language

CONTENTS

Spanish	**361**
Pronunciation	361
Gender & Plurals	362
Accommodations	362
Conversation & Essentials	362
Directions	363
Health	363
Language Difficulties	364
Numbers	364
Shopping & Services	364
Time & Dates	365
Emergencies	365
Transportation	366
Travel with Children	366
Aymará & Quechua	**367**

The official language of Bolivia is Spanish, but only 60% to 70% of the people speak it, and then often only as a second language. The remainder speak Quechua (the language of the Inca conquerors) or Aymará (the pre-Inca language of the Altiplano). In addition, a host of other minor indigenous tongues are used in small areas throughout the country. English won't get you very far in Bolivia but, fortunately, it's not difficult to learn the basics of Spanish. You might not be able to carry on a deep and meaningful philosophical or political discussion after a short course or self-teaching program, but you'll have the tools you need for basic communication.

SPANISH

Spanish courses in Bolivia are available in La Paz, Cochabamba and Sucre for those who want to learn the language in greater depth while in the country.

For a more comprehensive guide to the Spanish of Bolivia than we can offer here, pick up Lonely Planet's *Latin American Spanish Phrasebook*. Another useful resource is the compact *University of Chicago Spanish Dictionary*. For words and phrases for use when ordering at a restaurant, see p46.

PRONUNCIATION

Spanish spelling is phonetically consistent, meaning that there's a clear and consistent relationship between what you see in writing and how it's pronounced. In addition, most Spanish sounds have English equivalents, so English speakers should not have much trouble being understood if the rules listed below are adhered to.

Vowels
a as in 'father'
e as in 'met'
i as in 'marine'
o as in 'or' (without the 'r' sound)
u as in 'rule'; the 'u' is not pronounced after **q** and in the letter combinations **gue** and **gui**, unless it's marked with a diaeresis (eg *argüir*), in which case it's pronounced as English 'w'
y at the end of a word or when it stands alone, it's pronounced as the Spanish **i** (eg *ley*); between vowels within a word it's as the 'y' in 'yes'

Consonants
As a rule, Spanish consonants resemble their English counterparts, with the exceptions listed below.

While the consonants **ch**, **ll** and **ñ** are generally considered distinct letters, **ch** and **ll** are now often listed alphabetically under **c** and **l** respectively. The letter **ñ** is still treated as a separate letter and comes after **n** in dictionaries.

b similar to English 'b,' but softer; referred to as 'b larga'
c as in 'celery' before **e** and **i**; otherwise as English 'k'
ch as in 'church'
d as in 'dog'; between vowels and after **l** or **n**, the sound is closer to the 'th' in 'this'
g as the 'ch' in the Scottish *loch* before **e** and **i** ('kh' in our guides to pronunciation); elsewhere, as in 'go'
h silent, ie never pronounced

j	as the 'ch' in the Scottish *loch* (written as 'kh' in our guides to pronunciation)
ll	as the 'y' in 'yellow'
ñ	as the 'ni' in 'onion'
r	a slap of the tongue against the palate (like the 'd' in 'ladder'); at the beginning of a word or after **l**, **n** or **s**, it's strongly rolled, though some Bolivians pronounce it as the 's' in 'pleasure'
rr	very strongly rolled
v	similar to English 'b,' but softer; referred to as 'b corta'
x	as in 'taxi,' except for a very few words when it's pronounced as **j**
z	as the 's' in 'sun'

Word Stress

In general, words ending in vowels or the letters **n** or **s** have stress on the next-to-last syllable, while those with other endings have stress on the last syllable. Thus *vaca* (cow) and *caballos* (horses) both carry stress on the next-to-last syllable, while *ciudad* (city) and *infeliz* (unhappy) are both stressed on the last syllable.

Written accents will almost always appear in words that don't follow the rules above, eg *sótano* (basement), *América* and *porción* (portion). When counting syllables, be sure to remember that diphthongs (vowel combinations, such as the 'ue' in *puede*) constitute only one. When a word with a written accent appears in capital letters, the accent is often not written, but is still pronounced.

GENDER & PLURALS

In Spanish, nouns are either masculine or feminine, and there are rules to help determine gender (there are of course some exceptions). Feminine nouns generally end with -**a** or with the groups -**ción**, -**sión** or -**dad**. Other endings typically signify a masculine noun. Endings for adjectives change to agree with the gender of the noun they modify (masculine/feminine -**o**/-**a**). Where both masculine and feminine forms are included in this language guide, they are separated by a slash, with the masculine form first, eg *perdido/a*.

If a noun or adjective ends in a vowel, the plural is formed by adding **s** to the end. If it ends in a consonant, the plural is formed by adding **es** to the end.

ACCOMMODATIONS

I'm looking for ...	Estoy buscando ...	e·*stoy* boos·*kan*·do ...
Where is ...?	¿Dónde hay ...?	*don*·de ai ...
a hotel	un hotel	oon o·*tel*
a boarding house	una pensión/ residencial/ un hospedaje	*oo*·na pen·*syon*/ re·see·den·*syal*/ oon os·pe·*da*·khe
a youth hostel	un albergue juvenil	oon al·*ber*·ge khoo·ve·*neel*

I'd like a room.	Quisiera una habitación ...	kee·*sye*·ra *oo*·na a·bee·ta·*syon* ...
double	doble	*do*·ble
single	individual	een·dee·vee·*dwal*
twin	con dos camas	kon dos *ka*·mas

How much is it per ...?	¿Cuánto cuesta por ...?	*kwan*·to *kwes*·ta por ...
night	noche	*no*·che
person	persona	per·*so*·na
week	semana	se·*ma*·na

full board	pensión completa	pen·*syon* kom·*ple*·ta
private/shared bathroom	baño privado/ compartido	*ba*·nyo pree·va·do/ kom·par·*tee*·do
too expensive	demasiado caro	de·ma·*sya*·do *ka*·ro
cheaper	más económico	mas e·ko·*no*·mee·ko

Does it include breakfast?

¿Incluye el desayuno?   een·*kloo*·ye el de·sa·*yoo*·no

May I see the room?

¿Puedo ver la habitación?   pwe·do ver la a·bee·ta·*syon*

I don't like it.

No me gusta.   no me *goos*·ta

It's fine. I'll take it.

OK. La alquilo.   o·*kay* la al·*kee*·lo

I'm leaving now.

Me voy ahora.   me voy a·o·ra

CONVERSATION & ESSENTIALS

In their public behavior, South Americans are very conscious of civilities, sometimes to the point of ceremoniousness. Never approach a stranger for information without extending a greeting and use only the polite form of address, especially with the police and public officials. Young people may be less likely to expect this, but it's best to stick to the polite form unless you're quite sure you won't offend by using the informal. The polite form is used in all cases in this guide;

where options are given, the form is indicated by the abbreviations 'pol' and 'inf.'

Hello.	*Hola.*	*o·*la
Good morning.	*Buenos días.*	*bwe·*nos *dee·*as
Good afternoon.	*Buenas tardes.*	*bwe·*nas *tar·*des
Good evening/ night.	*Buenas noches.*	*bwe·*nas *no·*ches
Goodbye.	*Adiós.*	a·*dyos*
Bye./See you soon.	*Hasta luego.*	*as·*ta *lwe·*go
Yes.	*Sí.*	see
No.	*No.*	no
Please.	*Por favor.*	por fa·*vor*
Thank you.	*Gracias.*	*gra·*syas
Many thanks.	*Muchas gracias.*	*moo·*chas *gra·*syas
You're welcome.	*De nada.*	de *na·*da
Pardon me.	*Perdón.*	per·*don*
Excuse me.	*Permiso.*	per·*mee·*so
Forgive me.	*Disculpe.*	dees·*kool·*pe

How are things?
  ¿Qué tal? — ke tal
What's your name?
  ¿Cómo se llama? — *ko·*mo se *ya·*ma (pol)
  ¿Cómo te llamas? — *ko·*mo te *ya·*mas (inf)
My name is ...
  Me llamo ... — me *ya·*mo ...
It's a pleasure to meet you.
  Mucho gusto. — *moo·*cho *goos·*to
The pleasure is mine.
  El gusto es mío. — el *goos·*to es *mee·*o
Where are you from?
  ¿De dónde es/eres? — de *don·*de es/e·res (pol/inf)
I'm from ...
  Soy de ... — soy de ...
Where are you staying?
  ¿Dónde está alojado? — *don·*de es·*ta* a·lo·*kha·*do (pol)
  ¿Dónde estás alojado? — *don·*de es·*tas* a·lo·*kha·*do (inf)
May I take a photo?
  ¿Puedo sacar una foto? — *pwe·*do sa·*kar oo·*na *fo·*to

DIRECTIONS

north	*norte*	*nor·*te
south	*sur*	soor
east	*este/oriente*	*es·*te/o·*ryen·*te
west	*oeste/occidente*	o·*es·*te/ok·see·*den·*te
here	*aquí*	a·*kee*
there	*allí*	a·*yee*
block	*cuadra*	*kwa·*dra
street	*calle/paseo*	*ka·*lye/pa·*se·*o
mountain	*montaña/cerro/ nevado*	mon·*ta·*nya/*se·*ro/ ne·*va·*do
mountain pass	*paso/pasaje/ abra/portachuel*	*pa·*so/pa·*sa·*khe/ *a·*bra/por·ta·*chwel*

How do I get to ...?
  ¿Cómo puedo llegar a ...? — *ko·*mo *pwe·*do ye·*gar* a ...
Is it far?
  ¿Está lejos? — es·*ta le·*khos
Go straight ahead.
  Siga/Vaya derecho. — *see·*ga/*va·*ya de·*re·*cho
Turn left.
  Voltée a la izquierda. — vol·*te·*e a la ees·*kyer·*da
Turn right.
  Voltée a la derecha. — vol·*te·*e a la de·*re·*cha
I'm lost.
  Estoy perdido/a. — es·*toy* per·*dee·*do/a (m/f)
Can you show me (on the map)?
  ¿Me lo podría indicar (en el mapa)? — me lo po·*dree·*a een·dee·*kar* (en el *ma·*pa)

HEALTH

I'm sick.
  Estoy enfermo/a. — es·*toy* en·*fer·*mo/a (m/f)
I need a doctor.
  Necesito un médico. — ne·se·*see·*to oon *me·*dee·ko
Where's the hospital?
  ¿Dónde está el hospital? — *don·*de es·*ta* el os·pee·*tal*
I'm pregnant.
  Estoy embarazada. — es·*toy* em·ba·ra·*sa·*da
I've been vaccinated.
  Estoy vacunado/a. — es·*toy* va·koo·*na·*do/a (m/f)

I'm allergic to ...	*Soy alérgico/a a ...*	soy a·*ler·*khee·ko/a a ... (m/f)
antibiotics	*los antibióticos*	los an·tee·*byo·*tee·kos
peanuts	*los manies*	los ma·*nee·*es
penicillin	*la penicilina*	la pe·nee·see·*lee·*na

SIGNS	
Abierto	Open
Cerrado	Closed
Comisaria	Police Station
Entrada	Entrance
Información	Information
Prohibido	Prohibited
Salida	Exit
Servicios/Baños	Toilets
Hombres/Varones	Men
Mujeres/Damas	Women

I'm ...	Soy ...	soy ... (m/f)
asthmatic	asmático/a	as·ma·tee·ko/a
diabetic	diabético/a	dya·be·tee·ko/a
epileptic	epiléptico/a	e·pee·lep·tee·ko/a

I have ...	Tengo ...	ten·go ...
altitude sickness	soroche	so·ro·che
a cough	tos	tos
diarrhea	diarrea	dya·re·a
a headache	un dolor de cabeza	oon do·lor de ka·be·sa
nausea	náusea	now·se·a

LANGUAGE DIFFICULTIES

Do you speak (English)?
¿Habla/Hablas (inglés)?   a·bla/a·blas (een·gles) (pol/inf)
Does anyone here speak English?
¿Hay alguien que hable   ai al·gyen ke a·ble
inglés?   een·gles
I (don't) understand.
Yo (no) entiendo.   yo (no) en·tyen·do
How do you say ...?
¿Cómo se dice ...?   ko·mo se dee·se ...
What does ... mean?
¿Qué quiere decir ...?   ke kye·re de·seer ...

Could you please ...?	¿Puede ..., por favor?	pwe·de ... por fa·vor
repeat that	repetirlo	re·pe·teer·lo
speak more slowly	hablar más despacio	a·blar mas des·pa·syo
write it down	escribirlo	es·kree·beer·lo

NUMBERS

1	uno	oo·no
2	dos	dos
3	tres	tres
4	cuatro	kwa·tro
5	cinco	seen·ko
6	seis	says
7	siete	sye·te
8	ocho	o·cho
9	nueve	nwe·ve
10	diez	dyes
11	once	on·se
12	doce	do·se
13	trece	tre·se
14	catorce	ka·tor·se
15	quince	keen·se
16	dieciséis	dye·see·says
17	diecisiete	dye·see·sye·te
18	dieciocho	dye·see·o·cho
19	diecinueve	dye·see·nwe·ve
20	veinte	vayn·te
21	veintiuno	vayn·tee·oo·no
30	treinta	trayn·ta
31	treinta y uno	trayn·ta ee oo·no
40	cuarenta	kwa·ren·ta
50	cincuenta	seen·kwen·ta
60	sesenta	se·sen·ta
70	setenta	se·ten·ta
80	ochenta	o·chen·ta
90	noventa	no·ven·ta
100	cien	syen
101	ciento uno	syen·to oo·no
200	doscientos	do·syen·tos
1000	mil	meel
5000	cinco mil	seen·ko meel
10,000	diez mil	dyes meel
50,000	cincuenta mil	seen·kwen·ta meel
100,000	cien mil	syen meel
1,000,000	un millón	oon mee·yon

SHOPPING & SERVICES

I'd like to buy ...
Quisiera comprar ...   kee·sye·ra kom·prar ...
I'm just looking.
Sólo estoy mirando.   so·lo es·toy mee·ran·do
May I look at it?
¿Puedo mirar(lo/la)?   pwe·do mee·rar·(lo/la) (m/f)
How much is it?
¿Cuánto cuesta?   kwan·to kwes·ta
That's too expensive for me.
Es demasiado caro   es de·ma·sya·do ka·ro
para mí.   pa·ra mee
Could you lower the price?
¿Podría bajar un poco   po·dree·a ba·khar oon po·ko
el precio?   el pre·syo
I don't like it.
No me gusta.   no me goos·ta
I'll take it.
Lo llevo.   lo ye·vo

less	menos	me·nos
more	más	mas
large	grande	gran·de
small	pequeño/a	pe·ke·nyo/a (m/f)

Do you accept ...?	*¿Aceptan ...?*	a·sep·*tan* ...
American dollars	*dólares americanos*	do·la·res a·me·ree·*ka*·nos
credit cards	*tarjetas de crédito*	tar·*khe*·tas de kre·dee·to
traveler's checks	*cheques de viajero*	che·kes de vya·*khe*·ro
I'm looking for the ...	*Estoy buscando ...*	es·*toy* boos·*kan*·do ...
ATM	*el cajero automático*	el ka·*khe*·ro ow·to·*ma*·tee·ko
bank	*el banco*	el *ban*·ko
bookstore	*la librería*	la lee·bre·*ree*·a
drugstore/ chemist	*la farmacia/ la botica*	la far·*ma*·sya/ la bo·*tee*·ka
embassy	*la embajada*	la em·ba·*kha*·da
exchange house	*la casa de cambio*	la *ka*·sa de *kam*·byo
general store	*la tienda*	la *tyen*·da
laundry	*la lavandería*	la la·van·de·*ree*·a
market	*el mercado*	el mer·*ka*·do
post office	*el correo*	el ko·*re*·o
supermarket	*el supermercado*	el soo·per·mer·*ka*·do
tourist office	*la oficina de turismo*	la o·fee·*see*·na de too·rees·mo

What time does it open/close?
¿A qué hora abre/cierra? a ke *o*·ra *a*·bre/sye·ra

I want to change some money/traveler's checks.
Quiero cambiar dinero/ cheques de viajero. kye·ro kam·*byar* dee·ne·ro/ che·kes de vya·*khe*·ro

What is the exchange rate?
¿Cuál es el tipo de cambio? kwal es el *tee*·po de *kam*·byo

I want to call ...
Quiero llamar a ... kye·ro ya·*mar* a ...

airmail	*correo aéreo*	ko·*re*·o a·e·re·o
customs declaration	*declaración de aduana*	de·kla·ra·*syon* de a·*dwa*·na
letter	*carta*	*kar*·ta
registered mail	*certificado*	ser·tee·fee·*ka*·do
stamps	*estampillas*	es·tam·*pee*·lyas

TIME & DATES

What time is it?
¿Qué hora es? ke *o*·ra es

It's one o'clock.
Es la una. es la *oo*·na

It's seven o'clock.
Son las siete. son las *sye*·te

---

midnight	*medianoche*	me·dya·*no*·che
noon	*mediodía*	me·dyo·*dee*·a
half past two	*dos y media*	dos ee *me*·dya
now	*ahora*	a·*o*·ra
today	*hoy*	oy
tonight	*esta noche*	es·ta *no*·che
tomorrow	*mañana*	ma·*nya*·na
yesterday	*ayer*	a·*yer*
Monday	*lunes*	*loo*·nes
Tuesday	*martes*	*mar*·tes
Wednesday	*miércoles*	*myer*·ko·les
Thursday	*jueves*	*khwe*·ves
Friday	*viernes*	*vyer*·nes
Saturday	*sábado*	*sa*·ba·do
Sunday	*domingo*	do·*meen*·go
January	*enero*	e·*ne*·ro
February	*febrero*	fe·*bre*·ro
March	*marzo*	*mar*·so
April	*abril*	a·*breel*
May	*mayo*	*ma*·yo
June	*junio*	*khoo*·nyo
July	*julio*	*khoo*·lyo
August	*agosto*	a·*gos*·to
September	*septiembre*	sep·*tyem*·bre
October	*octubre*	ok·*too*·bre
November	*noviembre*	no·*vyem*·bre
December	*diciembre*	dee·*syem*·bre

TRANSPORTATION
Public Transportation

What time does	¿A qué hora	a ke *o*-ra
... leave/arrive?	sale/llega ...?	sa-le/ye-ga ...
the bus	el autobús	el ow-to-*boos*
the plane	el avión	el a-*vyon*
the ship	el barco/buque	el *bar*-ko/*boo*-ke
the train	el tren	el tren

airport	el aeropuerto	el a-e-ro-*pwer*-to
bus station	la estación de autobuses	la es-ta-*syon* de ow-to-*boo*-ses
bus stop	la parada de autobuses	la pa-*ra*-da de ow-to-*boo*-ses
luggage check room	guardería/ equipaje	gwar-de-*ree*-a/ e-kee-*pa*-khe
ticket office	la boletería	la bo-le-te-*ree*-a
train station	la estación de ferrocarril	la es-ta-*syon* de fe-ro-ka-*reel*

I'd like a ticket to ...
Quiero un boleto a ...   kye-ro oon bo-*le*-to a ...
What's the fare to ...?
¿Cuánto cuesta hasta ...?   kwan-to kwes-ta a-sta ...

student's	de estudiante	de es-too-*dyan*-te
1st class	primera clase	pree-me-ra *kla*-se
2nd class	segunda clase	se-*goon*-da *kla*-se
single/one-way	ida	ee-da
return/round trip	ida y vuelta	ee-da ee *vwel*-ta
taxi	taxi	tak-see

Private Transportation

I'd like to	Quisiera	kee-*sye*-ra
hire a ...	alquilar ...	al-kee-*lar* ...
4WD	un todo terreno/ un cuatro por cuatro	oon *to*-do te-*re*-no/ oon *kwa*-tro por *kwa*-tro
car	un auto	oon *ow*-to
motorbike	una moto	*oo*-na *mo*-to
bicycle	una bicicleta	*oo*-na bee-see-*kle*-ta

pickup (truck)	camioneta	ka-myo-*ne*-ta
truck	camión	ka-*myon*
hitchhike	hacer dedo	a-ser *de*-do

Is this the road to ...?
¿Se va a ... por esta carretera?   se va a ... por es-ta ka-re-*te*-ra
Where's a petrol station?
¿Dónde hay una gasolinera/un grifo?   don-de ai oo-na ga-so-lee-*ne*-ra/oon *gree*-fo
Please fill it up.
Lleno, por favor.   ye-no por fa-*vor*

ROAD SIGNS

Acceso	Entrance
Aparcamiento	Parking
Ceda el Paso	Give Way
Despacio	Slow
Dirección Única	One-Way
Mantenga Su Derecha	Keep to the Right
No Adelantar/ No Rebase	No Passing
Peaje	Toll
Peligro	Danger
Prohibido Aparcar/ No Estacionar	No Parking
Prohibido el Paso	No Entry
Pare/Stop	Stop
Salida de Autopista	Exit Freeway

---

diesel	diesel	*dee*-sel
gas/petrol	gasolina	ga-so-*lee*-na

I'd like (20) liters.
Quiero (veinte) litros.   kye-ro (vayn-te) lee-tros
(How long) can I park here?
¿(Por cuánto tiempo) puedo aparcar aquí?   (por kwan-to tyem-po) pwe-do a-par-kar a-kee
Where do I pay?
¿Dónde se paga?   don-de se pa-ga
I need a mechanic.
Necesito un mecánico.   ne-se-*see*-to oon me-*ka*-nee-ko
The car has broken down (in ...).
El carro se ha averiado (en ...).   el ka-ro se a a-ve-*rya*-do (en ...)
The motorbike won't start.
No arranca la moto.   no a-*ran*-ka la mo-to
I have a flat tire.
Tengo un pinchazo.   ten-go oon peen-*cha*-so
I've run out of gas/petrol.
Me quedé sin gasolina.   me ke-de seen ga-so-*lee*-na
I've had an accident.
Tuve un accidente.   too-ve oon ak-see-*den*-te

TRAVEL WITH CHILDREN

I need ...	Necesito ...	ne-se-*see*-to ...
Do you have ...?	¿Hay ...?	ai ...

a car baby seat	un asiento de seguridad para bebés	oon a-*syen*-to de se-goo-ree-*da* pa-ra be-*bes*
(disposable) diapers/nappies	pañales (de usar y tirar)	pa-*nya*-les (de oo-*sar* ee tee-*rar*)
a highchair	una trona	*oo*-na *tro*-na

infant milk formula/powder	leche en polvo	le·che en pol·vo
a potty	una pelela	oo·na pe·le·la
a stroller	un cochecito	oon ko·che·see·to

Do you mind if I breast-feed here?
¿Le molesta que dé   le mo·les·ta ke de
de pecho aquí?   de pe·cho a·kee
Are children allowed?
¿Se admiten niños?   se ad·mee·ten nee·nyos

AYMARÁ & QUECHUA

Here's a brief list of Quechua and Aymará words and phrases. The grammar and pronunciation of these languages are quite difficult for native English speakers, but those who are interested in learning them will find language courses in La Paz, Cochabamba and Sucre.

Dictionaries and phrasebooks are available through Los Amigos del Libro and larger bookstores in La Paz, but to use them you'll first need a sound knowledge of Spanish.

Lonely Planet's *Quechua Phrasebook* provides useful phrases and vocabulary in the Cuzco (Peru) dialect, but it will also be of use in the Bolivian highlands.

The following list of words and phrases (with Aymará listed first, Quechua second) is obviously minimal, but it should be useful in the areas where these languages are spoken. Pronounce them as you would a Spanish word. An apostrophe represents a glottal stop, which is the 'non-sound' that occurs in the middle of 'uh-oh.'

Hi.	Laphi.	Raphi.
Hello.	Kamisaraki.	Napaykullayki.
Please.	Mirá.	Allichu.

Thank you.	Yuspagara.	Yusulipayki.
Yes.	Jisa.	Ari.
No.	Janiwa.	Mana.

It's a pleasure.
Take chuima'hampi.   Tucuy sokoywan.
How do you say ...?
Cun sañasauca'ha ...?   Imainata nincha chaita ...?
It is called ...
Ucan sutipa'h ...   Chaipa'g sutin'ha ...
Please repeat that.
Uastata sita.   Ua'manta niway.
Where is ...?
Kaukasa ...?   Maypi ...?
How much?
K'gauka?   Maik'ata'g?

distant	haya	caru
downhill	aynacha	uray
father	auqui	tayta
food	manka	mikíuy
mother	taica	mama
lodging	korpa	pascana
near	maka	kailla
river	jawira	mayu
snowy peak	kollu	riti-orko
trail	tapu	chakiñan
very near	hakítaqui	kaillitalla
water	uma	yacu

1	maya	u'
2	paya	iskai
3	quimsa	quinsa
4	pusi	tahua
5	pesca	phiska
6	zo'hta	so'gta
7	pakalko	khanchis
8	quimsakalko	pusa'g
9	yatunca	iskon
10	tunca	chunca
100	pataca	pacha'g
1000	waranka	huaranca

LANGUAGE

Latin American **Spanish**

Quechua

Also available from Lonely Planet:
Latin American Spanish Phrasebook,
Quechua Phrasebook

Glossary

For a glossary of food and drink items, see the Food & Drink chapter, p46.

abra – opening; refers to a mountain pass, usually flanked by steep high walls

achachilas – Aymará mountain spirits, believed to be ancestors who look after their *ayllus* and provide bounty from the earth

aduana – customs office

aguayo – colorful woven square used to carry things on one's back, also called a *manta*

albergue – basic guest house

alcaldía – municipal/town hall

Altiplano – High Plain; the largest expanse of level (and, in places, arable) land in the Andes, it extends from Bolivia into southern Peru, northwestern Argentina and northern Chile

Alto Perú – the Spanish colonial name for the area now called Bolivia

anillos – literally 'rings'; the name used for main orbital roads around some Bolivian cities

apacheta – mound of stones on a mountain peak or pass; travelers carry a stone from the valley to place on top of the heap as an offering to the *apus;* the word may also be used locally to refer to the pass itself

apu – mountain spirit who provides protection for travelers and water for crops, often associated with a particular *nevado*

arenales – sand dunes

artesanía – locally handcrafted items, or a shop selling them

ayllus – loosely translates as 'tribe'; indigenous groups inhabiting a particular area

Aymará – indigenous people of Bolivia; 'Aymará' also refers to the language of these people; also appears as 'Aymara' or Kolla

azulejos – decorative tiles, so-named because most early Iberian *azulejos* were blue and white

bajones – immense flutes introduced by the Jesuits to the lowland indigenous communities; they are still featured in festivities at San Ignacio de Moxos

balsa – raft; in the Bolivian Amazon, *balsas* are used to ferry cars across rivers that lack bridges

barranca – cliff; often refers to a canyon wall

barranquilleros – wildcat gold miners of the Yungas and Alto Beni regions

barrio – district or neighborhood

bloqueo – roadblock

bodega – boxcar, carried on some trains, in which 2nd-class passengers can travel; also means wine cellar

bofedales – swampy alluvial grasslands in the *puna* and Altiplano regions, where Aymará people pasture their llamas and alpacas

boletería – ticket window

boliche – nightclub

bolivianita – a purple and yellow amethyst

bolivianos – Bolivian people; also the Bolivian unit of currency

bombas de gasolina – gasoline pumps

bus cama – literally 'bed bus'; a bus service with fully reclining seats that is used on some international services, as well as a few longer domestic runs; it's often substantially more expensive than normal services

cabaña – cabin

cama matrimonial – double bed

camarín – niche in which a religious image is displayed

camba – a Bolivian from the Eastern Lowlands; some highlanders use this term for anyone from the Beni, Pando or Santa Cruz departments (oddly enough, the same term applies to lowlanders in eastern Tibet!)

cambista – street moneychanger

camino – road, path, way

camión – flatbed truck; a popular form of local transportation

camioneta – pickup truck, used as local transportation in the Amazon Basin

campesino – subsistence farmer

cancha – open space in an urban area, often used for market activities; soccer field

casilla – post-office box

cerrado – sparsely forested scrub savanna; an endangered habitat that may be seen in Parque Nacional Noel Kempff Mercado

cerro – hill; this term is often used to refer to mountains, which is a laughably classic case of understatement given their altitudes!

chacra – cornfield

chalanas – ferries

cha'lla – offering

chapacos – residents of Tarija; used proudly by *tarijeños* and in misguided jest by other Bolivians

chaqueo – annual burning of Amazonian rainforest to clear agricultural and grazing land; there's a mistaken belief that the smoke from *el chaqueo* forms clouds and ensures good rains

charango – a traditional Bolivian ukulele-type instrument

chichería – bar specializing in *chicha*

cholo/a – Quechua or Aymará person who lives in the city but continues to wear traditional dress

chompa – sweater, jumper
chullo – traditional pointed woolen hat, usually with earflaps
chullpa – funerary tower, normally from the Aymará culture
cocalero – coca grower
cochabambinos – Cochabamba locals
colectivo – minibus or collective taxi
Colla – alternative spelling for *Kolla*
comedor – dining hall
Comibol – Corporación Minera Boliviana (Bolivian Mining Corporation), now defunct
contrabandista – smuggler
cooperativos – small groups of miners who purchase temporary rights
cordillera – mountain range
corregidor – chief magistrate
cruce – turn-off
cruceños – Santa Cruz locals

DEA – Drug Enforcement Agency, the US drug-offensive body sent to Bolivia to enforce coca crop-substitution programs and to apprehend drug magnates
denuncia – affidavit
derecho – a right; a privilege provided in exchange for a levy or tax
dueño/a – proprietor

edificio – building
EFA – Empresa Ferroviaria Andina; the new private railway company, also known as FVA, or 'Ferroviarias Andinas'
ejecutivo – executive
Ekeko – household god of abundance; the name means 'dwarf' in Aymará
enclaustromiento – landlocked status
Entel – Empresa Nacional de Telecomunicaciones (Bolivian national communications commission)
entrada – entrance procession
esquina – street corner, often abbreviated *esq*
estancia – extensive ranch, often a grazing establishment

feria – fair, market
ferretería – hardware shop
ferrobus – passenger rail bus
flota – long-distance bus company
frontera – border
futból – soccer
FVA – Ferroviarias Andinas; see EFA

garapatillas – tiny ticks that are the bane of the northern plateaus and savanna grasslands
guardaparque – national park ranger

hechicería – traditional Aymará witchcraft
hoja de ruta – circulation card

hornecinos – niches commonly found in Andean ruins, presumably used for the placement of idols and/or offerings
huemul – Andean deer

iglesia – church
Inca – dominant indigenous civilization of the Central Andes at the time of the Spanish conquest; refers both to the people and to their leader
ingenio – mill; in Potosí it refers to silver smelting plants along the Ribera, where metal was extracted from low-grade ore by crushing it with a mill wheel in a solution of salt and mercury

jardín – garden
javeli – peccary
jefe de la estación – stationmaster
jipijapa – the fronds of the cyclanthaceae fan palm (*Carludovica palmata*)
jochi – agouti, an agile, long-legged rodent of the Amazon basin; it's the only native animal that can eat the Brazil nut

Kallahuayas – itinerant traditional healers and fortune-tellers of the remote Cordillera Apolobamba; also spelled 'Kallawaya'
koa – sweet-smelling incense bush (*Senecio mathewsii*), which grows on Isla del Sol and other parts of the Altiplano and is used as incense in Aymará rituals; also refers to a similar-smelling domestic plant *Mentha pulegium,* which was introduced by the Spanish
Kolla – the name used by the Aymará to refer to themselves; also spelt *Colla*
Kollasuyo – Inca name for Bolivia, the 'land of the Kolla,' or Aymará people; the Spanish knew the area as Alto Perú, 'upper Peru'

La Diablada – Dance of the Devils, frequently performed at festivals
lago – lake
laguna – lagoon; shallow lake
lancha – motorboat
legía – alkaloid usually made of potato and quinoa ash that is used to draw the drug from coca leaves when chewed
licuados – fruit shake made with either milk or water
liquichiris – harmful spirits who suck out a person's vitality, causing death for no apparent reason
llanos – plains
llapa – see *yapa*
llareta – combustible salt-tolerant moss (*Azorella compacta*) growing on the *salares* of the southern Altiplano that oozes a turpentine-like jelly used by locals as stove fuel; also spelled *yareta*

GLOSSARY

loma – artificial mounds
lucha libre – freestyle wrestling matches

Manco Capac – the first Inca emperor
manta – shawl, also called an *aguayo*
mariguí – a small and very irritating biting fly of the Amazon lowlands; the bite initially creates a small blood blister and then itches, sometimes leaving scars
mate – herbal infusion of coca, chamomile, or similar
menonitas – Mennonites of the Eastern Lowlands, Paraguay, northern Argentina and southwestern Brazil
mercado – market
mestizo – person of Spanish and indigenous parentage or descent; also architectural style incorporating natural-theme designs
micro – small bus or minibus
minifundio – a small plot of land
mirador – lookout
mobilidad – any sort of motor vehicle
moto-taxi – motorbike taxi; a standard means of public transportation in the Eastern Lowlands and Amazon Basin
movilidades – anything that moves (in terms of transportation)
mudéjar – Spanish name for architecture displaying Moorish influences

ñandu – rhea; a large, flightless bird also known as the South American ostrich
nevado – snowcapped mountain peak

orureño/a – Oruro local

paceño/a – La Paz local
Pachamama – the Aymará and Quechua goddess or 'earth mother'
pahuichi – straw-thatched home with reed walls; a common dwelling in the Beni department
paja brava – spiky grass of the high Altiplano
parrilla – barbecue
parrillada – plate of mixed grilled meats
peajes – tolls sometimes charged at a *tranca*
peña – folk-music program
piso – floor
pollera – traditional *chola* skirt
pongaje – feudal system inflicted on the Bolivian peasantry; abolished after the April Revolution of 1952
pullman – 'reclining' 1st-class rail or bus seat; it may or may not actually recline
puna – high open grasslands of the Altiplano
punto – privately run phone offices

quebrada – ravine or wash, usually dry
Quechua – highland (Altiplano) indigenous language of Ecuador, Peru and Bolivia; language of the former Inca empire

quena – simple reed flute
queñua – dwarf shaggy-barked tree *(Polylepis tarapana)* that grows at higher altitudes than any other tree in the world; it can survive at elevations of over 5000m
quinoa – highly nutritious grain similar to sorghum, used to make flour and thicken stews; grown at high elevations
quirquincho – armadillo carapace used in the making of *charangos;* nickname for residents of Oruro

radiales – 'radials'; the streets forming the 'spokes' of a city laid out in *anillos,* or rings; the best Bolivian example of this is in Santa Cruz
reais – Brazilian unit of currency (R$) pronounced 'hey-ice'; singular is *real* pronounced 'hey-ow'
refugio – mountain hut
río – river
roca – rock

salar – salt pan or salt desert
salteña – filled pastry shell
sarape – poncho
saya – Afro-Bolivian dance that recalls the days of slavery in Potosí; it's featured at festivities
seringueros – rubber tappers in the Amazon region
SERNAP – Servicio Nacional de Áreas Protegidas, government-run environment agency
singani – a distilled grape spirit (local firewater)
soroche – altitude sickness, invariably suffered by newly arrived visitors to highland Bolivia
surazo – cold wind blowing into lowland Bolivia from Patagonia and Argentine pampa
surtidores de gasolina – gas dispensers/stations

Tahuatinsuyo – the Inca name for their entire empire
tambo – wayside inn, market and meeting place selling staple domestic items; the New World counterpart of the *caravanserai*
tarijeños – Tarija locals
taxista – taxi driver
termas – hot springs
terminal terrestre – long-distance bus terminal
thola – small desert bush
tienda – small shop, usually family-run
tinku – traditional festival that features ritual fighting, taking place mainly in the north of the department of Potosí; any blood shed during these fights is considered an offering to Pachamama
totora – type of reed, used as a building material around Lake Titicaca
trago – alcoholic drinks, not including beer and wine
tranca – highway police post, usually found at city limits
tranquilo – 'tranquil', the word most often used by locals to describe Bolivia's relatively safe and gentle demeanor;

it's also used as an encouragement to slow down to the local pace of life

tren expreso – reasonably fast train that has 1st- and 2nd-class carriages and a dining car

tren mixto – very slow goods train; most passengers normally travel in *bodegas*

trufi – collective taxi or minibus that follows a set route

vicuña – a small camelid of the high *puna* or Altiplano; a wild relative of the llama and alpaca

viscacha – small, long-tailed, rabbit-like rodent *(Lagidium viscaccia)* related to the chinchilla; inhabits rocky outcrops on the high Altiplano

Wara Wara – slow train on the Red Occidental that stops at most stations

yagé – a hallucinogenic drug used by certain tribes of the upper Amazon

yapa – bargaining practice in which a customer agrees to a final price provided that the vendor augments or supplements the item being sold

yareta – see *llareta*

yatiri – traditional Aymará healer/priest or witch doctor

zampoña – pan flute made of hollow reeds of varying lengths, lashed together side by side; it's featured in most traditional music performances

The Authors

ANJA MUTIĆ
Coordinating Author, Southern Altiplano

While growing up in Croatia, New York-based Anja Mutić had a deep fascination with the ancient civilizations and mysterious rainforests of South America. In 2002, she spent six weeks traveling around Bolivia, immediately enchanted with its remote landscapes and indigenous cultures. She descended into the mines of Potosí, swam in Inca hot springs, found herself in the midst of a coca peasants' roadblock and got lost in the Amazon. For this book, she was repeatedly hit by water balloons leading up to Carnaval. Still, she'd go back in a snap.

KATE ARMSTRONG
La Paz, Lake Titicaca

Kate first wandered to Bolivia during a year-long backpacking trip through South America. Captivated by the country's flavors, she holed up in Sucre to study Spanish and inadvertently joined a folkloric dance troupe after two ungraceful *cueca* lessons in her hiking boots. She returns regularly to Bolivia to search for the perfect *salteña*, hike in the highlands and brush up on her *castellano*. When not wandering the markets of La Paz, the Altiplano or Amazonian jungle, Kate is a freelance writer in Australia.

PAUL SMITH
The Cordilleras & Yungas, Central Highlands, South Central Bolivia & the Chaco, Santa Cruz & Gran Chiquitania, Amazon Basin

From an early age, and with a vague and naive ambition to be the next David Attenborough, Paul dreamed of exploring the remotest corners of South America in search of wildlife. After spending two months at the Beni Biological Station as a student, that dream started to come true but, with David Attenborough still going strong, he changed his career plans, became a travel writer and moved to South America (Paraguay) permanently in 2003. While researching this edition, Paul spent a night on a bus in a mosquito-infested swamp somewhere between Rurre and Riberalta, overcame his fear of light aircrafts in Pando, learnt how to take his *singani* like a man in Tarija, and saw his first Red-fronted Macaw in Saipina.

CONTRIBUTING AUTHOR

Dr David Goldberg MD completed his training in internal medicine and infectious diseases at Columbia-Presbyterian Medical Center in New York City, where he has also served as voluntary faculty. At present, he is an infectious diseases specialist in Scarsdale NY and the editor-in-chief of the website www .MDTravelHealth.com

LONELY PLANET AUTHORS

Why is our travel information the best in the world? It's simple: our authors are passionate, dedicated travellers. They don't take freebies in exchange for positive coverage so you can be sure the advice you're given is impartial. They travel widely to all the popular spots, and off the beaten track. They don't research using just the internet or phone. They discover new places not included in any other guidebook. They personally visit thousands of hotels, restaurants, palaces, trails, galleries, temples and more. They speak with dozens of locals every day to make sure you get the kind of insider knowledge only a local could tell you. They take pride in getting all the details right, and in telling it how it is. Think you can do it? Find out how at **lonelyplanet.com**.

Behind the Scenes

THIS BOOK

This 7th edition of *Bolivia* was researched and written by Anja Mutić, Kate Armstrong and Paul Smith. Anja served as the coordinating author, writing all of the front and back chapters as well as researching and writing the Southern Altiplano chapter and the Potosí section of the Central Highlands chapter. Kate Armstrong covered the La Paz and Lake Titicaca chapters. Paul Smith covered the following chapters: The Cordilleras & Yungas, South Central Bolivia & the Chaco, Santa Cruz & Gran Chiquitania, Amazon Basin, and most of the Central Highlands. Dr David Goldberg MD wrote the Health chapter.

The 6th edition was written by Kate Armstrong, Vesna Maric and Andy Symington. The 5th edition was written by Andrew Dean Nystrom and Morgan Konn.

This guidebook was commissioned in Lonely Planet's Oakland office, laid out by Cambridge Publishing Management, UK, and produced by the following:

Commissioning Editor Kathleen Munnelly
Coordinating Editors Elizabeth Anglin, Thomas Lee
Coordinating Cartographer Owen Eszeki
Coordinating Layout Designer Paul Queripel
Managing Editor Katie Lynch
Managing Cartographer Alison Lyall

Senior Cartographer Ross Butler
Managing Layout Designer Sally Darmody
Assisting Editors David Carroll, Michala Green, Victoria Harrison, Dianne Schallmeiner, Ceinwen Sinclair, Kelly Walker
Assisting Cartographer Dennis Capparelli
Assisting Layout Designer Trevor Double
Cover Katy Murenu, lonelyplanetimages.com
Indexer Marie Lorimer
Internal Image Research Sabrina Dalbesio, lonelyplanetimages.com
Project Manager Melanie Dankel
Language Content Annelies Mertens

Thanks to Shahara Ahmed, Lucy Birchley, Evan Jones

THANKS
ANJA MUTIĆ

Thank you to my inspiring father who waited for my return from Bolivia to Croatia before passing to the other side. Tata, I dedicate this book to you. *Hvala mama*, Hoji and my whole family in Croatia, Barcelona and New York for their support. I profusely thank my editor Kathleen and everyone at Lonely Planet for their understanding and sympathy during a difficult time. Many thanks to my coauthors Paul and Kate. *Gracias* to Dirko and Virna in Sucre for their incredible kindness

THE LONELY PLANET STORY

Fresh from an epic journey across Europe, Asia and Australia in 1972, Tony and Maureen Wheeler sat at their kitchen table stapling together notes. The first Lonely Planet guidebook, *Across Asia on the Cheap,* was born.

Travellers snapped up the guides. Inspired by their success, the Wheelers began publishing books to Southeast Asia, India and beyond. Demand was prodigious, and the Wheelers expanded the business rapidly to keep up. Over the years, Lonely Planet extended its coverage to every country and into the virtual world via lonelyplanet.com and the Thorn Tree message board.

As Lonely Planet became a globally loved brand, Tony and Maureen received several offers for the company. But it wasn't until 2007 that they found a partner whom they trusted to remain true to the company's principles of travelling widely, treading lightly and giving sustainably. In October of that year, BBC Worldwide acquired a 75% share in the company, pledging to uphold Lonely Planet's commitment to independent travel, trustworthy advice and editorial independence.

Today, Lonely Planet has offices in Melbourne, London and Oakland, with over 500 staff members and 300 authors. Tony and Maureen are still actively involved with Lonely Planet. They're travelling more often than ever, and they're devoting their spare time to charitable projects. And the company is still driven by the philosophy of *Across Asia on the Cheap*: 'All you've got to do is decide to go and the hardest part is over. So go!'

SEND US YOUR FEEDBACK

We love to hear from travelers – your comments keep us on our toes and help make our books better. Our well-traveled team reads every word on what you loved or loathed about this book. Although we cannot reply individually to postal submissions, we always guarantee that your feedback goes straight to the appropriate authors in time for the next edition. Each person who sends us information is thanked in the next edition – and the most useful submissions are rewarded with a free book.

To send us your updates – and find out about Lonely Planet events, newsletters and travel news – visit our award-winning website: **lonelyplanet.com/contact**.

Note: we may edit, reproduce and incorporate your comments in Lonely Planet products such as guidebooks, websites and digital products, so let us know if you don't want your comments reproduced or your name acknowledged. For a copy of our privacy policy visit lonelyplanet.com/privacy.

and generosity and Jhonny Montes in Potosí for being such great help. I also thank Liz Rojas, Fabiola Mitru, Javier and Janette, Chris Sarage and Christian Schoettle.

KATE ARMSTRONG

Muchas gracias to a team of medics and nursing staff, without whom I wouldn't have arrived home safely: Dr Jordan and Dr Silvia, Dr Nels Calderon, Dr Casanovas and Dr Wayrar, Rebecca, Froddy, Maritza, Katalina and Ferminia. Further thanks to the team at AIG, particularly Ben, Paul, Shannon and Rory. Thank you Griselda Tordoya of Aerolineas Argentinus, Rolando Illanes Vera (*te quiero*) and my friends at ICBA, plus Monica Aguilas, Tom Ellman and Alix Shand. All my lifesavers at Hotel Rosario: Ximena, Fernando, Rosita, Alex and Omar at reception; and Eduardo, Benito, Gabriel, Rolando, Juan Carlos, Caesar and Apolinar. For crossing the 't's and dotting the 'i's in unexpected circumstances, and much more – Alistair Mathew and Sebastian Terrazas. As always, to Kathleen Munnelly, plus my fellow scribes, Anja and Paul. Finally, hearty appreciation – in every respect – to Eduardo and Vania Zeballos for their generosity of spirits (and fresh veggies!), Stephen Taranto and Clea, and Martin Stratker and Katty, for their generosity of, well, everything.

PAUL SMITH

Thanks to everybody I met in Bolivia, especially: Trent and Rosario in Samaipata for helping set the record straight on Samaipata; Bennett, Eli and everybody at Armonia – keep up the good work; Gustavo Gutierrez at FAN for dogged determination and details; Louis and Travis in Sorata; Liz Rojas in Sucre; Javier Quiroz in Trinidad and the Bolivian *migraciones* official who didn't understand his job properly and nearly landed me in hot water on my way home! Special thanks

of course to Kathleen, Kate and Anja for their patience and for being a great support network (hopefully resulting in a great book) and to Mum and Dad for all their usual help!

OUR READERS

Many thanks to the travelers who used the last edition and wrote to us with helpful hints, useful advice and interesting anecdotes:

A Nelleke Aben, Evan Abramson, Kate Adlam, Jorge Jaime Aguirre Ramirez, Thien An Tran, Merieke Arts, Bruce Atherton **B** Marco A Ayllon Bueno, Stelios Bafaloukos, Thomas Baumgartner, Maguy Bechetoille, Lina Behrens, Donna Belder, Iain Bisset, Stefan Boeni, Thomas Bohn, David Boldt, Isabelle Bomba, Anita Bonnema, Isabelle Bovey, Shaina Brassard, Louis Brescia, Jeremy Brock, Mark Brooks, Erik Bruns, Stefan Buballa, Daniel Buck, Keiran Buckley, Mirtha Bustamante **C** Heather Carratt, Samuel Charache, Charlotte Booth, Lionel Chok, Arthur Clegg, Donal Convery, Augustine Corcoran, Manuel Corral Valero, Brian Corrigan **D** Benjamin Dangl, Yvonne Danson, Ben De Castelet, Hans De Schryver, Martin J De Vries, Helene Destailleur, Romain Devemy, Patrick Dondlinger **E** Stefan Edling, Jim Evans **F** Michael Fernando, Pascal Ferrat, Marian Feunekes, Frauke Finster, Charlotte (Sarika) Frey, Inge Fuchs **G** Elias Gardner, Rebecca Gasser, Annabelle Gauberti, Eddie Gerrard, Jim Grahamm, Emily Gray, Scott Greene, Fred Grote **H** Tore Haaland, Martin Hanzalek, Megam Harward, Klara Hermanns, Susa Herzog, Matej Hojdar, Joh Horst, Gretta Howard, Ann Huston **J** Cameron James, Luise Jarl, Jessica Jormtun **K** Mike Knowles, Christine Koch, Matti Kuosmanen **L** Yael Lachkar, Vivian Lackovic, Barbara Lauener, Morgan Lehman, Silvia Leto, Peter Lo Schiavo, Montse Lopez, Parker Love, Rene Luethi, Guenther Lutschinger **M** Doris Maeso, Lucas Maillette De Buy Wenniger, Ellen Mannion, Nikolas Marggraf, Daniel Mckay, Nicole Medema, Dorien Meijerink, Bart Meijs, Marion Miazzo, Pascal Mora, Thor Morales, Peter Mouldey, Joy Murray **N** Emma Naylor, Seagan Ngai **O** David O'Brien, Jana Olejnikova, Marion Opdam **P** Odette Perik, Aaron Price **Q** Phil Quayle **R** Katja and Jens Radon Kahnert, Jerome Richard, Karen Robacker, Ben Rosner, Mieke Ruyzendaal **S** Josef Saller, Hilary Sanders, Katheryna Sansone, Joost Schouppe,

Peter Schramm, Theodore Scott, Jauregui Schiffelmann, Alan Shenuit, Peter Simmonds, Izidora Skracic, Charlotte Skrubbeltrang Madsen, Justina Southworth, Paul Spizman, Galen Stahle, Kelly Stiller, Anna Strub, Sibylle Studer, Helga Svendsen **T** Erik Thomann, Robin Thompson, John Tuckwell **V** Mariska Van Cuijk, Max Van De Ven, Eveline Van Drielen, William Van Haverbeke, Bart Van Hoof, Marieke Van Meerten, Carla Van Zetten, Guido Vandorpe, Anniek Visser **W** James Waterman, Tony Watton, Erwin Wesenhagen, Nicole Willburn, Sam Wilson, Thea Winnips, Edric Wong **Z** Foteini Zafeiriou, Andrew Ziebro, Kathrin Zorn.

ACKNOWLEDGMENTS
Many thanks to the following for the use of their content:

Globe on title page ©Mountain High Maps 1993 Digital Wisdom, Inc.

Index

See also separate GreenDex, p391.

4WD tours 168-9
4WD vehicles 58

A
acclimatization 58
accommodations 328-9, *see also individual locations*
activities 54-9, 329, *see also individual activities*
    top 10 15
Afro-Bolivian people 34, 131
agoutis 50
agrarian reform 29, 34
agriculture
    slash-&-burn 52, 53
    soybean 44, 52
Agua Blanca 147
aguardiente 45
Aguas Calientes 291
Aiquile 207
air travel 342-5
    airlines 342-3, 346-7
    children 330
    climate change issues 343
    deep vein thrombosis 353-4
    departure taxes 342, 347
    internet resources 343, 344
    jet lag 354
    tickets 343-4
    to/from Bolivia 342-5
    within Bolivia 346-7
Akamani Sacred Hill 148
Alasitas 76, 77, 103, 332
alcohol 44-5, 190, 203
alligators 50, 318
alojamientos 329
Alpaca Works 204-5
alpacas 50, 147
Altiplano 13, 21, 49, *see also* Southern Altiplano
altitude sickness 55, 358
Amazon Basin 294-327, **296**
    bird-watching 309, 318, 320, 321
    climate 295

hiking & trekking 309
history 295
jungle & pampas tours 303, 304
travel to/from 295, 297
wildlife watching 300, 303, 304, 308, 309-10, 318, 320
Amboro National Park 51, 275, 276-8, **277**, 7
anacondas 50
Ancohuma 144
Andean cats 50
animal bites 358-9
animals 49, 50-1, *see also individual animals*, bird-watching, wildlife watching
    endandered & rare species 50-1
    feeding 55
    sacred 52
anteaters 51, 259, 318
ants 320
Apa-Apa Reserva Ecológica 129-30
Apacheta Chucura 125
api 44
Apolobamba national park 51, 146-7
Aqualand 268
Aquaquiza 178
Árbol de Piedra 176
archaeological museums
    Ethno-Archaeological Museum 313
    Museo Arqueología y Antropológico de los Andes Meridionales 167
    Museo Arqueológico (Cochabamba) 194
    Museo Arqueológico (Samaipata) 281
    Museo de Arqueología y Paleontología 247
    Museo Nacional de Arqueología 70
archaeological sites, *see also* Inca sites, rock paintings
    Charazani 146
    Copacabana 99
    Coquesa 176
    Curahuara de Carangas 165
    El Fuerte 279-81, **280**
    Iskanwaya 140
    Isla Pariti 115
    La Paz 93-6
    Llanos de Moxos 317

Pasto Grande 132
Pukara de Tuquipaya 278
Quila Quila 227
architecture 39-40
Área Natural de Manejo Integrado Nacional (Anmin) Apolobamba 51, 146-7
Argentina 25
    travel to/from 185, 257, 345
armadillos 50, 259
art galleries, *see* museums & galleries
arts 37-41, *see also individual arts*
Atahualpa 23
ATMs 334-5
Aucapata 140
avalanches 55
Aymará people 23, 32, 34, 73
    culture 32, 35, 36, 77
    festivals 76, 96
    language 367
ayullu 33

B
Bahía Kona 110
banks 330
Banzer Suárez, Hugo 26, 27
bargaining 14
Barrancas 180
Barrientos Ortuño, René 25, 26, 205
bartonellosis 357
basilicas, *see* churches & basilicas
Batea Q'ocha rock paintings 208-9
bathrooms 55, 339
bats 300, 320
bears, spectacled 51, 147, 255, 276
beer 44-5
begging 33
Bendicion de Movilidades 102
bicycling 347, *see also* mountain biking
Biocentro Güeme 267
biodiversity 58
birds 49, 316
    books 50
    see also condors, flamingos, macaws
bird-watching 59
    Amazon Basin 309, 318, 320, 321
    Cañón de Torotoro 208
    Cordillera Apolobamba 147
    El Nido de los Condores 283

000 Map pages
000 Photograph pages

Lomas de Arena 268
Parque Nacional Amboró 276
Parque Nacional Sajama 165
Reserva Biológica Cordillera de Sama 254
Reserva Nacional de Flora y Fauna Tariquía 255
Reserva Privada de Patrimonio Natural de Corbalán 259
Southwest Circuit 176, 177
boat travel, *see also* canoeing, kayaking
  cargo boats 300, 324, 347
  ferry services 347
  river boats 322, 324, 325, 347
boat trips
  Amazon 300, 306, 307, 309, 314
  Lake Titicaca 99, 107, 109
  Quijarro 292
boats, reed 109, 114
Bojorquez, Abraham 39
Bolívar, Simón 24, 189, 190, 211, 214-15
Bolivian hemorrhagic fever 357
bolivianita 49
books, *see also* literature
  birds 50
  food 42, 43
  health 353
  history 21, 23, 25, 26, 31
  travel 14, 54, 56
border crossings
  Argentina 185, 257, 345
  Brazil 293, 327, 345
  Chile 345-6
  Paraguay 258, 346
  Peru 116, 346
Brazil 24-5
  travel to/from 293, 327, 345
Buena Vista 273-6
bus travel
  dangers 347
  to/from Bolivia 345
  within Bolivia 347-8
business hours 330, *see also inside front cover*
butterflies 130, 132
Butterfly Pool El Mirador 302

C
Cabeza del Cóndor 143
caimans 309-10, 318, 320, 321
Calacala 162-3
cambio 335
camiones 349-50

Camiri 259-60
campesinos 32-3, 35, 133, 173, 297
camping 328
Candelaria 223
canoeing 58, 253, 306, 309, *see also* kayaking
Cañón de Palca 92-3
Cañón de Torotoro 208
Cañón del Pilcomayo 258-9
Capachos hot springs 162
capybaras 50
car travel
  driver's licenses 348
  private drivers 348-9
  rental 349
  road rules 349
  to/from Bolivia 345
  within Bolivia 348-9
Caranavi 140
carbon offset schemes 343
Cárdenas, Victor Hugo 27
Carmelite nuns 195-6
Carnaval 15, 39, 157, 249, 268, 332
Carrasco national park 51, 300
Casa de la Libertad 211, 214
Casa de Murillo 71
Casa Dorada 247
Casa Günther 133
Casa Nacional de Moneda 231
casas de huéspedes 329
cash advances 335
Cassidy, Butch 186-7
Castillo de Moisés Navajas 248
Catarata Ahlfeld 321-2
Catarata Arco Iris 322
Catarata El Encanto 321
Cataratas del Suton 291
cathedrals
  Aiquile 207
  Cochabamba 196
  Concepción 287
  Copacabana 102
  La Paz 67, 70
  Oruro 156, 158
  Potosí 231
  Riberalta 324
  Santa Cruz 267
  Sucre 215
  Tarija 248
  Trinidad 312
Catholicism 35
cats, Andean 50
caves
  Cueva Cóndor 138
  Cueva de los Monos 278

Cueva del Diablo 178
Gruta de las Galaxias 178
Gruta de Lourdes 107
Gruta de San Pedro 133
Gruta de Umajalanta 209
cell phones 337-8
Cementerio de Trenes 167
Central Highlands 49, 188-242, **189**
  climate 190
  history 189-90
  travel to/from 190
Centro de Ecología Ch'aska 180
Cerro Calvario 103
Cerro Corazón de Jesús 181-2
Cerro Kopakati 103
Cerro Tunari 201-2
Cerro Uchumachi 119
Chacaltaya 93
Chacaltaya glacier 52
Chaco 25, 244-5, 256-60, **244**
Chaco War 25, 244-5
Chaga's disease 357
Chaguaya 254
Cha'lla 111
cha'lla blessings 102, 157, 234
Cha'llapampa (Isla del Sol) 111
Cha'llapampa (Yungas) 126
Chapare 297-301
charango 38
Charazani 144, 146, 148
Charcas 189
Chari 146
Chataquila 226
Chaunaca 226
Ché Guevara, *see* Guevara, Ernesto
Ché Guevara Festival 284
Ché Trail 283-6
Chica people 180
Chicaloma 132
chicha 190, 204
chicha cochabambina 45
Chicha Festival 204
child labor 34
children
  health 359-60
  traveling with 330
Chile 24
  travel to/from 345-6
Chimane people 310
Chincana ruins 111-12
Chipaya people 179
Chiquitano people 286
cholas 25, 32, 36, 37
cholera 91, 354
cholos 25, 32, 36, 37

Choquekhota 128
Chorros de Jurina 255
Christmas 333
Chucura 125
chullpas 115, 162, 165, 178, 226
Chulumani 129-33, **130**
    accommodations 130-1
    food 131
    sights & activities 129-30
    travel to/from 131-2
churches & basilicas, *see also*
    cathedrals
    Basílica de San Francisco 248
    Basílica Menor de San Lorenzo 267
    Capilla de la Virgen de Guadalupe
        216
    Capilla de Lajas 253-4
    Capilla de Nuestra Señora de
        Jerusalén 233
    Iglesia & Convento de San
        Francisco 196
    Iglesia de la Merced 233
    Iglesia de la Recoleta 196
    Iglesia de los Santos Desposorios
        274
    Iglesia de San Francisco (La Paz) 71
    Iglesia de San Francisco (Sucre) 217
    Iglesia de San Juan 248
    Iglesia de San Lorenzo de Carangas
        233
    Iglesia de San Martín 232
    Iglesia de San Pedro 205
    Iglesia de San Roque 248
    Iglesia de Santa Domingo 196
    Iglesia de Santa Mónica 217
    Iglesia Matríz 206
    Jesuit Mission Church 290-1
    Templo Nuestra Señora de la
        Merced 216
cinema 38, 40-1
climate 13-14, 330
climate change 343
climbing, *see* mountaineering &
    climbing
cloud forest 130, 277, 300
Cobija 326-7
coca
    Coca Museum 70
    cultivation 28, 34, 118, 297, 298
    eradication measures 27, 28, 297
    organic 46

000 Map pages
000 Photograph pages

traditional uses 22, 23, 24, 44,
    234, 298
Cochabamba 190-201, **192**, **202**
    accommodations 197-8
    courses 196
    dangers 194
    drinking 200
    emergency services 191
    entertainment 200
    festivals & events 196-7
    food 198-9
    history 190-1
    internet access 191
    medical services 191
    money 193
    postal services 193
    shopping 200
    sights 194-6
    telephone services 193
    tourist information 193
    tours 196
    travel to/from 200-1
    travel within 201
Cochabamba Valley 202-5
Codo de los Andes 278
coffee plantation tours 275
Coimata Falls 255
Coipasa 178
Colcha K 176
Colchani 173, 174
Colocolo 149
community values 33
Concepción 287-8
Condoriri Massif 143-4
condors 50, 147, 255, 283
consulates 331-2
Convento de San Felipe Neri 216
Convento de San Francisco 232
Convento de Santa Teresa
    (Cochabamba) 195-6
Convento de Santa Teresa (Potosí) 232
Convento de Santa Teresa (Sucre) 217
Copacabana 99-107, **100**
    accommodations 104-5
    dangers 101, 102
    drinking 106
    festivals & events 103-4
    food 105-6
    history 99
    internet access 101
    medical services 101
    money 101
    postal services 101
    shopping 106
    sights 102-3

telephone services 101
tourist information 101-2
tours 103
travel to/from 106-7
Copacabana Beach 102-3
Coquesa 176
Cordillera Apolobamba 144-50, **145**
Cordillera de Kari Kari 242
Cordillera de los Frailes 223-7, **225**
Cordillera Occidental 49
Cordillera Quimsa Cruz 150
Cordillera Real 49, 141-4, 8
Coroico 119-24, **120**
    accommodations 122-3
    activities 119-22
    courses 122
    drinking 124
    food 123-4
    shopping 124
    travel to/from 124
costs 13, 14, 335
courses
    language 74, 122, 196, 217, 361
    music 74
Cráter de Maragua 226
credit cards 335
Cretaceous Park 215
criollos 24
Cristo de la Concordia 196
Cueva Cóndor 138
Cueva de los Monos 278
Cueva del Diablo 178
Culpina K 180
cultural experiences
    Chipaya villages 179
    Jalq'a villages 224
    Parque Nacional Amboró 275
    Parque Nacional Madidi 306-7
    San Pedro Prison 67
    Santiago de Okola 115
    tinku fighting 237
culture 32-41
Cumbre Kiayansani 149
Cumbre Sunchulli 149
Cumbre Tambillo 148
Cumbre Viscachani 148
Curahuara de Carangas 165
currency 335
Curva 147, 148
customs regulations 331
cycling, *see* bicycling, mountain biking

D
dance 39
Dance of the Devils 157

dangers 331, *see also individual
    locations*
    4WD tours 168-9
    bus travel 347
    drugs 67, 334
    fake immigration officials 266
    fake police 66, 211, 266-7
    fake taxi drivers 66
    fireworks 102
    hiking & trekking 54
    hitchhiking 349
    kidnapping 66, 102
    mine tours 233, 234, 235
    mountaineering & climbing 55
    prison tours 67
    propane heaters 329
    scams 67
    wildlife 320
Day of the Dead 45, 77, 179
deep vein thrombosis 353-4
deforestation 52, 53
dengue fever 354-5
departure taxes 342, 347
Día de la Madre 332
Día de los Desposorios 274
Día de los Muertos 45, 77, 179
Día de los Reyes Magos 332
Día de Todos los Santos 333
diarrhea 358, 359-60
dinosaur tracks
    Cordillera de los Frailes 226-7
    Sucre 215
    Torotoro 208
directions, asking for 33
disabilities, travelers with 339
discount cards 331
dolphins, pink river 50, 309, 318, 321
dress, traditional 37
drinks 44-5, *see also* water, wine
    alcoholic 44-5, 190, 203
    nonalcoholic 44
driver's licenses 348
driving, *see* car travel
drug trafficking 28
drugs 67, 298, 334, *see also* coca

E
economy 33-4
ecotourism 306-7
education 33
Ekeko 77
El Alto 73
El Angosto 186
El Balneario 291
El Cairo 274

El Camino del Oro 136-8
El Cañón del Duende 186
El Cañón del Inca 186
El Choro trek 124-6, **125**
El Chorro 302-3
El Chorro Grande 258-9
El Día del Mar 32
El Fuerte 279-81, **280**
El Gran Poder 15, 76
El Mausoleo del Ché 284
El Nido de los Condores 283
El Pueblito 283
El Sillar 186
El Vagante 119-20
El Valle de la Concepción 254
El Vergel 208
electricity 329
embassies 331-2
emergencies, *see inside front cover*
employment 340-1
environment 49-53
environmental hazards 358-9
environmental issues 52-3, 343
Escalera del Inca 110
Estrecho de Tiquina 116
etiquette 32, 46
evangelical movements 35
Exaltación de la Santa Vera Cruz 236
exchange rates, *see inside front cover*
ExpoCruz 268

F
Faro de Conchupata 158
Fawcett, Colonel Percy 54
Fería de la Fruta 206
Fería de Muestras 326
Fería del Charango 207
Fería Regional del Pescado 299
ferry services 347
Festival de la Wallunk'a 204
Festival of Skulls 36
festivals 332-3, *see also* food festivals,
    individual festivals & locations
    top 10 15
Fiesta de Compadres 249
Fiesta de la Cruz 15, 104, 332
Fiesta de la Ñatitas 36
Fiesta de la Uva 254
Fiesta de la Virgen de Candelaria
    104, 332
Fiesta de la Virgen de Chaguaya 254
Fiesta de la Virgen de Guadalupe 218
Fiesta de la Virgen de las Nieves 144
Fiesta de la Virgen de Urkupiña 15,
    197, 203

Fiesta de las Flores 248
Fiesta de Leche y Queso 254
Fiesta de San Bartolomé 15, 129,
    236
Fiesta de San Lorenzo 253
Fiesta de San Roque 248
Fiesta del Espíritu 235-6
Fiesta del Santo Patrono de Moxos
    15, 311
Fiesta del Señor de Burgos 206
Fiesta del Señor Santiago 209
film 38, 40-1
fires 55, 320
fireworks 102
fishing 258, 297, 300
    festival 257
flamingos 50, 165, 176, 177, 255
floating reed islands 107
Flower Festivals 204, 248
folk medicine 149, 227, 358
food 42-8, 333
    customs 46
    eateries 45-6
    festival foods 45
    glossary 46-8
    street food 42-3, 46
    top 10 eats 15-16
    vegetarians & vegans 46
food festivals
    Chocolate Festival 274
    Coffee Festival 274
    Fish Festival 299
    Fruit Festival 206
    Ham & Cheese Festival 248
    International Festival of Cheese &
        Wine 268
    Milk & Cheese Festival 254
    Potato Festival 204
    Rice Festival 274
    Trout Festival 204
forced labor 34
fossil sites 208, 226-7
foxes 50, 259, 320
Franciscan Convent of San
    José 205
fruits 44
Fuenta del Inca 110
futból 35

G
galleries, *see* museums & galleries
garapiña 203
gay culture 33
gay travelers 333
geography 49-50

geysers 164, 176
glaciers 52, 142-3
global warming 52
Gold Digger's Trail 136-8
gold-mining 139, 148
government travel advice 331
Gran Chiquitania 286-93, **262**
Grape Festival 254
Gruta de las Galaxias 178
Gruta de Lourdes 107
Gruta de San Pedro 133
Gruta de Umajalanta 209
guanacos 50, 163
Guanay 139
Guaraní people 267
guarapo 203
Guayaramerín 323-4
Guevara, Ernesto 26, 259
    Ché Trail 283-6
    festival 284
    museum 283

H
H1N1 virus 352
healing tradition 149, 227
health 352-60
    children 359-60
    environmental hazards 358-9
    folk medicine 149, 227, 358
    infectious diseases 354-7
    insurance 352
    internet resources 353
    vaccinations 340, 353
    women 360
heat exhaustion 359
hemorrhagic fever, Bolivian 357
hepatitis A 355, 360
hepatitis B 355
Heroínas de la Coronilla 196
Heyerdahl, Thor 114
hiking & trekking 54
    Amazon Basin 309
    Chulumani 130
    Copacabana 107, 109
    Cordillera Apolobamba 147-50
    Cordillera de los Frailes 224
    Cordillera Quimsa Cruz 150
    dangers 54
    El Camino del Oro 136-8
    El Choro trek 124-6, **125**
    Isla del Sol 110-11

La Paz 74, 91-3
    Mapiri Trail 138-9
    Mizque 206
    Parque Nacional Amboró 276-8
    Parque Nacional Sajama 163
    Parque Nacional Tunari 201
    Reserva Biológica Cordillera de
        Sama 255
    Reserva Biosférica del Beni 309
    Reserva Nacional de Flora y Fauna
        Tariquía 255-6
    responsible trekking 55
    Sorata 134-5
    Takesi trek 127-9, **127**
    Trans Cordillera trek 134
    Tupiza 181-2, 186
    Yunga Cruz trek 129
    Yungas 119-20, 124-6, 127-9,
        130, 134-5
Hilo Hilo 149
history 21-31
    Early, Middle & Late Horizons
        21-2
    independence 24
    Morales era 25-31
    political conflict & change 28-31
    Spanish conquest 23-4
    territorial losses 24-5
hitchhiking 349
HIV/AIDS 357
holidays 333-4
Horca del Inca 103
horseback riding 58-9
    Parque Nacional Amboró 276-8
    Tupiza 182
    Yungas 120
hostels 328-9
hot springs 59
    Aguas Calientes 291
    Capachos 162
    Potosí 242
    Sajama 164
    San Xavier 287
    Termas de Charazani Phutina
        146
    Termas de Obrajes 162
    Termas de Polques 176
    Termes de Talula 227
hotels 329
Huaca Huañusca 186
Huallpa, Diego 23
Huarina 115
Huayculli 205
Huayna Potosí 141-2
Humaca 226

I
ice-cream parlours 46
iglesias, see churches & basilicas
Illimani 142-3
immigration 342
Inca people 21, 22-3, 98, 99, 295
Inca sites
    Cochabamba Valley 203-4
    Copacabana 103
    El Fuerte 279-81, **280**
    Incallajta 205-6
    Isla de la Luna 114
    Isla del Sol 109-12
    Isla Kalahuta 115
    Llama Chaqui 209
    Tiahuanacota Inca cemetery 109
    Tupac Katari Mirador 73
    Yungas 128
Inca Trail, *see* Takesi trek
Inca Tribunal 103
Incacancha 148
Incallajta 205-6
Incamachay 226
Inca-Rakay 203-4
Independence Day 77, 104, 333
indigenous groups 12, 29, 34
    Afro-Bolivians 34, 131
    Aymará 23, 32, 34, 73
    Chica 180
    Chimane 310
    Chipaya 179
    Chiquitano 286
    Guaraní 267
    Jalq'a 224
    Kallawaya 146, 149
    Kolla 22, 32, 99
    Moxos 310, 311
    Quechua 32, 33, 34, 35, 36, 37,
        367
indigenous religions 35-6
Ingenio 138
ingenios 233
insect bites & stings 359
insurance 55, 334, 352
international money transfers 335
internet access 334
internet phone calls 339
internet resources
    air tickets 344
    airlines 343
    environment 53
    film industry 38
    health 353
    La Paz 64
    mountaineering & climbing 55

music 38
planning 16
Irupampa 226
Irupana 132
Iskanwaya 140
Isla Cáscara de Huevo 177
Isla de la Luna 114
Isla del Pescado 175-6
Isla del Sol 109-14, **108**, 6
Isla Incahuasi 175-6
Isla Kalahuta 115
Isla Koa 98
Isla Pariti 98, 115
Islas de Wiñaymarka 114-15
itineraries 17-20
    Amazon 19, **19**
    culture & nature 17, **17**
    national parks 20, **20**
    Peru, entering from 18, **18**
    transportation, means of 20, **20**

J
Jach'a Avalancha 57
jaguars 50, 51, 256, 259, 276, 318, 320
Jalq'a people 224
Japapi 110
Jesuit Missions Circuit 287-91
Jesuits 286, 295
jet-skiing 253
jungle tours 303, 304

K
Kacapi 128
Kalamarka 39
Kallawaya people 146, 149
Katari, Tomás 227
kayaking 58, 204, 297, see also
    canoeing
kidnapping 66, 102
k'oa ceremonies
    Cochabamba 200
    Oruro 156
Kolla people 22, 32, 99
Kusijata 103

L
La Angostura 204
La Diablada 157
La Festividad de Nuestro Señor Jesús
    del Gran Poder 15, 76
La Higuera 285-6
La Pajcha 283
La Paz 60-96, **62-3**, **68-9**, **76**, **90**
    accommodations 77-81
    activities 74

courses 74
dangers 66-7
drinking & clubbing 84
El Alto 83
emergency services 64
entertainment 84-5
festivals & events 76-7
food 81-4
history 61
internet access 64
itineraries 65
medical services 65
money 65-6
postal services 66
shopping 85-7
sights 67, 70-4
telephone & fax 66
tourist information 66
tours 74-6
travel to/from 87-8
travel within 88-9
La Virgen Morena del Lago 99-100
Lago Caimán 321
Laguna Anarilla 179
Laguna Blanca 179
Laguna Cañapa 179
Laguna Celeste 178
Laguna Chalalán 306
Laguna Chillata 134
Laguna Colorada 176, 8
Laguna Glacial 134
Laguna Guinda 179
Laguna Hedionda 179
Laguna Isirere 310
Laguna Jiskha Huara Huarani 128
Laguna Normandia 309-10
Laguna Tuni 143
Laguna Verde 176-7
Laguna Volcán 278
Lagunas de Kari Kari 241-2
Lagunillas 147, 148
Lake Titicaca 97-116, **98**
    climate 98
    history 98
    lake excursions 99, 107, 109
    travel to/from 99
language
    Aymará 367
    courses 74, 122, 196, 217, 361
    food vocabulary 46-8
    glossary 368-71
    Quecha 32, 33, 367
    Spanish 361-7
Las Cuevas 278
Las Islas Flotantes 107

Las Misiones Jesuíticas 287
Lauca 165
leafcutter ants 320
leeches 359
legal matters 334
leishmaniasis 320, 357-8
lesbian travelers 333
literature 34, 41, see also books
lithium reserves 30
Llama Chaqui 209
llamas 34, 50, 147, 163
    fetuses 34, 36
    llama trains 163
Llanos de Moxos 317
logging 52, 308, 318
lomas 317
Lomas de Arena 268
Los Espejillos Community Project
    278
Los Lípez 176-7
Loza, Remedios 36
lucha libre 35, 73
lustrabotas 70

M
macaws 208, 255, 316
Madidi National Park 51, 306-7, 308
malaria 355-6, 360
Mallasa 90
Mamani Mamani, Roberto 39, 40
Mapiri 139
Mapiri Trail 138-9
maps 334
Maragua 226
Marka Pampa 111
markets
    Cochabamba 194
    La Paz 70, 71-2, 73, 7
    Sucre 221
    Tarabuco 222-3
    Tupiza 182
mate de coca 44
measures 329, see also inside front
    cover
Mecapaca 90-1
Media, see newspapers, radio, TV
medical checklist 352-3
medical insurance 352
medical services 354, see also
    health
medicine, folk 149, 227, 358
Melgarejo, Mariano 205
Méndez, José Eustaquio 253
Mendoza, Alonzo de 61
Mesa, Carlos 28

INDEX

metric conversions, *see inside front cover*
micros 350
Mina Caracoles 150
Mina Chojilla 129
Mina San José 158
Mina Viloco 150
mine tours 158, 173, 233-5
minibuses 350
mining
  gold 139, 148
  silver 23, 173, 227, 229-30
  tin 150, 153, 155
Mizque 206-7
mobile phones 337-8
mocochinche 44
money 14, 334-5, *see also* costs, *inside front cover*
money changing 335
Morales, Evo 12, 28-31, 32, 33, 155
motion sickness 354
motorcycle travel
  to/from Bolivia 345
  within Bolivia 348
mountain biking 57-8
  Grand Avalanche Mountain Bike Race 57
  La Paz 74, 75, 93
  organised trips 57
  Parque Nacional Torotoro 210
  Sorata 57, 135
  WMDR (World's Most Dangerous Road) 75, 121
  Yungas 120, 124
mountaineering & climbing 54-6
  agencies & guides 56, 141
  Cordillera Quimsa Cruz 150
  Cordillera Real 141-4
  dangers 55
  guidebooks 56
  maps 55-6
  mountain rescue 55
  Oruro 158
  Parque Nacional Sajama 163-4
  Parque Nacional Tunari 201-2
  Reserva Biológica Cordillera de Sama 254
  volcanoes 178
Moxos people 310, 311
Muela del Diablo 91-2
Murillo, Pedro Domingo 71

000 Map pages
000 Photograph pages

museums & galleries, *see also* archaeological museums
  Alcaldía museum 133
  Arte el Aire Libre 72-3
  Casa de la Libertad 211, 214
  Casa de Murillo 71
  Casa Nacional de Moneda 231
  Centro de Ecología Ch'aska 180
  Ché Museum 283
  Coca Museum 70
  Cuartel-Museo 259
  Kallawaya cultural museum 146
  Museo Antropológico Eduardo López Rivas 156
  Museo & Convento de San Francisco 232
  Museo & Convento de Santa Teresa 232
  Museo Coquesa 176
  Museo Costumbrista Juan de Vargas 71
  Museo de Arte Contemporáneo 72
  Museo de Arte Sagrado 267
  Museo de Etnografía y Folklore (La Paz) 72
  Museo de Etnografía y Folklore (Sucre) 214
  Museo de Historia Nacional 267
  Museo de Historia Natural Alcide d'Orbigny 194-5
  Museo de Instrumentos Musicales 72
  Museo de la Catedral (Copacabana) 102
  Museo de la Catedral (Sucre) 216
  Museo de la Coca 70
  Museo de la Recoleta 216
  Museo de la Revolución Nacional 71
  Museo de los Niños Tanga-Tanga 216
  Museo de Metales Preciosos 71
  Museo de Pariti 115
  Museo de Santa Clara 216-17
  Museo de Textiles Andinos Bolivianos 72
  Museo del Charango 207
  Museo del Litoral 71
  Museo del Poncho 103
  Museo Étnico 111
  Museo Etno-Folklórico 267
  Museo Franciscano Frey Francisco Miguel Mari 248
  Museo Guaraní 267

  Museo Gutiérrez Valenzuela 217
  Museo Kausay Wasi 176
  Museo Lítico Monumental 94
  Museo Mineralógico 156
  Museo Misional 288
  Museo Moto Méndez 253
  Museo Nacional del Arte 70-1
  Museo Patiño 156
  Museo Sacro, Folklórico, Arqueológico y Minero 156
  Museo San Francisco 71
  Museo Tambo Quirquincho 71
  Museo Taypi 103
  Museo Textil Indígena 214
  Museos Universitarios 217
  Museum Casa Arte Taller Cardozo Velasquez 156
  Pachamama Wasi 208
  Templete Semisubterráneo 73
music 38-9
  Afro-Bolivian 131
  chapaco 249
  contemporary 39
  courses 74
  festivals 38, 268
  International Festival of Baroque Music 15, 268
  internet resources 38
  tinku 237
  traditional 38-9
musical instruments 38-9
  museum 72
Muyuloma 254

N
National Mint 231
national parks & reserves 51, 52
  Apa-Apa Reserva Ecológica 129-30
  Área Natural de Manejo Integrado Nacional (Anmin) Apolobamba 146-7
  itineraries 20
  Lomas de Arena 268
  Parque Machía 297
  Parque Nacional & Área de Uso Múltiple Amboró 275, 276-8, **277**, 7
  Parque Nacional Carrasco 51, 300
  Parque Nacional Madidi 306-7, 308
  Parque Nacional Noel Kempff Mercado 318-23, **319**
  Parque Nacional Sajama 153, 163-5, **164**
  Parque Nacional Torotoro 207-10
  Parque Nacional Tunari 201-2

Parque Nacional y Área Natural de Manejo Integrado Aguarague 258-9
Reserva Biológica Cordillera de Sama 254-5
Reserva Biosférica del Beni 309-10
Reserva de Vida Silvestre Ríos Blanco y Negro 318
Reserva Forestal Chimane 309, 310
Reserva Nacional de Fauna Andina Eduardo Avaroa 153, 173
Reserva Nacional de Flora y Fauna Tariquía 255-6
Reserva Privada de Patrimonio Natural de Corbalán 259-60
Santuario Chuchini 317-18
Nevado Candelaria 178
New Year 76, 77
newspapers 329
Noel Kempff Mercado national park 51, 318-23
Núñez del Prado, Marina 38

O
Ocabaya 132
Ojo del Inca 242
opening hours 330
orchid nursery 297-8
Oriente 261-93
climate 263
national parks 263
travel to/from 263
Orquidario Villa Tunari 297-8
Oruro 153-63, **154**
accommodations 158-9
activities 158
Carnaval 39, 157
dangers 156
drinking & entertainment 160-1
emergency services 155
food 160
history 153, 155
internet access 155
medical services 155
money 155
postal services 155
shopping 161
sights 156, 158
telephone services 155
tourist information 155-6
tours 158
travel to/from 161-2
travel within 162
otters, river 50, 318, 320

P
Pachamama 35-6, 45
Pachamama Wasi 208
Padcaya 254
painting 40, see also rock paintings
Palacio Portales 194
Palca Canyon 92-3
Palca Valley 149
pampas tours 303, 304
Pantoja, Miguel Alandia 40
paragliding 59
Paraguay 25
travel to/from 258, 346
Parque Bolívar 217
Parque Cretácico 215
Parque Histórico Santa Cruz la Vieja 291
Parque Machía 297
Parque Nacional Amboró 51, 275, 276-8, **277**, 7
Parque Nacional Madidi 51, 306-7, 308
Parque Nacional Noel Kempff Mercado 318-23, **319**
Parque Nacional Sajama 51, 153, 163-5, **164**
Parque Nacional Torotoro 51, 207-10
Parque Nacional Tunari 201-2
Parque Nacional y Área Natural de Manejo Integrado Aguarague 258-9
passports 339, see also visas
Pasto Grande 132
Patiño, Simón 155, 204
Paz Estenssoro, Víctor 25, 26
Paz Zamora, Jaime 26
home of 254
peccaries 50, 276, 318
Pelechuco 149-50
Peru, travel to/from 116, 346
phonecards 337-8
photography 336
Piedra Grande 149
Pilko Kaina 110
pink river dolphins 50, 309, 318, 321
Pizarro, Francisco 23, 189
plague 356
planning 13-16
government travel advice 331
health 352
internet resources 16
itineraries 17-20
plants 51-2, 256
Pocitos 256
politics 12, 25-31

ponchos 103
pongaje 25
population 34-5
posadas 329
postal services 336
Potato Festival 204
Potolo 227
Potosí 23-4, 227-42, **228**, **241**, 6
accommodations 236, 238-9
drinking 240
emergency services 230
entertainment 240
festivals & events 235-6
food 239-40
history 229-30
internet access 230
medical services 231
money 231
postal services 231
shopping 240
sights 231-5
silver mining 23, 227, 229-30
telephone services 231
tourist information 231
tours 233-5
travel to/from 240
travel within 241-2
pottery 205
prison tours 67
public holidays 333
Pucará 284-5
Puerto Almacén 317
Puerto Suárez 13
Puerto Varador 317
Puerto Villarroel 300-1
Pujllay 15, 223
Pulacayo mines 173
Pumamachay 226
pumas 50-1, 256, 259
Punata 204-5
puro 45

Q
Quebrada de Palala 186
Quebrada Palmira 186
Quebrada Thajo Khasa 208
Quechua people 34, 35, 36, 37
language 32, 33, 367
quena 38-9
Quetena Chico 179-80
Quijarro 292-3
Quila Quila 227
Quillacollo 202-3
Quimsa Cruz 150
quinoa 43, 44

R
rabies 356
radio 329
rainforest 52, see also Amazon Basin
reed boats 109, 114
reform, agrarian 29, 34
religion 35-6, 45, 52
Reserva Biológica Cordillera de Sama 254-5
Reserva Biosférica del Beni 309-10
Reserva de Vida Silvestre Ríos Blanco y Negro 318
Reserva Forestal Chimane 309, 310
Reserva Nacional de Fauna Andina Eduardo Avaroa 51, 153, 173
Reserva Nacional de Flora y Fauna Tariquía 255-6
Reserva Privada de Patrimonio Natural de Corbalán 259-60
residenciales 329
responsible travel 55, 306-7
restaurants 456, see also individual locations
rheas 50
Riberalta 324-5
Rincón de la Victoria 255
Río Beni 301, 7
Río Choqueyapu 61, 91
Río Coroico 121-2
Río Coscapa 126
Río Huarinilla 122
Río Isama 276
Río Jucumarini 126
Río Macuñucu 276
Río Madre de Dios 326
Río Mamarani 138
Río Quillapituni 137
Río Quimsa Chata 129
Río Solacama 132
Río Surutú 274
Río Takesi 128
Río Unduavi 132
Río Yani 138
river boats 314, 322, 324, 325, 347
river otters 50, 318, 320
road rules 349
Roboré 291-2
Rocas de Dalí 177
rock paintings
  Batea Q'ocha 208-9
  Calacala 162-3

000 Map pages
000 Photograph pages

Cordillera de los Frailes 226, 227
Villa Mar 180
rodeos 248
rubber plantations 324
Ruiz, Jorge 40-1
Rumi Campana 158
Rurrenabaque 301-7, **302**
  accommodations 303-4
  drinking & entertainment 305
  eating 305
  internet access 301
  money 301-2
  shopping 305-6
  sights & activities 302-3
  telephone services 302
  tourist information 302
  tours 303, 304
  travel to/from 306-7
  travel within 307

S
safe travel, see dangers
Sajama national park 51, 153, 163-5, **164**
Salar de Chiguana 176
Salar de Coipasa 178, **175**
Salar de Uyuni 173, 174-7, **175**, 6
salt
  extraction 173, 174
  flats 173, 174-7, 178
  hotels 174
Sama Biological Reserve 254-5
Samaipata 278-83, **279**
San Andrés festival 206
San Borja 308-9
San Buenaventura 307-8
San Cristóbal 180
San Ignacio de Moxos 310-12
San Ignacio de Velasco 288-9
San Jacinto Reservoir 253
San José 139
San José de Chiquitos 290-1
San José de Uchupiamonas 306-7
San Juan 176
San Juan festival 76
San Lorenzo 253-4
San Miguel de Velasco 289-90
San Pablo de Lípez 180
San Pedro prison 67
San Rafael de Velasco 290
San Vicente 186-7
San Xavier 287
Sánchez de Lozada, 'Goni' 12, 26, 27
Sanjinés, Jorge 41

Santa Ana de Chipaya 179
Santa Ana de Velasco 290
Santa Barbara 274
Santa Cruz 263-73, **264-5**
  accommodations 268-9
  dangers 266-7
  drinking 271
  emergency services 266
  entertainment 271-2
  festivals & events 268
  food 269-71
  history 263, 265
  internet access 266
  medical services 266
  money 266
  shopping 272
  sights & activities 267-8
  telephone services 266
  tourist information 266
  tours 268
  travel to/from 272-3
  travel within 273
Santa Veracruz Tatala 196-7
Santiago de Chiquitos 291
Santiago de Okola 115
Santuario Chuchini 317-18
scams 67
sea fossils 208
Semanta Santa 104, 332
Serrano Ham & Cheese Festival 248
shoeshine men & boys 70
shopping 336-7, see also individual locations
  bargaining 14
Siles Zuazo, Hernán 26
silver mining 23, 173, 227, 229-30
Sipe Sipe 203
slash-&-burn agriculture 52, 53
slavery 131
sloths 50
snakes 359
soccer 35
social welfare system 33
Sol de Mañana 176
solo travellers 337
solstices 52, 96
Sorata 57, 121, 133-6, **134**
South Central Bolivia 243-60, **244**
  climate 245
  history 244-5
  travel to/from 245
Southern Altiplano 151-87, **152**
  climate 153
  history 153
  travel to/from 153

Southwest Circuit 173-87
  tour operators 168-9
  travel to/from 177
southwestern Bolivia 165-73
souvenirs 337
soybean agriculture 44, 52
spectacled bears 51, 147, 255, 276
sports 35, *see also individual sports*
standards of living 32-3
steam locomotives 167, 173
street food 42-3, 46
street vendors 34
strikes & public demonstrations 27, 118, 331
student travelers 331
Sucre 210-22, **212-13**, 8
  accommodations 218-19
  courses 217
  dangers 211
  drinking 221
  entertainment 221
  festivals & events 218
  food 219-21
  internet access 211
  medical services 211
  money 211
  postal services 211
  shopping 221
  sights 211, 214-17
  telephone services 211
  tourist information 211
  tours & activities 217-18
  travel to/from 221-2
  travel within 222
Sucre, Antonio José de 24, 189, 215
sunburn 359
Sundance Kid 186-7
Supay Huasi 227
swimming holes 119, 255, 274, 291, 297, 321

T
Takesi 128
Takesi trek 127-9, **127**
talismans 36
tap water 359
tapirs 50, 256, 259, 276, 318
Taquesi trek 127-9, **127**
Tarabuco 222-3
Tarata 205
Tarija 245-53, **246**, **252**
  accommodations 249-50
  drinking & entertainment 251
  emergency services 245
  festivals & events 248

food 250-1
  history 245
  internet access 247
  money 247
  sights 247-8
  tourist information 247
  tours 248
  travel to/from 251
  travel within 251, 253
Tariquía Flora & Fauna Reserve 255-6
taxis 350
  fake taxi drivers 66
telephone services 337-9, *see also inside front cover*
Templete Semisubterráneo 73
Templo del Inca 111
Termas de Charazani Phutina 146
Termas de Obrajes 162
Termas de Polques 176
Termes de Talula 227
textiles 37-8, 146, 221, 223, 224, 226, 240, 272
  museums 72, 214, 223
theater festivals 15, 268
thermal springs, *see* hot springs
time 339
tin mining 150, 153, 155
tinku fighting 237
tipping 333
Tiquina Straits 115-16
Tiquipaya 204
Titi Khar'ka 99, 109, 112
titi monkeys 50
Titicachi 109
Tiwanaku 21-2, 39, 93-6, 115, **95**
toilets 55, 339
Tomatitas 255
Torotoro national park 51, 207-10
Totaizal 310
Totora 206
tourist information 339, *see also individual locations*
tours 350-1
  Cochabamba 196
  coffee plantation 275
  Copacabana 103
  jungle & pampas 303, 304
  La Paz 74-6
  mines 158, 173, 233-5
  Oruro 158
  Potosí 233-5
  prison 67
  Rurrenabaque 303, 304
  Santa Cruz 268

Sucre 218
Tarija 248
triathlon 58, 182
Tupiza 182-3
Uyuni 167-9
wineries 253
Train Cemetery 167
train travel 350
  Trans-Chiquitano train 292
  trains, steam 167, 173
Trans Cordillera trek 134
transportation 342-51
  air travel 342-5
  bus travel 345, 347-8
  fare hikes 86
  itineraries 20, **30**
  train travel 350
  travel to/from Bolivia 342-6
  travel within Bolivia 346-51
traveler's checks 335
trekking, *see* hiking & trekking
triathlon tours 58, 182
trimate 44
Trinidad 312-17, **313**
Trout Festival 204
trufis 350
tubing 58
Los Tumbos de Suruquizo 287
Tumichucuá 324
Tunari national park 51, 201-2
Tupac Katari Mirador 73
Tupac Yupanqui 99, 110, 153, 205
Tupiza 180-7, **181**, 5
turtles 50
TV 329
typhoid fever 356
typhus 358

U
Ukamau y Ké 39
Untucala suspension bridge 140
US–Bolivia relations 12, 30, 31
Uyuni 13, 165-73, **166**
  accommodations 169-71
  dangers 167
  emergency services 167
  festivals 169
  food 171-2
  internet access 167
  medical services 167
  money 167
  sights & activities 167
  tourist information 167
  tours 167-9
  travel to/from 172-3

V

vacations 333-4
vaccinations 340, 353
Valencia 90-1
Valle de la Luna 89-90
Valle de las Ánimas 92
Valle de los Machos 186
Vallegrande 283-4
Valles de Rocas 180
vegetarian & vegan travelers 46
Ventilla 128
Vesty Pakos Zoo 90
vicuñas 38, 50, 147, 163, 255
video systems 329
Villa Albina 204
Villa Mar 180
Villa Remedios 132
Villa Tunari 297-300
Villamontes 257-8
Villarroel, Gualberto 70
Viracocha 22, 114
Virgen de Urkupiña 202-3
Virgen del Carmen 77, 333
Virgen del Rosario 333
visas 339-40
viscachas 50, 147
visual arts 40
Volcán Licancabur 177, 178
Volcán Ollagüe 176, 178
Volcán Sajama 164
Volcán Tunupa 176, 178
Volcán Uturuncu 178
volcanoes, climbing 178
volleyball 35
volunteering 196, 217, 281, 297, 341

W

walking, *see* hiking & trekking
War of the Pacific 24
water
  drinking 359
  pollution 52, 55, 91
weather 13-14, 330
weaving, *see* textiles
websites,
  see internet resources
weights 329,
  see also inside front cover
whitewater rafting 58
  Amazon Basin 297
  Río Unduavi 132
  Yungas 121-2
wildlife watching 59,
  see also bird-watching
  Amazon Basin 300, 303, 304,
    308, 309-10, 318, 320
  Chaco 256
  Cordillera Apolobamba 147
  jungle & pampas tours
    303, 304
  Parque Nacional Amboró
    276
  Reserva Privada de Patrimonio
    Natural de Corbalán 259
Willkakuti 332
wine 45
  Grape Festival 254
  International Festival of
    Cheese & Wine 268
  production 253
  wineries 253

witch doctors, *see yatiris*
WMDR (World's Most Dangerous
  Road) 75, 121
wolves 51, 320
women in Bolivia 36
women travelers 337, 340
women's health 360
work, paid 341
World's Most Dangerous Road
  75, 121
wrestling 35, 73

Y

Yacuiba 256-7
Yampupata 109
Yani 138
yatiris 73, 77
yellow fever 356-7, 360
yoga 122
Yolosa 126
Yolosita 126
Yumani 110-11
Yunga Cruz trek 129
Yungas 49, 118-40
  climate 118
  history 118
  travel within 118-19

Z

ziplines 126, 307
Zongo Valley 121
zoos
  Jardín Zoológico, 267
  Vesty Pakos Zoo 90
  Zoo El Refugio 281

INDEX

GreenDex

GOING GREEN

Sustainable travel is still a new concept in Bolivia, but one that's growing fast. Many entrepreneurs have jumped on the bandwagon, but the tricky task is recognizing a truly sustainable operation that has Bolivia's environmental and cultural values in high regard. Our authors have highlighted choices that contribute to sustainable tourism in Bolivia, whether it's by using alternative energy, helping to preserve the environment, supporting sustainable development of local and indigenous communities or promoting Bolivia's cultural and architectural heritage.

You can help us improve this list by sending your recommendations to talk2us@lonelyplanet .com.au. To find out more about sustainable tourism at Lonely Planet, head to www.lonelyplanet .com/responsibletravel.

accommodations
   Armonia eco-lodge 316
   Armonia lodge 316
   Candelaria Ecoalbergue 275
   Chalalán Ecolodge 306
   Ecolodge del Lago 104
   Hacienda El Cafetal 275
   Mapajo Lodge 307
   Palla Khasa 112
   Posada Ecologica 276
   Probioma 278
   Prometa albergue (Tajzara) 254
   Prometa albergue (Tariquía) 256
   Refugio Volcánes 275
   San Miguel del Bala 307
   Santiago de Okola 115

   Tarapari La Paz 80
   Urpuma Ecoturismo 126

activities
   Biggest Canopy in Bolivia 307
   FAN office 279
   Fundación Amigos de la Naturaleza 266
   Fundación Pueblo 128
   Gruta de San Pedro 133
   Jalq'a communities 224
   Los Espejillos Community Project 278

eating
   Alexander Coffee & Pub 83

   Mosoj Yan 199
   Pastelería Amanecer 221

shopping
   Ajllay Wasi 221
   Alpaca Works 204
   Artecampo 272
   ASOPEC 283
   Centro Cultural Tacana 307
   Centro de Arte y Cultura Guaraní Ñandereko Ñomai 272
   Inca Pallay 221
   Irupana 86

sights
   Candelaria museum 223

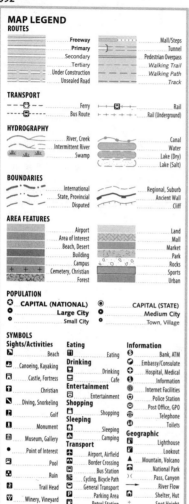

MAP LEGEND

ROUTES

- Freeway
- Primary
- Secondary
- Tertiary
- Under Construction
- Unsealed Road
- Mall/Steps
- Tunnel
- Pedestrian Overpass
- Walking Trail
- Walking Path
- Track

TRANSPORT

- Ferry
- Bus Route
- Rail
- Rail (Underground)

HYDROGRAPHY

- River, Creek
- Intermittent River
- Swamp
- Canal
- Water
- Lake (Dry)
- Lake (Salt)

BOUNDARIES

- International
- State, Provincial
- Disputed
- Regional, Suburb
- Ancient Wall
- Cliff

AREA FEATURES

- Airport
- Area of Interest
- Beach, Desert
- Building
- Campus
- Cemetery, Christian
- Forest
- Land
- Mall
- Market
- Park
- Rocks
- Sports
- Urban

POPULATION

- ○ CAPITAL (NATIONAL)
- ● Large City
- ● Small City
- ◉ CAPITAL (STATE)
- ◉ Medium City
- ◉ Town, Village

SYMBOLS

Sights/Activities
- Beach
- Canoeing, Kayaking
- Castle, Fortress
- Christian
- Diving, Snorkeling
- Golf
- Monument
- Museum, Gallery
- Point of Interest
- Pool
- Ruin
- Trail Head
- Winery, Vineyard
- Zoo, Bird Sanctuary

Eating
- Eating

Drinking
- Drinking
- Cafe

Entertainment
- Entertainment

Shopping
- Shopping

Sleeping
- Sleeping
- Camping

Transport
- Airport, Airfield
- Border Crossing
- Bus Station
- Cycling, Bicycle Path
- General Transport
- Parking Area
- Petrol Station
- Taxi Rank

Information
- Bank, ATM
- Embassy/Consulate
- Hospital, Medical
- Information
- Internet Facilities
- Police Station
- Post Office, GPO
- Telephone
- Toilets

Geographic
- Lighthouse
- Lookout
- Mountain, Volcano
- National Park
- Pass, Canyon
- River Flow
- Shelter, Hut
- Spot Height
- Waterfall

LONELY PLANET OFFICES

Australia
Head Office
Locked Bag 1, Footscray, Victoria 3011
☎ 03 8379 8000, fax 03 8379 8111
talk2us@lonelyplanet.com.au

USA
150 Linden St, Oakland, CA 94607
☎ 510 250 6400, toll free 800 275 8555
fax 510 893 8572
info@lonelyplanet.com

UK
2nd fl, 186 City Rd,
London EC1V 2NT
☎ 020 7106 2100, fax 020 7106 2101
go@lonelyplanet.co.uk

Published by Lonely Planet Publications Pty Ltd
ABN 36 005 607 983

© Lonely Planet Publications Pty Ltd 2010

© photographers as indicated 2010

Cover photograph: Lake Titicaca, Andes Mountains, Pete Oxford/ Minden/Emerald Images

Printed by Fabulous Printers Pte Ltd
Printed in Singapore

Mixed Sources
Product group from well-managed forests and other controlled sources
www.fsc.org Cert no. SGS-COC-005002
© 1996 Forest Stewardship Council